MW01120655

# INSTALLATION THEORY

*Installation Theory: The Societal Construction and Regulation of Behaviour* provides researchers and practitioners a simple and powerful framework to analyse and change behaviour. Informed by a wide range of empirical evidence, it includes an accessible synthesis of former theories (ecological psychology, activity theory, situated action, distributed cognition, social constructionism, actor-network theory and social representations).

'Installations' are the familiar, socially constructed, apparatuses which elicit, enable, scaffold and control – and make predictable most of our 'normal' behaviour; from shower-cabins or airport check-ins to family dinners, classes or hospitals. The book describes their three-fold structure with a new model enabling systematic and practical analysis of their components.

It details the mechanisms of their construction, resilience and evolution, illustrated with dozens of examples, from restaurants to nuclear plant operation. The book also provides a detailed analysis of the processes of creation and selection of innovations, proposing a model for the maintenance and evolution of social systems.

SAADI LAHLOU is Chair in Social Psychology at the London School of Economics and Political Science, in the department of Psychological and Behavioural Science, of which he was formerly Head. Trained initially as a statistician and economist, then a student of Serge Moscovici, he developed methods in large surveys, text mining, participative design and digital ethnography. Lahlou directed the Consumer Research Department of the Centre for Lifestyles and Social Policies (Crédoc, Paris), the Laboratory of Design for Cognition at EDF R&D (a whole building instrumented as a living lab), and was a member of the board of the Commissariat Général du Plan (French Prime Minister's office). He has written more than 150 papers, books and published reports.

# INSTALLATION THEORY

*The Societal Construction and Regulation of Behaviour*

SAADI LAHLOU

*London School of Economics and Political Science*

CAMBRIDGE
UNIVERSITY PRESS

# CAMBRIDGE
## UNIVERSITY PRESS

University Printing House, Cambridge CB2 8BS, United Kingdom

One Liberty Plaza, 20th Floor, New York, NY 10006, USA

477 Williamstown Road, Port Melbourne, VIC 3207, Australia

314–321, 3rd Floor, Plot 3, Splendor Forum, Jasola District Centre, New Delhi – 110025, India

79 Anson Road, #06-04/06, Singapore 079906

Cambridge University Press is part of the University of Cambridge.

It furthers the University's mission by disseminating knowledge in the pursuit of education, learning, and research at the highest international levels of excellence.

www.cambridge.org
Information on this title: www.cambridge.org/9781107137592
DOI: 10.1017/9781316480922

First published 2017

Printed in the United Kingdom by Clays, St Ives plc

*A catalogue record for this publication is available from the British Library.*

*Library of Congress Cataloging-in-Publication Data*
Names: Lahlou, Saadi, author.
Title: Installation theory : the societal construction and regulation of behaviour / Saadi Lahlou.
Description: New York: Cambridge University Press, 2017. | Includes bibliographical references and index.
Identifiers: LCCN 2017034651 | ISBN 9781107137592 (hardback)
Subjects: LCSH: Behavioral assessment. | Psychology, Applied. | BISAC: PSYCHOLOGY / Applied Psychology.
Classification: LCC BF176.5.L35 2017 | DDC 303.3/7–dc23
LC record available at https://lccn.loc.gov/2017034651

ISBN 978-1-107-13759-2 Hardback

*To Aaron Cicourel*

# Contents

# Figures

# *Plates*

# *Foreword*

I awake at 5 AM, sparked by birdsong, when, with weathered familiarity, I arch my right hand over my head to my bedside table where, on a pile of books I read nightly, I grasp my glasses, lifting them up and onto my face. I tiptoe from the bedroom so as not to disturb my partner's sleep and make for the kitchen, where I run water into a kettle and press its button to boil. Today is Friday, April 28, 2017.

A priority on my to-do list is writing the Foreword to this fiftieth and last book to appear in the thirty years of our Cambridge University *Learning in Doing* book series. LSE Professor Saadi Lahlou's *Installation Theory* brings a fresh framework to analyse behaviour, and a theory of societal evolution; it connects the minute gestures of action as-we-live-it to aggregate historical change.

Installation theory (IT) is a synthetic theory explaining how humans construct systems that support and format behaviour. 'How is it', he asks, 'that we creatures of free will, despite our differences, despite our biographic differences, all comply to "behave" in society as expected? And how is it that we manage so easily to behave adequately even in new contexts?' To provide detailed answers to these perennial questions, he has 'installations' serve as our unit of analysis for the nexus of societies, cultures and individuals. This focus on installations then enables coordinated answers to the two classical research questions for human development at the heart of the social sciences: How does society regulate the behaviour of its members? How do individuals choose their behavioural path in a situation? Answering each, the reader finds, enlightens the other.

Because focus on detail is essential to understand the determinants of behaviour, which is a sum of details, because understanding what an installation is requires getting into the nitty-gritty of everyday actions, let me describe what I do while the kettle heats the water. Please bear with me.

I interweave other activities as the water is boiling; I grab a blood pressure cuff, collect my smartphone, turn on Bluetooth as I sit, mounting the cuff; I press the Start button on my iHealth app, which channels my take-blood-pressure activity. After the cuff inflates and the reading is produced, I take it off and return it to its charger. The water is boiling now.

I place three tablespoons of coffee into a filter (from a nearby jar in which I keep a tablespoon), pouring the boiling water languorously into a Japanese coffee-dripping device, savouring each burst of its dark-roasted scent. I flip over a five-minute sand clock I installed on the kitchen counter the night before in anticipation of this morning's caffeination ritual. There is then time to walk across the kitchen, don my slippers, walk down the twelve steps to the front door, unlock and open it and walk the sixty steps to the street curb of my home, where the morning papers have arrived. I collect them and return to the house, bounding up the steps. Ready to enable the coffee now brewed to drip, I lift the clear plastic device and sit it upon my cup. As the bottom rim of the device touches the coffee cup's rim, the cleverly engineered bottom of the coffee dripper rises, and the coffee fills my cup. I dump the grounds for recycling and rinse and reset the coffee-filtering device into a sink-side draining rack. I open the fridge, the filled coffee cup in my other hand, pour a dollop of cream from the fridge, and now the calm I have been seeking to launch the morning can begin.

In all that just happened, my home and kitchen installations, including me as a key component, have performed several activities cooperatively; I was acting, but I was also guided and scaffolded by the rest of the installation's components.

Now I settle myself into my habitual right corner of the black couch, turning on my nearby lamp, and my day can start. I pull a bound leather journal from my side table. I sketch the day's arc in a list: it must set out my priorities and primary time chunks of the day and estimate where I will devote my energies. I check the weather forecast hour by hour by launching my iPhone's Accuweather app. It tells me it will get quite warm today, 78 F, by 2 PM. This will affect my schedule planning, as I expect to run to the gym I use 1.5 miles away, do a weight workout, and then run home, where I will continue writing.

I have learned to avoid the pull of checking email before setting priorities, so I've placed my phone facedown so I will not be tempted to open it up before I have completed my list-making. In the journal itself I create an installation (keep reading . . .); I sketch a list of what I hope to achieve in the day. I estimate the hours I wish to spend on each task. For each I envision the percentage of my energy expenditures for the day which I imagine it will consume. This is a new habit, begun in 2013 after I suffered a massive stroke which reduced my available mental energies each day and impaired my left inferior peripheral vision so that I can no longer drive or ride bicycles for safety's sake. Otherwise fine, I walk everywhere for exercise and for contemplation. The need for energy estimates for the day is so I'll avoid my prestroke tendencies to be captured in each of the things I begin doing each day, running my clock out by making progress toward all of them that I pursue. With less overall energy to expend, I must be more strategic, so tranching my energies, guided by a priority queue and scribed time estimates, is key. Because of this increased awareness of detail, I am especially sensitive to Lahlou's description of how the context scaffolds and constrains behaviour, and how I create as well as use the installations I live in.

To begin, I look around the table and the floor for cues I have left myself to the things I'll need to do today. Last night I sketched a few words on each of several coloured sticky notes about things to do, and I have four different stacks of papers on the floor by the couch, each representing a major cluster of tasks: materials for a course I'm teaching on media multitasking, learning and the brain, the IT book manuscript, Stanford University long-range-planning documents, student papers and journal manuscripts needing attention. These assets I scan, filtered by my emerging priorities from the knowledge integrations and values-sifting my brain engages in during the prerising times of consciousness. The items that still matter make it onto my evolving list of today's to-dos. Any items needing calendaring I render on my smartphone calendar app, which synchs to my desktop calendar.

What exactly is an installation as Lahlou defines them? Installations are smaller units than society is; they are specific, local, societal settings in which humans are funnelled to and expected to behave in a predictable way (such as the aforementioned bedroom, kitchen, roadways, gym and, shortly, the restaurant). Installations are ubiquitous; collectively, they are the main loci and devices through which the continuous reproduction of society and culture occurs at a micro-level through daily practice. But installations are not reducible to or to be confused with physical settings. Those in a culture spontaneously identify them and, because they have been socialized to do so, know what to do in them. Installations, you see, have three component layers – distributed at physical, psychological and social levels – that are linked into a single functional bundle. Lahlou explains that although installations have a functional coherence and are a deliberate production of societies, they are distributed in their nature and assemble only at the moment and point of delivery of activity, just as ingredients assemble and transform as expected in a chemical reaction.

For envisioning the redundancy of installations, consider the customs installation of an airport, an assemblage of our embodied competences in queueing behaviours upon arrival, the material physical barrier channels and the customs agents and associated authority and regulatory apparatus. I presume your competency in airport customs using this example. Yet installations, although channelling, are nonetheless nondeterministic – variabilities in behaviours occur with the leeway of caprice. An agent's free will make its way into installations through selecting goals, in choosing which installation one will participate in and in performing the details of action inside socially allowable limits for the installation (e.g., which dish I order in a restaurant). Furthermore, agents do not only use standard installations; they also create their own and use them to frame their own behaviour, as I do in my home or with my arrangements to sort out priorities and organize my day, as I have described earlier.

Continuing my saga, after writing the first part of this introduction, weightlifting at the gym and musing over the morning's ethnographic notes, I walk to a fish market to order a dish. While waiting, I use my phone's Notes app to draft a series of reflections on how my morning's observations relate to IT. The three layers of Lahlou's IT framework are affordances, embodied competences and social regulation. Layer 1 deals with the *Objective Material Environment*, made up of affordances in the material environment (which scaffold behaviour); Layer 2 is *Embodied Interpretive Systems*, the competences expressing the embarked agency of the subject, who is part and parcel of the installation (which produces behaviour); and Layer 3, *Social Regulation,* is made up of institutions and formal and informal rules (which regulate behaviour).

A first observation on the beginning of my day is how intertwined in the behaviours of my account are the first two layers: getting and donning my glasses from the bedside, preparing the coffee with its multiple steps and devices, taking a trip outside to collect a morning paper, rummaging my stacks, establishing my priorities for the day in my work journal, writing these very words on my computer. Less obvious but no less channelling my behaviours were five different instances of social regulation in this brief, dramaless morning: my tiptoeing out of the bedroom – so as not to wake my partner; my putting away both the blood pressure cuff and the coffee filter system – to avoid clutter; adhering to the social norm of recycling my coffee grounds – to provide biodegradable waste; and my calendar synching – which is socially regulated in how I am making accessible to others I need to be coordinating with when it is that I am occupied and when I might be available. The combination of these three layers of components, at the point of delivery of action, naturally channels my behaviour. And I could be sharing scores of other event sequences that unfolded in my running, road crossings with traffic lights, gym entry, workout and locker room procedures, restaurant ordering and eating scripts; all analysable and redesignable with the guidance provided in this IT book.

In Lahlou's book, indeed, the three layers shaping human behaviour and their operationalization in research and practice are used for analysing installations to understand, manage or redesign them. That these three layers of installations coalesce to function with momentum as a single system provides redundancies and produces their resilience.

With installations at the centre of the theory for understanding and intervening in how humans construct systems to support and format behaviour, how do installations work as what Lahlou calls 'a behavioural backbone architecture for society'? They 'channel' behaviour by offering users a restricted choice of alternatives, limited by three distributed layers of determinants at material, embodied interpretive and social levels, which provide behavioural feedforward and feedback. Each installation layer induces or allows specific behaviours and provides limited degrees of freedom to act. The guiding path is continuously produced as action unfolds. Thus, installations operate as a behavioural attractor where choices left to the person are often minor. The combination of the three layers makes this channelling system resilient and enduring. If we can understand how installations have their effects, we should be enabled to modify behaviour, collectively and individually. We could then intervene by reframing components singly or in combination: redesigning material contexts, educating participants, modifying institutional or regulatory systems.

The reader will find upon inquiry into the text that IT uniquely integrates a phenomenal range of theories, across the social science disciplines of psychology, sociology, anthropology and economics, and further incorporates the already interdisciplinary cognitive sciences. IT has been informed and iteratively developed through its grounding in extensive analyses of video-recorded activities produced in natural settings, of users of technology, broadly defined, and professionals in a diversity of occupations, so as to understand their decision-making and actions. At the root of this richness lay multilayered analyses of the digital ethnographic data of human activities and interactions that Lahlou and colleagues have captured in situ with the aid of 'subcams' – miniature subjective cameras worn by research participants as they conduct their everyday life, thus yielding first-person perspectives on action in situ and enabling replay interviews where participants who wore the camera comment on their own film.

These data on how and why people act in real-world situations have been used to provide unprecedentedly detailed and insightful accounts into the psychological states of participants as they are interacting with the physical, social and representational stuff of their environments.

Installation theory is ambitious in intent and fine-grained in execution, seeking to be nothing less than a simple and robust framework for both analysing all manner of behaviours and changing them using design and policy interventions. The framework is connected to many other current accounts of similarly vexing issues, such as activity theory, distributed cognition, ecological psychology, situated action, social constructionism, actor-network theory, social representations and the like (which are also presented in the book). Yet it provides a unique vantage point in its integrative powers and range of examples from which it has been constructed. The dozens of real-world examples encompassed in the book illustrate the value of IT. The behaviour settings studied range from shopping and family meals to cycling on the urban street, changing a flat tire, getting a dental filling, white-collar work, waiting restaurant tables, surgery, nurses dispensing medications, master chef apprenticing, and nuclear plant operations.

The pluripotent nature of IT should yield generative fruits for many disciplines and societal roles, including designers, engineers, managers, consultants, policymakers, social scientists, educators and students. Perhaps even more fundamentally, anyone concerned with the real-world contexts of cognition and action, their own and those of others, will benefit from reading this book.

IT is also an ambitious academic theory, whose delicious intricacies await the reader, of the stability yet continual evolution of societies, culture and their constitutive installations, emboldened with particularities I can say little about here. Lahlou provides a vision of the endurance and evolution of societies as reproducing piecemeal and in a distributed manner by means of installations. This academic theory of societal evolution – its spawning of variants and its selection mechanisms – is advanced by study of the examples of scientific progress and innovation processes in industry.

Such evolution combines endurance (day-to-day reproduction) and change (longer-term continuously modifying form). Lahlou argues that installations not only channel behaviour but are essential to reproducing society and culture, since they are the very devices by which culture reproduces through daily practice. The resilience of installations, coming from their redundant threefold structure, is key in socializing novices, who find themselves induced into the correct practice and therefore learn how to behave while participating in installations. IT shows how installations, in practice, enable people to *learn in doing.*

Lahlou describes the reproduction cycles of embodied competences, of material objects in the physical layer and of institutional rules emerging from power struggles among stakeholders. Participants in and stakeholders of installations change them in betterment loops for improved experience and satisfaction. He shows how the construction and endurance of installations reflects power struggles and compromises of interests, how they evolve spontaneously and how their evolution can be channelled by deliberate design. He articulates several mechanisms that select from the variants which are produced, from thought experiments to reality trials to the power struggles of competition. His account provides for dual aspects of the mechanisms for the long-term evolution of installations in society – the three semiautonomous component layers of installations evolve independently with their own technical (re)production logics and constraints, but the installations also evolve conjointly, in the composite splendour of their entirety. There may also be crossed effects, where design of one layer may be influenced by what happens in another layer, since individual humans circulate between installations and their embodied competences are constructed within and for diverse installations.

Satisfyingly, the IT book itself is organized as an installation; it provides different levels of structure to align with different reading goals: browsing mode and reading mode. Takeaways and abstracts appear in bold font to capture browsing attention, much like the copasetic page summaries in the text margins popular in philosophy books in the nineteenth century.

Lahlou avers that IT has pragmatic value. He provides some examples of application for behavioural change, which is his main goal, and that will likely become a core application of IT. As a learning scientist trained in developmental psychology, philosophy and the cognitive sciences, working on the complexities of K–12 STEM education and learning with technologies for thirty-six years, I am especially keen to bring IT into close contact with the interdisciplinary learning sciences and technology design. I foresee three specific strategies for that enablement.

The first will be to employ IT for describing and analyzing the situated experiences of people learning in the many different contexts in which learning scientists investigate learning processes and outcomes, from schools and universities to museums, communities and homes. While unsurprisingly, echoes of Dewey, Piaget, Vygotsky, Bruner and Situated Learning are manifest in IT, I have legions of reasons to anticipate that

Lahlou's IT brings unique leverage to tackling these issues in powerfully new ways.

The second strategy is leveraging IT as a design and intervention framework for creating and researching the processes in use and consequences of learning technologies and learning environments of every kind more broadly over the life course, not only for formal education but in informal learning and for learning online.

A third approach will be analyzing the ways in which IT aligns or conflicts with extant learning theories, pedagogical frameworks, and educational policymaking for building equitable learning opportunities and adaptive capacities in educational systems for learners and teachers. I eagerly anticipate these activities with a large community of colleagues keen for such an encompassing and generative theory as Lahlou has developed.

In short, as an explanatory and intervention-ready account of how installations, in practice, enable people to learn in doing, I believe Lahlou's IT serves as a fitting crown to the Cambridge University Press's *Learning in Doing* series.

I hope you grant me forbearance for exposing in this Foreword the skins of my installations du jour when you also find resonance, as you are reading Professor Lahlou's book, with your reflections on the installations you use and build throughout your own daily living. As you will experience, IT is a handy toolkit for sharpening our awareness and understanding of the fine-grained fabric of how we act-in-the-world – and how we can design for change.

Roy Pea
*Stanford University*

# Acknowledgements

I was helped for the substance of this book by friends, colleagues and students so numerous that I can only give here a warm collective acknowledgement. Friends, colleagues, students, a big thank you for your support, your intellectual and technical input and all the rest of it!

My teachers and mentors kindly supported me again for this project, especially Aaron Cicourel, who taught me field work, among other things. Aaron, this book owes a lot to our discussions, thank you also for your generous mentoring all these years. George Gaskell has been there for me in times of need. George, many thanks for your good advice. Alas Serge Moscovici, my PhD supervisor, and Jean-Claude Abric, my habilitation director, departed this world too early and only saw the first sketch of this book. Serge, Jean-Claude, I wish you were still with us.

An extra thank you to colleagues who read the book and contributed to its current form at various stages of production, from first draft to launch. Your input seriously improved the book —and especially Roy Pea's suggestions that made me completely re-write some sections: Ai Yu, Alex Gillespie, Aliénor Lahlou, Antoine Cordelois, Bonnie Heptonstall, Bradley Franks, Cathy Nicholson, Champa Heidbrink, Charles Lenay, Charles Stafford, Claude Fischler, Claudine Provencher, Denise Baron, Denise Jodelet, Elena Samoylenko, Elinor Ochs, Frédéric Basso, Gretty Mirdal, Jana Uher, Jim Hollan, Johannes Rieken, Jorge Correia Jesuino, Lucia Garcia-Lorenzo, Marina Everri, Marshall Buxton, Martin Bauer, Maximilian Heitmayer, Monica Zhang, Paulius Yamin-Slotkus, Peter Dieckmann, Philippe Fauquet-Alekhine, Pierre-Emmanuel Godet, Robin Schimmelpfennig, Roy Pea, Sandra Obradović, Simon Luck, Sophie Guéroult, Sophie Le Bellu, Terri-Ann Fairclough, Tom Reader, Valérie Beaudouin, Valery Nosulenko, Vivian Loftness, Volker Hartkopf, Zoe Jonassen —and of course C.U.P.'s anonymous reviewers and editorial team: David Repetto, Daniel Brown, Fred Goykman, James McKellar, Kanimozhi Ramamurthy. Diana Witt made the index.

Finally, I am grateful to several institutions:

The London School of Economics and Political Science, whose generous sabbatical policy enabled me to take a year off-teaching to write; also for a Seed Fund grant.

The European Commission EURIAS senior fellowship programme, for a year of invited residence at the Paris Institute for Advanced Studies, with the support of the French State managed by the Agence Nationale de la Recherche, programme "Investissements d'avenir" (ANR-11-LABX-0027-01 Labex RFIEA+).

The Paris Institute for Advanced Studies team led by Gretty Mirdal, who have been supportive and kind beyond imagination.

The CNRS for a DRA grant (programme CADEN, UMR 8037/8177 EHESS-CNRS).

The EDF R&D Division for solidly funding the building and operation of the Laboratory of Design for Cognition for 10 years.

# Introduction

Most sections of this book are easy to read and illustrated with real-world examples. Nevertheless, a few sections include more technical discussions which connect this work with the literature. Their presence is necessary for the scholarly reader, but not indispensable for understanding the argument. For example, Chapter 3 provides an abstract of five important streams of theories which are relevant for this book, but its reading is not essential to those who already know them: different readers have different needs.

**I encourage the reader to switch into browsing mode in the moments where the detail of the text may appear too stodgy, and then to switch back into reading mode.**

**The book was written precisely with this possibility in mind, with takeaways and abstracts in bold font to facilitate browsing and resumption of reading.**

**There are introductory overviews and a final takeaway in each chapter, and even in each major section. The conclusive chapter also includes a detailed takeaway in Section 9.1**

This book provides a simple framework to analyse and change behaviour.

In lectures, bus stops, workstations, shops, dental practices, family dinners and so on, behaviour is locally *channelled* by mechanisms that induce subjects to behave in an 'appropriate' way to reach their goals, to cooperate and to minimize social confrontation. A substantial part of our activity in society takes place in such settings, 'installations', which are a natural behavioural unit. Installations are specific, local, societal settings where humans are expected to behave in a predictable way. These units are spontaneously identified as such by members of a culture, socialized from childhood, who thus 'naturally' know what to do in them. Installations channel behaviour by offering users a limited choice of alternatives, limited by three layers of determinants at material, social and embodied level. These determinants provide behavioural feedforward and feedback.

The book first presents a threefold ***framework*** and methods for analysing these installations to manage or redesign them. Installations have three layers: *affordances in the material environment, embodied competences in the subject and social regulation.* The subject is part and parcel of the installation, which is therefore a compound functional unit that assembles at the point of behavioural delivery, such as a chemical reaction or a cooking recipe. Entering an installation is subjectively experienced as being in a 'situation' that has a momentum of its own: one feels naturally *driven* to do what is appropriate. The components of the installation in the three layers are linked into one single functional bundle; they scaffold, produce and regulate a specific normative behavioural sequence.

Each layer of an installation induces or allows specific behaviours and gives only certain degrees of freedom to act; their threefold combination in a local situation leaves an even more limited path for action. That guiding path is continuously created as action unfolds, as for a player driving an avatar in a video game. Therefore, installations operate as a behavioural attractor where the choices left to the subject are often minor (e.g. which drink you choose from a menu). The way each layer contributes to channel behaviour will be explained in detail. Their combination makes this channelling system resilient and enduring. Understanding their effects enables us to modify behaviour.

Installations benefit from continuous, gradual, cultural improvement to provide efficient support for activities. As a result, subjects behave in a predictable and efficient way; social cooperation is possible and externalities are optimized. By structuring behaviour, installations provide a backbone for societies and organizations. Installations do not overtly regulate what people feel or think (what they *experience*), but in practice they regulate, and support, their behaviour (what they *do*) for a wide range of mundane activities by providing an envelope for 'appropriate' behaviour.

Of course, individuals do have leeway and initiative; there is more than one way to skin a cat. Every interaction or activity is unique in the way participants live it at the microscopic level: no two family dinners are exactly the same and we never step in the same shower twice. Still, in practice, the variations are usually in the details. Installations facilitate the 'paradigmatic' learning and execution of an array of such variations within a frame; they account for the similarity-with-minor-adaptive-variants that we observe in practice, and that make life in society predictable and easy. The variability of behaviours is also a source of innovation, and as a result, installations undergo change on a sociohistorical scale.

Although it is obvious that there are individual differences, there are also striking commonalities in the way people behave. Installations are precisely addressing that second aspect and account for how these similarities are constructed in spite of all the reasons for difference.

This simple analytic framework provides a robust tool for design and policy intervention in the real world; extant layers (and how to analyse these) are presented in detail and illustrated with dozens of real-world examples.

The framework is useful for designers, consultants, managers and policymakers, as well as for social scientists or students. Read Chapters 1, 2, 4 and 8.

The book also presents, grounded in the aforementioned framework, an ambitious ***theory*** of the endurance and evolution of societies and culture, for an academic audience. It shows how installations evolve naturally, and extracts from this evolution principles and mechanisms usable for deliberate interventions and change. It is argued that installations are the main loci and devices through which the continuous reproduction of society through daily practice occurs, and so they can be a powerful instrument for regulation and policy.

In a nutshell, installations, because of their redundant threefold structure, have enough resilience and regulatory power to channel 'appropriate' behaviour even in novice or reluctant subjects. As a consequence, novices *learn by doing*: subjects are socialized into cultural skills by being channelled into experiencing appropriate practice, within local installations. Such appropriate practice is then embodied by subjects: installations literally *inform* subjects by having channelled them. In turn, subsequently, experienced subjects become part and parcel of the societal reproduction process: they act as helpers and vigilantes who contribute to regulate other people's behaviour through the social layer.

Participants and stakeholders operate installations on a daily basis. But they are not only passive users. They also change installations for improved experience and satisfaction. Various institutional and technical selection mechanisms involving reality trials, thought experiments, external representation, competition and power struggles ensure global societal coherence of this distributed process; these are described herein.

The endurance and evolution of societies therefore emerges as a distributed process in which material culture and representations reproduce piecemeal and mostly locally, following an original mechanism of betterment loop through *monitored dual selection and modification* of installations, a process that is more resilient and faster than biological evolution. Its driving forces, regulation loops and operation are described therein.

As evolution is a combination of stability and change, the mechanisms producing evolution are presented separately before being combined in a single model. It appears that societal change in general and the evolution of installations is mostly constituted of control and selection loops which frame innovations. These ensure continuity of the new with the old. The bulk of innovation and change is tested in simulation trials in 'external representations' before being confronted with reality tests. This spares time and cost, compared to biological evolution. The processes of scientific progress and industrial innovation are used as detailed examples, among many others.

The power of the demonstration of the theory resides in a detailed explication of the full chain of genesis, reproduction and selection of installations' components, from the macro societal level of institutions to the micro-level of local interaction and neurons. It is illustrated by many empirical cases.

Installation theory is a synthesis weaving together a series of other theories in psychology, sociology, anthropology, economics and cognitive science. This integration has been made possible by the use of powerful data collection techniques, including digital ethnography, to capture activity data from the very perspective of the actors (with wearable video cameras). These techniques enable unprecedented in-depth analysis of the psychological states of subjects as they interact with their natural environment. The empirical material comes from very diverse real-world situations, from family dinners and shopping to emergency medicine and nuclear plant operation, as well as from ten years of experimentation in the largest industry living lab in Europe.

This theory is proposed as one more step in the long series of scientific efforts to account for the endurance and evolution of societies. It is presented in Chapters 4, 5, 7 and 9.

Chapter 3 presents some important theories used in building the framework, especially ecological psychology, activity theory, situated action, distributed cognition, social constructionism, actor-network theory and social representations. The informed reader can skip it.

Section 6.1 presents a perspective on scientific publication that may be of specific interest for PhD students and their supervisors.

# CHAPTER I

# Installation

## A Synthetic Theory to Explain How Humans Construct Systems That Support and Format Individual Behaviour

This book addresses the question of how societies empower and control individuals to behave in a 'correct' way.

It describes *installations* in which, even though they are creatures of free will, humans are induced to behave in an overall predictable and standardized manner. Restaurants, escalators, shoe shops, cinemas, family dinners, basketball matches, toilets, voting booths, intensive care units and open-plan offices are some examples of installations. They have a momentum of their own. They elicit, frame, channel and control individual behaviour. The chapters show how to analyse installations, how they work, how they are constructed, how they evolve and how to change them.

Installations have been partly described in social science under various names: behavioural settings, 'dispositif', frame, etc. Installation theory is their first systematic analysis from the pragmatic perspective of design and intervention.

The book provides a simple and robust framework, grounded in extensive empirical analyses of real cases.

This first chapter introduces the problem with some simple examples (air travel, road traffic). It then clarifies our research questions (how humans manage to accomplish complex tasks in society, how social regulation is implemented in practice). It also provides an overview of the book's content and an outline of each chapter.

Let us start with a mundane experience many of us share.

I travelled by plane recently. I arrived at the airport and queued to check in. On demand, I showed documents to get my boarding pass. Then I was channelled through customs, security and the boarding area, through corridors, signs and the instructions of specialized personnel. Finally, I walked into the plane through the jet bridge. Then I sat at my assigned seat. I fastened my seat belt. I stayed seated for the whole flight.

You know the process, don't you?

What happened in fact? I executed a series of complex action sequences, in a succession that enabled me to be transported to a faraway place and empowered me to fly over the oceans at hundreds of miles per hour. Still, my contribution and agency in the process remained limited, even though I acted willingly. I came with the goal of my final destination, and some embodied competences about travelling; the rest was provided by the context. Many actions were executed by other components of the system (e.g. flying the plane). And my own behaviour was guided and controlled almost all the way. The choices I made myself were few, and I was actually given only a few alternatives, e.g. the choice of drinks the flight attendant offered me.

I was not the only one to behave like this. There were other fellow passengers, of diverse age, gender, nationality, etc. But although they all were – I assume – creatures of free will, each and every one of them behaved in a manner similar to my own, regardless of their individual final purpose, values, biological characteristics, cultural origin, dispositions and socioeconomic specifics. Each may have had a different personal psychological *experience* of the flight, different desires and emotions; each may have given a specific meaning to this journey. In the detail they may each have acted according to their own biographic peculiarities. But, roughly, our outward *behaviour* was very similar, and our acts towards other persons and objects were conventional and predictable. We all were, willingly, funnelled, scaffolded and controlled to *behave as airline passengers*. The strange part is that I had never been to that specific airport or used that airline before; but even though that specific context was new to me I had no problem behaving efficiently.

How is it that we, creatures of free will, despite our differences, despite our biographic differences, all comply to 'behave' in society as expected? And how is it that we manage so easily to behave adequately even in new contexts?

As the following chapters explain in detail, as I travelled, I was channelled through specific local 'installations' that framed my behaviour: the airline website, the check-in counter, the waiting line, the customs post, the security area, the waiting lounge, the corridors, the plane, etc. These settings are not just spatial places; they are populated with other actors or agents and they are ruled by institutions. The combination of these components is a cultural reactor that predictably produces 'appropriate' behaviour (we shall clarify that term), simultaneously empowering and controlling participants: it regulates[1] behaviour with feedforward and feed-back loops. From airport to airport we were channelled and empowered by culture and society all the way; in the end we all cooperated and 'did the right thing'. Each of us acted differently, but overall these differences remained in the detail.

That predictability is a functional condition for cooperation: should a passenger arrive late at the plane door, the whole flight would be delayed. Interestingly, the status of will and freedom in such situations is ambiguous. We do act in a certain way because we want to reach the end goal, but what we do to reach it we do not necessarily do happily (e.g. boarding a crowded train to reach the airport); we are free to think what we want, but not free to act as we would prefer.

In this channelled state, which is neither fully automated nor deeply reflexive, the question of free will is not really relevant; it is rather a means–end issue. As a matter of fact, the 'decisions' in such a state are not merely an individual process, but rather the result of a distributed process in which society has framed the situation and guides individual choice along a narrow range of alternatives only. When I pass a test, when I board a train, when I queue for my bowl of soup, when I undress for the shower, I behave in installations; sometimes I follow my own will, sometimes I don't. Most of the time my freedom addresses only some aspects of the process. In large-scale societies, we spend a substantial part of our lives in such channelled states, as creatures of bounded free will, enjoying the semi-freedom that is the price of getting the benefits of society.

This channelling phenomenon is the central topic of this book. We shall study in detail the nature, structure and dynamics of the devices that regulate human activity in society at local levels. Let us call them ***installations***. In passing, we shall see how they constitute a behavioural backbone architecture for society.

Apart from airports, from the cradle to the grave, which ultimately are also situations in which our behaviour is tightly framed and restricted, we find ourselves to be actors in a multitude of relatively standard sketches, of 'repisodes' (see Glossary): 'the Elevator', 'the Haircut', 'a Beer at the Pub', 'Checking E-mail'. Some sketches we experience hundreds of times ('an occasional drink' might turn out to be quite frequent), some a single time (baptism and rites of passage), some a few times only, perhaps in different roles (as a child, then as a parent; as a learner, then as a teacher), but always we conform to a socially and culturally attached script. We chain

---

[1] Regulation is here taken in the generic sense rather than in the legal sense.

and weave such small behavioural sequences that tend to constitute an essential part of the fabric of our daily lives: think about your day today and consider how little of it escapes such scripts....

Of course, humans are not robots, and installations do not rule *every* aspect of life; they mostly rule *the functional aspects of behaviour,* especially those that matter for practical cooperation. For example, at a family dinner, the content of the conversation or the nature of the menu (potatoes or beans?) may not matter for the functional result of the family being fed, with a fair distribution of food available and reinforcement of family cohesion. Such aspects (conversation, menu) will vary in content. But many other aspects of the dinner as a script in that specific family will remain similar from one dinner to another. This permanency makes the meal a predictable activity and enables cooperation of participants.[2] In the same vein, 'a lecture' or 'an exam' in a given university tends to follow one of a few scripts only, in a very standard manner, even though the content matter might be very different (e.g., philosophy or marketing). Installations account for the normative aspects we observe in these activities.

For each of these standard scenes, our society and our culture have prepared and provided the appropriate stage, with its actors and props, but also the execution skills (each actor knows his role) and the script. Those constitute the frame of the experience, the scaffolding and engine of any social activity and the conditions for performance without which we could not behave satisfyingly. *An installation encapsulates all the components that produce such a scene. It is the functional entity for a segment of activity.* That is why it is a relevant unit for analysis and intervention regarding behaviour. We are here specifically interested in the installations that support the standard scripts of ordinary life. If we want to manage and change them, it is necessary to understand how such installations operate *in detail* (at physical, psychological and social levels): how they are constructed, how they endure and how they evolve.

The etymology of the word *installation* is to put someone in position.[3] This process involves situating a person simultaneously in a geographical location, in a psychological state and in a social role and status. As did

---

[2] That is why, when one dinner diverges massively from the standard practice, which does happen, it will be considered 'exceptional' to that norm by the participants. In some way, it does not count as a 'normal' dinner; it cannot be used as a reference for future practice and expectations.

[3] Originally, the word designated the process of solemnly inducting an ecclesiastic into office by seating them in an official stall (from medieval Latin *installare*); this was generalized to the installation of a political or military dignitary, or of oneself; then to ship apparatus set-up and home furnishing;

many words ending in '-ation', built on verbs in the participle past, 'installation' came to designate the process as well as the product of this process.[4]

A key intuition of installation theory can be traced back to Stanley Milgram's comment describing his famous obedience experiment (Milgram, 1963). In that experiment, ordinary people were induced to give massive electric shocks to other people, supposedly to help them learn. Most participants did inflict the maximum shock, a (literally) shocking result. In his 1965 film, *Obedience*, describing the experiments at Yale University, Milgram comments:

> Many people not knowing much about the experiment claim that subjects who go to the end of the board [the maximum, 480 Volts shocks] are sadistic. Nothing could be more foolish as an overall characterization of these persons. The context of their actions must always be considered. *The individual* upon entry in the laboratory **becomes integrated into a situation that carries its own momentum**. (Milgram, 1965: 39'12"–39'30"; emphasis added)

Just as Milgram's installation induced subjects to perform behaviours beyond their will (Milgram, 1963, 1974), many mundane installations within society *frame and induce* our behaviour. Such installations account for a large part, possibly the majority, of our daily activities.

Let us be clear: first, not *every* behaviour is channelled by some installation. And even in installations people may behave atypically: thirty-five

---

coming to the contemporary general meaning of setting things in place in a proper arrangement (Littré, 1885).

[4] *Installation* is a term often used in the vocabulary of art, referring to three-dimensional set-ups designed to induce a specific effect on the spectator who enters it, and where the spectator is part of what he or she observes. The art installation includes physical components, but it also plays on the interpretive systems of the spectator.

'We do not really know what installation art is or agree on what we are talking about when we speak of installation art, even as we create works that bear its name … Upon entering an installation, one not so much suspends reality, in the common phrase of the arts; rather one enters an entirely new world of the artists' own making. A reality of its own exists in the work of art and a world that, through the act of entering it, one becomes a part of. For the time one is within an installation, this is the world and the world is it. The essence of this sort of installation art is that, unlike a painting for instance, one not only looks at it but actually enters it, travels through it' (Bestor, 2003). As Cicourel (personal communication, 2016) notes, 'installation', in art, is a fleeting usage in which an undocumented phenomena, or more complex conceptual thought or activity, is represented as an abstract visual/auditory, perhaps imaginative presentation by a unique, temporary, real time performance that can include hypothetical, material, auditory and/or machine or human performance for a fleeting audience. The installations we describe in this book are very different in construction, nature and intent, although they share something with artistic installations in that they are multilayered devices that, deliberately, locally create some cognitive attractor, inducing intended effects in the participant/spectator.

We are not interested here in artistic installations, but rather in mundane and ordinary installations; the spirit of inducing the person entering into a specific mindset is the same, however.

per cent of participants did *not* fully comply in Milgram's seminal experiment; while driving, many people do not strictly conform to traffic regulations. So individuals do keep some leeway; we will come back to this.

Nevertheless, these breaching behaviours remain the exception. And, in practice, most of our daily behaviours are scaffolded and constrained by such installations, which we hardly even notice. As Alfred Schütz noted,

> [T]he member of the in-group looks in a single glance through the normal social situations occurring to him and ... he catches immediately the ready-made recipe appropriate to its solution. In those situations his acting shows all the marks of habituality, automatism and half-consciousness. This is possible because the cultural pattern provides by its recipes typical solutions for typical problems available for typical actors. (Schütz, 1944: 505)

As we shall see, installations are more than the cultural patterns in Schütz's sense, but Schütz's remark about automaticity and half-consciousness is essential.

Then, in making decisions, individuals sometimes operate some rational choice between the alternatives given to them. Economics, and especially microeconomics, tries to model these decisions with a rational *Homo economicus* who would attempt to maximize expected utility by computing and comparing the value of alternatives. There have even been attempts to force *every* decision into that rational framework; Gary Becker's 'expanded theory of individual choice' is an extreme example (G. S. Becker, 1996).

Recently, behavioural economics attempted to reintroduce the other aspects of *Homo sapiens* with a more realistic perspective than the *Homo economicus* model, and indeed closer to the projects of the founders of economics (Smith [1759] 1976); it studies the heuristics used by humans in such choices (e.g. Kahneman, 2011; Kahneman, Slovic, & Tversky, 1982).

The approach we take here is more social and cultural; it is complementary: we shall study how the choices presented to individuals in their everyday life are framed by society – so to say, upstream from behavioural economics, which studies the choices within these given frameworks. Looking in more detail at how humans behave in these socially framed settings, we will also be able to account for behaviours for which 'economic' calculation comparing expected utilities is not realistically applicable: how to behave at a dinner, while driving, at the dentist, etc. As we shall see, in many situations the choices left to the subject are quite limited.

Installations are not a marginal phenomenon: in large-scale societies, as mentioned earlier, we spend most of our life in these systems that make our behaviour so amazingly predictable. Sometimes, as with the example of air travel, we are simply chaining sequences of action in successive installations. Often the succession is less automatic and leaves more space for personal initiative: the Bedroom, the Bathroom, the Kitchen, the Street, the Bus, the Elevator, the Office, the Cafeteria, the Meeting Room, etc. are all installations that frame successive episodes in one's workday, but the actor has some leeway; for example, one might ride a Bicycle instead of the Bus, or walk up the Stairs instead of taking the Elevator. Nevertheless, in each installation, the behaviour will be predictable, at least in broad terms.

The freedom to use installations differently has some limits. In prisons, in hospital traumatology departments, in some mental institutions, one will meet people who encountered problems in attempting, willingly or not, to behave a bit too far outside of the path of culturally appropriate behaviour. For example, not following the appropriate behaviour in road traffic may soon lead one to a hospital ward or jail – installations in which, by the way, participants' behaviour is then especially restricted.

Society works because everyone plays their role. This seems so natural to us that it goes without saying; but it does not happen by chance. That people know what to do in every mundane circumstance, that they are actually able to do it and that the context affords and supports it – all that is the result of massive preparation by society, of an 'installation' of these behaviours.

In many aspects, we are here dealing with what is the nature of 'Culture' and 'Society'; these structured and quasi-stable ways of locally organizing the interactions of humans with their environment (including other humans). Of course, there are major cultural differences between different societies, and within 'one' society there are many different subcultures. Installations will naturally, by construction, differ substantially in form and content across culture and history, just as the style of houses changes in different areas, but the generic principles of their construction and operation are assumed to remain similar.[5]

In this field of research we can find monuments of science: 'capital-T' Theories that stand as landmarks to account for behaviour, socialization, social thought, cultural practice or social construction. Among many prominent authors, think of the works of Durkheim, Dewey, Piaget, Lewin, Parsons, Mead, Schütz, Moscovici, Bourdieu, Berger and Luckmann, Goffman, Bateson, Bruner, Geertz, Vygotsky, Giddens, Tomasello, Morin

---

[5] Nevertheless, this theory has been constructed from observations, experiments and interventions in large-scale industrial societies only; its validity in small-scale societies remains untested.

or Latour.[6] And there are many others. The very multiplicity of these landmarks and the fact the reader will probably be surprised not to find his or her own favourite on the aforementioned list[7] show the problem remains open, even though considerable progress has been made already.

We shall address the problem here with a different approach, from the other side of the mountain so to speak. Unlike some of the works cited in footnote 6, which often rely on generic, custom-built or anecdotal examples, we shall ground our analysis in a range of precise empirical material. And rather than relying on observations of individuals in the lab or on what they declare in interviews or questionnaires, we shall analyse actual *natural activity of humans in situation*, including the material, social and institutional context. In this approach, we follow the bottom-up, grounded path of microanalysis of situations (Cicourel, 1974; Hutchins, 1995a; Moles & Rohmer, 1976) rather than adopting the overarching spirit of philosophical inquiry, or using the aggregate perspective of statistics, or building on secondary analysis of literature. What encouraged me to venture on such an ambitious endeavour, and after so many intimidating predecessors, on top of benefitting from their own work as scaffolding, is that I could use new techniques providing empirical material that is more detailed and solid than that available to many colleagues.

Indeed, the analytic work mobilized a powerful data-collection technique, subjective evidence-based ethnography (SEBE). SEBE uses first-person perspective recording with body-worn video by the actors themselves, showing how they live their lives as usual, and then in-depth interviews with the participants while reviewing these recordings ('replay interviews'). So first we can see (and hear) the actual action from the situated perspective of the subjects, in faithful detail. Then we can later investigate what they thought in the moment as they re-enact it mentally, with their episodic memory powerfully cued by the recordings of their action from their very own perspective. This gives us, at last, a proper access to what people think as they act in real-world situations, an indispensable condition for analysing properly the determinants of action.[8]

The SEBE technique, described in Section 2.2, provides greater precision in the analysis of activity in natural settings. It is for social scientists

[6] Bateson, 1972; Berger & Luckmann, 1966; Bourdieu, [1972] 2013; Bruner, 1990; Dewey. 1929; Geertz, 1973; Giddens, 1984; Goffman, 1974; Latour, 2013; Lewin, 1948; Mead, [1934] 1972; Morin, 2008; Moscovici, 1961; Parsons, 1954; Piaget, 1926; Schütz, 1976a; Tomasello, 1999; Vygotsky, 1978.
[7] For example, what about Tylor, Weber, Simmel, Marx, Leroi-Gourhan, Huxley, Jonas, or Elias?
[8] That is a dream that psychology abandoned more than a century ago because of the difficulties of getting accurate and reliable data with classic introspection techniques (Wundt, 1912,149–151).

the equivalent of what the microscope was for biologists when it was invented: a tool giving the possibility to explore phenomena in microscopic detail. This vivid, reliable and extremely fine-grained material sheds new light on old issues and enables a step forward to be taken.

The empirical data were collected over two decades and include hundreds of hours of video recordings of natural activity in homes, public places, workplaces, industrial plants, hospitals, training facilities, restaurants and shops,[9] and also from a large industry intervention, for which we constructed a whole building specially designed for natural experiments and observation; we continuously recorded, for ten years, employees living and doing their normal work and also testing and adapting to new devices or systems (Lahlou, Nosulenko, & Samoylenko, 2002, 2012).

*The argument that will be developed based on these data is as follows: societies funnel their members into specific, expectable behaviours with local 'installations', specific scaffolding and regulation systems that assemble, in context, components distributed at physical, psychological and social levels. These entities bundle into behavioural attractors whose result are standardized and satisficing sequences of behaviour. Although installations do not determine the detail of the inner psychological experience of subjects and leave them some freedom to act differently, they regulate their behaviour, and in doing so they ensure the smooth operation of society and cooperative coexistence. So installations are local systems that scaffold and regulate behaviour.* The existence of such systems has been described in theory (Giddens, 1984, for instance); here is now their description in practice.

*Furthermore, it will be argued that installations do not only channel behaviour; they are also essential in the reproduction of society and culture because they are the very devices by which culture is reproduced through practice. The resilience of installations, coming from their redundant threefold structure, is key in socializing novices, who find themselves induced into the correct practice and therefore learn how to behave while doing so.*

We shall examine how the installations endure (interestingly, practice contributes to their reproduction), how their construction reflects power

---

Neuroimagery is now another attempt to do the same, but the technical limitations currently exclude capture of real-world activity.

[9] Examples are policing (Phelps, Strype, Le Bellu, Lahlou, & Aandal, 2016; Rieken, 2013), consumer decision-making (Gobbo, 2015), nuclear plant piloting (Fauquet-Alekhine, 2016a, 2016b), coming home (Cordelois, 2010), industrial maintenance (Le Bellu, 2011), family education (Lahlou, Le Bellu, et al., 2015), etc.

struggles and compromises of interests, how they evolve spontaneously and how their evolution can be channelled by deliberate design.

An idea that will be developed is that societies do not reproduce by block, but rather piecemeal, by the local reproduction of installations, which are in practice the elemental reproduction units. To take a metaphor, society does not reproduce as a whole organism, it reproduces cell by cell. Installations are these cells, or at least some of them – those that reproduce 'normal' behaviour. Installations are therefore functional *and* reproduction units of culture and society. We will get into the detail of these cells and their reproduction.

**The overall picture of a society that emerges is therefore, rather than a monolithic structure, myriad local functional systems of scaffolding and regulation, overlapping, nested, often replicated from one another, but still with some degree of local independence.**

**This theoretical framework has been designed with real-world intervention in mind.** Installation theory is intended as a tool for those who want to change the world into a better place, or more modestly to manage in a sustainable way some parts of the world: organizations, territories, big or small. It aims to provide change agents with a pragmatic tool to empower subjects for specific activities, or conversely to control or avoid certain behaviours. The framework should also help academics engaged in real-world analysis and intervention.

In our troubled times, where unsustainable human behaviours are driving our societies towards collapse, it is of paramount importance to understand why people behave the way they do, and how they can be funnelled into performing a different type of behaviour, e.g. to help fill the intention-behaviour gap. Another world is possible, but a better world will emerge only if we seriously work on modifying our behaviour, and this requires robust analytic tools to guide intervention. Governments are aware of the issues, so behavioural change units and policies for nudging are being created in various places; a lot of good work has been done, but so far we are somewhat lacking a systematic theoretical backbone; a lot more work is necessary. I hope this theory will contribute to the endeavour of creating a theory for 'nudging' (see Glossary).

This framework is new as a synthesis, but it builds on many previous works by scholars from various disciplines, of which the main ones are also presented in the book (Chapter 3). Some of these works come from very different philosophical and empirical filiations, as well as from different sociohistoric and disciplinary backgrounds. The final result is composite and has its own autonomous logic and structure based on this new unit of unit of analysis: the *installation*.

The claim of this theory is that it is applicable to real-world settings where 'everything interacts with everything else' and allows for a breaking down of their complexity into simpler units tractable for analysis and intervention. It claims robustness rather than elegance. With it, when we analyse the determinants of a given activity, we can sort out what is relevant from what is not in the forest of potential variables, tell the wood from the trees and grasp concrete handles for intervention.

## 1.1. In Society, Individual Behaviour Appears Standardized and Predictable in Many Situations

The notion of *installation* addresses the same phenomenon as the notions of 'behaviour setting' (Barker, 1968), 'frame' (Goffman, 1974) or 'dispositif' (device) used by Foucault (Foucault, 1975); namely, that some socially constructed device induces individuals into performing specific and predictable behaviour. It is in a direct line with Kurt Lewin's field theory and dynamic psychology, which states that a person immersed in a given environment will experience a field of psychological forces that will drive the person's actions, these forces being mediated by the way that specific person interprets the situation (Lewin, 1935, 1936). Some of the many theories addressing that issue –e.g. scripts (Schank & Abelson, 1977), or the theory of reasoned action (Ajzen & Fishbein, 1980)– will be discussed in Chapters 3 and 4. But although the phenomena are well identified, the current theories are not handy for interventions to modify behaviour.

It is obvious to anyone who has ever participated in a Religious Worship Service, a Basketball Game or an Award Ceremony (examples of behavioural settings given by Barker) that behaviour in such circumstances is usually predictable and limited to a narrow range of possibilities. Even though, in the detail, variants and combinations are infinite, the envelope is strict. Of course there can be exceptions, but in general people don't play ball during religious services or award ceremonies; the rules of basketball remain the same match after match.

In a given setting (say, a Bus Stop, a Court Session, a Chiropractor's Office) different people will behave in the *same manner* (with minor variations) whatever their age, gender, social class, religious or political opinion, personality factors, personal history, etc.

Conversely, a given person's behaviour will vary *according to the settings* (e.g. at the Dentist's or at a Funeral) in a predictable manner. Rather than depending on the person's individual characteristics, the person's behaviour will be dictated by the situation's standing programme, and in that situation by the role endorsed (e.g. dentist vs patient).

To state it simply: *the power of such structures locally supersedes all classic psychological or sociological variables.*

This does not mean classic variables are useless. The faithful will go to religious offices, atheists more rarely. But once in a religious office the participant (even the occasional atheist) will be caught in a behavioural attractor. Indeed, in the detail, some individual dispositions will affect the style of behaviour. But the pattern of the overall behaviour in installations remains predictable. Such guidance by the context is especially the case for habitual behaviours.

As stated above, this idea is not new, and Roger Barker's work demonstrates how prominent such formatting settings are in our daily lives. In his monumental study of a small Midwest town in the United States, Barker minutely recorded for decades the behaviour of all inhabitants, thereby providing us solid statistics about mundane behaviours. For example, Barker counted (Barker, 1968: 129) that in one year the 830 inhabitants spent 1,125,134 hours in the 884 *public* 'behavior settings' of the town, which amounts to an average of 3 hours and 45 minutes per day and per inhabitant.

This includes, for example: 1,984 hours in Bus Stops; 544,449 hours in Latin Classes; 1,356 hours in Moving Pictures Shows; 26,435 in Religious Worship Services; 443 hours in Telephone Booths; 1,489 in Volleyball Games; 974 hours in church Weddings and 21 hours in civil Weddings. These figures are aggregated by type ('genotype') of setting: the 884 behaviour settings fall into 220 genotypes (e.g. there are in the town several occurrences of the genotypes Beauty Parlour and Auction Sales).

While it is difficult to appreciate the extent to which Barker's survey is exhaustive, and the amount of time spent in behaviour settings that are not public (for example, activities at home or alone at work were not counted), Barker's count shows that channelled behaviour in such constructed settings accounts for a substantial amount of our waking social life – probably the largest part. Understanding how such installations work, and how to design and change them, is therefore of paramount importance for those interested in improving the way we live.

Unfortunately, Barker's theory came with a taxonomic approach that limited its applicability, as we shall see shortly. Additionally, it was designed for description rather than for intervention and change management, which are purposes of this book. Because of this focus on intervention, installation theory is less descriptive and more functionalist than most previous theories, including Barker's. What is lost in taxonomic capacity and formalism is gained in flexibility and usability in the field: practitioners cannot always apply a strict and cumbersome formalism.

There are some important differences between 'installations' and 'behavioural settings'. Both distinguish between individual and context, but installations extend across that border: the individual subject is considered part and parcel of the installation, and contributes to it with their own agency. For example, 'a Restaurant' or 'a Family Dinner' are 'installations' for eating; each induces and supports specific eating scripts, but the participants are an *essential* part of them, they are actors and not just users.

In the literature, the sociological and psychological notions of *norms* also address the social aspects of the process of behavioural channelling that we study here. The notion of *habit* and its variants describing embodied dispositions (habitus, attitudes, etc.) address some psychological aspects of the process. But norms are only one of the layers of societal control (and, as we shall see in Section 4.4, only a part of that layer). While the notion of the norm is very relevant for our problem, it misses a crucial aspect of the process of producing normal behaviour, the role of material artefacts. The same goes for habits: although they are considered to be embodied in humans, they occur only in specific contexts – characteristics that are outside the individuals – and so habits can hardly be defined independently of the settings in which they occur. Furthermore, the notions of context and dispositions alone cannot account for behaviours; as we shall see, there is a third layer: institutions.

The incompleteness of psychological theories that focus on a single locus of control of behaviour (e.g. attitudes, social norms) partly accounts for the very slow progress in understanding how our society works. On the practical side, it accounts for the accent being placed mainly on creating new norms, by law or education, in our efforts to change society. In this respect, such a classic vision, because it misses a crucial dimension,[10] can be just as toxic as the incomplete neoclassic economic theories when they directly inform political action.

---

[10] Of course, the resources that practitioners have can vary; they may not be able to address all the relevant dimensions, and have to make do with what they have, or wait indefinitely to make all the changes until conditions are favourable. But often some dimensions are not even considered because they are not in the theories in use.

## 1.2.   An Example: Road Traffic, Showing How the Three Layers of Behavioural Determination Operate as a Single Regulation System

While installations have a functional coherence and are a deliberate production of societies, they are *distributed* in their nature and the three layers assemble only at the point of delivery of activity, just as ingredients assemble and react as in a predictable manner in a chemical reaction. The structure of installations as described by this theory is somewhat unusual in social science. It combines material (physical) components with immaterial ones, and these components are distributed over ontologically different support layers. Therefore, its study must cross disciplines; this might be another reason why installations have never been studied systematically (if we except Barker), although they are ubiquitous. To understand how installations work we must think differently from the classic subject/environment divide. The example that follows – the Urban Street – will clarify.

When I manage to cycle in heavy traffic, it is the emergent result of simultaneously using the affordances of the road, of mobilizing embodied skills and of being protected by the traffic rules that prevent cars from driving me off the road. Society has constructed the built environment (the road), trained me to embody skills (cycling, reading traffic signs) and created control institutions (police, rules of the road). Individually, none of these layers produces traffic: when I am at home reading, I still carry with me, embodied, the competence of cycling, although it is not relevant nor operant *then*.

But these three layers *when assembled locally* become an installation that produces 'traffic'. Then, on one hand, these three layers guide and scaffold my own individual behaviour, enabling me to reach my goal destination safely. On the other hand, they make me a predictable road user to others, so we finally all together co-construct a 'normal' traffic flow at societal level. The same mechanism that 'nudges' and empowers me as an individual actor is also a mechanism of control of the traffic at an aggregate, collective, level. In fact, nudge is not a strong enough word; it would be more appropriate to say that I am 'channelled'.

The Urban Street is an installation; this installation is not located within the physical world only or inside my nervous system alone; it is *distributed* in the built environment, in educated and disciplined bodies, in institutions and their enforcing agents. It is so in a systematic and intentional way. It is only when these components assemble in situ (me in the traffic) that they emerge as a coherent empowering, nudging and controlling set-up that funnels my behaviour by adequately pulling the strings of my psychological mechanisms.

So the three layers are linked in one single functional and intentional perspective: producing a correct behaviour. Obviously, the different layers (roads and vehicles, driving competences, rules of the road) did evolve as a single bundle, each informing the other in a gradual historical evolution. None makes sense in the absence of the others.

The composite nature of the installation, spanning across individual and context, may appear a bit destabilizing to the reader. We humans have a natural tendency to consider as an entity *something that 'goes together'* in space. For example, solid objects (a chair, a car), or a geographic area (a room) or a set moving together (a crowd, a suit). We acknowledge the existence of entities that move together spatial and material components (e.g. a person with body and mind, a society with people and culture, an organization with assets and rules), but that makes us uncomfortable in epistemic terms when we have to relate their components (e.g. body/ mind) because they belong to different epistemic systems. An installation is an even stranger entity because it assembles only intermittently, when in operation, and also because it coalesces components of a very different nature in three realms: material, embodied and social. These components refer to different ontological domains: matter, interpretation and relation. But while this may appear as a problem in theory, it is not in practice: common sense considers as coherent entities such strange epistemic compounds as 'a Town', 'an Automobile Race' and 'a Dinner'.

The components, as said above, assemble at the point of action, and that makes description difficult. Most of the time the installation is in a *potential* state, and only at the point of delivery, which is where the actor acts, does the installation coalesce and unfold as such. Take the metaphor of a player driving a car in a video game. The road that guides the player continuously unfolds on the screen before the player, but it is continuously created as a path only by the presence of the player himself at that point. If the player takes a turn at some junction, a road will still unfold before him as he progresses. Still these roads are not the result of the player's sole fantasy or decision: they guide the player, they bring in events and tasks to be done; if the player drives off the road he is eliminated. The road is created as a path for the player by the system, but it is locally adapted to the player's situation as a mechanical result of his position and actions. Like the installation, the video game road exists all the time potentially as components, but it is constructed as 'real' only at the point of delivery, as a stage for the player's activity. I use the video game as a metaphor to show

how installations are emerging where the subject *is*, because the subject is an essential component of installations. But such video games were created with our world as a model so the resemblance is perhaps not fortuitous. Think of the earlier example of the cyclist in traffic.

In fact, more and more of the settings that we live in, and the installations thereof, are digital, and in the future it is likely that the video game type of installation I just described will be more than an illustration and a game, but rather the standard type of setting in which we live our lives. This makes little change for installation theory: the affordances will simply be digital. But for the sake of simplicity and demonstration, most examples in this book will use material settings.

So, on one hand our society's installations appear to us, natives of our culture, as natural common-sense units (a Street, a Conference, a Shop) and we all know how to act in them; on the other hand when we want to examine them in more detail we realize their ontological structure and the way they operate are not so easy to analyse with our usual scientific frameworks and notions.

The installation is a functional unit. What gives it its meaning and unity is the activity it supports; that activity matches (in principle) the goals of its participants. The installation assembles the various components that are needed to perform the activity;[11] it does so with guidance and control mechanisms that enable and ensure correct articulation and sequencing of components. Again, not everything is an installation: when I walk in the woods, I am not in an installation.[12] But in urban life, where society cannot afford for individuals to behave erratically, installations are ubiquitous.

We are not interested here in unusual events and strange experiments; rather, we address the bulk of day-to-day life, the mechanisms that create and maintain the 'normal' operation of organizations and societies, the smooth running of everyday life: how our daily life is constructed and organized, how we manage to make some behaviours so natural that we perform them without even thinking in the 'channelled state' described earlier. A good society, a sustainable organization, are not made of continuous turmoil and invention; rather, they are a flow of millions of seemingly effortless and natural small actions that appear almost miraculously

---

[11] And that is why participants come, and participate willingly, into installations: to perform a given activity.

[12] Some of my students object that the Woods can be considered installations for hunting. I would not go that far.

compatible, coordinated and expected. That is no small achievement and of course it does not happen by chance.

Installations can be massively efficient: in 2012, there were respectively 5 and 6.5 fatalities per *billion* vehicle-kilometre in Germany and France (OECD/ITF, 2014: 22). Even with a high estimation of 60 km/h as an average driving speed, this would mean a fatal accident occurs only every 2 million hours of driving. In other words, someone who spends her life driving, every day and for 8 hours per day, would statistically have a fatal accident only every 1,100 years, the equivalent of going 7,700 times round the Earth. Not even our best-built machines can claim such dependability. Such is the scale of installations' control power and efficiency.

I will attempt to put their mechanisms in a clear light to explain *how, in practice,* societies provide typical solutions to typical problems.

I know that is already a bold claim. In fact, I claim even more:

### 1.3.  The Research Questions: How Do Individuals Choose Their Behavioural Path in a Situation? How Does Society Regulate the Behaviour of Its Members?

Installation theory is ambitious because it addresses a phenomenon that simultaneously clarifies two grand questions, sociological and psychological:

- *How, in practice, is the continuous predictability and efficient control of the behaviour of millions of individuals constructed, which in turn is necessary for smooth operation of societies?*
- *How can individual humans make sense on the fly of the rich, ambiguous and complex environments of society and take appropriate action (keeping in mind humans are cognitive misers)?*

Both problems (operation and evolution of societies; determinants of individual behaviour) have long been studied; the more they are studied the more complex they appear. Because these questions also include a dynamic question: How do societies manage to function even though they continuously change? Not only does the boat stay afloat, but it does so while changing shape.

In a nutshell, these are the core questions of the disciplines of sociology, psychology and anthropology; they should also be core questions for economics and political science. Therefore, if daring to address *one* of these questions can be considered pretentious, claiming to build a theory that addresses *both* may appear naïve – or worse.

I did not expect to address such grand questions, but it turns out that installations link them symmetrically. *These two questions are easier to deal with together than separately, as each one enlightens the other because they are two sides of the same coin.*

Indeed, if we think of road traffic, it is obvious that both problems (individual driver behaviour and global traffic) evolved together. Their form, as well as the implements society constructed, constitutes one single fabric. Rules of the road and driver behaviour are not independent, they must be considered as a bundle because one explains the other and vice versa.

In other words, this book ventures to propose a single theoretical framework for how individual behaviour is linked to societal construction. It describes the nature and function of structures that simultaneously support and socially regulate individual behaviour: 'installations'. And it attempts to do so in further realistic detail than previous approaches. Of course, the framework is connected to currents and theories that account for various aspects of the same problem: ecological psychology, activity theory, situated action, distributed cognition, social constructionism, niche construction, actor-network theory, social representations, and a few others. But although each of the aspects bundled here has, separately, been well described in the literature, each theory tends to overlook some aspects of the problem. In addition, one issue with general macrotheories[13] is that they often take as a scale of empirical study the society at large; this makes it impossible to study in detail the mechanisms of determination of action, which are by nature local. Installations are a unit of analysis at a smaller scale, where the mechanisms can be more easily unbundled.

Installation theory does not claim to be revolutionary, complete, exact or true; some parts are original, other parts simply weave existing theories together. Because it is grounded in real-world practice, the theory claims to be operational for practitioners faced with the pragmatic needs of understanding and bettering real-world systems, for those who design and run the installations (change agents, politicians, managers). What gives it its specific pragmatic value is the way it cuts the infinite complexity of reality into easily identifiable components upon which one can act, to tune the system or change it.

To support such interventions, we will explore how the principle of the natural evolution of installations can, to a certain extent, be harnessed to

---

[13] For example, Talcott Parsons' theory of the social system (Parsons [1951] 1964), introduces, to explain action, the interpenetration of three layers (cultural system, social system and personality) very similar to installations' layers.

produce deliberate change, and we will illustrate this with examples from product and service design, organizational change and public policies.

## 1.4.   This Book's Structure

Chapter 2, The Problem of Human Action and the Problem of Social Regulation: Two Sides of the Same Coin, provides a fresh perspective on the problem, one that sets the frame for the pieces of the jigsaw puzzle that are assembled in the book. *This chapter provides an overview of the theory.* **The hurried reader can read this chapter 2 and go directly for the summary of the theory in Chapter 9**.

Chapter 3, Theoretical Frameworks Grounding Installation Theory, briefly describes key theories that address our problem: ecological psychology, activity theory, social constructionism, distributed cognition and actor-network theory, social representations and shared mental models. The informed reader can skip that literature chapter and go straight to Chapter 4, where the detailed description of the new theory starts.

Chapter 4, The Structure of Installations, provides a model of installations and lays out their threefold structure. Behaviour is guided and controlled at three levels, each of which delineates 'possible' patterns for action in a situation. Appropriate behaviours are at the intersection of the three delineated zones. The model integrates the theories described in Chapter 3. It does not substitute former theories; rather, it situates them in a larger framework that clarifies which aspect of the problem each theory addresses best. Chapter 4 is full of examples.

Chapters 5, 6 and 7 address the evolution of installations.

Evolution is a combination of endurance (day-to-day reproduction) and change (modification in the longer-term). Chapter 5 addresses the first aspect (endurance), Chapters 6 and 7 the second (change).

Chapter 5, Endurance of Installations: The Reconstructive Cycle of Practice, describes the process of day-to-day reproduction of installations *without evolution*. It is essential to first understand the process of identical reconstruction to later understand the process of evolution. The mechanisms of regeneration and resilience described are essential tools for those who are interested in maintaining real-world systems – managers and politicians, for example.

Chapter 5 also shows in detail how, in installations, practice reproduces structure and vice versa. The picture that emerges unveils a solution that is at the scale of the problem – grand, and perhaps somewhat chilling in the degree of control it unveils.

Chapters 6 and 7 address the issue of the longer-term historical change and evolution of installations. The generation and selection of changes follow a process more sophisticated than the natural selection of biological species. This complex process, 'monitored dual selection', is faster, safer and more cumulative. In dual selection, objects are selected twice, in actual practice and in 'thought experiments', with the support of external (reified) representations. This dual selection is furthermore under the control of communities. This social construction process is described in detail and illustrated with examples.

Chapter 6, Selection Mechanisms in Societal Evolution: Two Cases—Science and Industry, provides concrete examples of innovation in science and industry to illustrate typical cases of mechanisms, which is described in Chapter 7. This section shows the importance of external representations and tools in cumulative evolution.

Chapter 7, The Evolution of Installations, provides a general model for the evolution of installations, layer by layer, and the mechanisms of evolution that go across layers (drift, crossed-impact, innovation). The regulating role of institutions is explained and the function of external representations is specified.

These 'natural' mechanisms can be, to some extent, harnessed by managers and change agents to maintain or change installations.

Chapter 8, Redesigning Installations to Change Behaviour, is more applicative and addresses the 'how-to' question with four examples illustrating how installation theory can inform change in management, consumer science, design and policies. These are *illustrations*. As a note to the hurried reader, this chapter alone is not enough to grasp the theory and how-to; you need to read more of the book.

Chapter 9, Conclusion, is a summary of installation theory and includes some comments on how to use it.

CHAPTER 2

# The Problem of Human Action and the Problem of Social Regulation
## Two Sides of the Same Coin

**This chapter provides an overview of installation theory.**

**It explains why simultaneously addressing the two big questions we tackle (regulation of societies, determination of individual behaviour) is easier than considering them separately.**

**It then describes the type of data in which the theory is grounded: first-person video recordings of activity in a real context, obtained through miniature video cameras worn by the subject, and in-depth introspective discussions about what happened while re-viewing the tapes with the participants themselves.**

**In using this technique we benefit from microscopic detail in the analysis of behaviour in real-world situations.**

The daily operation of a city relies on a complex organization in which each participant must play their role in due time and place, in a predictable manner. The failure of individuals to perform 'as expected' incurs costs, and possibly provokes catastrophes. A single car accident usually creates a traffic jam, and automobile traffic is just one example among thousands of systems that must run smoothly and continuously: energy, telecommunications, kindergarten and more – generally every production and service.

Societies are thus confronted with the problem of keeping the behaviour of thousands, sometimes even millions, of humans predictable and within limits of what is considered acceptable. That is no trivial endeavour. The human body and psyche, which have remained the same as they were tens of thousands of years ago, were selected for a life in very different conditions: small-scale societies of hunter-gatherers. Humans, like other primates, tend to be emotional, selfish, aggressive, easily distracted and cognitively limited: refer, for example, to the reduced size of our working memory – about seven items (Miller, 1956), or our inattentional blindness – we don't notice what we don't expect to see (Mack & Rock, 1988), etc.

In practice, as we noted earlier with traffic statistics, accidents appear amazingly rare considering that a single moment of inattention or wrong behaviour could provoke one (think, again, of driving – but also of chemical plants or hospitals). *How do societies, in practice, manage such a continuous and efficient control of millions with often conflicting interests?* That is our first research question.

Conversely, individuals are confronted with an arduous problem: they must continuously react properly, and immediately, to a complex environment. The difficulty of producing robots capable of doing what humans do easily every day illustrates how complex that problem is. Every second, each of our fellow humans must be able to interpret the environment on the fly and take appropriate action. Consider again the example of traffic: drivers – and cyclists even more so – must continuously make micro-decisions that may each have serious consequences, possibly life or death ones. What enables me to perform the proper behaviour, in synchrony with other stakeholders of the situations? The flow of traffic is ever different, it requires an ever-different situated and adapted reaction. To paraphrase Heraclitus, 'No-one ever exactly steps in the same situation twice'. If everything flows, how do we manage to perform adequately in ever-different situations? *How can humans make sense on the fly of rich, ambiguous and complex environments and take appropriate action?* That is the second question we shall consider here.

As suggested in the Introduction, these two questions are connected; in fact, they are two sides of the same coin: the socialized human in a culture.

As for many important phenomena, a wealth of concepts and theories have been proposed in the literature, e.g. 'affordances', 'disciplining institutions', 'settings', 'frames', 'structures', 'habits', 'structuration', 'socialization', 'dispositifs', 'assemblages', 'environments', 'mediating structures', 'niches', 'infrastructure', 'channels', 'codes', 'norms', 'dispositions', 'habitus' and so forth. We shall use elements of this toolbox.

We shall assemble them in a single framework constituted of three layers: *the material environment (the physical space), embodied[1] competences and*

---

[1] I use 'embodied' in the simple sense that these competences have been incorporated by the subjects (e.g. how to ride a bicycle). They are not abstract concepts; they are inscribed in the flesh and emerge as cognitions, emotions and movements. I wanted to include what is mental as well as what is physical; this does not mean that I take position in the heated discussions about embodiment and the mind-body problem, e.g. between emergentists and representationalists. I simply did not want to invent another term when there are already so many. I am concerned here with an empirical

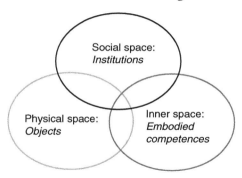

Figure 2.1. Sustainable behaviours are the ones supported by the three layers of the installation, in a zone here represented as the intersection of the three ovals.

*social regulation.*[2] Each layer contributes to the determination of the behaviour; nevertheless, each layer alone leaves considerable degrees of freedom and therefore is an incomplete explanation of behaviour. But when the layers operate concurrently, as the degrees of freedom they leave are not in the same directions, their combination leaves only a small tunnel of possibilities for the subject. This results in predictable behaviours. Most theories address only one or two of these layers; installation theory considers them together.

Figure 2.1 provides a simple illustration: each oval represents the possibilities for behaviour left open to the subject by a given layer. As the three layers operate concurrently, the array of possibilities left to the subject is reduced to the intersection of these three ovals; it can become very small, often limited to a single behavioural path with minor variations allowed.

For example, a while ago I went to Dr Kovarski's dental clinic to get a filling. The *material environment* (the dentist's chair and its headrest) restricted my movements. My *embodied competences* (of my role as a compliant patient) made me restrict my limb movements even more and stay still and silent even in the few moments I felt pain. Finally, the social regulation of the dentist's orders ('open your mouth', 'spit', 'let me know if you feel any pain', etc.) guided my behaviour in detail regarding what I was still allowed to move (my head, face and mouth) so that I could play my role properly in the process. Had any of these layers been missing, the dentist

approach rather than epistemic discussions. For further detail on the use of embodiment in cognitive science and enactivism see Section 5.2.3.

[2] These layers are of a different epistemological nature, which is somewhat unusual in a single theory framework. We deal with this later, especially in footnote 37 and in Section 4.4.4)

could not have played his role and the whole session would have failed. Seen from a larger perspective that includes the whole installation (the chair, the dentist, the patient, the instruments, etc.) we see that the various layers operated in combination to produce a specific outcome (tooth filled, thank you Dr Kovarski).

The dentist is also constrained and guided by the three layers. The embodied competences he mobilizes are different, he uses different parts of the material environment (e.g. the X-ray machine) and for him I am part of the social layer, guiding his actions with my oral responses and other signals. This remains the same installation: e.g. I am aware of the rules he follows, I expect him to embody the right skills, and the drill he uses is the same that I feel on my tooth. For me as a patient, Dr Kovarski is another component of the installation, just as for him as a dentist I am a component of his installation. Agency is distributed; the relevant unit of analysis for what happens here is the Dental Clinic. Take away one single component (patient, dentist, drill, know-how) and the tooth-filling operation cannot happen. Dr Kovarski and I happen to be long-time friends, but that has only a minor influence in that specific technical process where we play our parts as components of the Dental Clinic installation.

*Mutatis mutandis*, other installations (the Religious Worship Service, the Basketball Game, or the Award Ceremony) will restrict my degrees of freedom to some behaviours only, each installation within its own specific and predictable repertoire. The channelling operates through specificities of the material environment, of the situated tuning of my own psychological processes and, finally, of local social regulation. As one can see, the installation assembles as a complete functional unit only at the point of delivery, when the actors come into it. Without the participants who bring in their body and embodied competences, and who provide feedback during action, the process would not happen: no Basketball Game without players.

Because the installation is distributed over three layers, its boundaries are necessarily fuzzy in any projection (e.g. in space, in time, in knowledge, in law). But the installation is not a scientific construct of the researcher; it is a 'natural' unit for behaviour. Common sense recognizes the existence of the installation as a functional entity and gives it a single name (e.g. Basketball Game).[3]

---

[3] Even though its exact boundaries are difficult to trace (does the Basketball Game start when the referee whistles, when the team comes on the field or when the public enters the stadium?) the installation is considered as a single unit by its users, by regulations, by commerce, etc. Just as it is functionally difficult to separate epistemically a single biological cell or organ from the tissue and

The actual extension of an installation does not immediately fit our intuition. For example, 'a Train' includes a railway network as well as the ticketing system; 'a Poll' includes laws, polling stations and citizens. To some degree, installations are nested, because an activity is constituted of smaller segments of activity: there can be as many smaller installations as there are subsegments of the larger activity: the Train Station, the Ticket Office, the Train Platform, the Voting Booth, etc. Each supports one segment of the larger activity. The scale of detail we consider depends on our purpose; if what we scientists consider an installation is not recognized as a natural behavioural setting by participants, it is probably a wrong unit of analysis. If the theory does not bring an interesting insight, the same: better use another theory to analyse the phenomenon.

The functional role of installations is the reason for their existence and endurance. They fulfil a societal need for the correct performance of a given behaviour (transport, governance, etc.) As long as their function is not supported by something more efficient, they will endure.[4] If another type of installation emerges that satisfices that function better, they will evolve.

## 2.1. The Three Layers of Determination of Human Behaviour

Installation theory combines three layers of determinants (material, embodied, social) that have so far been separated by the disciplinary approach, even though in practice they operate as a bundle. The various

organism it is embedded in and in which it is constructed, it is difficult to isolate completely an installation from its societal context. The fuzziness of the installation at its margins is actually the condition for its interactions with the rest of the social system; it interacts and intersects with the system in three dimensions. Simondon has clarified this issue with the notion of *individuation* as a process, where the resulting individual (object) is considered as an emerging solution to some necessity or incompleteness in a larger system, that process being inseparable from the form and nature of the individual (Simondon, [1958]2013). In our case, we must search for the principle of individuation of an installation in the behaviour that is the final cause of the installation and the reason for its existence, maintenance and evolution; as the traffic is for the road, healing is for the dental clinic or cooking for the kitchen. Such fuzziness may appear problematic to the purist or the philosopher in the formalization of a theory, but in practice it is not an obstacle to using the construct: for example, even if the exact limits of an organ (the stomach) in the body, or a part in an engine (the carburetor), are in theory not so clear-cut (e.g. should their definition include part of their command system?), the practitioners – surgeon, mechanic – are happy to use their approximate definition in their diagnoses and interventions.

4    I must make clear that 'efficiency' should be taken in the sense of satisfying in the psychological sense, and not as a functional optimization. Emotions, among other things, play an important role. For example, Paulius Yamin-Slotkus notes that when he was a student in Bogotá, although there was a shorter bus route to get to his university, he preferred, as most people did, to take a much longer route that didn't go through some of the rougher neighbourhoods, out of fear of being robbed. [Please note all the following examples about Colombia in this book, which provide an interesting intercultural contrast, were kindly given by Paulius].

components of an installation, which are carried by different substrata, emerge together as a functional unit only when they locally assemble in action. As a bundle they were gradually constructed, and only as a bundle can they be understood. Also, because they occur together only in situ, their interaction can be observed properly only during actual situated practice. That makes it difficult to study in a laboratory, so one has to get the data from the field.

As a bundle the layers occur in practice because they are linked by a series of mechanisms that will be detailed shortly. What is crucial to understand is that the unit of analysis will be the *installation*, not the individual subject, nor the 'context' nor the institution. This way of approaching things takes a while to sink in, because we are used to attributing agency to people, perhaps to objects or organizations, but not to such hybrid compounds.

I will show how installations have a momentum[5] of their own and enough resilience to funnel even noncompetent subjects into specific behaviours: they are foolproof. They are, as Giddens says of social structure, "both constraining and enabling" (Giddens, 1984: 25, 169, 177, 179). Most often, individuals will find themselves performing a specific behaviour without having taken a conscious or explicit decision to do so. Installations 'nudge' (Thaler & Sunstein, 2008) people below the radar of consciousness; and if that is not enough they *constrain* them. In this way, installations supersede the subject's individual will, not so much by force (even though they can do in some instances), but usually because they bypass the individual, conscious, reflexive decision-making system.[6] That is why installation theory can be considered a theory of nudging.

At a higher structural and symbolic level, Émile Durkheim noted the logical necessity for society to impose common categories of thought on its members to enable life in common (Durkheim, 1912: 29–30). There are what he called 'social facts': in these, it is the society as an entity that imposes some ways of thinking (and acting) on humans:

> Thus there are ways of acting, thinking and feeling which possess the remarkable property of existing outside the consciousness of the individual.

---

[5] By this I mean that once assembled, the installation results in a specific behaviour emerging spontaneously, as if some action potential were triggered: the installation operates as a behavioural attractor. Consider the metaphor of a chemical reaction taking place when reactants are combined.

[6] Kahneman, after Stanovich and West, called in pedagogic simplification 'system 1' the fast, associative process of thought in which we automatically match a situation to a response, and 'system 2' the slower and deliberative process we use in conscious decision-making (Kahneman, 2011; Stanovich & West, 2000). What we describe here is more a system 1 type of process.

Not only are these types of behaviour and thinking external to the individual, but they are endued with a compelling and coercive power by virtue of which, whether he wishes it or not, they impose themselves upon him. (Durkheim [1895] 1982: 51)

Durkheim's claim here is that society (rather than the individual mind) is the right level on which to search for the ultimate cause of such facts – and that is what makes sociology indispensable in the study of human behaviour. As he aptly noted, individuals themselves may be unconscious of that social determinism. Often indeed, that determinism is not exerted by immediately visible external forces, so sociology must unveil them. It has been argued that the mediation happens through the internalization by the individual of the value systems, representations, and rules – a form of alienation; and there is evidence for this. That is the socialization process. But how does such internalization occur?

There has been considerable debate over the mechanisms that produce this shared order in society, a heated debate, of which Mary Douglas (M. T. Douglas, 1986) provides an interesting historical account by showing how the ideas of Durkheim and Fleck (Fleck [1935] 1979) met strong resistance, especially from the tenants of a liberal view and of rational, self-interest–driven behaviour. Indeed, in society individuals are led to behave in a cooperative way that may be inconsistent with their own personal interests: they do accept the constraints imposed by society. This old discussion chimes with the notions of social contract (Rousseau, 1796), voluntary servitude (La Boétie [1575] 1993),[7] Hobbes' commonwealth (Hobbes, 1651) or liberty (Mill [1859]1999). That debate is heated perhaps because we, as individuals, do not like to be reminded that our free will is not so free, but rather determined by a series of conventions we absorbed naturally during our education. The issue of free will inevitably comes to the fore when I discuss my findings with colleagues (agency vs structure, autonomy vs socialization). We all, as individuals, share a natural and spontaneous rejection of constraints, and many of us are rebels inside to some degree or at some moments;[8] we don't like to be controlled, not even the idea of being controlled. But we must face the facts and look objectively at the determinants of our activity. As Goethe's character Ottilie noted: 'No one is more a slave than he who thinks he is free without being so' (Goethe [1809] 2005: 133).

---

[7] The other title of La Boétie's 'Discourse on voluntary servitude' is 'le Contr'un' (against'one), which in French sounds like 'le contraint' (the constrained).
[8] Perhaps that is why so many people wear tattoos?

Psychology and anthropology, among other sciences, have vastly contributed to clarifying the debate: it is now clear that there are many processes by which children acquire the skills, language, attitudes and more generally the habitus and even food preferences[9] of their peers, carers, subculture and culture in which they live. This does not deny that there are biological universals on top of which culture is built. More about this in Section 5.2.

Installations contribute to socializing us, but do not suppress free will; they merely guide and control *behaviour*, which is the external, overt, manifestation of activity (see Glossary). When I drive my car, installations have little control over what I think or choose to listen on the radio, as long as I drive properly and respect the rules of the road. Perhaps commercials on the radio will try to influence what is left of my free will, but that is not a case in point. In their controlling aspect, installations seem to follow more or less the principle that 'my right to swing my fist ends where your nose begins': it is action in the real world that matters, because what a society minimally requires for its smooth operation is that people locally *behave* in a cooperative way, *however they feel about it*. Of course, the leeway left to each individual will depend upon power struggles and one's position in society: some can swing their arms more than others. This aspect will be discussed in Chapters 4–7.

I was not very happy myself to realize, through detailed analysis of daily behaviour, the degree to which we are alienated by society in the way we act. Yes we are creatures of free will; that is precisely why there are installations: to channel the behaviour of creatures of free will. Life in society comes with limitations on free will; there is a trade-off. We are all well aware of the role of law in the regulation of behaviour. But laws are only part of one of the three layers of regulation of behaviour. These layers are at the same time limiting and empowering. The coin of alienation has two sides: one is control but the other is empowerment.

We shall have a fresh view on the problem because we start from empirical data collected at the point of delivery of behaviour, with a new investigation technique. Unsurprisingly, empirical evidence will confirm most of what the literature already contains. Unfortunately, it will demonstrate how behaviours are perhaps even more socially determined than has been suspected before. Happily, it will shed some light on how the design process occurs and provide a few handles to curb it deliberately. In passing, we learn something new about the nature of social regulation, at which points

---

[9] Birch, 1999.

it happens, and its nature. What is unveiled is a construct of a hybrid ontological type, the installation, a composite that operates simultaneously in
three different epistemic dimensions. This bizarre nature accounts for the
fact that such a construct, which projects poorly in our classic categories,
has remained so far elusive despite being ubiquitous, as I suggested in the
Introduction.

An installation is a behavioural attractor, some kind of *cognitive trap*
which, once entered, results in the subject feeling and behaving in a specific way. Part of the cognitive trap resides in the subject herself.[10] Being in
an installation switches on the individual into a specific mode and mindset, priming some competences and interpretive frameworks over others.

One may wonder why individuals comply, why they engage voluntarily
in installations that are so obviously constraining devices. The answer is
simple: at the moment we enter the installation we are motivated to get a
result. We want to get a toothache fixed, so we sit in the dentist's chair; we
need to go somewhere, so we stand calmly in the crowded bus; and so on
and so forth. So, in the moment and for the purpose that motivates us, we
accept the constraints of that specific installation, we implicitly acknowledge a social contract. But then the long run is mostly made up of linking
small such channelled segments of behaviour and we end up behaving in a
socially controlled way for most of our time in public spaces.

In an installation, action is distributed. For example, in the activity of
preparing breakfast at home, we observe on a Sunday morning that in
that specific French family,[11] as Mother sets the table, Father tells Son to
go and buy Croissants, Coffee Machine brews Coffee, Bottle contains the
Orange Juice, Alarm Clock wakes up the Daughter, etc. As we can see,
some components exert action in a passive way (Bottle containing Orange
Juice); some are active, but merely mechanically relay reified human intentions (Alarm Clock, Thermostat); some are conscious and act with a clear
and defined purpose (Mother setting up the table); some act with a goal
that is not their own (Son); some control others' behaviour (Father giving
instructions to Son), etc.

If we consider the installation from the perspective of one specific
human participant, we realize that their own behaviour is continuously
guided by myriad components and feedback from the rest of the setting.

[10] This is a general feature of traps. For example, consider a mouse trap: the drive of the mouse for the
cheese that serves as bait and the mouse's movements are an essential part of the device's design and
operation.
[11] This family follows one of the standard French models of 'breakfast' (Lahlou et al., 1995).

For example, Mother will set up the table according to what is the local family breakfast institution (that is the set of behaviours that are locally the rule in this specific community for that type of situation): she knows that Daughter usually sits at this specific seat and that she takes cereals; but that Father sits at the opposite seat and drinks coffee, therefore she will put a bowl here and a mug there. When Daughter and Father come to sit, they will naturally take their usual preferred food and drink, and the table is installed for that. And in doing so, they reinforce their existing habits, thereby comforting Mother into setting the table in a similar fashion the next day.

The development of action in that scene relies on a series of minute feedforward and feedback loops.[12] Participants anticipate certain response from the installation, and the satisfaction of anticipations relies on the fact that the set-up and the other actants – humans and objects – indeed provide the appropriate conditions and fit. When one knows how long it takes to rehearse a theatre play or a film scene to get the appropriate effect, one can measure the power of the mechanisms at work to install the proper décor, props, costumes and scripts that enable us to flawlessly link, in a 'normal' day, a continuous series of such scenes (at home, on transport, at work etc.), while hardly even thinking of what we do. We can do so only because the various settings in which we find ourselves as we navigate in our world scaffold and guide us in an efficient manner. The scene is set, we know our role. We are in the first status of the existence of individuals, which Dewey described as where an individual

> belongs in a continuous system of connected events which reinforce its activities and which form a world in which he is at home, consistently at one with its own preferences, satisfying its requirements. Such an individual is in its world as a member, extending as far as the moving equilibrium of which it is a part lends support. (Dewey, 1929: 245)

*A contrario*, think of how disoriented and puzzled we may find ourselves in unknown settings, in the other possible status of the individual 'at odds with its surroundings' (say, having breakfast for the first time with Inuits in their igloo), and how much we would then have to pay attention, to deliberate, to guess, to inquire, to experiment and to need help to behave appropriately.

---

[12]  These loops are not confirmation loops only; they can be corrective when necessary. Should Mother forget the bowl, then Daughter would probably make a corrective comment; should Mother try to hang the mug in the air above the table instead of putting it on the table, then the physical environment will remind her that this is not a correct place. The installation has built-in feedback capacity.

Now, think how often we find ourselves doing things we did not intend to do. This happens in our mundane life, such as when buying useless items in a supermarket. It is also true at work; e.g. processing our emails instead of doing what we had planned. A survey of 500 office workers in a large corporation showed that 49.9% of participants would fully agree or rather agree with the statement 'I cannot manage to do in the day what I had decided to do' (Lahlou, 2010a). That is because even though what participants had planned to do was a priori reasonably doable, the installation induced them to do other things.

Indeed, situations act as cognitive attractors (Lahlou, 2000), sometimes funnelling us like puppets into doing things beyond our will, although in such a subtle way that we cannot say we are being forced. And we are not completely aware of how this happens; we don't even remember clearly because that was done in autopilot mode. That is precisely what Schütz, cited in Chapter 1, described as 'habituality, automatism, and half-consciousness'. Indeed, 61.5% of the participants in the same office survey just cited agreed with the statement 'It happens to me that I come back home from work exhausted but wondering what I've been doing all day'. Perhaps that feeling is familiar to the reader too; I venture that it is the result of having being 'channelled' all along the day.

Installation theory has a family resemblance to many other previous 'capital-T' Theories. It is a new avatar of the grand Lewinian project of a field psychology (Lewin, 1935). Lewin's field theory pictured that behaviour results from a totality, a dynamic field, the situation in which the person is immersed. Its main equation is $B = f(P, E)$: Behaviour (B) is a function (f) of the person (P) and the environment (E). This environment of action, the internal motives and goals, combined with how the situation was perceived, produce a set of forces and internal tensions that the subject tries to resolve through action.

The spirit and intuitions of installation theory are similar, but the modelling differs. We benefit from eighty more years of progress in psychology and cognitive science.[13] Our current approach must be situated in line with

---

[13] It seems that the model Lewin was trying to set up in his 'topological psychology' was in fact what we now call dynamical systems, but that formalism was not readily available in 1935; it developed and became popular in the 1960s and 1970s. The state of a dynamical system can be represented by a point in an appropriate phase space (a geometrical manifold, also called state space). A function determines how future states follow from the current state; this function has for arguments the point coordinates and the time. Therefore, Lewin's approach was unfortunately hampered by a series of technical confusions; e.g. the term 'B' in his equation should rather be (P', E') – the 'next' state of the system – as the proper formalism must be a description of the successive states of *the whole system* in time, rather than of the successive states of the individual within the system.

societal psychology (Himmelweit & Gaskell, 1990; Howarth et al., 2013), a psychology that studies humans in their natural environment and includes in its scope the psychological influence of context, institutions and culture in general – a line started by Lewin himself.

Installations do not account for *all* human behaviour, nor for *the whole* society. Some of the mechanisms described are general, but the theory is designed to study (let us keep to this short definition for the moment) specific, local, societal settings where humans are expected to behave in a predictable way. Installations channel behaviour by offering users a limited choice of alternatives, limited by three layers of determinants at material, social and embodied level. These levels provide both feedforward and feedback.

That is not a theory of the context; it is a social-psychological theory because humans are part and parcel of the installations, given that one layer of installation is embodied.

We want to analyse the detail of the interaction between the various components and, in case of a problem, to identify immediately what layer is involved, for which section of the behaviour, why the problem occurs and eventually how to fix it. To do this, we need to follow step by step the activity in its natural setting, and to access the various layers for analysis.

That is precisely what subjective digital ethnography provides. The next section describes that technique and illustrates it with some examples.

## 2.2. Our Microscope: Subjective Evidence-Based Ethnography

*Behaviour* is what subjects do, as described from the outside by an external observer. It is an external description of 'objective' phenomena.[14]

*Activity* is what subjects do and how they make sense of it. It is goal-oriented, and it includes subjective experience of action: the action seen from the perspective of the subjects in their own 'phenomenological tunnels'. Activity includes the objective deeds of the subjects, but also their internal, 'covert' intentions, interpretive processes and thoughts.

To understand behaviour or activity, of course we should capture the context in which subjects act and to which they react. When we are interested in *activity*, we must capture both what subjects 'objectively' do

---

[14] For a recent review of definitions of behaviour, see Uher (2016b), who defines behaviour as 'external changes or activities of living organisms that are functionally mediated by other external phenomena in the present moment'.

Figure 2.2. Subcams worn by research participants. *Left*: Anaesthetist Kirsten Gjeraa, MD, Danish Institute for Medical Simulation (DIMS), Capital Region of Denmark, and University of Copenhagen, Denmark, and surgeon, seen from the nurse's perspective. *Right*: Cadet police officer Tore Seierstad during training for intervention, seen from the perspective of the trainer (from Lahlou, Le Bellu, & Boesen-Mariani, 2015). A black and white version of this figure will appear in some formats. For the colour version, please refer to the plate section.

(movements, utterances) and what they 'subjectively' do (intentions, goals, emotions, reasoning)

Subjective evidence-based ethnography (SEBE) was designed for this dual purpose. Therefore, the data collection consists of the two steps described below.

First, participants[15] wear miniature video cameras on a pair of glasses, known as 'subcams' Lahlou, 1999), as they perform their ordinary activities (e.g. eating, nursing, policing, piloting nuclear plants, etc.) in their natural setting (the researcher is not present): Figure 2.2.

The device itself, the subcam worn by participants, is unobtrusive: all the participants declared that they forgot it after a few minutes and behaved as usual.

The protocol, detailed in (Lahlou, 2006, 2011a), includes a series of ethical precautions to ensure participants have full control over their data all the way, so they don't need to worry about recording 'something wrong'.

One of the important ethical precautions we take is that participants go away with their recording and are asked to have a look at it first to make sure they are OK with the researchers seeing it. It is repeatedly explained to participants that because researchers have an excess of material, it is no problem if participants wish to delete the recording or parts of it, and that they should do so if they wish, without having to explain why; and of course they can withdraw at any point of the research. In addition, we do not need to observe on tape actual failures or mistakes or misbehaviour: we can get

---

[15] In this technique we refer to subjects as 'participants' because they participate in analysing the primary data.

just about the same information simply by observing near misses and failures repaired at the last minute (both being, in the end, demonstrations of proficiency by the participants), and by asking participants 'what problems they tried to avoid' when they comment on their own good practice.

Preserving the face of participants and ensuring that they cannot be harmed from participating in SEBE is a key concern for us, which of course supersedes all other objectives of our research: one single small failure to safeguard participants' interests and our entire field would be burnt. That is why we are far more selective than participants (who in practice almost never censor their tapes) and cut out from the replay interviews moments that could appear embarrassing.

This protocol is constraining for the researchers, but as a result participants feel at ease, secure, and in control. Participants always report they enjoy the replay interviews very much and often volunteer for more and to recruit other participants.

The participants' opinion is that the activity they recorded was natural and 'as usual'. We are of the same opinion, having watched many moments that participants probably would not have filmed if they had remembered they were wearing the camera, for example some non–politically correct comments or jokes among colleagues and utterances they probably would not like their boss or acquaintances to hear. Of course we erase these moments even though the participants leave them on the recordings. Still, some moments remain where the protocol does have an influence, e.g. in the first moments of close interaction with people who notice the camera and need it to be explained,[16] but these moments are brief and few.

First, the subcam films produce provide a remarkably precise and accurate account of what the participants did, saw, heard, said etc., captured from their own perspective in high-definition and stereo (Figure 2.3, *left*).

Second, the participants watch their own first-person perspective 'subfilm' with the researcher and comment in great detail on the why and how of their actions (Figure 2.3, *right*). That is called the 'replay interview'.

This collaborative cognitive analysis is extremely detailed because participants are re-immersed in their own perception-action loop, from their own perspective, provided with the context, and with kinetic cues in the flow of successive actions recorded with a high quality. The replay interview is what makes SEBE powerful: it elicits re-enactment and enables accessing the subjective aspects of activity. As they review the recordings,

---

[16] We prepare the participants with a set of ready-to-use responses for such situations. Interestingly, the response 'Oh, I am filming *my own activity* as a part of a psychological research' seems to satisfy very well and usually ends queries.

Figure 2.3. Screenshot from a subcam film of a power plant technician centring a gasket during the maintenance of a pump valve (*left*, from Le Bellu, 2011, snapshots extracted from video appendix). Replay interview of an obese person commenting on her subcam film and remembering how she felt as she tried on a vest and saw herself in the mirror of the fitting room of a department store (*right*, from Lahlou, Urdapilleta, Pruzina, & Catheline, 2012). A black and white version of this figure will appear in some formats. For the colour version, please refer to the plate section.

participants are put back in the flow of their activity. They thereby access their multimodal memory of the events ('episodic memory': Tulving, 1972, 2002) and are able to describe their mental states at the time with amazing accuracy (Lahlou, 2011a; Lahlou, Le Bellu, et al., 2015). Similar effects of situated interviewing on recall have been described in embodied cognition literature, especially regarding the positive influence of kinetic cues (Barsalou, 2009; Cole, Hood, & McDermott, 1997; Dijkstra, Kaschak, & Zwaan, 2007). First-person perspective also facilitates remembering the experience from the 'I' perspective, with an actor's mindset, attention to concrete actions and emotions, whereas a third-person perspective elicits a more self-distanced and abstract or normative perspective (Libby & Eibach, 2011). By enabling these insights SEBE addresses two common oversights in current psychology pointed out by Valsiner (2009b): the dynamic flow and the effect of the immediate context of action.

Below is an extract of a replay interview. The participant, Monica, was preparing an omelette with onions, tomatoes and peppers for breakfast, in a house that is not her usual home. Here she comments as she watches with a researcher (Tereza) a clip in which she is cutting vegetables off a board.

[On the subcam film: participant's hands cutting with precision sections of spring onion.]

MONICA: There is a madness in this procedure. This is a very small knife and as I have said I don´t have that many options [in this house]... Back home I would probably take another one. And also this chopping board has like a line along the edge, which makes the cutting more challenging ... So I just wanted to line up my onions so that I can do like [a] couple of [them] sliced rather than do it separately. So I kind of changed my cutting style so that it adapted to my tools.

TEREZA: Because here it seems that you cut it but you decided that pieces are too big so you are cutting them again...

MONICA: Yes, I did, because I was trying to just line them up to do as many [as possible]... [Participant expressively shows cutting with her hands to the researcher.]

[On the film: hands take tomato, then put it back and take pepper instead.]

TEREZA: What is that?

MONICA: Oh, that is... you know like the tomato has this juice and seedy bits... I did not want to deal with it now so I started to cut the drier ingredients first. (Vrabcová, 2015, 79)

As we can see with this example, participants remember well and can account for even minuscule actions and decisions because the context of their actions is presented to them in great detail (and when necessary in slow motion).

In another example[17], this doctor comments on a subfilm in which she tries to do an intubation (during training) but she cannot introduce the tube in the trachea; so she looks into the trachea with a video laryngoscope but can't see anything because the view is obstructed:

SAADI: Can you remember what you were thinking at that point?

DOCTOR: I'm thinking: it can't be true! I can't get, er, I can't get a view! [gestures to indicate introducing the laryngoscope]. I'm thinking well, I'm OK, he [patient] is saturating at eighty-three [blood oxygen], which is not good, but is not worse than what we started out with; and then I'm thinking: well, is he not enough sedated? Because he has a tachycardia of one twenty-nine; it's actually pretty much... It might be the ephedrine; and then it might be that he's not sedated enough. But this would normally just close up [shows her throat] uh, the vocal chords; it would not [gestures her hands around her neck and cheeks and tenses her chin to mimic the patient's state] give the whole [grins; Figure 2.4] that tension like he has, as I feel.

As we can see, although the vital parameters of the patient varied considerably during the session, the doctor remembers them precisely for the given moment she comments upon; her expressions and gestures provide an insight into how she empathized with the patient. This gives a vivid account of her mental processes at the time, and demonstrates acute recall.

---

[17] See Lahlou et al., 2017.

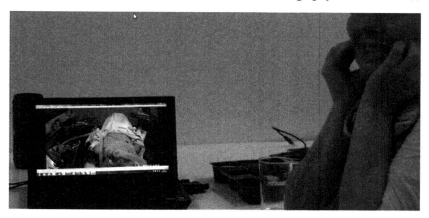

Figure 2.4. Doctor describing what she thought during an episode of trying to intubate a patient in a difficult airway case; she expresses with gestures the state of the patient with a constricted trachea and throat as she empathizes with that patient. A black and white version of this figure will appear in some formats. For the colour version, please refer to the plate section.

The replay interview itself is also video-recorded and analysed afterwards by the researchers in detail, together with the subcam recordings. The validity of analyses is finally checked with the participants themselves and sometimes even with other protagonists of the same scene and/or experts of the domain in cross-interviews.

This technique solves most of the issues of classic introspection;[18] it also enables the recording of natural interaction with objects and other people in great detail, even in places hardly accessible to the researcher, such as private interaction, family or professional settings. The most exciting part, for both researcher and participant, is the peeling frame by frame, layer by layer of the many cognitive factors involved in the most apparently simple and mundane acts. In doing so, participants discover how amazingly sophisticated are the mental processes that underlie their activity, and the myriad parameters they successfully and effortlessly juggle, given that they are usually experts in what they do (from slicing onions or taking the bus to piloting nuclear plants). That is a very rewarding experience for the ego, and accounts for the sustained involvement and high level of collaboration of participants, which in turns enables detailed analysis.

---

[18] For example, oblivion of details, reconstruction rather than remembering, impossibility of checking the accuracy of what the subject says.

SEBE is to social science what the microscope was once to biology: a technique that enables us to understand the structure of phenomena in microscopic detail.

The method requires preparation and care because it takes a while to build trust with participants,[19] which is of course the key to good analysis. The results are worth the effort. Because we work *with* the participants, the level of explication and the grain of description of the phenomena correspond to 'natural' thought and objects as understood by the participants rather than as a result of the researcher's fantasy. This helps to avoid (some of) the pitfalls of biased interpretation and recondite scientific constructs.

Through detailed analysis of many types of situations with this powerful lens we were able to gradually understand what, *in practice*, are the determinants of day-to-day action. A lot of candidate factors that were important *in theory* appeared to have, *in practice*, a second-order importance, whereas some others were indeed found to be crucial. Looking at evidence is easier than speculation. As happens so often, a new observational instrument makes science simpler; having a powerful data collection instrument makes a big difference.

Let us now see how this technique sheds light on installations using the example of Eva, a receptionist in a nonprofit organization dedicated to vocational training. This example is deliberately short: Eva wore the subcam for an afternoon, and we focused the analysis on a short moment when she greets an incoming visitor, a segment of activity lasting 50 seconds, on a Wednesday afternoon from 15:01:32 to 15:02:22.

Figure 2.5 gives an overview of the setting as the receptionist presses the button that opens the door to a visitor, and also the view from the perspective of the receptionist, who is wearing a subcam.

As Maslow noted, the situation cannot be the sole determinant of human action, the motivations of actors must also be taken into consideration:

> The situation or the field in which the organism reacts must be taken into account but the field alone can rarely serve as an exclusive explanation for behavior. Furthermore the field itself must be interpreted in terms of the organism. Field theory cannot be a substitute for motivation theory. (Maslow, 1943).

That is why, in the replay interviews, we continually ask participants to make their goals explicit for each segment of the action.[20] We explain to

---

[19] See how that is done in Jonassen (2016) and Lahlou, Le Bellu, et al. (2015)
[20] We use the framework of activity theory, see Section 3.2.

Figure 2.5. The reception installation. *Left*, seen from the third-person perspective, the receptionist presses the button that opens the door to the visitor. *Right*, the same scene as seen from the receptionist's point of view. A black and white version of this figure will appear in some formats. For the colour version, please refer to the plate section.

the participants what we are looking for in the interview, in a transparent manner. We consider participants to be co-researchers rather than 'subjects of observation'; we need their insights and for that they must feel completely at ease and in control.

Here is how the interview starts, before we start looking at the tape in detail:

SAADI: First I'll explain how it works. You have recorded your activity with the subcam. Now we will review your tape, focusing on moments that seem more interesting, richer in terms of 'professionalism'. Then, I'll ask you what your goals were, what you wanted to do, what you needed to avoid. The purpose of this is to understand the mental processes, the decision processes you use, for us to be able to teach how it works to trainees. This kind of film can be used in training. In the sequence that we will review together, you were at the reception for a couple of hours. To begin with, describe to me how it goes in general, what you do when someone arrives at the reception.

EVA: First, I try to identify the person through the videophone to see if I know or not the person, whether it's a delivery man, an appointment, etc. All this in order to anticipate the reception phase. The individual rings, I open it, he comes in. There are several possibilities since we receive different audiences including youth. Either it is young people who come to the training centre, or they are visitors coming to meet an admin, or project leaders, or deliverymen. The person usually simply comes to the desk and states that she has an appointment. From there, I either direct her to the person with whom she has an appointment or to the training centre or I get mail or packages in the case of a deliveryman.

Now here is what happens in terms of behaviour in that short sequence where Eva receives a visitor:

15:01:32–15:01:33: Doorbell rings on Eva's videophone.

15:01:32:-15:01:34: Eva looks at her counter on the videophone, which gives an image of the visitor, then with her right hand she presses the release button that opens the door.

15:01:36–15:01:37: Visitor rings again (he has not understood door is now unlatched; Eva's counter is not visible from the outside).

15:01:37–15:01:40: Eva presses the release button again.

15:01:40–15:01:45: Visitor enters, passing two glass doors, looks around.

15:01:45–15:01:46: Eva: 'Hello Sir?'

15:01:48–15:01:50: Visitor: 'Hello. I have an appointment with Mr S—'.

15:01:50–15:01:53: Eva: 'Certainly. Please make yourself comfortable on the sofa, I will him call right now'. (Eva points at the sofa with the left hand and takes her phone with the right hand.)

15:01:53–15:02:01: Visitor turns around, sees sofa, and goes to sit there. Meanwhile, Eva types the extension of Mr S— and waits for him to respond.

15:02:02–15:02:05: Eva (to Mr S— over the phone): 'Your appointment has just arrived. I make him wait. Are you coming down?'

15:02:05–15:02:09: Mr S—: (Inaudible, tells Eva to send the visitor up the stairs to him)

15:02:10–15:02:13: Eva (to Mr S—): 'Okay, very well'. Eva hangs up the phone.

15:02:14–15:02:18: Eva (turning to visitor, pointing at the stairs with her left hand) 'Please go up the stairs, Mr S— will meet you up the stairs'.

15:02:15–15:02:21: Visitor: 'OK' (gets up, goes towards the stairs).

15:02:21–15:02:22: Eva (to visitor): 'Have a nice day!'

15:02:22: Visitor starts climbing the stairs and disappears from sight, as Eva turns back to her desktop screen to process emails.

Although the sequence is short (fifty seconds), the replay interview lasted thirty-eight minutes. This length shows how much psychological and cultural substance there is behind such an apparently simple behavioural sequence.

In the replay interview, Eva described the various elements of the situation that she took into account to act and the components of the installation that she used to reach her goals. Among those were some specific ones, such as the fact that she identified this specific visitor as a frequent visitor and therefore could open the door right away, but also more generic ones, such as the general mindset and skills of a good receptionist. As we shall see, we not only learn about how the installation worked in that specific

Figure 2.6. The replay interview: *Left*, Eva shows the various elements of her workstation on the subcam recording at 15:01:43. *Right*, a screenshot from the subcam at 15:02:02 where Eva's workstation is clearly visible (note in the background the visitor waiting on the sofa near the staircase). A black and white version of this figure will appear in some formats. For the colour version, please refer to the plate section.

case, but also how it works in general and even in some exceptional cases. This emerges naturally in the discussion as Eva describes how she operates and why.

In the following extract, Eva explains some built affordances of her workstation that scaffold her work (physical layer), as she points them out on the video (Figure 2.6).

EVA: So here is the internal extension number list because all the numbers are not listed on the switchboard keyboard. There also various informations with respect to phone calls if there is a request for information, when I must refer people to an email address ... At the reception, we also do mail registration, you have to scan the paper mail and email it. Depending on the content, it has to go to specific persons so sometimes we put reminders for ourselves.

She also explains her tricks of the trade (competences) using artefacts:

EVA: I make piles [of incoming mail] and I have my little techniques: the documents that are turned upside down are processed, those that are not turned are not processed yet ... when recording the mail we use different plastic folders for each department that allow classifying documents and avoiding mixing things up.

In the next extract, we can hear how Eva not only mobilizes built affordances of her workstation (the room planning on her desktop computer), but also her embodied professional competences to deal with the case of visitors who come but do not know exactly why (which, as she says, happens two or three times per week with young people coming for an interview or a training session):

EVA: Sometimes there can be more than thirty to forty young people arriving at once.

SAADI: And in those cases, how do you...?

EVA: First, you need to stay cool. With the room planning, we know in which rooms they need to go. You have to ask them for what meeting or otherwise you can look directly on their summonses ... usually they come but they do not necessarily know who they visit. Then you ask if it's for a job search, if it is for a registration for a course ... they know they have to come here, that they have a meeting but they do not know ... they are often late so they call to know, because often to get here from the metro station they are lost.

SAADI: So you monitor them from the metro station?

EVA: Some, yes.

SAADI: Okay... I thought that the receptionist just had to be nice, ask people why they are there in order to guide them but actually it is a very small part of the job...

EVA: That is the visible part of the job. After, there is what is behind, like management. I happened to get young people who arrive here tired, exhausted, on the verge of passing out. Generally, I sit them, serve them an orange juice and reassure them. When they come here, they are generally a bit stressed because they come here for recruitment, it is understandable.

SAADI: You make sure that they arrive in good condition for their meeting?

EVA: Yes, it's better for them; and for the person hosting the meeting it is better than having people who do not feel well and will disturb the progress of the meeting.

Finally, the next extract shows some of the institutional rules that must be followed to behave correctly:

SAADI: Are there any rules or norms to be observed in this work?

EVA: Yes, always be available, smiling, clean, well presented as you are anyhow the first vision that people have of the company, it is you who are seen first and not another...when recording mail, there are things that are more or less confidential; we must know to whom they must be dispatched, who can manage it, not to disclose; we are required to have some discretion.

It turns out that the reception is the interface of the organization with the outside world, dispatching visitors and deliveries with a political judgement that requires a thorough knowledge of the whole organization and its members. This requires considerable attention, self-control and face work from the receptionist; she must at all times remain smiling and affable despite being continually interrupted by dozens of phone calls, visitors and endless urgent requests to fix minor details or provide information.

These short extracts cannot do justice to the complexity of the job and its detailed description by Eva; more examples of detailed analyses of installations will come later, especially in Chapter 4. Nevertheless, we can see from this minimal example how SEBE enables us to extract the various material components that scaffold the activity (video control on the door, desktop computer, lists and Post-its), the embodied skills (self-control, knowledge of the organization, experience of what to do in critical moments) and institutional rules, formal and informal (who has access to what, mail registration procedures, presentation and interaction style). These elements go beyond the specific scene that has been recorded and analysed and will be precious to the change agent who wants to design a better Reception.

The reception installation includes Eva with her skills, her counter with its many artefacts, and institutional rules. The visitors immediately understand the setting of Eva at her counter as a 'Reception' installation they can (and should) use for check-in and orientation, and they behave accordingly. They play their part in the installation correctly, politely explaining to the receptionist the motive of their visit, waiting in the assigned seat, and following her instructions.

The major surprise from our real-world observations, a bitter surprise for a social scientist, is the importance in the determination of behaviour of the material layer of things, concrete objects, the physical infrastructure; and then the almost continuous regulation of behaviour by others and society. That makes interactions very predictable. Of course, the subjects do demonstrate free will, intentions, emotions, reasoning, etc. But their importance in the determination of *behaviour* in installations appears, in most cases, less important than many psychological models would suggest.

The following chapter briefly reviews the main theoretical frameworks on which installation theory draws.

# CHAPTER 3

# Theoretical Frameworks Grounding Installation Theory

**This section presents a selection of theories that are relevant to our problem. It briefly presents ecological psychology, activity theory, distributed cognition, actor-network theory, and social representations. Each of these theories addresses some aspects of human behaviour in society; nevertheless, each leaves aside some important aspects of it – especially in the perspective of interventions to modify behaviour.**

**These theories are important per se; they also constitute pieces of the jigsaw puzzle that installation theory assembles in one single framework. Their reading is useful to situate installation theory but not indispensable to understand it. The informed reader can skip this section and go straight to Chapter 4, perhaps after reading the takeaway at the end of the chapter.**

To some degree, every theory in social science can claim that it contributes to the description of the determinants of individual behaviour and/or the nature of society. In fact, most of them actually do.

Usually theorists are modest and their theories encompass only a single aspect of the dual problem we tackle in this book. On the other hand, they are often generic in their scope, trying to explain 'behaviour' or 'decision' whereas we are interested here specifically in the very frequent but also very specific case of behaviours that have been framed by society to follow a specific script and are channelled by socially constructed devices.

I cannot do justice here to the vast literature that could be considered relevant. As I indicated previously, there are too many theories. I had to make choices and select only a few, based not so much on their individual quality or elegance, but rather on how they can be assembled to fit the current project. Needless to say, my ignorance and personal preferences are limiting factors.

I found myself confronted by unexpected dilemmas. It seems that for a theory, the epistemological quality, the academic fitness and the pragmatic value are not necessarily on a par. There are trade-offs. Epistemic purity and cleanliness come at the cost of neglecting some aspects that do not fit well in the formal or philosophical frame, and fine theories in this dimension end to develop parts that may have great philosophical importance but little practical relevance (see phenomenology). Academic sophistication comes from completeness; it forces us to integrate some famous but obsolete frameworks as well as recent but hollow references; it is hardly compatible with transdisciplinarity. Focusing on pragmatic aspects (and this includes intelligibility and teachability) brings the author to oversimplify and, also, often, results in the theory being informed mostly by a few fields and techniques well known by the author.

We restrict this chapter to five important streams of general frameworks that have contributed to installation theory: ecological psychology, activity theory, social constructionism, distributed cognition (and actor-network theory) and social representations. I quickly summarize their findings below. Each framework is a major corpus per se, each has generated thousands or even tens of thousands of publications and many subtheories. I feel more at ease with some substreams than others, for their authors are my friends or colleagues, and therefore my account is inevitably biased. The following sections give a brief overview of the theories, provide pointers to the main works of interest for the reader who wants to dig deeper, and then focus on the specific aspect of the theory that is relevant for the issue of installations.

A takeaway at the end of the section helps the reader already familiar with these theories to skip this chapter.

## 3.1. Ecological Psychology

*In the framework we set up, ecological psychology is useful for our problem because it provides concepts, methods and findings regarding the relation of subjects to the objects of their natural environment, especially the material objects.*

Ecological (aka environmental) psychology (Barker, 1968; Gibson [1979] 2013) is a tradition of studying behaviour in natural settings, which naturally gave great importance to the context. Most useful for our problem are the notions of *affordances* (Gibson, 1950, 1963, 1982) and *behaviour settings* (Barker, 1968).

According to James Gibson, subjects perceive *directly* the behavioural possibilities that the environment affords them; e.g. a chair is 'seatable on', an apple is eatable, one can walk on rock but (usually) not on water and so on.

> Roughly, the affordances of things are what they furnish, for good or ill, that is what they *afford* the observer... they are *ecological*, in the sense that they are properties of the environment *relative* to an animal ... Affordances do not cause behaviour but constrain or control it. Needs control the perception of affordances (selective attention) and also initiate acts. An observer is not 'bombarded' by stimuli. He extracts invariants from a flux of stimulation. (Gibson [1967] 1982)

For example, the climbability of a stair in bipedal mode is limited by the riser (the height of the step) because of the maximum degree of leg flexion. Beyond this, the subject must climb in quadrupedal mode (with hands and feet). William Warren showed experimentally that the maximum riser height is eighty-eight per cent of the leg's length; and indeed participants' evaluations of the climbability (by looking at stairs) closely corresponded (0.89) to the critical ratio of 0.88 predicted by the biomechanical mode (Warren, 1984). Affordances account for how subjects perceive the pragmatic potential of their environment.

Roger Barker was a postdoctoral student with Kurt Lewin. He later set up an observational psychological field station in a small rural town (Oskaloosa, Kansas, anonymized as 'Midwest') from 1947 to 1972. There, he methodically observed and inventoried the behaviours of 'free-ranging persons' in natural ecological units such as drugstores, school classes or the bridge club meeting.

Barker's approach is certainly the closest to installation theory; he regretted that '[w]e lack a science of things and occurrences that have both physical and behavioural attributes' (Barker, 1968: 19). He considered that 'the environment is seen to consist of highly structured, improbable arrangements of objects and events which coerce behaviour in accordance with their own dynamic patterning' (Barker, 1968: 4).

Barker's *behaviour settings* are 'stable, extra-individual units with great coercive power over the behaviour that occurs within them' (Barker, 1968: 17). Behaviour settings can be classified into genotypes; for example, the Chaco Garage and the Eastman Garage have the same genotype. Barker sets up a smart test to check similarity: Can the different units perform if the main performers are swapped (Barker, 1968: 80–9)? For example, would Attorney Wiley be able to run the Attorney Wolf practice, and vice versa; could a Presbyterian Pastor operate efficiently in the Methodist Church Worship?

Barker's endeavour includes a descriptive, natural history approach. He made impressive taxonomic efforts to define precisely the various parts of behaviour settings. Description criteria are extensive and specific, to allow for empirical observation and even some measurement: e.g. temporal and geographic locus, population, occupancy time, action patterns, programme, degrees of (social) pressure, authority system, etc. Each comes with its own classification: e.g. for 'penetration' of participants, six zones from onlooker to single leader. Barker also measured the availability and use of behavioural settings:

> On Thursday, April 16, 1964, at 5:00 AM, early-rising Midwest inhabitants had immediate access to these behavior settings: Streets and Sidewalks, High School Parking Lot, Telephone Booths, Coin-operated Laundry, Park, Lake, Open Golf Play, Elementary Upper and Lower School Playgrounds, and Cemetery. These ten settings identify the public environment of the town at this time. Behavior in the town's public areas, therefore, was limited to walking, cycling, driving and parking automobiles, laundering clothes, telephoning, playing a variety of games, fishing, picnicking, inhabiting the cemetery, and to social interaction in these settings, e.g., conversing, in the case of pairs of groups or inhabitants. Four other settings were immediately accessible upon taking appropriate action at their boundaries, Hotel, Fire Station, County Jail and Sheriff's Residence, and Sherwin Funeral Home.
>
> Between 6:00 and 6:59 AM five more behavior settings were added to Midwest's environment: two paper delivery routes, Pearl Café, Gwyne Café, and School Garage. And between 7:00 and 7:59 Midwest's environment was expanded by 40 behavior settings of the following genotypes: Animal Feed Mills, 1; Barbershops, 2; Beauty Shops, 1; Building, Construction and Repair Services, 3; Cleaners, Dry Cleaning Plants, 1; Clothiers and Dry Goods Stores, 1; Day Care and Home Nurseries, 1; Drugstores, 1; Factory Assembly Shops, 1; Farm Implement Agencies, 2; Fire Stations, 1; Furniture Stores, 1; Garages, 2; Grocery Stores, 2; Hallways, 2; Hardware Stores, 2; Kennels, 2; Laundry Services, 1; Lumberyards, 1; Nursing Homes, 1; Restaurants, 1; School Administration Offices, 2; School Offices, 1; Service Stations, 4; Staff Lounges, 1; Variety Stores, 1; Water Supply Plants, 1.
>
> Midwest's environment was increased further between 8:00 and 8:59 by the addition of 75 behavior settings ... On April 16, 1964, Midwest provided its inhabitants with 193 behavior settings. (Barker, 1968: 104–5)

For Barker, the milieu and the behaviour are in a reciprocal relation: the milieu is around ('circumjacent') and surrounding the behaviour. There is a 'synomorphy' (similarity of structure) between the milieu and the behaviour; their elements are in correspondence, so their segmentations correspond, in a nested manner. The behaviours are described in nested units and subunits, depending on the scale at which they are observed.

Barker's work was an inspiration for many, as a vision and as an endeavour.[1] But his theory itself does not seem to have been appropriated and used as it was designed, in its descriptive detail, perhaps because it is too precise and therefore heavy. It used thresholds of per cent of measures that are often difficult to operationalize; the concepts are somewhat specific to American culture and not always easy to manipulate. For example, his description of the test of whether two settings have the same genotype has three steps, and:

> The first question in connection with step 3 is: What performers incorporate within themselves the total program of the synomorph? (Barker, 1968: 86).

This excessive specification of Barker's theory may explain why it did not thrive, even though the idea is very strong, and also relevant for design. For example, it is rediscovered in an influential paper in the human computer interaction community, although Barker is not cited, with the notion of 'place': 'a place is a space which is invested with understandings of behavioural appropriateness, cultural expectations, and so forth. We are located in "space", but we act in "place"...' (Harrison & Dourish, 1996; see also Dourish, 2006). This is also the case with Giddens' notion of 'locales': 'locales are not just places but settings of interaction' (Giddens, 1984: xxv); as he notes:

> it is useful to speak of role only when there are definite settings of interaction in which in the normative definition of 'expected' modes of conduct is particularly strongly pronounced. *Such settings of interaction are virtually always provided by a specific locale or type of locale in which regularized encounters in conditions of co-presence take place.* (Giddens, 1984: 86; italics mine)

As my supervisor, Serge Moscovici, once told me in confidence, explaining the success and longevity of his social representations theory: a theory should keep some degree of vagueness to survive a long time. Perhaps

---

[1] I am especially impressed by the performance and endurance of Barker's observation station, as one who has led, on a much lower scale and in easier conditions, a similar attempt at systematic observation and analysis (ten years of 24/7 observation of activity, but only in a single building, specially constructed for ubiquitous activity recording, with twenty-first-century equipment, full cooperation of all inhabitants, in the context of the wealthy and generous Research and Development division of the French national power utility, EDF [Lahlou, 2009; Lahlou, Nosulenko, et al., 2012]). The problem with the systematic ecological approach is that it is heavier than experimental lab work or ambulatory observation.

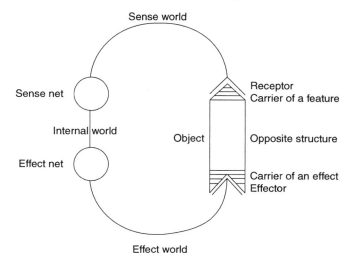

Figure 3.1. Uexküll's functional loop (Uexküll, -1934, 1992: 324).

Barker's theory was too precise. Anyway, the general idea behind Barker's theory is the same as for installation theory: some settings repeatedly and predictably generate similar behaviour, even with different people, and this comes with nested structural properties that correspond to the content of the behaviour. But the way installation theory describes these settings is different. Barker's approach is structural rather than functional. Installation theory is interested in the purpose of installations, and considers their structure as a means to reach the goal, so structure is not so important and is subject to change and evolution. Barker's theory, because his analyses are based on description rather than on intention, is well suited to classification and census at a given time, but it is difficult to use when one wants to change the system. Moreover, as we saw, Barker defines the behaviour settings by two 'synomorphic' dimensions, the behaviour programme and the context, whereas installation theory distinguishes three layers that are each potential targets for intervention.

Another important concept is Uexküll's functional loop (Figure 3.1). Jakob von Uexküll (1864–1944) was a visionary biologist who can be considered one of the fathers of ethology. He described the organism as connected to its environment by functional loops that connect an interpretation system (internal to the organism) and external objects that display both a 'carrier of significance' (which triggers the organism's interpretive response) and a 'carrier of the effect' (to which the response applies).

Only the functionally relevant environment, specific to that organism (its *Umwelt*), is perceived by the organism (Uexküll, 1934, 1992).

For example, take the common hard tick (Ixodidae), a parasite often found on dogs. How do they get there? The sweat of mammals (including dogs) contains butyric acid. When it senses butyric acid, the tick stops clinging to the branch where it dwells and – or so it hopes – lands on some hairy skin into which it then dips its head to suck out blood. Because mammals are hairy, the tick can get a firm grip on its prey. Because they have hot blood, a simple temperature sensor guides the tick to where to dig its head in to access blood. When the tick misses a prey, it climbs, driven by positive phototropism. The tick ends its climbing at the edge of a branch, and there it clings and quests until it smells butyric acid and restarts its foraging cycle, which can be very long.[2] The tick can therefore be described as a simple but efficient system with robust innate interpretive competences. These embodied competences selectively interpret affordances in the tick's environment to take actions that are relevant for the tick's existence.

Uexküll's approach to the relation of an animal to its environment, more informed philosophically, is epistemologically more solid than Gibson's or Barker's because it focuses directly on the *coupling* between object and subject; the functional loop is neither subject-centric nor environment-centric. This perspective of considering the perception-action loop as a single functional unit is essential to understanding the nature of organisms and of the psyche, and of *meaning*. As Dewey noted in his classic paper on the reflex arc:

> the reflex arc idea, as commonly employed, is defective in that it assumes sensory stimulus and motor response as distinct psychical existences, while in reality they are always inside a coordination and have their significance purely from the part played in maintaining or reconstituting the coordination…(Dewey, 1896)

We will see in Section 5.2 how the unity of this loop is preserved and exploited by installations in the learning process, in 'maintaining or reconstituting the coordination'. Nevertheless, to describe the synchronic operation of installations, in practice the notion of affordance is more useful as a pragmatic concept for change agents because it provides a handle on where to act (e.g. redesigning the affordance of the object), and therefore we will

---

[2] Uexküll reports that ticks remained alive for eighteen years without eating at the Zoological Institute of Rostock.

use affordances here to describe the physical layer of the environment, even though I prefer Uexküll's theory (Uexküll's model of the functional loop of perception and action becomes valuable, though, when we consider interpretation and embodiment, in Sections 4.3 and 5.2).

Let me make more explicit why we should prefer to use affordances in our framework; this may clarify what I meant earlier by assembling pieces of theory that fit well in the perspective of a robust framework.

The idea that things in the environment have some kind of agency, and an active influence on our behaviour, is very old in psychology. In 1926, long before Gibson, Lewin expressed it very clearly with the intuitive notion of 'valence':

> it is common knowledge that the objects and events of our environment are not neutral towards us in our role of *acting* beings. Not only does their very nature facilitate or obstruct our actions to varying degrees, but we also encounter many objects and events which face us with a will of their own: *they challenge us to certain activities...* A stairway stimulates the two-year-old child to climb it and jump down; doors, to open and to close them; small crumbs, to pick them; the chocolate and a piece of cake want to be eaten... The intensity with which objects and events challenge us varies greatly. The shadings of such challenge range from "irresistible temptations", to which child as well as adult yields unthinkingly and against which self-control is little help if at all, to those which have the character of "command", to the weaker "urgings" and "attractions", which can be easily resisted and become noticeable only when the person tries to find something to do. The term "valence" comprises all these shadings. (Lewin [1926] 1999: 95)

Lewin notes that objects with positive valence press us to approach them, and those with negative valence press us to retreat from them. But '[i]t is much more characteristic for valences that they press towards definite *actions*' (Lewin [1926] 1999, ibid.).

Now comes what is problematic both in Lewin and Uexküll's frameworks: 'The valence of a structure is usually not constant, but depends greatly - in its kind and degree - of the internal and external situation of the person...' (Lewin [1926] 1999: 95). Lewin provides an enlightening example:

> For instance, someone intends to drop a letter into a mailbox. The first mailbox he passes serves as a signal and reminds him of the action. He drops the letter. The mailboxes he passes thereafter leave him altogether cold. In general, the occurrence of the occasion (referent-presentation) as a rule has no effect once the intentional action has been "consummated". (Lewin [1926] 1999: 84)

Although the concept of valence makes perfect sense in a phenomenological perspective, unfortunately using it in practice is problematic, because the valence will change with the situation. To deal with this issue, Lewin has to change the nature of the object and index it by the situation.

> The valence of an object is as much a part of its essence as its figural Gestalt. In order to avoid misunderstandings, it would be better to speak not of changes of valence of the object, but of different structures which are only figurally and externally identical. A structure whose valence has changed with the change in situation -for example, the mailbox before and after mailing the letter- is psychologically a different structure. (Lewin [1926] 1999: 101)

That may be correct philosophically, but it yields a complicated model, too complicated to use in practice.

The valence itself cannot be 'calculated' without the internal state of motivation and *satiation* in the subject. Therefore, to calculate the valence, we need to know both something about what type of actions are challenged by the object and in what state of motivation the subject is. The first set is the concept of affordance, and the second is the concept of motive as it appears in activity theory (see Section 3.2). In fact, it is precisely because of this problem that Gibson set up the notion of affordance. 'In contrast [to Lewin's *Aufforderungscharakter*] the affordance of something is supposed *not* to change as the need of the observer changes' (Gibson [1967] 1982: 409; original italics). I therefore find it more economical and clear to have a framework that uses these (affordances and motives) as building blocks. In other words, to cover our problem, it can sometimes be more efficient to patch together smaller theories than to use vast frameworks, however beautifully crafted the latter are.

To sum up, while there are excellent theories describing the kind of agency emerging in the interaction between the subject and the environment as a compound construct, installation theory settled on keeping those (subject and environment) separate in the model. Let us take a metaphor: a geologist's hammer (pointed on one side, flat on the other) is a wonderful tool and the result of long development and craftsmanship; it can both break and crush small rocks with its flat end, and shatter larger ones with its pointed end. But if one wants to do fine work, it's better to use a mace and a chisel (Figure 3.2), which is what the mineralogist and the sculptor do – even if the latter tools are more primitive.

More approaches attributing decisive influence to the environment, appeared later in cognitive science, especially 'situated action' (Lave, 1988; Suchman, 1987) or psychology with 'situated social cognition' (Smith &

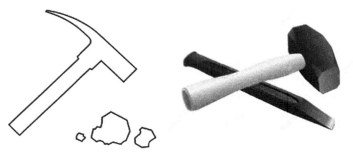

Figure 3.2. Geologist's hammer (*left*). Mace and chisel (*right*).

Semin, 2004, 2007). They highlight the emergent nature of cognition and action under the influence of context as opposed to the effect of an individual plan, although they do not deny the existence of plans, but see them as higher level resources to position oneself in proper situations rather than a set of detailed instructions. A famous example by Suchman describes the activity of canoeing:

> When it really comes down to the details of getting the actions done, in situ, you rely not on the plan but on whatever embodied skills of handling a canoe, responding to currents and the like are available to you. (Suchman, 1988).

The intuition here is that, at a given moment, the current situation supersedes plans in determining the behaviour. This does not mean that global plans do not exist, but simply that *locally* one has to work with the given situation.

In the same vein, Herbert Simon's famous example of 'the ant on the beach' attributes the complexity of the ant's trajectory not to the ant, but *to the beach* and the local obstacles it presents to the animal, resulting in detours: 'on that same beach another small creature with a home at the same place as the ant might well follow a very similar path' (Simon, 1996: 51–2).

Although these theoretical streams are loosely connected historically, they all point to the structuring influence of the context, especially the physical context, on behaviour. That may appear obvious to the reader, but this approach is somewhat at odds with mainstream psychology theories that study general mental processes in laboratory experiments and tend to locate the 'locus of control' within subjects, the latter being the main unit of analysis. This is consistent with the *fundamental attribution error*

(Jones & Harris, 1967; Ross, 1977): the human tendency to explain some-one's behaviour by the individual's characteristics rather than by external factors. After all, theorists are humans too, and therefore scientific theories bear the mark of the biases and preconceptions inherent to the human psyche (Uher, 2014a).

Ecological psychology provides us with a piece of framework that links the objects of the built environment to the subjects in an 'interpretive loop' that produces actions out of situations. It highlights the fact that some of the momentum of the action is generated by the setting itself rather than by the actor's intentions. Indeed, when I am in the corridor of the Underground, a member of the crowd in the rush hour, I cannot chose my speed and I have to go with the flow. When I am canoeing, sitting an exam, going to the doctor, using the toilets in the plane, dining at my in-laws, it is the same; and more generally, in most mundane situations my free will is limited to some minor options once I have entered the installa-tion and I have to go through a plan I did not design – or be prepared to bear unpleasant consequences.

But the context is not only constraining, it is also empowering. François Jullien, in discussing the Chinese notion[3] of *shì* (勢) introduces a series of considerations on how *position* in (geographical or social) space comes with a series of empowering affordances (Jullien, 1995). A very simple example, classic in military strategy, is that a position at the top of a hill is ben-eficial in a battle to anybody who occupies that position (Tzu, 2009: 28, 32). Similarly, a high social position will automatically provide potential agency to its owner (e.g. being the emperor), regardless of the person. The potential is associated with the position. In the same vein, we could say that the installation represents some accumulated potential, which the user will be able to transform into action. Perhaps action will even trigger itself as a result of the presence of the subject. This reminds one of the topological formulation of Lewin's dynamic psychology, which considers the subject as positioned in 'force fields'.

Michael Turvey and Robert Shaw introduced the notion of *effectivity*, symmetrical to affordance, to describe this other side of the dynamic sub-ject/environment fit. While the affordance is what the context affords the subject and is a property of the environment seen from the perspective of the subject, effectivity is the action capabilities that an organism has in that particular environment.

---

[3] 勢 is not easy to translate: situation, position, location, circumstance, power, disposition, potential...

> The term effectivity is offered to complement the term affordance ...The effectivity of any living thing is a specific combination of its tissues and organs taken reference to the environment. By this conception, an animal is defined as a set of effectivities, or an effectivity structure (Turvey & Shaw, 1979: 205–6)

With this notion, we can understand that a given environment both provides and empowers (increases, decreases) effectivity of the subject in specific directions. For example, a prison decreases the effectivity to move, a car increases the effectivity to move. The environment is in a complementary relation to the subject. A fish has more effectivity in water, and a pilot in a cockpit – but a fish in a cockpit or a pilot in the water would have little effectivity.

An empirical illustration of both these notions – effectivity and *shì* – comes from analysis of decision-making in the medical operating room. Figure 3.3 shows the design of such a setting. The positions at the head of the patient and at bedside are especially important. At the headside, the doctor and nurse have access to more information and an overview of the situation, because they are close to the vital signs monitors and can directly assess the state and reactions of the patient with touch, hearing and sight. They have more effectivity for decision-making in these hotspots.

And indeed, different levels of effectivity go with different behaviours. Analysis of cognitive tasks[4] shows that both doctors and nurses tend to execute more cognitive tasks involved in decision-making when they stand in these two strategic places, and especially at the headside, as seen in Figure 3.4. That is because affordances for decision-making are best in that position of the installation. In fact, the installation is *designed* for that, as is obvious from the position and orientation of the vital signs monitor display.

We can see here that the production of action depends on the agency both of the objects present in the context and of the position of the subject. Although naive psychology tends to be subject-centric and ecological psychology highlights the role of the context, we must conclude that action irremediably results from both. If we want to consider action, the coupling and fit between subject and environment, we must adopt a systemic view that accepts that their relationship in action goes both ways (Dewey, 1929). Models that focus only on the subject's internal mental processes and take

---

[4] In that study by my student Monica Zhang, nine physician-nurse pairs were observed in a simulation centre throughout an identical scenario of managing a patient with a difficult airway that brought the team, after trying various types of intubation, to finally decide on a tracheotomy.

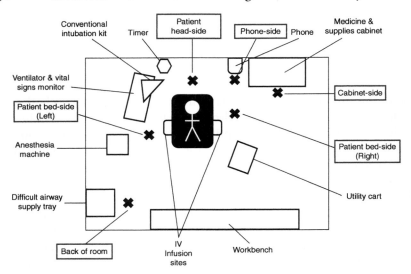

Figure 3.3. The intensive care unit simulation room layout with labelled equipment. *X*s represent possible locations of the physician or nurse-anaesthetist. (Zhang, 2015: 30). Subjects perform more decision-making tasks when located at head side or bedside.

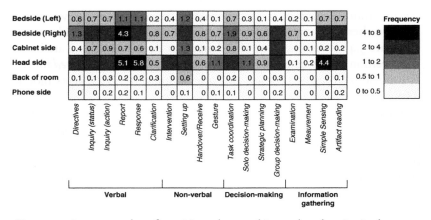

| | Directives | Inquiry (status) | Inquiry (action) | Report | Response | Clarification | Intervention | Setting up | Handover/Receive | Gesture | Task coordination | Solo decision-making | Strategic planning | Group decision-making | Examination | Measurement | Simple Sensing | Artifact reading |
|---|---|---|---|---|---|---|---|---|---|---|---|---|---|---|---|---|---|---|
| Bedside (Left) | 0.6 | 0.7 | 0.7 | 1.1 | 1.1 | 0.2 | 0.4 | 1.2 | 0.4 | 0.1 | 0.7 | 0.3 | 0.1 | 0.4 | 0.2 | 0.1 | 0.7 | 0.7 |
| Bedside (Right) | 1.3 | | | 4.3 | | 0.8 | 0.7 | | 0.8 | 0.7 | 1.9 | 0.9 | 0.6 | | 0.7 | 0.1 | | |
| Cabinet side | 0.4 | 0.7 | 0.9 | 0.7 | 0.6 | 0.1 | 0 | 1.3 | 0.1 | 0.2 | 0.8 | 0.1 | 0.4 | | 0 | 0.1 | 0.2 | 0.2 |
| Head side | | 5.1 | 5.8 | 0.5 | | | 0.6 | 1.1 | | 1.1 | 0.9 | | | | 0.1 | 0.2 | | 4.4 |
| Back of room | 0.1 | 0.1 | 0.3 | 0.2 | 0.2 | 0.3 | 0 | 0.6 | 0 | 0 | 0.2 | 0 | 0 | 0.3 | 0 | 0 | 0 | 0.1 |
| Phone side | 0 | 0 | 0.2 | 0.2 | 0.1 | 0 | 0 | 0.1 | 0 | 0.1 | 0.1 | 0 | 0 | 0.2 | 0 | 0 | 0 | 0.2 |

Frequency: 4 to 8; 2 to 4; 1 to 2; 0.5 to 1; 0 to 0.5

Verbal — Non-verbal — Decision-making — Information gathering

Figure 3.4. Average number of cognitive tasks per subject and per location in the room during a scenario involving difficult intubation (*N*=18 subjects: 9 pairs physicians and nurse) (Zhang, 2015: 41). The lines corresponding to bedside and headside exhibit a higher frequency in most types of tasks, as visible by their darker tone.

it as the unit of analysis, such as attitudes (Allport, 1935) or the theory of planned behaviour (Ajzen, 1991), are not wrong, they are just incomplete.

We encounter here an epistemological issue that will we come across for the whole of this book, namely that theories are rarely true or false, rather they are local and incomplete. Here, clearly the subject is key, but the environment is key *also*.

In passing let us comment on the fact that different theories with a family resemblance have been proposed to address the question that we tackle here. The difference can be subtle, as between Uexküll's *functional loop*, Gibson's *affordance*, and Lewin's *valence*; nevertheless some phenomena may be described better by some theories, and not so well by others. For example, Gibson's affordance theory has difficulties taking into account learning or satiation, whereas Lewin's valence or Uexküll's functional loop are difficult to operationalize for design purposes. A theory is usually better in the small empirical domain where it was grown, and the further we go from this seminal terrain the weaker the theory gets.

Finally, to encompass a wide area, a theory has to be vaguer and tends to become less predictive. This is a difficult trade-off: if too large and vague, the theory does not cut. But very precise theories often go with a very narrow domain of application. Installation theory is on the large and vague side: it should be used as a framework and works well as a first approach to the phenomena at a systemic level; it opens clear avenues. But the smaller streets must then be examined in more detail with specific, local, theories.

## 3.2. Activity Theory and Scripts

*Activity theory enables us to cut a behavioural sequence into shorter homogeneous goal-oriented segments. We can then separate the influence of the context (the given conditions) from the efforts of the subject (who tries to reach her goal in these given conditions). In such segments an analysis with installation theory and its three layers is straightforward to carry out.*

Activity theory originally developed in the Soviet Union in the 1930s as an ambitious psychological approach to human life that ranged from neurophysiology to philosophy. It considered the whole development of subjects and their higher mental processes in society. Its founders were Sergei Rubinstein and Alexei Leontiev, but it is closely connected to the neuroscience of Alexander Luria and the cultural psychology of Lev Vygotsky (Leontiev's mentor). 'The socio-cultural perspective was to overcome the divide between, on the one hand, human mind, and on the other hand, culture and society' (Kaptelinin, 2013).

Indeed, in line with the Vygotskian perspective, most now agree that individual development is inseparable from its milieu, which the subject gradually assimilates through interaction and practice, an idea that is core to socialization theories. Also – and this is more Rubinstein's contribution – in the course of activity, what is internal to the subject is inseparable from what is external because consciousness or action are processes connecting both 'inside' and 'outside'. This echoes what we saw in the previous section.

Activity theory takes the perspective of the subject (anthropocentric) and studies the relation of the subject to the objects he or she encounters in the course of activity in the real world. Among other activities, originally activity theory addressed in particular work; which was of course a key value in the Soviet context. Therefore, activity theory was confronted by the necessity of accounting for individual behaviour (and development) in a culturally mediated social reality (e.g. work) and also for the relations of subjects with objects. The cultural-historic perspective of activity theory bears the mark of the materialist and dialectic approach of Marx, which was pervasive at the time of its construction. Activity usually has an object that it transforms.

Activity theory developed for almost half a century with a limited echo in the West,[5] fostered by the importance of studying work and education in Soviet Union. In the 1980s it finally spread to Scandinavia and the literature in English.

Activity theory now comes in many different shades (Rogers, 2008). Leontev and Rubinstein already had different views (Leontiev, 1976, 1978; Nosulenko & Rabardel, 2007; Rubinstein, 1922); their many followers inside the USSR and their followers outside each set up their own stream as well (Bedny & Meister, 1997; Bødker, 1991; Engeström, 2000; Wertsch, 1981). Most recent versions published in the West, due to a reliance on texts published in English (for historical reasons, only the works of Leontev were translated [Mironenko, 2013]) ignore a key aspect of Rubinstein's original theory, which focused on the subject as an active agent of self-construction with a self-actualization project.

So, among these many variants, I present here a version developed by Nosulenko and colleagues in line with Boris Lomov's engineering psychology at the Russian Academy of Sciences, and with Boris Ananiev's filiation (Barabanschikov, 2007; Lahlou et al., 2012a; Le Bellu, Lahlou, Nosulenko, & Samoylenko, 2016; Lomov, 1981; Lomov, Belyaeva, & Nosulenko, 1985; Nosulenko et al., 2005). This version has been simplified and made robust

---

[5] With a few exceptions, especially among the French ergonomists.

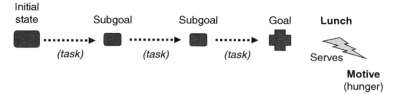

Figure 3.5. A simplified version of activity theory.

to serve operational purposes (activity analysis in an industrial context), so it lost some of the philosophical and existential characteristics of Rubinstein's seminal work.

In this version, subjects (individual or collective) are driven by *motives* and try to reach *goals*.

A goal is a representation of the desired final state. The subject tries to reach his goals in the given conditions (the context).

This goal is usually reached through a series of steps. At each step, the subject tries to reach a subgoal. For example, the subject driven by hunger (motive) may decide to leave his office to go for a meal at the cafeteria (goal). The whole trajectory is the activity (Figure 3.5).

> So activity appears as an oriented trajectory from a given state ("conditions given") to a consciously represented expected state ("goal"). Attaining the goal satisfies the motives of the subject. The trajectory of activity is a succession of small problems to be solved ("tasks"), which can each be seen as reaching a local subgoal. The operator solves each task by taking *actions* (consciously controlled motoric or mental moves) and *operations* (automatic, routinized moves taking place beyond the threshold of consciousness). At each moment, the subject is confronted to the possibility of taking a different local route to reach the final trajectory, and may do so opportunistically in consideration of the local conditions given at this point. (Lahlou, 2011b)[6]

The objects encountered are perceived from the perspective of the current activity.[7] In the example above, the subject may want to have a meal (goal) because he is hungry (motive). He will go to the cafeteria and take spaghetti. Then subgoals may be: going to the cafeteria, choosing food, and so on. Objects encountered will be considered from the perspective of the goal: a colleague met on the way may then be evaluated as a lunch partner. In

---

[6] 'Action', 'task', 'operation', etc. have definitions that vary between authors, and a comparison of these variations alone would take another book. We will stick with the definitions given here.

[7] Note how this addresses the problem of satiation highlighted by Lewin, in Section 3.1.

practice, a goal may serve several motives (e.g. for lunch: nutrition, sociability), and a motive may be satisfied by different goals (e.g. for hunger: lunch or a snack). Subjects may opportunistically switch an activity segment for another to improve satisfaction and efficiency. For example, the colleague met on the way may be recruited for lunch, and then that lunch can simultaneously serve several motives (e.g. feeding and sociability).

The definition of motives remains somewhat fuzzy. While it is easy to point to some motives (e.g. hunger, esteem, sex) it is less easy to provide a clear-cut operational definition. They refer, obviously, to the same phenomenon Sigmund Freud called drives, and to the object of the many works on motivation theory – to which I even tried to contribute myself with no success (Lahlou, 2010a). To keep it simple here, let us say that motives refer to some internal state of incompleteness in the subject, with a vague connotation of what behaviours could extinguish this feeling of incompleteness.[8] Motives tend to become more salient the more they are unsatisfied, and the most urgent ones tend to supersede others in orienting behaviour.[9] What is important to keep in mind is that we constantly carry all our motives with us, that we tend to opportunistically satisfy them when we find a possibility offered and that our behaviours strive to keep as many motives as possible below the threshold of urgent demand, therefore continuously sending us into quests for objects, situations or behaviours that can satisfy them. A goal is an end point of such a specific quest.

A motive can be satisfied by different goals (e.g. a sandwich or a big meal can satisfy hunger). This accounts for changes in trajectories ('if the restaurant is closed I'll buy a sandwich'). A goal can satisfy one or several motives

---

[8] Internal vs external states are ontologically connected to active vs reactive behaviour. Let us consider the reaction (reflex, interpretation) and proaction (desire, initiative) properties of bodies. While the former (reaction) can be considered an interpretation by the subject of the situation outside of his body, the latter (proaction) can be considered an interpretation by the subject of the inner situation of his body, inside the skin. So what we call action or reaction would be the same type of interpretive mechanism, but triggered respectively by internal or external states of affairs. It is all about 'a difference producing a difference': a difference between my current organic state and some set point will result in a drive to act (e.g. low blood sugar results in hunger); a difference between my expectations and my perceptions will produce an attempt to adjust (e.g. my destination is still a hundred meters away; I continue to walk). These are simplistic examples of matching the current situation to a single preset goal in a simplified setting; as we know, life is more complex because we have many simultaneous goals and motives, because we live in a rich, ambiguous and continuously changing environment, and above all because actual activity is the continuous linking of proaction and reaction; so it is challenging to point at what an 'original cause' of the behaviour would be.

[9] The various attempts to hierarchize motives – the most famous being Abraham Maslow's (1943) – have all encountered severe setbacks in empirical observations, and the reader now can guess this is because the notion exclusively considers the embodied aspect, which is only one dimension of the determination of behaviour.

(a business lunch can be satisfying for my hunger and my business). As the situations unfold into new given conditions, subjects opportunistically and creatively curb their behavioural trajectories to reach attainable goals and satisfy their motives.

Our version of activity theory is kept simple for easy use. Some authors propose more sophisticated versions of activity theory (e.g. Engeström & Bannon, 2009; Engeström, 2000; Kuutti, 1991). But whichever way this is represented, activity is some trajectory where at each step a new state-of-things must be produced, by bringing in new objects, taking away others and recombining or transforming the present objects. In the end, these successive transformations lead to a final state-of-things (hopefully) matching the goal and satisfying motives. The objects could be a tool, some material (e.g. food, wood, money) or other humans. For example, for the goal 'breakfast' we may want to change the position of a piece of metal (bring cutlery on the table), the state of some material (transforming eggs from raw to cooked) or the willingness of a participant to perform some action (partner to fetch croissants).

Our ideal formalism to describe such a trajectory would be *dynamical systems*, where activity is represented as a trajectory in a 'phase space', a multidimensional space where each possible state of the system is represented by a point (Daucé, 2010; Katok & Hasselblatt, 1996). A function describes the time dependence of that point in the phase space. An installation would then be described as a dynamical system whose basin of attraction is the performance of the specific behaviour that is the raison d'être of the installation. Unfortunately, dynamical systems is a heavy formalism; therefore, we will do our best to avoid getting too far into mathematizing – a flaw that limited the dissemination of Lewin's field theory and which may be poisoning current mainstream economics as well (Romer, 2015).

Activity theory is an excellent tool to describe and account for behaviour of free-ranging subjects in any type of setting; it highlights the smart, generic competences of subjects to deal with the conditions they encounter and use them opportunistically to reach their goals; how they adapt their strategies locally to the terrain. But although every course of activity is genuinely different because it depends on the context, it is a fact that our activities tend to be somewhat repetitive, because we tend to keep the same motives and also because we tend to act in the same environment, often with the same protagonists. Our lunches, showers, journeys to work, etc. have a family resemblance and tend to follow roughly one of only a few templates. As we live these repisodes, we learn these templates.

Interestingly, from a different research stream comes the notion of 'scripts' (Schank & Abelson, 1977; Tomkins, 2008). When a person is asked to describe, out of context, an activity she performs often, she comes up with an ordered sequence of actions (see examples below).

In Silvan Tomkins' original formulation, which starts from nine primary innate affects and how they assemble with events to activate memory, scripts are generic sequences of stimulus-affect-response ('scenes'). Such scripts that have struck us in past experience we tend to reactivate in similar situations, in some dramaturgic metaphor. Scripts are 'sets of ordering rules for the interpretation, evaluation, prediction, production, or control of scenes'. (Tomkins, 2008: 669). They are emotionally coloured patterns of activity, but remain incomplete because the details must be filled in with auxiliary information by the elements of the actual context of action (Tomkins, 2008: 669–70).

Roger Schank and Robert Abelson used the term to define more stereotyped and generic sequences, in the hope to use them as a framework for artificial intelligence computer programmes.

> A script, as we use it, is a structure that describes an appropriate sequence of events in a particular context. A script is made up of slots and requirements about what can fill those slots. The structure is an interconnected whole, and what is in one slot affects what can be in another. Scripts handle stylized everyday situations. They are not subject to much change, nor do they provide the apparatus for handling novel situations, as plans do. For our purposes, a script is a predetermined, stereotyped sequence of actions that define a well-known situation. (Schank & Abelson, 1975)

For example, the script of the restaurant would start with:

> Scene 1: Customer enters restaurant; Customer looks for table; Customer decides where to sit; Customer goes to table; Customer sits down.
>
> Scene 2: Ordering Customer picks up menu; Customer looks at menu...

And so forth.

Interestingly, members of a given subculture provide very stereotyped scripts when asked to describe such behavioural sequences Bower and colleagues asked one hundred and sixty-one Stanford psychology undergraduates to describe four usual activities and compared the descriptions:

> what is surprising is how much agreement there is in the "basic action" language that people use to describe the activities. This uniformity is reflected in how few of the events were mentioned by only one person. For example, in the restaurant script, of 730 actions mentioned in total (types times tokens), only four were completely unique (given by a single person). Similarly, the

ratio of unique mentions to total events was 4/704 for Lecture, 26/814 for Grocery, 26/770 for Getting up, and 36/528 for Doctor (which had the fewest subjects and least chances for overlap). (Bower, Black, & Turner, 1979)

Here, for example, is the sequence obtained for 'attending a lecture,' where the items in capitals were mentioned by at least 55% of subjects:

ENTER ROOM, Look for friends, FIND SEAT, SIT DOWN, Settle belongings, TAKE OUT NOTEBOOK, Look at other students, Talk, Look at professor, LISTEN TO PROFESSOR, TAKE NOTES, CHECK TIME, Ask questions, Change position in seat, Daydream, Look at other students, Take more notes, Close notebook, Gather belongings, Stand up, Talk (Bower et al., 1979)

Activity theory provides us with a piece of a framework that links the internal motives of the subject to the objects he or she encounters. It also enables us to describe what happens along a temporal axis, with logic and a vocabulary (goals, motives, constraints) that are at the level and grain of common-sense language. This Activity theory's framework will feed methods for empirical investigation and design (Nosulenko & Samoylenko, 2009; see also Chapter 7).

Scripts provide a description of typical sequences of activity. They show how individuals have embodied a specific competence to perform a given activity in a given installation, generic enough to adapt to various specific installations as long as these provide the appropriate props (e.g. chairs, notebook) and roles (professor, students) and the subject has the right motivation.

It is noteworthy that individual scripts seem to be standardized in a given homogenous population. We shall see later that installation theory explains this quite simply by the fact that such populations learn the same scripts not just because they share the same subculture, but more precisely because they all use similar installations.

## 3.3. Social Constructionism

*Social constructionism provides us with a piece of a framework that accounts for the genesis and transmission of large social systems through the mediation of socially constructed objects.*

Indeed, social constructionism, which is an approach rather than a theory, has in common with cultural psychology (already influential on activity theory) the transmission of cognitive skills, representations and behaviour habits through cultural and social processes; for example, a transmission and co-construction through discourse and discussion. I shall also boldly include in this section references to Erving Goffman's symbolic interactionism and Antony Giddens' structuration theory because these theories enlighten the same part of the picture.

The core idea here is that reality-as-we-know-it is the product of social construction, so it does not exist per se independent of how we understand it and reproduce it through our social interactions. Social construction-ism also comes in many different shades, from the empirically oriented grounded anthropological to the radically critical post-modernist, where almost everything is language (and in some extreme politicized versions, all is the result of evil power games). It is difficult to find an encompassing definition that would satisfy all parties.

While social-psychological models naturally focus on how individual mechanisms produce social systems when aggregated, social construction-ism also highlights the reverse mechanism, by which social systems inform individual activity.

Peter Berger and Thomas Luckmann popularized the idea of the con-tinuous reconstruction of societies and highlighted the role of education of individual members in this reproduction. Their theory mostly focuses on the co-construction of knowledge, customs and social roles and how these in turn become institutionalized and reproduce themselves and their conditions of 'reality' (Berger & Luckmann, 1966). Material objects, when they are mentioned, are considered almost exclusively for their symbolic value; their impact on behaviour is not considered in the theory, in con-trast with ecological psychology.

> social order is a human product, or, more precisely, an ongoing human pro-duction... Social order is not part of the 'nature of things', and it cannot be derived from the 'laws of nature'. Social order exists only as a product of human activity... Both in its genesis (social order is the result of past human activity) and its existence in any instant of time (social order exists only and in so far as human activity continues to produce it) it is a human product. (Berger & Luckmann, 1966: 59–60)

Giddens in his *structuration theory* (Giddens, 1984) highlighted the two sides of this reconstruction: whereas individual behaviour results from societal structure, human action also reproduces (that is, sustains *and* modifies) the structure.

> One of the main propositions of structuration theory is that the rules and resources drawn upon in the production and reproduction of social action are at the same time the means of system reproduction (the duality of struc-ture). (Giddens, 1984: 19)

Giddens takes the following enlightening example: 'Thus one of the regular consequences of my speaking English in a correct way is to contribute to the reproduction of the English language as a whole' (Giddens, 1984: 8). Essential for our problem here is the fact that societies do not reproduce as a block, but rather piecemeal as distributed system of installations.

> It is always the case that the day-to-day activity of social actors draws upon and reproduces structural features of wider social systems. But 'societies' ... are not necessary unified collectivities. 'Social reproduction' must not be equated with the consolidation of social cohesion." (Giddens, 1984: 24) The [localized contexts of day-to-day life] are probably much more important in respect of the reproduction of large-scale institutional continuities than are [larger locales – regions, nations, etc.] (Giddens, 1984: 367)

Again, here objects are not given much attention, even though Giddens is well aware of Gibson's work, for instance. That is because the main discussion is about social construction of the social, and the physical layer is out of focus.

The idea that 'the social' frames 'the individual' has been present since the origin of sociology (Durkheim, 1912, [1895] 1982). It is one of the fundamental findings of sociology and comes under many forms and theories in the literature. Pierre Bourdieu expresses it with the notion of 'habitus':

> [Habitus] expresses first the result of an organizing action, with a meaning close to that of words such as structure; it also designates a way of being, a habitual state (especially of the body) and, in particular, a disposition, tendency, propensity, or inclination" (Bourdieu [1972] 2013: 214)
>
> [habitus is] a system of lasting and transposable dispositions which, integrating past-experiences, functions at every moment as a matrix of perceptions, appreciations and actions and makes possible the achievements of infinitely diversified tasks.(Bourdieu, 1972, 2013: 82–3)

This framing, because it occurs in the education of new generations, not only propagates knowledge, skills and habitus, but also reproduces social classes, a process that has been both well demonstrated and criticized; Bourdieu shows how the social reproduction mechanism also reproduces inequality (Bourdieu, 1979).

Central for us here is the idea that reproduction of societies occurs through practice, by the members of society, in the practice of the situations. A metaphor for this would be how a path is constructed in a forest: the first person finds her way into the undergrowth and leaves a trail. The followers use the same trail and as they do it becomes a path, and maybe at some point it becomes a road. The fact many European main roads follow the same path as the ancient Roman *viae* illustrates this gradual reconstruction and hysteresis. Path-dependency is a general feature of societal evolution, as we detailed in Chapter 7

Social constructionism accounts for the following boot-strapping mechanism: the installed basis of society frames and controls everyday situations; it frames them with enough stability and momentum to present individual members with what seems to be a stable state, to which they must adapt and conform. Thereby, in maintaining this inertia and coherence, societies enable the emergence of the 'ratchet effect' (Tomasello, 1999), by which culture accumulates and increases the skills of individuals.[10]

Material culture and institutions play a key role in creating this stable environment that educates, nudges and scaffolds. *Niche construction theory* (Lewontin, 2000) is a biological version of the same idea (this time involving the material layer), which describes how social animals (e.g. termites, beavers), by modifying the environment, create their own milieus which then become an ecological heirloom and asset for successive generations. Vygotsky's cultural-historical theory, starting from a study of early human development, fleshes out the processes by which, in its interaction with its social environment, the infant subject actively elicits the elements that are necessary for its development and in this process internalizes them. By this process (which we come back to in Section 5.2) the subject's culture gets embodied into the individuals. That is not only done mechanically, it is also the purpose of a deliberate process of framing: education, which is detailed in Section 5.4.3. As Durkheim notes bluntly:

> it is patently obvious that all education consists of a continual effort to impose upon the child ways of seeing, thinking and acting which he himself would not have arrived at spontaneously. (Durkheim [1895] 1982: 53).

To run modern large-scale societies, we need massive education. It now takes almost two decades to train a standard competent adult; 'majority' status is in many countries only reached after 18 years of age. Education does not only happen during childhood, it is a continuous and ambient process. Cognition and culture are mutually constructive, that co-construction must be understood from an evolutionary perspective (Franks, 2011).

---

[10] A ratchet is a dented piece that keeps a spring wound. A ratchet effect means that the current state serves as a basis for the construction of the next, the system is prevented from going back. For Tomasello, a beneficial cultural trait or competence that has been acquired by some individuals of the population will, by imitation, be transferred to the rest of that population and not be lost; therefore, the new generation starts from a higher tooth of the ratchet: culture is cumulative.

This continuous process of reproduction through practice has been described by researchers who studied interaction by observing people in mundane situations, such as Alfred Schütz, Harold Garfinkel, Aaron Cicourel or Erving Goffman. Among the fascinating work of Goffman, especially relevant for us are the 'frames of interaction', which describe how the setting signals to the actors what scene they are in, and how each actor plays his or her role according to the script (Goffman, 1974).

> Given their understanding of what it is that is going on, individuals fit their actions to this understanding and ordinarily find that the ongoing world supports this fitting. These organizational premises -sustained both in the mind and in activity - I call the frame of the activity. (Goffman, 1974: 247)
>
> definitions of a situation are built up in accordance with principles of organization which govern events -at least social ones- and our subjective involvement in them; frame is the word I use to refer to such of these basic elements as I am able to identify. That is my definition of frame. My phrase "frame analysis" is a slogan to refer to the examination in these terms of the organization of experience. (Goffman, 1974: 10–11)

Goffman describes in great detail how the interaction between the actors prompts, mediates, supports, monitors and controls other actors' play (Goffman, 1959, 1961b, 1967, 1969, 1971). Especially significant for our purpose are the 'repairs', those actions by which an actor helps another actor who failed to play her role properly by bringing the interaction back onto the track of normality.

Goffman shows with pleasant examples and anecdotes how talk, posture, props and action in general are not only a means for the individual's activity, but also a part in the larger distributed performance, because each individual utterance is usually a prompt or a reply to some other actor. Goffman demonstrates that actors *always* expect such frames in social interaction, and he describes how individuals acknowledge their existence and behave accordingly, how they keep each other within the frame, play with these frames ('keying'), fake them, stage them, break them and so on. The notion of frame is heuristic; it also has the right degree of 'vagueness' to ensure longevity and wide use.

One limitation is that, as Goffman honestly puts it: 'I am not addressing the structure of social life but the structure of experience individuals have at any moment of their social lives.' (Goffman, 1974: 13). So his work focuses on the social construction of interaction in the moment; but what produced the frames in the first place, and how their content is learned by actors is not the case in point. The nature of the empirical material used by Goffman, mostly (exquisitely narrated) anecdotes and news stories rather than properly recorded field observation or direct capture of experience from the protagonists themselves, renders difficult a precise and systematic treatment. As Cicourel notes,

> All of Goffman's descriptive statements are prematurely coded, that is, interpreted by the observer, infused with substance that must be taken for granted, and subsumed under abstract categories without telling the reader how all of this was recognized and accomplished. (Cicourel, 1974: 24)

Producing a functional theory of the social was not the purpose here, and Goffman's work and dramaturgical metaphor are inspiring and demonstrate the extreme sophistication and subtlety with which actors can *play*, in all senses of the term, with the frame and with each other. The frame appears as a constraint and as a resource at many different levels; and although it does guide action and is necessary for cooperation, it does not straitjacket the actors.

Abraham Mole's 'micropsychology' is, in the same vein, an attempt, this time more psychological, to provide a microdescription of how action is constructed in actual practice, from the subject's perspective, e.g. what happens in people's minds when they queue, buy flowers or wait for the bus. Here again, analysis shows that apparently 'small' details in the context can become pivotal for the whole action, e.g. lack of parking space near the shop results in a trade-off between parking far away and being late, or risking getting a parking ticket (Moles & Rohmer, 1976: 56–7), creating 'microanxiety' in both cases. Note in passing how such microanxiety acts as an embodied reminder of a social rule; we come back to this question in Section 4.4.

The social-constructionist perspective is part of a wider, sociological, family of thought that considers the individual as the product of a larger context rather than as a self-standing finished product that would be the result of the natural development of human genetic potential. This perspective leads us to consider the cultural context as constitutive of the human nature, in ontogeny and in phylogeny as well; this has philosophical consequences for what we consider the nature of humanity to be. Jerome Bruner summarized in a striking way the gist of this conception of Man *designed* by evolution as a versatile cognitive platform for combining tools and connecting to a socially constructed context:

> Man's use of mind is dependent upon his ability to develop "tools" or "instruments" or "technologies" that make it possible to him to express and amplify his powers. His very evolution as a species speaks to this point. It

was consequent upon the development of bipedalism and the use of spontaneous pebble tools that man's brain and particularly his cortex developed. It was not a large-brained hominid that developed the technical-social life of the human; rather it was the tool-using, cooperative pattern that gradually changed man's morphology by favoring the survival of those who could link themselves with tool systems and disfavoring those who tried to go on big jaws, heavy dentition, or superior weight. What evolved as a human nervous system was something, then, that required outside devices for expressing its potential. (Bruner, 1968: 24–5)

A consequence emerges from this literature: to understand action, one must, inescapably, get into a minute level of description of the context. Studying the dispositions of the individual is not enough. What is the matter at hand is essential to understand action. As Moscovici used to say, '*What* men think determines *how* they think, and not the opposite'. Just the same, what men do determines how men do it.[11] The processes of action are not only based on generic cognitive mechanisms, they are dependent upon the *content* of the action as well. Action is not just context-dependent for secondary aspects, it is by its very nature a response to the context, or an attempt to modify the context or object, and therefore it is *context driven,* not *object driven.* The context is not just a décor, or the stage or a variable; it is the very weft of the fabric of activity.

As we see in the next section, distributed cognition takes us even further into detail. The problem with real settings and actual interaction is the profusion of elements necessary to take into account to explain properly what happens.

That can be somewhat scary for the researcher. A marginal aspect, but essential to the career researcher, is that such analyses become difficult to publish: if the sole description of the context and the phenomenon takes seven thousand words, how can I include it in an eight-thousand-word journal article? A deeper fear is to get lost in the material: at what level of detail should one stop? Describing a situation could be expanded to an infinite level of detail, as shown by the example of the massive "Natural History of an Interview" (Birdwhistell, 1971; Leeds-Hurwitz, 1987). This classic study by Gregory Bateson's group at Palo Alto analysed four short videotaped scenes over a fifteen-year interdisciplinary project. The manuscript was so massive – some of the tables had up to 143 entries – that it was never published. In the same vein, the sophisticated codification systems of conversation analysis developed by ethnomethodologists and pragmatists

---

[11] In fact, the determination goes both ways.

(Sacks, Schegloff, & Jefferson, 1974), who insist that this is the proper way to code verbal interaction, are so heavy that they may discourage many a brave reader. For those who are accustomed to the simple designs of lab experiments in which variables are few, and known beforehand, all this can appear uncontrollable, too complex, heavy, and anyway too difficult to publish. As the fox of Aesop's fable said to the grapes that he thought were too high for its reach: 'Oh, you aren't even ripe yet! I don't need any sour grapes'.

But in practice, only some details of this complex situation are relevant. It is not necessary to get into microscopic detail for *everything*, as the Palo Alto seminar mentioned above did. My group and I daily use video recordings, and usually only a few minutes per hour of tape need to be coded in detail for a given research question. Analysing thick descriptions of real-world data is like diving into a cold lake: from the outside, it seems unpleasant; and if one only puts a toe or a foot in the water, it seems one will never go in because it feels so chilly. But if one does indeed get into the water, the discomfort quickly disappears, and it is surprisingly pleasant to swim in there. Of course it is funnier if you know how to swim, if you have a technique.

In precisely this manner, the installation framework describes how these mechanisms of situated action, which have been described in principle at general and societal levels, work *in practice* and in detail for the local production of specific behaviours. This framework helps to sort out the various elements in this profusion of determinants, therefore facilitating the work. It provides a systematic approach and a checklist for the researcher or practitioner to tackle the problems in a Cartesian way, by separating them into simpler pieces, but without destroying the organic structure of the whole. It also helps to select, among the many possible levels of analysis suggested by Goffman or Birdwhistell and colleagues, or Barker's long list of variables, what is relevant for the problem at hand.

## 3.4.   Distributed Cognition, Actants

*Distributed cognition and actor-network theory provide concepts and findings that allow a systemic description of installations. Although they come from different horizons, they both highlight how nonhuman components of the system have agency in the activity process. Because installations operate as a heterogeneous compound of humans, material objects and immaterial constraints, the notions developed by these theories will come in handy.*

Distributed cognition delimits cognitive processes by the functional relationships between the components involved rather than by limiting them to the body of a specific actor. In doing so, it uncovers that:

- Cognitive processes may be distributed across the members of a social group.
- Cognitive processes may involve coordination between internal and external (material or environmental) structure.
- Processes may be distributed through time in such a way that the products of earlier events can transform the nature of later events. (Hollan, Hutchins, & Kirsh, 2002: 176)

Edwin Hutchins observed the activity of pilots and demonstrated that what flies a plane is not a pilot alone but the whole cockpit, including instruments, checklists, maps, etc. (Hutchins, 1995b). In the same vein, he showed how fixing position on a ship is the product of a whole team of humans using instruments, rules of thumb and other artefacts (Hutchins, 1995a): cognition is 'distributed', in its content as well as in its process.

Hutchins was originally interested in 'how information is represented and how the representations are transformed and propagated through the system' (Hutchins, 1995a: 287). In each component of the distributed cognitive system, these representations may be locally processed in the component's own format. Communication from one component takes place in the open and is therefore observable, which enables a good understanding of the process, unlike what happens inside the black box of the human skin, where we only have indirect access to processes. For example, when the pilot reads the altitude on the altimeter and spells it out loud to the copilot, or when the pelorus operator on the navigation bridge aligns the compass hairline with a landmark on the coast and shouts a bearing into the microphone for his colleagues in the pilothouse, who then use it to draw the bearing and fix position, we can *observe* what data are used and how they are transformed.

The information, when it transfers from one support to another, may change format or 'representational state'.

A representational state is a particular configuration of an information-bearing structure, such as a monitor display, a verbal utterance, or a printed label, that plays some functional role in a process within the system. Processes of the activity system propagate representational states across diverse media and thereby achieve effects within the environment. (Hazlehurst, McMullen, & Gorman, 2007)

Hutchins, after Pea, calls 'mediating structures' the artefacts used by humans as information processors.

In conducting such analysis, distributed cognition continues and develops a tradition of research that observes how human artefacts tend to incorporate something of the human culture that created them, and that in turn the artefacts will help, support or guide users in their activity through their culturally constructed properties. This idea emerged in various forms, in history (Leroi-Gourhan, 1965), philosophy (Simondon, 1989), psychology (Vygotsky, 1978), cognitive science (Pea, 1994) and design (Norman, 1988). Hutchins' work is enlightening because it shows, in detail and with real-world cases, how distribution operates. The exercise shows first the extent to which information is processed outside the human mind (Hutchins rightly says 'outside the skin') by *mediating structures* such as cockpit instruments, checklists and charts, which was Hutchins' main point.

> Language, cultural knowledge, mental models, arithmetic procedures, and rules of logic are all mediating structures too. So are traffic lights, supermarkets layouts, and the contexts we arrange for one another's behavior. Mediating structures can be embodied in artifacts, in ideas, in systems of social interactions... (Hutchins, 1995a: 290–1)

Mediating structures are purposefully designed to facilitate information processing. In practice, live humans appear to play a relatively minor role, especially in large sociotechnical systems; at least if we simply count the number of operations, artefacts do a lot of the work. What I find even more important, which can be understood only when one actually reads Hutchins' book and papers, and which does not appear in second-hand descriptions of his theory, is how highly complicated the processes are in practice. It takes many pages just to describe the activity, because there are so many steps and objects involved. His description of the remembering of the speeds on a simple aircraft (the MacDonnell-Douglas MD-80) during descent, takes more than seven thousand words, four figures and a table in the short paper version (Hutchins, 1995b); describing the apparently basic process of fixing position on a ship takes fifty-eight pages (plus the introduction describing the situation that was studied in the book in the introductory chapter, 'Welcome Aboard', which takes forty-eight pages). Hutchins' work demonstrates how naive it is to hope that modelling real-world actions through psychological models is possible by using only a few boxes and arrows in a figure or data model. When we set up laboratory experiments, we use only a few generic variables, but reality is more complex by several orders of magnitude. Moreover, the influence of local artefacts is omnipresent, which makes generic models hazardous. When looking at real processes, we understand why brains have billions of cells. They are necessary to deal with real-world phenomena, which are made of more than a few boxes and arrows.

The original theory of distributed cognition was concerned only with 'cognitive' processes and the use of information, but it is now obvious that action itself is distributed, and agency as well (Lahlou, 2017). Just as with piloting a plane, baking a cake is a distributed activity that relies on the *action* of many nonhuman 'objects' such as the Mixer, the Yeast, the Oven and so on. That is why we must also mention actor-network theory here.

Actor-network theory (ANT) comes from a very different tradition and was developed, from the longitudinal perspective of understanding how innovation develops, by Michel Callon and Bruno Latour at the Centre de Sociologie de l'Innovation, in Paris. Callon, Latour and colleagues are interested in the how the confrontations of various actors produce the emergence of innovations, conventions, compromises. The researchers were induced into considering the various strengths and influence of actors, and because these are not proportional to the physical size of actors themselves, but rather to the network of forces for which they are a proxy, they became interested in the process of translation (see Glossary), by which an actor becomes such a proxy for a larger network.

This is why an actor can be considered as a network, and vice versa: hence the notion of 'actor-network'. As the theory is itself distributed in the papers that gradually shaped it, and is not always easy to grasp, a quick history of its construction is necessary.[12] Latour's first studies of laboratory activity (Latour & Woolgar, 1986) showed that a good deal of the scientists' activity consists in making the objects express their characteristics through experimental interactions and instruments, characteristics that are then *translated* into *inscriptions* in symbolic format – for example, scientific reports, charts, etc. (hence the first name of 'sociology of translation' for the theory). The positions expressed by objects then circulate as statements in a sociotechnical network, where they can be taken into account in political, economic and social controversies (e.g. the ozone layer has a growing hole; pesticides can be dangerous for humans, etc.). Such statements do not originate only in the object, but in the sociotechnical network (labs, scientists, etc.) that expresses it. That network is an actor (hence ANT).

---

[12] See Callon (2001) for an enlightening summary.

The theory is multiform and has vast epistemic ambitions that do not concern us here. We shall in fact use here only a minor aspect of that theory, the notion of 'actants'. In empirical studies by this group it appeared necessary to take into account how some nonhuman entities defend their conditions of existence in the various arenas and controversies where change is negotiated between stakeholders. Confronted by the need to account for nonhuman 'actors', the authors of the theory came up with the notion of 'actant' (Akrich, Callon, & Latour, 2006), a generic term that can include acting humans and material objects alike:

> An "actor" in AT [Actor-Network Theory] is a semiotic definition -an actant-, that is, something that acts or to which activity is granted by others. It implies no special motivation of human individual actors, nor of humans in general. An actant can literally be anything provided it is granted to be the source of an action. (Latour, 1996)

Any object with motoric capacity can be an actant, but also computer programs, files, and even static objects, as they can scaffold or obstruct the action. For example, a wall is an actant in the action of detaining a prisoner, and it complements a larger system, including wardens, laws, files and locks, which together perform this activity. Therefore, the operation, and especially the amendments, of the system studied will have to take all actants into account. The final compromises and institutions emerge from controversies in public arenas where all these actants are convoked, argue, negotiate, and confront in power struggles and complex games of alliances.

A nice example is the process of domestication of Scallops in the Saint-Brieuc Bay (Callon, 1986). Scientists and Fishermen tried to cultivate a decreasing population of Scallops with a new system in which 'larvae are anchored to collectors immersed in the sea where they are sheltered from predators as they grow'.

*Fishermen* are represented (translated) by their union representatives. Fishermen and Scientists had to 'negotiate' with many actors of the system, including the Sea currents, the Parasites and the Scallops themselves, who were not keen to reproduce in the conditions the Scientists initially created. Fishermen and Scientists had some tough conversations because Scientists wanted Fishermen to wait until Scallops had repopulated enough before harvesting them. Scallops are *actants*, represented (*translated*) by the Scientists in discussions with the Fishermen.

Some aspects of that theory are applicable to studying the daily operation of societal installations. For example, detailed analysis of the scientific process of making a map of the soils in the Amazon forest will necessitate processes of representation and translation of the physical soils into the representation as a pedologic map. This is done with and by various instruments that 'say' something about states-of-things – e.g. the 'Chaix Topofil ref. I8237', the 'pedocomparator' or the 'Munsell soil color chart' – (Latour, 1993).[13] That is very similar to Hutchins' 'mediating structures'.

The agency of nonhuman actants is not limited to their affordances and the knowledge accumulated in them through cultural-historical processes. They can embed interpretive and reasoning capacity. As Roy Pea notes:

> Intelligence does not need human hardware (the nervous system) to run; it is independent of hardware. The consequence is that an intelligence system (that is, a system that has the programs needed for achieving intelligent performances) need not be based in the nervous system. (Pea, 1985)

One fascinating perspective emerging from the development of computers and robots is that nonhuman actants will become more and more numerous, autonomous and pervasive, but also more intelligent. Cognition (and intelligence) will therefore be more widely distributed.

Finally, let me recall the obvious: cognition is distributed not only in objects, it is also distributed across humans and therefore other humans are cognitive resources in action. Human societies are organized to store and retrieve this information that is distributed across humans (Roberts, 1964; Roqueplo, 1990). As we will see in installation theory, other humans are also important 'distributed' components in making decisions and determining action.

That distributed action of 'others' is not only efficient in determining action in situ at a given moment (e.g. by serving as a model to imitate, by collaborating or obstructing). It is also a key factor in the genesis of the self of an individual (Mead [1934] 1972), and therefore of how we learn roles and behaviours. We return to this in Section 7.5.

Pea, with his notion of 'distributed intelligence', combines the various layers presented here and highlights their structuring influence on activity, an idea installation theory develops:

---

[13] Latour in this paper describes in great detail all the operations executed by a group of pedologists making a map of the different soils near Boa Vista, Brazil. It becomes apparent that the final product is the result of various translations of the phenomena by a series of instruments and people. For example, the topofil [a measuring device] will transform a walked physical distance into a measurement for the map, the pedocomparator will enable the comparison of soil samples to build categories, the colour chart will enable the qualification of a sample with a reference colour, etc. The map is the final product of all these actants.

On close inspection, the environments in which humans live are thick with invented artifacts that are in constant use for structuring activity, for saving mental work, or for avoiding error, and they are adapted creatively almost without notice. These ubiquitous mediating structures that both organize and constrain activity include not only designed objects such as tools, control instruments, and symbolic representations like graphs, diagrams, text, plans, and pictures, but people in social relations, as well as features and landmarks in the physical environment. (Pea, 1993: 48)

### 3.5.    Social Representations

*Social representations theory is a piece of a theoretical and methodological framework that provides an empirical description of the structure and distribution of shared representations, and sheds some light on how they are constructed.*

In Chapter 2, regarding breakfasts and Inuit, we evoked the existence of shared mental representations that locally enable a standard interpretation and a collaborative performance of situations by subjects. Without such shared understandings, most installations would not work, because their design takes as a prerequisite that the embodied interpretation systems of human users are similar across the population of users. For example, the polling station installation requires that participants know what Democracy, a Vote and a Ballot are. Playing a symphony requires all the members of the orchestra to share a common musical code and the representations of the symphony.

Many theories have focused on the structures that individuals mobilize to make sense of situations and objects, such as mental models (Johnson-Laird, 1983), simuli (Minsky, 1985), scripts (Bower et al., 1979; Schank & Abelson, 1977), mental images (Bower, 1972), relevance (Sperber & Wilson, 1986), perceptual systems (Barsalou, 1999), etc.

Social representations theory (Moscovici, 1961, 1976, 2008) studies how such constructs emerge as *common objects* for a society (Clémence, 2002; Doise & Palmonari, 1986; Herzlich, 1969), how they are distributed across individuals (Sperber, 1996) and their connection to practice (Abric, 1994; Guimelli, 1994b; Jodelet, 1991; Lahlou, 1998). As Moscovici notes, social representations are

> a system of values, ideas and practices with a twofold function; first, to establish an order which will enable individuals to orientate themselves in their material and social world and to master it; and secondly to enable communication to take place among the members of a community(Moscovici, 1972: xiii)

Social representations theory differs from other theories regarding mental structures by its sociogenetic stand: the representations are a way to approach social thinking; the theory is interested in the social genesis of representations and in their role in communication and construction of the world. It is also interested in representation as a *process* leading to action. The field is characterized by an anthropologic and multimethod approach, with substantial use of qualitative techniques and triangulation (Apostolidis, 2003). Rather than focusing on simple objects that can be studied in laboratory conditions, as most cognitive theories do, it also tackles complex, socially loaded objects, such as illness, madness, science, democracy, etc. (Kalampalikis & Apostolidis, 2016; Kalampalikis, Bauer, & Apostolidis, 2013)

At the moment of acting, human actors in a given society display an amazing proficiency to react appropriately to the situation. Any 'normal' individual will know how to use the myriad artefacts and navigate the complex situations that continuously come their way. 'Simple' activities like taking the bus, dining in a restaurant or buying shoes (Gobbo, 2015) require the subject to have incorporated a vast library of representations (Bus, Restaurant, Shoes but also Laces, Seats, Money and so on).

Moreover, these representations are not idiosyncratic: they are similar enough across individuals of a society for them to behave in an adapted manner in the situations usually encountered. Each person hosts a portfolio of representations and other embodied interpretive structures that enable the individual to deal with the situations encountered. Each of us knows what a bicycle, a hospital, a train, a dinner, etc. are. We can identify them, we know how to behave with them. These structures are to some degree similar from individual to individual, they are 'what every person knows'. Different people will independently refer to a given phenomenon (e.g. a hat, tea, a baby) with the same name; they will also independently display similar behaviour towards it in similar conditions (e.g. wear the hat; drink the tea; take care of the baby).

This similarity enables cooperation about a common referent. People are able to communicate about objects, which shows again they share some representation of them: if I ask my neighbour to 'pass me the tea', she will pass me the liquid and not the hat nor the baby. That is not just because the individual representations are similar, but also because they are known to be so; because we *assume* they are 'shared' (common knowledge, common sense). This enables them to be *conventions* for social construction, that is, some behavioural rule (or interpretation) everyone applies and expects others to apply (see Glossary).

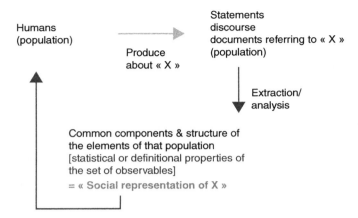

Figure 3.6. The empirical process of describing social representations from empirical data. Human populations produce *observables* about an object *X*, in the form of free association, discourse, written documents, drawings and so on. The researcher extracts from this material, with analytic techniques, common components and the structure of the set of these observables. These common features amount to an intensional description of the set of observables. Individual mental representations of the population of human subjects are assumed to have the same features (structure, content) deduced from the set of observables.

> So if a convention, in particular, holds as an item of common knowledge, then to belong to the population in which that convention holds -to be party to it- is to know, in some sense, that it holds." (Lewis, 2002: 61)

This accrues such representations with the power of descriptive social norm, as one then assumes being expected to use the common representation.

The empirical issue for social representations theory is to make explicit the content and structure that are common to all these individual representations. Such [content + structure] is what social representations theory wants to describe. The natural way to proceed is to study many instances of such individual representations, which should contain the common content and structure, and to compare these individual representations to find the common features, or take out such features from the material. In the structural branch of the theory of social representations (Abric, 2003c; Flament, 1994; Guimelli, 1994a), the content and structure of the social representation are then described by these common features (Figure 3.6).

Social representations can be studied in several ways, from ethnographic observation to various types of interview and questionnaire, discursive analysis, dialogical analysis, sorting vignettes and so on (Duveen & Lloyd, 1993; Jodelet, 1991; Marková, 2012; Potter & Edwards, 1999;

Uher, Werner, & Gosselt, 2013; Wagner et al., 1999). The manner of study is not trivial because, in the process of collecting the content and structure of individual representations, various types of biases and loss in translation can occur. For example, some unconscious aspects may not be made explicit, aspects that may be poorly projected in language or other media for collection, e.g. motoric or emotional aspects (Lahlou, 1998) or aspects that subjects consider to be politically incorrect to express (Abric, 2003b).

Social representations theory provides methods to describe empirically the content and structure of any common-sense notion in a given culture, e.g. what is 'work' (Flament, 2007) or 'AIDS' (Joffe, 1995). The structural approach developed by Jean-Claude Abric and colleagues (Abric, 1994; Flament, 1994; Guimelli, 1994a) distinguishes the core (central) 'elements',[14] indispensable for recognizing the general object (Moliner, 1994) from peripheral 'elements' that enable the representation to be adapted to local contexts (Bataille, 2002). Various techniques (Abric, 2003c; Flament, 1962) enable the components of the representation to be extracted from discourse about the object. These techniques are often based on statistical comparison of individual mental representations to extract the common traits across a population (see Figure 3.6). They can also be functional tests, where variants of representations are proposed to the subject, to determine what traits are indispensable for recognizing the object the representation refers to (Moliner, 1993, 1994); e.g. is 'a job' necessarily a paid activity?

Some people consider the notion of internal representation epistemologically at odds with the possibility of emergent behaviour, more specifically enaction (see Glossary). In fact, this stand is often based on an outdated, naive, definition of representation (as some image of a real world that people would reproduce in their brain), or that internal representation is some kind of symbolic token that is the object of some computation. But representations are also a process. As Jodelet writes of social representations, they

> are approached as together ['à la fois'] the product and the process of an activity of appropriation of a reality external to thought and of a psychological and social elaboration of that reality. (Jodelet, 1989: 45; my translation)

Whereas the structural approach focuses on content, representation as a process (of re-representing the object when the subject is dealing with it) is best studied with more qualitative and ethnographic techniques. That

---

[14] In fact, we should here understand 'components'. 'Elements' is a confusing term in this context, as will appear later in this section in the discussion of individual vs social representations.

is because the 'representing' is an emerging and situated process of sense-making, where the subject reconstructs the object in a cultural situation. Denise Jodelet, one of the main authors in the field, describes situations as 'semiosis situations',[15]

> That is, a system of sense production according to which the institutional and social context where the representations are construed affects the elaboration of a 'representational system' within which the representations of the situation, of the task and of the partner are linked. (Jodelet, 2013)

The field of social representations has devoted substantial study to the content, structure and distribution of such 'shared' mental structures, and their link to the construction of meaning and action, but the theory remains in some aspects a bit fuzzy. I must clarify here the distinction between individual representations (IRs) and social representations (SRs).

IRs and SRs are different in nature and logical type: an SR (of a 'thing') in a population is the *set* of IRs of that 'thing', representations housed by the individual members of that population (you, me, my mother, etc.) The current SR of 'a hospital' in the United Kingdom will then be the set of 60 million IRs of what 'a hospital' is for each of the 60 million United Kingdom residents. That way of defining social representations is a clean epistemic solution to the problem of the relation between IR and SR. It yields the same results as the classic (but fuzzy and implicit) definition of a social representation of an object as the 'common' content and structure that individuals 'share' in their mental representations of an object. Indeed, when a set is described, it is done so usually *in intension* (discussed shortly) as the list of common properties of the elements of the set. And in practice social representation specialists do extract these common properties by comparing individual representations, which is precisely extracting a representative sample of the set of individual representations – implicitly acting as if the social representation were that set.

Considering SRs as sets it is necessary to take an evolutionary perspective (Lahlou, 2015), because it is through variation of individual representations that the social representation evolves, just as a natural biological species (e.g. finches) evolves as a population through the variation of individuals.[16]

---

[15] Referring to Schaff's sign-situations, situations in which participants understand the common signification of the sign (Schaff, 1969: 196)

[16] In his studies on the 'contagion' of ideas, anthropologist Dan Sperber developed an epidemiological approach to representations; strangely it is rarely cited in SR literature. What he calls 'cultural representations' are very close to the notion of SR, even though here too the distinction of logical

If we consider the set of individual representations about an object (in the very general sense of a 'thing' e.g. Hat, Democracy, AIDS, Eating[17]) we can compare them statistically and see what they have in common. We know by personal experience that indeed they have something in common because we can communicate. The *set* of individual representations in a population can be *described* by what these representations have in common.

There is a difference in *logical type* (Russell, 1908; Whitehead & Russell, 1962) between individual (mental) representation and social representation. This difference is similar to the one between *token* and *type* in logic (you can eat a specific apple, but you cannot eat the APPLE type; one individual can have her own individual mental representation of a hospital, but she does not embody the full social representation of the hospital). Technically, a class (here: social representation) is of a logical type *higher* than its members (here: individual representation). A class cannot contain itself as a member; a social representation cannot be an individual representation. As sets, social representations have properties that the individual representation does not have.[18]

Mathematically, in the theory of sets (Cantor, 1874; Halmos, 1974; Runde, 2005) a set can be described in *intension* or in *extension*. An *intensional* description defines a set by some properties of its elements (e.g. a rule or semantic description; necessary and sufficient conditions). For example, an *intensional* definition of 'birds' could be 'animals with wings': $\{x \in animals: x\ has\ wings\}$.

An *extensional* definition explicitly lists all the individual elements of the set. An *extensional* definition of 'birds' would be 'the physical set of

---

type between individual and social representation is unclear. 'Among the mental representations, some – a very small proportion – are communicated, that is to say, bring their user to produce a public representation which in turn leads another individual to construct a mental representation of similar content to the initial representation. Among the representations provided some – a very small proportion – are communicated repeatedly and may even end up being distributed in the whole group, that is to say have a mental version in each of its members. We call cultural representations such representations that are widely distributed within a social group and inhabit this group durably. Cultural representations as defined are a fuzzy subset of the set of mental and public representations housed by a social group'. (Sperber, 1996: 50; my translation)

[17] I use 'object' here in the same general sense Schütz sometimes used the term 'thing' : 'in its broadest sense, covering not only corporeal objects but also "ideal" –mental- ones'.. (Schütz, 1960, 1976c, 9)

[18] One must remain careful, though, in using mathematical formalism too exactly here, because for one thing, individual representations are a moving target: they are fuzzy and change all the time in number and detail (panta rhei!). The idea that we should consider the set as a type, although useful for the issue of social representation, has some technical and metaphysical limitations. See *The Stanford Encyclopaedia of Philosophy*, section 'Type and Token'(https://plato.stanford.edu/) for a detailed discussion.

all animals that are called birds on the planet': {all individual pigeons, all individual eagles, my parrot, etc.}.

Social representations, as any set, can therefore be defined in intension or in extension. In practice, because of the huge size of the set, they are defined in intension. This definition is empirically obtained through statistical techniques.

Individual mental representations are observable empirically, for instance by asking a sample of individuals to talk about the object (e.g. 'If I tell you "democracy", what comes to your mind?'). From this sample we can extract (through content analysis) a description of the elements of the set and infer statistically the intensional definition of the set. For example, Lheureux and colleagues (Lheureux, Rateau, & Guimelli, 2008) find the SR of 'studying' to contain the following cognitive components: *Knowledge, Investment, Diploma, Culture, Future, Work, Job, Long term, University*; they obtained this through questionnaires filled in by a sample of students. I studied the social representation of 'eating', separately from the analysis of definitions of 500 terms related to eating in a dictionary, and of 1,600 live human subjects' free associations. The results from both corpuses were identical: the social representation of eating in the French adult population at the end of the twentieth century consists of six components: *Desire, Take, Food, Meal, Fill-up,* and *Living* (Lahlou, 1998: 26–39).

The nature of the components of a social representation[19] poses some epistemic problems because each component is itself a social representation; e.g. in the social representation of 'studying', its component 'diploma' is a social representation per se. From this perspective a representation is a fractal object that is hardly dissociable from the whole linguistic and cultural system (Lahlou & Abric, 2011). Nevertheless, in practice the structural approach developed by Abric and his school (Abric, 1994, 2003a; Guimelli, 1994b; Moliner, 1994) provides a first-level breakdown into components that is satisfying for operational purposes (e.g. marketing, policy design).

What distinguishes a social representation from a mere set of individual mental representations that would be similar in content? The answer stems from the functional aspect of social representations. SRs emerged to facilitate cooperation about an object of the lifeworld. Therefore, they all point to the same empirical phenomenon 'out there' and their content is the

---

[19] Which, by some unfortunate and confusing terminology, were called "elements" in the literature, although it should be clear by now that the elements are the individual representations, and components are traits of the *intensional description* of the social representation.

result of the operational effectiveness of the content of the representation, which must match the 'objective' characteristics of the object in question; this match is verified through trials of practice.

In addition, it is crucial that IRs not be independent of each other, and that they crossbreed and reproduce as members of the set (there is discussion, controversy, influence, education). Finally, this set of individual representations is linked by the representation *process* to their object, which is another source of interdependency and which is described in more detail in Chapter 5. The representations contribute to the construction of their objects, they are not passive images of them. This is why SRs differ from 'memes' (Dawkins, 1976), and more generally why social representations theory is different from the naive approach of 'shared' representations, which considers a set of multiple replicated occurrences of a single representation distributed over a population. This latter simplistic view misses some crucial points, as just stated in the preceding paragraph.

This last misconception is well described by Harré:

> The weight of an army is a distributive property, while its organization is a property of the collective. As far as I can see, the concept of *représentation sociale* is used by the French school as a distributive property of groups. (Harré, 1984)

Let us be fair: this inaccurate distributive interpretation of social representations theory is widespread among many users of the theory, and it has been often noted that there is a real ambiguity in the core texts regarding the epistemic status of SRs (Billig, 1988; Jahoda, 1977; McKinlay & Potter, 1987; Potter & Edwards, 1999; Potter & Litton, 1985; Potter & Wetherell, 1987). The fact that most descriptions of representations are done in intensional mode did nothing to help clarify the issue. I hope it is now clarified. Most important to note is that this formal definition of SRs as sets of IRs provides solid epistemological ground for all techniques that describe SRs based on surveys on samples of IRs.

The heart of the matter is that there is no opposition between the individual and the social. Of course, individual representations are inherently social, because they are socially constructed. Nevertheless, they have some autonomy. Conversely, even though the social is constructed by an aggregate of individuals, it has some autonomy (it will survive even when individual members die) and it has emergent properties at the level of its logical type (e.g. structure, internal variability) Individual and social is another example of the chicken-and-egg issue.

Furthermore, as the representations are taken into the communication processes that occur around the construction and use of the object, these communications have an influence on the structure and content of representations (for example, their anchoring in previous relevant concepts). More generally, as the objects are involved in larger issues (e.g. conflicts of interest, power struggles between groups of stakeholders interested in the object) the representations are also impacted by these issues. Added to that, as discussed in Sections 5.1 and 5.2, the social representations are part of the reproduction cycle of the objects, and you understand that social representations entail in their nature much more than similar symbolic content across individuals. They must be considered as a bundle with the object they refer to and with the population that houses them, because the representations are always representations of something, by someone (Jodelet, 1989: 43)

## 3.6.   Takeaway on the Theories and Some Comments

### 3.6.1.   *Takeaway on Theories*

**Ecological psychology considers the effect of context on perception and action: affordances in the context elicit and support action (a chair will invite sitting), but such action remains mediated by the internal conditions of the subject.**

**Cognition and action are situated and distributed. Elements of the context will be involved in processing information about the situation, as well as performing activity (it is not the pilot alone who flies the plane, but the whole cockpit, with all its navigation and command instrumentation). A situation must be considered as a bundle to account for what happens. Nonhuman actors (actants) contribute to what happens, directly or through human mediation.**

**Activity appears as an oriented trajectory from a given state ('conditions given') to a consciously represented expected state ('goal'). Attaining the goal satisfies the motives of the subject. The trajectory of activity is a succession of small problems to be solved ('tasks'), which can each be seen as reaching a local subgoal. The operator solves each task by taking *actions* (consciously controlled motoric or mental moves) and *operations* (automatic, routinized moves taking place beyond the threshold of consciousness). At each moment, the subject is confronted by the possibility of taking a different local route to reach the final trajectory, and may do so opportunistically, given the local conditions at that point.**

Members of a culture have similar individual representations of the usual objects of that culture, whether material objects or concepts; these shared 'social representations' enable communication and cooperation. Their common structure can be empirically extracted by comparing individual representations.

The theories noted here revolve around a few ideas. These are consistent with the intuitions of Kurt Lewin about field theory and of Stanley Milgram when he describes his famous 'obedience experiment': the context (objects, other people) has a massive influence on behaviour; *the situation has a momentum of its own.*

At the moment of action (synchronic aspect) the context informs the behaviour of subjects; it actively contributes to this behaviour; this contribution is distributed and performed by various actants; these actants incorporate some socially constructed intention, by design. Individual 'normal' subjects are somehow equipped with competences to adequately interpret these contexts and make use of this environmental contribution, to satisfy their motives in the conditions given. Psychologically, the situation provides a nudge to behave in a specific way.

The situation at a given moment (the synchronic aspect just described) is the result of a historical 'social construction'. The reproduction of society is based on the daily operation of practice; the interpretive systems (representations) are distributed and reproduced by practice and education. Repeated experience of situations produces a stable disposition (habitus) in the subjects; in turn, subjects reconstruct the environment according to what they need to support their dispositions.

For example, consider eating habits. People of a given culture learn to appreciate a certain type of cuisine; then they organise their procurement and preparation systems (shopping habits, kitchen) to prepare this type of cuisine, which will also shape the next generation's practices. More generally, representations and world visions learned through experience and practice become self-fulfilling predictions through the reconstruction of their environments by subjects.

### 3.6.2. *Some Comments on the Limitations of Psychological Theories of Action*

All this sounds realistic, but it takes us away from a classic psychological model of the individual person as the source of behaviour and as the best unit of analysis to explain and predict behaviour. Compare what we saw above with, for example, the popular theory of reasoned action

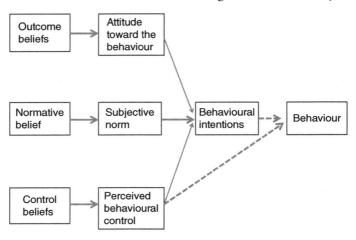

Figure 3.7. The theory of planned behaviour (from Ajzen, 1991). For ease of presentation, crossed influence between antecedents and possible feedback effects of behaviour on the antecedent variables are not shown.

(Ajzen & Fishbein, 1980; Fishbein & Ajzen, 1975) and its update, the theory of planned behaviour (Ajzen, 1991), which are centred on the subject and consider action as the result of rational calculation, based on the assumption that the best predictor of a behaviour is the intention of the subject to perform it (Figure 3.7).

Although these theories do make sense at first glance, we see upon closer inspection that the influence of the context and of other people does not fit easily in the model, and that such a model, although excellent for making questionnaires and surveys, is not adapted to the description of actual behaviour in context.[20]

A more realistic approach was the TOTE (Test Operate Test Operate Exit) model that pictures the subject performing a recursive loop in which the current state is tested for congruity with the state that it is tested for (Miller, Galanter, & Pribram, 1960: 26), e.g. 'is the meal cooked yet?' Unfortunately, most refinements of such mostly 'psychological approach', however smart – for example, Bandura's self-efficacy model (Bandura, 1986) – keep the individual subject as the unit of modelling. While such models are aware of the importance of the context, they internalize it in the individual as, e.g. 'perceived behavioural control' in the model just

---

[20] A meta-analysis of 185 empirical studies showed that the theory of planned behaviour could explain 27% of the variance for the behaviours (Armitage & Conner, 2001).

cited, or norms, as if the context only acted via the perception the individual has of it.

As a matter of fact, that is wrong; or rather, incomplete. The context also acts directly and its impact is paramount. The context can act regardless of the subject's reflection: for example, if there is no bread, but only rice, the subject will not eat bread but eat rice, and this in the most predictable manner. And even if this child does not want to go to school, well, as we all know, in the end the child will go anyway. *In practice*, in many cases, if we really want to change a given behaviour (eat rice vs bread) the efficient variable, the locus of control, the target for intervention, are not necessarily in the subject; they can just be in the environment, however unethical – and let us say it, *inhuman* – this approach may appear. Of course the context will at some point be reflected in the subject's experience. As Kurt Lewin hypothesized in light of the results of his famous seminal food study, people come to 'like what they eat rather than eat what they like' (Lewin, 1943: 47).[21]

In a similar way, attitude, which Allport defined as 'a mental and neural state of readiness, organized through experience, exerting a directive or dynamic influence upon the individual's response to all objects and situations with which it is related' (Allport, 1935), actually seems to vary with the context. Bohner and Schwarz's review 'suggests that attitude judgments are constructed on the spot, based on the information and inference rules that are most accessible at that point in time' (Bohner & Schwarz, 2001).

Psychological theories tend by construction to take the psyche, and often the individual psyche, as their object of study, and therefore they tend to locate most causes of behaviour in the psyche. Using only psychologizing theories to account for action would be like trying to understand a scene by looking at it through a distorting mirror. But the subject is caught into a constructive spiral with its environment.

Representations cannot be considered apart from the context, nor from their functional orientation for a specific subject, because that is why and how they are constructed in the first place. 'part of the meaning of the term representation is the rule or the rules required to use it for the purpose it was intended' (Turvey & Shaw, 1979: 207). The logic is to have some operational efficiency of the coupling (subject + environment) to reach the goal. A 'satisficing' solution ('good enough') must be obtained. In other

---

[21] This is only the first of a few unsettling facts that we shall stumble upon as we take a unit other than individuals as the focus of study. The locus of control, the design logic, the selection factors, the decision processes do not necessary lie in the hands and will of individual subjects.

words, the success of a coupling subject-environment is measured by the outcome of their synergy: does it produce a 'good' result? Well, the proof is in the pudding.

In practice, and somewhat at odds with psychologizing theories, it seems that the most influent components of our complex sociotechnical systems, what makes behaviour predictable, are not so much what is inside the subject, but rather the installations that funnel behaviour. To quote Herbert Simon again: 'on that same beach another small creature with a home at the same place as the ant might well follow a very similar path' (Simon, 1996: 51–2). In large societies, this first impression must be mitigated. It is often easier to modify the physical environment or the rules than peoples' representations, which are massively distributed across millions of individual brains.

That reality is problematic when it comes to interventions. The most popular models[22] used in intervention studies are the theory of reasoned action (discussed in Section 3.6.2) and its variants, the Prochaska model, social norms, and, increasingly, types of nudge, as listed in (Sunstein, 2016). But nudge is often limited to a series of local applications of some known biases and influence mechanisms in decision-making, such as the preference for the default condition in a choice or the availability bias, rather than a formal theoretical framework. Very few approaches take into account more than one or two of the three layers highlighted by installation theory.

The problem goes beyond the number of layers taken into account. What makes real-world behaviour difficult to study is that the nature of the determinants depends massively on the situation.

For example, when people queue up to wait for the bus, it is the social rule and how strongly it is enforced in given culture that matter more than the configuration of the terrain at a specific bus stop. On the other hand, in choosing between different brands of coffee in a supermarket aisle, embodied competences will be more important than social rules. Therefore, a good model acknowledges that the various layers of determination apply differently in different situations: that is what installation theory tries to do. What is constant is that all three layers will be influential, but the local shape of the determination model depends on the specific case.

[22] According to a large review by Davis and colleagues (Davis, Campbell, Hildon, Hobbs, & Michie, 2015), the most used models are the theory of planned behaviour (13%) (Ajzen, 1991; Ajzen & Fishbein, 1980), Prochaska's transtheoretical model of behavioural change, especially in the health domain (33%) (Prochaska, Wright, & Velicer, 2008) ; social cognitive theory (11%) (Bandura, 1991), and the information-motivation-behavioural-skills model (7%) (Fisher, Fisher, Bryan, & Misovich, 2002). The social norms approach is also popular (Cialdini, Reno, & Kallgren, 1990; Goldstein, Cialdini, & Griskevicius, 2008; Tankard & Paluck, 2016).

It is a fascinating exercise to look at models of behaviour built by colleagues when you construct one yourself. The models all are 'right' in some sense, but they address only some aspects of the problem because of the way they define the unit of analysis. My feeling, relating to models of behaviour, is that they tend to make their own task difficult by (a) not taking the whole situation as a unit of analysis; and/or (b) by mixing components from different time frames, which are difficult to observe. Taking the situation as a unit of analysis respects the old rule of the unity of action, time and place. It is also prudent to use only constructs that can be empirically observed.

For the reader interested in the exercise, footnote 23[23] provides a list of some of the more influential of these models, following the taxonomy proposed by Darnton (Darnton, 2008a).

So, generic models encounter issues when they try to encapsulate the determinants in a single schematic series of boxes containing variables linked with causal arrows suggesting linear relations. That is not the case of

---

[23] Economic assumptions: Expected utility theory (Jevons, 1871). Behavioural economics: Principles of hyperbolic discounting, framing, inertia (Dawnay & Shah, 2005); Bounded Rationality (Simon, 1955);Tversky & Kahneman's judgment heuristic (Kahneman & Tversky, 1974); prospect theory (Tversky & Kahneman, 1979); system 1/system 2 cognition (Stanovich & West, 2000).

Information: (Information) deficit models; awareness interest decision action (AIDA) (Strong, 1925); value action gap (Blake, 1999).

Values, beliefs and attitudes: (Adjusted) expectancy value (EV) theory (Atkinson, 1957); theory of reasoned action (Fishbein & Ajzen, 1975); health belief model (Rosenstock, 1964); protection motivation theory (Rogers, 1975); schematic causal model of environmental concern (Stern, Dietz, Abel, Guagnano, & Kalof, 1999); value-belief-norm theory (Stern, Dietz, Abel, Guagnano, & Kalof, 1999); elaboration likelihood model of persuasion (ELM) (Petty & Cacioppo, 1986); MODE (motivation opportunity determinants) model (Ewoldsen, Rhodes, & Fazio, 2015; Fazio, 1990).

Norms and identity: Norm activation theory (Schwartz, 1977); norm neutralization theory (Sykes & Matza, 1957); focus theory of normative conduct (Cialdini, Kallgren, & Reno, 1991; Cialdini et al., 1990); theory of normative social behaviour (Rimal & Real, 2005); self-categorization theory (Turner & Oakes, 1986; Turner & Reynolds, 2012); social identity theory (Tajfel, 1974; Tajfel & Turner, 1979);

Agency, efficacy and control: Theory of planned behaviour (Ajzen, 1985, 1991); theory of self-efficacy (Bandura, 1977, 1978); theory of fear appeals (Hovland, Irving, & Kelley, 1953; Tannenbaum et al., 2015); model of pro-environmental behaviour (Kollmuss & Agyeman, 2002);

Habit and routine: Theory of interpersonal behaviour (Triandis, 1977); prototype/willingness model (Gibbons, Gerrard, & Lane, 2003);

Emotions: Affect heuristic (Slovic, Finucane, Peters, & MacGregor, 2002); risk as feelings model (Loewenstein, Weber, Hsee, & Welch, 2001).

External factors: Theory of consumption as social practices (Spaargaren, 2011; Spaargaren & Van Vliet, 2000); theory of structuration (Giddens, 1984).

Self-regulation: Control theory (Carver & Scheier, 1982); social cognitive theory of self-regulation (Bandura, 1991).

Societal factors: needs-opportunities-abilities model (Vlek, 2000; Vlek, Jager, & Steg, 1997); main determinants of health model (Dahlgren & Whitehead, 1991)...

This list is incomplete and always will be, however remarkable the reviewing work of Darnton, itself building on thirteen other reviews, and the same goes for other admirable comprehensive reviews.

all models, but the most classic ones tend to do so, as visible in Darnton's review of more than eighty of them (Darnton, 2008a, 2008b). This limits their applicability to the empirical domain for which they were first designed.

Clearly, behaviour is influenced by the context and by other people. Nevertheless, detailed observation reveals that the way in which human behaviour is channelled and regulated by the situation is detailed, tight and continuous, literally almost second by second and inch by inch. The examples provided in Chapter 4, even though considerably simplified for brevity, provide a taste of this impact of external determination on individual activity.

The situation is uncomfortable for psychologists because psychology's comfort zone of study is what happens in the mind, not outside. Still it is obvious that some crucial variables operate outside of this mental zone. And as Lewin noted, the influence of 'nonpsychological' factors on perception and action 'makes it impossible to disregard them in psychology' (Lewin, 1936 : 29).

The situation is similar and symmetrical for other disciplines: each discipline holds some pieces of the jigsaw puzzle – conversely, the psychological aspects of human cognition are out of their reach. And the division of scientific labour does not work well because in actual phenomena, unlike in disciplinary models, all the aspects are connected. Reality is dispiritedly undisciplined.

It is worth mentioning that there have been major theoretical efforts to bridge the macro (social) and the micro (psychological) aspects; among the most prominent are Alfred Schütz's phenomenological sociology (Schütz, 1962, 1970a, 1976a, 1996, 2011, 2013) and Aaron Cicourel's cognitive sociology (Cicourel, 1974, 2002). This book owes them a lot, especially Cicourel, who has been my mentor for so many years. Schütz and Cicourel provide insightful descriptions of interaction, with a level of detail and erudition beyond my capacity. Installation theory builds on their findings and takes steps to simplify the system of description to make it usable by ordinary researchers and practitioners for real-world intervention.

Indeed, although there may be some agreement on a constructionist approach, a key practical issue for the purpose of research is how to describe the situation, which is manifold and discouragingly complex. At this point, most general theories tend to become evasive. Alfred Schütz in his description of the lifeworld states:

> Closer analysis shows that the concept of a situation to be defined contains two principal components: The one originates from the ontological structure of the pregiven world.[24] ... The other component... originates from the actual biographical state of the individual, a state which includes his stock of knowledge in its actual articulation. (Schütz, 1970b: 122)

We will use these two components, the physical world and the embodied experience, and add a third, the social. Indeed, the way a situation is defined is not the individual's sole choice, and there are a series of 'correct' rules to be followed in interpreting the situation. These rules are a social construction, and it is in them, as well as in his own experience, that the actor will find guidance. As Cicourel notes,

> [t]he actor must be endowed with mechanisms or basic procedures that permit him to identify settings which would lead to 'appropriate' invocation of norms ... [they] function as a base structure for generating and comprehending the behavioural (verbal and nonverbal) displays that can be observed. (Cicourel, 1974: 27)

These procedures and norms enable the actor to play the appropriate role in the situation. Cicourel calls them 'interpretive procedures'; they are shared by all actors and 'enable the actor to generate appropriate (usually innovative) responses in changing situated settings'. (ibid: 27). Although such procedures are shared across participants, and refer to structures at a sociological level, they can generate locally appropriate variants that integrate the specificity of the situation and of the performer. Cicourel compares these structures to Chomsky's (1965) deep linguistic structures (as opposed to surface structures that would compare to performed behaviours), and the play between the normative procedure and its local translation into a specific behaviour to the Meadian dialectics on the (socially constructed) 'me' and the (idiosyncratic) 'I' (Mead [1934] 1972). Such interpretive procedures are crucial because they are the locus where (immanent) social structure is translated into (situated) individual behaviour.

As we can see, the problem we tackle is tough, and the chances of making a simple theory appear low. Even the great Kurt Lewin, who attempted, in his dynamic psychology (Lewin, 1948), a topological description of the lifeworld as a manifold, was somewhat unsuccessful.

The next chapter presents an attempt in the same spirit as Lewin but with a less ambitious and simpler formalism; it also benefits from the work

---

[24] Schütz means here the material world.

of the many researchers, Lewin included, who have made progress in the field since 1936. Chapter 4 explores how taking an object of intermediate size, such as the installation, considerably facilitates analysis of the transition between macro and micro. Having access to the relevant microscopic data also makes investigation considerably simpler.

# The Structure of Installations

This chapter describes the structure and nature of installations.

It first sketches their threefold structure, and then details each of the layers: the material environment, the embodied interpretive competences, the social regulation. It addresses, from the perspective of the actor, how activity is determined by these three layers of components, locally acting jointly as 'installations'.

It illustrates the content of these layers with examples from activities such as changing a flat tyre on a roadside, tightening a bolt in a nuclear plant, taking orders in a four-star restaurant, preparing medications for patients in a hospital, intubating a patient in an intensive care unit and searching a suspect in a stop-and-search police procedure.

Section 4.1 gives an overview of installations' structure; Sections 4.2, 4.3 and 4.4 describe their three layers of components.

The last part of each section is dedicated to the operationalization of the concepts: how the researcher can in practice extract these components from the empirical material.

Section 4.5 shows how the redundancy of these layers makes installations *resilient*. That property will turn out essential for societal reproduction.

Picture society as a pointillist image, a wider picture made of thousands of little dots (Figure 4.1). This is how images are reproduced in modern processes such as photography and printing.

Installation theory is about is *how things happen* at the level of these little dots, the microscopic level of society, all the places where specific behaviours happen (the counter, the bus, the religious office, etc.). The

Figure 4.1. A halftone printed image at increasing levels of magnification. A black and white version of this figure will appear in some formats. For the colour version, please refer to the plate section.

dots in this metaphor are the installations, these *micro-settings* where human *activity* is constructed and channelled; the situations where individual needs, desires and will combine with the reality of the context to produce a behavioural outcome. A society is the combination of all these microscopic, local devices that produce behaviour. Installation theory is about analysing society at ground level, not from a bird's eye view. Human beings' social life is a trajectory joining such dots, as the individuals link along a chain the behaviours that constitute their daily activity. In each of these spots, as in a funfair ground, our fellow human beings enter some attraction where they behave and experience more or less what they expected to get there.

And at each of these spots they learn or relearn how to behave in such attraction. Each of these spots is where practice is (re)produced locally, not completely independently of the rest of the spots of course, but still mostly based on the local conditions. And each of these spots is not one little homogenous block, but the combination of layers (Installation theory simplifies it as three layers); just as in printing or photography one coloured dot is obtained by the superimposition, the combination, the coalescence of three layers of primary colours. The resilience of society is due, in part, to the relative redundancy of these three layers, which induce and sometimes force the participant to behave appropriately.

So society is not constituted of individuals only. Individuals and their embodied competences are indeed one layer of this system. The two other layers are the material environment and social regulation. In social science, it is often considered that humans are the single material from which societies are made. Describing societies with this layer does indeed provide an image, but this remains an incomplete, monochrome description, which

Plate 1. Subcams worn by research participants. *Left*: Anaesthetist Kirsten Gjeraa, MD, Danish Institute for Medical Simulation (DIMS), Capital Region of Denmark, and University of Copenhagen, Denmark, and surgeon, seen from the nurse's perspective. *Right*: Cadet police officer Tore Seierstad during training for intervention, seen from the perspective of the trainer (from Lahlou, Le Bellu, & Boesen-Mariani, 2015).

Plate 2. Screenshot from a subcam film of a power plant technician centring a gasket during the maintenance of a pump valve (*left*, from Le Bellu, 2011, snapshots extracted from video appendix). Replay interview of an obese person commenting on her subcam film and remembering how she felt as she tried on a vest and saw herself in the mirror of the fitting room of a department store (*right*, from Lahlou, Urdapilleta, Pruzina, & Catheline, 2012).

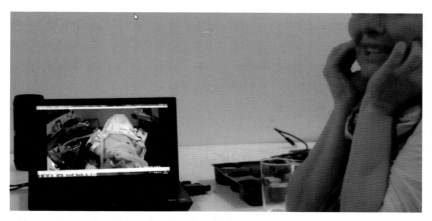

Plate 3. Doctor describing what she thought during an episode of trying to intubate a patient in a difficult airway case; she expresses with gestures the state of the patient with a constricted trachea and throat as she empathizes with that patient.

Plate 4. The reception installation. *Left*, seen from the third-person perspective, the receptionist presses the button that opens the door to the visitor. *Right*, the same scene as seen from the receptionist's point of view.

Plate 5. The replay interview: *Left*, Eva shows the various elements of her workstation on the subcam recording at 15:01:43. *Right*, a screenshot from the subcam at 15:02:02 where Eva's workstation is clearly visible (note in the background the visitor waiting on the sofa near the staircase).

Plate 6. A halftone printed image at increasing levels of magnification.

Plate 7. Changing a flat tyre: Finding an affordance for the jack and cranking.

Plate 8. The technician sets the value of the torque on the torque wrench (*left*). During tightening, when the set value is reached, the wrench beeps and lights a red signal diode (*right*). (From Le Bellu, 2011; snapshots extracted from video appendix.)

Plate 9. Nurse tries to scan the barcode of a drug. The individual glass container (*1*) has a barcode (*2*) that is not recognized (*3*). Nurse looks methodically on the box containing the bottles (*4–7*), finally finds the barcode on one side (*7*) and scans successfully (*8*).

Plate 10. Equipment sterilization. The nurse takes a wiping cloth (*1*), cleans the digital assistant (*2*), then the keyboard and workstation area (*3*), then once the procedure is complete she checks into the dispensation programme (*4*) and scans her ID badge to authenticate (*5*). Finally, she takes off the gloves and washes her hands (*6*).

Plate 11. The nurse nudges the patient into learning the procedure. Patient puts forward arm (*1*), nurse scans bracelet (*2*), later patient puts forward arm again (*3*), but the nurse gently puts it back on the bed (*4*) because there is no need to scan the ID bracelet again.

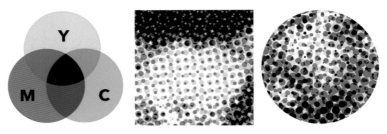

Plate 12. Halftone printing. *Left*, the effect of combining three primary colours (yellow, magenta and cyan). *Centre*, magnification of halftone dot print with primary colours-magnification of the neck of the character on Figure 4.1. *Right*, magnification of the bouquet of lily of the valley in Figure 5.12.

Plate 13. Chef Frederic Martin adapts his technique to fill the bowls with soup from one day to the next and uses the 'piston' instead of a ladle.

Plate 14. The apprentices volunteer to help and try to reproduce what they saw the chef do the day before. Apprentice 2 sprinkles the pepper (*1*) and asks if they should pour the oil (*2*). She tries (*3*) and the chef gives verbal feedback. For the next batch of twelve bowls (*4*) they all manage alone and the chef does not comment.

Plate 15. Example of a litho print (*left*) obtained by the superimposition of four layers (*right*): cyan, magenta, yellow and black – also called 'Key').

Plate 16. A view of the open space offices in the K1 building. The RAO meeting room, with the Tabec screen during a videoconference (*right*).

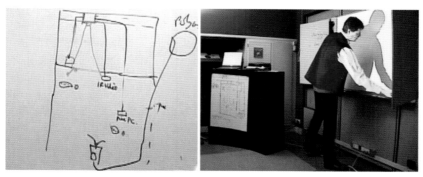

Plate 17. First draft of the Tabec (*left*). First prototype with direct projection (V-01) showing the problem of the user's shadow. (From Lahlou et al., 2012.) This picture and all the Tabec illustrations that follow are reproduced with the kind agreement of Lavoisier Publications, Paris.

Plate 18. Broadening the Tabec. Here we see the new screen attached for tests before the enlargement of the wall opening, visible in the back. This allows size comparison between Tabec V-02 and Tabec V-03. (From Lahlou et al., 2012.)

Plate 19. Double projection from a single source (V-03). The seam between the two sources (vertical line in the middle of the logo) is very visible and unpleasant. (From Lahlou et al., 2012.)

Plate 20. Tabec V-04: Double projection from two independent sources (2002). (From Lahlou et al., 2012.)

misses some crucial aspects that come from the combination of the three layers.[1]

In practice, everything relates to everything else to some degree. Actor, objects, representations, institutions and most variables of a system are connected by transverse, longitudinal, functional, sociohistoric and genetic (etc.) relations. In a system, isolating the parts destroys the very nature of the system. Still, a handy theory should be simple and separate the parts to break down the problem into tractable units. That is a tricky trade-off.

Where on the phenomenon one traced the delineating lines of theory (how one distinguishes what one considers the relevant components), that may not make a big difference when it is for description purpose only, but it can make a huge difference when it comes to cutting the phenomenon along those lines for practical purposes such as intervention.

Indeed our problem here was to produce a theory that is usable for action, not just for description. Inevitably, there are trade-offs in the way we artificially cut the system into subsystems and sketch the model. As the reader will learn, installation theory is simple, but at the cost of some epistemic approximations and quite a bit of redundancy. Still it works in practice, and for practice indeed it is designed. As said already, I do not try to, as Barker did, provide a systematic description system for classification of installations. I believe that the limits of installations are fuzzy, and that there are too many different kinds. Rather I provide a framework and a method fit to analyse any particular installation.

## 4.1. Components of Installations Are Distributed over Three Layers

In human societies, the determinants of human behaviour are distributed. They lay in the subjects (motives, goals, preferences, habits) and in the context (artefacts, rules, other people). As Roy Pea noted, 'When I say that intelligence is distributed, I mean that the resources that shape and enable activity are distributed in configuration across people, environments, and situations.' (Pea, 1993: 50).

Because that distribution is difficult to study, because its components are scattered, we need operational units of study. Installations are these

---

[1] The elemental unit of analysis in social psychology is the social-psychological Triangle of Ego, Alter and Object. There is no such thing as an isolated human (there is always an Other to consider); relations with others (and life in general) are about Objects. Any study of human life, at any level, must therefore include this triangular approach. This is why we use three layers of analysis, in which individuals, other people and objects are always considered together as a system.

units. They are local and functional units that can be empirically studied; they are also relevant units for intervention.

**Installation theory describes installations as a combination of** *three layers of components that assemble locally to produce activity.* **These components are not of the same nature and are not physically located in the same substratum. Some are in the physical setting, some embodied in the subject, some in the social fabric. But when they meet in the same space-time locus, their conjunction triggers a predictable development. The specific combination of the three layers emerges to the subject as a specific 'situation'; this situation is usually recognized as an instance of a typified situation and interpreted as such with the usual script (e.g. 'eating at the restaurant'; 'waiting in line'), with minor adaptations to fit the local specificities (e.g. eating with chopsticks; taking a ticket and listening for one's number to be called).**

Together, the various components in the three layers form a 'coalition' (Turvey, Shaw, & Mace, 1978), that is, an integral functional system, one that has operational closure. In other words, their combination acts as an autonomous operational unit; it contains all necessary resources and mechanisms to perform its purpose.[2]

Installations tend to be localized as the point of delivery of activity (a Shop, a Gallows, a Lecture, a Service Station) Most of them are easily recognizable and named by the typical member of the culture (the native); they are associated with a specific, stereotyped, behaviour that the native predictably performs naturally and spontaneously upon entry in the installation. Some installations might move along with the subject (e.g. a Bus, a Plane). Some may be hard to localize in space (e.g. a Social Network such as Facebook). But most of the time the physical layer of the installation occupies a fixed area of space and time, and this 'place' is used to describe the whole installation *to where* people would go, or *in which* things would happen (a Restaurant, Toilets, a Bedroom, a Concert, a Board Meeting). *This metonymic reduction of installations to a place in current language is revealing but misleading.* The place alone is not a complete functional

---

[2] The notion of operational closure, as a self-maintaining system, is of course blurry (see Glossary). There is no such thing as a system that is independent from its environment, and wherever the border is set we shall realize that in fact what is out of the border still impacts the system. Also, operational closure exists at many embedded levels in any system: there are always some coherent 'parts' with some degree of autonomy and endurance. After all, animals are made of atoms. And there is a subtle margin between what is a 'satisficing' performance of purpose, a configuration of the system that meets some minimal criteria, and 'better states', which are slightly different configurations that perform better on the criteria just described, but would require some transition cost from the present state. A lot happens in that blurry territory, the whole story of life perhaps.

system. An installation is not reduced to the 'context': it includes the participant as a key engine, along with other stakeholders and participants, directly or indirectly.

The installations of the World guide subjects into their activity track, at three levels: objective material environment, subjective embodied interpretative systems and social regulation. Let us explore these three levels in detail.

## 4.2.   Layer 1: Objective Material Environment

This objective layer is in the physical context, the material environment. This is a given ('*data*') to the subject and external to him; what Schütz calls the pregiven world (see Section 3.6). Buildings, chairs, bicycles, apples are examples from this layer. Most of these objects are constructed artefacts: 'the built environment'. They were constructed, with deliberate intention, as a setting or instrument for activity; e.g. a hospital ward, a hair dryer, a bus.

### 4.2.1.   *The Material Layer and its Affordances*
### *in Theory (with Examples)*

Let us call 'objects' these material things for the sake of simplicity. An object is not necessarily, like apples or chairs, some material entity that appears connex and rigid. An object, for an actor, is an entity that is, as a whole, relevant for action. For example, a set of scuba-diving gear, a suit, a uniform are 'objects', even though they are made of distinct parts. So are 'a hospital', 'a car' and 'a government'. Uexküll defined an object as 'that which moves as a unitary whole' (Lorenz, 1935, quoting Uexküll). We could make this more precise by saying an object is for the observer *what appears to act or being acted upon as a unitary whole*. By this we understand that the boundaries between an object and a setting can be fuzzy. It does not matter. What is relevant is their connotation for action rather than their precise physical boundaries.

The affordances (see Section 3.1) of physical objects inform, support and constrain activity. For example, a table signals a location for a meal and supports the dishes, but also constrains the space where food manipulation takes place. We know this when we set the table for a dinner, and in occasion carefully plan the affordances (placement) to funnel social performance. The shape of tables is known to influence the nature and outcome of meetings (Abric, 1999): it is no accident if King Arthur's table was designed round. More generally, the idea that the built environment is a way to influence behaviour is as old as Feng shui, one of the five arts of Chinese metaphysics; the extreme view is known in the West (and criticized) as 'architectural determinism' (Broady, 1966). More recently Christopher Alexander's now classic 'pattern language' helps to build physical enclaves appropriate for a given activity (e.g. 'corner grocery', 'a place to wait', 'Zen view'). It provides architects with 253 problems and hypotheses of 'what arrangement of the physical environment will work to solve the problem presented' (Alexander et al., 1977: xv). For workspaces Hartkopf and colleagues (Hartkopf, Loftness &Aziz, 2009: 65 et seq.) provide a classification of seven types of collaborative places.

Affordances of installations are constructed on purpose. In this perspective, the objects can be considered implanted in the installations to provoke *stigmergy*. Stigmergy (see Glossary) is how individuals can effect (stimulate) the behaviour of others through the modification of artefacts. Stigmergy was originally discovered as the mechanism by which social insects coordinate action without communicating directly. For example, how termites, by depositing building material at a specific place, chemically induce other termites to deposit at the same place, which results in a column and, scaling up, in the end into a termitary (Grassé, 1959). Unlike insects, humans are able to use stigmergy *intentionally* in a variety of situations, and also combine it with communication (e.g. through annotations and signs). For example, in cities trash bins are implanted in the streets so people deposit their garbage instead of dirtying the pavement. As Susi and Ziemke note: 'a number of agents, interacting with each other and their common environment, achieve some collaborative activity, which is (to some degree) mediated by artefacts' (Susi & Ziemke, 2001).[3]

Affordances are interpreted as connotations of activity by the subjects. Objects can act directly as barriers or scaffolds (a wall, a chair). They also act as bearer of signification and trigger a cascade of interactions coupling the setting and the subject if they bind with a matching receptor in the subject (the interpretive structure that has affinity with the object): a service station sign is significant for the motorist and may trigger the motorist to drive in. In other words, objects have a potential for activity, but this potential will realize only if an interested actor comes into their field of

---

[3] Stigmergy is not always positive. Roy Pea (personal communication, 2016) noted that ex-New York City mayor Rudy Guiliani, in his late-1980s cleanup action of the city, showed that graffiti, trash, broken windows, traffic light squeegee hustlers, all foster a lawless, crime-oriented set of subsequent behaviors, and that suppressing such traces from the public space diminishes 'me-too' vandal behaviour.

Figure 4.2. Changing a flat tyre (extracts from a subcam film):
Awareness of problem (*1*), stopping (*2*), diagnosis (*3*). A black and white version of this
figure will appear in some formats.

potential, just like a magnet only has visible effects if some magnetizable object comes close. This is an intuition that grounded Lewin's dynamic psychology (Lewin, 1948).

This layer of installation is distributed in the physical environment, in the form of objects, which are the material components of installations. As just stated, the placement of these objects in the physical context is usually the result of deliberate intention to elicit or support a specific behaviour (or to prevent it).

Let us consider some examples in the course of a mundane activity: changing a tyre. This example will show that in practice, this layer is more sophisticated than the in classic example of the chair. The structure and content of the spare tyre compartment in the car's boot, some parts of the car and specific sections of the roadside provide the physical layer of the installation for the activity 'changing a tyre'.

All figures are extracted from a film in first-person perspective provided by a SEBE protocol (see Chapter 2), in which researcher Sophie Le Bellu confronted the driver with his videotaped activity and asked him to comment on his behaviour (see also Lahlou, 2010b). As we describe the action and the effects of the physical layer, we also, in passing, mention some interventions of the other layers of the installation.

Here and below we refer to figures in the following format: images should be read from left to right, then line by line. So Figure 4.2:1 refers to the first image of Figure 4.2 (the one on the left, where the driver holds the driving wheel).

The driver first realizes that there is something wrong because the car does not react normally (embodied interpretation skill). He pulls to the right (Figure 4.2:1) to stop on the roadside as soon as he sees a space for parking. Note that these parking spaces have been especially designed by road builders precisely to afford such emergency stops, and are often signalled as such. That is a nice example of affordance built on purpose in the environment.

Figure 4.3. Changing a flat tyre: Taking the vest from the car boot and
placing the triangle. A black and white version of this figure will appear in some formats.

As he parks, the driver switches on his warning lights (institutional rule, embodied by the driver, reified by the warning switch on the dashboard) (Figure 4.2:2).

Notice how this action, because it is crucial for the safety of the whole system, is compulsory (by law) and redundantly scaffolded by all layers.

The driver checks the tyre Figure 4.2:3) sees it is flat; then goes to the boot to get a replacement tyre (constructed physical affordance). Before he takes out the tyre, he opens the repair kit, which contains the tools (tyre wrench, folding jack) but also a folding signalling triangle and a fluorescent reflective vest. The triangle is a conventional sign for danger in road traffic symbolism. The reflective vest is compulsory in some countries.

Because the repair kit is above the tyre, the driver must remove it to access the tyre. In doing so he is nudged to open the kit, with the happy result that the driver is prompted to use the vest and the triangle, which will protect him and the car, before he continues with the rest of the activity. Indeed, the driver puts on the vest and unfolds the triangle and places it on the road behind his car (Figure 4.3).

Interestingly, we see here that the structure of the tyre compartment and the repair kit provide indications about what to do, but also in which order to do it. As the driver watches the section of the film depicted in Figure 4.3, during the replay interview, he comments:

> - DRIVER: This is the emergency bag ... I only have to remember to go to that one single emergency bag and in this bag I will as I open it ... [Gestures as if something jumps from the bag to his face] things will tell me what I have to use. I would probably have forgotten putting on the ... the jacket if I hadn't seen it in the bag; same goes for the gloves.

Indeed, the bag also contains protection gloves. The driver puts them on – which will avoid getting his hands dirty. The driver then takes the replacement tyre out of the boot and puts it on the ground near the flat tyre; he also puts there the folding jack, which he found attached to the

Figure 4.4. Changing a flat tyre: Bringing in the replacement wheel.

Figure 4.5. Changing a flat tyre: Finding an affordance for the jack and cranking. Note that the images in this Figure are tilted because the driver is bending his head to have a better view under the chassis, so the camera affixed to his glasses is tilted too. For the colour version, please refer to the plate section.

tyre compartment as he took the tyre out (Figure 4.4). Here again, he has been guided both in content and sequence of process by the affordances that unfold before him as the action progresses. The maker of the car has designed the spare tyre compartment as a self-contained physical support layer for changing a tyre; it contains all the necessary scaffolding and displays, accessible in an ordered sequence that guides the user.

The driver then unfolds the jack and inserts its upper part in a small mortise in the lower part of the girder in the chassis that will prevent the jack from slipping (specially constructed affordance; Figure 4.5). The driver has to look under the chassis to find the affordance (Figure 4.5:1). He does not exactly know what he is looking for, except that it must be some kind of ridge or structure that fits the top of the jack. When he thinks he's found it he checks that it matches the top end of the jack (Figure 4.5:2) before starting to turn the crank to elevate the jack (Figure 4.5:3).

And so on and so forth: the driver changes the tyre; puts the flat tyre in place of the spare tyre in the boot compartment; takes off the gloves, jacket and triangle; and returns all the components to the boot in the reverse order. Then he gets back in the car, fastens his seat belt and drives away (Figure 4.6, Figure 4.7 and Figure 4.8).

No further detail of the activity is needed; I assume the reader knows the procedure. But, interestingly, although you probably know how to proceed in context, you may not be able to describe exactly the full sequence of operations outside of context. We'll come back later to this interesting point.

Figure 4.6. Changing a flat tyre: Replacing tyre, tightening bolts. A black and white version of this figure will appear in some formats.

Figure 4.7. Changing a flat tyre: Finishing tightening bolts with foot, storing flat tyre and tools. A black and white version of this figure will appear in some formats.

Figure 4.8. Changing a flat tyre: Back in car (*1*), fastening seat belt (*2*), leaving (*3*).

The role of the components in the material layer is obvious here, as well as some embodied competences. Interestingly, most of the procedural calls to embodied competences (e.g. tightening a bolt) come from the affordances as they unfold. The user only needs a vague knowledge of the script (e.g. go and get the spare tyre in the boot, then exchange it for the flat one): as he tries to perform, the details of what has to be done become obvious from the situation and its affordances. The actor is guided step by step and scaffolded by the installation, in space at a fine level of detail for movements; and in time for the order of succession of operations. Material components also contribute to enforcing the regulation, as we saw here for safety rules with the warning lights, the triangle and the jacket that will protect both the driver and other oncoming drivers. This example illustrates how in the detail operates what Julia Black calls the regulation by 'technologies' (Black, 2002), in which she includes the design of the built environment. We see again and again throughout this book that components of installation have aspects of both facilitation and control.

Figure 4.9. The technician sets the value of the torque on the torque wrench (*left*). During tightening, when the set value is reached, the wrench beeps and lights a red signal diode (*right*). (From Le Bellu, 2011; snapshots extracted from video appendix.) A black and white version of this figure will appear in some formats. For the colour version, please refer to the plate section.

Especially remarkable is that the process works even in some cases in which the driver does not know and has never executed the action before, as was the case here for fitting the jack into the mortise under the girder. With a bit of local exploration and fiddling the driver quickly finds the fit. We'll come back to this amazing resilience of the system to the lack of knowledge of the subject.

The affordances often signal the turning points of action, with a system response that triggers the next step. In the tyre example, when tightening up the bolts, it is when a given bolt becomes too difficult to tighten that it is time to go to the next. And then, when the last bolt is tightened, there is no more affordance for tightening and it is then time to put back the trim, and so on.

In contrast, let us look at the example from Chapter 2 of the technician changing a valve gasket, (Figure 2.3). Once the technician has changed the gasket, he puts back the other section of the valve on top of the gasket and bolts it to the bottom section, with the gasket in between (Figure 4.9:1). Quality control requires that all bolts be tightened *exactly* with the same strength, to create an even pressure on the gasket (these valves are used in nuclear plant cooling circuits; the safety rules are very strict). Therefore the technician tightens the bolts with a digital torque wrench that displays the torque value. The wrench beeps and a red diode lights up when the torque reaches the set value (Figure 4.9:2). This signals the technician that he can go to tighten the next bolt. Note that the difference in the performance of tightening, which is much more precise in the valve case, is not obtained by increased competence of the operator, but rather by the sophistication of the installation that provides more detailed feedback (the diode) and explicit rules formalized in an algorithm (see Glossary).

Here's another example of when a change of the affordances signals the need for new action. French sommelier Christophe Martin showed me the process of decanting an old wine, which consists in carefully pouring the wine from the bottle into the decanter without transferring the sediment of solidified polyphenols that has accumulated on the side of the bottle as it laid ageing for years in the cellar. When asked during the replay interview: 'And when do you stop pouring?' he explained that, by observing the sediment in transparency, backlit with a candle, he can see when some particles start moving from the deposit; this is for him the signal to stop pouring and pass to the next step. Here again, the context signals by its affordances when to go to the next step, but it requires more embodied competence by the subject to interpret it correctly.

A well-designed installation provides the subjects with different affordances as the action unfolds. This can be done in many ways, the simplest of which is that appropriate action of the subject produces a change of the system that creates the affordance for the next step, as we saw in the decanting example. In more complex installations, signalling (e.g. to synchronize different participants or create advance warning) may be used: that is for example what is done with traffic lights at a road intersection.

Institutional work and influence through social interaction is not immediately apparent in the changing tyre sequence and is developed in Section 4.4. They would have been more visible if a policeman had been involved. Nevertheless a closer look at the reflective vest illustrates the omnipresence of norms controlling the genesis and form factor of the artefacts: This vest is recommended by the European Transport Safety Council and conforms to EN-471 European Norm for High Visibility Standard, as well as to the European Council Directive of 21 December 1989 on the approximation of the laws of the Member States relating to personal protective equipment (89/686/EEC) and especially its article 2.13: *Personal Protection Equipment in the form of clothing capable of signalling the user's presence visually*. We could go on and on: every detail of this artefact is the result of a complex historical social construction, submitted to social control and norms. The same goes for the driving behaviour, the traffic regulations, the dashboard switch for the warning lights, the specifications of the tyres, the road and the bolts.

Institutions can be more or less local, but they locally reflect in the affordances. For example, Patrick Bertron, chef at the prestigious Bernard Loiseau restaurant in Saulieu, France, explains how they set up in the kitchen a system of rules for managing the orders, using tickets to follow the progression of the preparation and service of the various plates at each table. The system is necessary to manage dozens of tables, each with several

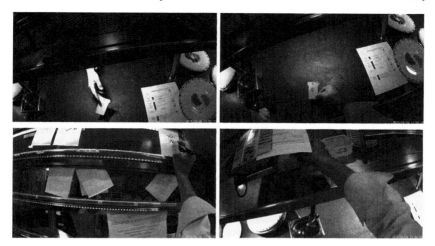

Figure 4.10. Following the dishes orders in the kitchen with a system of rules and note-cards in a gastronomic restaurant. Ticket with table and course number to send is brought in from the dining room by the waitress (*1*), taken by the chef (*2*), decoded with the menu Post-it and announced to cooks, then Post-it is annotated (*3*). Finally, the ticket is put in dedicated plastic box (*4*).

guests and several courses, with dishes for each guest, all eating together and expecting that all dishes arrive simultaneously at the right temperature on each table. Not too early because the customers must have finished the previous dish, but not too late, to avoid making them wait. This even though each dish ingredient needs different preparation time and precise cooking – for example, the vegetable may take longer to cook than the fish, and the sauce is prepared separately. In such a restaurant, perfection is the rule. This imposes some complicated constraints on the timing and sequence of operations and a very tight coordination of countdown to launch the cooking of each ingredient at the right time. Here is how they do it, with the use of annotations and affordances of the physical layer.

As the waiters come in the kitchen to signal when the plates can be started (based on how they assess and anticipate the progress of the meal at the table), the orders are transcribed on a small ticket (and here 9/2 means second course for table 9) handed to the chef (Figure 4.10:1). The chef reads from another Post-it note on a board (Figure 4.10:2) the nature of the orders for that table, and announces out loud to all the team 'gentlemen, the nine, a hot foie gras at the menu and a bream at the menu!' meaning that table 9 has ordered two second courses: a foie gras and a bream, so the cooks can start preparing, with the quantity appropriate for the fixed price menu – a tad less quantity than 'à la carte' orders. The chef annotates the Post-it note to signal the dishes have been started (Figure 4.10:3) and puts the ticket in the 'processed' container, a plastic box (Figure 4.10:4).

As dishes progresses from order to preparation to being sent to the dining room, the Post-its move on a special board and finally the names of dishes are crossed off on the Post-it when the dishes are sent to the dining room. This provides a dashboard view of the current state of orders. It also regulates labour division and avoids conflicts between waiters and cooks, because sometimes there was confusion (e.g. 'table 2, course 3' instead of 'table 3, course 2') and the clients would wait. Then there would be dispute among staff over who was responsible for the loss in translation.

> We were tired of fighting like cats: Who is right, who is wrong? Who spoke clearly, who heard or misheard? So we made these little tickets and since that day, oddly, there's never been an error. (P. Bertron, commenting on his subcam recording)

Here again, as for the torque wrench, the affordances are linked to the institutional rules and facilitate execution according to what is expected. These affordances are meaningful, and efficient, in the specific system of the installation but they can hardly be understood in isolation of the other layers.

Finally, we must note that, to execute a specific apparently 'single' activity, the subject must use many different tools and artefacts. That is obvious in the video recordings of our examples above. It is also in clerical work: to draft a client email to schedule a conference call, the paralegal observed by Cangiano and Hollan (2009) needed her calendar, her email folders and a web-based database. The installation brings all these necessary resources in the same place (along the behavioural track) to make them easily accessible. That is why the structure and contents of the installation match the functional requirements of the activity.

### 4.2.2.   Operationalization of the Material Layer in Research and Practice

How can we access and describe the physical layer empirically?

Affordances are often constructed by humans in the built environment and in material objects, with specific intentions. They can be described in functional terms, and natural language provides a detailed vocabulary to describe the shapes and properties of objects.

In the practice of research it is easy to discuss with participants what objects are relevant to their actions, and what affordances they perceive and use. Many objects are also accessible to direct measurement and recording, and often the rationale and plans of their constructions are explicit and available (manuals, blueprint, procedures etc.). So in research practice this layer of determinants is well suited for empirical capture and study. Methods such as 'perceived quality' quantified analysis through verbalization (Nosulenko, 2008) strengthened the arsenal of psychological techniques to explore and measure the perceived functional properties of objects.

Therefore the first layer of determination of action is rather easy to access empirically. It is immediately visible and measurable; furthermore humans have developed precise symbolic systems of reference to describe these determinants in shape and function (language being the most notable, which subsumes sophisticated systems of categorization and classification). Finally, human observers, because they are humans, tend to naturally interpret affordances for humans. To some degree, because many affordances are based on physically measurable parameters (e.g. shape, frequency, weight), their perceived quality for activity (Nosulenko & Samoylenko, 2001, 2009) is measurable by instruments.

In other words, this first layer of constructs in installation theory has some solid empirical handles. That is not always the case in social science: think of constructs such as 'habitus' or 'attitude'.

This possibility to empirically access, by external observation, the very components described in the theory is an important aspect of installation theory. It suggests there will be a minimal loss in translation in the course of operationalizing the theory in practice. In practice, observing the installations in use enables one to understand and describe which components of the context are relevant. But because the details are paramount, video recordings, preferably in the first-person perspective, provide a better view. The participation of the subjects themselves in the description, in the tradition of ethnography, provides a better understanding, as well as the names of the relevant objects, affordances, and the meaning the participants give them in an 'emic'[4] manner.

---

[4] Emic refers to a description in terms of the actor, whereas etic refers to a description by an observer in culturally neutral terms (in practice: scientific). The emic/etic refers initially to the difference between phonemics and phonetics. Phonemes are elementary units of sound distinguished by the speakers of a given language; phonetics focuses on the physical description of the sound of human speech: the categories used for lexical or grammatical description of words by linguists are different. More generally, the categories used to describe phenomena in one's own culture may differ from those used in an external description. For a longer discussion, see Headland, 1990; Headland, Pike, & Harris, 1990; Lahlou, 2011a; and Pike, 1967.

### 4.3. Layer 2: Embodied Interpretive Systems

One can only do what is afforded by the present environment as described in the previous section. This first, physical, level of determination affords a tree of possible behaviours.

But not everything that is possible will be realized. For example, I could stand up on this chair, but I don't. I could also dance in the bus, pee in the garden, eat cats or beat children; I don't do that either. There are, beyond affordances, other determinants that limit what I actually do.

Let us therefore look at this essential protagonist, the subject, who carries the second layer of determinants of activity: *embodied interpretive systems*.

This is a long section, because it describes the long chain from the macro (institutions, societal rules) to the micro (neurones). We won't get into the neuroscience details of the micro – that would take many books and is beyond my capacity – but I give some indications to show the direction of travel. This section is long also because it contains many illustrative cases to ease the reading.

#### 4.3.1. *The Embodied Layer and Interpretive Systems in Theory (with Examples)*

Just as a mousetrap uses the mouse's appetence for cheese, and the mouse's motor capacity is a crucial component of its operation, an installation uses the embodied interpretive systems of its participants as the engine of its operation. There may be nonhuman agency in the system, but the human contribution is paramount in executing the behavioural sequence. Think of an elevator, a ticket booth, a football match: they cannot operate without human participation and input. That human participation, in a specific situation, is driven by embodied interpretive systems that connect the perception of the situation by the subject into action by the same. For example, as I am driving my car in town, I see the traffic light turn red; I push the brake pedal to stop. In my past experience I have learned 'something-about-traffic-lights-that-guides-my-action-when-I-encounter-one'; and I carry around that 'something' with me in my body.

So by *embodied interpretive systems* I mean interpretation structures internal to the body, usually known as reflexes, skills, knowledge, representations, mental models, experience, habitus, common sense and so forth. Under this term we must also include the *dispositional* properties of the body that have their own orientation and dynamics: *drives, reflexes, propensity, inclination,* etc. Whether these originate in the very biological structure of the body (hunger), are culturally acquired (artistic taste), result from life experience (disgust of ketchup) or are a mix the of these (sexual orientation, food preferences) does not matter at the moment of action: in fact most dispositions have mixed origin and result from a combination of innate organs and learning through life experience. So every individual embodies different, idiosyncratic, interpretation processes. But as we saw in Section 3.5 (with social representations theory) all individuals in a given culture tend to have similar idiosyncratic interpretation processes; i.e. all drivers stop at the red light (or at least they know they should).

The very process of interpretation of a situation or object is an emergence of an *action* through some spiralling, abductive, loop between the subject and the situation. The deeper neuroscience digs into the problem the more we discover that 'perception' itself is informed by intentions, even at the level of individual neuronal activity or the sensory cortex (Alexandrov, 2008). It is likely that many if not all parts of the brain (and the body) are involved in *any* interpretation of action, *that every human act is a total neurophysiological act*, to paraphrase the famous (and often misused⁵) notion of 'total social fact'. This makes it difficult to distinguish between various types of embodied interpretive competences. Let us simply consider here that the individual body carries a series of interpretive systems, which map a given situation (state of the body, position in a larger setting, object of attention) into a specific action (emotion, thought, movement) of the body.⁶

Often these interpretive competences are automatic: the subject cannot help transforming what is perceived 'out there' into a conventional object. When I see this vertical plank covering an opening in the wall, barring my way to the next room, I cannot help but see 'a door' and my hand moves automatically to the handle. Similarly, I cannot help but understand as

⁵ 'That is to say, in certain cases [facts that] involve the totality of society and its institutions ... and in other cases only a very large number of institutions...' (Mauss, 1990: 100). Emile Durkheim's *Rules of the Sociological Method* introduced the notion of social facts (Durkheim [1895] 1982). Mauss' 'total social phenomena' refer to systemic exchange systems, and Durkheim's notion of social facts (which influenced Mauss) contains the idea that individual action is influenced by society as a whole. Although the ideas are indeed originated in these texts, the expression of total social fact for the systemic idea that a specific fact involves a projection of the total social system seems to be an anachronistic elaboration. See Wendling (2010) for a detailed analysis.

⁶ I have called 'lata' (from *latum*, the participle past of the Latin verb *ferre*: to carry) these interpretive structures the subjects carries embodied (Lahlou, 2000; also see Glossary). Lata are opposed to data, what are given to the subject in the situation. We must use the notion of 'lata' in Section 7.3.1 to distinguish the material neural structures from the processes they underlie. But there are already enough neologisms in installation theory, so rather than introducing neologisms, at this point, I'll stick to 'embodied interpretive systems'; we must use the notion of lata after Section 5.2.3.

informative speech what I hear spoken in my native language; whereas if the same person spoke in Swahili or Berawan, languages I cannot understand, I would hear nothing but meaningless sounds. For example, when I teach to large audiences at the London School of Economics, usually thirty to sixty different nationalities are represented in the room. When I say out of the blue 'Que ceux qui parlent français lèvent la main s'il vous plaît', most people simply do not understand what I said, and for them I just uttered meaningless sounds. But a few hand always rise because those who speak French automatically understood what I asked in French ('Those who can speak French please raise your hand'). Section 5.2 describes these interpretive structures and their genesis in more detail.

Automaticity of interpretation can lead to mistakes when the cues are not correct, and these mistakes are not immediately detected precisely because automaticity happens in autopilot mode. An interesting example is domestic accidents by accidental poisoning. Some cleaning or hygiene products are packaged like foodstuffs (e.g. shampoos or cleaning products containing fruit extracts etc.) and there are numerous cases of consumers drinking them by accident. Basso and colleagues showed with functional neuroimaging that these products evoke cortical taste inferences and are likely to be unconsciously categorized as edible, hence triggering absent-minded, automatic, ingestion in some cases, especially when they are stored in the kitchen (Basso et al., 2014).

Habits are another, often motoric, automatic interpretation system. That may seem a truism, but habitual behaviour tends to be repeated: past behaviour is a good predictor of future behaviour. Ouellette & Wood (1998) point at reasons such as automaticity and dispositions. This correlation is not pure tautology; repetition *builds and strengthens* habits in a positive feedback loop.

> [There] is consensus that habits are acquired through incremental strengthening of the association between a situation (cue) and an action, i.e. repetition of a behaviour in a consistent context progressively increases the automaticity with which the behaviour is performed when the situation is encountered. (Lally, van Jaarsveld, Potts, & Wardle, 2010)

But repetition does not happen by chance. One is, by one's life conditions, regularly led into similar situations. In fact, our days are often rather similar: we take the same transport, at the same time, work in the same place, eat in the same place, etc. Habits are not compulsive acts like twitching; they are proven solutions for recurrent tasks. Put me in a habitual situation and I (my body) is likely to execute a habitual behaviour. Habits result from executing the same behaviours in similar settings. In people's lives, similar situations tend to occur repeatedly (see Glossary: repisodes). Unsurprisingly, people tend to behave similarly in these repisodes, even though in the details they show some adaptive creativity (Glăveanu, 2012).

Indeed, 'similar' means not necessarily the exact same setting in the same place, but can refer to similar settings in different locations like kitchens, cashier's desks, movie theatres. For example, Tereza Vrabcová, studying students moving house across continents for their studies, noticed that some habits came along; e.g. storing the bread in the fridge, a habit transferred from a Chinese kitchen to a UK kitchen when moving over (Vrabcová, 2015: 89). According to (Wood, Quinn, & Kashy, 2002) between one-third and one-half of our behaviours are habits. Although an exact figure would be meaningless considering the vague definition of 'habits', I would agree with Wood and colleagues' range of the estimation. A huge amount of our behaviour is habitual, and a huge amount of our behaviour occurs in installations (see Barker's statistics in Section 1.1).

At biological level, interpretive competences probably take the form of some preferred path of activation in the nervous system that is evoked by a specific state of the subject or stimulus, such as a goal.

> frequent and consistent performance of a goal-directed action in a specific situation facilitates the ease of activating the mental representation of this behavior (and hence the resulting action itself) by the situation. (Aarts & Dijksterhuis, 2000)
>
> … the situation can activate mental representations of normative behaviors automatically. And once activated, these representations provide the knowledge necessary for guiding one's own situationally appropriate behavior. (Aarts & Dijksterhuis, 2003)

Such preferred activation paths are connected with the re-enactments that can be imaged when presenting the stimulus to a subject in an fMRI scan. I will not get into the details here;[7] this is just to point out that psychology and neuroscience have some ideas about how this embodiment is fleshed in the neural system. Perhaps in a few decades we will have a more precise and independent description by an external observer of the physical correlates of our phenomenal experience of the world. So far, the best access we have is still through what the subjects communicate verbally or nonverbally of their experience. Therefore, the best practice to date is to capture all we can objectively record during action (e.g. body-worn video and sensors) and

---

[7] For more details, see Section 5.2.4, especially 5.2.4.2.

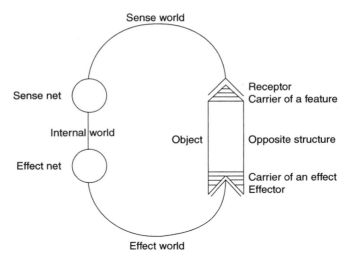

Figure 4.11. Uexküll's functional loop (from Uexküll, 1934, 1992: 324).

combine these 'objective' data with the subjects' own comments on what happened based on a collaborative analysis of the recorded data with the subject, as in the SEBE techniques.

Let us consider again Uexküll's functional loop (Figure 4.11), schematizing how the subject interprets the environment. Structures inside the organism (left side of the figure) couple with structures outside the organism (right side of the figure) to produce the perception-action loop of behaviour. In the previous section we described in the physical layer the 'objects' that are in the physical environment of the subject, which carry affordances for perception and action. What we describe now as 'interpretive competences' are the left side of the loop on the figure: the structures that inside the subject connect perception (sense) to action (effect).

These interpretive systems are the contents of the human black box that produce a response when exposed to a stimulus. The patterns of responses to a given situation can be of evolutionary origin (e.g. innate reflex loops). They often are constructed and/or modified by training (acquired skills, representations, knowledge).

This layer of installation (interpretive systems) is distributed over individual human minds and bodies by means of experience, education and exposure to discourse (media, advertising, etc.)

Here is an empirical illustration from research with Marianne Hald Clemmensen and Peter Dieckmann (Dieckmann, Clemmensen, &

Lahlou, 2017). In the process of preparing medications for the patients (a process we will re-use several times to spare the reader the burden of getting to know in detail too many activities), nurses must scan each product to ensure that medications given to the patient indeed match the physician's prescription (which is kept in a database). This check is done by presenting the barcode of the product to a laser scanner, and the scanner beeps when it recognizes the product – a system known to reduce dispensing errors (Poon et al., 2010).

In the case pictured in Figure 4.12, a nurse is confronted with a product whose barcode the scanner does not recognize (Dieckmann, Clemmensen, & Lahlou, 2016). In this instance, the routine of finding the affordance (barcode) on the packaging, followed by scanning it, fails: the scanner does not beep (Figure 4.12:1–3). This absence of positive feedback warns the nurse something is wrong and interrupts her default routine procedure loop. Fortunately the nurse has a more complex representation of the product than the scanner has. She knows that every product in the hospital pharmacy must have a valid barcode. She also knows by experience, as most nurses of that hospital do, 'which medications are not recognized by the system and make the software crash' –not the case for this product. Therefore she guesses that the correct barcode is not on the individual small glass container but rather on the larger, outer packaging that contains the individual dose units. She looks at every side of this larger cardboard packaging (Figure 4.12:4–6) for a barcode until she finds it on the smaller side of the packaging (Figure 4.12:7), which she then scans successfully: 'beep!' (Figure 4.12:8). The installed coupling (affordance/competence) produced the correct outcome after the repair to the procedure was initiated by the nurse.[8]

---

[8] According to Bernstein's theory of movement (Bernstein, 1947), the key determinant of motor action consists in matching the actual mental image with the image necessary for the future – the goal-image. The most important feature of the subject of human actions is the fact that the transformation of input information about an object into the suitable action upon the object is made in the form of mental reflection. Psychological processing of information is seen as a process of confrontation of exteroceptive information flow (of information sequentially supplied, in the course of action, from the object) with informational groundwork (relevant information about the objects deposited in the memory of the subject and organized as more or less persistent information entities referred to the different objects of the outside world and at the same time, interrelated and interacting with each other) (Oshanin, 1973). This is consistent with the perspective of 'systemic cognitive neuroscience' which grounds goal-oriented action theories in neuroscience (Alexandrov & Sams, 2005). Unlike the gestalist view, Oshanin shows the object of activity is not perceived as a single shape, or affordance, but as a multilayered structure of interrelated elements and features with diverse potential action connotations, which the subject explores for relevance in horizontal or vertical depth as he or she performs goal-directed activity, extracting matching operative images, the relevant elementary features. Oshanin calls this dynamical monitoring process, which is continuously

Figure 4.12. Nurse tries to scan the barcode of a drug. The individual glass container (*1*) has a barcode (*2*) that is not recognized (*3*: barcode reader light is red, no sound). Nurse looks methodically on the box containing the bottles (*4–7*), finally finds the barcode on one side (*7*) and scans successfully (*8*: barcode reader light is green, beep sound). A black and white version of this figure will appear in some formats. For the colour version, please refer to the plate section.

analysing and diagnosing the state of the object ('what is happening') compared with the expected outcome ('what is supposed to happen') to produce 'what is to be done', the psychological function of the objective of the system (психологической функциональной системы предметного действия: ПФСПД). In this process the subject switches from one aspect of some properties of the object to other properties to ground action. This has design implications for improving the operator's efficiency by adapting the affordances of the object as it is presented to the operator, as Oshanin did for the displays in industrial plants.

This simple example illustrates how actors rely both on affordances and on internalized representations that guide their action (here, exploring the packaging until finding the desired affordance matching the search image). This redundancy makes the installation resilient to defects and errors, as is the case here when affordances fail: one failing layer is substituted by the other. We see in passing the key role of humans in fixing the limitations of the automated systems and managing exceptions to procedures. As Boris Lomov noted (Lomov, 1963: 19, 21, 22) the role of humans in the system is precisely to do what machines cannot do and to regulate and control; the more complex the system the more difficult the fixes and the higher the necessary competences. The redundancy of embodied skills and physical affordance in installations (in the medication case, for product recognition, between the labels on the product and in the prescription, as well as on the barcode and in the database, but also in the medical knowledge of the nurse) appears as a safety feature and a way to handle shortcomings of one layer or the other.

Representations include the 'how to use' the objects; for example what is, for the subject, a medication, a web browser, a babysitter, or a self-service restaurant. Upon identifying a given object, the subject then has some expectations: inferred properties that come with the object in its standard representation. In the barcode example, the nurse's behaviour exhibits a search from which we can infer she has a 'search image' (Uexküll, 1992: 373–7): she searches the packaging for something that looks like a barcode; when she finds it she presents it to the barcode reader. We observed similar behaviour from other nurses in similar circumstances, and this will not surprise you, reader, because the other nurses work in similar medication rooms (there is at least one per hospital department); Barker would say the nurses work in the same 'genotype' of behaviour settings. As we expect, all trained nurses in that hospital will also have embodied a similar search image for barcodes (a series of small parallel black lines of varying width). This exemplifies a more general phenomenon that is crucial for installation theory: all members of a community seem to 'share' similar representations of the objects that are commonly encountered in that community. This is true to such an extent that we can rely on the fact that thousands of simple but also complex objects will be interpreted in a similar way by various people. A proof of that is that I wrote a book with the expectation that you could make sense of all these representations signified on paper; which you actually do, reader.

Considering the fact that embodied interpretive systems are not, like software, copied directly from memory to memory, but learned individually by each body through its individual experience of the world, the presence of similar interpretation systems in different bodies can appear somewhat mysterious. It can be accounted for by the fact that different human bodies have a similar base structure and that each has been 'embodied' with similar interpretive structures by getting through similar experiences, and by mechanisms that ensure that different bodies will interpret similarly a given situation, by *correcting* inappropriate interpretations. Which is precisely what installations do: this concept is explored in detail in Section 5.2.3 and especially 5.2.3.4.

Social representation theory deals with these common social constructs (see Section 3.5). Every 'normal' member of a community naturally knows how to use the objects, as beautifully described by Schütz and Goffman (e.g. Schütz, 1944; Goffman, 1971). Only strangers to this community will find some difficulty in interpretation, because they lack this familiarity and common sense. Here, all Danish nurses know that each and every hospital drug must have a barcode.

The barcode example is very specific, but there are many representations of a more general scope, which are designed to funnel members of a society into a certain type of behaviour by indicating what is to be done in a certain circumstance. For example, in their professional installations doctors are trained to see patients as 'patients' rather than as people; teachers see students as 'students' (and vice versa). Interestingly, by doing so, these representations avoid people perceiving other affordances that also exist but would be problematic socially. In the case of doctors or teachers, this limits the affordances for interaction that would get into the way of playing their roles correctly, for example emotional involvement that could interfere with professional evaluation of the case at hand.[9] While that is obvious for the representation of roles, the same phenomenon occurs for *any* object for which there is a social representation.

Chapter 5 explores how education in general, and ideological frameworks such as religion in particular, install in people interpretive systems of the world that foster certain generic behaviours (e.g. collaboration) and hamper others.

Societies must face the following problem: a few individuals performing incorrect behaviour can cause considerable harm or negative externalities, for example in the case of violent or abusive behaviour. Although it is

---

[9] On a more dramatic scale, the dehumanizing preparation propaganda by organizations such as the Third Reich, or the radio station Mille Collines in Rwanda in 1993–4, which presented the targets of genocide as vermin – and the same has been done for other genocides – had a similar effect: they presented the victims as acceptable targets for killing (Sémelin, 2007).

always possible to punish and repress by making it physically impossible for the perpetrators to backslide (e.g. through imprisonment), it is a costly measure and does not fix the damage done; it is more economical to prevent it. The best way to do so is to make sure that such damaging acts are *unthinkable* or *unnatural*. At least they must be forbidden and blamed; they should provoke in the performer disgust, shame, and other unpleasant emotions to create a psychological barrier.[10,11]

That is precisely what culture tries to do, and it usually succeeds. Nevertheless, if some members realize that such behaviours are feasible, stopping them becomes difficult. Epidemics of suicide (Phillips & Carstensen, 1986) are an illustration of such an effect. It is likely that the display of violence or pornography has such an uninhibiting effect; at least this is what most communities believe since they censor it in films. Nevertheless epidemic proof of 'copycat' effects are difficult to make (Van den Bulck, 2008). Anyway, education is a process by which cultures systematically implement the 'correct' representations in individuals in the hope that they will behave accordingly. We return to these issues in Section 5.4.

In societies the power of this embodied layer is visible in the relatively small amount of crime and deviance that needs to be dealt with by explicit social control, just as there is a surprisingly small number of traffic accidents: e.g. considering the huge number of opportunities for theft, theft is very infrequent. In addition to mutual regulation, self-regulation is massive, and has been acknowledged by many authors. Sigmund Freud noted the existence in the human psyche of a 'super-ego', 'the moral agency which dominates the ego' (Freud, 1926), which he considered to be an internalization of the culture's values and 'parental prohibitions and demands' (Freud, 1923; Laplanche & Pontalis, 1973:435–6;). Howard Becker noted how outsiders feel strong inhibitions to perform deviant behaviour and 'strong impulse to law-abiding'; especially the first time they act against the rules (Becker, 1966: 27–9). They must resort to a series of 'techniques of neutralization' (Sykes & Matza, 1957) to avoid guilt and shame because

---

[10] Some authors consider that there are some innate bases to morality, which would inform such rules – the so-called Nativist position. Even if this position holds true for some behaviours, the great diversity of what is allowed or forbidden in different societies suggests that most such rules and morals depend on the social system. For example, killing people (as long as they belong to the right category), beating spouses or children, torture, mutilation and other behaviours that seem revolting to some readers were or are part of normal behaviour in other circles.

[11] Creating a taboo around specific behaviours, especially murder, was attempted in practice by Mockus when he was mayor of Bogotá, Colombia, at the level of a whole city (Mockus, Murraín, & Villa, 2012; Yamin-Slotkus, 2015).

they still feel the need to answer the social demands for conformity: hence the construction of justifications and rationalization of delinquents, which facilitate their transgression.[12]

A striking aspect of that embodied layer of installations is how widely its components are shared by the various members of a population. Any standard member of a society is able to recognize immediately thousands of situations or objects; to name them and explain how to behave with them: a train, a cup of tea, a football team – anything. The members of a society are like millions of computers with the same huge library of pro-grammes installed in each memory, with only minor variations of versions. When one thinks of it, this result of the reproducing and installing cultural machinery is fantastic and almost unbelievable; but it is an empirical fact.

### 4.3.2.  Operationalization of the Embodied Layer in Research and Practice

How can we get empirical access to this embodied layer of the installation?

In research practice the components that we described in this section, embodied competences, are more elusive and difficult to capture and record than are the material objects described in Section 4.2. Physical and psychophysic competences are rather standard among humans: in Section 3.1 we use the example of competence to climb stairs based on the flexion of the knee. Perception is studied by psychophysics and is already more complex because it is influenced by learning processes and the experience of the subject. There are some difficulties here. It is hard to know how relevant a measure is outside of ecological conditions. As Lazurskii noted:

> There is no doubt that for each individual the manifestations of any elemen-tary function (concentration of attention, straining of the will, interest, ...) are determined not only by his psychoneural organization but also by the routine external conditions under the influence of which these functions are ordinarily performed.(Lazurskii [1916] 1997)

Gestalt theory studied pattern recognition and showed that it is a holistic process. The more we know about perception, the more we realize that the interpretation processes are abductive loops where embodied interpretive structures preformat the capture of data. For example, a process as simple as speech recognition, an operation routinely and effortlessly performed

---

[12] For example, denial of responsibility, denial of injury, denial of the victim, condemnation of the condemners, appeal to higher loyalties (Sykes & Matza, 1957).

by most humans, is still, at the time this book is written, stumbling on a series of technical problems when done by machines. The vocalization process depends on many local conditions: someone will pronounce differently the same phrase in a quiet office and in a noisy café. Therefore, there are virtually millions of possible sounds corresponding to a given word: Humans manage, but machines still have some difficulty.

Low-level competence is very difficult to explore and model, because its nature is of massive and dynamical neural networks. Fortunately (and paradoxically) higher-level competences are easier to model and survey. One reason behind this paradox is that one of the functional requirements of 'higher' mental processes is that they must be common and communicated, so by construction they are easily projected in natural language. In fact, language is the natural expression of these higher-level patterns and competences. We have simple words to designate complex phenomena (a dog; a hospital), and this system of coding is both available to our subjects and understandable by researchers.[13] So fortunately we come back to something that is easily observable empirically: representations, which are, as their name suggests, reformulation of phenomenological presentations (what we perceive of phenomena) into some symbolic system that humans can easily process. We are especially interested in those representations that are not idiosyncratic to one individual, those that are used in communication and other social activities: social representations.

Because of the variability of individual representations, the social representation is usually described by scientists in intensional format, as an 'ideal type'. Indeed

> those "ideas" which govern the behaviour of the population of a certain epoch i.e., which are concretely influential in determining their conduct, can, if a somewhat complicated construct is involved, be formulated precisely only in the form of an ideal type, since empirically it exists in the minds of an indefinite and constantly changing mass of individuals and assumes in their minds the most multifarious nuances of form and content, clarity and meaning. (Weber, 1949: 96–7).

It so happens that ideal types are also what ordinary people, not only scientists, use to inform their day-to-day behaviour, as discussed in Section 5.2.

---

[13] We will not get here into the detail of how far this stands philosophically; this has extensively been discussed by Wittgenstein (Wittgenstein, 1921). The limitations of nominalism are not so problematic here, because what we want is to have some satisficing and operational coding system for the phenomena, even if not true and exact.

Psychology has developed a range of techniques to obtain representations from the subjects themselves (Bauer & Gaskell, 2000; Flick, 2007). Qualitative techniques gather discourse during interviews or focus groups about the object or activity, and then extract the main components through content analysis or thematic analysis (Attride-Sterling, 2001). Open-ended questions in questionnaires can provide a less detailed content but on larger populations, and can be analysed with post-coding. Finally, text mining (Lebart, Salem, & Berry, 1998) can be applied to such responses in natural language, or to sources of text that discuss the matter (transcriptions of interviews, press articles, blogs, etc.)

Social representations theory has developed robust empirical methods to describe the contents of social representations (Abric, 2003c; see also Section 2.1.5). This is noteworthy because, although many theories deal with such shared cognitive constructs (e.g. scripts [Bower et al., 1979; Schank & Abelson, 1977], mental models [Johnson-Laird, 1983], categories [Rosch, Mervis, Gray, Johnson, & Boyes-Braem, 1976], social representations theory is by far the one that has developed the more systematic and explorative approaches in general psychology.[14] Some are automated (Lahlou, 2003) and can describe social representations precisely and without having to rely too much on the intuitions of hypotheses by the researcher. This is useful to map the repertoire of shared representations that are embodied in a population.

One practical issue in data collection is that there such representations are numerous.[15] Considering that number, subjects have at their disposal a vast toolbox of preconceptions and patterns they can use to make sense of the world. Therefore it becomes important, in a given situation, to understand *which* representations are mobilized.

Analysis of mental processes in situ requires different methods than the mapping of social representations. We need to confront the subject to the object-in-context to get an account of what are the evoked interpretations that were indeed mobilized in the act.

Many techniques have been developed for that purpose, especially in ergonomics. The most efficient are based on confrontation of the

---

[14] Education is facing a similar issue when trying to assess the results of teaching, and is still struggling with large-scale assessment, although there is progress (Mislevy, 2010).

[15] As Kalampalikis notes, 'Naming amounts to confer and socially share meanings on a specific object (real or ideational) in a particular socio-cultural and historical context' (Kalampalikis, 2006; my translation). Therefore the vocabulary of a language gives an estimation of the number of social representations in a population. For example in English, the vocabulary of an educated adult is somewhere between 10,000 and 30,000 words, depending on authors (Anglin, 1993; D'Anna, Zechmeister, & Hall, 1991; Zechmeister, Chronis, Cull, D'Anna, & Healy, 1995).

subjects with their own record of activity: self-confrontation (Cranach & Kalbermatten, 1982), self-confrontation with course of action (Theureau, 1992), crossed self-confrontation (Clot, Faïta, Fernandez, and Scheller, 2001), cued recall debrief (Omodei, Wearing, & McLennan, 2002), explicitation interviewing (Vermersch, 1994), subjective re situ interviews (Rix & Biache, 2004). The general idea is to use some stimulated recall (Lyle, 2003) to help the subject make explicit the mental events underlying the activity.

Other techniques without direct confrontation with the recordings include giving instructions to an alter ego (Oddone, Re, & Briante, 1981). The 'talking out loud' protocols derived from protocol analysis (Ericsson & Simon, 1996) are interesting but hardly usable in social situations; they also slow down considerably the natural action.

We recommend SEBE (Lahlou, 2011a; Lahlou et al., 2015b), which uses as primary evidence first-person recording by subcams, miniature video cameras worn at eye level, and a 'replay interview' self-confrontation protocol based on activity theory (see Chapter 2). SEBE enables exceptional quality of recall of what happened during action in this psychological layer of the installation, thereby making it accessible to scientific investigation.

In the following extract of a replay interview, a young doctor ('FT', two years of experience) explains how she usually talks out loud during surgery in the operating room for the benefit of her colleagues and her own:

FT: Because I'm so new I think I verbalize everything I'm thinking, and then people can input on it, and they know what I'm doing. And they also know that I'm not just standing there panicked, you know, that I'm actually thinking that something's happening. Because sometimes you see people who don't verbalize at all and you wonder if anything is going on at all. So I do it all the time. And for my own sake as well, because it sort of orders things.

RESEARCHER: So it's a way of you saying 'you can trust me'?

FT: Yeah, and also 'you know what I'm doing, you can stop me if you are thinking I'm completely out of loop'. (Heptonstall, 2015: 27–8)

This extract points at two ways of getting access to the embodied layer of the installation:

- Replay interviews enable accessing the reasons behind participants' behaviour, and their representations, by using natural language;
- Participants use the same symbolic format, natural language, to communicate relevant information and coordinate action with other participants;

therefore by recording the situation itself we have direct empirical access to relevant processes and contents of this embodied layer.[16]

Although this may sound trivial, the issue is not about getting information about participants, but about the *installation*, of which the participant is a component. The contents of the representation can be captured as they become apparent in the distributed cognition processes of the installation, when the contents are transmitted, or when the participants make them explicit to the researcher during the replay interview. A first set of data is collected in the installation (that is: the coalition, in situ, of the three layers in action). For the second set of data, although the replay interview is recorded after the fact, the procedure is such that the participants are reimmersed in the global situation by reviewing their first-person recording to reaccess and make explicit the same embodied competences that were used in situation.

Situated data collection is important for analysing installations. That is also the type of data collection made by conversation analysts, ergonomists, designers, and some organizational developers. The techniques are well known and productive; nevertheless they require trust and cooperation of the participants and detailed qualitative analysis and are therefore time consuming.

The nature of installations makes it difficult to collect data on them in a 'laboratory' setting; rather, an observation system must be implemented over the installation as it is in its natural ecology, transforming it in a 'natural experiment'. So far, because observation techniques were time consuming, difficult, and expensive, there have been few systematic attempts to do so. Alexander Lazurskii launched the idea of natural experiments in 1916 (Lazurskii [1916] 1997), but died too early to make long-term observations on the personality development of children, as he had planned (Brushlinskii, Kol'Tsova, & Oleinik, 1997). The most prominent research is Barker's endeavour, observing a small Kansas town for two decades. In the same line, but on a smaller scale, with colleagues and generous funding from EDF Research and Development Division I set up a whole building to observe office work, and recorded activity 24/7 for a decade at the Laboratory of Design for Cognition (Lahlou et al., 2012a); we never reached the exhaustiveness of Barker's work. Field labs and natural experiments will

---

[16] In this case, the subject talks out loud spontaneously. We do not recommend the talking-out-loud protocols, because they tend to slow the subject's action and are inapplicable in most interaction situations.

certainly develop in the future with the progress of embedded sensors and ubiquitous recording devices.

In conclusion, regarding data collection, the content of the second layer of installations, embodied competences, is classic material for psychologists who have developed a wealth of methods to operationalize data collection and analyse such data in symbolic format, mostly using natural language. The focus on installations, rather than on the individual dispositions per se, makes us advise using data collection techniques in situ, preferably video-ethnographic, during installation use.

## 4.4. Layer 3: Social Regulation

Not everything that is both possible and desired will be realized: a third level of determination, social, will cut off more branches from the tree of possibilities. Indeed, embodied knowledge of how to use the affordances is not always sufficient to execute *appropriate* behaviour.

Some people might do something wrong and provoke (by ignorance, personal interest) negative externalities for themselves or others. *Institutions* (as a set of rules) are a social answer: they create and enforce rules to control misuse or abuse; they set common conventions enabling cooperation (e.g. all motorists should drive on the same side of the road). Important functions of institutions are to regulate externalities and to coordinate the behaviours of communities. They produce and enforce regulation; they also try to anticipate possible consequences of changes, or foster changes; therefore selection of appropriate behaviour, as well as encouraging or forcing evolution of the social system in specific directions, is their business.

Ideally, as a good member of society, I should have embodied the norms and be spontaneously inclined to act as is adequate: remember how the driver described by Moles (Section 3.3) feels micro-anxiety when thinking of parking in a forbidden place; in the same vein, entering a library automatically tends to activate the situated norm of being silent (Aarts & Dijksterhuis, 2003). But that anxiety also comes from the menace of negative feedback. Social regulation usually comes with the possibility of sanctions. That is why, for instance, electricity companies keep cutting power on those who don't pay, even though detailed accounting analysis shows the administrative and technical aspects of the procedure usually cost the company more than the sums it recovers from the cut client (Reymond & Lahlou, 1996: 64–72).

The existence of sanction reminds *all actors* that there is a contract (Cochin & Dupont, 1995) that must be respected. Without such sanctions and reminders, it is likely that many individuals would not fulfil their obligations in the social division of labour that is necessary for the smooth operation of society.

As we know very well, even if we dare trying to do odd things, some others, directly or indirectly, will bring us back on the right path. This level of the installation is where *other stakeholders* regulate our activity. This can be to foster it or to hinder it. This may be because these others are directly involved in the process or because they take in externalities, positive or negative. This may just be because they feel they should intervene because we are not behaving correctly, and it is their right and duty to put us back on track, for the sake of the group.

Sanctions do not need to be physical, as in the case of power cut, or jail as when breaching some legal norms. Most of the time, there are, for those who deliberately breach informal social norms, a social sanction by ostracism or avoidance (Elster, 2007: 355); these are efficient because the individual sanctioned loses benefits attached to group membership.

In sum, there are, among possible behaviours, some that *Others* (as a group, as a community or as a society) think are the correct ones, for one reason or another. The third layer is made of the mechanisms by which this *Other* locus of control of our behaviour operates. Let us now detail how this is done.

### 4.4.1.   *The Social Layer in Theory (with Examples)*

In this layer the behaviour of a given individual is socially regulated by others. This third regulation process is less easy to localize than the regulation by the two previous layers, which were clearly located in space (the physical environment, or the body). Indeed, social regulation can:

(a)  be direct through the feedforward or feedback of other participants in the same scene ('do this; don't do that');
(b)  be internalized by the individual ('if I chat the teacher will punish me');
(c)  come in the form of anonymous devices or signs (the traffic light, the police officer's whistle).

For practical reasons of data collection and intervention I suggest we consider that the essence of this social regulation lays the *institutions*, i.e. the set of standing rules locally applicable. All the regulating manifestations discussed earlier (direct social interaction, internalized norms, artefacts) are only different local forms of expression of these institutions.

As Dewey notes:

> The essence embodied in the policeman's whistle is not an occult reality superimposed upon a sensuous or physical flux and imparting form to it; ... it's essence is the rule, comprehensive and persisting, the standardized habit, of social interaction, and for the sake of which the whistle is used. The pattern, archetype, that forms the essence of the whistle as a particular noise is an orderly arrangement of the movements of persons, and vehicles established *by social agreement* as its consequence. (Dewey, 1929:, 190–91; italics mine)

The key difference with individual interpretive systems is that these rules are social in nature and origin; they were set up by, and sometimes with, Others.

There are various means of social regulation: embodied norms, physical reminders, peer influence, intervention by specialized personnel... All these are means to enforce socially constructed rules.

For example, take road traffic again: I normally stop at a crossroad to yield priority; in fact, it has become an embodied reflex. This may be because I have embodied such rules that are social conventions: what others expect me to do. Also, traffic signs may be planted there as a physical reminder. Furthermore, I can see others doing it as the whole traffic flow halts there. If I do not stop, other users will probably honk or otherwise signal their disapproval. Finally, a police officer might intervene. Or all of the above.

But in practice, it is the *rule* that is predictive; *it is the rule that summarizes the content of the various forms of social influence above.* And the set of rules in place for a given situation is usually rather easy to determine, because they are by nature public and known, even when implicit.

> For example, in Western large-scale societies, the rules for getting access to public transport, such as a place in the bus (and more generally for order of access to a service, such as health care in a hospital) are (a) prove entitlement (a ticket); (b) first come, first served; (c) modulated by social status (some categories may jump the queue or get priority access to seats); (d) in case of doubt or conflict the provider will arbitrate. As an illustration, in public transport the rules for entitlement and status priority (a and c) will be displayed in situ; whereas rules b and d are embodied as a result of education and will be accessible to the researcher as they can be easily described upon inquiry by adult native informers.

The ways by which the influence of the rules is conveyed can be, as stated earlier, manifold.

This section will clarify terminology and the relations between the various entities involved in the social regulation of installations. The general mechanisms of social regulation (political, economic and so on) are beyond the scope of this book.

### 4.4.1.1.   *Communities, Organizations, Institutions*

There are many things that I don't do, even if I technically could and would have the competence (and perhaps sometime the desire) to do, e.g. cheating, jumping the queue, swearing, yelling.[17] My behaviour follows some social rules.

> All social groups make rules and attempt, at some times and under some circumstances, to enforce them. Social rules define situations and the lands of behaviour appropriate to them, specifying some actions as "right" and forbidding others as "wrong." When a rule is enforced, the person who is supposed to have broken it may be seen as a special kind of person, one who cannot be trusted to live by the rules agreed on by the group. He is regarded as an *outsider*. (Becker, 1966: 1)

As groups get more organized, activity gets more regulated. Rules make behaviour predictable; they facilitate collaboration (working together with a common goal); they reduce transaction costs (negotiations to agree on respective behaviours). This has the great advantage of making plans possible, building trust (belief in the prediction of other's behaviour) and more generally enable cooperation (common performance even though goals may differ, as opposed to competition) and labour division on a total scale. It even regulates competition by providing common frameworks for the limits of competing behaviours. That provides a feeling of security to participants,[18] and enables sparing the cognitive efforts and precautions necessary to survive in an anomic world. Institutions guarantee that we can safely walk in the streets or enter a shop without the fear of being robbed.[19] Institutions prescribe behaviours.

---

[17] One could consider that I don't do it because I have a normative representation of what is to be done, and this is true; nevertheless this normative aspect does not seem sufficient per se since there are many attested cases of nonnormative behaviour. Prisons are full of people who broke the law. And when I am alone in a train compartment I may behave differently than when it is full: for instance I may put my bag on a seat instead of between my feet. So there must be another explanation for why such behaviours usually do not happen.

[18] Wondering 'what is going to happen next ?' is one of the fundamental sources of anxiety of human beings (Stafford, 2007). Installations address that issue at least in the short term.

[19] Different countries or even different neighbourhoods (and different installations) can have different levels of danger. But competent subjects are usually able to differentiate this and modify their behaviour accordingly (i.e. the people that live in Bogotá know very well in which neighbourhoods or even in which sections of the street they can take their cell phone out of their pocket, and in which ones they can't).

I must first clarify the notions of *institution, organization* and *community*. These are not easy notions and a literature review of these notions independently would take us very far and create confusion, because authors do not agree. I will stay short and functional and propose a matching set of definitions. The three notions should be defined together because they are not only related but mutually constitutive.

**Communities** are groups of humans with common interests (e.g. sharing a resource, a need, or a territory) who recognize each other as members of the same group, are aware of their common fate and have developed some institutions and organization. That is, they have set some rules (formal or informal) relating to the behaviour of members, and they have set up categories of members with different roles and statuses (some labour division). Usually communities consider themselves as perennial, that is, they not only consider that they currently share interest, but construct a common future and a common past (which may both be fantasized but exist at least as founding stories and myths).

The rationale here is naturally that, because of their common interest, it is in the advantage of members to organize in order to leverage the global efficiency of the group, which can then, for example, increase the availability of the resource; or to limit unproductive conflict between members. Indeed, as game theory (Neumann & Morgenstern, 1944) shows, in many cases knowing how the other will act in given circumstances results in globally more beneficial decisions if participants cooperate – typically, the prisoner's dilemma (Tucker, 2001). Conversely, not cooperating may produce results that are detrimental to the community as a whole. The 'tragedy of commons' where individuals each trying to maximize their own interest end up depleting a common resource (Hardin, 1968) is such a case.[20] A system of roles and statuses is precisely a series of behavioural rules in which everyone knows who should do what in given circumstances.

The system of roles and statuses in a society sets up rules of behaviours that spare the burden of deciding and negotiating time and again who should do what in a given circumstance; that is what we call rights and obligations. 'A right is a legitimate expectation entertained by a person in one position with respect to the behaviour of a person in another position. From the point of view of the other person this claim represents an obligation.' (Davis, 1948: 87, in Cicourel, 1974: 20)

---

[20] Everyone unlimitedly sending their cattle to graze in the common pasture, to take advantage of this free resource, finally exhausts the resource, resulting in everyone's disadvantage.

The role/status system makes people's behaviour predictable; therefore planning and cooperation become easier. The reciprocal awareness of what we are supposed to do is essential in society. As Schütz noted: '*A social relation between contemporaries consists in the subjective chance that the reciprocally ascribed typifying schemes* (and corresponding expectations) *will be used congruently by the partners.*' (Schütz [1932] 1976b: 54)

**Organizations** seem similar to communities, because they include groups of humans with common rules of behaviour, with roles and statuses. But they are fundamentally different because they start from the other end. Community starts with a common need of its members; they are organized around the members' needs and in the end, even if some members suffer, that is for the common good of members. Organizations have a *goal* and members serve that goal; so the ultimate rationale is to reach the goal. We can the define organizations as *sociotechnical entities combining people in an explicit structure with labour division to reach a goal.*[21]

In that perspective, here again, behaviours of the parts of organizations (humans, machines, subgroups) must be predictable for other elements to maximize efficiency. This reduces transaction costs between parties (Coase, 1937, 1960; Williamson, 2007). Organizations therefore create sets of behavioural rules, and these rules are often explicit.

Note that because organisations involve humans as their members, these members come to share a common interest as members of organizations and therefore tend to become *communities* with the characteristics described earlier.[22] Conversely, communities tend to create organizations devoted to the welfare of the community (e.g. political, economic). So the actual landscape becomes complex because roles, rules and representations are interwoven.

---

[21] We may here compare organizations (which have human parts) with the excellent definition of *organisms* by the great (and humorous) biologist William Wheeler in his speech at the Marine Biological Laboratory, Woods Hole, Mass. on August 2, 1910: 'a dynamic agency acting in a very complex and unstable environment... An organism is a complex, definitely coordinated and therefore individualized system of activities, which are primarily directed to obtaining and assimilating substances from an environment, to producing other similar systems, known as offspring, and to protecting the system itself and usually also its offspring from disturbances emanating from the environment. The three fundamental activities enumerated in this definition, namely nutrition, reproduction and protection seem to have their inception in what we know, from exclusively subjective experience, as feelings of hunger, affection and fear respectively. (Wheeler, 1911). In this definition, Wheeler included colonies such as those of social insects. As we can see, organisms, because their effort is aimed at their own survival ('conatus'), are closer to communities than to organizations, whose effort is in principle aimed at delivering an output.

[22] That is an evolution that is often criticized in bureaucracies, or trade unions.

Finally, **institutions** are a set of behavioural rules applied by a group of individuals in a given context, and of which these individuals are aware. Definitions of institutions in the current literature tend to focus on their prescriptive aspects 'as systems of established and prevalent social rules that structure social interactions' (Hodgson, 2006).

Hamilton's classic definition of an institution shows how relevant it is to our problem of installations, which are set-ups for activities:

> [An institution is] a cluster of social usages. It connotes a way of thought or action of some prevalence and permanence, which is embedded in the habits of a group or the customs of a people... our culture is a synthesis or at least an aggregation of institutions, each of which has its own domain and its distinctive office. The function of each is to set a pattern of behavior and to fix a zone of tolerance for an activity or a complement of activities. (Hamilton, 1932)

While 'institution' seems in theory a very simple concept, it encompasses in practice much more than merely logical 'if/then' predicates. The very definition of an institution includes implicitly the group that operates it. Furthermore, to be able to define, understand and enforce the rules requires a community, an organization and a set of shared representations and understanding. A simple rule such as 'you cannot cultivate on someone else's land' requires, in practice, a complete system of land ownership, signalling, transmission, litigation and enforcement. Therefore, institutions become in common practice and language undistinguishable from the contextual bundle in which the rules apply. For example, 'a hospital' is an institution.

Institutions are inseparable from those who generate, steward and marshal them: a specific group of people. If these people disappear, so do the institutions. As Geoffrey Hodgson notes,

> institutions are simultaneously both objective structures "out there" and subjective springs of human agency "in the human head." Institutions are in this respect like Klein bottles: the subjective "inside" is simultaneously the objective "outside". (Hodgson, 2006: 8).

This idea that institutions are simultaneously objective and subjective has a family resemblance with Varela's notion of enactment and operational closure:

> A system that has operational closure is one in which the results of its processes are those processes themselves. The notion of operational closure is thus a way of specifying classes of processes that, in their very operation, turn back upon themselves to form autonomous networks. (Varela, Thompson, & Rosch, 1993: 139).

Therefore I prefer defining an institution not independently from the community that supports and enforces it.[23] This is a functional perspective that considers that institutions are patterns of behaviour that emerged as collective solutions to a given problem, and are maintained as a status quo by the stakeholders.

Because, as we saw earlier, communities and organizations need to construct a set of behavioural rules to endure, we should not be surprised to see that communities and organizations usually have an institutional side, and vice versa.

**Note that the way institutions operate can be manifold: by constraint of other members, by embodiment of the actor herself, through explicit regulations and laws, and even through material devices (see the example of the wall and the prisoner).** *But the ultimate cause of all these effects is the rule itself; the avatars through which it is enforced are only proximate causes.*

The rules are constructed, but they are not arbitrary and usually have been created as a solution to a problem.[24] At social level the domain-local communities of interest (users, providers, public authority) set the patterns of objects, the rules of practice and so on, in a way that is acceptable by the community. For example, the price of bread may be fixed to prevent abuse; as well as the purity of milk. Or there may be rules for sharing food within a household. One main reason for this phenomenon is that actions may have social costs (Coase, 1960), also called 'negative externalities', that are not immediately apparent to local players; the distance to effect may be in space or time and therefore the ultimate effect has to be avoided (or produced) by a proximate cause: the behavioural rule. Institutions create rules that make these distant constraints proximate (present) to local users, therefore avoiding the emergence of behaviours that are not sustainable at group level. The rules may require or forbid. Often they do both and specify what should be done (deontic rules). For example, although we could drive, and pass, on any side of the road, only one side is allowed in a given country.

As we just saw, communities, organizations and institutions are often coalesced or at least overlapping. Nevertheless, distinguishing them remains important in functional grounds because in the end what drives

---

[23] This goes against a trend that explicitly tries to differentiate the rules from the players. Here again, things come as a bundle.
[24] This effect may have been unconscious to those who effect the rule. See Mary Douglas' discussion on Elster's (Elster, 1983: 57; see also Glossary: functional explanation) criteria for functional analysis (Douglas, 1986: 33–43).

the evolution of these different entities is different: the group's interest is the raison d'être of the community; the efficiency in the perspective of the goal is the essence of organizations; institutions are set up in order to enable proper coordination of participants and predictability of their behaviour in a specific context. Communities and organizations set up installations to channel behaviour, and the behaviour in these installations is supposed to abide by the rules.

**Institutions are the deep nature of the third layer of installations, however diverse is their manifestation in enforcement and nudging**.

What is the relation of organizations and communities to installations? They manage and own the installations. For example, a restaurant, a hospital, a shop, are owned by organizations. A street, a family dinner are owned by communities. Communities may set up organizations to run their installations, as is the case for hospitals, or streets. Some people, some groups, have power and ownership over the physical layer, and authority to set the rules. Often, they are also in charge of transmitting the competences. We will come back to this important question when we study the evolution of installations, in Chapter 6. But we need not here get into the detail of how 'official' rules are constructed or formalized. Such rules are only a subset of the vast system of regulation that tells individuals what they are supposed to do, and which extends from some very loose and vague principles based on local tradition to precise laws enforced with heavy sanctions.

The nature and domain of application of these regulations vary. But in a specific installation the set of regulations in force is usually rather clear for participants, including which community is in charge. What matters for our problem here is that:

(a) rules and regulations exist that convey what is considered as correct behaviour in a specific installation (behaviour as deemed acceptable by institutions);

(b) individuals are aware of the existence of such regulations, if not always of their detail;

(c) it is an empirical fact that most individuals comply most of the time, by behaving correctly;

(d) there are enforcement bodies (e.g. the police) who are socially entitled with control and sanction power to deal with those who refuse to apply the rules and behave in an incorrect manner.

We are interested here in how the regulation in the social layer operates in general in installations, not in the detail of how it operates for a specific rule.

#### 4.4.2. *The Mechanisms of Operation of Institutions: Imitation, Influence and Persuasion; Role and Status; Conformity and Zeal; Instruction and Guidance; Vigilante Effect; Force and Menace; Seeking Guidance*

What are the mechanisms in the social layer? There are many; what matters for our point here is that they exist: institutions are enforced in many ways.

In this section I review some of the natural mechanisms by which humans regulate each other's behaviour.

What must first be understood is that rules are not only controlling, they are also empowering and necessary for life in common; and people understand that. Therefore individuals, however frustrated they can feel about a particular rule in a particular instance, are *motivated* to follow rules in general. Even marginal or criminal groups set their own rules. Therefore the use of brute force or direct constraint for enforcement is (happily) often not necessary because individuals tend to follow the rules on their own. This helps institutions to be accepted by individuals.

#### 4.4.2.1. *Imitation, Influence and Persuasion*

We mentioned in Chapter 1 Milgram's comment about his obedience experiment, that 'the situation has a momentum of its own'. The power of installations can be so strong that it forces people to do things in contradiction with their value system. The Utrecht studies (Meeus & Raaijmakers, 1995) that substitute 'modern', administrative, violence for Milgram's experiment's physical harm confirm the effect and show that Milgram's experiment mostly relies on *institutional* power. In practice, subjects do as they are told by influential others invested with *authority*. We all experienced the coercive power of institutions and rules: the army, the police or the school, for example; but any powerful corporation can mould individuals' behaviour to such a degree that they execute perfectly coordinated movements, as in a march.

Humans have inherited from their evolutionary past a spontaneous tendency to be influenced by leaders. This must have been an adaptive advantage that facilitates social animals to act as troops, to all go together in one direction, to combine efforts, etc. There are many obvious advantages to being a group, especially in a hostile environment.

The proneness to influence by leaders can take many forms: admiration, imitation, mimetic desire, obedience, etc. This innate tendency results in individuals with high status or authority[25] not needing to physically coerce others into compliance: giving orders, or even merely suggesting, may suffice.

Beyond that inclination to follow leaders, all humans also come (likely again for evolutionary reasons) with a natural tendency to be influenced by their peers in the group, like fish in a school or birds in a flock. In humans, the impact of peers on individual behaviour is not only motor, it is also cognitive; it can take several forms, among which are *imitation, persuasion* and *influence*. Those forms can be mixed in practice.

***Imitation*** is the phenomenon where an individual replicates, consciously or not, the behaviour of others. The nature of the mechanism is not fully known and is probably multifactorial. There is neurophysiological evidence that, when a subject observes another acting, the brain of the observer activates motor structures similar to the ones activated for action by the observee, and that a specific system (the motor neuron system) is activated (Gallese, Fadiga, Fogassi, & Rizzolatti, 1996; Rizzolatti & Craighero, 2004; Rizzolatti, Fadiga, Fogassi, & Gallese, 1996). Although this discovery was the source of many speculations (and is still discussed per se), it seems only natural that seeing action would activate the representation of that action in one's brain, which is necessarily connected to the relevant motor neurons. Whatever the interpretation, this finding chimes with the common-sense knowledge that when we see someone doing something we feel some sort of resonance of their action in ourselves, and some urge to do the same. We smile back, for example. By acting the same (e.g. in posture, or facial mimics) we also feel the same, as noted by William James (James, 1890: 305 et seq.). Adam Smith based his theory of moral sentiments on the principle of sympathy,[26] by which we tend to spontaneously share other peoples' emotions. More generally, emotional contagion (Elfenbein, 2014) and even mimetic desire (Girard, 1985) have been reported frequently among humans of the same group. As James noted: 'man is essentially *the* imitative animal. His whole educability and in fact the whole history of civilization depend on this trait' (James, 1890: 279). We have evolved as social animals, and our

---

[25] This authority can be real (coming with the actual power of enforcing others) or gained through proximal cues such as visible strength, aggressiveness, assertiveness, dominant posture or signs of high status as per the local culture (uniforms, accent, etc.)

[26] 'Upon some occasions sympathy may seem to arise merely from the view of a certain emotion in another person. The passions, upon some occasions, may seem to be transfused from one man to another, instantaneously and antecedent to any knowledge of what excited them in the person principally concerned ' (Smith [1759] 1976: 11)

physiology includes a massive system devoted to intraspecific communication. We have at least twenty facial muscles used for mimics, not to mention the muscles used in producing language, and most other muscles are involved in taking postures, to which other humans are extremely sensitive, as they are to eye gaze. In humans, the eye's white sclera contrasts with the pupil, providing an especially salient signal of eye gaze compared with other mammals and even other primates, facilitating joint attention. So, humans are a communicating species by design, equipped with many signalling systems to facilitate joint attention and learning, including of course language.

*Influence and persuasion* are two processes by which conspecifics make us adopt a given behaviour.

> *Persuasion* to perform a target behaviour changes the representations
> and attitudes of a person towards something; as a consequence
> the person adopts the target behaviour on their own, consciously.
> Persuasion uses rational arguments, or heuristics.
>
> *Influence* results in people complying with the target behaviour,
> but not necessarily as a result of a deliberated decision or will.
> Influence often plays on cognitive dissonance (felt discrepancy, e.g.
> between action and beliefs: Festinger, 1957), and more generally on
> consistency. For example, the subject feels compelled to perform
> a given behaviour to align what he does now and what he did
> before to remain consistent. By making salient the need for such
> consistency, influence can be exerted. See Cialdini(2009) and
> Joulé & Beauvois (2002) for excellent reviews of influence processes
> in consumption and business.

The power of group influence has been much studied and demonstrated in social psychology. In their seminal experiments, Muzafer Sherif and Solomon Ash showed that the opinion expressed by other members of one's group can determine the perception that an individual has of an object (Sherif, 1935) and the statements an individual expresses about a phenomenon (Asch, 1951).

In Asch's famous 'lines' experiment, subjects are asked to evaluate, in turn, which of three lines has the same length as a reference line. The task is easy: no subject, alone, makes mistakes. But the experiment is run in groups. What subjects do not know is that all the other participants in the experimental group are confederates of the experimenter, and they deliberately and unanimously provide wrong answers. A large proportion[27] of the naive participants follow suit and give at least once a wrong answer, against the evidence of their own senses, in order to be consistent with the group. Even more surprising, the influence of the group is so strong that some subjects come to believe that what they say is what they actually perceive, rather than acknowledging the influence of the group.

Kurt Lewin's key finding that is still used today in change management relies precisely on this influence of the group:

> Experience in leadership training and in many areas of re-education, such as re-education regarding alcoholism or delinquency (Lewin & Grabbe, 1945), indicates that it is easier to change the ideology and social practice of a small group handled together than of single individuals. One of the reasons why "group carried changes" are more readily brought about seems to be *the unwillingness of the individual to depart too far from group standards*; he is likely to change only if the group changes. (Lewin [1947] 1959: 204, italics mine)

Symmetrical is the unwillingness of the group to see the individual member depart from group standards: the group takes action against the maverick. The determination of the actor's behaviour by 'others' can take several forms, from gentle nudging to brutal constraint by force. Imitation, influence, communication and various types of feedback and physical action are all forms of this regulation that can be exerted directly by other individuals present on the scene or mediated by various devices.

Minority influence also exists: Moscovici and colleagues (Moscovici, Lage, & Naffrechoux, 1969) showed that a minority that is consistent can curb the majority's attitude and representations. A general explanation of influence is cognitive: if one wants to know what is 'right', it seems a good solution to follow suit with the majority, or with those who seem to be very sure of what they believe. And in both cases, one will rally strong social support.

Take, for example, ordering the meal in a restaurant: in communication with the waiter or the sommelier, and with other guests, the discussion that takes place involves influence and persuasion, and perhaps imitation as well. Our behaviour in installations is regulated in detail by such mechanisms. If necessary, these may produce adjustments so that the activity

---

[27] The figures depend on variations of the experimental conditions. In the initial experiment, more than two-thirds were influenced, some more than others. Only one subject out of four remained completely independent (Asch, 1951: 181).

takes place in an appropriate way and produces a satisfying outcome for the parties involved.

### 4.4.2.2.   *Role and Status*

Social regulation towards what one should do comes not only from the outside; it takes place through internalized structures as well; that is where role and status intervene. These are learned expectations about which behaviour people should have in a given situation.

We are able to take the perspective of others, not just of one specific Other, but the perspectives of the various possible stakeholders. This gives us the knowledge of what is 'generally' expected from us as an actor in a specific situation. In other words, we take into account what Mead calls 'the generalized other'. Mead argues that the key mechanism is what he calls 'the conversation of gestures' in which 'gestures implicitly arouse in the individual making them the same responses that they explicitly arouse in other individuals to whom these gestures are addressed'; hence, the internalization of external conversations of gestures would be the essence of thinking, and of the creation of significant symbols (Mead [1934] 1972: 47).[28]

> It is in the form of the generalized other that the social process influences the behaviour of the individual involved in it and carrying it on, i.e. that the community exercises control over the conduct of its individual members; for it is in this form that the social process or community enters as a determining factor into the individual's thinking. (Mead [1934] 1972: 155)

As these generalized other's expectations become internalized as a norm, we internalize various roles.

Self is the mosaic of roles that people can/know how to play, and this is constructed through experience. This process is described in more detail in Section 5.2. As a result of our own experience, we acquire the capacity to project our own embodied interpretation systems onto others and to 'understand' their perspective.

> social things are only understandable if they can be reduced to human activities; and human activities are only made understandable by showing their in-order-to or because motives [because] I can imagine that I myself would perform analogous acts if I were in the same situation, directed by the same ... motives ... The prototype of all social relationships is an inter-subjective connection of motives... I presume that this meaning for them,

---

[28] I must say I am not fully convinced by Mead's argument, although I believe that his notion of the 'me' as socially constructed is a very powerful and heuristic insight.

these actors, corresponds to the meaning their act has for me. (Schütz, 1960, 1976c: 13–15, passim)

and

I apprehend the contemporary only mediately, by means of typifications ... My knowledge of the world of contemporaries is typical knowledge of typical processes. (Schütz, 1932, 1976b 42, 44)

Because individual experience comes from immersion in the common world, also because humans share innate biological motives and structure and are capable of empathy, each individual becomes, in a given society, a specific individual instance of 'generalized other' embodying the society's institutions, and therefore similar to the individual others. This socially constructed self drives and controls ourselves from the inside.

Stoetzel defines **the role (of a person)** as *the set of behaviours that others can legitimately expect from the person.* The notion of status, as Stoetzel described (Stoetzel, 1963: 178) is also very relevant in that respect.[29] Stoetzel defines the status symmetrically to the role*: the status (of a person) is the set of behaviours that person can legitimately expect from others.* Therefore, roles and statuses define the same thing as institutions: what behaviours are expected in a given situation. But they define it from the perspective of the subject: the role is what one should do; the status is what one can expect others to do in relation to him.

The legitimacy comes from the institutional nature of roles and statuses: they are socially validated and not only the result of a local psychological contract between participants. Institutions, in one single movement, create roles and statuses. A role is then the set of behaviours the institution prescribes to a specific individual; status is the set of behaviours prescribed by the institution to others, regarding that individual. That definition is more restrictive than other classic notions of status that encompass both roles and status as described above. For example, 'A person's status is designed here as a collection of her rights, duties, and dispositions at a given moment, relative to other members of the social group' (Enfield, 2013: 76). Interesting in Stoetzel's definitions is their operational quality in terms of behavioural rules ('institutions').

---

[29] The notions of role and status have been debated in psychology and sociology for more than a century (Bates, 1955; Coutu, 1951; James, 1890; Lewin, 1935; Linton, 1945; Mead [1934] 1972; Parsons, 1964) and one can find many variations in their definitions between authors. (For a detailed review see Rocheblave-Spenlé, 1969.) For the sake of simplicity, we adopt here the definition given by Stoetzel.

These two notions as defined by Stoetzel are handy in installations, where role and status are partly defined by the local context. For example, a person entering a Shop will know her role, and status, as Client. Often, in organizations, these roles and statuses are formally described in various documents and conduct codes.

### 4.4.2.3.　*Instruction: Generic Learned Compliance and Certified Skills*

Individuals come into installations with some generic social skills and interpretive systems, which are the result of education. These differ from specific functional skills (such as making a knot or using a phone) in that they are social skills, generic rules about how to behave with others; this especially includes inclination to compliance, respect of authority, politeness, reciprocity, communication. The maxims of conversation[30] are an example of such generic rules in communication. Many of such competences are acquired through *instruction*, educational processes deliberately organized by society. These competences facilitate interaction and leverage the influence of other people's feedback and institutional rules in installations.

Indeed not all knowledge is specialized knowledge specific to an installation; many competences are used across installations, whether they were learned in another specific installation or through more generic forms of education.

There are behaviours that have no rewarding quality for the individual herself but only for the collective. For example, some behaviours are designed to avoid negative impacts on others; like keeping your litter with you in the street until you find a garbage can, or staying silent in a library or simply obeying the orders of the authorities in charge. Instructional systems usually include this aspect of making sure the competences for such 'socially positive' behaviours are embodied, and competences to avoid 'socially negative' behaviours as well. This includes learning about obedience to authority in general. Foucault has given vivid analyses of how institutions like hospitals and prisons use discipline to turn individuals into docile bodies (Foucault, 1975).

Education is about implementing in individuals general skills and interpretation competences that are of transverse use in a society, often across

---

[30] Maxim of quantity: Make your contribution as informative as is required (for the current purposes of the exchange); do not make your contribution more informative than is required. Maxim of quality: Try to make your contribution one that is true: do not say what you believe to be false; do not say that for which you lack adequate evidence. Maxim of relation: Be relevant. Maxim of manner: Be perspicuous: avoid obscurity of expression; avoid ambiguity; be brief (avoid unnecessary prolixity); be orderly (Grice, 1975).

installations (e.g. politeness, manners, mores, communication skills, compliance). Training is more about implementing in individuals specific professional skills that regard production. Instruction tends to be compulsory and not linked to immediate material reward; it is a requisite for living in society. Education usually uses a reward/punishment system to train individuals to embody the adequate skills. Here also the law of effect (see Section 5.2.3.3) is used to transfer into the body the 'correct' interpretation systems.[31] This embodied knowledge about social interaction, constructed by society, is expected from the participants in installations and often key to their operation. For example, politeness rules, and the restraint of aggressive behaviour, are necessary for smooth operation of crowded public transport. Installations often explicitly remind their users of these rules of behaviours with posters, public announcements, etc. In large-scale societies, proper education is so important that it has been dedicated specific instructional systems with dedicated personnel ('teachers').

Formal education systems ('instruction') award a series of statuses (e.g. rituals of passage in small-scale societies, diplomas in large-scale societies) Most instructional systems *certify* the embodied competences acquired, the certification marked by some rituals and public ceremony. This takes different forms in different cultures. In large-scale societies, students get diplomas upon graduating from universities; in some smaller-scale societies, the body itself is used as a canvas to write one's autobiography on the body (Schildkrout, 2004) and there tattoos or scarification may signal experience or competence. The competences learned include knowledge about authority; for example that one should listen to elders or other figures of authority. The rituals usually enable the subject to enter officially the social distribution of labour in exchange for redistribution of material resources (a job, a status) and hence open rights to founding family and reproduction.[32]

Note that these certification systems in fact certify two things: the first is that the awardee does have some technical competence. The second is that the awardee passed successfully through the often stringent social process that is usually necessary to get the competence (and often there is no other competence than having being compliant through the whole

---

[31] Note how society manages to link the reward system of professional training to positive feedback loops of meeting a goal (status, salary, means of living) whereas education to avoid negative behaviours is, by nature, often repressive.

[32] Although this system almost systematically applies to males; in many cultures females, even though they also are subjected to training, may not be as systematically subjected to public rituals where their competences are celebrated. That is a topic for reflection but one we cannot tackle here.

process). The award is therefore a certificate of citizenship and compliance that attests that this member is aware of, and ready to abide by, the local cultural rules.

What is interesting regarding installations is that these formal certifications of competences can be required to access some installations. One cannot enter the traffic as a motorist unless one has a driving licence, etc. The social system as a whole, and installations in particular, can work only if individuals do learn the adequate competences to play their role in the labour division, or at least agree in principle to comply with the local social rules that are given to them in the moment of action.

As a result of all the above, each adult member of the society knows their role in the installations they usually are part of, or at least they have the generic competence and compliant mindset that enables them to understand and apply the injunctions they may be given on the spot. In other words, **social regulation ensures that appropriate embodied competences are present in the participants of an installation so that local guidance is possible. Competent members of a society come into installations with a generic, second-order type of competence: they know rules about rules and social interactions.**

### 4.4.2.4.   *Vigilante Effect in Interpersonal Feedback*

Because we know our role, we each become an individual representative of the 'generalized other' to others. Sociology and psychology have insisted on the role of control that others exert on us (as the 'Other'). But that coin has two sides: another obvious implication is that *each of us*, continuously, is the 'Other' to everyone else. *I* represent the generalized other for the person next to me in the bus line. **Each of us, in the way we react to others with encouraging or reproving postures, mimics, speech, actions, continuously reminds others of how they should behave, in the name of 'society'. And as we do this, we feel right. Let me call this the 'vigilante effect'.** *That is how the corrective feedback is provided in installations by the participants themselves.*

As we just saw, *the generalized other is also a generalized self, the basic character of a culture.* Such typical cultural selves vary from culture to culture. But in our own culture, we can then become controllers to others because we know what 'the correct way to do' is. By being controlled we learn what must be done and then we act as controllers to others (as parents, as managers, colleagues, etc.)

Here is an example. Elinor Ochs and her group studied socialization in family meals. They show the diverse forms the social feedback takes:

> Through mealtime communication, more experienced participants engage less experienced interlocutors in the collaborative construction of social order and cultural understandings. In some cases, the sociocultural messages are conveyed explicitly to the less experienced participants through speech activities such as directives, error corrections, and assessments. In other cases, sociocultural orientations are socialized through less direct strategies such as irony, inference, pragmatic presupposition, metaphor, and noticeable silences. Both direct and indirect communicative strategies can co-occur in the same mealtime and can be embedded in genres such as prayer, storytelling, and planning at the meal. (Ochs & Shohet, 2006)

For example, the way young Adam learns the rules that one family member should not take more food at the expense of other family members is illustrated by in the following example:

MOTHER:  (quite annoyed) Adam? There are other people at this table. Now you put back two of those peaches! (0.6 second pause)
ADAM:  Okay okay. (Ochs & Shohet, 2006)

We see clearly here in passing why institutions are so necessary: the spontaneous inclination of human beings (here, greed) is not always compatible with harmonious collaboration and social life, and must be channelled.

Harold Garfinkel's smart 'breaching experiments' are another classic and spectacular illustration of this social control process. Garfinkel induced students to behave inadequately in mundane situations (Garfinkel, 1964); e.g. behaving at home like a guest instead of as a member of the family (being very polite, reserved...). This provoked very strong negative reactions from their families. We see there again how every loyal member of a community (here, the other family members) can become a controller for others.

Common sense as well as experiments shows that punishments are inflicted by individuals to those who do not respect the norm. People seem ready to incur some costs for that, at least as long as the costs are weak for the punisher (e.g. gossip, ostracism) or are shared and centralized, whereas there is only scarce evidence that the vigilantes are ready to incur heavy cost for punishing (Guala, 2012). Most of the time, in large-scale societies, it is enough for the vigilante to suggest he could call in the collective policing force to be a credible menace, at low cost.

There is also some neurological evidence that people experience satisfaction from providing altruistic punishment (Quervain et al., 2013). Such behaviour of altruistic punishment is usually approved (unless when considered excessive) and positively valued by other members of the community.

Generally we all believe that others are normal, are controllers, and we behave the same.

Stanislaw Lem, in one of his novels (Lem [1971], 1976), comes up with a nice parable. I considerably simplify the story here:

> In some fictitious future, planet Earth is worried that planet Cercia, inhabited by humanoid robots, plots against Earth. Therefore, brave spy Ijon Tichy is sent to Cercia disguised as a robot, wearing tin armour. He starts to live in Cercia, acting as a robot and pretending to be one, in constant fear of being discovered and killed as a spy. But because robots do not eat Tichy must on a regular basis surreptitiously go to the countryside to eat berries (and satisfy other biological needs). To his surprise, he realizes that he is not the only robot to feed in the bushes. It finally turns out that *all* the 'robots' on the planet are in fact human spies disguised as robots, each one believing all others are robots and fearing to be discovered; but the original robots had long since rusted.[33]

In the same way, one could argue that all of us feel compelled to act according to the social rules, even if we personally would perhaps prefer to act otherwise, because we believe that the others genuinely act according to the social rules, believe in them and abide by them, and that terrible things will happen to us if we do not behave correctly. And indeed others will remind us of the rules when we go astray. Fear is a powerful motivator for compliance, and it is often used in governance. This happens in installations on a daily basis: in queues, for example, but also in a work context in shops or factories where failure to comply may have severe implications. There is usually someone around whose social duties include control (parent, boss) and if this control fails a good citizen may take over.

I remember vividly that when I was a child, I once tried to cross a street in Geneva while the light was green. There was no car in sight on either side of the street for at least half a kilometre; nevertheless a Swiss lady who happened to be there put her hand on my shoulder and pulled me back on the pavement.

**This distributed vigilance results in a strange situation where not only are we controlled and constrained by others, but also where we do the same and control others. This comes with membership in a society, and enforcing the rules in others is part of 'good citizenship'. This does not only mean repressive control, but also support to others, meeting expectations and 'participating' in a general sense.**

---

[33] I have often thought that everyone is a child disguised as adult. Deep inside, we all know we are impostors to some degree, but we tend to believe the others are not; and indeed they behave overtly as if they were genuine and loyal social subjects – as did Ijon Tichy; in fact as we all do ourselves.

This duty of care to one's society requires a lot of attention and tension, because we all are involved in the maintenance and operation of many installations (at work and in the family being usually the most prominent) where we are expected to play our roles.

> Interestingly, Simon Evans, studying Second Life, showed such set of social obligations is inescapable in any social setting. Second Life is a virtual world where there are almost no rules, where users can create themselves a new life with avatars they design as they wish (anything from a sexy creature to a hairy tree). But Evans found that some Second Life 'residents' (what users call themselves) after a few years of playing roles, become plagued with social chores in Second Life. These chores are obligations of attention and care that arose from the social connections, networks, roles and status that they had constructed in Second Life. Some of the obligations are practical, such as paying rent for (virtual) land; others are more social, concerning friendships or intimate relationships (Evans, 2015: 150–1):
>
> 'I guess it was because I had made friends with people on my old av[atar] that wanted to do things that I didn't want to do anymore, but I didn't have the heart to unfriend them because they were nice'. (Cited by Evans, 2015: 492)

Ironically, the residents' success in creating another identity afresh to free themselves from the constraints and chores they had in the real world resulted in constructing another set of similar social obligations with the other avatars. There is no such thing as a free lunch: participation in *any* society comes with the obligation to play the roles of the generalized – and specific – other. As we act in a society, even a virtual one, every transaction changes what we are and our relations with others, it creates 'feelings of personal obligations, gratitude and trust' (Blau, 1964: 94); a member of a society cannot escape the web of these social obligations and feelings resulting from being a participant.

We saw in a previous section that the generalized Other controls us from the inside, as we embody roles. We just saw that the generalized Other, personified by each of us, also attempts to drive and control others from the outside. In a way, the massively controlled surveillance societies that were the Soviet Union or communist China in their worst totalitarian years, where everyone feared denunciation of neighbours and even parents, illustrate the general mechanism of distributed social control that is in action in every society – though more moderately. This mechanism is ubiquitous and operates at the high level of value systems, but also at the microscopic level of everyday practice.

Although installations certainly cannot be compared to small dictatorships, we can nevertheless see there in action, at a mild level, continuous and vigilant social control mechanisms by 'others' and self that ensure that the behaviours performed are appropriate.

### 4.4.2.5.  *Conformism and Volunteered Compliance*

Social psychology has demonstrated in many laboratory experiments how individuals conform to the norm and do as others do. This has been attributed to social influence coming from others (Asch, 1951; Sherif, 1935), to accept judgements from others as evidence about reality or to avoid sticking out and being identified as different (Deutsch & Gerard, 1955). That is correct.

But observation of real life shows some individuals often go beyond mere conformity and 'overdo it'. The zealous torturer, the sucker-up, the champion, the courtier are familiar characters that all have in common showing more than mere compliance to the rules or the cause: they volunteer 'exemplary' compliance. Many installations occasionally house such individuals who loudly display their 'correct' behaviour. Such can be observed in situations where hierarchy is relevant: some individuals conspicuously display their agreement and respect of the rule to pass as 'good citizens'. They agree with the authority in charge, and even anticipate zealously what they think is the expected behaviour.

By displaying such behaviour the zealous individual claims and displays his belonging to the group, in the hope of gaining some personal advantage or simply to avoid being singled out as an outsider. In acting in such an exemplary manner, individuals expect to gain a certificate of good membership and recognition of their contribution by other members of the community or its authorities.

Not only does this objectively result in the conformist individuals respecting the rule, but it does set at a higher level the social norm and therefore has an impact on the behaviour of others, who take this social norm into account.

As an example, in one organization I worked for, employees had noticed that the head of department was more available for an informal conversation when he arrived early in the morning. Because these morning conversations were an opportunity to solve their problems and also to advance their career, some individuals started coming in very early – at 7:45 AM instead of 9:00 AM. Because the boss was arriving early precisely to do his work without being disturbed, he started coming earlier and earlier; but then the courtiers did the same and the situation escalated. As other members of the department arrived at the standard hour and saw several colleagues already at work, they felt obliged to come early; gradually everyone started arriving early. This created an absurd situation where the majority of this specific department was present at a very early hour, much before everyone else in the other departments of the facility. At that point the head of department decided to halt the process and launched a collective project called 'Work better, work less hours' and stopped coming early.

Conformism and its extreme form, voluntary compliance, is different from being influenced, because it is driven by the individual. It may come from internalization, but also from purely strategic purposes. Whatever the reasons, such behaviour results in enforcing the norms in installations.

### 4.4.2.6. *Seeking Information and Guidance*

Especially interesting is the case where a participant in the installation does not know the rule yet. This is also crucial for learning how to use installations.

In practice, we can observe that, in case of uncertainty or doubt over what to do, humans actively try to get behavioural information from others, and are open to their influence. Novices in an installation spontaneously ask for direction (e.g. at the information counter, or asking some official or staff). Or they simply ask (or follow) another user who seems to be assured in his behaviour.

This practice is also visible when one analyses in detail the interaction records of a face-to-face semidirective interview: the interviewed subject tends to continuously check the nonverbal (and sometimes verbal) response of the researcher to assess whether they are giving 'good' answers; and that even if they are supposed to say what they think without constraint, and that in principle 'every answer is right as long as it is sincere and spontaneous'. This effect feeds the conformity bias and the inevitable influence of the researcher on the responses obtained (Nickerson, 1998; Rosenthal, 1966).

In cooperative action targeted at an object, I observed, by equipping participants with subcams, that they continuously alternate their gaze, *in synchrony*, towards the object, then towards the partner for eye contact, in an amazing attentional ballet. Eye contact enables each partner to decode the facial mimics and posture of the other and ensure that 'they are on the same page', with a shared representation of the situation. Peripheral vision and the prosody of speech probably indicate to each partner the moment when the other starts looking at him. This control mechanism can supersede and even repair verbal content when the latter is faulty (Lahlou, 2008a: 120–4). This example shows at a microscopic level the permanence and resilience of the mechanism of social verification and control by others during activity.

Eye-tracking measures show this triadic joint-attention mechanism is critical for collaboration and learning (Schneider & Pea, 2013, 2014).

As for the previous mechanism, this is at the initiative of the subject and not a feedback or feedforward by Others. These mechanisms contribute to the good operation of installations.

### 4.4.2.7.  *Force and Menace*

We have noted the existence of special bodies for control and enforcement (e.g. police and controllers); their active intervention remains exceptional. Most of the time their mere *existence* is sufficient to prevent what they are supposed to fix and I will not detail their action here; but they need to be mentioned briefly.

As moderate reminders and negotiation are not always enough, in addition to mild feedback systems, and to deal with more serious conflicts, communities usually maintain some dedicated policing forces entitled to force by physical constraint or punishment those who do not comply to behave, if necessary. As Bittner notes, police is for situations where there is 'something-that-ought-not-to-be-happening-and-about-which-someone-had-better-do-something-now!'(Bittner, 2005: 161). Even then, because of the costs of using force, the mild approach is preferred when sufficient. Johannes Rieken provides detailed examples of how the police regulate behaviours, in his research based on the analysis of first-person video recordings of actual rounds by the officers themselves.

> Officers are conscious that members of the public [MOP] are more likely to conform to the law in their presence. Several times cyclists push their bikes through the visual field of the officer on the recording ... [In the SEBE replay interview] Officers point out that this is a reaction to their presence: 'I can guarantee if we would not have been there he would have been cycling.' ... For officers, their gaze is a consciously used tool in the toolbox of policing practices. In another situation, an officer recorded a taxi blocking the traffic and comments. 'That guy just stopped, the taxi you know, blocking the road up. So I gave him a little stare when he went past me'... Therefore, officers at times deliberately aim to be seen to see. They are aware that this communicates to MOP that the offence they are committing is noted and thus more likely to be followed-up on. The expectation is that the MOP will then in turn self-regulate in order to avoid the officer getting involved. (Rieken, 2013: 187)

This low-key approach (aka 'discretion') in using legal power avoids formal interventions that would cost more. It relies on the fact that members of the public have been implanted with the appropriate embodied interpretive skills. We can see from the extract above that police officers take for granted that this competence is implanted and that the 'generalized other effect' will do the job.

Public space is more controlled than private space. One reason is that there are fewer enforcers in private space. But the key reason for this laxer control of private space is that society tries to avoid the *public display* of 'precedents' that may serve as an example of deviance, and as a proof that deviance is both feasible and tolerated. Such control and subsequent censorship avoids public display of undesired changes in the reproduction of society, and that in particular avoid inappropriate behaviour takes place in installations that would produce a malfunction or drifts in the same. We detail the role of institutions on this point in Section 5.4.

### 4.4.3.  *An Example, with Medication*

All these systems of social regulation combine, and come on top of the two other layers. As words alone can hardly render how detailed is the level of control, we must here get into description and use imagery.

Let us use again the example of medication dispensing in a hospital, mentioned in Section 4.3 (Dieckmann et al., 2017). Several times a day the nurse (or the pharmaconomist) prepares trays that contain the medications that will be administered to each patient. The nurse consults software that displays all her patients' prescriptions. We described in Figure 4.12 how the nurse, for each medication prescribed, takes the appropriate container from the shelf and checks it with the barcode scanner.

We are now interested in showing institutions in action. We must therefore first describe the *procedure*, of which the next steps are as follows:

The nurse prints small stickers with barcodes corresponding to the prescriptions, and sticks them onto plastic dispensing cups. There may be several cups if the patient has to take medicine several times during the period covered by the nurse's round, with different-coloured lids (e.g. green for 8:00 AM and pink for 12:00 AM). The nurse takes the appropriate quantity of medication (e.g. two pills), puts it in the respective dispensing cup, and puts the cups in a tray, in a specific cell marked with the patient's bed number (Figure 4.13). Therefore, when she arrives at the patient's bedside, she knows what she has to deliver and at which bed. This is in principle analogous to preparing and posting a traced parcel for a client following an online order, except the nurse plays all the roles of the shop, the expedition service, the carrier, the post and the postman. As noted earlier, real-world installations are sophisticated. We

Figure 4.13. Preparation of medication for dispensing seen from the nurse's perspective. For each patient in turn, nurse puts validated patients cups in tray (1) in the cell marked with patient's room and bed numbers (e.g. 8-2).

can see here, in passing, distributed cognition in action and gauge the degree of collective construction that was necessary to produce such an installation, from nurse training to the elaboration of artefacts and rules involved. Although this case might seem complicated because it involves technology, experience shows that a high degree of complexity is present in most of our mundane actions. So please don't jump page; follow along with me.

The trays are put on a trolley (Figure 4.14:1) which the nurse takes into the room during her rounds. Before she goes to deliver the trays, *the nurse cleans her workstation* (we'll come back to that segment later). She then leaves the medication room to visit each patient in turn.

*She then checks that she is giving the right cup (Figure 4.14:2) to the right patient by reading the patient's barcode on a bracelet each patient wears on the wrist (Figure 4.14:3) and checking it matches the barcode on the cup* (which also enables knowing the name, in case the nurse has forgotten). (This is analogous to a courier delivering a parcel and requesting a signature from the recipient.) The digital assistant (Figure 4.14:4), which carries the detail of the medications and their timing, enables the nurse to have an informed conversation with the patient and assess the patient's reactions to the treatment.

As we can see, the hospital is a complex installation that includes many smaller installations such as the medication room, the trolley or the patients' rooms. Let us focus on two moments where social control operates: first (a) in a series of institutional rules that is both embodied by the participant and enforced by the community; then (b) through direct social interaction that teaches a novice patient the procedure.

Figure 4.14. Medication dispensing seen from the nurse's perspective. Bringing in the tray (1), checking medication cup (2), nurse scanning patient's barcode bracelet (3), posology control on digital assistant and discussing with patient (4).

(a) First example: equipment sterilization (Figure 4.15). This is a compulsory rule and procedure that comes from the hospital (the organization). The nurse does know the procedure and executes it automatically, going to the sterilization station, taking a wiping cloth from the wall dispenser (Figure 4.15:1) then wiping the digital personal assistant (PDA) and the workstation (Figure 4.15:2 and Figure 4.15:3); then she must log into her PDA to start the next steps (Figure 4.15:4). Only once this step is acknowledged and authenticated (Figure 4.15:5) can the PDA turn into the dispensation mode required to perform the process of drug delivery to the patients. The nurse can then clean herself (Figure 4.15:6).

Note the presence of the disinfection station near the door, which both supports the action of cleaning and reminds nurses to clean before they leave.

We see here the three overlapping determinants in the installation: the affordances in the disinfection station near the door, the embodied procedure in the nurse, and the institutional control gateway reified in the PDA. *The organization acts here at several redundant levels to make sure that the rule is applied.* The affordance of the sterilization station at the door reminds the nurse and affords the cleaning (physical layer). But this would

Figure 4.15. Equipment sterilization. The nurse takes a wiping cloth (*1*), cleans the digital assistant (*2*), then the keyboard and workstation area (*3*), then once the procedure is complete she checks into the dispensation programme (*4*) and scans her ID badge to authenticate (*5*). Finally, she takes off the gloves and washes her hands (*6*). For the colour version, please refer to the plate section.

probably be reminded by colleagues present in the medication room if necessary, because they will act as loyal enforcers ('vigilante effect').

As a matter of fact, I was myself stopped at the door of the medication room before entry by one of our participant nurses and asked to sterilize my hands. In other circumstances I have been reminded orally to wash my hands, put on blouse and sterile slippers upon entry in hospital rooms during my field work, by hospital personnel and even by my fellow researcher colleagues who were not part of the hospital but had embodied the rule.[34]

This example shows the intervention of the generalized colleague as a behavioural enforcer, either in direct feedback, or through artefacts

[34] Similarly, in a previous employment in the power generation industry I had to go through the stringent process of complete clothes change (among other procedures) when accessing specific zones

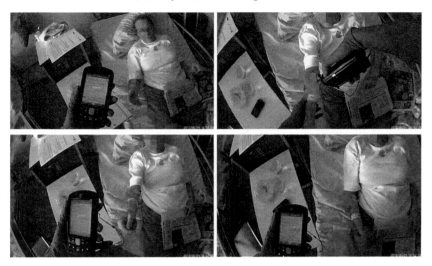

Figure 4.16. The nurse nudges the patient into learning the procedure. Patient puts forward arm (*1*), nurse scans bracelet (*2*), later patient puts forward arm again (*3*), but the nurse gently puts it back on the bed (*4*) because there is no need to scan the ID bracelet again. For the colour version, please refer to the plate section.

(posters) or through the embodied role. Only when the embodied role is not sufficient does the external feedback intervene and call to order; nevertheless there are more subtle cues to engage one into performing the right behaviour, and this can manifest by example (colleague washing their hands before coming in the room), reminding about the rule (there are signs reminding about hygiene procedure all over the hospital) or simply signalling the affordance to trigger the embodied reflex (as does the position of the cleaning station that is inevitably seen as one gets close to the door).

(b) Second example: patient education (Figure 4.16), we see how the nurse gently corrects and nudges the patient into doing the right moves to comply with the procedure. By this experience the patient learns the procedure for subsequent rounds. Here the nurse operates as the generalized other teaching the novice patient the expectations of her role, as described below.

of nuclear plants; and in the early days I was always guided by specific personnel or simply other colleagues present in the changing room.

Let us continue with Figure 4.16 the action that was described in Figure 4.15. As stated earlier, checking that the right drug is administered to the right patient requires that the nurse scans the patient's barcode bracelet.

But here, the patient, a novice (as a patient), spontaneously presents her bracelet *twice* to the nurse. Once before getting the drug and then the nurse scans the bracelet as expected in the procedure (Figure 4.16:2, which is the same as Figure 4.15:3). But also, unexpectedly, the patient spontaneously presents her bracelet *once again* after having received the drugs (Figure 4.16:3). That second time is not necessary and is not in the procedure: the patient has already been checked. Therefore the nurse gently moves the patient's arm back (Figure 4.16:4) and explains to the patient that this second scanning is not necessary.

Here the nurse acts as part of the installation to correct the patient's behaviour. As a result the patient learns the rule and how to play her role correctly. Let us note this important point: *in the same movement with which the nurse corrects the patient's behaviour to channel it back into the installation's appropriate behaviour, she teaches the patient what the right behaviour is.* That is the key property of installation's resilience, coming from the redundancy of control layers. Here, the patient's embodied competences are inadequate, but the nurse's are correct. The nurse's competences compensate for the patient's incompetence (regarding this specific procedure). The resulting behaviour is correct *and in the same movement the patient's embodied competences are updated* for further behavioural sequences. The installation is self-corrective.

People usually behave as expected and therefore need not get corrective feedback once they have embodied the correct interpretive systems. But the controlling forces are always latent to funnel us into the correct behaviour, if necessary. When the self-regulatory mechanisms do not seem to apply, the social control intervenes to bring the individual back on track. This is especially visible in children, because in that case the calling back to order usually includes an explicit description of the desired behaviour rather than just a hint or reminder. We'll come back to this learning process in Section 5.2.2.

Nevertheless it should be noted that this social channelling often encounters resistance, especially in adolescents.[35] Of course there may be

---

[35] In their work on families and adolescents, Marina Everri and colleagues present different forms of interactions that account for the ways in which competences, power and distances, the three fundamental dimensions of family functioning, are negotiated. The stance-taking process analysis

conflicts of interest between stakeholders and power struggles; precisely these are some of the drivers of the evolution of installations.

We saw with these examples that in installations the social regulation, which enforces correct behaviour as defined by institutions, can occur through many ways (direct interpersonal feedback, self-regulation, etc.) Because these ways are many, it is easier, to describe and address the social regulation layer, to find which are the institutional rules that are enforced by these various means.

### 4.4.4. *Social Regulation Takes Many Forms; by Addressing Institutions We Capture It at Its Root*

The other people who influence us do not have to be physically present at the moment of influence: their perspective is reified into institutions, which are sets of rules. The mention of the institutional character of a rule is usually enough to produce compliance, by evoking the group that instituted and enforces it. As individuals learn these rules, the third level of installations (social regulation) seems to act sometimes through others, sometimes through the actor's embodied rules. But in both cases, even though the *proximate* cause (others, or rule) is different, the *ultimate* cause remains the same: the institutions.

Because of these various modes of intervention (direct or indirect) this third level of installation is not as clear-cut as the other two (physical affordances, embodied interpretive systems), which can be easily located in physical space.

Our problem here is not to highlight the fact that social influence is important, which we all know, but to address social regulation in such a way that we can act upon it. Hence we should focus on *institutions*, which are the rules 'designed for others' rather than on the interaction or feedback, even if it is at that latter level (individual feedback) that rules often operate in an observable manner. Institutions act upon one individual, $X$, through other individuals' actions on that individual $X$. They also operate through embodiment of rules by the subject and artefacts.

While installation theory considers for the sake of pragmatic simplicity the institutional layer as separate from the others, we can see that in

---

has shown that both parents and children engage in 'manoeuvres' to deconstruct and reconstruct family balance, in what Everri calls 'micro-transitions'. In adolescence it is clear how parents attempt to channel children's behaviour but children resist it, or even try to channel parents' behaviour by opening negotiations or what Everri calls oscillations (Everri, Fruggeri, & Molinari, 2014).

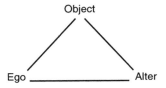

Figure 4.17. The psychosocial triangle (Moscovici, 1984).

fact it is deeply entangled with the two other layers, just as the two first were entangled with each other, but there is no room for that discussion here.[36]

Institutions have *purpose* (maintaining established order, controlling externalities, saving transaction costs); therefore considering them addresses the problem at the right place, *political*, and yields a functionalist view of the system considered. This is handy for managing continuity, or change. Remember that a theory is a model with a purpose, and not reality itself.[37]

The basic structure of social psychology is the 'psychological triangle' (Figure 4.17) including ego (the subject), the object (of activity), and alter

[36] Of course, institutions are also objects, and there are representations of institutions. And individual representations are also constructed by institutions. The distinction between the three layers is a gross pragmatic simplification. Because each of the layers is, in its genesis, co-constructed by/ with the others there cannot be a clean epistemic cut. Models are not the phenomena, but only a simplified and practical way to deal with them; and in this respect the installation framework is no exception. We made here a trade-off between simplicity and precision. Installation theory is an epistemological collage: its various parts are not connected with the same philosophical underpinnings. At times it seems to use realism (assuming there is a physical layer), and at times relativism and phenomenology (because affordances are relative to the subject and perceived in an intentional perspective) then constructivism when it comes to the social layer. Although this may shock some straight theorists and philosophers, the proof is in the pudding. As a matter of fact, we humans do not in practice construct all our knowledge and beliefs in a single way. Some knowledge comes from direct experience, some from inference, some from communication, etc. Nevertheless, when it comes to act in practice, we draw on all these forms of knowledge at once, in a pragmatic way, whatever their origin. The compound nature of installation theory reflects this diversity. Similarly, the toolbox of a mechanic may contain tools made of different material (steel, wood, aluminium, etc.), of different brands and bought at different times in different shops. But when it comes to repair, the mechanic will not limit himself to tools of a single brand or metal. In early times, in art, techniques were separated: a picture would be sculpted or painted, and if painted only one method was used, e.g. oil paint *or* watercolour. Now many artists use mixed methods to render complex effects. Anyway 'If the researcher sticks dogmatically to a specific kind of epistemology, be it dialectics, positivism or constructivism, he might tend to adapt the interpretation of his findings to that specific epistemology and reject everything that does not fit into the pre-given conception'. (Marková, 2008). '[The scientist] therefore must appear to the systematic epistemologist as a type of unscrupulous opportunist ...' (Einstein, 1949: 684)

[37] 'A map is not the territory' (Korzybski, 1933:750); We can only hope for some similarity of structure between what is represented and its representation.

(the socius). Social psychology claims that none of the binary relations can be considered in isolation of the third term.

So it is no surprise that we find 'the others' as a key layer of influence in installations.

Nevertheless, the issue of where we put the other (alter) in the model is tricky. Alter can be considered an object for ego, or an instrument, or a more distant stakeholder. There are many ways to build the model; each with good arguments. I chose to make the social regulation a separate layer because of the pragmatic purpose of the model: it provides the components one has to act upon to change the system.

Finally, this social layer is more complex than the two others because it is far from being purely functional. The institutional feedback often comes through direct interaction with fellow humans, be they specialized personnel or simply good citizens. But relation to other humans in action is specific because we are social animals and our cognitive system treats humans differently from other objects; generally there are more emotions involved. It matters that what we interact with is human or not.[38] In practice interaction with humans seems to take over other types of negotiating with the environment; for one thing, humans seem to have a greater presence (salience) in situations and they attract our attention automatically.

A comment of a police officer describing her stop-and-search procedure in a replay interview of an actual arrest illustrates an interesting exploitation of this effect. Olivia (not her real name) explains why she continuously talks to the member of the public as she searches him:

> 'I talk to them when I am searching as well. It distracts them when I have a go at their pockets and it makes it easier for me to find something because they are concentrating on what I am saying'. (cited by Rieken, 2013: 178)

Our relations with other humans are not purely functional and goal-oriented in the perspective of activity; they are tainted with intraspecific, 'animal', motives. We cannot avoid entering into relationships with other humans *as other humans*, and we have an innate need to situate ourselves in relation to them in intraspecific terms: that is regarding group belonging, hierarchy, sex or relationship demands (e.g. help, aggression). This tendency is supported by the very sensitive and always-on innate systems for producing and sensing pheromones, posture, facial expression, verbal

---

[38] The very notion of the Turing test (and the attention it attracted) shows that knowing (or believing) that another human is in the loop influences the way we behave.

sounds – and possibly even motoric intention (Rizzolatti et al., 1996). The bank teller, the police officer, the teacher are not only function bearers, they also are 'persons', whose personal style and characteristics influence us. For example, the way politicians move their body, irrespective of what they say, makes the public attribute them qualities that may contribute to their election (Koppensteiner, 2013; Koppensteiner & Grammer, 2010). The same goes for groups: they are not 'just' an association, a corporation; they are perceived in terms of kin and in-group/out-group, friend or foe, beyond their functional nature for the activity at hand (Tajfel, 1970, 1974, 1982). This comes from our nature as social animals: it is not 'rational'; it is the inbuilt consequence of our evolutionary past. That is why the social layer of nudge and control of our activity is tainted with a different emotional tone than our interactions with the physical layer of affordances.

In addition, other humans act as intentional units, at individual and group level and this has specific consequences: they actively try to influence the actor's behaviour; they have a theory of mind – that is, they address the actor at a symbolic level. For one thing, they signal the actor potential consequences of her acts, and display what their own potential reactions to the actor's actions are. They explicitly forbid some actions, which is the same as advertising strong negative reactions and sanctions if the actor acts. This is important because the actor knows and expects this, and uses these signals as feedback on her own actions. For example she will try to guess the motives of others, and monitor their reactions to orient her own behaviour. This is one more reason why relations with other humans are to be considered separately in the model.

### 4.4.5.    *Operationalization of the Social Layer in Research and Practice*

How can we access and describe the social layer empirically?

In practice, determining the nature of social influence and control means 'finding the rules'. Indeed, it is rather easy in practice to spot the *social rules* that funnel behaviour and to identify their *institutional source* in order to act upon them.

Rules can be found empirically in formal regulations: law, codes, instruction manuals, decrees, orders, norms, licences, rulebooks, algorithms, etc. They can also be stated by the individuals themselves, when asked; members of a community or organization know the rules, even when they

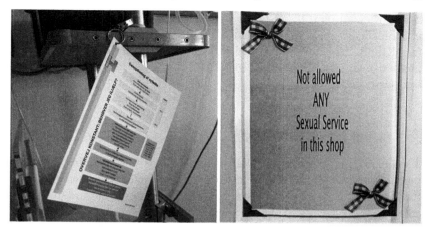

Figure 4.18. Procedures and rules displayed in the environment. *Left*, a neonatal resuscitation procedure, tagged to equipment in a training ICU (intensive care unit) in a Danish hospital. *Right*, a sign posted on the wall of a Chinese massage parlour in London.

are informal. Sometimes the rules are made available to participants with signposts.

Figure 4.18 shows two examples of rules displayed in behavioural settings, an intensive care unit and a massage parlour. Of course these signs are redundant with the performer's embodied competences, and we could extract (more or less) the same rules from interviewing them. The redundancy, which in practice increases resilience of the installations to the inadequate initiatives of novice participants, is a boon for the researchers: it enables them to extract the rules from diverse sources.

Every full member of a community is aware of the existence of the institutions; perhaps not everyone knows them all in detail, but at least there is awareness of their existence. That awareness makes each individual attentive to social feedback from those who are supposed to know the institutions in detail. This knowledge makes the researcher's task easier: another simple way to get the rules is simply to ask people what the rules are in that installation: 'What is one supposed to do in that situation? Are there rules that one is supposed to follow? Are there things that are forbidden?'

It does not matter if there is some redundancy between the three layers in our analysis when our final purpose is to understand what happened and how to act. We have seen that there is a vast array of practical techniques for social influence and control in installations; the important thing is that they all tend towards the same goal: funnelling behaviour so that it conforms to the socially constructed norm of the group who rules the installation. Therefore in the end it is the institution (the rule) that is the predictive factor of behaviour; the institution is also the target for change interventions.

### 4.4.6. *Takeaway on Social Regulation: External Organizational Control and Internal Social Drives Combine to Enforce Institutions*

The operation of institutions takes many forms: imitation, influence and persuasion; role and status; education and guidance; vigilante effect; conformity and volunteered compliance; seeking guidance and force and menace.

Within these operational forms there are two types. One is the *external* control of individual behaviour by Others, through feedforward, feedback or anticipation by the subject: influence and persuasion, education and guidance, force and menace. This external control is an expected feature of any community because of the necessity of cooperation and avoidance of negative externalities.

The other type is at the initiative of the subject: imitation; conformity and volunteered compliance and seeking information and guidance. Those voluntary forms of regulation are attributable to our psychology as social animals who need and seek group belonging, social support and recognition and compete for hierarchical positions.[39] The dual nature of role and status reflects this mechanism by which we gain a position in the group through playing by the rules. We can see how the installations draw on natural psychosocial drives to activate the third layer of social regulation; the 'social' uses the 'psychological' as a device, but that psychological has a social motive.

As noted already, many of the rules are already contained in the representations, which are by nature normative (Guimelli, 1998). Rules can also, as we saw above, be embodied in artefacts. But institutions come with a specific physical control layer of these rules; they enforce them with special personnel. And furthermore, as we saw, every loyal member of the community tends to serve as a rule-enforcer vigilante and bring others back on track. This makes the institutional control redundant and ubiquitous.

---

[39] Interestingly, two extreme (and therefore socially disturbing) forms come with a strong desire for participation and affiliation: the volunteer and the vigilante. It should be no surprise that they can come together in the single character of the fanatic ('more Catholic than the Pope himself').

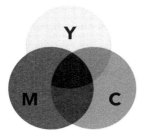 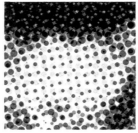 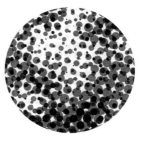

Figure 4.19. Halftone printing. *Left*, the effect of combining three primary colours (yellow, magenta and cyan). *Centre*, magnification of halftone dot print with primary colours-magnification of the neck of the character on Figure 4.1. *Right*, magnification of the bouquet of lily of the valley in Figure 5.12. A black and white version of this figure will appear in some formats. For the colour version, please refer to the plate section.

## 4.5. The Three Layers Combine as a Single Functional System and Their Redundancy Makes Installations Resilient

Let us take again the metaphor of printing where images are produced as the result of thousands of small dots of varying tone and size. Halftone printing is a process whereby colour is obtained by combining locally dots of three primary colours: yellow, magenta and cyan (Figure 4.19).

As the eye coalesces these small dots the effect is to see a single dot of a single colour, which depends on the mix of the basic colours. The size of the dots can vary as well as their overlap, so the final effect provides a dominant colour in a given area. This is illustrated by the circle on the right in Figure 4.19, which is a magnification of the bouquet in figure 5.12, showing the detail of the leaves –mostly green, and of the flowers –mostly white. Just the same, the influence of a given layer may be more or less important in a given installation. When I climb a staircase the physical affordances are paramount; when I read a book my interpretive competence is paramount; when I participate in a graduation ritual the social rules are paramount. But an installation is always, to some degree, a coalition of the three layers.

But let us not push the metaphor too far. An installation is not a dot. The metaphor of printing is only a metaphor. It reminds us that installation theory is only a representation of the phenomena, as are all theories. The map is not the territory, whatever the number of colours used to represent the territory.

We have seen in the last three sections what layers installations are made of. Although these three layers do have some independence and are distributed over different substrata, installations still have some autonomy as coherent constructs. This coherence comes from their functional orientation to produce one specific type of behaviour, and makes them considered as a whole by humans. The coherence also comes from interweaving into the construction the three layers, which are taken into positive reconstructive feedback loops, as described in Chapter 5: Endurance of Installations. This interaction between the three layers also provides a redundancy that contributes to the resilience of installations.

Now we investigate this resilience in more detail. Let us start with some curious findings.

We have been conducting, with students and colleagues, fine-grained observation of people's behaviour in daily situations with SEBE (e.g. Glăveanu & Lahlou, 2012; Le Bellu, Lahlou, & Le Blanc, 2009; Le Bellu, Lahlou, & Nosulenko, 2010; Rieken & Lahlou, 2010). We obtained detailed accounts of why they behaved the way they did.

The observations confirm that a substantial amount of individual activity is conducted in a somewhat autopilot mode, where subjects merely chain routine behaviours and let the installations guide them.

Another result is that in many cases participants are unable to provide a complete account of their activity without being put back in context. When they are interviewed outside of context and asked to describe their routines, some steps are missing – usually steps that are made by the rest of the installation anyway.

For example, when an expert was asked to describe the process of sending an email with a PDA and a phone,[40] the expert described nine tasks. But in fact, as he performed the process afterwards, we observed sixteen tasks: the nine he had described *and seven more*. Those unplanned operations accounted for 58% of the actual task duration (Lahlou et al., 2002). For example, although the expert mentioned 'activate infrared port' he forgot to mention 'enter password'. That is understandable. In context, the subject is prompted to do some tasks by the context, in this case by the PDA, which 'asks': 'select an account!', 'enter password!'. Although the subject needs to remember the tasks that are done at his own initiative, he does not need to remember the other tasks because the rest of the installation automatically reminds him to complete those

---

[40] That was the height of technology at the time, in 2000. The user had to connect the PDA to the telephone by infrared, and the phone would send the message written on the PDA. Now these elements are combined in smartphones, following Deforge's technological law of 'fusion of components', by which the evolution of industry-made objects tends to combine in one single structure separate components of the same object; this enables saving matter, energy and space (Deforge, 1985).

tasks. Therefore the script that the subject has in his memory does not need to be complete; the missing chunks are filled in by the rest of the installation.

Not only the subject does not need to know how to perform what the installation does, but even the knowledge that some operations have to be performed is not necessary because they are signalled in situ. All that the subject needs to know is how to react to the prompts of the installation. To use the dramaturgic metaphor dear to Goffman, an actor learning how to perform a play only needs to learn her own part, and also the moments, or the prompts from other actors, when she must utter each sentence or act. If we interview that actor about what the other actors say, she might have only a vague idea of the content. Both the learning and the competences are distributed over the actors.

In decay, as well analysed by Cicourel, the environment (caregivers, robots, etc.) plays an increasingly vicariant role in a person's performance. As individuals lose the competence to perform themselves, because of dementia, for example, caregivers do more and more of the action (Cicourel, 2012). Partners of individuals afflicted with dementia create both the questions and the answers in conversation to compensate for the defective competences of the other. If we see this situation from the perspective of the healthy partner, (s)he is increasing embodied competence to behave in this new installation (the household with a demented partner) to compensate for the decreasing competences of other components of the installation (here, the demented partner).

This brings us to an interesting point: even subjects who do not know the script well are able to perform an activity as long as the support from the installation is sufficient (see the example of the novice patient and her ID barcode scanning in Figure 4.16, and the example of the driver discovering how to fit the jack under the car when changing a tyre in Figure 4.5). In actual practice we can often observe that subjects with a deficient competence, e.g. novices, beginners, apprentices, still manage to perform the task required. Also, it happens that even competent subjects make mistakes or, more often, approximations (e.g. out of tiredness or inattention), but somehow the installation brings them back on track (see the example of my forgetting to wash my hands when entering a hospital room). This can be through repairs performed by other participants, warnings or specific instructions given by others, or simply because the physical part of the installation contains affordances for repair or correction of the incorrect sequence. This process requires from the subject only some generic competence for repair, e.g. the capacity to notice signals, understanding, compliance and the ability to ask for help and support (the 'educated' generic competences we pointed at in Section 4.4.2.3).

This property of installations can be called *resilience to incompetence* (of participants). ***An installation will be resilient to incompetence if it is able to produce satisficing behavioural sequences even if the competence of some participants is deficient.***

This property enables learning the installation in situ, through practice. That is a fundamental property for the reproduction and evolution of installations, because it enables creating the embodied skills de novo in new people by the rest of the installation. In fact, more generally installations seem to be able to regenerate some of the components of one layer from the components of other layers.

Figure 4.16, where the nurse gently explains to the patient that she should not present again her barcode bracelet *after* the medication was given, is a low-key example of a resilient installation. There, the novice patient learns the proper procedure by trial and error, and the error is corrected by a knowledgeable participant, in fact here precisely the nurse who interacts with her. The examples provided in Section 4.4.2.4, of the parents firmly reacting to Garfinkel's students' attempts to behave inappropriately (Garfinkel, 1964) and the policemen staring at potential offenders, also illustrate resilience where control is exerted by other humans.

The two other layers of installation also participate to resilience. The most powerful is probably the physical layer, not only because it 'naturally' suggests some behaviour, but most importantly because it does *not* afford an infinity of other behaviours and thereby excludes them. A simple example is the wall, which prevents anyone from crossing the space it delimits; another is the lock, which can prevent from trespassing all but those who hold the key. Prisons and asylums are enlightening examples because these 'total institutions' have been designed especially to control the behaviour of inmates and other residents – and their study produced some of the most interesting work in the study of 'installed' behaviour (Foucault, 1975; Goffman, 1961a).

A remarkable property of physical objects is their capacity to remain. They can continuously and independently provide their affordance; which is not the case for humans: compare a wall and a warden in their respective capacity to keep a prisoner in a given place.

Many mechanical systems have been invented to be resilient to incompetent users. European norm EN 28317:199 regulates re-openable packaging (e.g. corrosive or poisonous domestic cleaning products) to make them safe, especially to little children. Most firearms and dangerous electric tools have a safety lock; many products are tamperproof, etc.

The more educated and homogeneous a population, the more behaviour control is spontaneously exerted by individuals themselves, and therefore the less the installations need to be resilient.

The differences of control systems for urban public transport in various countries are especially revealing in this perspective. At the time of writing, entry onto the Paris metro and in most London underground stations is physically limited by the affordances of turnstiles where passengers must validate some kind of pass or ticket to get through, and it is physically very difficult if not impossible to get through without paying. In contrast, in Copenhagen, entrance is completely open, and the passenger is expected to remember to validate his pass or ticket on specific sensor poles. In Prague the validation system was so discrete that I could not even find where to show my transport pass, and I still do not know how it works.

Even educated personnel can have failures. Therefore institutions create procedures that secure objects or systems against errors or malpractice; for example, operators in nuclear power plants must lock valves in position after control or intervention, and seal the lock with a specific safety pin, tracing indications on what operation has been done -although all operators are trained. When there is high risk, procedures include specific checklists:

- In French nuclear power plants, operators must confirm that the ID number riveted on the equipment matches the number prescribed on the work order; this avoids the operation being done on the right valve but in the wrong building, for example.
- In surgery, a sign is drawn on the organ or limb to be operated to avoid surgery being done on the left eye instead of the right eye, for example.
- In aviation, the pilot and copilot must read out loud a preflight checklist that ensures double-checking that all systems are OK. In fact the very presence of a copilot is a redundancy to provide more system resilience.
- In fast trains, specific feedback systems control the alertness of the driver.

A classic trick to make installations resilient is to create compulsory control points at certain steps of the procedure. Another is to have the same step done twice and to compare results: see above airplane checklists, but there are also double signatures in finance, double keys for safes and repeated entry for the creation of new a password.

These controls on execution are on-the-fly control. But most societies also set up preventive control measures. Regular equipment checkups

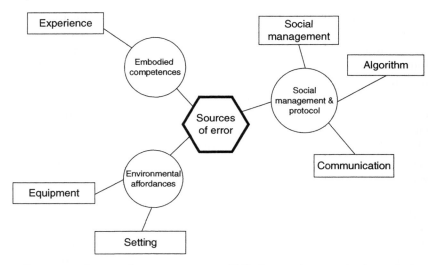

Figure 4.20. Sources of error in managing a 'difficult airway' scenario by the medical team in an ICU (from Heptonstall, 2015: 25).

ensures physical affordances are functional (e.g. compulsory periodic control of automobiles or fire extinguishers). Certification of competence (see Section 6.5.1) verifies that adequate embodied competence was acquired. Personnel training and continuing education ensures that competences are operational and up to date (e.g. licence, professional diplomas, professional habilitation). Finally, but more rarely, institutional cleanup is done through legal regulations combing to make sure the rules are not obsolete.

The three-layered structure of installations allows for redundancy and is therefore a defence mechanism against failure in one of the layers.

Bonnie Heptonstall, studying decision-making in intensive medical care, shows how the sources of error in the process can come from any of the various levels of the installation (Figure 4.20).

But the other layers can 'repair' when a mistake occurs in one dimension. For example, in one case studied by Heptonstall, the patient's state suddenly deteriorates and the doctor realizes he may have to do a tracheotomy (surgical intubation through the throat, something the teams prefer to avoid). The nurse calls for help ('an ear, nose and throat specialist') over the phone. At this point the laryngoscope[41] stops working (physical layer

---

[41] The laryngoscope is an instrument that enables looking into the larynx as well as inserting in it the intubation tube.

failure). The doctor identifies the source of the problem (dead battery)and the nurse fixes it (repair by embodied layer):

NURSE: *[into phone]* Yes, hi, this is [ *her name*] from the ICU. Is it possible for you to come and help us, ear, nose, and throat, because we have a difficult intubation on a patient here in the ICU and we've already sedated him. I don't know what we're anticipating, hopefully not a trach, but maybe just a -

DOCTOR: I want a trach ready [he means: the tracheotomy equipment tray]

NURSE *[into phone]*: My doctor says that if you take trach tray with you, that will be good. Okay, fine, I will get it ready for you then, but we really need your help. Thank you so much. Bye. *[Hangs up phone]*

NURSE: Okay, ear, nose, and throat is coming. And the trach... I'll just prep that in case we need it.

[video laryngoscope batteries die]

DOCTOR: And now this is gone. We have any more battery?

NURSE: Oh, God. I don't know. It doesn't look like it.

DOCTOR: BP [blood pressure] is falling. Is he aspirating?

NURSE [looking into the laryngoscope]: There's no light in this.

DOCTOR: It's not broken, we just need more batteries.

NURSE: This one.

DOCTOR: Yes, but I cannot get a proper...

NURSE: God, is there a way to get another one of these?

DOCTOR: Is help coming?

[Nurse checks drawer, finds another video laryngoscope tool]

NURSE: It's okay, we fixed it. Is this too long?

DOCTOR: No. (Heptonstall, 2015: 60-1)

So here the humans act as the resilient layer and fix the system. In a similar occasion in the ICU with the same difficult airway scenario, we observed the reverse, the physical layer fixing failures of the competences: the team is reminded of another possible action plan because they *see* another type of intubation instrument on the instruments tray. The visual affordance fixed the loss of human memory of the procedure.

James Reason's 'swiss cheese' model (Figure 4.21) used in risk analysis and accidentology, especially in the medical and aerospace domains, presents the defence layers that a system has against failure ('defensive filters') as slices of swiss cheese, where the holes are latent failures: if these holes are aligned, the accident may occur (Reason, 1990, 2000).

As we see, the various layers of an installation act as such layers of defence as well as action scaffoldings.

Figure 4.21. The swiss cheese model of how defences, barriers and safeguards can be penetrated by an accident trajectory (from Reason, 2000).

Often there is redundancy between the layers of the installation. Let us observe lines in an airport passport control: the physical setting is designed for queuing in line with specific affordances (e.g. socket-mounted retractable belts), a sign reminds the visitor to wait in line to make sure the context is interpreted correctly ('please wait in line', 'stand behind the yellow line'), and live agents control the area, orienting people into the lines according to their type of passport as they arrive from the corridor. It does not matter so much by which layer of the model the rule is captured by the analyst, as long as it is identified. Once the process is identified ('wait in line in order of arrival; first come, first served'), the detail of how it is applied to the participants can be investigated more easily, and as stated earlier it probably operates simultaneously along more than one dimension. (Remember the earlier examples of double signatures, double keys, repeated entry for a password, etc.)

So in fact, installations are 'triplicated': the same action is scaffolded/ funnelled at the three levels of the installation simultaneously.

Redundancy has a cost, but this 'belt and suspenders' aspect of installations seems to me the expression of a need for resilience. When one looks into more detail, one sees that the redundant aspects are usually the ones for which failure to behave adequately could bring catastrophic consequence or negative externalities (and therefore conflict and cost). It is obvious for the case above: people can get aggressive when passed in a line. But if we look at other examples already cited, such as the automobile warning lights (Figure 4.2) or the sterilization station (Figure 4.15) we can see that redundancy is designed there also to make sure that potential accidents for which the possibility is not immediately obvious to the subject are avoided. In this respect, installations perform some duty of care for the members of society, exhibiting the two sides that were evoked in Chapter 1: as they guide individual action, they also make sure this action is not detrimental to others and to society at large.

From such mechanisms we can better understand what makes an installation strong and resilient: it is the combination of the various layers. Conversely, behaviours are all the more likely to happen if they are supported by more layers.

Therefore, 'sustainable'[42] behaviours are the ones that are compatible with the three layers of the installation. If we use the graph with the three ovals (Figure 2.1) to describe sets of behaviours that are affordable (physical space oval), imaginable (embodied space oval) and socially acceptable (social space oval), the sustainable behaviours are the ones at the intersection of the three ovals. These behaviours are sustainable for two reasons: the first is that, because they are supported by the three layers, they are easier to perform, and possibly the load of execution and control will be distributed over the three layers. The second reason is that these behaviours, because they are controlled by three layers simultaneously, are always executed in the same way. This means that they are maintained the same when reproduced, and that is a definition of sustainability and endurance.

Nevertheless, despite of all its layers, not all behaviours performed in an installation are sustainable. It is possible to have a behaviour that is not compatible with affordances of the installation – by spending an extra effort or accepting damage to self or installation (e.g. forcing a door). It is possible to have a behaviour that is not socially acceptable – by incurring the social costs and risks (e.g. fighting the authority in charge). It is even possible to have a behaviour that is unthinkable – by accident or mistake; although this usually has some consequences in the person's psychic life (e.g. as a colleague once did, driving in the morning, with your toddler in the back seat, straight to the office instead of stopping by the kindergarten, and then leaving the forgotten child locked in the car for hours in the

---

[42] Here I mean *durable*, having the capacity to be sustained in time; not necessarily ones that have a small ecological footprint.

company car park). But such behaviours are rarely sustainable. Sustainable behaviours are the ones that are compatible with the three layers. Usually there is some leeway, and this margin enables local adaptations.

There is also another important possibility. We have so far described sustainable installations, where the three layers tile in a coherent manner. But that is not always the case. The layers can be contradictory and may have no sustainable intersection. In such a situation, any behaviour will be problematic. For example, some parts of the installation have been designed with a specific content of the third layer in mind, but in fact the actual third layer in force in the installation is not the one expected.

In Colombia (in a state of civil war at the time of writing), formal education follows models and values similar to those in force in Europe and the United States. Nevertheless, in everyday life, the actual values in use can be different. For example, in a lot of contexts, the use of violence and even homicide can be justified under certain conditions (such as to protect your family or entering a gang), even when clearly forbidden in both the law and the predominantly Catholic value system.

Likewise, being 'clever' often means knowing how to con or take unjust advantage of the system and can be considered as the social role model, whereas being a good citizen' and 'being a good student' in a more traditional sense is a synonym of being a fool (a popular saying from a song goes: 'the astute lives of the fool, and the fool lives of his parents').

Some researchers have linked this to the violent history of the country (see Duque, Toro, & Montoya, 2010): gang members and drug dealers can become powerful role models (lots of money, power and capacity to defend themselves and their families) and those who act as vigilantes and try to regulate others directly or through authorities are often killed[43] (Paulius Yamin-Slotkus, personal communication).

In such contexts, many installations are dysfunctional. As a matter of fact, when we want to change installations, it can be precisely because in their current state they are dysfunctional, at least in the eye of the change agent. Colombia may appear a specific case, but in many areas the state

---

[43] Because of the prevalence of these contradictory norms, for the same specific activity, a subject can be influenced by several regulatory systems at the same time. To address this issue and pacify the city, Antanas Mockus, mayor of Bogota, designed interventions by cultural agents, aiming at influencing social-norm perceptions; that is, the perceptions one has of what most people in a certain context think is acceptable or is the right thing to do. Such an approach is advocated by Tankard and Paluck (2016). Some of these interventions are listed in Section 8.5. Mockus' framework divides motivation into three main types (interests, emotions and reasons) and regulatory systems into three types as well (legal norms, social norms and moral norms). The idea is to suppress the discrepancies between law, morale and culture to limit motivational conflict (Mockus, 2002; Yamin-Slotkus, 2015).

of war is a permanent or frequent regime. In such cases or during sharp historical transitions, institutions are destabilized and installations are not as neatly regulated as is presented in installation theory. To some degree, degraded regime is the normal state of affairs, but usually the degree of degradation is less acute than as described in the Colombian case.

Anyway, if we want to change behaviours, we must change the components of the installation to enable and support the new behaviour. This can be done through innovation of design and building new affordances in the material environment. It can be done through education and training for the embodied layer. It can be done through political work and institutional change for the social layer.

Careful analyses of current installations, and of which components influence what aspects of behaviour, are the way to go. Once the components are identified, changes in the installation can be made. At any given moment, some components will be easier to change than others.

### 4.6. Takeaway: The Resilient Power of Installations and Its Limits

**A substantial amount of our life in society takes place in the setting of installations – specifically constructed societal settings where humans are expected to behave in a predictable way. Not all behaviours are funnelled by an installation, but that is frequently the case especially for routine activities. Most structures of the built environment that are behavioural arenas become installations when actors step in: restaurants, kitchens, plane cockpits, theatres, toilets, lectures, offices, etc.**

**The components are distributed over three different layers: affordances in the physical environment, representations and other interpretive competences embodied in the persons and social regulation of institutions exerted directly or indirectly by Others.**

**Often these components are redundant. This redundancy is a guarantee of resilience; it enables the installation to have a momentum strong enough to funnel the behaviour of persons even with limited or faulty competence. The installation has a momentum of its own; it channels people's behaviour in a predictable way.**

**We have seen how the three layers of installations (physical affordances, embodied interpretive systems, social influence and control) prune the tree of possibilities to leave only few alternatives to the subject. In this way, the subject's behaviour is channelled, and often the subject does not even have to make decisions because apparently 'there**

**is no alternative', or the alternatives are only minor variations of interpretation in a behavioural course.**

Installation theory resonates with many previous scholarly works and especially with Lewin's. As Lewin states when commenting on the life space as the totality of possible events:

> from both the theoretical and practical point of view the most important characteristics of a situation are what is possible and what is not possible for the person in this situation. Each change of the psychological situation of the person means just this – certain events are now 'possible' (or 'impossible') which were previously 'impossible' (or 'possible'). (Lewin, 1936: 14)

In other words, in that model, how the subject perceives a situation determines what the subject believes is possible or impossible and the subject acts according to this belief. **What we have shown with our model is that in societies, installations construct 'situations' that leave only a few possibilities to the subject. This is how regulation occurs and how is avoided the potential mess of each individual continuously inventing his own ways. The subject's awareness of that societal control is important but not indispensable; most of the time the subject will think he acts of his own volition.**

The three layers of components are very similar to Lewin's initial modelling of what 'facts' are in the life space: Lewin talks about quasi-physical, quasi-social and quasi-conceptual facts to highlight that what is determining the behaviour are *subjective* interpretations of facts (Lewin, 1936: 24-27). Installation theory is a somewhat more systematic and pragmatic framework to operationalize these components.

**This provides a theoretical framework to the approach of using 'nudge' (Thaler & Sunstein, 2008) to support public policies; although we are more radical because installations can use the full range of funnelling style from 'light touch' and avoidable incitation (which was the original nudge concept)[44] to compulsory, enforced and unescapable constraint. The model therefore also includes, realistically, unethical and inhuman situations; as we know, such situations alas occur and must be accounted for by the theory.**

---

[44] 'A nudge, as we will use the term, is any aspect of the choice architecture that alters people's behavior in a predictable way without forbidding any options or significantly changing their economic incentives. To count as a mere nudge, the intervention must be easy and cheap to avoid. Nudges are not mandates. Putting fruit at eye level counts as a nudge. Banning junk food does not.' (Thaler & Sunstein, 2008: 6)

Installations are not only interesting for society because they enable behaviours and funnel them in a specific way. From the perspective of the user, they also enable building habits and therefore a gain of efficiency. As noted by (Wood et al., 2002)

> Stable contexts facilitate this propensity to perform repeated behaviors with minimal cognitive monitoring. Although no situation ever completely maps onto earlier experiences, responses proceed quickly without limiting processing capacity to the extent that the current environment is similar to the one in which the behavior was performed in the past.

Installations are precisely such 'stable contexts'. Therefore installations are a comfortable environment for users, and a cognitively economic one.

**Installations must not be reduced to or mistaken for the material setting (the built environment, the stage, the device), because installations are fully assembled only when in this setting step in the actors with their embodied competences, and the institutions.** Those who study innovation are well aware of the classic effect of 'function creep' where a product or system designed for a specific purpose ends up being used for something different by the end users. The SMS, which was designed for communicating between technicians to check the good operations of the network and is now used for different purposes, is a classic example; but when people use a farm to have a rave party, or the coffee machine as a social hub, the phenomenon is the same (see Akrich, 1998, for other examples). The content of a given layer may be multipurpose; it is the assembling of several layers that produces the installation.

**Remarkable and somewhat unexpected is the redundancy of installations, as exemplified by the example of the queue at customs.** A physical barrier channels people in a narrow corridor, humans have embodied the notion of queuing in line by order of arrival, finally an agent (or the customs officer herself) is usually there to enforce that people actually do queue. In theory, one should be enough. But **that redundancy is the key to resilience and also sustainability of the installation. This resilience enables challenged participants to perform in a satisfying way. In particular, this enables to train novices into the correct competence.**

**Installation theory simply builds on the insight that societies inscribe guidance and control in the components susceptible to being involved in a given behavioural sequence. Most animals cope with the conditions to them given, with the innate skills inherited through genetic evolution. Humans install their environment and deliberately adapt the resources so as to support and funnel the behaviour of others and**

**their own.** Although that trend is present to some degree in most animals especially for their dwelling (nests, burrows, etc.) this adaptive tendency has been multiplied by human's capacity to imagine new possibilities, and to store and transmit the result of successful innovations.

But that insight is useless in practice: if we want to analyse and intervene, it is too general. Installation theory uses the minimal threefold framework for description and therefore describes installations as three-layered for the ease of description and analysis. The truth is that we could unfold installations in as many folds as we want. I believe that three folds cover the main dimensions and are already somewhat redundant because the three realms are not independent. But two realms are not enough.

Let us take a tree metaphor. When we say a tree is made of three parts, the roots, the trunk and the branches, that certainly does not account for all what the tree *is*, but that is a practical first-approach model for the lumberjack and the gardener. Installation theory is a handy simple model for change agents; as all models it will stay incomplete; so the equivalent of good lumberjacks and gardeners will *also* draw on other models. It is clear that root, trunk and branches are not independent and that limits are blurry because each only makes sense as a part of the whole tree. Nevertheless, even though each component is not so clearly defined, the fact of having a name for that part enables us to analyse better and communicate the complex relations among the parts of the tree and between the tree and its environment, and to act on the tree. That is the use of a model. The actual, real, system of activity scaffolding is more complex than the simple model proposed by installation theory, but that model is of great help to deal with the actual phenomenon.

**Installation theory is of course very schematic. It is deliberately so to enable a first orientation in the complex sociotechnical systems that change agents must deal with; it provides *a simple checklist for analysis and agenda for intervention: check the influence of the three layers, one by one, for each step of the behaviour considered.* That enables understanding of why people act in a specific way in specific situations, and to reframe the components accordingly: by (re)designing material context, education/training of participants, or institutional change and political action.**

**Sustainable behaviours are the ones fit with installations. Therefore if we want to change the world or, more modestly, one of its subdomains, it is clear that action limited to a single layer of determination – for example a new product or a campaign – will hardly be enough to change alone the behaviours of people.**

Finally, we must consider the limitations of the framework. I agree with Valsiner, who regrets that the definition of psychology has sometimes been restricted to 'a science of prediction and control of behaviour' (Valsiner, 2009a); psychology should not be neglecting the cultural-historical aspects nor the phenomenological, subjective, intentional and creative nature of the human psyche. Installation theory focuses on the structures (installations) that make behaviour predictable; these structures exist precisely because humans are free agents with a rich mental life, whose behaviour and thoughts must be channelled and controlled to some degree to allow the smooth operation in society – that is a sad price to pay to benefit from the advantages of culture. Installation theory should not be understood as a way to predict human behaviour in general; rather it examines which socially constructed structures make behaviours predictable.

I already warned in Chapter 1 that, as every theory, Installation theory is neither complete, nor exact, nor true; it is only a practical and heuristic tool to deconstruct the determinants of behaviour in installations. It does not apply to everything: *not everything socially constructed is an installation*, although some of my enthusiastic students seem to believe otherwise. Installations are socially constructed settings where behaviour becomes predictable. Of course the limit is blurry because mechanisms used in installations are general behaviour control and support mechanisms and they are used also for one-off interactions; but the theory loses explanatory and heuristic power the further it is used from its original terrain of application – on top of all its other imperfections.

Another limitation is the degree to which an installation can be expected to be predictive of behaviour. As Warde notes, behaviour is heavily dependent upon the local context, because reasoning is local. But that does not mean the classic sociological or psychological variables are useless; rather they account, at a higher level, for the frequency with which particular types of individuals will get exposed to a specific type of installation, where they then will be caught in the installation's situational logic (see Warde, 1997: 202). These higher determinations are above the level of explanation of installation theory.

Also, installations do not completely specify the detail of the action. For example, in a supermarket, installation theory will be useful to explain and probably quite accurate to predict how consumers enter, stroll in the aisles, put products in their trolleys, queue and pay at the cashier's; but it will be of little help to predict which brand of soup or flavour of soda a given consumer will put in her trolley. Installations frame the behaviour, but only to some degree and they leave some room for variability.

Therefore, even though the control and guidance are intense, this does not mean that the behaviour in a given installation will be exactly identical in every case. For example, we observed in a systematic way nine doctor-nurse teams in an identical ICU installation to the one described in Figure 5.2; with an identical scenario of patient's condition quickly deteriorating, using a simulation room at the Danish Institute for Medical Simulation. Although all the teams used a globally similar protocol and ended up with the same (correct!) medical intervention after trying the same possibilities, each case was slightly different (in terms of timing, internal communication, requests of resources and so on).

Cicourel's description of two types of *context* is illuminating in this perspective.

> [The larger] use of the term "context" includes an institutionalized framing of activities or ways that group-derived prescriptive norms pressure and/or channel people with designated titles, presumed competencies, duties or responsibilities into certain physical spaces at certain times in order to engage in a finite number of specifiable activities. Within this institutionalized context or framing of activities, emergent processes of talk appear that creates a more narrow view of "context" in the sense of locally organized and negotiated interaction. (Cicourel, 1992).

Installations provide or restrict the *larger* context framework, but within that framework participants still have leeway. The detail of what actually happens is also the result of many other factors (e.g. participant's motives, history). Although societal control by installations on individuals is intense, continuous and detailed on *some* dimensions, *it is never total* and some margin is left to the creativity of actors to play the system, as long as they stay within certain limits.

**The next chapter examines how installations endure. This book introduces two main ideas. The first is a framework that describes how individuals are framed into appropriate behaviour by installations, and that is described in Chapters 1 through 4. The second idea is that installations are the device by which society reproduces itself through practice, in a distributed manner. Installations, in that perspective, constitute and construct society and culture at the micro-level. Subsequent chapters show how these installations endure, how they are continuously reconstructed and therefore how society is continuously reconstructing itself.**

# CHAPTER 5

# Endurance of Installations
## The Reconstructive Cycle of Practice

This chapter is where the installation framework turns into a theory. It describes how installations are reconstructed through practice. In doing so, it addresses the first aspect of evolution: endurance (the second aspect is change, which is considered in Chapters 6 and 7).

This chapter starts with a sketch of the general cyclical process by which installations produce practice, and practice produces installations (Section 5.1).

In the three subsequent sections (5.2, 5.3 and 5.4) we examine the reproduction of each layer, starting with embodied competence. The layers are not addressed here in their usual order; the embodied layer is described first because of its key role in the reconstruction process.

Installations are resilient as a result of some redundancy of their three layers. This redundancy enables them to induce even incompetent (e.g. novice) subjects to behave appropriately. In doing so, participants learn in doing. The embodied layer is therefore reproduced by the two others. Learning processes at relational level (by legitimate peripheral participation, intent community participation, instruction, education or trial and error) are described, as are feedback and embodiment processes that account for the inscription of competences at the neuronal level. This concept is illustrated in Section 5.2 with examples of learning in the fields of nursing, cooking and eating.

Then the reproduction of material objects (Section 5.3) and the reconstruction of communities and institutions (Section 5.4) are more briefly described, highlighting the role of the latter in regulating the reproduction system. Material objects and their representations are taken in a chicken-and-egg process where each is created after the other, under the control of institutions. Again, a layer is reproduced with the aid of the two others.

Finally, as institutions gradually emerge through practice, they are also a product of the other layers (practice creates norms).

I use the words reproduction and reconstruction more or less indifferently here to describe the mechanisms by which installations endure and replicate in *almost* identical form. As the reader will see, the mechanisms are a bit of both.

The chapter concludes with an overview of the whole process and a takeaway (Section 5.5). It shows how societal conditioning and control of behaviour are continuous and distributed processes; how they take place at a scale that is so massive and systematic that brainwashing and totalitarian regimes may appear almost benign and amateurish in comparison. This section also introduces the notion of the 'betterment loop', which is frequently encountered in the process of social reconstruction and which accounts for stability and optimization.

Let us first summarize in a paragraph the previous chapters. The framework of installation theory describes 'installations': specifically constructed societal settings where humans are expected to behave in a predictable way. Shops, conference rooms, roads, hospital wards and dinner tables are installations. Installations have a momentum of their own; they funnel people's behaviour in a predictable way, according to the local goals of the installation. This is obtained by constructing a bundle of components which, when assembled, are interpreted as a specific situation and behavioural setting by subjects, and operate as an attractor that results in the expected behaviour. We categorized these components in three realms (physical, embodied, social).

Lewin (Lewin, 1936: 55–6) warned against explaining a behaviour by anything else than the present situation of the system concerned ('systematic concepts of causation'). So far we have followed Lewin's advice. We explained in detail how installations nudge, scaffold, funnel and control people's behaviour in a situation at a given point in time. These components seemed sufficient to provide a (rough) explanation of behaviour, possibly even predictions.

But behaviours evolve, it is a historical fact. We do not eat, dwell, work or travel as we did in the Middle Ages. Today's conference rooms and hospital wards differ from what they were a century ago. We must therefore examine how installations change. Lewin (ibid.) calls 'historical concepts of causation' what accounts for how the situation itself was constructed. In other words, at a given moment a given installation generates specific behaviours; but installations evolve in time. *How do installations evolve?* That is the question addressed in this chapter and the next.

As the reader can imagine, answering this question is a daunting task, because every case is specific and path-dependant. Nevertheless, installations (and more generally our world) are social constructions; by looking at *how that construction happens in practice* we will sketch some general mechanisms of the social construction of installations. These generic mechanisms combine with local conditions to produce specific historical developments.

For all things social (and biological as well), endurance is not the result of passive inertia, but rather of continuous reconstruction. Evolution happens because this reconstruction is not strictly identical from generation to generation[1].

Studying how things happen at a given moment in time (see Chapter 4) is the *synchronic* study of installations (e.g. what happens when I check in for my flight that specific Friday at noon). It must be distinguished from the *diachronic* aspect, which is the study of installations over time (e.g. how airport check-in evolved over the last decade).

Because the mechanisms are several and their combination is somewhat complex, we start with the simpler case of mere reproduction without change; this will make visible the process of social (re)construction. We shall see how synchronic use of the installation reproduces practice *and the installation*. That is the purpose of the current chapter, to show how the diachronic stability of installations is constructed.

I must start this chapter with a warning, and an apology. Much of what is presented here may be obvious to the reader, or at least well known because we all, as members of society, have personally experienced the mechanisms that I shall describe. The list is long, and perhaps cumbersome, but that is because the mechanisms are many indeed. Although each of them is well known, their study has so far been distributed over different scientific fields and disciplines. The current chapter attempts a synthesis that will build a global image from all these scattered pieces. The pattern

---

[1] So beyond the reconstructive processes, evolution combines (at least) two processes: morphostasis and morphogenesis. In morphostasis, more or less another word for homeostasis, perturbation to a system are taken as noise requiring minor adjustments to keep the system within the operational limits of its current state. In morphogenesis, the perturbations result in system transformation and durable change of structure.

that appears describes in detail the linkage between macrostructures of society, the micro-structures of the neural system of individuals and the characteristics of objects or institutions. The purpose here is to detail the long and complex chain of mechanisms that produce the reproduction of behaviours. As the reader will see at the end of the chapter, the final picture is both amazing and somewhat chilling, because of the level of distributed, often redundant, micro-control it reveals.

The process by which installations reproduce themselves is a fascinating hybrid cycle involving human populations and material objects. Some of its aspects have family resemblance with the life cycle of insects, but it brings ecological efficiency and resilience a step further than any biological species.

I first provide an overview of the global process in Section 5.1, then step into more detail in Sections 5.2 and 5.3 to show how the embodied competences and the material objects are continuously reciprocally reproduced. Section 5.4 provides a description of the regulating role of communities, organizations and institutions in trying to keep the installations identical through their reproduction process. The role of system feedback is explained. Finally, the process of embodiment is presented in a way that clarifies how the social structure can inform a neural structure.

## 5.1.   An Overview of the Standard Reproduction Cycle

The general structure of the reproduction mechanism of installations and behaviours is a cycle. Not all reproduction mechanisms are cycles; for example, cell division, budding, tillering (plant reproduction from grow shoots, sprouts, rather than from a seed), photocopying are not.

What is specific here is that installations and behaviours are part of the same cycle, and reconstruct each other continuously. Giddens' example about the fact of speaking English contributing to reproducing the English language as whole (Section 3.3) is an illustration of such continuous reconstruction. The reproduction process is simultaneous and continuous, as in M. C. Escher's famous lithograph of hands drawing each other (Figure 5.1). The same goes for installations.

When I queue correctly, when I drive properly, I contribute to reproducing the queue institution or the rules of the road. But as we can see, mere *behaviour* is not enough to reproduce the installation as a whole in its three layers. My own driving behaviour as a motorist does not, for example, directly reconstruct the traffic lights. Because we went into painstaking detail of social mechanics we cannot be satisfied by general theoretical

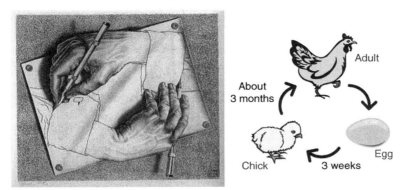

Figure 5.1. *Left, Drawing Hands,* Maurits Cornelis (M. C.) Escher, 1948. Lithograph, 28.2 x 33.2 cm. *Right,* the chicken-and-egg cycle.

answers evoking a principle of 'practice reconstructing practice'. How does it happen *in detail?* 'Capital-T' Theories such as social constructionism or structuration remain evasive regarding the detail of the process. They are not wrong, but they lack detail. Saying that 'practice reproduces practice' is like saying chickens reproduce chickens. We want more detail in the description of the mechanism.

In nature many biological organisms cannot reproduce by themselves; they need another species to contribute to the reproduction process. For example, viruses use the biological factory of their host to reproduce; the same with some symbiotic or parasitic species.

Casting is another kind of reproduction process, mechanical, used to produce copies of material objects: a mould (or matrix) is made of the original model that is the exact negative of the original model, e.g. by covering the model with plaster. Then this mould is used to cast copies, e.g. by pouring metal into the matrix. The matrix serves as a scaffolding to provide the adequate pattern to the cast while it takes shape. This mechanism can also become cyclical because from the model another object, similar to the original model, is created and can then be used as the new model for future casts, as in reproducing a key in several exemplars.

As we shall see, the reproduction cycle of installations has characteristics in common with each of these very different processes: casting, chicken-and-egg, symbiosis or parasitism.

Although we should be careful with metaphors, we can see that the mould/cast mechanism has some analogy with the installation/behaviour mechanism. Behaviours shape installations because installations are designed after their pattern; in turn installations produce behaviours. For example, we build toilets based on the idea of supporting a specific behaviour; but then these toilets channel this specific behaviour again. Depending on the details of the behaviour that serves as a model, the toilets will be different: in some countries people use paper, in some others they use water, and the installation usually supports either one or the other custom, rarely both – the well-travelled reader knows exactly what I mean.[2] So, specific behaviours generate supporting installations, and then these installations are supposed to generate this specific behaviour.

Once the reproduction cycle is started, it is not necessarily easy to change: see the example of road traffic. If the United Kingdom wants to change left-hand drive to right-hand drive, both behaviours and installation must change simultaneously.[3]

But just as casting is a much more complicated process than what I just described, the reproduction cycle of installations and behaviours is also more complex.

On the one hand, people experience installations and learn behaviour through practice in these installations. On the other, installations are constructed to mould behaviours. So at first sight this reproduction cycle appears similar to casting, where installation would be the mould and behaviour the model and the cast. But installations are not made of one single piece; they are composed of three layers of components: material objects, embodied competences and social regulation. These layers do not reproduce with the same mechanisms, and the reproduction of each layer uses components of the other (a bit like the virus using the genetic material of the cell).

The following sections detail the reproduction mechanism of each layer in the ideal situation where reproduction is strictly identical. This is an

---

[2] Oshlyansky and colleagues (Oshlyansky, Thimbleby, & Cairns, 2004) showed drawings of light switches to UK and US subjects: UK subjects thought the 'down' position of a light switch indicates the light is 'ON'; for their US counterparts it was 'OFF.' The well-travelled reader may have experienced the fact that some of their embodied competences are only adapted to specific environments. For example, many continental Europeans look for cars on the wrong side of the street when they come to the UK. I myself almost killed my good colleague Jaan Valsiner (and myself) by driving on the wrong side of the road during a conference in a foreign country. Happily Jaan has good reflexes.

[3] An old joke suggests being cautious in the change process, by starting with trucks and taxis only for the first week, then generalizing to all vehicles the next week. More seriously, in 1970 General Ne Win decided overnight to change the traffic rules in Myanmar from left-hand drive to right-hand drive. This resulted in accidents (e.g. people getting off the bus in the middle of the traffic because the doors were on the wrong [new] side). And still today in Myanmar, many years after the change, many old cars have the steering wheel on the right, which is impractical for seeing oncoming traffic.

ideal case, but can be considered a valid approximation for a given place and a short duration of time.

## 5.2.  Reproduction Cycle of Embodied Competences

This section explains how the installations reproduce embodied competences in humans. We first consider how subjects embody competences through practice, then how the installation provides feedback to the subject to make sure the subject embodies the *correct* practice. What is key to note is that because installations are resilient, first-time users, whose embodied competences are yet lacking, are still channelled into behaving appropriately (by the two other layers), so they learn in doing, they are socialized into the proper way.

Because this section is a bit dense, let me summarize the argument before we start. It is quite simple: humans *learn* the 'correct' way to behave, and that is why they behave correctly. But there are many ways to learn; all are involved to some extent in the general learning process, although on different occasions. Furthermore, societies have come up with devices that ensure that people learn 'the right things', and not something else: that is the difficult part, because humans can learn very easily, so they could learn 'different' ways. We therefore look here not only at the learning mechanisms, which are well studied in psychology, but also more specifically at how in actual practice the *correct* things are learned. Installations are one of the devices that produce that effect, and their three layers are involved in the process.

### 5.2.1.  *Learning Processes in Humans*

What is the mechanism of reproduction of cultural patterns?

Tomasello and colleagues (Tomasello, Kruger, & Ratner, 2010) consider that cultural learning takes three forms: 'imitative learning, instructed learning, and collaborative learning'. We may add trial and error, which can take place even if other humans are absent, because the context can carry culturally constructed indicators (refer to the case of the driver positioning the jack in the 'changing tyre' example in Figure 4.5). Ordinarily, how to behave in an installation (eating in a restaurant, waiting in a queue, buying clothes in a shop) can be learned in one of several ways: in situ by trial and error, in situ with help from someone who knows (including imitation) and off-site by formal instruction.

### 5.2.1.1.   *Trial and Error and Exploration*

One issue with learning is, paradoxically, the exceptional capacity of humans for learning, as illustrated by the size of their brain and especially their neocortex. Humans learn from experience. The succession in time of a stimulus and an unconditioned (innate) stimulus can create a conditioned reflex, such as e.g. fear of needles following a painful injection. Behaviour is also function of the *consequences* of past behaviour: e.g. behaviours that proved satisficing in the past are used again when similar situations occur; behaviours that entailed punishment tend to be avoided later. This is called *operant learning* (see Glossary: Operant conditioning). Therefore, any exposure to a situation is an occasion for learning. This results in people being able to acquire strange habits.

> My colleague Patrick (now a respected professor of sociology in an Ivy League university) has a sharp mind and is a fast learner, but on one occasion, he learned too fast. Before his doctorate he worked in my lab, and one day I entered his office for a morning conversation. As we talked, he turned on his Macintosh Plus.[4] At the time these machines took a while to boot, and a small icon of a smiling Mac appeared on the blank screen for a few seconds while the operating system was loading. I was surprised to see Patrick interrupt a sentence to quickly click on the icon as it appeared, and I asked him why he did so. He answered that this was to boot the machine. As a matter of fact, I knew that clicking had no effect, because the icon was not sensitive, and I told him, which surprised him. In that exchange we discovered that the first time he had turned on his Mac, he had clicked on the icon, and had assumed ever since that this was a necessary step because he had always seen the machine boot after that. He must have done it many times before we talked, and because he is a fast man the procedure had always been the same, always with success, leaving him unaware that this gesture was unnecessary. We both laughed, and I think Patrick stopped doing this.

Patrick's example is an innocuous instance of attributing causality to sequential correlation (*post hoc ergo proctor hoc*); the same may account for some superstitious behaviour.

Some examples or perseveration in the first practice learned with procedural rationality can be more worrying because they restrict individuals' behaviour or may marginalize them.

> In my early twenties I dated a young woman who, as I eventually discovered, insisted on keeping her panties on while having sex. After a few sessions, as I found that such a practice was somewhat strange, not to mention

---

[4] These were the first desktop computers with a graphic interface, in the 1980's.

damaging to clothing and to other things as well, I dared to inquire: why? It turned out that the girl's first partner, an older man, had had this fantasy, which the girl had hence taken for normal practice. In that case, again, exposure to the possibility of a different practice to attain the desired result changed the person's behavioural pattern; but I was amazed at how long the behaviour learned by initial exposure had remained repeated. Still, as in Patrick's case, the person was a smart individual (now vice-president of a large corporation).

As long as the behavioural solution satisfies, subjects may continue to use it. Some individuals may even show a surprisingly limited appetence for exploring outside their routine:

> My car was equipped with an alarm system that included blocking the ignition; the alarm would turn off when I unlocked the doors with the remote control, a small key-holder with three buttons. The ignition block system would automatically turn itself on again when the engine stopped. I found that impractical because when the car stalled, or when I turned off the engine but stayed in the car, to start the car again I had to relock the doors to unlock them and hence the alarm, by pressing the remote door-opening button *twice* before turning the ignition key. I always considered that a design flaw. Not so long ago I went to a garage to have the car stereo loudspeaker changed. As I did my double button pressing to start the engine, the mechanic looked at me and said 'Er... sir; you know, you don't need to press that button twice; there is another specific button on the remote to unlock the ignition'. And indeed, that was the function of that third button on the remote whose function I had sometimes wondered about. To my embarrassment I must admit that I had had that car and its alarm for ten years. I think the mechanic must have had on his face the same expression I had when I told Patrick about the computer booting icon.

Other, more consequential, examples of 'mis-learns' are well known, such as the effects of domestic violence in adulthood as a consequence of being abused in youth by violent parents (Bailey, DeOliveira, Wolfe, Evans, & Hartwick, 2012; Hetzel-Riggin & Meads, 2011). The very qualification of such cases as health problems, perversions or stories worth mentioning highlights, in contrast, that most of what we usually learn is actually the correct *standard* procedure.[5]

---

[5] This perhaps also enlightens the nature of crossing a border or breaking the rules for socially forbidden behaviour, or for behaviours that are 'secret' (not performed in public space and therefore not well known by the nonmembers). Because these forbidden behaviours are unknown grounds, when the subject is confronted by them (often forced, or asked to perform them by outsiders) there is strong reluctance because of the interdiction, fear of the unknown and mere incompetence to perform. Then once the behaviour is performed (e.g. killing someone) suddenly the behaviour becomes simple to perform and anxiety is gone. But in absence of other role models, there may

The key mechanism is as follows: the first successful behaviour that has been learned by a subject in a given situation tends to become the default choice for future behavioural path in similar settings. The first experience is determinant, as is the first impression of people, because they cast the mould in which subsequent situations will be processed and, as long as this produces an acceptable result, reinforced (reinforcement learning).

This phenomenon of initial learning creating a path-dependency in future choices, which seems evident, has also been demonstrated experimentally (Shteingart, Neiman, & Loewenstein, 2012). The consequences of this simple fact, which is a direct effect of the physiology of our neural system, are immense. As a result there is a strong bias for the reproduction of previous behaviours by the same subject. And if the first behaviour has been learned by observing another subject, then, through transitivity, whole populations may adopt the same behaviour and successive generations will reproduce it, as long as it satisfices.[6]

Indeed, the spontaneous way humans usually[7] operate is not by trying to calculate 'the' optimal solution for the problem given ('substantive rationality'), but rather by using 'procedural rationality' (see Glossary: 'rationality'); that is, applying some previously known generic procedure or heuristic that worked in a previous similar situation. That is a good heuristic because our rationality is anyway bounded by our limited cognitive capacity, so we cannot 'optimize' by finding the best solution; therefore we use an algorithm (Simon, 1955).

People naturally think inside the box rather than 'outside the box'. We use whatever we have at hand that seems to do the trick, a process Claude Lévi-Strauss called 'bricolage' – and this applies to mental tools as well as to material ones (Lévi-Strauss, 1962: 26 et seq.)

That process may, in fact, not necessarily be one of conscious deliberation. Daniel Kahneman (Kahneman, 2011) popularized the notion of 'System 1' vs 'System 2' introduced by Keith Stanovich and Richard West

---

be perseveration of stereotypic behaviour, especially when the subject is socialized in a marginal community where this behaviour is developed within the framework of local cultural norms, as is well described for marihuana smokers by Howard Becker in his remarkable book, *Outsiders* (Becker, 1966).

[6] In their first eight weeks in the army, young recruits modify their psychological contract (the tacit expectations they have about the army, how they should behave and what they can expect in return) which gets closer to the veterans'. (Thomas & Anderson, 1998)

[7] I except here specific occasions framed to test the capacity of *Homo sapiens* to use substantive rationality, such as games, mathematical or philosophical problems, formal school exams or laboratory experiments.

(Stanovich & West, 2000: 658–60).[8] System 1 represents automatic, often unconscious, operations whereas System 2 represents controlled, deliberative operations. System 1 is highly contextualized, personalized and socialized, whereas System 2 is decontextualized and depersonalized. Of course System 2 is still mostly procedural rationality: even an expert chess player or a seasoned travelling salesman will not attempt to calculate all the possibilities to decide 'the best' next move.

Procedural rationality has the advantage of carrying in itself a pragmatic algorithm when that process involves a course of action (procedure), which is usually the case: 'do as usual', or 'do as you did last time'. As the procedure is rolled out and action unfolds, as long as the result seems to satisfice, or in the absence of available alternatives, the subject perseverates in action. If something goes wrong the situation may be reassessed and other processes summoned, and if these do not satisfice either then the subject may start looking for more creative alternatives and escalate in reasoning strategy (Rasmussen, 1983).

The natural process of trial and error is some kind of exploration of possible behaviours, and capitalizing on the outcome for future occasions. This exploration can be systematic, trying out different alternatives, especially when the risk is low and time is available, as in games, but that is rarely the case. Usually trial is oriented. More often trial and error is made in the vicinity of a model behaviour: the subject has a vague idea of how to behave, but does not know the detail, or has experienced similar situations, but not exactly *this* one. For example, I know how to take breakfast, but in this specific country and family where I am a guest I do not know exactly what is the correct procedure, so perhaps I will arrive too early or too late the first day, and sit at the wrong place; in this rented car I will fumble with the controls of the radio until I find the right tuning and volume.

Play is, especially in children, a way to learn by trial and error without serious consequences. Gregory Bateson describes how play, an important learning process observable in many animals, entails learning. Play enables testing behaviour and seeing what outcomes it produces, in a nonrisky context where explorative behaviour is tolerated and even encouraged, because these behaviours are framed as 'not for real' (Bateson, 1972: 138–48). As Bateson aptly notices, in play what is *selected* as valid, as adapted to a given situation, are small *behavioural sequences*. The criterion for selection is the feedback of the context (here, the reaction of the Other):

---

[8] Which clarified and summarized an important series of dual-processing models (see especially Posner & Snyder, 1975).

> It is rather simple to see a first level of discovery by human player, A, who has a finite number of alternative actions. These are evolutionary sequences, with natural selection of, not items, but patterns of items of action. A will try various actions on B and find that B will only accept certain contexts. That is to say, A must either precede certain actions with certain others or place certain of his own actions into time frames (sequences of interaction) that are preferred by B. A "proposes"; B "disposes". (Bateson, 1979: 137)

Play is a pleasant learning process based on individual initiative that provides learning through trial and feedback. Let us note that a lot of this feedback is socially provided by conspecifics. During play, children learn roles.

More generally, exploration leads to an operational result that is an input for operant learning (see the beginning of this section); it can also produce feedback from others. Such feedback then results in the same: positive or negative input for learning. The important thing to note here is that learning takes place in a context, and that context's response determines the outcome of the activity; therefore the context conditions the learning of the 'appropriate' way.

In unknown settings, where there is no solution ready, humans tend to refer to the closest similar setting known, or to look around to see what others do and then imitate this. This imitation strategy reinforces the cultural transmission and replication effect discussed earlier.

To apply this to installations: novice participants may use trial and error to test how they should behave. The response of the installation will impact their future behaviour; they will in the future tend to reproduce the behaviour that finally worked. This behaviour, as we saw in Chapter 4, will have been channelled by the installation so that it is normally the 'appropriate' behaviour.

### 5.2.1.2.  *Observation and Imitation*

Learning by observation is present in many primates (Bruner, 1972; Itani, 1957; Kawai, 1965; Van Lawick-Goodall, 1968) and humans are no exception. Interestingly, human children seem more prone to imitate slavishly than chimpanzees (Horner & Whiten, 2005).

*Social learning theory* describes the process in humans (Bandura, 1977); it shows that learning process in humans does not need, like conditioning, to associate a reward (or punishment) with the associations learned. This can happen when they have observed the positive consequences of the behaviour on the person observed ('vicarious reinforcement', 'causal learning', 'emulation'), or simply by imitating the procedure itself.

Children often learn by hanging around and looking at adults doing, in what Barbara Rogoff called 'intent community participation' (Paradise & Rogoff, 2009). We come back to this in Section 5.4.2.

Imitation is a key process in learning; we can learn by observation only (to some extent), even without direct communication. The studies of the 'mirror neuron system' suggest that humans (and other primates) have some capacity for empathy with the motoric movements of other people. It seem we can somehow feel the movements of others (Gallese et al., 1996; Rizzolatti & Craighero, 2004). Whatever the exact mechanisms involved, the facts are solid: humans can (and do) spontaneously learn how to reach a given result by simply observing other humans acting, and they tend to act the same.

For installations, learning by imitation can occur when the novice observes other participants in the same role behaving appropriately. For example, I learn by silently observing how other guests behave in this restaurant, how people dress (or undress) on this specific beach, how my colleagues talk to the client.

But in humans, unlike most animals,[9] intentional pedagogy is frequent and is enhanced by verbal interaction (e.g. explanation) and social support; therefore, examples of how to do something are usually deliberately given to the novice. We come back to this point in Sections 5.4.2 and 5.4.3.

### 5.2.1.3.  *Learning During Development*

Although learning processes have been extensively studied in the psychology of development, it is especially among those who seriously take into account the role of the environment (vs focusing on the subject's maturation as the source of development) that we find the most relevant concepts and findings for our problem; e.g. Lev Vygotsky and Jerome Bruner.

Vygotsky (Vygotsky, 1978), then Bruner (Bruner, 1978, 1984; Wood et al., 1976), developed the notion of a *zone of proximal development*, that is the set of behaviours a learner can perform with the help of someone more skilled, but not without this help. Bruner and his group called 'scaffolding' the action of the helper in such situations (see Pea, 2004 for a critical review of the concept). One important distinction Pea brings is the fact that scaffolding is made by another actor, who 'fades' his support as the

---

[9] Although there is evidence of nonhuman animals' behaviour that amount to scaffolding, and teaching in a large sense, these are very rare (Whiten, 1999). It seems that the intention to educate that is routinely acknowledged in humans is not easily observable in other species, if even present at all.

learner progresses. For example, at first the parents hold the spoon to the feeding child, and then finally the child holds it himself.

During development, the novice gradually embodies the competences performed in this zone of proximal development. In doing so, the novice gradually expands his area of competence. The former zone of proximal development becomes part of the comfort zone, and now beyond the new border a new zone of proximal development will become the stage for further development. The accumulation of such competences, as we describe them in relation to the capacity for behaving properly within an installation, creates a portfolio that is characteristic of an individual, and reflects both his culture and his own experience.

General theories of child development, because they are focused on the individual, tend to highlight the internal determinants of development, as in Jean Piaget's theory of individual stages of development (Piaget, 1955); or to create models that are subject-centric, such as the ecological systems theory (Bronfenbrenner, 1979).[10] These models are interesting for clinical psychology and counselling, but we can hardly use them here because our focus is different, and we consider another unit than the individual: the installation. But the general mechanisms of development are very relevant to our problem.

Piaget described two important mechanisms in the learning process: *assimilation* and *accommodation*. These address aspects of the embodiment of experience as a relation between the already embodied interpretive structures of the individual (cognitive schemata) and the environment. The rationale is that the subject, when confronted by a new situation, tries to interpret it with her existing portfolio of competences. The identification of the new object with some existing pattern in the portfolio is *assimilation* (the 'reality' is considered the same as the former representation). In this process, of course, the object's perception is slightly modified and some of its specificities may be discarded to match the preexisting pattern. *Accommodation* is the opposite mechanism: the subject adapts her cognitive schemata to the incoming data. If the existing pattern does not work (e.g. the representation does not match, the action does not yield a satisficing result) then the pattern is modified, as the lens of the eye 'accommodates' by changing its shape to produce a sharp and contrasted image of what is looked at.

---

[10] Which distinguishes four subject-centred trundle environments that shape development: microsystem, mesosystem, exosystem and macrosystem.

Interestingly, this dual mechanism that either modifies the object perceived to match the model pattern, or modifies the model to match the
object has been identified in various forms and names in psychology and
cognitive science.

Dissonance theory (Festinger, 1957; Festinger, Riecken, & Schachter,
1956) describes how individuals confronted by a discrepancy between their
beliefs and reality either change their beliefs or reconstruct reality. As a
result the (re)constructed belief is consistent with the (re)constructed reality. The embodied interpretive competence is adapted to the (constructed)
reality.

Simon's procedural rationality describes how subjects first try to use
available routines, their preexisting interpretive processes, and change their
approach to consider afresh the problem space only if these do not produce
a satisficing result (Simon, 1957).

> [Humans] use selective heuristics and means-end analysis to explore a small
> number of promising alternatives. They draw heavily upon past experience
> to detect the important features of the situation before them, features which
> are associated in memory with possibly relevant actions. They depend upon
> aspiration-like mechanisms to terminate search when a satisfactory alterna-
> tive has been found. (Simon, 1976: 136)[11]

As a result, the subjects use processes that are 'satisficingly' (good enough)
adapted to reality.

Rasmussen's 'skills, rules and knowledge' model describes how workers
first try to solve a problem with the tacit routine approach, then escalate to
trying more and more sophisticated strategies[12] and finally try new creative
approaches if this does not work (Rasmussen, 1983). In doing so, the operator addresses the system at different levels of abstraction and detail, but
in complex cases especially the reference to the goal is explicit (Rasmussen,
1985). As a result, the final subject's strategy solves the problem.

Modelling the process by which analysts interpret data (Lahlou, 2003),
I described interpretation as an *abductive* process by which the analyst
gradually adjusts the successive candidate models *and* the empirical results

---

[11] Interpretation of projective tests such as the Rorschach inkblot test, or the similar Zulliger test, is
based on the principle that individuals approach an unknown stimulus with their 'usual' interpretive structures and especially defence mechanisms; therefore, how they interpret the ink blots gives
the psychologist a glimpse of these processes (Rausch de Traubenberg, 1970).

[12] Rasmussen was originally interested in man-machine systems; he distinguishes three types of
behaviour in the operator: *skills-based* ("rolls along without attention or control"), *rule-based* ("goal-
oriented but structured by feedforward control through a stored rule"), *knowledge-based* (-in unfa-
miliar situations. "a useful plan is developed -by selection- such that different plans are considered
and their effects tested against the goal") (Rasmussen, 1983).

until they match 'enough' (to publish). The subject constructs his model based on the previous knowledge of the domain analysed. In this movement, a new model and a set of observations that are considered valid occurrences of the model are created simultaneously.

These theories illustrate in different contexts a similar general human approach to dealing with phenomena and situations. Humans use existing competence as a default approach, and adapt that competence in a trial-and-error process when it does not work, or in the hope to get a better result, and then capitalize on the new experience acquired in modifying the model for future use.[13]

Let us call this strategy the *betterment loop*, because this works as a continuous recursive loop, updating the interpretive structure (representation or practice) through practice. Importantly, the trial-and-error process is not random. Trials are oriented by informed guesses based on the already acquired knowledge. The betterment loop is an *abductive* strategy for improvement; it considers whether a small variation based on 'educated guess' would be a better solution; that solution is then tested and the result incorporated in the knowledge stock, eventually leading to changing the default solution to the improved variant.

This strategy provides gradual improvement in continuity with the previous stock of knowledge. In doing so it attempts to map an existing template of interpretation to actual objects. The model created through experience is continuously updated with the results of new experience. What must be noted here is that regarding action-in-the-world *the betterment loop does not simply improve the object; it improves both the object and the model used by the subject to act upon reality.*

This notion of a betterment loop, used here to show how subjects adapt to the existing environment, also comes in handy in Chapter 6, which considers evolution. The general idea is to systematically explore variants that satisfy 'better' than the current solution, then chose a 'better' solution, substitute it for the current state, and reiterate ad infinitum. In the process, the model used to generate new solutions is also updated and improved.[14]

---

[13] This is consistent with Norman's seven stages of human action: 1. goal (form the goal); 2. plan (the action); 3. specify (an action sequence); 4. perform (the action sequence); 5. perceive (the state of the world); 6. interpret (the perception); 7. compare (the outcome with the goal) (Norman, 1988: 41). What happens is that at stage 7, the subject takes on board the results from lessons learned and uses them to improve action, immediately or the next time. It is also consistent with Dewey's model of thought, which can also be considered as a cycle: solving the problems that previous experience and routine alone cannot satisfice to solve creates ideas and solutions that can be used in future situations (Dewey, 1910).

[14] This same family of processes has been identified many times, under many names and by many authors, and it is used also in machine learning, for instance the algorithms of retropropagation

Interestingly, in such processes, the exact form of the 'best' solution may not be fully known, but some features of it are, and there are at least some criteria for comparing whether a solution is 'better' than another. Although that seems to provide very little leverage with which to proceed, this marginal criterion is enough to produce progressive procedures. Put bluntly, we do not really know what would be an ideal world or situation, but we are able, *when we try something new*, to compare two outcomes and decide which is preferable, and that seems enough to drive progress. Of course these procedures may be prone to the limitations of the hill-climbing algorithm,[15] which is that they can find an optimum only in the vicinity and may miss optima of a very different form.

But the first consequence of such betterment procedures is that they create stability by reinforcing the existing processes as long as these satisfice; and this reinforcing mechanism is our concern in this chapter.

I am not interested here in the biological detail of how this happens at a neural level. What is important to understand is that, through interaction with the installation, the subject constructs an embodied interpretive competence that enables her or him to perform the expected role in the context of that installation.

As we saw in Section 4.5, an installation is resilient enough to mould the behaviour of the subject even if he does not yet know his part well. This may come from affordances and reminders or indications in the physical world, or from corrective feedback from others: remember the example of

---

developing neuron networks. The latter are simply a mathematical implementation of the law of effect, reinforcing or modifying the structures, depending on how well they produce the desired result. In management, Chris Argyris developed the double-loop model of learning, as opposed to the single-loop model (Argyris, 1976). In the single-loop model, decisions are made to keep the organization functioning within the standard domain and rules of operation (as in a thermostat regulating temperature); in the double-loop model, the organization accepts the questioning of its own theories, policies and objectives in an attempt to progress towards a better set of operating rules and regime. Whereas the idea of 1) astabilizing cycle and 2) long-term modification are also part of the betterment loop, double-loop learning in Argyris' perspective mostly focuses on interpersonal games of decision and power, and the material layer is absent. As a matter of fact, organizations as well as installations do exhibit more long-term positive evolution than predicted by the rather pessimistic stance of the double-loop model. One reason for this is the positive ratchet effects of improvement in the physical layer, of accumulation of knowledge and of procedures that compensate for the zero-sum or destructive result of power games between actors and the fact that actors deliberately hide or bias information that might get in the way of their interests.

[15] The hill-climbing algorithm starts with a given solution, then attempts to find a better solution by small changes. If the solution is better, a change is made to the new solution; this is repeated incrementally until no further improvements can be found. The name comes from the situation of being on the side of a hill and trying to escalate it by choosing the one step that enables the hiker to get higher, and then reiterating the process. The hiker thus gets to the top, where a maximum is reached. But one can only get to the top of the local hill and may miss the next higher mountain: it is a local algorithm.

the nurse who is reminded to sterilize by the cleaning station or by signs on doors; the example of my colleagues explaining me how to put on a protection suit in the nuclear plant; the example of the nurse gently teaching the patient when to present her barcode bracelet. These are examples of the betterment loop through which installations produce a 'better' (more correct) competence in the subject.

Early education in childhood (or formal training) provides in development similar, often tighter, scaffolding to provide elementary generic skills that may be used further on, such as walking and language. Think of how kids learn how to ride a bicycle. First the parents hold the child as she learns to pedal, then one day the stabilizing wheels are taken off, then one day the child is allowed to ride her bike in the quiet street. And finally, she rides in the traffic: the same basic skill is reused, and modulated, in various installations.

For an individual, acquiring common sense is a product of education in the local culture, a long and gradual process described by developmental psychology. The constructionist approach describes development as a dialectic process between the child and its environment. Assimilation and accommodation (Piaget, 1926), proximal development (Cole, 1984; Vygotsky, 1978), scaffolding (Wood et al., 1976), storytelling (Bruner, 1987, 1991), etc. are some of the many paths that have been described in this complex process. Experiencing the situations, under the guidance and scaffolding of others, generates 'anticipation schemata' (Bruner, 1974) of what should happen or be done in similar occurrences; these interpretive systems are then inserted into the previously acquired social representations by anchoring and objectification (Moscovici, 1976). In this process, the novice (e.g. the child, the apprentice) gradually builds up a portfolio of representations and skills that are adapted responses to the object (how to recognize it, predict its reactions, evaluate its use for various activities, etc.) These structures are internalized, 'embodied'. Developmental studies suggest that identity development is distributed; specifically, it emerges from the texture of different interactive configurations occurring in families (Everri & Sterponi, 2013)

The structures acquired, schemata, enable orientation and exploration, and in this process they are continuously renewed and adapted to the actual environment 'out there'. Neisser defines a schema as

> that portion of the perceptual cycle that is inside the observer, modifiable by experience, and somehow specific to what is observed; The schema accepts information as it becomes available, and is changed by that information ... schemata are not passive; they direct movements and exploratory activities

of many kinds that make more information available, by which they are further modified. (Neisser, 1978: 97)

This notion, developed in Neisser's 'perceptual cycle', by which the subject orients itself in its environment (Neisser, 1976), recalls (amazingly!) closely Uexküll's functional cycle (Uexküll, 1934, 1992) but the extract above makes more explicit the process by which these schemata continuously update as the subject interacts with his environment, a point that Uexküll did not develop.

Exploration is key in that it builds the necessary variability of the perception and the response in a paradigmatic learning process (see Section 5.2.4). Motoric response must be able to cover a continuous array to be adapted to the variety of incoming situations. Every apple I take has a slightly different form and dimensions, but I manage to take any of them efficiently. This results from my capacity to interpret as 'apple' an infinite variety of different exemplars, as long as they stay within certain limits; and from my capacity to produce movements that fit most forms of apples. As I grab more apples, both these competences for recognition and action expand by capitalizing experience.

By repeating experiences during exploration and play, the subject learns what the limits are between the basins of attraction of various categories, and therefore how to allocate an adequate response to each in an ever more detailed way: apples should not be eaten in the same way as oranges, then they should not be eaten in the same way as quinces, etc.

All these learning mechanisms are not only used, but also leveraged by installations, as discussed in Sections 5.2.1.5 and 5.2.1.7

### 5.2.1.4. *Instruction*

Educational behaviour is frequently observable at many levels in humans: in parenting, in schools and between peers. All human societies have set up procedures by which those who do not know are deliberately induced to acquire the desired behaviour. Education and instruction are the most visible forms of that framed learning (see Section 4.4.2.3). Although the distinction is blurry, instruction is the activity of transmitting knowledge (teaching) and has this transmission as a purpose; whereas education is a general process of producing a competent member of society and may more generally happen also as a by-product of other activities. In another sense, education is more about transmitting generic symbolic knowledge and value systems (what things are and should be: what and why), whereas instruction is about transmitting explicitly the know-how of technical processes (how to do things: how, when).

There, the subject is presented with representations of the desired behaviour, and a teacher usually controls to ensure that the content has been learned. This mostly happens 'offline', away from mundane activities, in dedicated installations such as lectures, but can also take the format of 'initiation' in various cultures. Therefore, this formal education often happens away from the installation the representations refer to, 'in theory' (as opposed to learning through practice). It can also occur through media (books, television, the Internet). It also happens more and more through films and simulators, which are a form of simulated peripheral or direct participation (see Section 5.2.1.5). Offline education is economical because it can be broadcasted by one teacher to many students simultaneously, which is more difficult to do for education through practice, given that installations are often designed for only one single user at a time in each role.

Interestingly, new forms of education attempt to get closer to natural experience in situ by providing multiple, distributed material scaffolding and motivation (Puntambekar & Hübscher, 2005; Puntambekar & Kolodner, 2005).

Here is an example, from the training of police cadets in Norway.[16] A patrol of two is looking at their subcam tapes during a replay interview with the SEBE method. One of the officers is watching his first-person recording where he is preparing to enter a room in which the patrol has been told there is a suspect. As he remembers what he was thinking at the moment of action, helped by the cues provided by the recording, it becomes clear that the training videos he has seen in offline lectures are used as a template to inform his behaviour, and that he refers to the role distribution as provided in the training: 'number 1' and 'number 2' who have different actions to perform in such situation [italics mine]:

SAADI: what's in your head at that moment? Is that a vision of [his partner, in the role of 'number 1'] opening the door, is that a sequence? Let's look at it, I'm sure you ... yeah. Just try and put yourself back into your shoes and...

OFFICER: I remember when we started at the, you know, the cross. I remember that I thought I could stand behind the corner if I needed to, you know, the... the corner over there. And I remember thinking that... what distance I should have to the door, if I should go closer or if this distance was appropriate. *I remember thinking back to the movie that you showed in the auditorium, and I tried to compare my distance to the distance the guy in the video had. And try to compare it to my distance...*

---

[16] See Phelps et al., 2016; Stangeland, 2016.

SAADI: OK. So did you have the image of the video in your head at that moment?
OFFICER: Yeah.
SAADI: OK. Was that like, did you see the whole video, or...?
OFFICER: No, I thought of, you know, the point in the video where number 1 starts to secure the door. Yeah.

We can see here how instruction had immediate effects on the performance of behaviour; and how the visual examples provided during training are used as a reference for actual situations, in mental visualization, without passing through the stage of symbolic rule (e.g. an explicit measure of the distance in metres).

An important aspect of education is that it structures the delivery of knowledge piecemeal, in such a way that it can be more easily combined in a cumulative manner. For example, novices learn one specific domain or theory, or one tool, at a time. Indeed, observation and explanation are not sufficient beyond a certain stage of complexity, and the competences must be acquired by chunks, then combined to produce sequences of a higher complexity. As Bruner puts it:

> Unless the child can master the subroutines, the demonstration of the whole task is about as helpful as a demonstration by an accomplished skier to the beginner. (Bruner, 1972)[17]

Then, at some point the novice gets into 'practice', which usually takes the form of the peripheral participation described in Section 5.2.1.5. Learning how to drive is an example of this process. Novices must first learn the rules of the road, which are presented as typical situations, and what to do in these (e.g. which cars to let go first at a crossroad, what to do when passing another vehicle). Then they need to embody the practice further in the actual context of the road traffic, in the actual installation of instructional vehicles.

Education processes are usually sanctioned with some type of title or diploma (e.g. driving licence). These are an entitlement, or a condition, to be admitted to perform unsupervised in the actual arena. Such precautions support the resilience of installations, as noted in Section 4.5, by populating them with a majority of competent users —who can then also provide proper control and feedback to others.

---

[17] The division of knowledge into specific sections that can be assembled and the construction and proper delivery of courses are difficult tasks; therefore, education does not only accumulate knowledge about things, but also knowledge and experience about pedagogy. It is a major societal achievement and mobilizes considerable resources (see Section 5.4.3).

So, as we can see, a lot of learning happens outside the actual installations where it will be put to use. This is an important limitation to the claim that installations are the main locus of reproduction of practices.[18] Nevertheless, this offline learning usually happens in specific installations (schools, training centres) dedicated to the activity of instruction. Furthermore, the final step of learning usually occurs in actual installations, 'on the job' (driving in real traffic, doing an internship, building one's own canoe).

### 5.2.1.5.   *Legitimate Peripheral Participation on the Job and Intent Community Participation*

In practice for humans the most common learning occurs 'on the job' or 'in life': in situ, through interaction with the installations in a social context (family, peers, caregivers, educators) The process has been well described for the professional context as *'legitimate peripheral participation'* (Lave & Wenger, 1991; Wenger, 2000, see Glossary): there, the novice gradually builds know-how by participating in the activity, first by only observing competent others, later by supervised acting and being given more and more autonomy to perform by colleagues and the organization. The similarity of Vygotsky's scaffolding in the zone of proximal development for the learner (already described) and learning by peripheral participation is noteworthy.

This goes beyond mere technical skill-building for a specific installation, as Stafford shows with the biographic examples of a teacher and a merchant in a rural Chinese village. It is a lifelong process, entangled with the local culture and the individual's personal, social and moral developmental history, in which the learner does not only embody 'production techniques', such as calligraphy or haggling, but also more subtle, informal competence, ethics and habitus, 'enchanting skills' such as 'how to behave like a respect-inducing teacher, how to competently seduce potential customers' (Stafford, 2004).

The mechanism of peripheral participation (see Section 5.4.2 on the role of communities in organizing that process) describes for complex installations how in practice this learning happens gradually and step by step, under the control of others who let the subject get involved in the next step only when they feel she is ready. Let us see it in this section from the perspective of the individual subject.

---

[18] We shall see that competences for a given installation may also be learned in another one, for example, learning how to eat at the cafeteria is often done by eating at home.

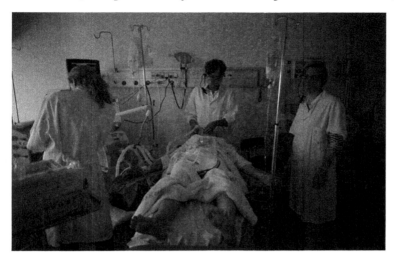

Figure 5.2. General setting in the operating room. Nurse standing at the head of the patient, doctor standing next to the arm (at *right*).

Here is an example of the very moment the novice, having seen several times the action performed by someone else, now does it herself for the first time under supervision. To save the reader a cumbersome explanation of context in exotic installations, let us use another case of the intubation sequence in an ICU described in Figure 3.3 (Section 3.1) and discussed elsewhere (Lahlou, Dieckmann, Zhang, & Heptonstall, 2017).

A doctor and an anaesthesia nurse are preparing to intubate a patient, with a specific procedure called rapid sequence induction. The doctor realizes that the anaesthesia nurse has never done it herself before, only assisted. But now they are only two with another very novice nurse in the operating room, and the doctor needs the help of the anaesthesia nurse, so the doctor guides the nurse into performing the task herself. The situation is depicted in Figure 5.2 where the nurse is ventilating the patient.

In the following sequence, the doctor realizes in utterances [5–6] that the nurse has never done the rapid sequence induction herself. She then instructs the nurse in utterance [7] as to the general process she must follow: injecting into the patient specific drugs that the doctor has just prepared in syringes. In [9] the doctor gives the go-ahead, then they physically switch positions and the nurse is now in front of the instruments she must use. In [10] the nurse acknowledges she is ready to follow the doctor's instructions. In [11] the doctor gives the instructions: what to inject and in which order. In [12] the nurse describes what she is going to do and asks for confirmation that she has well understood. In [13] the doctor confirms. As a result the nurse has now herself performed the right sequence of operations.

[1] DOCTOR: Yes. Okay, so what I'm going to do is we're going to try on a regular intubation and a rapid sequence induction and if we're in trouble, we have the Larynx Mask and then we have the Glide Scope. But I'm not... Is it on? *[Fiddles with Glide Scope]* Yep, it's on.

[2] NURSE: Vital signs are still the same. Rapid heart rate, it's at 84 and blood pressure. Maybe I'll just switch that to *[Presses monitor screen]* Auto, two minutes. Are you satisfied with that?

[3] DOCTOR: Yes, please.

[4] NURSE: Alright. Yeah?

[5] DOCTOR: But you did not intubate, correct?

[6] NURSE: No, no, I've never done it, but I've assisted in many intubations.

[7] DOCTOR: You've assisted. So what I want you to do is give what I've taken off, okay? [Doctor here refers to the syringes that she has prepared next to the patient's arms, and that she wants the nurse to inject the patient with]

[8] NURSE: Yup. *[Talks to patient]* Are you with us? Can you hear what I'm saying, Hans? *[To Doctor]* Still nonresponsive. I'm looking in his eyes (...) Okay. Equal pupils.

[9] DOCTOR: Okay. So I'm ready to take over. [As the nurse is currently at the patient's head, ventilating him with a hand device, Doctor and Nurse need to switch position, Doctor to intubate the patient, while nurse will inject the medications in the patient's arm]

[10] NURSE: Okay, I'll go and you tell me what kind of medicines you want.

[11] DOCTOR: Yes. *[Points to syringes]* And I put them so this is what you give first and then you give 10 millilitres and then you give Ephedrine afterwards.

[12] NURSE: Alright. So this one first? The whole thing?

[13] DOCTOR: Yes, the whole. (Heptonstall, 2015: 56–7)

One essential aspect of learning in copresence in the installation itself is the capacity to create and learn common ground by associating one's own representations, signs and embodied experience with things present in the shared reality, thereby binding them with the embodied experience and with the signs of others, in what Herbert Clark calls mutual knowledge or common ground (Clark & Marshall, 1981; Clark & Wilkes-Gibbs, 1986), and Schütz calls a 'we-relation'. Copresence leaves little ambiguity regarding 'what is the case', what is referred to and what is named what.

> Therefore, I am always able to check the adequacy of the schemata by which I interpret your utterances and expressions by pointing to an object in the world within our common reach. This is an eminently important

Figure 5.3. Chef Frederic Martin adapts his technique to fill the bowls with soup from one day to the next and uses the 'piston' instead of a ladle. A black and white version of this figure will appear in some formats. For the colour version, please refer to the plate section.

circumstance in the building up of my stock of knowledge and for my practical adjustment to social reality. (Schütz [1932] 1976b: 31)

Here is another example.

Chef and cuisine Professor Frederic Martin is doing the service for a banquet of thirty-five, helped only by two apprentices; he did exactly the same menu for another group the day before, with the same two apprentices. The day before, he used a ladle to pour the cold soup (the first course) in the bowls; but although this technique is appropriate for a few bowls, as usually happens in a restaurant, it is not the best one for serving a batch of twelve identical bowls (which is all that fits on the preparation table in the space beside the large soup container). Indeed, the liquid may drip from the ladle on the way because some bowls are far from the larger container, and then some bowls may look messy, which is unacceptable.

Therefore the chef has modified his technique and is using a special device, a kind of funnel, the 'piston' (Figure 5.3), which is of course more complicated to set up. We can see here how even the expert continues to adapt and learn by trial and error. He comments to his apprentices:

CHEF: *[Talking to apprentices]* So we will test the piston, we'll see what happens...

[He tries, and it works quite well]

CHEF: *[Talking to apprentices]* Here we are using a technique that is somewhat slower but much more precise. [To himself] I think it's worth it.

The soup (poured in the bowls over a julienne of green apples and cucumbers) is served with grissini, topped with a small sprinkle of spice and a few drops of olive oil. These ingredients must be added after the soup is poured.

Figure 5.4. The apprentices volunteer to help and try to reproduce what they saw the chef do the day before. Apprentice 2 sprinkles the pepper (*1*) and asks if they should pour the oil (*2*). She tries (*3*) and the chef gives verbal feedback. For the next batch of twelve bowls (*4*) they all manage alone and the chef does not comment. A black and white version of this figure will appear in some formats. For the colour version, please refer to the plate section.

As the chef is pouring the cold soup into the bowls, the apprentices spontaneously volunteer to help him by adding these ingredients, as they saw the chef doing the day before. Apprentice 1 puts the grissini in the bowls, Apprentice 2 takes pinches of Espelette pepper, and asks: 'I put two pinches?' the Chef answers, 'Yes, please'. The other one takes the oil bottle.

APPRENTICE 2: Shall we put the oil also?
CHEF: Please do.

[Apprentice2 moves the oil bottle over the bowls]

CHEF: Yes, go on, slowly. No, you don't need to put the finger. Go slowly. Go slowly. Test yourself on one dish.

[The apprentice pours a few drops]

CHEF: That's it. You've got enough. Five or six drops will be enough.

When they have finished the first batch of twelve bowls, they set up another batch of twelve. The apprentices then spontaneously fill in the bowls with the grissini, pepper and oil without asking, having now learned the procedure, while the chef fills the bowls.

These examples show how people learn on the job, and what peripheral participation means. As a result, a nurse learned to perform rapid induction, and two apprentices learned in a few minutes too many things to express easily in one sentence.

The techniques used by experts to teach novices (or rather, to help them learn) are very diverse. They vary with the tasks and include, as we saw above, motor as well as verbal guidance. Studying the professional education of dental hygienists, Becvar-Weddle & Hollan (2010) showed in detail how experts use motor guidance, demonstration and modelling, but also embodied conceptual metaphors.

Naturally the nurse, or the apprentices, have already previously embodied through education and direct experience a considerable amount of interpretive competences, and among them language. Learning is continuous throughout life, and continuously updated, in a progressive, cumulative, combination of reinforcement and adaptation. A substantial amount, possibly the majority, of learning takes place during early development – which in our societies can continue until adulthood: it takes almost two decades in our culture to consider an individual to be competent enough to be a citizen, an autonomous member of society, one who does not need further supervision.

The type of learning shown in these examples in a professional context occurs in very similar ways in any other context (family, public space, etc.). Barbara Rogoff, who studied in detail how Mayan children learn informally by participating in adult activities, through 'observing and pitching in', calls it 'learning through Intent Community Participation'. The primary motivation there is not learning a specific professional skill, but rather contributing and participating to the community, with an intense experience of belonging and emotional involvement:

> In the family and community settings ... children participate in the same activities of the everyday life of the community as do adults, contributing in real ways as they learn about their shared economic and social reality. Their motivation derives from their integration in the same economically and socially valued activities that other members of the community are involved in. Their useful and purposeful integration into the social sphere of work and community life allows for an underlying coherence and groundedness of the educational experience. (Paradise & Rogoff, 2009)

Rogoff describes with a wealth of examples from detailed ethnographic observation in small scale communities how, during participation in everyday activity, children learn through keen and attentive observation of their elders, by receiving from them comments and advice, or getting guidance when they pitch in to contribute to the activity. The use of stories and narratives, present in these settings as well as in industrial organizations

(Patriotta, 2003), is ubiquitous in support of transmitting experience and rationales.

This analysis highlights, in contrast to the Piagetian notion of learning stages, the importance of situated and goal-directed learning: learning how one should act in a specific situation according to role and function. Although the terms used are different, the rich empirical material connected by anthropologists feeds the argument that such learning occurs by participating in the context of *installations*, and is put to use later in similar *installations*.

> The unit of analysis used in sociocultural theory – the whole activity – helps researchers to focus on the goals that people pursue by thinking and to understand how people's participation in one activity relates to their participation in another. The idea is that individuals handle later situations according to how they relate to prior ones in which they have participated. (Rogoff, 1998)
>
> This view of cognition moves beyond the idea that development consists of *acquiring* knowledge and skills. Rather, a person develops through *participation in* an activity, *changing* to be involved in the situation at hand in ways that contribute both to the ongoing event and to the person's preparation for involvement in other similar events. (Rogoff, 2003: 254)

Interestingly, in contrast with the Western schooling system, there are virtually no 'drop-outs' in such a communal learning systems: children are motivated enough to learn all the necessary community skills (Spindler & Spindler, 1989).

As a result of this situated learning in the installations, in practice the novice embodies, through performing them, a large repertoire of possible behaviours, which are, through variation and combination, an empowerment to perform an infinite series of possible different behaviours. In this perspective, we must underline, as Ochs and Schieffelin note about language socialization, that 'novices' participation in practices is '*promoted but not determined* by a legacy of socially and culturally informed persons, artefacts, and features of the built environment' (Ochs & Schieffelin, 2012: 22). As noted in Section 4.6, the individual actor has an open choice among an infinite set of possibilities – as long as they remain minor variations around what is the expected norm.

By providing a standardized set-up for repeated experiences of small 'correct' variations of the same activity, installations provide an ideal learning ground for novices. By involving gradually the novice through peripheral participation, the actors of the installation make sure that the competences already learned are sufficient to keep the new experience in the proximal zone of development, where learning is possible. By remaining vigilant scaffolders, the other components of the installation ensure that the new actions the novice performs finally are 'correct'.

In doing so, installations ensure that the multimodal experience of performing satisficing behaviour within the installation is made available to the novice, and that this multimodal experience, which will inform the novice's further behaviour, is indeed 'correct'. **Installations leverage the effect of learning by first exposure to implement the appropriate competences in novices. They also provide novices with concrete examples of the allowed range of variation in that specific installation.**

### 5.2.1.6. *Continuous Reciprocal Feedback and Ubiquitous Control*

The construction of a person is the result of education, imitation and exploration and all the processes described in earlier sections, alone or in combination. We learn to embody the multiple roles we play in the various installations, from the family table to our professional position. All the mechanisms just described contribute to implementing the embodied skills and interpretive competences.

But the stability of society does not merely reside in the fact that each individual was inculcated once with the correct competence. The most powerful mechanism is the distribution of feedback by ubiquitous control. Indeed:

(a) our behaviour is continuously *reinforced and updated* in the correct behaviours of others, even as adults and experts;
(b) we continuously reinforce others into the correct behaviours.

Processes (a) and (b) are two aspects of the same phenomenon of reciprocal human feedback.

There is also a process (c): material feedback (how objects react to our actions).

The three contribute to the homogenization and stability of practices and embodied competences. We look in more detail at process (c) in Section 5.2.2; let us focus here on processes (a) and (b): reciprocal control.

The construction of the 'me' (Mead [1934] 1972: 175) is the way individuals embody their societal role. I described in Section 4.4.2.2 how the mechanism, described by Mead from the perspective of the subject, has wider implications than appear at first sight when it is considered from a second person's perspective, and from a bird's-eye view. It generates a generalized mechanism for controlling others, as each of us comes to embody the 'generalized other' character to our fellow men, as illustrated by Stanislas Lem's parable of the man who pretended to be a robot. *We understand better now after these sections on learning how this process works in practice: it is because humans learn from each of these interactions that the control is so powerful*, not just because each corrective interaction constrains the behaviour into the correct format at the time of the interaction. When I honk at the driver before me who does not start immediately as the traffic light becomes green,[19] I not only induce him to do so *now*, on this specific occasion; I also reinforce his conditioning to do the same for *all future traffic lights*. I also reinforce his tendency to honk at others on the same occasions.

We have already mentioned Foucault's 'disciplined bodies' as the result of supervised exercise, and Bourdieu's notion of habitus as systems of acquired dispositions. In every situation we learn 'what is correct' through social feedback, whether formalized in education or simply by our fellow humans' reactions to our behaviour: reprobation or approval, disincentive or encouragement, blame or recognition. As a result, we learn what is expected, and it is much easier to comply with expectations because resisting is an uphill battle. These dispositions endure because they are continuously reinforced by others. Just like Baudelaire's 'L'héautontimorouménos',[20] we become our own tormentors, our own censors, as a result of conditioning; but we also become our fellow men's censors – or rather, vigilantes. And to those who may object that I exaggerate, please consider how tough we can be as parents in the domestication of our own children, and how hard we can be on ourselves in the control of our own drives; consider how miserable we sometimes feel as we frustrate children – 'for their own good!' – or ourselves, from fulfilling desires that we strongly sympathise with.

**No one is better placed than ourselves to control our own behaviour, because we have first-hand knowledge of our behavioural intentions and the capacity to modify them as well. Therefore, the solution found by society to control individuals by self-control is at the same time splendidly simple and extremely efficient.** Freud had already noted this mechanism with his notion of the superego, this internalized moral Other that criticizes and censors, giving us the ego-ideal as a model of behaviour. **The way societies work is by making each participant a vigilante of**

---

[19] A joke goes that the definition of 'one second' is 'the time it takes before a Parisian driver honks at another driver who does not drive off immediately as the light turns green'.

[20] 'I am the wound and the dagger! I am the blow and the cheek! I am the members and the wheel, Victim and executioner! (The man who tortures himself [Baudelaire, 1857: 123–4; translation by William Aggeler]).

herself and others; and by making 'being a good citizen' and 'being a good student' become the pride of individuals. Their goal is to comply with the model. Our whole education system, our initiation rituals, are based on this: making us follow social role models. And it works because humans are vulnerable to this by the nature of their primate heritage, as we have already noted: humans are by design communicative animals prone to conspecific influence. And it works so well because we are also continuously reinforcing each other in the correct behaviours.

**In sum, the same mechanisms of distributed, subsidiary control where each participant regulates his or her own behaviour and the behaviour of others are not only, as shown in** Section 4.4.2, **a way to keep the behaviours correct on the fly, they are also a mechanism of reinforcement and education that feeds and reconstitutes itself. Installations do not only channel behaviour, they channel learning in doing.**

### 5.2.1.7. *Installations Are Omnipresent in Learning Processes*

In peripheral participation, the subject first sees, then imitates, and then tries, under the continuous control and feedback of more experienced people. The teaching process ensures that the novice has performed the right behaviour, thereby closing the perception-action loop and embodying the subsequent circuits with the appropriate reinforcing reward signals of satisficing result and appraisal from the teacher and bystanders. Each of us on occasion acts as a control agent for others. In practice, the various forms of learning are combined – conditioning, imitation, etc. Finally, as a result of experience, embodied competence is produced. That competence in turn produces the appropriate cultural behaviour, the one that is expected in the installation. Embodied competence has been transferred from the expert performers or teachers to the novice. From the perspective of the installation there has been a reproduction of the embodied layer in a new body. **This reproduction does not occur directly from embodied competence to embodied competence alone; it is reproduction *through the installation*, by practice, and all the layers of the installation contribute to the channeling.**

**Here we saw concretely what is meant by 'reproduction by practice'; we can also see that the embodied layer needs the two other layers to be reproduced.**

Good installations are designed in such a way that affordances guide the exploration by trial and error into a valid domain and provide clear feedback. For example, the tuning button on the radio and its coupling with display and sound naturally suggest exploration, restrict it to relevant bandwidth and display the quality of tuning with sound clarity. Often, the presence of other users of the installation naturally provides the novice with a set of examples of available possibilities and the acceptable range of variability. For example, how people can behave in a night club, in a swimming pool or how to dress for a black tie reception; the merely visual feedback that is provided to the exploration of the novice can be complemented by social feedback by the other participants.

> For example, at my first black tie event at the London School of Economics, I was complimented on the choice of my tuxedo by a British colleague; then the same colleague kindly explained to me that I should learn to tie my bowtie myself rather than use a preknotted one.

As we see, the role of the installation in giving feedback to the novice as to whether his behaviour is correct is crucial for learning; but as discussed in Chapter 4 it is precisely the nature of installations to provide guidance and feedback.

Now, in practice, what responses is the environment providing? In this section we examined the learning process: trial and error and exploration, observation and imitation, learning during development, informal education, instruction, legitimate peripheral participation on the job and intent community participation, continuous reciprocal feedback and ubiquitous control. Now let us look at the contents, the finer detail of what these processes are made of, and the forms of response that the installations provide their participants as they act.

### 5.2.2.   *System Feedback and Feedforward on Individual Behaviour*

Environmental response is crucial in making sure the subjects embody the correct practice. Installations are in this respect conditioning devices that provide the appropriate response to reinforce correct behaviour and prevent inappropriate behaviour, in this specific occurrence and in the future. This can take two forms: material affordances and social feedback or feedforward. Both are connoted with *value* in terms of functional success or failure, social reward or punishment.

**The first type of installation's response to the subjects' action[21] is affordance.** Feedback from sensory exploration is feedforward for though

---

[21] And in action I include here perception, which is an explorative action of the senses. At this early stage the feedback of the installation can prevent some actions and incite others.

and action. Some actions can be done, some others simply cannot. I try to open the door by pushing it, it does not move: bah! I pull, it opens: wow! The affordance has provided me in the first case with functional failure, and in the second with functional success. This shows how the TOTE model (Miller et al., 1960, see Section 3.6) can provide learning.

Functional success is a key criterion for evaluation of behaviours and installations. What gets me closer to the goal has positive value, what gets in the way has negative value. So the first type of response provided by the environment is functional success or failure: Did I reach my goal? That provides operant learning.

In practice, affordances are often preventive. A good design signals what can and should be done and excludes what should not be done – even if it *can* be done. As Norman showed, a good door handle displays by its very shape whether it should be pushed or pulled (Norman, 1988: 10). In machine tool design, 'barrier guards' are implemented to limit accidents by physically preventing users (workers) from reaching the danger area (e.g. hot or moving parts, blades, etc.)

**The second type of response is social feedback.** The feedback of others on our behaviour does influence us. We naturally tend to prefer agreeing with others (unless it is clearly against our own interest).

Conspecific feedback is a major determinant of the action of social animals. Humans, as other social animals, have developed a rich system of communication by mimicry and posture (Darwin, 1872). This system is innate in humans too, at least for facial mimicry, for which a complete repertoire can already be observed in newborn infants (Challamel, Lahlou, Revol, & Jouvet, 1985), and their interpretation in terms of attitude and intention as well as emotional correlates is common to most known human cultures ('universals': Eibl-Eibesfeldt, 1967). This repertoire was probably initially developed to communicate emotions and intentions among conspecifics, and nowadays humans still use it with subtle gradations of social pressure.

And of course language, another human universal, possibly also developed initially for other purposes (Dessalles, 2007), is massively used as a feedback and control system whether in oral or written form ('stop!'; 'say thank you!', 'meet your annual objectives'). Language is very developed in humans, who are probably the only species to have also developed it in graphic symbolic form. This rich repertoire is continuously used in communicative acts that feedback conspecifics in a 'light-handed' form of social control: a small comment may be sufficient to bring the other back on the correct track.

Social influence has been widely studied in social psychology from its origins. Classic experiments show how influence can modify the way we perceive stimuli (Moscovici et al., 1969; Sherif, 1935), express judgements (Asch, 1951) or act (Meeus & Raaijmakers, 1995; Milgram, 1963). In fact, every individual continuously monitors the impact of their actions by evaluating others' reactions and seeking feedback. I have already mentioned this effect several times.

But, curiously, influence has usually been studied from the perspective of *receiving* influence. Nevertheless, people also actively *seek* influence, especially in a situation of uncertainty. In natural situations, social influence can be observed on many occasions when individuals observe how others behave before engaging in the behaviour themselves, or they explicitly ask for advice, as well as getting spontaneous instructions from parents ('don't pick your nose!'), advice from benevolent protagonists ('this sauce is for the fish') or directions from specific agents (information kiosks, professional helpers, stewards). The latter are often the result of a request by the subject herself. This is especially visible in international installations such as airports or venues where cultural variations are expected and/or users are suspected of being first-time visitors. There, individuals expect to get such support from the installation, and conversely all cultures consider that providing novices with information on how to behave is a natural duty of every loyal member, and their need and request for information is expected and welcome. Therefore, influence is a possible effect of an active information search by the subject. The latter may even be an ultimate cause for the evolutionary selection of human susceptibility to influence.

On the receiving end, we should not be surprised that sources that are legitimated by the installation are more influential regarding the activity concerned, since that legitimation is a guarantee that the person is familiar with the process, and perhaps also familiar with the process of informing novices. A person who displays signs of belonging to the installation (warden in uniform, salesperson with a badge, person standing in official stall such as a booth of some kind, etc.) will automatically be considered as a better potential informer and a source of legitimate authority on 'how things are done here'. Because it is in the collective interest that everyone behave correctly, many installations have set up the information for novices as a capacity of some of their layers; for example, information booths in airports and malls, maps in the underground and name plates in streets, warning posters on walls and more generally the politeness rule that requires us to kindly respond to orientation requests by strangers.

Every interaction is a source of feedback. Goffman provided ethno-graphic descriptions of how individuals conform to their expected role and 'face', but also how conspecifics employ mechanisms of control and 'repair' to put back on track interactions that go astray (Goffman, 1959, 1971, 1974). Ethnomethodologists have studied in great detail, especially in conversation analysis, how participants monitor the interaction process to make sure everything goes 'as it should'. 'Repair mechanisms for dealing with turn-taking errors and violations are obviously available. For exam-ple, if two parties find themselves talking at the same time, one of them will stop prematurely, thus repairing the trouble' (Sacks, Schegloff, & Jefferson, 1978: 11). Feedback mechanisms include of course verbal indica-tions in utterances, but also eye contact, nods, postures, mimics, huhs, etc. (Goodwin, 1995; Sacks, 1992; Schegloff, 1982). These mechanisms are used not only to monitor the consistency of the interaction, but also more simply its contents. If someone behaves inadequately, every interaction they have with other (correct) participants will provide feedback to the misbehaver with a profusion of warning and negative signs, verbal and nonverbal.

Such mechanisms are not limited to conversation; they are active in most social interactions. Their degree of activation varies and escalates with the incompetence or the resistance of the person to be corrected. Any reader who has children or remembers what it is like to be a child knows exactly what I mean. In some situations the tolerance is low and the sub-ject who does not behave properly is stopped, possibly taken off the scene, or even punished.

Conversely, those who behave well get positive and encouraging signs, especially if it is obvious to other participants that the subject is in the phase of learning the installation. Those who behave well and use the installation on a regular basis in an exemplary way may be offered some privileged sta-tus, access or terms of use. Examples are the 'regulars' in a café who benefit from special attention by the personnel, or the gold-status members in an airline or hotel chain who are offered priority services. Those individuals may even be offered the chance to participate in monitoring the installa-tion (typically by providing complaints or suggestions for improvement). They are also likely to become spontaneous informers for novices.

Because feedback is produced through experience, its meaning for the organism is inevitably connected with the state of the organism at the moment it is received. This connects the response of the environment to a complex network of mindset, intentions, emotions and action that was the state of the subject in the situation in which the feedback was received.

Therefore, the 'external' response of the cultural system becomes internalized as embodiment weaved inextricably into the idiosyncratic and situational components of the subject's own developmental history.

> What layers up within the individual is not culture per se but rather experiences patterned by culture. This layered nature opens the space to conceptualize movement in mind as the emergence of new ideas, the expression of agency or subjectivity, or the possibility to enrich the social and cultural environment ... [Internalization is] a complex layering up of experiences and responses occasioned by diverse, and potentially contradictory, social settings and cultural guidance structures. (Zittoun & Gillespie, 2015)

So far in this section, we examined feedback and feedforward provided by installations. But this orienting response is more than the mere display of correct behaviour and involving participants in doing described in previous sections. That is the other side of the learning loop: once subjects have been induced into performing a behaviour within the installation, usually an appropriate one, by example, imitation, etc., then the installation provides feedback to transform this experience into operant learning. **By providing the positive approval of other participants, and the reward of reaching the goal, the installation closes the loop of learning. In a word, the installation channels the subject into doing the correct behaviour, then rewards the subject for having behaved properly; as a result of these two successive experiences the subject learns the appropriate ways and embodies the experience into an embodied competence. Installations combine providing the framed opportunity for experience, and the appropriate feedback. They combine stigmergy and operant conditioning.**

So these are the *value mechanisms* that produce embodiment, and we see that installations frame these mechanisms all along the way.


### 5.2.3.    *Embodiment*

But how does that feedback produce *embodiment* in the subject? In this section I attempt to describe the process of embodiment and then show how installations leverage it to inscribe in the human bodies some components that are necessary for their smooth operation.

#### 5.2.3.1.    *Embodiment as Inscription in the Body Structure*
The notion of embodiment is often seen in psychology as a reaction to a narrow vision of cognition where the mind is considered merely as a computational device. Proponents of this notion advocate a reinsertion of

emotions, proprioception, and more generally all bodily states, into cognition and decision-making. (See, for example, Basso, Guillou, & Oullier, 2010, and Oullier & Basso, 2010, for discussions of this concept in the field of economic decision-making.) Embodiment is currently investigated with brain-imagery techniques. The roots of the notion of embodiment involve phenomenology, learning processes and the very nature of what it means to be an organism.

The problem we tackle appears simple to describe in common-sense terms, but complex to study in its biochemical detail. What we know from common sense as well from sophisticated neuroscience research is that every bit of life experience modifies the individual.[22] This means that something has changed in that individual's body: that person has *embodied* something, a change that may influence future behaviour. Of course science would like to *localize* these changes in the body, and describe them. And in general, science would like to match specific functions, or changes, with the material structures involved, perhaps in the hope this would finally anchor solidly psychology, and through it all human sciences, into hard science.

That endeavour seemed attainable when we discovered that experience changed the structure of neuronal connections in the brain. It seemed that memory would simply be a set of synapses between neurones. Association in experience, which is known to bind things in the mind, would correspond to binding neurones in the brain. Ramón y Cajal's seminal works on synapses (Ramón y Cajal, 1895) and Freud's (Freud, 1895) first neuroscience works suggested experience would be embodied in the form of stable neuronal pathways or circuits that would locally correspond to that experience, as a result of synaptic concurrent activations and 'reverberations' during the experience (Hebb [1949] 2002: 61–3).

It seemed only a matter of time until we could identify the neuronal circuits involved in a specific activity or thought, as the investigation techniques got better.

Alas, the more neuroscience and psychology dive into the complexity of the brain, the more this goal seems to recede. Indeed, thought, as well as action, perception and more generally all cognition are never independent from the context of activity. Although the simple neuronal circuit model just presented above is not wrong in its principle, it appears the detail is much more complicated.

---

[22] Even remembering is in fact reinscribing (and therefore possibly modifying) our memory.

For example, when I catch my cat in the kitchen to keep it from eating the ham on the table, my action is a continuous monitoring process of what I do guided by the desire of holding the cat but also of saving the ham, and I continuously adapt to the situation I perceive. In that process, unfortunately, my whole body and my whole brain seem to be involved and it is difficult to limit to only a specific part of the brain the activations related to what I am doing, or to abstract these from my intentions at that moment. This means that *all* these structures will probably be involved when I think, later, of a 'cat' when my brain activity is explored by my colleagues with brain imagery in search of what cells 'fire' during re-enactment. The issue is, of course, what is specific to 'cat' in the sum of all my experiences with cats (what about the ham?). As a consequence, the delimitation of what neural structures correspond to what 'thought' is difficult. More specifically for our problem, installations, work in situated cognition demonstrates that it is difficult to abstract a competence from the context in which it was acquired (Lave, 1988).

Furthermore, cognitive processes are dynamic processes rather than material structures. The *nature* of such processes is more of some resonance[23] between the excitation of the body structure and the context in which the body is; and the regulation mechanisms of that resonance seem to be based on comparing the actual output to expected output rather than the planning of an output then executing a plan – an intuition as old as Gestalt theory. And resonance mechanisms are not easy to study: *any* modification of *any* part of the system may have massive impacts on the overall result, which is why such resonating systems tend to be tuned 'by ear' in trying some small modifications until the expected result is attained: see how a piano tuner operates. That is why a purely structural approach appears a bold endeavour.

To take a metaphor, describing in detail the shape and structure of all the musical instruments in an orchestra, as well as measuring the volume in various locations as the orchestra plays, brings us only a limited understanding of music. To date, the musical score, with its notes expressed in symbolic format with tempo, metre, and articulation are still more useful in practice for the purpose playing the music; and that is what musicians use to communicate and learn.

In sum: the mechanism of embodiment is assumed to be a semistable modification of the physiology following experience, especially in the

---

[23] Or, as Lashley puts it, 'reverberation'(Lashley, 1951).

nervous system ('experiential selection', 'a secondary repertoire of functioning neural circuits is formed on the basis of existing neuroanatomy by
means of the selective strengthening and weakening of synaptic efficacies'
[Edelman, 2004: 159]). Although the overall mechanism seems well understood, the physiological detail appears more complicated than imagined
decades ago. The classic view, suggested by the pioneer neuroscientific
works of the twentieth century now seems, even though visionary and not
wrong in principle, somewhat simplistic and outdated. It is more likely
that what is created is not simply synapses and circuits but 'time-locked'
dynamical patterns (in space and time) (Damasio, 1989; Engel, 2010) and
involves the whole organism (Goldstein, 1934, 1995).[24] These resonating
structures are activated when the body finds itself in situations that to
some extent match the conditions in which the resonating structures were
created.

That latter view is closer to Barsalou's 'perceptual symbol systems'
(Barsalou, 1999); in this theory what matters are the connotations associated (in the brain) to some experienced state ('simulators'; those are re-
enacted and mobilized (e.g. in 'simulations': see Glossary) when a similar
state is to be dealt with. The notion seems consistent with the Freudian
definition of 'presentations', the objects of judgement of the mind: 'all
presentations originate from perceptions and are repetitions of them'
(Freud [1925] 1999). Minsky introduces the term 'simulus' to describe
'a reproduction of only the higher level effects of a stimulus' (Minsky,
1985: 70).

More generally, the 'System 2' with which we reason consciously is a
higher-level generalization and systematization of objects and situations
grounded in the 'System 1' embodied competences we construct as a result
of our daily experience of the world.

If we want to understand how individuals come to be influenced by
their past experience, we must study embodiment: how does experience
change the structure of the human body? There is a rich tradition of
work in this domain which is not my specialism; I skim it below and

---

[24] Andy Clark has an even more generous vision of the notion of embodiment; he highlights how the
very physical properties of objects are involved in action (e.g. the resistance of a surface, the nature
of the grip at the point of contact, etc.) and therefore the way real organisms work is by creating relevant coupling and control between themselves and their environment for performing ecologically
relevant action from the feedback they get, rather than creating some abstract representations and
then computing them (Clark, 1997). In this perspective, we should not only consider embodiment
aspects for the organisms, but also for all bodies in the physical sense ('material things') and this
view logically arrives at embodied embedded cognition, where the whole ecological system must be
considered.

highlight a few findings that are especially relevant for our problem, namely that:

- the embodied structures are multimodal, in particular they link perception, emotion and action;
- embodied structures automatically link together aspects (e.g. perceptual and motor) that have frequently been experienced together in previous activity;
- embodiment tends to induce automatically some mindsets and actions as subjects' bodies are put again in a situation they previously experienced;
- embodiment is influenced by emotions felt at the moment of experience or immediately thereafter.

These aspects are relevant for installation theory because they account for that mysterious 'momentum' which we have evoked several times, and which seems to seize and then drive participants automatically in installations, and makes installations 'cognitive attractors' (Lahlou, 2005) for the participants, turning subjects into engines for action.

The meaning of the term embodiment varies across fields and authors. For example, in pragmatics, it refers generally to 'the involvement and contribution of the body in interaction' (see Nevile, 2015 for a review).

In cognitive psychology, the concept of embodiment may sometimes appear to be reduced to the influence of the physiological state of the body on mental processes; e.g. how a given posture or sensation can influence our mental processes, and vice versa. For example, while shaking their head vertically (supposedly to test headphones), subjects tend to be more positive to a message than if they shake the head horizontally (Wells & Petty, 1980); because conventionally in that culture nodding vertically means approval and shaking horizontally means the opposite. In this perspective, embodied cognition is in opposition to the narrow view that cognition is what happens in the brain only, and shows that 'aspects of the agent's body beyond the brain play a significant causal or physically constitutive role in cognitive processing' (Wilson & Foglia, 2015). The 'embodiment thesis' states that:

> Many features of cognition are embodied in that they are deeply dependent upon characteristics of the physical body of an agent, such that the agent's beyond-the-brain body plays a significant causal role, or a physically constitutive role, in that agent's cognitive processing. (Wilson & Foglia, 2015)

Although this view is correct and supported by solid empirical evidence, the concept of embodiment has a wider scope and application. In a nutshell, *every* mental state has a bodily (and especially, neural) counterpart in terms of activation of bodily cells. There is no such thing as 'abstract' thoughts in humans; they are all produced, and experienced by a body as a whole. Experience is inevitably through the body. Because the body is one interconnected unit, and all that it learns is through experience, including the emotions and sensations experienced during that process, all knowledge is indissolubly grounded in total bodily states.

The organism is modified by experience: neural connections and other physiological systems undergo modifications as a consequence of activations during the subject's activity; that is how new patterns emerge and existing patterns are modified.

Subsequently, when individuals think about something, when they recognize an object, etc. they re-enact[25] some of the past, experienced, activation that correspond to these thoughts and objects. That is (to some degree) subjects undergo again the same *experience* they had in the first place. That can lead to acting the same.

Conversely, because of that correspondence between physiological activation and mental states, putting the body in a given state (e.g. shaking one's head, or smiling) induces the corresponding mental states and therefore induces a certain mindset and interpretation.

The learning does not have to be conscious or even deliberate. Below, Anne-Mette, an anaesthesia nurse, explains how she has embodied the signals given off by the vital signs monitoring systems:

SAADI: ... in nuclear plants, the operators don't even have to look at the controls, they just listen to the noise and they know everything's all right.
ANNE-METTE: Yeah, Yeah. That's what experience does. I can stand with my back against the screen [points at the monitor that displays the cardiac, respiration and blood parameters that are near the patient headside in the ICU,

---

[25] Embodiment must be situated in the perspective of enactivism, in which the organism creates its own world through interaction with its environment – and in the same movement maintains it existence as an organism.

> For Merleau-Ponty, as for us, embodiment has this double sense: it encompasses both the body as a lived, experiential structure and the body as the context or milieu of cognitive mechanisms. (Varela et al., 1991, 1993: xvi)

Enactivism is a difficult theory. I have presented here the idea that the individual is an interpretive system of its own milieu, and therefore from the individual's perspective the world is perceived as it is constructed by him. Conversely I have argued that the environment shapes and constructs the individual, as emerge, amid the individual's body, structures (which I called embodied interpretive systems) that are functionally coupled with the environment. They are functionally coupled with the environment in the sense that they enable the individual to perform adapted behaviours. Replace 'individual' with 'organism' and all these statements have a lot in common with enactivism and with Rubinstein's conception of psychology (Nosulenko & Rabardel, 2007). In the latter perspective, cognition is not influenced by the body; it is inseparable from the body because experience and being are one same thing.

refer to Figure 3.3 in Section 3.1] and actually listen to what the blood pressure is next time. Because I'm actually used to [hearing] 'Vuuut' and if it then goes on to 'Vuuiiiit', a bit more, I know the blood pressure is rising. So I don't have to turn around and see; I know it's risen. And I can hear in the saturation how the ECG [electrocardiogram] is. Because if suddenly it's running a bit faster, or unregularly [gestures], I, I know how the ECG is. These noises are in kind of my head [points at the back of her head] and I can respond to that. But that's what every experienced anaesthesiologist and nurse anaesthetist would do. Because they're used to working with the sounds. Not noise, sounds.

SAADI: What other parameters have you embodied?

ANNE-METTE: Noises from the surgical team; as well.

SAADI: Mmm?

ANNE-METTE: No noise, silence, that's not nice. Silences [lasting] a little while are not nice. Because then people really focus. Mmm *[Thinks]*. When people rush, when people open drawers very fast, it's not nice as well because now then something has to be rushed suddenly. *[Thinks]* Noises from the suction, the surgeon's suction 'hhscchhlluushhss' and if it just continues you have to *[she bends as if she were looking at the suction bag on the floor]* see how much blood is in there. And maybe that's the first noise, or indication of that the patient's bleeding you get; with that noise.

SAADI: Well... What else?

ANNE-METTE: Err. Very sharp orders. 'Call. Call another surgeon'.' 'Fetch the...' instead of 'Oh, would you mind to fetch the...' So these very sharp ones mean that people are under pressure.

What we see in this example is that through this mechanism of learning, patterns in the environment acquire a signification in terms of 'connotations for action', and a connection with a set of possible responses.[26] The nurse explicitly says it comes through long experience (in the ICU installation).

The notion of embodiment matches our common sense, but how it happens in detail is not so simple because of the complexity of the systems involved. A rich and growing body of literature examines the localization, activation patterns, processes and phenomenological aspects of

---

[26] The mechanism described here is in fact complex: the medics learn to recognize patterns that are significant for diagnosis, directly through their sensory organs (sight, hearing and so on) and augmented by such tools as the stethoscope, the laryngoscope or the monitor. As Charles Lenay notes, 'the difference between these devices and natural sensory organs is that they can be separated from the organism; but this separability can be greater or lesser, on a continuous scale which does not change anything in principle, ranging from the quasi-continuous use of an auditory prosthesis to the episodic use of a telescope.' (Lenay, 2012). On the scale of the extension of the self with artefacts that facilitate activity, external components of installations could be considered as being on the far end of very 'separable'.

embodiment (see Anderson, 2003; Niedenthal & Barsalou, 2005; Wilson, 2002 for reviews). We do not get into the detail here of this fast-moving field. The argument that I develop is as follows:

- The experience of executing a specific behaviour in a given installation creates in the individual's body some physical traces, some structural change;
- Depending on how worthy is the result and the feedback received from the installation (success/failure, reward/punishment), these traces later foster or inhibit the behaviour performed during that experience (Thorndike's law of effect, see Section 5.2.3.3.);
- As a consequence, an individual carries around in his body embodied structures ('interpretive competences') *fostering appropriate behaviour for the various installations he's been through.*

This is close to the classic story of conditioning. What research on embodiment brought, especially with imaging techniques, is how the physiological inscription takes place in the flesh, and where and how these inscriptions connect with the phenomenological experience of the subject. It showed the importance of the context, of multimodality, of emotions. It showed that there are no such things as 'amodal' concepts in an *individual* brain.[27]

I have alluded that the biochemical aspects of embodiment (localization, dynamics) are extremely complex and intricate, and that it will be long before we can map physiological structures and processes to phenomenological experience. Fortunately we do not need to know the biochemical detail to understand the process of reconstruction of installations. Just like the musician, we need to how to learn and play good music rather than how the muscles work or how the physics of violin strings connect to acoustics.

We are here interested in the real-world conditions in which embodiment takes place; *how and where, during everyday activity in the world, the creation of semistable psychic structures happens in detail, and how life in society frames this creation.* I argue that *installations* are the locus where much of the embodiment of everyday life competences happens; that installations are the societal instrument for conditioning individuals, the place and time where the imprinting of the body is done.

---

[27] Amodal means abstract from sensory or motor etc. modalities, as a pure concept. So if the notion of e.g. 'Dog' may be amodal on paper, for an individual person it is inevitably connoted with multimodal aspects of the person's own experience with dogs, as it is taken in a bodily interpretation loop.

In the description of the chain that reproduces structure from the global level of society to the micro-level of subjects, the notion of embodiment is the final link that describes how the capacity and will to perform 'appropriate behaviours' becomes embedded in individuals.

So embodiment is a simple word to express the complex process by which individual bodies incorporate the results of their sensory-motor experience in their lifeworld – experiences such as 'riding a bicycle', 'speaking English', 'tying a knot', 'playing poker' and 'taking the bus'. Embodiment is a complex process to study because a given object is always encountered and dealt with by the subject in the course of a specific activity. It entails that the object is encountered from some intentional perspective, with a goal and a motive, and in a specific state of arousal and emotion. The activation of the brain (and of the body) at the moment of experience depends on all these factors. The same physical mailbox, apple or chair can produce very different activations depending on the specific activity context in which they are experienced. At the moment of experience, the neural activations themselves are dynamic patterns whose oscillations and form depend upon the various parts of the body and the brain that have been moved by those different components (perceptual cues are bearers of the object, but also emotions and intentions, as well as the neuronal paths resulting from previous experiences with all the above). Although there will be some commonalities in the various experiences involving that physical object, they may be too crude to be of much use in understanding what the subject experiences.

*But precisely all installations of a specific type (e.g. all check-in counters, escalators, shops, etc.) reduce experiential variance. Because they provide again and again a rather standardized experience in terms of context, mindset and goals, they tend to reinforce the same global activations every time one acts through them.*[28]

**Conversely, as installations of the same type provide *again* a similar context and because participants come into them with a similar goal (e.g. when I come into the elevator, that is again with the intention of going up), entering an installation will likely reactivate the same overall mindset (e.g. being in an elevator and wanting to go up) and then trigger in a cascade the behavioural sequence learned previously**

[28] That is probably why empirical investigation shows that knowledge, as a capacity to solve problems with what one has learned (understanding of situation and knowledge of what to do), is situated, as said above: people show better ability to solve concrete problems in the real context than in an abstract laboratory situation (Lave, 1988).

in similar installations; hence the semiautomatic mode that we can observe when people act in these installations. In short, because of the nature of embodiment, being resituated in that same (or similar) context by an installation creates a powerful attractor for the 'appropriate' mindset and behaviour.

The embodied structures are the physiological basis for re-enacting the perceptual, motor and introspective states acquired during experience. An installation that provides conditions very similar to previous experience in an installation of the same type, by activating the same bodily structures, tends to produce the same activity patterns that were embodied in previous experiences.

### 5.2.3.2. *Terminology Clarification: Lata, Embodiment, Interpretation*

Embodiment is the process by which, physiologically, the traces of past experience in the environment become part of the individual self-body. Because they have become part of her organism, the subject can carry them around with her body into various installations. This mobility is a very important aspect because it makes part of the installations portable. When we analyse installations, it is useful to have a simple name for these embodied interpretive structures that are carried around and become part of local installations as subjects bring them along with their body.

But the term 'embodiment' may refer to several things:

(a) the embodied structure (a result, the experience has been embodied into physiological structure, neuronal paths);
(b) a construction process (the process by which experience is embodied into physiological structure);
(c) the process by which, at a given moment, physiological activation and mental states generate each other, in which phenomenological experience and neural activation are concomitant.

Although there are excellent philosophical as well as technical reasons to bundle the three (and these are laid out in the theory of enaction), that makes it very difficult to describe in detail the dynamics of the system. So we shall distinguish these three aspects.

Let us call *lata* the material embodied semistable structures (e.g. embedded at the level of brain cells).

*Embodiment* as I use the term here is the *process* of constructing lata in the course of life experience (through conditioning, education, practice).

*Interpretation* is the process of mobilizing lata, at one given moment, to act upon the world (perception-action loop), with its concomitant phenomenological counterpart of consciousness and experiencing.

Although similar notions have of course been described in the literature with various purposes in mind, we need to have here a coherent set of conceptual tools adapted to the analysis of installations and especially of their evolution.

Lata means what is carried by someone; it comes from *latum*, the passive past participle of the Latin verb *ferre*, to bear. Whereas data are what the environment brings to the subject in a given situation, lata are what the subject comes equipped with in her own body: representations, memories, schemata, skills, etc. Lata contrast with *data* (from the Latin datum, 'given'), which are carried by the environment.

Lata has a meaning close to Friedrich Hayek's 'maps'[29] and to Antonio Damasio's 'systems-level code' (Damasio, 1989); various authors have come up with a wealth of concepts attempting to designate the 'hardware' substratum of cognition and action, of which the exact nature still remains an object of research. In defining lata I stay cautiously vague because the nature of the physicochemical substratum is, I think, yet unclear. In particular I am reluctant at this stage to make a precise mapping between lata and specific concepts, especially when it comes to describing action.[30]

Lata do not, like 'representation', refer both to process and content. Lata are the embodied material structures (embedded at the level of nervous system, muscles, joints and so on); they are the structure that *produces* a re-enactment when activated, but they are not the re-enactment itself, which is a process. The lata are to 'interpretation' what physical wiring is to the electric circuit: the same material structure, but not under tension; they are analogous to the electronic memory of the computer when it is not being read; they are analogous to the violin when it is not being played.[31]

---

[29] A map is 'the semi-permanent connexions representing not the environment of the moment but the kind of events which the organism has met during its whole past' (Hayek, 1952: 115). The map is a 'semi-permanent apparatus of classification, [it] provides the different generic elements from which the models of particular situations are built. The term "map", which suggests a sort of schematic picture of the environment is thus really somewhat misleading. What the apparatus of classification provides is more a sort of inventory of the kind of things of which the world is built up, a theory of how the world works rather than a picture of it. It would be better described as a construction set which supplies the parts from which the models of particular situations can be built.' (Hayek, 1952: 130–1)

[30] Some more informed authors are bolder (Barsalou, 1999).

[31] An issue here is that re-enactment is not equivalent to the activation of a limited set of neurones; the input external to that set of neurones matters, because resonance has to be maintained by these

The lata are *latent* representation: they emerge as a representation when activated because they are a resonating structure. Lata resonate with external structures in online activity, e.g. when there is recognition in sensory exploration; they resonate with internal structures when there is offline re-enactment (in the absence of the object, as in imagination). In the process of lata being activated, representations and action emerge.

Lata *resonate* best in the very contexts in which they have been constructed (e.g. a given installation) and in contexts similar. They may still be activated in other contexts, and may produce satisficing results, to a certain extent.

*Interpretation* is the process of activating the lata in a given situation: if [*X*] then do [act: Interpretation(*X*)]. The 'act' could be doing something motoric with *X* (riding the bicycle, if *X* is a bicycle) or doing something mental about it (evaluating the worth of the bicycle) or both (talking about the colour of the bicycle). Usually, we link all these acts *with* the object: identify, understand and perform motoric action. **One should take 'interpretation' in the sense of both understanding and playing, as a musician would interpret a piece of music, or an as actor would interpret a role.** It is 'what to do if' one finds oneself in a specific situation: action is the very nature and purpose of interpretation, whether is it outward motor action or internally simulated in the mind[32].

Interpretation is a loop, because we continuously update our body with data from our environment, and continuously act upon the environment as an interpretation of these data, to adapt to the new environment that results from our action upon it. For example, as you read this book and reach the bottom of the page *so* you turn the page and *so* you get a new text to read; as I climb in the tree each time I stand on a higher branch new affordances for climbing appear to me and new fruits become visible and *so* I climb higher.

But that loop changes over time on short and long scales, because every activation is an experience in its own right, an experience that produces

external inputs. The activation of a specific set of neurones cannot be considered independently of the activation of all the rest of the neurones and more generally of the whole body (hormones, mass activation, modulation by other parts of the brain, etc.) and even the environment because of the holistic nature of embodiment and the interactive aspect of reverberation. One cannot sit "as in a chair" if there is no chair to scaffold the bodily activation. That is one of the difficulties for getting "realistic" re-enactments from a body straitjacketed in a brain scanner.

[32] 'Utilization of this motor approach immediately helps us to view the brain objectively for what it is, namely, a mechanism for governing motor activity. Its primary function is essentially the transforming of sensory patterns into patterns of motor coordination. Herein lies a fundamental basis for the interpretation, direct or indirect, of all higher brain processes including the mental functions.' (Sperry, 1952)

changes in the body. These changes can be so minor that they can be reconsidered as mere reinforcement of the existing lata as in executing some routine; they may in some cases be substantial, as in the case of psychic or physical trauma; or anything in between: minor changes, such as the calluses that developed on Roy Pea's fingers from playing electric guitar which then assist him in playing more forcefully and with greater control and nuance (personal communication, 2016).

Embodiment is the process by which the lata are constructed, reconstructed and possibly changed as the result of experience through activity. It is mostly an epigenetic process, occurring during development and life of relation in everyday activity.

We can now picture the loop at different moments to understand what is going on when a subject enters an installation.

Let us illustrate this based on Uexküll's functional loop. It took me a long time to realize that, to understand fully the functional loop, one must cut it and consider it in several phases. I will explain once the reader has gone through the next three figures and their explanation.

The functional loop describes the relation between the organism and its environment. From a phenomenological perspective, from the point of view of the organism, only exists the environment that is accessible to the organism's receptors and effectors (its *Umwelt*). That is, to use enactivist terminology, the world this organism enacts, the one that is meaningful for the organism. Objects exist for the subject through their affordances, which are their perceptual cue bearers and functional cue bearers.

Figure 5.5 shows Uexküll's functional loop. The object in the world, figured by a pointed cylinder on the right side of the figure, carries perceptual and functional cues. The subject's lata (figured by by spiky arcs on the left side of picture) couple with these cues through the body's receptors and effectors.

Let us consider the example of the shower:

> Yesterday I found a shower in my hotel room. I entered it and grabbed the lever that activates the water. It is one of those combined-command levers that you pull to command the water flow, and that you turn to adjust the temperature. Here, the more you pulled, the stronger the flow; and the more clockwise the hotter. But of course I did not know beforehand the exact correspondence between the position of the lever and the actual flow nor with the temperature and there was no clear indication on the lever.
>
> Because of previous experience in hotels, I put the lever in the middle position in the hope of getting warm water. But I stayed as far as I could from the flow because there was no reliable cue of what temperature I would

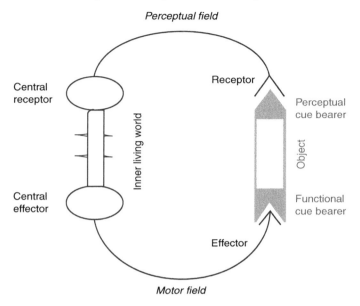

Figure 5.5. Uexküll's functional loop.

actually get; and I remembered previous unpleasant experiences. In doing so I was then *coupled* with the shower installation and in the mindset of starting the shower, and preparing to test the temperature of the water with my hand. We saw in earlier chapters how continuous practice maintains and reinforces interpretive structures (lata that link receptors to effectors in a loop). I took showers in hundreds of different installations in my life and I have therefore embodied such a loop. The shower situation activated that loop.

As I felt my grasp on the shower lever, as I coupled to the shower and got into the mindset for the activity of showering, I became part of an active installation. Cascading effects of my action would then unfold activity, including observable behaviour (e.g. pulling the lever in open position). This was made possible because showers are designed to be operable by such a lever, and because I had previously embodied the appropriate lata to operate showers from my past experience in similar installations.

But in the practice of life, the organism is exposed to varying objects and situations, and therefore the interpretive structures are updated: new neural connections are created, some are reinforced and others disappear. Lata are modified. *Embodiment* is the long-term effect that executing the loop has on the organism. It is a transition from a state of the organism to a new state of the organism, with updated lata. This is pictured in Figure 5.6.

> And in fact, as I pulled the lever slightly, the water came out burning hot and very strong. I quickly pushed the lever back, and positioned it towards 'colder' before pulling it again. Through this experience, I had updated my lata to deal with this specific installation. That is why this morning, knowing better from my experience yesterday, I carefully stayed out of the shower as I pulled the level to approximately the position that I had found comfortable yesterday, until the temperature was stabilized, before I stepped in the shower – having taken care to check the temperature with my hand in case that morning the temperature would be different.[33] As a benefit of this improved competence, I did not get burned and enjoyed a good shower, which confirmed to me that staying away as I opened the water and testing with the hand was a satisficing behavioural sequence: I will do the same tomorrow.

The update in my lata can be pictured as the bold spiky arc addition to the picture on the right side of Figure 5.6.

So, whereas embodiment is a process that is long-term modification of the quasi-stable interpretive loop by updating lata, *interpretation* is the use of the loop as it is at a given moment.[34]

**Interpretation is what happens as the organism performs the functional loop. The presence of the object in the environment of the organism impacts its senses. As the attention focuses, the organism proceeds to accommodate the data to its preexisting interpretive structures: there is an identification process. Interpretation takes place as the interpretive structures and their implicatures unfold; as re-enactments take place in the brain as activation spreads across neural pathways, as hormones are released, as emotions flow through the body, as conscience occurs and meaning emerges. Eventually, interpretation triggers motor response and some action can be observed.[35] Interpretation is the complete process, where the loop is activated, coupling the subject to its environment with its specific adapted interpretive structures. This is pictured in Figure 5.7.**

---

[33] To paraphrase Heraclitus, you never step in the same shower twice. The shower has changed, and you too: everything flows along the arrow of time. In practice, in some cases, as experience shows it may happen that in the 'same' shower cabin the temperature you get depends on how many people took a shower before you.

[34] As a side note, we can observe that I showed initiative in that installation and that my behaviour was not automatic all the way; I used my free will to mobilize protective strategies.

[35] In fact, motor impulse is probably launched before the interpretation reaches consciousness (Fried, Mukamel, & Kreiman, 2011; Libet, Gleason, Wright, & Pearl, 1983; Soon, Brass, Heinze, & Haynes, 2008)

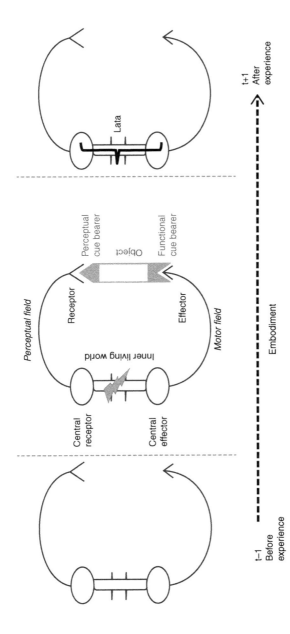

Figure 5.6. Embodiment and the functional loop. Embodiment is the process of updating the organism with new functional traces of experience that can be reused. The added bold spiky arc on the right of the picture shows the modification in the previous lata as a consequence of experience.

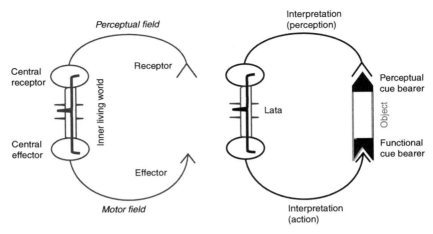

Figure 5.7. Interpretation and the functional loop. The presence of the object triggers an interpretation process by activating the functional loop.

What I did this morning in the shower was a local interpretation, activating my 'shower' relevant lata (updated yesterday) as I acted in the situation. As pictured on the right side of Figure 5.7, this interpretation involves the whole installation. I mobilized the specific embodied lata appropriate to *this* specific installation (bold spiky arc on the right side of Figure 5.7), even though I have a lot more available (as pictured by the other, grey and non-bold, arcs in Figure 5.7). The shower produced a response which I used to adapt my behaviour; and which I also used to update my lata. Next time I will be in a similar situation with this specific shower, or one with the same type of lever, I will probably mobilize this updated lata. That does not necessarily mean that I have destroyed my previous lata. Even though I have taken more than 15,000 showers in my life, my behaviour in a specific installation is not stereotyped and I have not lost the capacity to use a garden hose for a shower; I have simply expanded my paradigm[36] of showering. I assume the reader has embodied similar amazing competence.

*Behaviour* is what is observable of that loop as it is performed, from the perspective of an external observer; e.g. here the reader, if invited into my bathroom. *Activity* is chaining such loops, from the perspective of the subject (in this case me, whose internal states the observer is incapable to access directly).

---

[36] The notion of paradigmatic learning is detailed in Section 5.2.4.

What happens in an installation at a given moment, when the subject is active in it, is the *interpretation* loop (awareness, activation, action).

As interpretation is practice, each interpretation inevitably implies some (re)embodiment: just as every remembrance occurrence reconstructs the memory. So, every occurrence of practice reconstructs but also increases the competence.[37] Every use of the installation updates the lata a little, as shown by my modifying my behaviour the next day in the shower.[38]

And in turn, interpretation is the consequence of embodiment: it is because we have embodied interpretive structures that we can interpret phenomena and act appropriately. Lata are the physiological substratum for embodied competences activated in the installation.

Long-term history is built by the cumulated minute modifications each single process of interpretation (my 15,000 showers). But in one specific instance (the shower this morning), evolution is marginal and we can consider the system as roughly the same for that short span. Models that want to be too exacting and account for the fact that, in all rigour, the system is *continuously* changing its structure, become too complex and unusable even in these short spans of activity.[39] It is easier for practical purposes to distinguish a 'before' and an 'after' (the shower yesterday and this morning), an inside and an outside (what I experience 'inside' and the 'external' objects I perceive/act on), an individual and its environment (Saadi and the shower cabin), even though that is not epistemologically correct (since phenomenologically speaking all this shower episode was enacted 'in my mind').

That is why it is easier, in the model, to cut the loop and consider it at different times, as pictured in Figure 5.6 and Figure 5.7. The misunderstandings, and the ambiguity of some theories, come from the fact that the various concepts used do not necessarily address the same time frame. **Interpretation is synchronic; it considers how the organism reacts at one moment; whereas *embodiment* is diachronic and describes the evolution of the organism over time.**

Now we understand that the functional loop slightly changes every time an interpretation takes place, as lata are updated. The individual interpretations may stabilize the lata, they may also modify the lata.

---

[37] See Glăveanu (2012) for the role of this mechanism in increasing expertise in artists.

[38] In Piagetian terms: each new assimilation entails a small accommodation process.

[39] I mean here unusable for my own limited capacities and down-to-earth empirical concerns for application. The philosophical ambition and rigour of Varela, Simondon, Giddens or Schütz make their theories difficult to access and operationalize.

But when one looks at Uexküll's original schema, this dynamic aspect of change in the longer term does not appear immediately, because the arrows focus our attention mostly on the perception-action loop emerging during instant interpretation (synchronic) and not on the evolution of the lifeworld being constructed during longer-term *embodiment* (diachronic). In fact, the same figure as presented originally by Uexküll pictures *two* different processes with a single drawing, overlapping. There is (1) a synchronic loop that gets actuated in each interpretation, and (2) a circle that is the lasting structure enabling the emergence of that loop. The installation is that circle, and the activity is the loop. They each reconstruct the other. As I walk along the previous path in the woods I reconstruct it as a result of my trampling the ground; conversely, the previous path guides my trajectory.

Most theories, because they come up with models where the two temporal dimensions are figured in the same picture, tend to obfuscate the issue. While the full functional loop is indeed an exact model, it must be read at two levels of time to be fully understood. The models that combine the various time scales into a single phenomenon are correct in that an organism is indeed something that exists as a long-term structure precisely because it maintains that structure in the short term again and again, and that this structure is what simultaneously creates its enduring existence and the subjective world of that organism at a phenomenological level. But, as for the geologist's hammer metaphor (Figure 3.2), an epistemologically correct model is not necessarily the best to use for pragmatic purposes.[40] And because the environment and the subject are submitted to different constraints and different laws of evolution, it comes in handy to be able to distinguish them in the framework we use.

*In sum: installations construct the embodied competences in individuals (lata) by induction and reinforcement of appropriate behaviour, through repeated local and similar individual experiences. The accumulation of short-term interpretation loops in the course of activity constructs and stabilizes the semipermanent interpretive competences structures that we observe in full-grown members of a culture, their individual habitus.*

*This process is well adapted to the physiological mechanisms of embodiment, and facilitates appropriate relevant re-enactment in installations and therefore the performance of appropriate behaviour.*

---

[40] That is perhaps why most humans use naive realism for mundane activities.

***Installations, by repeatedly providing similar individual experiences, contribute to create stable and similar embodied competences in and across members of a culture who use similar installations.***

### 5.2.3.3. *Thorndike's Law of Effect*

We need this last physiological mechanism to get a full picture of how the processes by which the installation generates 'appropriate' behaviour. Indeed I noted earlier that practice stabilizes the data, but we have not fully explained what mechanisms operationalize that process, even though the description of the shower incident gave some clues: I learned to avoid being burned and to execute satisfying moves. Why? Because some experiences are more pleasant and satisfying than others.

We address therefore the part of the mechanism described in Section 5.2.3.1 with operant conditioning as: 'Depending on how worthy is the result and the feedback received (success/failure, reward/punishment), these traces will foster or inhibit the behaviour performed during that experience.'

Indeed embodiment comes with certain conditions. The construction of lata depends upon the *result* of the activity in the installation. Good results reinforce the lata, bad results do not. That is how 'appropriate' behaviours (vs nonappropriate) are embodied. We mentioned embodiment involves emotions; that is where they intervene, by reinforcing some behaviours and inhibiting others.

This last link completes the chain of reproduction from the installation to the embodied competence and provides a complete chain of mechanisms from the macro-level of society to the micro-level of the individual organism made of body cells that inscribe these social effects in the flesh.

According to the law of effect (Thorndike, 1911), responses that produced satisfactory results for the organism tend, by mere repeated association with the effect obtained, to progressively become established patterns and to occur again immediately in response to the same. Conversely individuals avoid repeating those responses that produced discomfort. The experiments on 'operant conditioning' (Skinner, 1938) popularized this link between feedback and the creation and reinforcement of specific responses to given situations.[41] The embodiment of the stimulus-response is obtained by biochemical modifications of the cells of the organism, and these can

---

[41] Operant conditioning should not be confused with classic conditioning, in which a stimulus A, when repeatedly associated with another stimulus B, in the end produces (more or less) the same response as stimulus B. For example, showing a light at the same time as food ends up with the light triggering salivation in dogs (Pavlov, 1927).

be empirically observed. These modifications are enduring, but they keep some plasticity and can be modified by new experience, as we could have suspected by observing how learning and memory work. Operant learning happens through the law of effect, which modulates the formation of lata. There are solid indications that dopamine is involved in this process, although the exact role of this hormone is still discussed and several models are proposed (Beeler, 2012; Berridge, 2007; Salamone, Correa, Farrar, & Mingote, 2007; Sutton & Barto, 1998; Wise, 1982).

This essential law of psychology (the law of effect) accounts quite simply for the mechanism of learning through practice. Humans tend to build expectations based on their experience. They learn probabilities of occurrence and respond according to correlations they previously observed (Estes, 1961; Sanford, Sherif, & Bruner, 1957). Positive outcome reinforces the lata bearing the behaviour just executed, negative ones inhibit it (whatever the exact pharmacologic mechanism involving dopamine is). This learning can result in performing specific actions in a given situation (e.g. saying 'thank you' when you are given a present), or not performing specific actions in a given situation (e.g. not pulling straight away to the maximum the lever of an unknown shower when you are in the shower cabin).

Let us consider this sad but enlightening comment posted on a blog by a former inmate[42]:

> I only spent just short of 18 months inside [jail] but it has a weird effect. Once released, I found myself stood by an unlocked door waiting for somebody to open it. Inside you never go through a door without it having being unlocked immediately beforehand. I don't consider myself to be institutionalised but little things like that make me think I was getting close. (Anonymous, 2014)

Here the subject himself described how unsuccessful experiences of trying to open prison doors extinguished his previously appropriate automatic impetus to open the doors encountered. The mechanisms of installations' feedback we described earlier feed the law of effect: appropriate behaviour produces satisfactory feedback (reaching goal and satisfying motive, social reward); inappropriate behaviour produces negative feedback (failure, social punishment). Clearly, society (the Others) includes some clear steer when it gives feedback. As a result, appropriate behaviour is learned and reinforced by positive feedback and inappropriate behaviour is

---

[42] Thanks to Elizabeth King for signalling this post to me.

discouraged by negative feedback[43]. Installations produce such 'valenced' feedback: try to jump the queue at the airport check-in and see what happens.

As said above, as a result lata are produced. The more often lata are activated, the more they become prominent (accessible) in the mind. This can be empirically evidenced by the descriptions or free associations of subjects on a given topic. We have shown for example that, although subjects in the French population shared a common representational structure of what 'eating' means, some parts of that representation were most salient (in verbal free associations) precisely in those subjects whose practice was often mobilizing these aspects. For example, those who went to the restaurant more often would more often come up with 'restaurant' as a free association to 'eating'; those who cook (compared with those who don't cook) associate 'butter' with 'cooking' rather than with 'sandwiches'; they also associate 'sugar' with 'cooking' rather than with 'coffee' (Lahlou, 1998: 187–9). Practice grows representation; just like right-handed tennis players grow larger right arm muscles as well as right-sided reflexes. This phenomenon is called 'trophism', a growth structured by what feeds it (Lahlou, 1998: 193). The structures that can be learned and embodied are not only constructed by positive feedback loops, but by negative ones as well, sometimes even faster. Both mechanisms contribute to delineate the path of appropriate behaviour: facilitating activation of what should be done, and inhibiting activation of what should not be done.

Interestingly, although people usually think of operant conditioning as the effect of 'stimuli' such as light or sound patterns, the seminal experiments were in fact done with (rudimentary) *installations*: Thorndike was studying hungry animals trying to escape from inclosures (Thorndike, 1911); Skinner had created a food-dispensing system ('operant conditioning chamber') where the rats or pigeons could receive stimuli, press a lever or a disk and get food – or electric shock (Skinner, 1938). This shows that animal subjects have no difficulty learning complex settings (as a compound) for a stimulus. That should not be a surprise because learning capacities are

---

[43] There is no such thing as positive or negative social feedback per se. The valence of the result must be considered in comparison with the motives and goals of the subject. Most subjects want to please and agree with others; therefore "positive" social feedback is usually rewarding. But that is not always the case (think of rebellious adolescents, for example). Also, even in absence of social feedback, the mere achievement of the goal or satisfaction of a motive is a reward. It is that subjective reward that feeds the law of effect. Therefore operant conditioning and learning are closely linked to motivation.

the result of the natural evolution of animals in ecological settings, which are complex systems rather than isolated objects. What is useful to learn in natural settings is how to react to complex and dynamic environmental situations, not to simple stimuli such as a dot on a screen as in the laboratory. The same goes for humans of course, and that is why they learn so easily in installations.

*In sum, installations operate as systems that induce subjects into performing some specific behaviour appropriate to the installation. In that process, installations ensure that subjects receive satisfaction for the appropriate behaviour (and positive feedback); conversely they often provide some unpleasant feedback to those who do not behave appropriately. This results, through biochemical processes, in subjects embodying the appropriate interpretive competences (lata). Installations therefore operate as educating devices that implement and reconstruct, through guided practice and conditioning response, the appropriate lata in the bodies of their individual users.*

### 5.2.3.4.  *The Standardization of Conditioning*

Now the mechanism of embodiment is set, let us see how societies manage to install *similar* embodied structures in all their members. Why do all members of a culture carry similar lata? I have suggested that installations are one of the important ways in which this happens, because installations provide similar experience to all people. Because installations are similar, members of a culture who practice in similar installations embody similar habitus.

We saw that embodiment occurs through actual repeated interaction, the successful ones and the failed ones that have been corrected. This can happen by experiencing reward and punishment through practice in installations. That can also happen by observing others doing (vicariant learning), or by learning through games and role play.

But that are not the only ways. Persons learn more than very specific and rigid behavioural sequences, or rules; they also learn more generic principles of action which they can adapt to local contexts. This happens in education, at school, but also in everyday activities in which these principles are pervasive and can be learned in interaction with others who apply them.

Leontiev provides an interesting example, from the notes of a Moscow teacher, S. A. Cherepanova, in which we can see that not only specific roles, but also more general principles, in line with local cultural value systems (in this example Soviet Russia) are acquired during play.

Igor and the other boys have built a big bus from chairs, while the girls play with dolls. I suggest to Igor to invite the girls to a bus trip. 'I am the conductor, I punch the passenger's tickets' says Galia. 'No, I want to be driver.' 'You were driving before; now it is my turn'. The teacher must now intervene. *I explain to the children that both drivers and conductors have their shifts, and that one rests while the other works.* The children like the idea of my trying to turn their play into the 'real thing'. 'Is this what happens with real drivers?' asks Vova. Peace is restored. Igor passes the steering wheel to the boy who relieves him, while Vania waits until he can relieve Galia, now acting as conductor. (Leontiev, 1961: 64; *italics mine*)

Situations of interactions with other humans include a number of relatively standardized encounters that derive from biological and social necessities. For some of them, evolution has built behavioural 'universals' (salutations, flirt, etc. see Eibl-Eibesfeldt, 1967: 428–52) and also inbuilt interpretation mechanisms to recognize and express emotions through mimicry and language, for which we have specific organs. But in the vast potential repertoire of possible responses for what is not innate (and even in cases to modify what is innate) societies have chosen to reproduce and allow only a small subset, and every loyal member of society will be quick to give negative feedback to conspecifics who perform outside of this culturally acceptable repertoire. For example, one should respond to a friendly salutation in the same way. One should share food at common meals. Children should respect elders, etc. These cultural elements are transmitted through practice in installations, and during the reiteration of correct performance. For example, Ochs and colleagues (Ochs, Pontecorvo, & Fasulo, 1996), in their analysis of family meals, show, through the detail of the interactions, how parents help children to learn and embody the proper way to behave (e.g. not to leave the table without finishing), but also how they inculcate a series of representations and value systems about what food is in different aspects (as nutrition, as a material good, as a reward, as a source of pleasure). These representations are the background of adequate behaviour.

Roles are the way individuals are trained into the embodied interpretive structures necessary for installations. Basically, the role is a series of ordered chunks of interpretation that enable individuals to play their functional part in a given activity, usually relative to some installation, but not always. Just as social representations are a collective construct that enables the predictable use of objects, roles are a collective construct that enable predictability in actions (behaviours legitimately expected from the subject) and functional cooperation. So the competences, embodied interpretive structures, lata, are acquired not as a separate series of information, but rather structured in a bundle as a role. This learning happens in situ for a professional role (specific contributions to the social division of labour), and connected with reward in status (ecological money for survival and reproduction). Individuals are also paid in pleasure 'currency', as well as with financial or material retribution (salary …), means of living, etc. Cabanac argues that pleasure is the single final currency for reward, the one that triggers the learning processes (Cabanac, 2003; Cabanac, Guillaume, Balasko, & Fleury, 2002).

As we see, learning can happen through various layers. A lot of the feedback ('this is OK', 'this is not OK') comes as a social response from other participants in installations, and the values (positive or negative) are often socially determined. But installations do not cover all cases.

*In other words,* **in general education as well as in installations, society sets up conditions in which individuals get exposed systematically to specific experience and feedback on their behaviour. This ensures that all the loyal members of a society share the same interpretive systems.**

**This is done by controlling the content of stimuli (situations) on one hand, and the feedback subjects receive on the other.** This is often mediated by the two other layers of components: built environment and social regulation. The built environment provides similar (and sometimes standardized) situations. The social pressure selects similar responses to behaviours, according to a set of value systems and templates that are socially determined (what is 'good' vs what is 'bad').

So far, we have explained, by looking at how things happen in practice, how individual competences for 'naturally' performing appropriate behaviours come to be present in members of a society, and how all these members share a similar habitus. In doing so, we have invented nothing new because all the mechanisms of learning, embodiment, education, etc. are well known and described in the literature. But **what we discovered as we went along is the continuous presence and importance of installations in these learning processes.** Installations therefore appear instrumental in this reproduction and conditioning process. Their similarity accounts for the similarity of experience and hence of competences embodied.

But then, why is there still also some individual variability in individuals? How is it that they do not react exactly the same in installations? That is what will be considered in the next section.

### 5.2.4.  *Behavioural Variation and Paradigmatic Learning*

One first and obvious reason for individual differences observed in behaviour is that individuals come with differences in their genetic capital and have similar but diverse experiences, so as a result they are different from one another.

But the same individual may also act differently from day to day in the same installation.

> To use again the shower example, in my next hotel, I will first recognize the local shower cabin as an exemplar of 'shower' despite its specificities. Then I may activate, depending on the local conditions (shape of shower handle, personal mood, lighting, angle of vision of the handle, etc.) any part of the lata accumulated in previous experience about 'showers', and even combine previous ones in a new activation path; and therefore produce a genuinely original behaviour that expresses my idiosyncrasies, my culture, my local mood, as well as factors in the specificities of that shower that morning.[44]

We can consider this as an expression of free will. What enables this? This section ventures that we learn, think and act in a paradigmatic way and that such paradigmatic variation enables operating 'roughly the same but different in the detail' in an extremely efficient manner.

A *paradigm* (see Glossary) is a set of entities that have some relation of functional equivalence in a given context. Initially, in traditional grammar, a paradigm is a 'list of forms from which we have to make a choice at a given point in the spoken chain' (Mounin, 1985: 7). For example, in the sentence 'Albert was driving his bicycle very fast', vehicles (car, motorcycle, horse) are the paradigm of the various words that can be substituted for 'bicycle' in that sentence and still make sense. They are the set of values that variable can take.

A paradigm will be the set of units that can commute in a given situation; the array of alternative possibilities at this point. For example, suffixes are a paradigm; so would be the various words describing 'places'. This notion was introduced by Ferdinand de Saussure: 'Thus a declensional paradigm is an associational grouping <which has the right to claim a unity>. Within this unity there is something which varies and something which does not vary; this is the character of all associational groups.' (Saussure 1909] 1997: 143a).

---

[44] See the notion of situated conceptualization (Barsalou, 2003). Also: 'meaning is reached by widespread multiregional activation of fragmentary records pertinent to a stimulus, wherever such records may be stored within a large array of sensory and motor structures, according to a combinatorial arrangement specific to the entity. A display of the meaning of an entity does not exist in permanent fashion. It is recreated for each new instantiation. The same stimulus does not produce the same evocations at every instantiation, though many of the same or similar sets of records will be evoked in relation to the same or comparable stimuli.' (Damasio, 1989)

In a nutshell, **individuals do not embody only one single stereotyped and rigid lata set appropriate to one single standardized installation.** Rather, as the result of repeated and ever-changing series of experiences, they embody a whole repertoire of slightly different possible pathways that enable them to *recognize* similar but slightly different situations and then to form appropriate but slightly different *interpretations*. In a given situation, subjects can therefore pick any of the above that satisfices the situation at hand. This may result in behaving slightly differently in the same situation.

As I have explained elsewhere in more detail (Lahlou, 1995: 138–40) learning tends to take place in a paradigmatic[45] way.

By comparing experiences, we group those that are similar, and gradually constitute a set of similar situations for which similar responses 'work'. This set of situations is subsumed into one single category (often labelled with a single word, e.g. 'shower', perhaps associated with a prototype); it is then associated with the same set of responses. In that set of responses, we then locally choose the most adapted one.

Let me illustrate with an empirical example, meals. Asked to freely associate to 'eating well', 1,600 French adults came up with various verbal responses (which differ from the associations to 'eating' described earlier because 'eating well' induces a normative mindset). These responses were processed with a descending classification algorithm, and produced several classes, among which one clearly is the 'classic French meal' format: first course, main course, cheese, dessert (Lahlou, 1992). That is typically the standard menu structure any French restaurant would propose for a meal when one chooses the fixed-price menu option.[46]

Interestingly, although some subjects' responses are exactly this standard generic expression (*'first course, main course, cheese, dessert'*), many responses are more specific descriptions of meals following such a structure: e.g. 'some mixed salad and meat with vegetables and green salad and a fruit' whereas other responses are a mix where very generic terms ('dessert') are mixed with more specific ones ('fruits') e.g. 'meat, vegetables, *dessert*, fruits, bread and the cheese'.

---

[45] Mounin argues that this is the way infants learn language, by associating a given word with a series of linguistic contexts (Mounin, 1963). A paradigm is the set of units that can commute in a given situation; the array of alternative possibilities at this point; that is why can talk about paradigmatic learning..

[46] 'Entrée, plat chaud, fromage, dessert'.

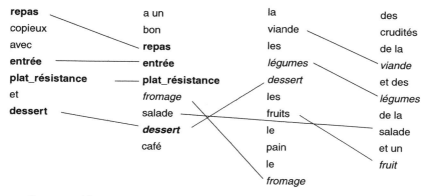

Figure 5.8. The paradigm effect: Example of the French meal as described in free associations by French adults. The original phrasing of responses by subjects is used, to show how the same paradigm can contain items that differ in every detail (no single word in common) but have the same meaning.

The descending classification algorithm, which creates clusters by separating what is different,[47] puts all these answers about standard French meals in the same cluster. With this sorting technique, they end up in the same cluster even though some of them have no word in common, as pictured in Figure 5.8, where the answer on the left side has no word in common with the answer on the right side. And indeed both respect exactingly, including in the temporal order of presentation of dishes, the classic French meal structure, although they describe it with different words.[48]

This illustrates how one single structure can subsume many different local forms. The classic French meal is a *paradigm*.[49] It is the set of all the 'correct' succession of dishes that appear acceptable for situations of eating together in that culture. The avatars of the paradigm respect the general structure, which is what characterizes it, so any of the elements can be

---

[47] Rather than aggregating what is similar, as would do e.g. ascending clustering algorithms, which put together what seems similar.

[48] In descending classification– here the one designed by Max Reinert (Reinert, 1983, 1987; and in English: Schonhardt-Bailey, Yager, & Lahlou, 2012: 509–13) such paradigms are preserved because the algorithm cannot 'cut ' the chains of similarity provided by the fact that some of these expressions have elements in common two by two, like the links of a chain. For details of the paradigm effect in classification seeLahlou, 1995: 148–53.

[49] This paradigm contains, nested, other paradigms. The French meal is a paradigm as all the forms of a food intake sequence that can appear acceptable for a French native in the (syntagmatic) course of the day. At a finer level, the dessert is the paradigm of all the sweet foods that can occur at the end of the (syntagmatic) sequence of a typical meal.

substituted by another that has the same function. For example, 'fruit' can be substituted by 'apple', 'pear', 'orange' etc.[50]

That is similar to what Rumelhart and Norman call schemata.

> Generic concepts are represented by schemata. These schemata contain variables: references to general classes of concepts that can actually be substituted for the variables in determining the implications of the schema for any particular situation. (Rumelhart & Norman, 1978: 41)

Having a paradigm enables one to mobilize with a single form (typically, a word) a whole set of possible variants. In this example, we see in passing how symbolic thought can match with empirical data: the symbol stands for the paradigm of all possible empirical phenomena it subsumes. This simple process accounts for our capacity to use symbolic format, and language in particular, to deal with the infinite variability of the world, by reducing what is variable to something stable enough to be manipulable (the concept, the symbol) and communicable, as pictured in Figure 5.9.

The full power of the paradigm appears when the paradigms are combined, because this process enables reducing the combinatory explosion that one would have to handle if manipulating the individual elements subsumed in the paradigm. When I ask my friend: 'Will you come for dinner?' I am proposing in five words an array of possibilities that has a million possible variations (e.g. the dessert might be fruit, cake, etc.) And my friend, when at the table, at the moment when he is invited to start eating, will have at his disposition a whole set of variants on how to eat, and will choose one of these variants according to what fits the local situation best.

At the moment of linking recognition to action, a reduction has occurred: paradigm S (situation: here 'meal') will induce several paradigms of action (paradigm A: e.g. 'eat', or 'refuse' or 'postpone' or 'leave'). Once the relevant generic paradigm is chosen (e.g. 'eat'), then a local adaptation can be made according to other contextual elements within the chosen paradigm (e.g. 'eat the noodles with chopsticks'),[51] and so on and so forth

---

[50] Some children's construction games (e.g. Playmobil®, where plastic characters can be assembled piecemeal [head, body, arms, costume etc.]) illustrate the same principle: different characters can be assembled but they always keep the same generic structure of 'a person' with a head, a body and four limbs.

[51] 'What is at first a habitual pattern for using sensorimotor activity to achieve some end later becomes a program in the sense that various « substitutes » can be inserted without disrupting the over-all act. Even a chimpanzee who is unable to get a hand into an opening to extract a desired object can substitute a stick in place of reaching. Or in skilled tool-using by humans the carpenter who forgets his plane can substitute a chisel in the smoothing routine, a pocket knife or the edge of a screwdriver, if need be.' (Bruner, 1966: 10)

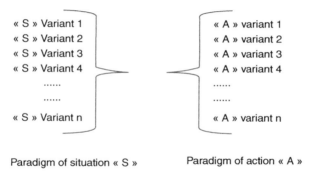

Figure 5.9. Paradigm of situation and paradigm of action. On the *left*, a paradigm of situations is represented as a set of all possible variants subsumed in the paradigm; that could be, for example, all the possible instances of 'a meal'. On the *right*, a paradigm of actions, which could be, for example, all the possible ways of eating (with knife and fork, chopsticks, fingers, etc.).

in a nested way and ever more detailed way (pick up this chicken bit separately with the chopsticks).

I showed elsewhere how the same subject, my colleague Antoine Cordelois, used, for the same dish and in the same meal sequence, three different ways to catch pitted olives with his fork in his salad,[52] depending on how the olives presented themselves regarding the position of the pitted hole and their stability in the surrounding vegetables.

This bundling of paradigms of situations to paradigms of responses is a remarkable process that constitutes the competence itself; it is a generalization process that, paradoxically, enables us to make responses more specific and well adapted by matching one large set of similar situational patterns (e.g. foods) to one large set of a functionally equivalent interpretations (e.g. ways of taking them). Instead of associating one single response with each single pattern, a set of possible responses is associated with a set of patterns. When a new situation arises, that specific situation is recognized,

---

[52] Piercing the olive through with the fork, sliding one spike of the fork through the central hole of the pitted olive, or lifting the loose olive along with a tomato slice (because an olive alone would roll off the fork) (Lahlou, 2012). In expertly acting so, my colleague Antoine unconsciously illustrated how each routine act is in practice a creative performance in its detail, an ever-new dance involving subtle arbitration between free will and the constraints resulting from the affordances provided in the conditions given. Such subtle adjustments are enabled by a long series of experiences acquired through similar but slightly different performances (the menu at the EDF R&D cafeteria is rather repetitive). We never eat twice the same pitted green olive, still they all are similar for us to capitalize competence.

by analogy, as a member of the set of similar situations, and then associated with the set of possible responses. That is the reduction of recognition. The latter set offers an array of possible behavioural paths that the
subject can mentally explore[53] and the pick the most well adapted (Mead
[1934] 1972: 98–9), or even create a novel one as a combination of previous responses (by simulation or simply by trial and error). In this second
step, there is extension of the set of possible behaviours. That reduction-
extension is what enables us to recognize chairs as sitting devices and sit
on any of them properly, although in practice each exemplar appears to
us in a slightly different shape, format, colour, perspective and lighting
conditions.

Local adaptation takes place through different mechanisms of coupling,
under motor micro-control of body segments, and finally at microscopic
level (say, the last millimetre) simply through the natural flexibility of the
body envelope.[54] As experiences of slightly varied situations occur, the
learning process transforms that set of situations into a single paradigm.
A paradigm is a set of objects that have some relation of equivalence – here
semantic and functional: things that fall into the same conceptual category
and that afford or call for the same interpretation.[55]

What has been said above can be generalized, beyond pattern recognition paradigms, to strategies of decision. Empirical research shows that
humans tend to use *heuristics*.[56] These heuristics often are more efficient
than strategies using more information (Gigerenzer, 2008). In a given situation, humans select what heuristics to use based on a series of criteria,
for example, what data are immediately available (Gigerenzer & Brighton,
2009). But also, as has been demonstrated by Rieskamp & Otto, (2006),
they choose on the basis of what they learned regarding the efficacy of a
specific heuristic in their previous experience. So here again, situated feedback is the key to learning.

So, returning to the betterment process outlined in Section 5.2.1 about
learning processes, we see that the evolution of the 'model' when a new
situation is encountered can take place by simply enlarging the set of
situations subsumed in the relevant paradigmatic set. Similarly, the new

---

[53] Freud describes this explorative simulation process that takes place in thought during the postpone-
ment of action, as some kind of 'palpation': 'experimental action, a motor palpating, with small
expenditure of discharge (Freud, 1925, 1976a).

[54] As a managerial proverb says, the bum takes the shape of the seat.

[55] Remember that by interpretation I mean a response that has both cognitive and motoric aspects.

[56] Heuristics are simple rules people use to make satisficing decisions or solve problems by using only
a small amount of the available or potentially available information.

learned response can also be a mere addition to the associated paradigm of responses, e.g. learning to eat a new type of fruit during a trip to a foreign country, which makes the 'fruit' category larger. We can also learn a new technique for peeling a given fruit, which can also be applied to other known fruits. In this way, accommodation does not make the subject lose all the adapted responses that he previously used for well-known situations, it only expands the subject's competence (of course, in some rare, extreme cases, the contour of the paradigm may change). Here is another example: when I travel to Japan or China and learn new ways of using toilets, this accommodation to a slightly different type of installation does not make me unlearn the use of European installations. Learning how to use a specific shower did not make me unlearn how to use the other showers. That is what is known as 'learning by accretion' (Rumelhart & Norman, 1978): adding new data in the paradigm category.

This mechanism of paradigmatic learning includes an array of possible minor adaptations that make the habitus robust to the local variations. It also labels situations (and responses) with higher-order conceptual and linguistic categories that can be used to verbalize them (e.g. 'a seat').

Finally, having a wide array of possible 'satisficing' interpretations available for a given situation also accounts for the variability observed in individual behaviour.[57]

It is interesting to note that **installations leverage this powerful cognitive tool that the paradigm is**. Indeed, installations facilitate paradigmatic learning, because they expose the subject to a variation of very similar set-ups that the subject can easily recognize as variants of the same (e.g. different streets, different family dinners, different lectures), therefore creating a paradigm. In turn this paradigm will help identifying as variants of the same new installations, those slightly different which have a family resemblance with the paradigm (a new street, a new family dinner, etc.). In the same movement of learning, installations associate to this paradigm a series of executable behaviours, again many variants and shades of the same (walking in this new street, eating in this new family dinner), which the subject will be able to draw from and combine when confronted, in the future, with similar installations. So a given type of installation (e.g. Street, Family dinner) frames a paradigm of behaviours.

---

[57] Basso argues, with some reason, that because brain processing is a parallel and reticular process, where there is competition and cooperation of different subnets, when one of these networks wins over it becomes the microworld of which we become aware and where we act (Basso & Oullier 2010.: 296–317). This produces (unconscious) discontinuities when activation switches from one attractor to another. Such processes can account at neural level for the observed variability.

**In short, an installation is interpreted, from the perspective of the actor, as a behavioural paradigm (a shower, a queue, a check-in, a reception, road traffic, a family dinner): what one is supposed to do in such situation. That paradigm is usually structured as a rather stereo-typed sequence of schemata that will occur in successive scenes.** That is what produces the 'scripts' such as the restaurant or the lecture that I mentioned in Section 3.2 when describing activity theory and scripts. The script appears as a syntagmatic chain, of which each link is a variable that has to be filled in by some local token (in the case of a lecture for a student: a chair, a professor, a talk, a notebook, etc.). Each token is an instance of a paradigm and can occur in different varieties (blue, red or grey notebooks, professors of psychology or of mathematics).

An installation readily provides the appropriate tokens to fill these para-digms along the course of activity; that is what makes it so easy to use.

**That is one answer to the issue we tackled above: how come we man-age to react properly in an ever-different world? Well, it seems that even if no one ever steps in the exact same situation twice, we often step into the same behavioural paradigm. Installations are the frames of such paradigms. Furthermore they provide the right tokens to fill in these frames as the subject looks for the missing pieces to complete the script.**

As the subject does so, a search image naturally forms as the lata-for-which-there-is-no-pragmatic-correspondent; for example, in attending a lecture, 'I miss something to take notes with'. The subject then looks around for something that satisfices the affordances of a notebook and pen, and fumbles in his bag to find something that matches, or gets it from fellow students.

**We can see how installations appear designed to match the natural structures of cognition. They provide the matching frame to action scripts. And that is not accidental: they have constructed these scripts to match their own frame in the first place.**

### 5.2.4.1. *Interpretation: Transforming Learning into Meaning*

Once the process of embodiment has taken place, interpretation becomes automatic. The world is not perceived as a raw form; rather, we always interpret it 'as' something that relates to our previous experience, alloyed with an 'effect tone', as Uexküll would say, or as 'affordances'. It then becomes almost impossible to perceive a phenomenon without this con-structed interpretation. For example, as already mentioned, we can listen to an unknown foreign language as 'sounds' (which we have great difficulty grasping and remembering), but when we hear someone speaking our own language we cannot help but hear words and process their meaning. It is the same with the example of the nurse automatically interpreting the sounds of medical equipment and alarms.

So do we with objects: we see 'a chair' rather than 'four sticks with a plate on top of them', and 'a ladder' rather than 'a set of sticks and holes'. And a chair means a 'sitting affordance' automatically; a ladder means 'affordance for climbing'. This meaning-construction process is so continuous and ubiquitous that it has become transparent to us. We don't realize how much it is socially constructed, except maybe when travelling makes us aware of cultural differences. This is what the social construction of the world does to our psyche: we become automatic interpreters of our perceptions in terms of taken-for-granted social constructs that guide our behaviour.

> So-called "normal" persons execute most of their daily actions without undue reflection upon social rules and expectations. Most of their dealings with the environment are automatized, somewhat like an experienced driver's movements. (Mirdal, 1984)

Mirdal's work shows how migration, because it changes the habitual setting and taken-for-granted basis for daily assumptions of the migrant, can create stress. Uprooted persons become strangers in their new environment and cannot trust their previously embodied competences to be efficient. In our habitual setting, only in some very unusual circumstances do we become aware of this constructed aspect of reality. Aldous Huxley, in *The Doors of Perception*, describes the experience of losing the interpretation layer and perceiving objects directly as forms and colours, under the influence of mescaline, a psychedelic drug:

> one bright May morning, I swallowed four-tenths of a gram of mescalin dissolved in half a glass of water and sat down to wait for the results ... A small typing table stood in the center of the room; beyond it, from my point of view, was a wicker chair and beyond that a desk. The three pieces formed an intricate pattern of horizontals, uprights and diagonals - a pattern all the more interesting for not being interpreted in terms of spatial relationships ... I was looking at my furniture, not as the utilitarian who has to sit on chairs, to write at desks and tables, and not as the cameraman or scientific recorder, but as the pure aesthete whose concern is only with forms and their relationships within the field of vision or the picture space. But as I looked, this purely aesthetic, Cubist's-eye view gave place to what I can only describe as the sacramental vision of reality. I was ... in a world where everything shone with the Inner Light, and was infinite in

its significance. The legs, for example, of that chair -how miraculous their tubularity, how supernatural their polished smoothness!

Huxley's own takeaway from his experience is that with the drug he recovered 'some of the perceptual innocence of childhood, when the sensum was not immediately and automatically subordinated to the concept.' He had accessed some primordial perception of things unfiltered by the 'reducing valve' of constructed cultural categories that reduce perception to a standardized interpretation, 'the carefully selected utilitarian material which our narrowed, individual minds regard as a complete, or at least sufficient, picture of reality':

> Every individual is at once the beneficiary and the victim of the linguistic tradition into which he has been born -the beneficiary inasmuch as language gives access to the accumulated records of other people's experience, the victim in so far as it confirms him in the belief that reduced awareness is the only awareness and as it bedevils his sense of reality, so that he is all too apt to take his concepts for data, his words for actual things. (Huxley, 1954 2011: 2-9, *passim*)

Just as we perceive things through their constructed affordances, we tend to perceive other humans through their roles. See for example how difficult it is to identify your butcher or baker when you come across them out of the context of their shop, in the street and without their professional clothes. You know you've seen that face somewhere, but who the hell is he? While in context, identification is immediate and transparent.

Here we must refer to the notions of ideal type and typification, key notions that enable identification and intersubjectivity. The concept of ideal type was initially coined by Weber; it described the way the scientist creates some pure mental constructs, devices that have no existence in reality but can serve as models that synthesize the typical traits of a class of phenomena.

> An ideal type is formed by the one-sided *accentuation* of one or more points of view and by the synthesis of a great many diffuse, discrete, more or less present and occasionally absent concrete individual phenomena, which are arranged according to those one-sidedly emphasized viewpoints into a unified analytical construct (Gedankenbild). (p. 90) ... Its function is the comparison with empirical reality in order to establish its divergences or similarities, to describe them with the most unambiguously intelligible concepts, and to understand and explain them causally. (Weber, 1949: 43)[58]

---

[58] The notion of an ideal type of something is close to 'in intension' (see Section 3.5) l definition of the set of all the instances of such 'something'.

Schütz explains how the scientist uses the ideal types as puppets: he puts these puppets in a setting that contains all the components of a situation in the social world relevant for the performance of the typical act under inquiry. The scientist then obtains a model of the social world, where action can be explained by the ideal-typical motives. (Schütz [1960] 1976c: 18). And he adds: 'it is the destiny of the personal ideal type to play the role the actor in the social world would have to adopt to perform the typical act' (ibid.: 18).

In fact, not only scientists proceed this way, all our fellow humans do typifications. individuals construct and update ideal types; they expect a person to perform as the ideal type would. And because of these expectations, the actor in the social world finally has to play it as the ideal type would, with only some margin of freedom as to how tightly they want to play their role. There is a fascinating bootstrap phenomenon at work here, where expectations become self-fulfilling prophecies.

We are able to interpret situations because we have embodied a portfolio of ideal types: the mother, the teacher, the clerk, the police officer, the doctor, the bus driver, etc. We 'bring into each concrete situation a stock of pre-constituted knowledge which includes a network of typifications of human individuals in general, of typical human motivations, goals and action patterns'.(Schütz [1932] 1976b: 29). We choose among ideal types to anchor the perception we get of a specific individual in a real situation, and we use the chosen ideal type as a model to predict her behaviour and to interact with her.

More generally humans tend to identify objects (chairs, buses, people) after their 'family resemblance' (Wittgenstein, [1953] 1986: 32), based on a categorization system centred around prototypes that have some specific qualities (Rosch et al., 1976). Of course, we are able to make the necessary minor adjustments to adapt to the local specificities; we know that individuals are not exactly the same as ideal types, and we gradually adapt the model in the light of actual experience (see Section 5.2.4. for the discussion about paradigmatic learning). Nevertheless, we tend to put objects in a specific category box, and then assume the object will behave as (and have the affordances of) the prototype (the ideal type/the stereotype). This explains why, once we have categorized something or someone, we tend to have expectations and prejudices: the implications for racism and stigma have been, alas, massively documented. What is true for roles and material objects (nurses, chairs) is true more generally for all types of phenomena that are perceived as a coherent entity, that is: something that has agency as a whole unit, *that acts together*, e.g. a train, a herd of cows, a married couple, a hospital – and of course installations. The latter are typically something 'that acts together'.

Language consolidates this categorization process. Once a phenomenon is identified, it is labelled in inner speech (and outer speech) under a specific name that conveys all the socially constructed assumptions, connotations and 'implicatures' (Grice, 1975; Sperber & Wilson, 1986) that go with the ideal type.

It has been suggested by anthropologist and linguist Benjamin Lee Whorf (Whorf, 1956), and demonstrated to some extent (Hunt & Agnoli, 1991), that a given language preformats the way individuals perceive reality, and orients and limits the way they think. Without getting into the complex and fascinating considerations coming from the fact that the very notions of space, time and causality may take different aspects depending on what tenses, modes and, more generally, grammatical structures are available in a given language (and they vary massively),[59] let us simply consider the fact that the more detailed the vocabulary one has, the more one is enabled to describe precisely the actions and the objects. Try to discuss manoeuvring a sailboat with a seaman or discussing your car's engine with a mechanic if you don't know the correct words!

A similar effect to Huxley's deconstructive experience of the ordinary fabric of life with mescaline is reported in Harold Garfinkel's breaching experiments, mentioned in Section 4.4.2.4. His students were instructed to 'spend from 15 minutes to an hour in their homes viewing its activities while assuming that they were boarders in the household', as if they were not aware of the implicit code of conduct (Garfinkel, 1964). The experiments are instructive in that they provoked strong reactions on the part of other (unaware) participants who reproved the participants for behaving inadequately. So far, no surprise: the reader will recognize the vigilante effect. But moreover:

> Students reported that this way of looking was difficult to sustain. Familiar objects -persons obviously, but furniture and room arrangements as well- resisted students' efforts to think of themselves as strangers. Many became uncomfortably aware of how habitual movements were being made: of *how* one was handling the silverware, or *how* one opened a door or greeted

---

[59] For example, and to build on what was stated earlier about how objects acting together can be considered as a single coherent unit, ancient Greek conjugation has a special *dual number* used when the subject is a pair. The same goes, for instance, with Hopi grammar, where animate objects can appear in singular, dual and plural number (LaVerne-Masayesva, 1978: 72–3). Also, ancient Greek considers a neutral plural as a singular: when describing a group of animals running, the ancient Greek says: "the animals *runs*" (τα ζῶα τρέχει).

another member. Many reported that the attitude was difficult to sustain because with it quarrelling, bickering, and hostile motivations became discomfitingly visible. (Garfinkel, 1964: 231).

We can see here that roles can become second nature, just as objects acquire a second nature. It is extremely uncomfortable to step out of a habitual behavioural paradigm, to go against one's habitus.

*In sum, the feedback mechanisms closely associate objects with a meaning in terms of action, in such a way that the object is automatically perceived according to its cultural interpretation (what it is supposed to be, how one is supposed to act with it). The orientation of material and social feedback alloys this interpretation with correctness, through reinforcement. This process applies to simple objects as well as to more complex installations. As a result, humans embody what should be done in an installation at a neurophysiological level, and in a situation the relevant interpretation (symbolic and motoric) automatically kicks in. The installation tunes the actor's mindset into a specific behavioural paradigm, and then supports and regulates this behaviour within the socially convened limits of what is considered appropriate behaviour.*

The paradigmatic nature of competence enables the minor local adaptations necessary for each specific local installation, and they are supplemented as necessary by the local automatic adjustments systems of the body. Typification enables symbolic manipulation of representations of the phenomena in internal simulation (brain processes) and communication with fellow human beings.

*We thus understand better what the interpretive competence layer is made of: it is the capacity, but also the automatic process, by which a given object or situation triggers a conventional cultural interpretation.* **Embodiment implements this automatic process in the individual's body through various learning processes (e.g. the law of effect). We also understand how the reproduction of competence happens: embodiment results in consistent feedback from the installation to the subject that rewards or encourages 'correct' behaviour and discourages, impeaches or reprimands incorrect behaviour.** *The key point here is the importance of installations as the locus and instrument of the embodiment of standardized lata into members of the same culture.*

On top of that, the primary encoding from experience is not the only and final product of experience. Internal processing continues offline as this experience is integrated into the rest of the mind. Annette Karmiloff-Smith, studying children and especially their building of mathematical competence, distinguished at least three phases of further processing, that she calls representation redescription (RR), by which the primary embodiment generates more abstract structures that can be used across empirical domains:

> The notion of RR attempts to account for the way in which children's representations become progressively more manipulable and flexible. Ultimately, this leads, in each domain at different times, to the emergence of conscious access to knowledge and children's theory building. RR involves a cyclical process by which information already present in the organism's independently functioning, special-purpose representations is made progressively available, via redescriptive processes, to other parts of the cognitive system, first within a domain and then sometimes across domains. (Karmiloff-Smith, 1994)

For example, the structures of social representations, as we can extract them from the discourse of individuals or cultural traces seem to map with the neural structures that link perception to action. Let me illustrate in the next section.

### 5.2.4.2.   *An Example: Eating*

I have described (see Section 3.5) how the content of the social representation of eating in the French adult population consists of six components: *DESIRE, TAKE, FOOD, MEAL, FILL UP,* and *LIVING*[60]. The basic components of this EATING representation were empirically identified by methods of verbal association among French adults in the late 1980s (Lahlou, 1998), and they were found almost identical in the statistical analysis of some six hundred dictionary entries associated with eating (Lahlou, 2003). Estelle Masson, using a different technique (content analysis of interviews) on a close enough population, found similar results (Masson, 2001).

The method used provided each component of the representation, each as a paradigm of words that illustrate the representations' content in the empirical material (text, speech). These words can be seen as the paradigm of the component, in the linguistic sense, that is to say all the words that could take the place of the component in specific instances. For example, the DESIRE component, which is a fairly generic drive, can emerge empirically in various local forms corresponding to particular instances of the general idea of DESIRE in specific circumstances: hunger, thirst, desire, curiosity, passion, trend, lure, instinct, etc.

---

[60] Each of these represents a paradigm of more specific entities, as is discussed shortly.

Specifically, our empirical analysis (Lahlou, 1998) showed that the DESIRE component subsumes the following traits (that is, words or their lexical roots): *desire, hunger, appetite, thirst, satisfy, envy, covet, satiate, satisfy, greed, soothe, devour, avid, hungry, grasping, content, need, ardent, curiosity, excited, eyes, passion, eye gaze, drive, attraction, glutton, experience, love, sex, instinct.* The full list includes tens of terms, which refer to some drive, appetite or hunger.

The class is generic in its content. It includes nonfood desires: *curiosity, greed, sexual desire.* Its intense and primitive character appears clearly with traits such as *greed, ardent, need.* The empirical analysis also brings an unexpected point, namely that are part of the same paradigm, not only concepts but objects or instruments (*eye gaze*), states (*hunger*) etc. Each of these terms is, in its own right, a form of that DESIRE node, and it is part of the representation of EATING. It is through the occurrence of such forms in the context (internal or external) that the evocation of the DESIRE node emerges in the subject.

Returning to the social representation of 'EATING', the basic components of EATING are, as indicated above: DESIRE, TAKE, FOOD, MEAL, FILL UP and LIVING.

We have already discussed DESIRE. The second class, whose features relate to an action operator, includes essentially motor characteristics or their instruments: *touch, grab, take, hands, nose, attack, embrace, kiss, cheek, bite, stomach, someone, seize, beat, lip, opening, finger, arm, pinch, enter, with, open, self, catch, pull, slap, hit, suck, fall, tongue, face, mouth, teeth*[61]

We are dealing here with an action-class, with agonistic connotation (*attack, bite, grab, beat, pull,...*) We called it TAKE. This appropriation class is loaded with violent, aggressive connotations: full of *teeth,* voracious *hands.*

The third class refers to FOODS; its features are a long list of edible things (we limited the list to the first seventy items, sometimes difficult to translate): *meat, bread, food, fruit, pasta, vegetable, animal, cook(ing), slice, boiled, plant, cut, salad, milk, tooth, piece, cost, canned, rat, digest, pork, eat, fish, dry, cheese, fat, vegetal, soup, beef, feed(ing), sugar, edible, juice, butter, toast, bread, liquid, herb, canned, sausage, feed(ing), mouth, lean, thick, drink, game, filled, rumin(ant) TECHN,*[62] *bird, fresh, grain, grill, flesh, green,*

---

[61] Because these words result from an automated statistical analysis of co-occurrences, a few items may be artefacts of the method.

[62] This metalinguistic marker occurs in the dictionary to signal technical terms.

*dog, small, ball, prepare(d), bake, leaf, cake, crust, pottage, swallow, crunch, flower, fine, beverage, hot.*

In other words, when a subject sees a 'fruit' (the fourth item of the list), that fruit is likely to be identified as a member of the 'FOOD' paradigm.

Other nodes are MEAL, which mainly occurs with a ritualized social sharing connotation; FILL UP, responsible for physiological connotations referring to a balance between too much and not enough; and finally LIVING, which refers to more general existential problems with social and moral aspects (good / bad). As seen, the content of the social representation is both very close to the physiological process of nutrition, and richer, because it also includes social components: MEAL, LIVING. Individual representations of EATING have that same content, with these components.

How does a representation produce action in context? I suggested that, in context, from the input of their senses and of their inner state, subjects identify some components of the representation. For example, picture a subject seeing a fruit and feeling hungry. The emergence of a representation is a cascade phenomenon, because the more components of the representation are present, the more the representation tends to complete itself by the strength of association of its components, each firing up the others. Therefore if several core components are present, there is a strong probability that the full essence of the representation emerges, so that finally the complete pattern is activated in the subject's mind. So, if I'm hungry and I see an apple, I already have two components of the representation present, because fruit is an exemplar of the paradigm FOOD and hunger is an exemplar of the paradigm DESIRE. Summoned by their association with these components other core components of 'eating' are evoked, and gradually the complete representation of 'eat' emerges, just as a hologram emerges as the proper sources of light interference are provided.

So, by association of ideas, and active exploration of the environment, the subject completes connected components, eventually searching for items to complete the missing components of the full pattern, to finally form a set of 'relevant' representations, matching this context. Relevant means here that some components of these representations are actually *present* in the context. These components present (e.g. this apple) in the context have a 'pragmatic correspondence' to the elements of the representation ('fruit'). They resonate with the representation of fruit.

So for example, the presence of an *apple* on the table, seen by a *hungry* subject, will simultaneously emerge as FOOD/fruit and DESIRE/hunger, both being components of the representation of EATING. The physical apple on the table resonates with the FOOD component of the representation; the gut feeling of hunger resonates with the DESIRE component of the representation. The mere presence of these components in the actual physical layer evokes and reverberates with elements in the embodied layer, then maintains this resonance; it triggers and sustains activation of the related lata.

Because these present components continue to steadily fire activations, it is likely that, gradually through the mere law of association, the rest of the components of the representation of EATING, which are associated with these firing components, will be convoked and start firing too. As a result EATING emerges as a global activated representation and remains salient as long as these two components (hunger, fruit) are present and maintain the resonance.

So, it appears that, when the subject actualizes 'relevant' representations, some of their components are precisely those components present in the context, which I just called 'pragmatic correspondents'. These pragmatic correspondents are likely to be those same ones that initially established the resonating correspondence between representation and context. This fact, which seems trivial in practice, *constitutes an economic and empirically elegant solution that humans have found to solve the thorny problem of the relationship between the symbolic level and pragmatic level of action. Those pragmatic correspondents become natural targets for action when the representation unfolds into motor action.* The subject takes *this specific apple* that is present in the context for a pragmatic target as a valid representative of the category FOOD which has to be TAKEn then ingested.

Because components of the symbolic system actually match the present components of the context, the coupling between the inner representation (embodied structure) and the outside context (affordances) is direct and simple. It is precisely the same targets of action that have fired the embodied competence components, and as long they are present the coupling through sensory organs and motors effectors can be maintained easily by attentional focus.

There is a resonance loop, passing through perception organs, between the bearers of signification for the material object and the matching lata in the subject. Re-enactment of similar past experience is evoked and sustained by the actual presence of the object. Awareness of the presence of the object emerges, consciousness establishes a connection between the inside of the body and the outside context, and interpretation is triggered. Motor action is then adapted by accommodating to the local situation at hand with minute adjustments. *Installations frame and facilitate this resonance.*

We can see here that the emergence and cascading of the representation's components are the same mechanism we described above as 'interpretation' emerging from the resonance between the lata and the data provided by the context. *The interesting point here is the pragmatic correspondence, by which the objects in the environment both elicit 'appropriate' embodied competence by activating the relevant components in the lata, and then keep activated the coupling with the competence as it unfolds until it naturally takes precisely these pragmatic correspondents as targets for motor execution.*

Once the relevant representations are selected and activated in the psyche of the subject, the articulation of the representation, that is its deployment as a programme of action, produces a programme adapted to the present situation, mobilizing the very components that are present in that specific context (in our example, *that* apple on the table). Indeed, representations can usually unfold into action programmes, because a representation is some user's manual of the object.

Now to the concrete example of implementation by a French adult subject. We can reasonably assume that the subject shares part of the French culture, so we consider that his individual mental representation of EATING contains, even if they vary slightly from the statistical norm, similar components to the social representation as described above, and associated in a similar fashion.

The subject is hungry: DESIRE is salient. It is 16h. The subject sees a fruit. The components DESIRE (hunger) and 'FOOD' (fruits) are present in the environment; one in the internal context of the subject (lata), the other in its external environment (data). These components are pragmatic correspondents in the sense that we have given above to this term (the presence in the context of material components that correspond to components of the representation).

DESIRE and FOOD evoke other components of the representation of EATING (activation by association). The representation of EATING is then convoked and completed. Note that the affordances of the situation guide the articulation of representation in the detail of cognemes[63] that instantiate the components of representation: the fruit is selected because it matches the specific affordances offered by the situation (there: *this fruit, rather than a FOOD in general*). In the detail of the TAKE paradigm we find the detailed components that will be selected, adapted to the affordances offered as a for this specific solid object, which can be grasped

---

[63] 'The "cogneme" would be the smallest, most basic unit of any theoretical construction in the domain of cognition' (Codol, 1969; my translation).

fully. Will be selected in sequence: hand, *finger, take, mouth, bite.*[64] The articulation of the components DESIRE/ TAKE/ FOOD/ FILL UP are a pragmatic programme that, applied to this specific and relevant *apple* present in the context, actually describes the concrete behaviour that occurs here: the subject grabs the apple, takes the apple to his mouth, and eats it.

I cannot provide a detailed description here, but at least I can provide some evidence that suggests what occurs in terms of neuronal activity and which areas of the brain are involved.

"The sight of food elicits a wide range of physiological, emotional and cognitive responses. Firstly, it is a cue for the body to prepare itself for subsequent food ingestion with accompanying anticipatory physiological responses, such as a cephalic phase release of insulin and changes in heart rate (Drobes et al., 2001; Wallner-Liebmann et al., 2010). Secondly, it can elicit emotional responses like a desire to eat (Ouwehand & Papies, 2010). It is thought that positive emotions, such as pleasure, evolved as a biological mechanism to promote behaviours that support survival, like eating (Berthoud & Morrison, 2008; van den Bos & de Ridder, 2006). Thirdly, the sight of a food gives rise to cognitive processes, such as memory retrieval and hedonic evaluation, based on information that was stored during previous experience(s) with the food (Berthoud & Morrison, 2008; Shin, Zheng, & Berthoud, 2009). In addition, exposure to food cues can trigger inhibitory cognitive processes like self-regulation, e.g. processes involved in resisting the temptation of palatable foods in order to maintain a healthy body weight (Kroese, Evers, & De Ridder, 2009; van den Bos & de Ridder, 2006)." (van der Laan, de Ridder, Viergever, & Smeets, 2011)

The activation of these regions is connected, in a way that fosters (feedforward) food intake when a hungry subject is exposed to food visual cues, and especially when seeing others grasping food.

The following study shows how hungry subjects react to seeing food objects being grasped (activation of hunger/DESIRE + FOOD + TAKE) activate the perception-action coupling mechanisms preparing the organism to behave, and which brain regions are involved (as opposed to satiated subjects who do not activate these regions as much).

Cheng and colleagues presented subjects with video clips of another person grasping objects or grasping food. Group 1 was presented such images when hungry, then when satiated. Group 2 had a meal before the first session. In hungry participants, presentation of video clips depicting an

---

[64] These will be selected and not, for example the sequence, f open, pull, lip, suck, which are also available in the paradigm but would be more suitable for drinking a carton of milk, for example.

individual grasping food elicited specific activation in the hypothalamus, amygdala, parahippocampal gyrus, orbitofrontal gyrus, and fusiform gyrus.

Parahippocampal gyrus, fusiform gyrus, amygdala, and orbitofrontal cortex are known to be involved in positive/appetitive stimuli in participants watching appetitive visual stimuli (LaBar et al., 2001; Morris & Dolan, 2001; Rolls, 2000).

The regions modulated by the hungry state were detected in the inferior frontal gyrus, the extrastriate body area (EBA), and the superior temporal gyrus in addition to the food/motivation-related regions (i.e., amygdala, orbitofrontal cortex, parahippocampal gyrus, hypothalamus, fusiform gyrus). The inferior frontal gyrus, the posterior parietal cortex, and EBA are involved in the mirror-neuron network, a neural system involved in perception-action coupling mechanism. Responses were stronger for observation of grasping food as compared with observation of grasping objects in the hungry state. In conclusion:

> the desire to eat leads to hemodynamic modulation not only in the neural circuitry involved in drive and motivation but also in the regions that are part of the mirror-neuron system, particularly the inferior frontal gyrus. This indicates that the motivational state of the organism affects neural systems involved in perception-action coupling mechanism. We speculate that the signals arising from the neural systems involved with drive (orbitofrontal cortex) and motivation (amygdala) enhance the activity in the mirror-neuron system to prepare the organism to behave (in this study, feeding behavior) in order to restore its homeostasis. Finally, our findings open up new direction in the investigation of the adaptive functions of the mirror-neuron system by showing that affordances from the external environment are determined not only by their physical properties but also by their internal state of the organism. (Cheng, Meltzoff, & Decety, 2007)

> Basso and colleagues showed twenty participants, who were instructed not to eat food for at least four hours before the imaging session, short movies where a hand was taking food from a plate (and nonfood objects also for contrast). With functional magnetic resonance imaging (fMRI) they observed, in all cases, activations of zones of the brain related to grasping (TAKE), which is no big surprise. For food objects, they also observed a robust activation of zones connected to FOOD across the gustatory processing areas (insula, opercular and orbital parts of the inferior frontal gyrus [IFG]), the limbic system (midbrain, thalamus, hippocampus, amygdala) and visuomotor areas (around the inferior and superior parietal lobules, and the middle occipital gyrus).

> The gustatory processing areas activated are located in the ventral reward pathway of the core eating network, especially the insula and the opercular and orbital parts of the IFG (i.e. lateral orbitofrontal cortex [OFC]), that

play important roles in representing taste and reward (Liu et al., 2016). Connected to the ventroposterior medial nucleus of the thalamus (Araujo & Simon, 2009), areas within the insula and overlying operculum are the main thalamocortical gustatory projection (Veldhuizen et al., 2011). These regions are supposed to be the primary gustatory cortex that represents taste property information and feeding-relevant interoceptive states (Avery et al., 2015; Small, 2010). In addition to the insula that is likely to store gustatory memories (Kobayashi et al., 2004) the lateral OFC operates as secondary gustatory cortex (Kringelbach & Radcliffe, 2005). It has been previously associated with memory enhancement for food items (Morris & Dolan, 2001), and is associated with the pleasantness of, and motivation to consume, food (Kringelbach, O'Doherty, Rolls, & Andrews, 2003), (i.e., a *'desire for food'* (Wang et al., 2004)

The limbic structures activated are the midbrain, the thalamus, the hippocampus and the amygdala. Limbic regions are known to be involved in both hedonic and homeostatic networks (Berthoud, 2006), and to contribute to taste and reward representations when participants are presented with visual food cues (Chen, Papies, & Barsalou, 2016; Killgore et al., 2003). The thalamus, at the top of the brainstem, through which interoceptive signals travel, is involved in the recollection processes that make the experience of retrieval vivid (Carlesimo, Lombardi, Caltagirone, & Barban, 2015). (Adapted from Basso et al., 2017; italics mine.)

In other words, being exposed to 'TAKE' and 'FOOD' activated cortical zones known to be active in 'DESIRE' and 'FILL UP'.

In short, seeing a hand taking food increases activation in brain areas known to be connected with food, grasping, taste, reward and more generally eating. Brain areas corresponding to FOOD+TAKE, activated by the presence of pragmatic correspondents in the context, recruit as they fire new areas that evoke other components of the representation of EATING: DESIRE and FILL UP. We see through imagery in the brain happens that same cascading process of coupling lata with data and unfolding this activation that we noted earlier in terms of the articulation of the representation and subsequent execution of behaviour.[65] We see how such cascading activation can lead to the emergence of the process of eating by articulating, in motoric mode, the components (grasping, bringing to mouth, swallowing, etc.). The behaviour unfolds according to the embodied standard interpretative script, guided by the re-enactment of lata and scaffolded by the rest of the installation, until the extinction of DESIRE or FOOD terminates the execution of the process by suppressing what caused its activation in

---

[65] Although in the fMRI study the subjects were not given the opportunity to act and were only presented images, so we do not have the complete sequence in imagery, only the onset.

the first place and maintained it by resonance between the pragmatic correspondents and the lata.

Now of course, the actual mechanisms are much more complicated than a mere coactivation by a simple law of association, and the sketchy description in the example is oversimplified and inaccurate in many aspects. Karl Lashley, in his classic paper on the problem of serial order of behaviour, which also showed the effect of the context and background state of the organism on the interpretation of a stimulus, demonstrated how the association principle is insufficient to explain the *sequence* of action (Lashley, 1951).

I presented this example to show that, for a given activity, the same components of the social representation (that is an entity at the societal level, which we obtained through empirical exploration of dictionaries) can be found in the individual at the symbolic level (through word association by live subjects) and finally at the neurophysiological level in brain activation. That is meant as an illustration of the coherence of the chain we attempt to describe, by which social structures are gradually transferred onto the neurological embodied level (e.g. what is edible, and how).

The scale of the phenomenon (the combinatory dynamic activation of a brain and body involving billions of individual cells connected by numerous biochemical and biophysical mechanisms) is out of proportion with the ridiculously small number of elements of our sketchy description (a few concepts only, translated into words). But at this stage of our knowledge we can only provide a vague and incomplete model, certainly inaccurate in detail.

Preparation of action and activation of the proper bodily organs and subsequent motor operation in the right sequence is a complex process that combines many cascading and overlapping perception-action loops. These mechanisms are modulated by learning: for example, young children have difficulty catching a moving ball with their hand. Similarly, novice tennis players are often unable to make a good serve, whereas experienced players have embodied the motor competence to produce a correct result, in a gesture that also includes respect for the institutional rules of the game. The detailed neurobiology of such processes is still an object of research, but clearly they are more complex than a mere stimulus-response reflex and include anticipation and feedforward (see Glossary). For example,[66] a subject catching a ball one-handed will finely adapt the position and

---

[66] For further discussion refer to the extensive literature on movement (e.g. Prinz, Beisert, & Herwig, 2013; Rosenbaum, Cohen, Jax, Weiss, & van der Wel, 2007)

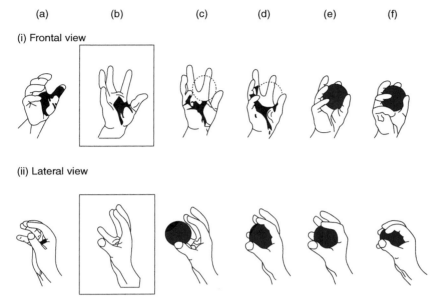

Figure 5.10. Six stages in the one-handed catching skill: *a*, The hand prior to the start of fine orientation movements. *b*, The hand after completing fine orientation, showing differentiation of the fingers. *c*, The hand as the ball centre passes between little finger and thumb. *d*, Contact between hand and ball. *e*, Ball held – grasp of flexion complete. *f*, Ball held – grip phase of flexion complete. From Alderson, Sully, & Sully, (1974: 223).

orientation of the hand about 150–200 ms *before* the ball reaches the hand; the grasp itself begins 32–50 ms *before contact* and ends 10 ms after (Figure 5.10).

Similar mechanisms of feedforward may be at work in interpersonal interaction (Wolpert, Doya, & Kawato, 2003). Nevertheless, for our purpose here we do not need to know the exact physiological detail of what happens: all we need to know is that experience produces some embodied 'interpretation' structure (lata) that has the capacity to couple efficiently with the environment given and to feedforward a functional and culturally correct response, and that these structures are strongly linked to motivation.

The first aspect described in the previous paragraph, the effect of experience, is the law of effect, which is supported by a series of solid experiments and by common sense.

The second aspect is illustrated by brain imagery investigations that show that stimuli in the environment provoke activation of matching structures in the brain. In a less sophisticated manner it is easily verifiable because people are indeed able to recognize and name which objects are present in their environment, and to take appropriate action (e.g. eating an apple that is on the table).

The latter, the link to motivation and goal orientation, also seems to be confirmed at a neural level (Alexandrov, 2008), and again we don't need to know the detailed neurochemistry of it to observe that it is an empirical fact. It is obvious that attaining the goal or satisfying the motive releases some positive reward that the nervous system acknowledges somehow and interprets as positive feedback for the behaviour that led to the goal.

**Installations are constructed in such a way that the relevant components (needed for appropriate processes to emerge in coupling between the subject and the situation) are made readily available at the point of delivery of behaviour.**

### 5.2.4.3. *Installation and Learning*
**In sum, experience of effects of actions produces lasting structures in the body that link perception, action and motives. Learning occurs, and in that process subjects embody interpretive structures that tend to associate a specific paradigmatic response with a given type of paradigmatic situation. The activation of these structures can be empirically observed at brain level. Installations are typically the place where such experiences and learning occur in the course of ordinary life. They are as well the behavioural paradigms where such learning is put to use.**

As we can see, installations do not only generate the correct behaviour, they also, as a result of 'normal' operation, generate in their users the embodiment of the competences necessary to perform the *correct* behaviour; and these embodied structures are the same as those that are activated during action. **The reproduction of the behaviours, of 'practices', and of competences does not come from behaviours alone. *The reproduction process needs the installations to frame the behaviours. Behaviours are continuously (re)generated by the installations, as in the mould/cast process.***

Of course, once the competences are embodied, they generate the behaviours at the contact of the installation, and the more the behaviours are repeated in repisodes the more solid the competences become, creating routines and habits. In this respect, a mechanical metaphor could be used: once an engine is started, it will continuously run, as long as there is fuel, and the necessary electric current is generated by the engine as it runs; only in the beginning was the kick-starter needed. Similarly, once the user has been taught a process by the installation, the necessary competence is implemented and will reproduce and reinforce itself through practice. But it has been necessary beforehand to ensure that the embodied competence is the *appropriate* competence, one that produces appropriate behaviour. In this process the resilience and controlling power of the installation, which as we have seen uses feedforward and positive and negative feedback to keep the behaviour within norms, is paramount.

We have now come to close the circle. Indeed what we have described are what Bourdieu calls 'the dispositions of the habitus', i.e. 'the schemes of perception and appreciation deposited, in their incorporated state, in every member of the group' (Bourdieu, [1972] 2013: 17). In other words, the social frameworks internalized by the individual. As we argued in Chapter 1, the psychological and the sociological are just two ways of looking at the same phenomenon, at two phases of the same reproductive cycle: of individuals through society, of society through individuals.

How these competences are wired in the physiology remains uncertain in the current state of the art: As typifications? As paradigms? As Perceptual Symbol Systems? As Representational Redescription? As redmet (see Glossary)? In extension with autopoietic processes? A mix of all of these? Never mind: the detail of this hardwiring aspect does not matter so much for our argument here.

**We have now detailed the complete chain of mechanisms that connect the installation to the behaviour and finally to the embodiment. In doing so, we have outlined the importance of material objects in that process, a role that has often been underestimated, if not completely overlooked, by many social scientists, because the focus of their study is mostly individuals and relations, rather than material objects.**

*Installations, by continuously providing the appropriate affordances, interpretations systems and social regulation at the point of delivery, channel the flow of activity in the correct track. They construct the walls of the phenomenological tunnel that keep the subject on the path of appropriate and correct behaviour. And in doing so, they reproduce the embodied competences of the subject for doing so in future similar situations. Because installations of a given type in a culture are similar (e.g. trains, launderettes, ticket booths), all members of a culture embody the similar, appropriate lata, which they are then able to use in the standardized installations provided by the culture.*

Not only were different disciplinary approaches necessary in our description because of the diverse nature of the media of that reproduction process (material objects, human individuals, societies), but we also required different theories and mechanisms because different levels of explanation need different models: there is a scale issue, since, in social science just as in physics or thermodynamics, the micro-levels and macro-levels cannot be well described in a single model.

Although the detail is a bit complex, the general idea is simple and has already been expressed in different ways by many authors: practice regenerates culture, and culture reproduces practice.

See for example Bourdieu's description of the same reproduction cycle, although it remains at a level too generic to make explicit the role of installations in the process:

> In short, the habitus, the product of history, produces individual and collective practices, and hence history, in accordance with the schemes engendered by history. The system of dispositions – a past which survives in the present and tends to perpetuate itself into the future by making itself present in practices structured according to its principles, an internal law relaying the continuous exercise of the law of external necessities (irreducible to immediate conjunctural constraints) – is the principle of the continuity and regularity which objectivism discerns in the social world without being able to give them a rational basis. (Bourdieu, [1972] 2013: 82)

One of the most complete descriptions of this mechanism is provided by Cicourel:

> Social structure, therefore, can be viewed as patterns of institutionalized, often bureaucratically organized, developmental, cultural and cognitive belief systems and activities, empirically grounded in daily life socio-cultural, political, economic, and emotional practices. Conceptual and empirical elements revolve around (often tacit, informal), routine "scaffolding practices" by individuals and groups within normative institutional settings. Such practices invariably consist of "representational re-descriptions" (Karmiloff-Smith, 1992), namely, memory-dependent re-descriptive devices that build on experiences and thoughts and go beyond the limitations of our immediate sensory capabilities. For example, the human ability to synthesize and compress or summarize experiences and thinking by producing cognitive schemata, cultural beliefs, emotions, speech narratives, artifacts, gestures, prosody, and other symbolic and physical mediums.(Cicourel, 2012)

All I did in the lengthy sections above was to make explicit in practical detail the mechanisms of this multilevel process, within a framework that enables such analysis in empirical cases despite their complexity. We needed to go beyond the level of symbolic description of these processes, and to *flesh out*, literally, how they operate in the bodies and in material and social context with concrete objects and interpersonal relations.

Empirical investigations among experts show that competence is not a rigid single mechanism that brings one single stereotyped response to one single fixed situation. Rather it is a flexible and adaptive process that is capable of producing a set of similar responses to a set of similar situations in such a way that the variation of the response fits the variation of the situation: there is more than one way to skin a cat. Building competence is the process of learning more and more such ways, each one adapted to specific conditions (e.g. specific cats), and therefore learning larger sets of situations and how to build adapted responses. Competences are paradigmatic, both in the dimension of the range of situations a given competence applies to, and in the dimension of how one acts in mobilizing a given competence in a specific case.

**To summarize simply: as we enter an installation, driven by our motives, we are channelled at three levels: affordances, lata, social regulation. As a result, we usually execute appropriate behaviour. If so, motive satisfaction and/or social feedback create or reinforce lata matching this specific behaviour in that type of installation. Installations frame the behaviour, and then provide reward so that correct behaviour is embodied.** *Installations operate as conditioning devices.*

Let me highlight again, as a final note, that physical installations usually are not unique, but exist in many similar exemplars with minor variations. Installations also come as paradigms. Cars are like other cars; chairs are like other chairs; roads are alike; even hospitals tend to have strong similarities. This has two consequences:

(a) **this similarity enables us to use installations easily: if you know how to drive *some* cars on *some* roads, you can drive *many* types of cars on *many* different roads because cars and roads are similar;**

(b) **this similarity with a small array of differences provides users experience that always stays within the acceptable limit of manageable differences, but still provides some variation that gradually extends the users' competence to a paradigm of 'roughly similar although not identical' situations and behaviours; therefore allowing participants to embody lata flexible enough to accommodate further small variation.**

*Installations operate as distributed opportunities for paradigmatic learning.*

**In short, as stated already, because humans tend to use similar installations, available in the public space, at least in a given culture, they tend to embody similar competences.** We all interpret in a similar way a conference room, a restaurant or a car. As a result we get what was described above as 'social representations': all members of a given culture have a similar individual competence regarding a given type of installation. That is because installations for a given activity tend to be similar in a given culture.[67]

So physical installations, in the same way as competences, come in an abundance of similar exemplars with minor variations.

But why do physical installations come in many *similar* exemplars? There must be something in the way the material layer is reproduced that results in that effect. What is the reproduction cycle of the material objects? Read on.

## 5.3.    Reproduction Cycle of Material Components of the Installation

Installations have a physical layer, made of physical objects: buildings, doors, lights, chairs, but also software, engines or food. Let us call that layer, for short, the physical installation. A physical installation is usually a combination of several, sometimes many, physical objects, and a given object is usually itself made of a combination of parts. To make things simple, we deal here with common objects and forget for the moment that they are made of parts. And installations being a combination of objects, what we say for the reproduction of objects is valid, *mutatis mutandis*, for physical installations.

Material objects in a society are mostly man-made. We therefore consider first the case of man-made objects, and will deal with 'natural' objects (such as the sun or the moon) at the end of this section.

Objects are not made at random, but after some pattern. The chair maker or the hat maker does not invent every new chair or hat from scratch. They use a representation of chairs, or hats, as a template. And that representation was made from a model chair, or a model hat; or perhaps as an ideal type drawn from a whole set of such objects. For example, in the chair factory there is a template of what is to be built; the hat maker has a book with all the hat models drawn on the pages.

---

[67] They may come in different subspecies, as for example different types of shops or meals, but that simply means that the activities supported are subspecies of one larger type of activity.

Sometimes, the template is a specific object I want to reproduce exactly: when I need a new door or table for my installation, I replace the old one with a new but similar one.

> Here is recent example of renewing my home dinner installation. Some pieces of cutlery were lost over the last ten years, probably thrown in the trash with food: eight coffee spoons and two fruit forks were missing. At some point, I ordered from the manufacturer in Italy a set of spoons and fruit forks to replace the missing items; I wanted the exact same model so as to complete a homogenous set. In doing so, I was reproducing my original installation, which was possible because the company does reproduce continuously, year after year, the same objects, based on a template that I could Google by its model name and check with the manufacturer's catalogue illustrations. And a few days later the exact copies of my lost cutlery arrived in the post, only a bit shinier and more polished than the used ones that sat in my kitchen drawer – and in fact also with a very small variation in the way the brand logo was engraved.

One may object that not all objects have a blueprint. Humans were able to make artefacts long before there were detailed symbolic representation systems. Even if the representation of artefacts and how to make them is very ancient,[68] those who undertook the craft construction of an object in many countries are known to have operated without a blueprint.

Nevertheless, the view that these illiterate craftsmen would not use a representation to guide their work does not stand against empirical evidence. If you go in a bazaar and see one of these craftsmen to order an object (e.g. a pot, a carpet), there will be a phase of discussion where the client explains what she wants, with very specific description (material, colour, size, shape, etc.). This discussion is usually based on objects on exhibit in the shop and samples of the material, which serve as a material catalogue of models and templates. In this phase, where the price and delay are also negotiated, client and craftsman clearly build together a shared representation of what is to be made, which serves as a model for the actual craft. The use of symbolic representation through drawing was also especially developed in architecture for large physical installations.

So physical installations, and objects, follow a chicken-and-egg cycle (see Figure 5.1 at the beginning of this chapter): from the model object, a representation is made, in the form of a sketch, a template, a model, a description, an architectural blueprint, engineering drawings, a circuit

---

[68] For example, there are technological representations in ancient Egyptian drawings of carpentry as early as 2400 BC (Olson, 2010), or of a watermill on a Roman sarcophagus (Ritti, Grewe, & Kessener, 2007).

diagram, a sewing pattern, a business process, etc., or simply a mental representation. Then, from that representation another object, similar to the first, is reproduced. Hence, we expect that there will be other similar exemplars of the objects we are used to, available to us when we need them.

In industrial development, the reproduction process historically became more and more sophisticated and looped to demand feedback. Marketing and sales services closely monitor and survey users to understand their requirements – how they think objects should be. Based on these requirements, adaptations are made in order for the product to match demand. These requirements are translated into 'specifications', which are a representation of the desired characteristics of the product that are a crucial element of discussion between the various stakeholders involved.

It is very important to note here that *in that process, representations of the material objects are systematically made. As a result, all man-made objects exist in two forms: symbolic (represented) and reified (material exemplars).*

During production, control and minor adjustment are made continuously in order to keep the product within these specifications of the model. This might be simply to compensate for the variation of the raw material and transformation process, or because the model changes as demand fluctuates (e.g. requesting more of a variety, colour or flavour). For example, to keep constant the taste of '100% natural, nothing added' orange juice despite the variation of maturation and taste of the oranges, producers must add (in very small, almost undetectable quantity) a cocktail of powerful essential oils that they adapt to each batch of raw material.

The process of adapting offer to demand is called 'design cycle' at an early stage of production (Figure 5.11), and then 'production cycle' and later 'quality control'. They all take the form of corrective feedback loops striving to make the reality match the model, but also building on previous experience. Hence, probably, the small difference in the way the brand logo was engraved in my new cutlery in the earlier example.

Conversely, the suppliers try to modify the user's representations and expectations to match the product they provide, through advertising or other kinds of publicity and 'public relations' (Bernays, 1928). They also try to influence or tamper with the social control system by lobbying the regulation authorities. In other words, there is also an effort to make the model (of what is desired) match the reality (of what is produced). We see here a dance that reminds one of the betterment process, but instead of it being oriented to modify the model to incorporate the variation of the reality, it tries to eliminate the variations of the reality to stay within the tolerance of the model.

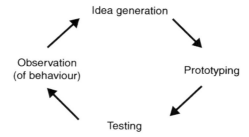

Figure 5.11. The design cycle.

I will not get into the detail of these processes here, because they are well detailed in consumer research, marketing and advertising textbooks (e.g. Haugtvedt, Herr, & Kardes, 2008; Kotler & Keller, 2009; Ogilvy, 1983). Lobbying is perhaps less extensively documented and taught, but it is nevertheless a massive and thriving activity: in 2013 there were 12,281 officially registered lobbyists for the US government, but in fact an estimated 100,000 with an annual spend of USD 9 billion (Fang, 2014), and about 30,000 for the European Commission (almost as many as the 31,000 staff of the Commission) influencing an estimated three-quarters of the regulations (Traynor et al., 2014).

The takeaway for our problem here is that there are two mechanisms of adaptation and accommodation of objects to the practices. Both mechanisms go in the direction of objects matching practices.

Objects exists in two forms, material (the physical token) and symbolic (the representation). For example, the hats exist as physical hats on people's heads, but also as drawings, plans and mental representations. Again, we find here a hybrid cycle: objects cannot reproduce by themselves; they need humans to make them in factories. Therefore, they are reproduced in a cycle of two successive forms, like the egg and the chicken: symbolic (the representation, the pattern) and material (the product, the material object).

Of course, in practice, the reproduction is not always exactly identical to the original. But we deal with this in Chapter 7 when we tackle evolution.

Installations follow the same process: indeed, when we want to duplicate an installation, we assemble the same components to produce a similar result. For example, work cubicles in a workplace are made with the same partitions, chairs, screens and lamps. Cars of the same model, or roads of the same type, are made in the same way. To some extent, this also applies to human components: firemen are trained to become firemen after the representation of what a fireman is; bus drivers, judges or soldiers are trained into a standard model, and even the dress is the same (uniforms).

Let us here highlight an important point that is necessary to understand what follows in the evolution section. Most man-made objects come in sets: there are many exemplars that are very similar. There is an abundance of chairs, of pens, of vending machines, of buses, of lamps, etc. Individuals in these sets are not strictly identical, but they are very similar, with minor variations; man-made objects are some kind of material paradigm.

I must at this point remind the reader of the theory of sets that was briefly sketched in Section 4.3. Just as representations could be described in extension (as a list of all the individual elements) or in intension (as a list of properties defining the elements of the set), objects can be defined in intension, for example by their function or their general pattern. It is this intensional definition that is used as a template to make the new objects. We can note here that since objects exist in two forms, symbolic and material, the set of similar objects (e.g. hats) can be divided into two sets: the set of symbolic representations and the set of physical exemplars. The first has a lot in common with what we called the social representation of the object; that is the set of all the individual representations of the object. But this set also includes all the external representations that are not embodied in humans: plans, written descriptions, pictures… Let us call this the societal representation of the object, to distinguish it from its subset ('social representations') that only contains embodied representations in humans.

Clearly, there is some correspondence between the material set of an object ('the collection' of these objects; e.g. all the physical hats on the planet) and the societal representation of this object (all the representations of hats on the planet). The two sets respectively generate each other. And this generation is made through humans or other actants (e.g. robots) who produce representations from objects, and then objects from representations. The similarity of objects of a given category (say, chairs) is understandable because they have been built after similar patterns (their representation). Finally, because objects are built on purpose for users, there is one supplementary mechanism that actively and deliberately produces some convergence between material objects and their representation. For example, physical chairs are built by chair makers who want the physical chairs to meet the expectations of the users, and therefore to fit their mental representations.

The case of 'natural' objects is not problematic. Many exist in large similar collections, and reproduce by natural means, alone or under human supervision (plants, animals or seasons). Seen from the users, there is not much difference with artificial objects as they get incorporated into an installation. Some are man-made, some are not. Unique natural objects that are durable (the sun, the moon) do not need to be reproduced, they simply remain. The problematic case is natural objects that neither reproduce nor remain (e.g. the ozone layer). This is an interesting problem that we cannot tackle here, but it is clear that when such objects are necessary for installations, their exhaustion, destruction or disappearance may end the existence of those installations. Humans have so far shown creativity in modifying installations to substitute the disappearing resources with some other component. Nevertheless, this did not always work out and collapse is a very possible consequence of disappearing natural resources (Diamond, 2005).

I will not get further in the description of the reproduction of material objects, as it would be another book, and some of its aspects are further detailed in Section 6.2. What matters for our discussion is that there is a reproduction cycle, through dedicated installations (workshops, factories), just as there are dedicated installations for the reproduction of embodied competences. I have sketched the mechanism by which objects and their representations are made to match, and reproduce, as two stages of one same cycle.

**We have also seen that most objects exist in vast collections of similar exemplars, with minor variations.**

At this point, we have fleshed out the mechanism of reproduction of embodied competences and of objects, two of the layers of the installation. But the third layer of installations, the social regulation, also operates in the reproduction process. In fact, it is crucial.

## 5.4. The Role of Communities and Institutions in the Installations' Reproduction Cycle

**Communities organize the transmission of competence described in** Section 5.2. **They do it in several ways: they control the expression of overt behaviour and representations in public space, they organize and supervise learning by peripheral participation, they manage instructional systems and many of the media that transmit knowledge (television, instruction manuals, ritual objects, etc.) and finally, they control the nature and form of material objects that are allowed in the public space with norms and law.**

The system of roles and statuses and the rules capitalize on previous experience regarding which behaviours produce what externalities. For example, when the nurse performs the sterilization routine that is part of her role, she is probably only vaguely aware that this hygienic routine builds on the works of John Snow, who first understood the nature of contagion by studying the epidemiology of cholera in London slums (Snow, 1855), the work of Louis Pasteur on asepsis (Le Fort, Pasteur, & Depaul, 1878) and the recommendations of Léon Le Fort: 'during rounds, I always wash my hands scrupulously before I touch a patient' (Le Fort et al., 1878: 282–3; my translation) etc. Here we see that installations capitalize on a vast sum of local experiences systematically collected by custom, science and law. This capital can be transmitted through education, but it is also reified in rules enforced by institutions, especially when the final consequences are not immediately visible by the individuals. We see here how *in practice* operates the ratchet effect (Tomasello, 1999: 37 et seq.) through which accumulated knowledge is passed from one generation to another: *institutions* select which behaviours are made compulsory. Setting a rule is an unexpected way of orienting evolution; indeed, a forbidding rule blocks possible evolution in the specific domain where the rule applies, by avoiding the emergence of variants.

That mechanism (deliberate conservation of some features) is not present in biological evolution. In nature, nothing selects out new mutations a priori. They will all be allowed to compete for fitness. In human societies (and this is even more salient in authoritarian regimes) some variants are eliminated a priori, and some variants are preserved even when they would disappear in natural competition. That comes from the intervention of institutions on potential evolution. The rationale for preserving some variants and eliminating some others is based on value systems – a different name for what is described in Section 7.3.1 as scales for the economies of worth.

I will not get into the detail of the reproduction of communities themselves – they are made of humans who reproduce their bodies by natural means, and then inscribe in these bodies the correct interpretive competences by the means described in Section 5.2. Of course their endurance as cultural entities is more complex than that but that would take too long a development here. I merely focus on the specific role communities have in the reproduction processes of the components of installations, and in the reproduction of installations as compounds. Although this section is inevitably somewhat redundant with regard to the others, because we describe the same phenomena from a different perspective, the analysis is necessary because it describes another locus of control, institutions, in which we can address interventions to change the world (or more modestly some specific installation).

### 5.4.1. *Control of Behaviour in Public Space*

I have mentioned several times already the controlling role of institutions in what is, or is not, allowed in public space. We saw how written regulations and signs explicitly state and display what should and should not be done (e.g. laws, work regulations, manuals of operations, compendiums of good practice, road signs, instruction labels). I described two aspects of this control: first, that it ensures only the correct behaviours are executed; second, that proper feedforward and feedback is provided to participants in general and novices in particular, producing operant conditioning.

The third aspect is to avoid a negative example being displayed to others, and therefore nip in the bud possible imitation that could create new streams of incorrect behaviour. This is why, when the incorrect act is public, the corrective feedback tends to be public also, for the edification of all. Foucault spends the three first pages of his book *Discipline and Punish* (Foucault, 1975) describing the painful public torture and execution of Robert-François Damiens, who attempted regicide in 1757: the more incorrect the act, the more public, the more exemplary, the punishment.

I mentioned in Section 4.4.2.7 the police officers giving looks to minor offenders, and in Section 4.4.2.4 the vigilante effect, with outraged reactions of the parents to Garfinkel's students as they tried to carry out their assignment in 'breaching experiments'. They are also visible manifestations of that control of public behaviour.

Vigilance and censorship, and their counterpart propaganda, or rewarding the correct and zealous, are important aspects of institutions. As we have already mentioned, special personnel is usually dedicated to surveillance and enforcement, with an entitlement to use coercion against forbidden practices.

### 5.4.2. *Communities of Practice and Intent Community Participation*

People who use the same installations usually tend to form communities of practice. Although this term remains fuzzy because such communities can take many forms, they are defined as follows:

> Communities of practice are groups of people who share a concern, a set of problems, or a passion about a topic, and who deepen their knowledge

> and expertise in this area by interacting on an ongoing basis. (Wenger, McDermott, & Snyder, 2002: 4)

Specialists insist on the fact that such communities emerge spontaneously and are difficult to control because of their informality. What is important is that:

> They may create tools, standards, generic designs, manuals, and other documents - or they may simply develop a tacit understanding that they share. However they accumulate knowledge, they become informally bound by the value that they find in learning together ... Over time, they develop a unique perspective on their topic as well as a body of common knowledge, practices, and approaches. They also develop personal relationships and established ways of interacting. (Wenger et al., 2002: 5)

Guilds and corporations had explicit formal structure, but this is not necessarily the case for communities of practice, which could just as well be a 'school' or artists, or users of a specialized online resource dedicated to open-source software development; or even a specialized online forum. It is during participation in the communities that situated learning takes place, as a socialized and emerging practice, and the competences learned remain to some degree linked to the context that scaffolds them, as opposed to 'internalization' of knowledge (Lave & Wenger, 1991: 48–9). The examples of the anaesthesia nurse or the cook apprentices (Section 5.2.1.5) are typically taking place in communities of practice.

In these communities of practice, status is gained by competence, and a system of learning by legitimate peripheral participation is more or less formally organized, by which the newcomers gradually gain competence through supervised practice. Therefore, communities of practice, also known as knowledge communities, enable and monitor the reproduction of competences by their transmission from expert to novice. This can take a long time.

> it is possible to delineate the community that is the site of a learning process by analyzing the reproduction cycles of the communities that seem to be involved and their relations. For the quartermasters, the cycle of navigational practice is quite short; a complete reproduction of the practice of quartermastering may take place every five or six years (as a novice enters, gradually becomes a full participant, begins to work with newcomer quartermasters who in their own turn become full participants and reach the point at which they are ready to work with newcomers). The reproduction cycle of the midwives', the tailors', or the butchers' communities is much longer. (Lave & Wenger, 1991: 97–8)

The authors of the concept strongly insist that a community is more than just a knowledge transmission system; it is a real human community where passion and motivation are key (refer to Rogoff's work cited earlier). The social aspects are not only key for motivation, they are also what gives strength to the social feedback systems that described in Section 5.2.2, and which communities of practice use liberally.

Communal reproduction processes also take place in families, and more generally in every community. Steps of competence are recognized by change in status, informal or formal. Examples of how institutions monitor the learning and reproduction cycle were provided with the figures of authority (the chef) making sure that no incorrect behaviour (such as dirtying the bowls) is performed in the open; of the doctor training the nurse; and indirectly of all the European norms informing objects, which in turn effect the individuals, by stigmergy, and provide them with guiding feedback.

### 5.4.3. *Education and Instruction*

This aspect of the action of communities is a most obvious process of cultural reproduction. We mention it in Section 5.2.1.4 from the perspective of the learner; but they are institutions per se. Schools, universities, but also all sorts of professional training organizations and processes are set up by communities to provide *instruction*; education by dedicated personnel. For example, the French education system, Éducation Nationale, was in 2013 the country's largest employer with a staff of more than 1 million and a budget of 145 billion euros, teaching 12.75 million students in some 64,000 teaching institutions – for a total French population of 66 million (MESNR-DEPP, 2014). Education is sanctioned by diplomas, certificates and other visible proofs of status. The government is not the only organizer of education; many other communities, for example religious or vocational, set up their own system.

The essence of this process was well described by Edgar Schein in his seminal study of a caricatured form of education, the 're-education' of prisoners by brainwashing: 'the crux of the Chinese approach has been to immerse the prisoner in a small group of other prisoners who are as or more advanced in their reform than he' (Schein, 1960: 2).

Not only is the normative way of seeing the world presented to the 'novices' as the only acceptable one, but that is done in a context where group pressure is intense, and deviation is punished. Although my presentation here and the comparison with brainwashing may seem excessive, we must admit that a substantial amount of our 'education' is done in relatively coercive contexts. For one, instruction is compulsory until the teenage years in most large-scale societies, where it occupies a substantial amount of the waking time of children. Parents and teaching personnel put considerable pressure on the novices; sophisticated systems of continuous evaluation have been elaborated to ensure compliance with the process and its correct embodiment. Education in that perspective includes a preventive brainwash against natural tendencies for aggression, greed, sexual predation and so on. Because societies are so successful in satisfying our basic needs, we tend to forget how strong the urges for such basic needs can be when they are not satisfied; that strength and the socially disruptive possibilities it entails are what justifies such systematic preventive social conditioning.

Of course, we all consider that education is a necessary process and has a positive value. Nevertheless, this process is enforced without consideration for the learner's acceptance; applied to other animals, we would call it taming. This process of conditioning is extremely costly for society, but on the whole efficient. Although the process is sometimes brutal and often stressful for the participants, it is necessary to fold the undisciplined primates we are into a standardized behavioural format that is indispensable for cooperative action.

Schools and other teaching installations are the visible part of the iceberg, but education also takes place in a distributed manner through the media (books, television, journals, newspapers and other online resources). The content of the media is usually controlled by specific communities who 'edit' and 'publish' these resources according to a series of more or less explicit criteria and value systems, which they enforce with often drastic procedures. The case of scientific publication must be especially telling for the reader. The very format of scientific publication is a way to ensure that the whole scientific community continues to work properly as a single system (Lahlou, 2014); this is discussed in detail in Section 6.1.1. But the selection, censorship, editing and publishing processes are just as selective and drastic for 'good art' and a 'good story' as for 'good science'.

In sum, societies organize the systematic implementation of some behavioural principles and rules that are used in installations.

This education provides competences and skills that are transverse to installations. Because we have so far emphasized the importance of installations in the learning process of embodied competence, we must strongly state again that practice is not the only way to learn. Knowledge can be transferred onto other media than the human body (e.g. documents, speech, cognitive artefact, etc.) and transmitted in that way. It is also essential for the cohesion of a society that participants (and objects) communicate and share some value systems, symbolic systems and rules. Some of these are learned and reinforced within installations through practice, but some are learned in instructional systems (and possibly reinforced through practice).

### 5.4.4. *Objects' Specification and Control*

Communities do not only control behaviour and training. They also control the built environment. For material objects, communities set norms and control practices.

We have already encountered the existence of norms for objects when describing the reflective jacket the driver must put on when changing his tyre (Section 4.2, Figure 4.3). This small example is the tip of a gigantic iceberg: every community and organization creates a series of institutions, more or less formally coded. Nation-states edict laws and regulations. For example, in the United States, the size of the Code of Federal Regulations (CFR) gives an idea of the scale of such regulations:

> The CFR has grown by more than 42,000 pages in the last twenty years. The most recent print edition contains 174,545 thrilling pages ...The print edition takes up 238 volumes, and the index alone runs 1,242 pages. The number of individual regulatory restrictions in the CFR topped one million in 2010. (Crews & Young, 2013).

The European regulation system, which is also proliferating, includes several degrees of strength, from 'regulation' (binding legislative act), 'directive' (legislative act that sets out a goal that all European Union countries must achieve), 'decisions' (binding on those to whom it is addressed, e.g. an individual company), to 'recommendations' that are not binding (e.g. pay structures for financial sector employees should not encourage excessive risk-taking) and even 'opinions' (allowing institutions to state their preference in the debate that leads to the formulation of regulation instruments).

Similarly, every community has sets of rules (institutions, see Section 4.4) and a substantial proportion of them regard the way artefacts should be made and maintained. Every organization of some importance that produces material artefacts has its own set of internal regulations regarding its process. These regulations try to encompass almost anything that matters to the community: the purity of water used to brew beer in Germany, the content of food composition labels, the size of fishable sturgeons in rivers, the width of doors in public buildings and so on.

This is not specific to modern Western societies. One can find the same detail in the regulation of medieval guilds for the specification of silk garments (Sharon Farmer, personal communication, 2014; and see Monnas, 1988) and as far back as we can go we find similar institutional control on human activity and on the objects humans build.

At a given moment in history, all the artefacts of the same kind have a strong resemblance, what we call style, to such an extent that this enables historians, art experts and archaeologists to date the artefacts and recognize their culture of origin. Part of this family resemblance is due to the state of the technique and the materials available at a particular time and place, as well described by Deforge (1985). Aspects of this resemblance are attributable to the fact that the makers shared the same social representation of the object to be made, used a similar technological principle (Simondon, 1989) and were part of the same community of practice. But aspects of it are also due to the communal regulation governing the construction of objects at that time and place, such as norms, laws, rules of trade, traditions and the like.

The reasons behind this regulation are several. We briefly mentioned externalities in Section 4.4: the regulation can be a way to safeguard some people from the unwanted effects that a certain type of production of artefacts would have on them; for example by polluting their territory (laws limiting pollution in industrial processes) or damaging their health (laws on drugs testing). This is prevention of undesired consequences, and in reproducing objects societies want to avoid the reproduction of past mistakes, or anticipated ones.

But there is another reason, more internal to the production system itself. The various stakeholders involved in the process of (re)constructing artefacts usually have diverging interests, e.g. because they compete for resources or clients, or because they have to share the value added in the production chain. Therefore, the pattern of a product is a compromise between the interests of the various stakeholders, established through a power struggle. Communities are the theatre of such compromise-building, which incurs substantial costs and investments by the participants, with confrontations, case building, settlements, etc. The result is a solution that is 'viable' in that it is both technically feasible and reflects the respective power of the stakeholders. That solution is usually some kind of a rule or norm. For example, incandescent light bulb manufacturers agreed in the 1940s to limit the lifespan of light bulbs to 1,000 hours rather than 2,500 so as to keep the sales at a high level. ***Patterns, norms***

*or patents are ways to maintain this compromise without having to re-*
*spend the costs of reaching an agreement every time some stakeholder*
*builds a new object.*

The norms can address the result or the process; they can be more or less descriptive, more or less formal. There are norms in the regulatory sense, such as the International Standards Organization norms. These written norms give precise specifications about the form and properties of objects. They result from long and heated discussions between experts mandated by the various stakeholders.

There are also social norms that are less explicit. Cialdini and Goldstein (2009) distinguish between descriptive and injunctive norms, whereby the former refer to what is commonly done in the situations and what informs people about an effective behaviour (what other people do, some kind of social proof), whereas injunctive norms refer to the valence of behaviours and informs people about what is commonly approved (what people ought to do).

From the perspective of the user of an installation, the important point is that in the global outcome, formal procedures and informal rules can both contribute to dissatisfaction if they are not followed as expected. For example, the analysis of failure in care in British hospitals shows that 'patient neglect' can come from procedural neglect *or* 'caring neglect', - which is a more subjective notion:

> Public concern with patient neglect can focus on the neglect of institutional procedures, for example failures in washing patients or documenting data, and these incidents can occur due to a variety of reasons (e.g. error, a lack of a caring attitude). However, significant concerns also focuses on the attitudes and orientation of staff that are attributed through instances of caring neglect (e.g. ignoring a patient, rudeness, failing to respond to seemingly minor requests) that violate public expectations of 'being cared for'. (Reader & Gillespie, 2013)

Laws, treaties, regulations specific to a trade, good practice, guidebooks, specifications of calls for tenders, recommendations, etc. are some of the various names under which the specifications for a given object are produced by communities. They can be extremely prescriptive, with potentially severe penalty for offenders – as in the laws about food safety; or they can just be a tradition and a support for those who want to act, as the traditional motifs of the decoration of Easter eggs in Romania (Glăveanu & Lahlou, 2012). Regulation of the physical objects produced is systematic and we can clearly see the institutions' regulation at work there.

But institutions also regulate in other, less obvious ways, by creating templates, formats, structures, categories in which actors must fit information, interactions, transactions, behaviours or material production.

Eymard-Duvernay and Thévenot called 'investments in form' the symbolic formats that result from this negotiation work between stakeholders, their seminal example being how the French statistical system classifies socioeconomic classes with reference to professional occupation (Eymard-Duvernay & Thévenot, 1983). More generally, an investment in form 'is as a costly operation to establish a stable relation with a certain *lifespan*' (Thévenot, 1984: 11).

These forms are used to 'format' situations and action. They help in the identification of situations (that is: choosing in which box of the form this situation is to be put, and to what ideal type it is to be assimilated). This results in categories, and procedures, that are typifications of situations and courses of action. For each ideal type of situation there are a series of possible courses of action to take (ideally, one only), typified by procedures. A procedure will prescribe what steps of action should be undertaken then, and in what order.

This is especially salient in sophisticated installations where in practice decision-making has been transformed into a diagnosis phase and a choice of procedures. And for a given diagnosis, the organization provides a list of possible procedures and even algorithms (see Glossary) to choose between them. For example, in hospitals or in police operations professionals are trained to apply such procedures, which become so familiar that they are often designated by their acronyms. In case of failure, personnel may face difficulties with their internal control instance if it is discovered that they did not follow the procedure.

Let us illustrate this with three cases that show institutional regulation of behaviour.

**Case 1:** Collaborative implementation of the control-command curve of a nuclear reactor during a test referred to as 'EP-RGL-4' (Fauquet-Alekhine, 2016b):

During one of the phases of this test fully structured by a procedure of several tens of pages, a testing technician has to carry out measurements in the control-command system with the help of a reactor pilot moving the control rods of the nuclear core (only pilots are allowed to handle control-command equipment). This enables the feeding of new values inside the control-command system afterwards and the improvement of the control of the reactor.

During this phase, the testing technician stands close to the pilot in front of the control panel in the control room. The technician reads the procedure step by step, asking the pilot to move the rods at a given level. In addition, to reduce the risk of misunderstanding to a minimum, they are required to apply three-way communication: every time the technician asks for an action, before acting, the pilot repeats exactly what he heard and the technician confirms using a dedicated expression 'correct' (or, in case of error, repeats what he expects) and while the pilot operates, the technician checks whether the action is as expected or not.

**Case 2.** Kirsten, an anaesthesiologist, is taking care of a case of chronic bronchopulmonary disease, whose blood oxygen is getting very low. She decides to go for intubation. In the course of doing so, she applies the algorithm that is recommended (which looks a bit like the one pictured on Figure 4.18, from the same hospital): first she tries with the standard (Fastrach) laryngoscope, then the video laryngoscope, then the laryngomask, and if none works, then she must go for tracheotomy. The doctor and the nurse must each make one attempt with the laryngoscope (to give a better chance since every practitioner operates slightly differently). Kirsten rehearses aloud the plan with the nurse, and they follow the procedure until tracheotomy.

In this case, the social layer is used not only through the procedure, but also because the doctor and the nurse communicate. Kirsten also checked whether the nurse agreed on her diagnosis and decision before she started the procedure.

**Case 3.** A police officer is called to a domestic incident. He finds the couple heavily drunk, the woman screaming and the man bleeding; but neither of them wants to make an allegation. Thus, stripped of any formal grounds to act on the assault that clearly occurred, the officer ultimately arrests the woman for 'breach of the peace' just to keep the two separated for the night and allow them to sober up.

Here is how the officer comments on the case: 'We are trying to establish what happened. So this guy is saying "the dog jumped up and hit me in the face" and that is where the blood comes from ... Because we had no allegations we are in a tough spot. Even we can quite clearly see that something has happened. We haven't got a victim or an allegation. There is not much we can do. So the lady was being quite verbally abusive and quite loud so it was decided to arrest her under a breach of the peace. Which means she comes here [in custody] gets to sleep it off. No more argument at the house anymore that night and hopefully once they both got some sleep and sobered up they go back and everything will be all right again. Fingers crossed. (Rieken, 2013: 116–7)

Here the law intervenes two times. The first time, it prevents the police officer from arresting one of the couple, because he cannot proceed unless someone makes a statement. But as the officer realizes that he must separate the couple, he uses another law, where in this case he can decide to arrest the woman (who seems to be the aggressor). Interestingly, we see that although institutional constraints may be strong, humans can be creative in using them. Of course this depends on the cases. In case 1, the operator has no choice. In case 2, the procedure can be amended, it is the doctor's decision.

The reader may wonder why such examples of investments in form as fixed procedures sit in this section. That is a deep question, and I am not sure myself. My intuition is that investments in form are halfway between objects and rules, and their production has a lot in common with the production of objects.

Just as the criterion for the reproduction of competences is the good end of its effect, operationalized by the positive reward to the individual (reaching the goal or getting good social feedback), the criterion for reproduction of an object is its fit to end-user practices (does it work?) and to the local production processes (is the sum of interests for those who make it available sufficient to compensate for the costs and impediments it takes to make it?). This is operationalized by the decisions taken by the regulation authority, who selects what form(s) of the object are acceptable. In many cases, as in the market system of economic life, the authorities simply transmit the demand of the end users, while introducing some filtering and modifications to limit negative externalities and to leverage some positive externalities (such as the investments of form that save a lot of transaction costs).

### 5.4.5.  *Authority, Rule Management and Governance: Reproduction of the Institutional Layer*

For a given system of rules, community members are expected to comply. Those who do not comply are either informally reminded by other members or summoned by specialized enforcing personnel (e.g. the police).

Finally, those who breach the conventions are punished and/or excluded from the community. There are often specific bodies, councils or tribunals that evaluate the cases, based on jurisprudence and previous cases, in order to rule.

The practical implementation of regulation of behaviours occurs through rules or processes that can determine whether this or that specific behaviour is acceptable or not. There are different ways to construct such rules/processes and publish them.

In practice, the construction of regulation is no trivial thing. There are many types of regulation; they vary by principle, by mode of construction, by format, by content, by degree of compliance expected, by degree of precision, by domain of application, by character; they are implemented with different strategies. Let us take the example of principles-based regulation (PBR):

> The rhetoric of PBR thus invokes, not deregulation, but a re-framing of the regulatory relationship from one of directing and controlling to one based on responsibility, mutuality and trust. Regulators and regulatees move from a directing relationship of telling and doing, to a relationship in which regulators communicate their goals and expectations clearly in principles and apply those principles predictably, regulatees adopt a self-reflective approach to the development of processes and practices to ensure that these goals are substantively met, and, critically, both trust each other to fulfil their side of this new regulatory bargain. (Black, 2008)

That type of regulation which relies on some degree of self-regulation by the target public differs in spirit and format from e.g. rules of the road, table manners, nuclear plant operating instructions or light bulb production norms; the latter are more directive. The existence of diverse approaches in regulation is understandable because of the variety of domains, but also of actors:

> Those who know what they are meant to be doing and are generally inclined to do it (the well intentioned and well informed) are best dealt with using a negotiating strategy, which is easier to do using principles. In contrast, those who do not know what they are meant to be doing and even if they did would not be inclined to do it (the ill-intentioned and ill informed) are best dealt with using a strategy that is more targeted, for which bright line rules[69] are more effective. (Black, 2010)

---

[69] A principle is more general than a bright line rule. For example: 'A firm must execute all orders of under 10,000 securities within one business day' is a bright line rule, whereas 'A firm must pay due regard to the interests of its customers and treat them fairly' is a principle (Black, 2008).

Law and political science; but also religion and ethics spend considerable efforts to construct 'proper' regulation.

All human communities put in place authorities in charge of *governance*. Governance is in charge of making sure the rules are applied; and also of adapting or changing the rules. There are many different kinds of governance, in the ways that they are defined, implemented, chosen and applied. Their study is in the realm of political science and beyond the scope of this book; nevertheless, it is key for our consideration here that *every installation is governed by some specific authority that is in charge of its maintenance and possibly its evolution.*

That authority (who is usually responsible for regulating the daily operations) will be the one that decides what physical objects are OK to use in the installation when the time comes to decide it (e.g. when components are damaged, obsolete or need replacement). That authority has legitimacy to rule this specific installation and therefore its influence is paramount. It is also usually empowered to enforce the rules in the domain of that installation, and therefore has power in that domain. We see here that knowledge, responsibility, power and legitimacy tend to go together with the authority in charge of the installation. This explains why some sources (those entitled with authority) have more influence over the subjects using the installation; and also why there are power struggles between stakeholders (to control or influence this authority) and how the disputes are settled (often by this authority). We look into the role of the authorities of the installation more in Section 7.5 when we consider evolution, because these authorities have an important say in what evolutions are fostered or hampered.

At any given moment, a community has a set of communal institutions about governance that constitute its political system. That includes laws, codes, unwritten rules, attribution of responsibility and decision-making power over domains, procedures for distributing the power and creating or amending rules and roles. In the course of daily governance and in the discussions and struggle occurring from various changes that must be dealt with, the political system evolves. This evolution is naturally connected to the other layers, i.e. because 'normal' practice tends to become formalized by law, or because new phenomena require ruling. So communities themselves evolve. I leave the vast study of the evolution of communities and governance outside of the scope this book, but this evolution has impact on local installations, as shown in Chapter 7, given that communities rule installations.

**What is to be noted from the this in a pragmatic perspective is that authorities who rule installations should therefore be the main target**

of interventions that aim at changing the social regulation layer; and also that when we intervene at this level we should be aware that we will get involved in a series of power struggles because behind each rule stands a hard-won compromise between interested stakeholders.

## 5.5.  Takeaway: Distributed Control, Distributed Reproduction

In the previous sections above we detail the reproduction cycle of installations and its components. In doing so, we give flesh to the idea that **practice regenerates culture, and culture reproduces practice. Although the idea appears simple, the mechanics of it combine a complex combination of concurrent processes, most of them involving installations.**

### 5.5.1.  *Reproduction of the Embodied Layer*

First, individuals learn through practice of the installations. Because installations are resilient to incompetence, novices manage to perform the correct behaviour, and in doing so get positive, reinforcing feedback. This results, through learning processes, in the embodiment of the correct competences, which can be traced to the inscription in their brain. Novices are helped because they may also get a formal education that prepares them to correct their performance and also social feedback on-the-fly from other participants in the installation.[70] More generally, the learning process takes place as the novice is gradually inserted into a community of practice with other users of the installation.[71]

In the course of this process, we recognized in various forms a similar approach to problems: using existing competence as a default approach, adapting it when it does not work and capitalizing on the new experience acquired for future use. We called such strategies the *betterment loop.*

---

[70] There is substantial redundancy in the social mechanisms that ensure the novice embodies the proper culture during development; see also (Valsiner, 2006: 44, 223, 355).

[71] 'In our view, participation at multiple levels is entailed in membership in a community of practice … It does imply participation in an activity system about which participants share understandings concerning what they are doing and what that means in their lives and for their communities … A community of practice is a set of relations among persons, activity, and world, over time and in relation with other tangential and overlapping communities of practice'. (Lave & Wenger, 1991: 98)

This accounts for how the structure of the installation, and its practice by the subjects, results in the subjects embodying the appropriate competences in their body and mind – therefore regenerating the 'embodied' layer of the installation. These competences are the automatic interpretation of the situation into a 'correct' response (action or thought) that becomes a second nature. The process could be compared to a very large scale and distributed brainwash. The resulting psychological layer serves individuals as a situational manual that they carry around with their body; it includes the cognitive skills, experiences and knowledge that allow them to take appropriate action in the situations they encounter, and especially in installations.

We have shown how many entities involved in the processes above can be considered as 'paradigms', sets of elements that are at the same time somewhat similar and somewhat different. Paradigms account for the flexibility and adaptability of embodied competences.

### 5.5.2.   *Reproduction of the Material Layer*

The physical layer of installations, material objects, undergoes a continuous reproduction cycle based on templates. A model or representation (plan, blueprint, formal description, specifications) is produced from existing material objects; then a new, similar object is produced based on this model. Within this production process, care is taken to suppress all emerging variability to produce an object as identical to the model as possible. Several mechanisms of control during design and production ensure that match between the symbolic and concrete formats of the object (the blueprints and the physical exemplars) and that the resulting objects are adapted to actual practice.

Objects also come in large quantities of similar but individually slightly different exemplars (cars, chairs, etc.).

### 5.5.3.   *Community Monitoring of the Embodied and Material Layer*

Finally, the two reproduction processes (of competences and objects) are monitored by communities. For the reproduction of competences, communities organize the embodiment processes in such a way that the competences embodied are the correct ones, transferred deliberately by the previous generation (e.g. in communities of practice, through instruction). They forbid and punish exemplarily any incorrect behaviour in public space to avoid those becoming precedents and inspiration. They make explicit what behaviours are correct with sets of rules, customs and laws.

Communities also rule the reproduction of material objects with norms and regulations. Creation of objects outside of these tolerances is forbidden; incorrect objects are taken away from installations or destroyed. In doing this, communities operate in a preventive and somewhat eugenic way. Communities create and enforce the rules with specific personnel devoted to control, like the International Standards Organization.

Finally, communities also exert direct control over adult individuals themselves, because even with these precautions some subversive behaviour may occur, and they establish governance systems from that perspective. These governance systems edict the rules and law; they come with ownership and control over installations and command of the policing forces. The rules reify semistable compromises between stakeholders with different interest.

And of course, communities also evolve.

Communities tend to try to organize the reproduction of the layers transversally as well as locally. Education systems such as schools are focused on the embodiment of generic competences that address all sorts of installations; generic economic regulations (e.g. commerce laws) tend to address all sorts of material production; finally, the legal system is concerned with everything regulatory and administering social feedback in general.

There are reasons for this effort of maintaining coherence across each type of layer (as opposed to by specific installation), but also some pure efficiency issues. It is sometimes easier to do the whole layer in one go. That is precisely what is done in physical reproduction systems like halftone printing or photo printing (Figure 5.12), which are printed in colour layer by colour layer.

As we see from this metaphor of printing, the global pattern can to some extent be recognized on each layer, but one layer alone gives an incomplete representation.

Although the general picture of society I have just summarized may appear totalitarian, in practice the exercise of this regulating power is not in the hands of a single tyrant, and there is no such thing as a master plan. The bulk of power and control are exerted in a distributed manner, locally, with *subsidiarity* (see Glossary), often by the very participants themselves. As we saw, for example, each of us acts as a self-controller, sometimes zealous, and as a controller for others

Figure 5.12. Example of a litho print (*left*) obtained by the superimposition of four layers (*right*): cyan, magenta, yellow and black – also called 'Key'). A black and white version of this figure will appear in some formats. For the colour version, please refer to the plate section.

(the vigilante effect). The social rules are constructed in common, as a result of political processes, and they reflect the respective power of the stakeholders in the construction process. How democratic the emerging results are depends upon the political structures of the society. The rules are often made explicit in the form of laws, norms and the like, but most of them remain informal local norms and know-how. Moreover, this controlling power is also, as Foucault had already understood, an enabling power – it is inseparable from knowledge and agency.[72]

A substantial amount of that power and control has been reified into affordances of constructed objects, and thereby delegated to non-human 'actants'. In the same vein, social influence has become reified into impersonal 'rules', which can be recalled by nonhuman media, actants and external representations.

The resulting regulation is continuous, detailed and thorough. It is efficient because it does not only operate *ex post* in suppressing the incorrect; it is preventive and quick to eliminate every potential exemplar of what could become a bad precedent.

There is, as mentioned several times, leeway and slack in the system. First, individuals are to a large extent free to choose which installations they enter and it is at this level that free will is most often exercised.

Then individuals retain a capacity to choose to perform different behaviours in a given installation. A first level of variation, tuning, is normal and expected, which is the local adaptation of behaviour

---

[72] With the proviso that there may be some contradiction in the rules or in the embodied interpretive systems, as described in the case of Colombia, where the moral and social norms were contradictory.

to specific conditions. A second level, diversity, includes behaviours that are expected and acceptable alternatives to the norm. A third level includes behaviours that contravene the norm and societies spend considerable energy to eradicate that third type.

There can be errors, innovation or deviance, depending on what layers they concern. Nevertheless, overall the behaviours appear rather standardized and controlled. Such a degree of agency and control is far beyond the capacity of any single authority: it would require a policeman for each citizen – and even then… The solution that emerged in societies goes a degree further: not only is everyone one's own controller, but he or she is also the controller for everyone else in their local environment – and especially in the installations they use. Every loyal member is expected to support and regulate others in the installations they use. The chore of helping and controlling is massively distributed. On top of that we have convoked nonhuman supports that scaffold[73] us all the way in our use of installations.

Subsidiarity is an essential characteristic of the process. The system can work flawlessly because control and scaffolding are exerted at the point of delivery – installations – rather than through some distant feedback loops.

Indeed, as we saw, regulation is distributed *locally* in the installations. The physical context provides material affordances, which open an array of possible paths. Social feedback suggests some privileged paths among these possibilities, and forbids others. Embodied competences enable the recognition of a framework for action in these patterns and generates a choice of next steps in these paths. As each step is taken, a new situation unfolds and the process of choosing an appropriate path considering the situation is reiterated, still within the tunnel of control. Between one step and the next, feedback enables an assessment of the step that has just been carried out. Did things go as expected? Am I progressing towards my goal as expected? Do I get positive social feedback? Based on this, I proceed to the next step according to what is expected. But I also update my expectations and competences. Therefore update of the system is also distributed.

---

[73] In scaffolding we can include even support that does not fade. In practice subjects can themselves 'fade' the use of the scaffolding devices when they have embodied sufficient competences. For example, the experienced and agile staircase user stops holding on to the banister, the expert does not use the user's instruction sheet, the professional photographer turns off the automatic features and uses his camera in manual mode.

We can now catch sight, in the process of the maintenance of installations, of the answer to our main research questions:

- How, in practice, is the continuous predictability and efficient control of the behaviour of millions of individuals (with often conflicting interests) that is necessary for smooth operation of societies constructed?
- How can individual humans make sense on the fly of the rich, ambiguous and complex environments of society and take appropriate action (keeping in mind humans are cognitive misers)?

Vast as the problems behind these questions are, they required a massive answer. That is indeed what societies provide: regulation is massively *distributed* in the very fabric of installations.

**Regarding the question of action from the perspective of the individual,** as noted by Klein and Calderwood (1991) **decision-making in natural contexts is characterized by 'high time pressure, uncertainty, and ambiguity, continually changing conditions, ill-defined goals, and distributed decision responsibilities'. The classic models based on the (more or less rational) calculation by the subject of the possible outcomes of the various alternatives of a tree of possibilities do not work in practice. We saw how installation theory proposes a model different from individual decision-making, a model where behaviour emerges as the result of distributed agency in the installation, which is both enabling and constraining. This process requires little rational calculation from the subject and capitalizes on previous experience to produce a correct outcome.**

In this respect, installation theory points to decision-making systems that are closer to the recognition-primed decision (RPD) than to the classic cognitive models such as the theory of reasoned action.

> The [RPD] model differs from standard models in that it begins with action based on the recognition of a situation as familiar or prototypical and posits a serial option evaluation strategy ... The model simply illustrates several types of recognitional decision strategies. A person understands a situation in terms of its familiarity to previous experiences. The judgment of familiarity to a given set of prior cases carries with it a recognition of goals that are feasible, cues that are relevant, expectancies to monitor, and actions that are plausible. The decision maker can use experience to generate a likely option as the first one considered. The evaluation of the option is through mental simulation to see if there are any pitfalls to carrying the option out. If these can be remedied, the option can be strengthened. If not, the option is rejected. If no pitfalls are envisioned, the option can be used. (Klein & Calderwood, 1991)

What is added here is *why* RPD can work in practice: because *installations* provide recognizable settings, where RPD is not only fostered but appropriate and correct, **as a result of accumulated sociohistoric experience capitalized in the installation. Installations frame the behaviour by providing situated choice among limited alternatives. We also saw how, with the paradigm effect, subjects can typify situations to be dealt with and choose from an array of alternative similar solutions.**

Finally, what installation theory adds is that, on top of this process, **there are also mechanisms of control by other participants to ensure the behaviour is correct all the way, and self-controlling conformity drives where participants actively strive to follow the socially correct script. And of course, reasoning and calculation can always kick in when the above fail to satisfice.**

**Regarding the first question (action from the perspective of society), the answer, is, as announced, the same: society (if we can impersonate such an emergent entity) constructs installations that locally channel individual behaviour in a resilient and distributed manner. Therefore, the answer is one of subsidiarity rather than central control. Things are taken care of locally. Individuals themselves are trained, and conditioned, into being part of these installations, as volunteer actors and as controllers. The process is somewhat similar to stigmergy, where individuals effect the behaviour of other individuals through mediating objects, but in this case other humans are also used as mediating objects.**

**In other words, the regulation system, both enabling and constraining, is reified and distributed at such a scale that it is continuous and ubiquitous.** *To some degree, almost every piece of the society and the built environment, every component of the material and symbolic culture, is participating in locally enabling and constraining some specific activity.* **This state of things is the result of millennia of continuous exploration and reconstruction where 'correct' solutions have been maintained by the ratchet effect of culture and others eliminated.**

**We can now judge the scale of this answer. It is indeed massive beyond imagination; it looks like some paranoid vision where everything around us conspires to help and control. The operation and regulation of societies actually involve the participation of *all* loyal members of the society, plus the built environment, plus the accumulated knowledge of all previous generations. These enormous resources are mobilized continuously everywhere, every second and every inch. They are mobilized in installations, which are run and controlled by**

their very local experts themselves, adding the precision of subsidiarity to the efficiency of labour division.

When one looks at the bewildering coercive and enabling power of such a regulating process, it becomes conceivable that indeed even the smallest of cogs in the machinery are empowered to operate correctly in a continuous and reliable manner.

**The system is (diachronically) continuously reconstructed through synchronous practice, not just through education of individuals, but by constantly regenerating the three layers of installations, in a distributed and local manner. This process is enabled by the resilience of installations, and the minor necessary adjustments often use the betterment loop.**

What is especially remarkable is the distributed nature of reproduction. This point deserves specific attention and has not so far been described. Society contains a very large number of local installations. We took as an introduction the metaphor of halftone printing, in which an image is represented by a series of points of various sizes, and where each point's colour is created by the superimposition of three dots of primary colours. We extended the metaphor in Section 5.5 by saying that the three local dots would be the components in the different layers. We saw at this point that the installation had a functional role: as the device where the local behaviours are channeled. Therefore, someone making her way in the social environment (the big picture) would *at each point of her trajectory* be channelled by the local installation, which acts as a behavioural attractor. That is the process we described in the introduction with the example of the airline passenger.

We have seen in this chapter that **these installation points also act as the reproduction points of society. Each installation reproduces itself, with the various layers having diverse but intertwined reproduction processes. What appears here is that these reproduction mechanisms are local – even though there may be to some degree interdependence with the global picture, and with other points, especially the similar ones. But this brings us to the amazing, and rather new, idea that societies do not reproduce as a whole, as an organism, as a structure, but** *point by point,* **locally and at different local pace. Let us call this** *distributed reproduction.* Contrary to a mechanical printing process, where the grid of each colour layer is reproduced on the whole sheet of paper in one single application (e.g. green, then red, then blue) **the reproduction of society takes place point by point, at a rhythm that is defined by local constraints.**

Of course, the third layer tries to impose some larger, e.g. national or global, level of reproduction, with laws applicable across a whole organization or nation *at the same time*. Of course, some education systems try to cast simultaneously a whole generation of individuals. Of course, mass media and mass production target large publics simultaneously. But the nature of social reproduction, and its spontaneous reproduction, rely massively on local and distributed practice in installations.

This has two consequences: resilience and diversity.

Now comes the other side of the problem: beyond reproduction, change. In such a controlled reproducing machine, what is the space left for free will, invention, creativity? How can evolution and change take place?

That, reader, is the focus of the next two chapters: Chapter 6, Selection Mechanisms in Societal Evolution: Two Cases, Science and Industry, and Chapter 7, The Evolution of Installations.

# CHAPTER 6

# Selection Mechanisms in Societal Evolution
## Two Cases: Science and Industry

**After having seen the massive feedforward and feedback forces that resist change, it is almost surprising that there is any change at all, but there is.**

**We must understand what enables change to come through, and for that we have to understand which are the selection criteria that halt some changes and let some others pass. We must also understand the forces behind the generation of potential changes.**

**The mechanisms of evolution that are described in Chapter 7 are complicated, so I thought it would be easier to start with examples to illustrate the societal mechanisms of generation and selection of changes.**

**In this section we study two cases, scientific progress and product innovation, to extract from this empirical material some principles used by society to select what makes changes acceptable, in the symbolic and material realms.**

Considering the complexity of the homeostatic control systems that rule societal management and reproduction described in the previous chapters, it is understandable that any responsible actor would be reluctant to step outside of the explored and safe routine of institutions to take the risk of changing something: 'if it ain't broke, don't fix it'.

And indeed, in organizations, when an 'improvement' is proposed that is not *absolutely necessary*, experienced managers usually cling to the unwritten principles of cautious inertia. Consider for example those principles that highly qualified high civil servants (informally) learn at ENA, the French national school of administration (elite institution and gateway to the highest political positions): 'MSWCI' ('My Successor Will Consider It') and 'NWOCNW' (No Waves, Old Chap, No Waves).[1]

The inertia of systems is visible in some odd designs, habits or rules. Three examples:

- The shape of wine bottles is not so much determined by what would be the optimal envelope of a container for liquids, but rather by what was technically feasible long time ago.
- 'A man who raises his hat in greeting is unwittingly reactivating a conventional sign inherited from the Middle-Age, when, as Panofsky [Panofsky, 1939: 4] reminds us, armed men used to take off their helmets to make clear their peaceful intentions'. (Bourdieu, 2014: 304)
- 'Democratic royalties' as observed in today's Europe are a sequel of political history where leadership was hereditary.

Change is costly because it means creation and destruction, by definition, as well as transaction costs between parties involved to reach a compromise. It does not come easy because of conflicts of interests, of uncertainty of outcomes, of disagreements and misunderstandings. Evolution is the result of struggles and compromises, which may include violent conflicts. It involves dialectic processes, or rather the combination of many multiparty confrontations, coalitions, discoveries, co-constructions etc.

Even in the absence of conflicts, change has a cost per se, as a process of reconstructing installations. When a professional cook changes kitchen, he loses 30% of his efficacy. One reason is the time spent to look for things (Frederic Martin, chef and professor of cooking, personal communication, July 2015). In a restaurant that operates with a menu, the kitchen works on the same dishes every day. When the menu is changed, the brigade needs several services, perhaps up to a week, to readjust. (ibid.).

Such considerations go against change; therefore homeostatic feedback may happen at two stages: first, a reluctance to act by anticipating overall harmful consequences or simply their possibility (see the 'precautionary principle' in the Glossary); second, a negative reaction (resistance, direct opposition, retaliation, countermeasures) by those negatively affected. The latter negative reactions are often the main source of reluctance to change, because they are anticipated by rulers, as well as the transaction costs the

---

[1] MSVC (Mon successeur verra ça) and PDVMVPDV (Pas de Vagues, Mon Vieux, Pas de Vagues). The flavour is vernacular; it is difficult to translate the mix of wisdom, detachment, cynicism, entitlement and icy humour these acronyms carry.

rulers will themselves incur in solving the ensuing conflicts of interests. Resistance can be considered a healthy reaction of the system, and an alert to the change agents signalling where the change creates problems – rather than a sign of the stubbornness of those impacted (Bauer, 1995; Dent & Goldberg, 1999; Lawrence, 1964).

Nevertheless, sometimes the course of history does force actors to change the installations; for example, when the climate changes, when epidemics arise, when the current system fails to satisfice. And even in the absence of accidents or shortcomings, we often feel the current system is not optimal, that something better could be done, that a better world is possible.

In sum, change is both risky and potentially beneficial. Societies, and individuals, are confronted with a contradiction: the simultaneous necessities to change and to stay the same.

Because installations are a pragmatic cultural solution to format and resolve problems and to maintain appropriate solutions, the construction of new installations, or the adaptation of existing ones, addresses the need for change. As we shall see, the evolution of a specific installation is affected by the above constraints issues on change because an installation cannot be abstracted from its societal ecosystem, because it uses shared resources and it impacts other installations.[2] To deal with these complex issues, a series of mechanisms for generating solutions and selecting those that are satisficing at both the local level of the installation and at the larger level of society have emerged. These mechanisms are the object of this chapter and the next.

I now illustrate of how creativity and selection happen in society with two cases: science and industrial innovation. Science is the business of changing the contents of the interpretation layer; innovation is more about changing the contents of the physical layer.

---

[2] That is a general issue in evolution: because the parts of an ecosystem are interweaved, a subsystem's characteristics integrate constraints from its larger ecosystem and result from its historical development. In biology, take the long neck of the giraffe species, for example; it results from a gradual and symmetrical escalation in the interaction with its food providers. Acacias have thorns to protect them from herbivory by such animals as goats and giraffes; thorns are larger in the lower areas of the tree that are more accessible to herbivores (Milewski, Young, & Madden, 1991). Reflecting on technology, Simondon came up with the notion of 'individuation', the genetic process in which something emerges as an individual object from its milieu and in relation to it (Simondon [1958] 2013: 79–82). As in the metaphor of the crystal grown from the latent forces in the saturated solution, the essence of the object lies in its individuating relation to the properties of its milieu. Individuation process is never-ending, even though one can observe metastable plateaus; for example (components of) technical objects may find some optimal form that remain similar for a long period (Simondon [1958] 1989: 27–35).

After we have seen these two examples we will know more about the mechanisms at work.

To maintain the reader's motivation after what must have been the painful exercise of reading Chapters 4 and 5, here is a preview: the case of science shows the importance of external representations (models) and coordination in the construction of knowledge; the case of industry illustrates why societies are obliged to exert an intense and reactionary selection in constructing new artefacts. These two aspects appear later as essential in the process of modifying installations.

I must apologize in advance for caricature, oversimplification, shallowness and incompleteness in my presentation the cases: they are intended to highlight some specific mechanisms to understand the evolution of installations, not to provide an accurate account of the nature of Science and Innovation, which are far beyond the scope of this book.

## 6.1. Science

Science aims to provide models of phenomena, models that are descriptive, explanatory and/or predictive. In a way, science is the ultimate human process for producing and transmitting interpretive competences about the world. That is worth taking a closer look.

Modern science is specific in that it seeks to control and trace the mechanisms of its constructive efforts; it organizes the social division of labour of scientists and the collective construction of their production (knowledge). Science is systematic and explicit, both in the way of classifying its findings and in the way they are sought. These systematic and explicit aspects help us understand the mechanisms at work.

A naive view of science is of the great scholar struck by the illumination of an 'insight' after a lengthy solo work, as allegedly Archimedes discovering a law of physics in his bathtub. A mainstream theory of science is that every new hypothesis is tested for validity by systematic empirical investigation before being incorporated in the framework of an existing theory. Sometimes theories change and are replaced by new frameworks that integrate better the sum of verified findings, including those that did not fit well in the previous framework (Kuhn, 1996). In principle, testing is done through confrontation of the hypothesis with empirical data, from direct observation or observation obtained through experiments, in such a way that findings are open to peer review. This systematic process of trial and verification is assumed to produce an objective progression of knowledge. In principle, again, there is a series of criteria that enable choosing the best theories: accuracy, consistency, scope, simplicity and fruitfulness (Kuhn [1973] 1977a: 321–2).

As shown for example by sociology of science (Latour et al., 1986; Latour, 1987), the reality of the process differs from the naive model, and also somewhat from the theory (Latour et al, 1986, Latour 1987). Science is above all a collective work of communities; it is based on technical objects, devices, institutions. There is indeed debate and controversy in various public arenas, but the social construction that results is path-dependent and involves many more parameters than simply whether a hypothesis is proved false or true, or how fruitful a theory can be. In practice, making such a decision is not straightforward (e.g. a first problem is *who* makes that decision).

Because there are many local cultures in science, and many ways of doing, empirical studies of how science is done highlight different versions; that makes it difficult to tell the wood from the trees. Therefore I ground my analysis on a process that is common to most natural sciences, and a key part of researcher's training: the structure of academic productions: publications.

A warning here: by no means should the following sections be considered an analysis of the global scientific system, which is complex, diverse, has evolved through history and has been aptly analysed by specialists elsewhere. I am merely focusing on one aspect, publication, and simplify its description to highlight some generative and selection mechanisms that are useful for our analysis of installation's evolution.

I show how the structure of the external representations (publications) reveals the mechanisms of generation and selection of new models, and how that labour is divided.

### 6.1.1.    *The Classic Scientific Format*

A classic (empirical) 'scientific' paper comes in the form of nine components, usually in the following sequence; although some are possibly aggregated into a single section, and minor variations are tolerated.

(1) Introduction: Describes the research question, and its importance, often in the form of a larger problem to address in the real world.
(2) Literature Review: Works in the author's discipline and subfield, which cites what other work addressed the issue, and describes their content succinctly.
(3) The 'Gap to Fill' in Literature: Specifies which specific unsolved challenges this specific paper will contribute to solve. This must include a

clearly formulated research question (small sentence ending with a '?') In some disciplines the questions should be formulated as hypotheses that can be verified.

(4) Materials and Methods: What empirical data and methods were chosen, and the rationale for this choice to address the research question. This section should be detailed enough to enable the reader to replicate the work or verify the results.

(5) Analysis: Application of the methods described in (4) to the material collected. Presentation of the results.

(6) Discussion: Comparison of results obtained in (5) with what is known from (2).

(7) Conclusion: What this research contributes to the question (1) and the state of the art (2) and how much it contributed to close the gap (3). Future research directions (what remains to be done to close the gap).

(8) Bibliography: References used that allow knowledge to be cumulative, so one can write (2) and (3) without having to repeat at length what is contained in the references cited.

(9) Appendices: More precise elements, relevant for checking the validity of the work, and which serve to successors who will work on the same question. They are set in the Appendix to keep the volume of the main body of the paper within reasonable limits, and in the format of the publication outlet.

When I was a PhD student, I was reluctant to use that formal structure, and I still observe that same reluctance among my own doctoral students now. This is because we have never been explained properly why we must put our communication in such a straitjacket.

This construction is indeed the direct result of the process of division of scientific labour. In fact *this structure is the minimal set of content that satisfices the necessity of collaborative and cumulative work; each section matches a functional requirement.*

Before I explain further, allow me to take the metaphor of science as a building construction site. Construction involves different bodies of complementary trades (e.g. mason, plumber) and in each trade often several workers. Assume I am a mason. Suppose my own endeavour is to build up a brick wall for the boiler room in the cellar of building #4. The 'problem' is to close that boiler room properly. That comes as a pragmatic gap to fill.

That boiler room is already half built by colleagues from another company who laid down the concrete floor. When I check in at the gate of the construction site, I must tell the guard what is my trade and in which building I am coming to do work. It is essential for me, and for other trades, that the work I do actually contribute to the final project. There is no need to build a wall where there is already one (e.g. in building #3). Once in building #4, my work must take into account what has already been done by colleagues, and be continued with materials relevant for the problem at hand (e.g. bricks). I must use appropriate methods to process that job material that comply with the rules of the trade and the regulations (e.g. stacking them with cement). And once my job is done, because others may continue the work (e.g. the painter), I must report clearly what remains to be done. A mason who does not respect these rules, however competent, would quickly be out of job, and other builders would not want to work with him, because the rules above are essential to successful collaboration. These are very general rules for collaboration in distributed labour, and, unsurprisingly, we find they must be applied in the collaborative and distributed endeavour that is science.

Science, just as building construction, is essentially a distributed work; this is what makes its strength. In that perspective, it is essential to respect the collective process. Because progress comes from a systematic and progressive accumulation, it is vital that each scientist respect the process. In particular, she must announce where she will place her bit, take into account previous work, operate according to common verifiable rules and account for her contribution in a way that allows subsequent capitalization. If we knowledge workers see more and further than our predecessors it is because we are, as Bernard de Chartres suggested, dwarfs perched on the shoulders of our giant predecessors,[3] the way we balance on each other's shoulders must be organized so that layers are stable. In such a large and distributed system, the individual work of each actor, drowned in such statistical mass, has little importance. As long as the gaps are identified and signalled, at some point someone will come and fill them. In fact, often the same gaps are filled several times, experiments replicated and models tested and retested, until the collective is certain that the filling is solid.

*In all this process, the existence of external representations (the publications) is essential to enable cooperation, confrontation and capitalization. Not only do external representations facilitate communication, but they enable representing the content of that communication into something that can be easily transferred (models). Furthermore they enable storing and capitalizing the*

---

[3] 'Nanos gigantum humeris insidentes'(Bernard de Chartres, oral communication to John of Salisbury, twelfth century, in Salisbury & McGarry, 1955: 167).

*models. This ensures that progress is made in a coherent manner and that the new tiles with the old.*

Let me take another metaphor, that of hunting wild boar. In this process a group of 'beaters' progresses in line, beating the bushes. Afraid, the animals flee, but in doing so they meet the hunters waiting in ambush at the other end of the forest, who shoot them. The key to success is the coordination of individual efforts, causing the forest to be combed in a systematic and comprehensive way. In this process, each participant contributes fairly simply, without needing much intelligence, but the result is an inevitable success – provided everyone does their share of work properly. Because the action is distributed it is efficient and powerful: one hundred stupid but disciplined beaters with a couple of not-so-smart-either shooters at the other end will produce many times more than the best hunter could ever do alone. Such is the efficiency of distributed action.

Labour division in science is afforded by external representations; they facilitate coordination and collating small pieces of knowledge which have been locally found. Labour division and coordination enable devolving what is to be done into small simple roles that can be executed with minimal competence. External representations enable leveraging collective intelligence.

What I intend to show with these metaphors is that science does not so much need geniuses or heroes but rather the systematic and coordinated work of many disciplined agents. *The intelligence is in the process, and the process is reified in the medium of external representations.* And if a great scientist of exceptional ability wants to contribute, she must do it within the rules of distributed work, otherwise her work will remain unused.

The standard academic document structure accurately reflects the constraints of the distributed and capitalizing processes I just described. The scientist must first explain in what spot, and in conjunction with which community, the work will be done (what building, which trade? – What problem, which discipline?) Then specify the exact nature of the work, why it is required in the larger division of labour (gap to be filled). Next, specify how and with what methods the work was done, so its quality can be known or controlled (materials and methods). Then describe the result of actual work (analysis) and, consequently, which part of the gap was filled and what remains to be done (discussion, conclusion). The bibliography attests to the care with which the work was inserted into the fabric of the prior work of the community; it is therefore an essential mark of the professionalism of the author, which is why it is often the first thing to be read by a colleague to locate the work at hand in the larger literature. We

| Intro + RQ | Be explicit in your research question. State which gap you fill |
|---|---|
| Literature review | Read predecessors. Cite sources |
| Material and methods | Explain what you did (be replicable) |
| Analysis | Present your results |
| Discussion | Discuss your findings in the light of literature |
| Conclusion | Make your contribution explicit. Highlight issues and limitations |
| Bibliography | Cite sources |
| Appendices | Stay readable |

Figure 6.1. Function of the sections of classic academic document structure. Adapted from Lahlou, 2014.

now understand why this situation and fit of the current work in the discipline's enclycopaedia of findings (the literature) is essential, because what counts is the progress of that enclycopaedia, not the local task exposed in that specific paper.

The rules of academic method (which is the gradual construction of an organized knowledge) may be summarized as follows:

- Please explain your research question (RQ);
- read your predecessors;
- specify which gap in the literature you attempt to fill;
- make explicit what you have done (ideally this should be replicable);
- compare what you found to the literature;
- describe the nature of your specific contribution;
- emphasize the limits of your approach and outline what future research is now necessary;
- cite your sources.

The various components of an academic paper correspond precisely to these requirements (see Figure 6.1).

We can now see that *the classic scientific communication piece is a proposition for a better version of what we already know, a reproduction with a small modification. It follows an algorithm that makes sure the new version matches reality better, but still tiles with most of the existing stock of models.*

It is not novelty that matters; it is how the new piece fits in and contributes. A large part of the document is used to show how the modification proposed can be inserted in the existing fabric of knowledge. Some papers are in fact pure confirmation of what is already known, without any novelty, and they are acceptable papers. But a paper that would only bring a new knowledge without showing how it can be inserted in previous knowledge is worth nothing; it is unusable in the scientific process.

An essential aspect of the knowledge produced is that a scientific paper usually contains comparison between a model of the phenomenon studied and empirical data. The discussion section is about constructing, refining or reconstructing such models. That empirical test of a match between the model and the object is an essential feature in the selection of new models.

A first thing we learn from this analysis of this evolutionary process is that *the intelligence resides in the process and in the format of the communications as much as in the human participants*. Science proceeds by selection of small variants and combination of the existing stock; external representations play an essential role in that process and their very format ensures that the generated material feeds into the selection process.[4]

We see here another instance of the betterment loop, where scientific models are gradually improved by trial and error.

### 6.1.2. *The Process of Scientific Selection*

The process of science, which is an idealized simplification of the mechanisms of social construction of knowledge in a regulated universe, gives an idealized view of the process by which knowledge in general evolves.

Bruno Bachimont, in his theory of the medium ('théorie du support') defines knowledge as agency for a specific goal: 'knowledge is the capacity to perform an action to reach a goal' (Bachimont, 2004: 65). Knowledge must necessarily be embedded in some structure (media); it can be transferred onto various structures until it is embedded in the actant who uses it to reach its goal. Here, the knowledge is the description of a model and

---

[4] In a way, this process for presenting novelty in the format that can be decoded by – and encoded in – the previous structure is an essential aspect of the evolution. We can compare this to the way reproduction occurs in biology: mutations must appear as a small modification of a DNA string, otherwise they cannot be taken into consideration. And the medium's structure is part of the reproduction process. To paraphrase Marshall McLuhan, the medium is the message. 'For the "message" of any medium or technology is the change of scale or pace or pattern that it introduces into human affairs' (McLuhan [1964] 1994: 8). That is what scientific communication does. The structure of the medium enables the collaborative work of distributed intelligence, at a larger scale and faster speed, by providing the keys to place the new in the existing, and to compare the variations. For interpretation processes to operate, the content must be grounded in the previously known. Therefore, the medium contains in its properties as a medium characteristics that scaffold and orient the process of interpretation.

of its domain of application, and the scientific paper is the medium. The model is a capacity to reach a goal in that it provides a paradigm to subsume a series of phenomena, and to infer certain pragmatic properties that can be used to deal with these phenomena.

Science attempts to create and improve knowledge. In its endeavour, it makes a systematic and institutionalized use of betterment loops and distributes it into multiple individual efforts through specialization. We have seen how publication proposes new models for phenomena to be selected as better solutions, locally or to contribute to a better overall understanding. They are presented in such a way that evaluation of their value and validation is made easy.

Indeed we find again the same recursive betterment process where the current stock of knowledge/interpretive competences are confronted with data, then, where it does not fit (the 'gap' in the literature) some exploration of minor variants is attempted (that is the new hypothesis, which remains close to the general theory framework and is tested using proven methods). When the result fits better, this is added or substituted to the stock.

In science this exploration is done massively and systematically, just like the line of beaters combs the forest when hunting boar. The number of published scientific papers since the beginning of publication is estimated to have passed 50 million in 2009 (Jinha, 2010). About one paper per minute is uploaded on the PubMed database alone. There were about 7.8 million full-time equivalent researchers in the world in 2013 (UNESCO, 2015: 32). Science is organized in disciplines and subdisciplines. There are specific repositories (publication) and trial systems (peer review) in specific installations (laboratories, academic departments, scientific journals). As we know, the whole process of publication is a process of verification of conformity and selection of the mass of locally produced papers. And these papers are structured as described above precisely to enable selecting them, sorting them and assembling the result in a systematic manner.

Let us note here some control mechanisms included in the scientific process, for resilience. We mentioned (Section 4.4.2) that societies set up certification systems as part of the resilience and quality control. Here are two. People are allowed to take part in the collective construction process only if they are proven to embody the necessary competences, which are demonstrated by the literature review section and the methods section. Furthermore, most researchers must pass an examination of their competence, the PhD, which is like a scientist's driver licence.

The nature of the doctoral thesis, its objective, is to verify the professionalism of the young researcher, and her ability to insert into the community to contribute to The Grand Collective Work (and not, as some believe, to write a Grand Individual Intellectual Work). Basically, what is important in this examination is that the candidate demonstrate that she knows how to properly fit a brick in the wall (rather than to build a castle, which is the endeavour of subsequent career). The thesis is a licence to do research in the scientific community without close supervision, just like the driver's licence entitles its owner to drive around alone on roads. When taking a driver's licence test, the important thing is to show one knows how to drive, not to drive the examiner somewhere in particular. As the British Psychological Society describes it:

> The primary purpose of PhD assessment is to determine whether the candidate is competent as an independent researcher in the discipline. (British Psychological Society, 2008)

The production of scientific knowledge is therefore based in the process of a systematic selection of scientific papers, based on the existing stock of knowledge, and from them to improve gradually the existing portfolio of models of phenomena in a coherent manner. Science is a process using betterment loops that has been distributed; and the structure of the elements that are communicated (papers) reflects the nature of that process. We should not be surprised to find betterment loops again; after all, scientist are humans, and they tend to 'model one problem solution on another, often with only a minimal recourse to symbolic generalizations' (Kuhn [1974] 1977b: 305).

Let us note that essential to the progress of knowledge, as noted by Kuhn, is the existence of 'knowledge communities' (Wenger, 1998) interested in solving a particular problem. In science these communities are the disciplines and subdisciplines. In principle, these communities apply distributed, and recursive, construction methods; they gradually build a shared vision and common paradigms, using controversy and various methods of trial and error.

Of course the betterment loop is not completely foolproof, it does not systematically produce 'better' results; as we see in the general model in Chapter 7, the selection systems used also involve power balance and are biased towards the value systems of the communities that hold authority.[5]

---

[5]  The generation and selection mechanisms used to produce and select new variants come with technical biases. These may result in sterilizing a research field after some years, by forcing new research to be exactingly in continuity with the current doxa, beyond what is reasonable or efficient. One can sometimes observe an effect similar to the 'sexy son' Fisherian runaway of the peacock's tail: new variants are selected on the basis of their excellent fit for reproduction rather than for their functional ecological fit (see footnote 2 in Chapter 7). For example, scientific papers that comply very well with

### 6.1.3.   *Takeaway on the Process of Scientific Progress*

To conclude this section: **science is an ideal case of evolving reproduction of knowledge. Knowledge is provided in the form of models, which are a form of paradigmatic representation subsuming a class of phenomena.** Models are similar in spirit and function to what has been described as interpretive competences, except they are embedded in external representations.

Science operates by using betterment loop – improving the stock of knowledge marginally by confronting models with reality and peers, that is: with the two other layers of installations. That is done in a distributed manner, each local community (subdiscipline) working on its local issues of concern. The process includes an empirical test of matching between the model in symbolic format and the empirical reality in the physical layer. Continuity with the previous knowledge base is essential, and controlled for.

The very format of scientific communication is in itself a framework that carries the affordances for the labour distribution over the community. The rigid structure of the medium that serves to communicate the change is part of the process of betterment loop: this medium is partly reproduction, partly introduction of a marginal change in the existing framework.

That selection process is reified in and supported by the very structure of the scientific publication which is itself an investment in form (see Glossary: Investments in form). **We see here that harnessing distributing intelligence is not just a matter of social rules, but also of objects construction (here documents, formats and models), which at this point should not be a surprise for the reader.**

Note that the process of communication ('publication') is here the process of reproduction *and selection*, simultaneously. The modalities of communication (in this case, the communication format, the medium) are weaving the threads of the reproduction about the content with the weave of social regulation and previous knowledge. The

---

the scientific format tend to shine in the review selection process, but have little added value in terms of scientific content or discovery; still they often outcompete more innovative but less conformist papers, as can be easily seen by anyone reading scientific journals. Typically, many papers are made for publication purposes only (reproduction fitness) rather than for the advancement of the discipline, e.g. by slicing research into 'smallest publishable pieces'. That situation is deplored by many authors. (For example, for the current drift of 'mainstream' psychology, see Toomela & Valsiner, 2010; or Romer, 2015 for the 'mathisation' of economics.

process is so intimately intricate that it is almost impossible to separate the layers in description. Here again, social regulation and the anchoring of what is reconstructed into the previous installation happens at microscopic and continuous level of detail. This microreconstruction is consistent with the subsidiarity principle at work in the process.

## 6.2. Innovation Processes in Industry

Science is not, in principle, concerned with the fact that the change it introduces might create 'a problem' for the current state of things. Innovation in industry is a trickier issue because organizations are by nature averse to change.

Some organizations are dedicated to creativity as a business (e.g. advertising, cinema or design). We shall not consider these, but rather 'ordinary' organizations (firms, administrations, governments and so on; not start-ups). There, creativity is challenged with the paradoxical injunction to set up something new, but to do so within the current rules and the culture of the organization. Thus, innovation is not about making plans for a new boat, but rather improving the boat while it sails at sea: business continues as usual during renovation.

This case is taking us closer to the problem of the evolution of installations. We shall look here at how this happens in detail.[6]

### 6.2.1. *Why Creativity Is a Problem for Organizations*

In managerial discourse, innovation (and creativity) have been praised, at least since the industrial revolution. 'Literally, it is impossible to read business journals or newspapers, attend business conferences, or read annual reports without constantly hearing about the importance of innovation' (Amabile, 1988: 124).

But the innovator jeopardizes the current state of things and hard-won compromises. Organizations include 'installations' and their components (built environment, embodied competences of members, institutional rules) are investments that the organizations are reluctant to change. That is why creativity in organizations is often praised but rarely welcome. Organizations are by nature averse to change, in fact they continuously strive to maintain things ordered and predictable. In that perspective creativity is disruptive of order and subversive to the organization and its

---

[6] This section is based on Lahlou & Beaudouin, 2016.

members. That is why 'resistance to change' has been noted by many (Alter, 1993a; Bauer, 1991; Dent & Goldberg, 1999; Kotter, 1996; Lawrence, 1964).

Still, organizations understand they must adapt to changes coming from their environment, and therefore make some changes that improve the state of things: 'innovation'. Innovation is slightly different from creativity: creativity produces new things and ideas; innovation is result-oriented production of improved products and solutions. *Creativity* 'is the production of novel and useful ideas by an individual or small group of individuals' whereas *organizational innovation* 'is the successful implementation of creative ideas within an organization' (Amabile, 1988: 126).

There are many definitions of creativity and innovation. Creativity is, as just stated, generally understood as generation of something new, while innovation is oriented change in some useful perspective. In organizations, the idea is to harness creativity to produce innovation. The following definitions by (Anderson, Potocnik, Zhou, Potocnik, & Zhou, 2014) illustrate this general approach:

> Creativity and innovation at work are the process, outcomes, and products of attempts to develop and introduce new and improved ways of doing things. The creativity stage of this process refers to idea generation, and innovation refers to the subsequent stage of implementing ideas toward better procedures, practices, or products. Creativity and innovation can occur at the level of the individual, work team, organization, or at more than one of these levels combined but will invariably result in identifiable benefits at one or more of these levels of analysis.

Of course there are many different definitions of the two terms, but the general idea is that in organizations, what is valued is improvement rather than novelty, and innovation rather than creativity. In fact, creativity is accepted in organizations because it is a necessary part of the innovation process. Nevertheless, as we shall see, innovation faces the same issues as creativity, as it is a disruption and menace to current practice and installations.[7]

---

[7] One might object: What about organizations dedicated to creativity: graphic studios, communication agencies, innovation consultancies, etc.? There, creatives, researchers, etc. are paid to be creative! A closer look shows that these organizations are in fact not creative for themselves, but for other, client, organizations. They exist because other client organizations have externalized to them those dangerous creative processes, as one solution to the problem, as discussed in Section 6.2.3. In practice, despite some spectacular peculiarities that are part of their business show and the necessities to keep individual creators motivated and operational, these organizations apply systematic procedures and can be just as averse to innovation in their own production processes as other organizations. For their own internal business processes these organizations tend to apply the classic production rules of labour division, specialism, incremental innovation and evaluation-by-the-demand-side.

For our purpose here, creativity addresses the generation of new variants, whereas innovation is the process by which some of these new variants are selected and incorporated into the system.

Section 6.2.2 explains why organizations need change, and their relation to creativity and innovation. Section 6.2.3 illustrates some types of solutions set up by organizations (Lahlou & Beaudouin, 2016) to deal with the problem. That is of interest because most installations are run by organizations; furthermore our point here is to understand how evolution of installations is *managed* by organizations as we are looking for the mechanism of installations evolution, what is at play in the trade-off between continuity and change.

### 6.2.2. *Organizations Are Naturally Averse to Creativity but They Need Change*

We have defined (Section 4.4.1.1) organizations as sociotechnical entities combining people in an explicit structure with labour division to reach a goal. In that perspective, behaviours of the parts of organizations (humans, machines, subgroups) must be predictable for other elements to maximize efficiency. The mainspring of organizations is to create a series of conventions inside their domain to reduce transaction costs between parties (Coase, 1937, 1960; Williamson, 2007). That is precisely why organizations exist: they are more efficient than random systems of coordination like the market.

To this effect organizations set up precise conventions, codes, roles and procedures, regarding all domains of activity within their limits (from procurement and production processes to human resources management). These conventions are costly to establish, they emerge through trial and error, fights, power struggle, controversies and compromises between the various stakeholders.[8] Every such convention represents sunk costs and often a long history of resolved problems and conflicts. They may not be the best solution, but at least one that is known to satisfice. They are 'investments in form' (Eymard-Duvernay & Thévenot, 1983; Thévenot, 1984; see Glossary: investments in form) and organizations rightly protect these investments against change until they appear not to work anymore ('if it ain't broke don't fix it'). They also make sure that these conventions are applied on a daily basis.

---

[8] See for example how financial regulation is influenced by power struggles between national regulation agencies -and their constituents (Black, 2008).

That is why organizations run control systems to ensure and enforce consistency in their operation and products. These rules can be tacit or explicit, but they always exist: an organization is a continuous fight for endurance of that structure and these conventions against the natural entropic tendency of things to disrupt and decay.[9]

The practice of a given organization impacts on interpretive competences, the local practice become the default framework for thought. These frames become a natural barrier against imagining ways of doing that would be different of 'the way we do things around here'. Interestingly, in their method to foster creativity with their C-K theory (Hatchuel & Weil, 2009), which tries to make people think outside the box, Armand Hatchuel and Benoît Weil found that the first obstacle to overcome is a tendency of 'fixation' of new ideas around what is the current way of approaching the problem (Agogué et al., 2014; Hatchuel, Le Masson, & Weil, 2011), so all their efforts focus on 'defixation'.

Rules and embodied interpretive systems are only two layers of what organizations are made of. Organizations contain a series of local installations that also involve a physical layer. For example, an assembly line is an installation, as is a call centre, an atelier, an accounting department, etc. As we saw, the specific combination of the three layers emerges to the participants (employees, providers, clients, members of the public, etc.) as a specific 'situation'; this situation is usually recognized by participants as an instance of a typified situation and interpreted as such with the usual script (e.g. 'assembling the product'; 'welcoming the client'; 'repairing the defective products', 'processing an invoice', etc.), with minor adaptations to fit the local specificities (e.g. different types of clients, specific form of damage)

Refer to any of the detailed examples in organizations we have used – the nurse dispensing medication, for example. We see that *even a small change at any step of the procedure has consequences in many other steps, layers, devices, etc.* Imagine for example that the coding system of medications is changed, or the labour division among nurses or the model of the PDA ... Although lots of people may have local creative ideas, any responsible manager would at least think twice before implementing them.

---

[9] Anyone who has ever been in a managerial position knows that rules should be respected at least officially, and that cases of exceptions are always dangerous: they may become 'precedents', jeopardizing the very existence of rules. Therefore, even when it is clear that the rules should not be applied in this exceptional case, that is rarely officially recognized and the situation is solved 'informally', that is, without leaving a track record. That is why actual practice is different from the book although everyone pretends it is not the case.

For many years, I held managerial positions in the R&D division of a multibillion-euro corporation and I have seen this syndrome in others and experienced it myself on both sides of the managerial line. The problem comes from the fact any local change jeopardizes several installations. Resistance then comes from various layers of any of these.

Let us take the example of videoconferencing over the Internet when it was introduced (Lahlou, 2007b). Videoconferencing requires that several rooms be booked at the same time in various sites connected in the videoconference. To make things easy and avoid double-booking, the meeting organizer should be able to do that booking in a single movement, even on sites that he does not belong to, and be sure that no one in a local site who 'owns' one of the rooms will do a double booking. But this collides with the institutional rule that a room should be booked by a person from the local facility, the one who has 'the right' to do so. Ripple effects also occur in other layers: videoconferencing changed what people can expect from meetings, e.g. getting in touch for informal resolution of issues rather than processing the agenda (Lahlou et al., 2012a) and this effects managerial embodied competences.

A good organization is one where the three layers of each installation are tuned to operate together: the physical setting has the best ergonomic affordances to support action, the operators have had the right training to operate predictably to well-tested protocols and the internal rules of good practice are followed in an exacting manner. This does not happen by chance: each installation (and an organization has many) is the result of a long history of investment, construction and tests.

Against that background, it is easy to understand that creativity, as the irruption of something different, and therefore unplanned and not intended in the rules, is problematic for the organization. The impacts of a change in any of the layers of an installation inevitably have rippling impacts in other layers and upstream and downstream in the process. For example, the organization will have to change the raw materials, the tools, the procurement procedures, operator training, instructions to the sales forces and the marketing strategy; amend the quality and security procedures and internal charts; reconsider employment contracts, the authorizations from the regulating authorities, the relations with the clients, the enterprise resource-planning parameters, etc. Risks and costs are unknown but potentially high, but the positive consequences remain uncertain. Any responsible agent or manager will therefore meet suggestions for changes with caution and oppose a series of arguments and countermeasures to avoid his or her own business and unit incurring the risk of negative externalities.

So, by nature, organizations are ordered, regulated and conservative. By nature, change jeopardizes current installations with unknown risk and cost.

But organizations need change. First, they need change when they must adapt to a changing environment. Second, even in a stable environment, organizations in a competitive system (for example commercial organizations in market economies) may need change to fight their competitors. This is even more the case in capitalist economies because 'creative destruction' is the easiest way to grow in saturated markets. In other words, the products must be changed, because mere replacement coming from natural (or even planned) obsolescence does not generate enough demand to keep the production growing.

> Capitalism ... never can be stationary ... The fundamental impulse that sets and keeps the capitalist engine in motion comes from the new consumers' goods, the new methods of production or transportation, the new markets, the new forms of industrial organization that capitalist enterprise creates. (Schumpeter [1942] 1962: 82–3).

Pushed by this systemic drive, most commercial organizations in our societies are engaged in a rat race where 'innovation' is a buzz word.


### 6.2.3.    Example of Organizational Solutions

The general approach taken by organizations, having understood that creativity and innovation are by nature incompatible with the rest of the organization, is to create some kind of a bubble where these activities can take place. An organizational membrane protects both the inside of that bubble from the rest of the organization and the organization from the subversive stuff that might be created within.

In practice, innovation is closely managed and controlled; creativity is carefully secluded from the rest of the organization and filtered. In modern organizations, specific people, places, times and formats have been designed to limit the risks of creativity. Researchers, 'creatives', creativity rooms, creativity moments, project mode and tests are some of the roles and devices that have been set up for this purpose.

The organizations consider creativity an activity for which specific persons have qualities and appetence. It also tends to believe that if the organization wants to get the results and transform them into economic value, it is a necessary evil to let these creators do their thing in their strange and wondrous ways. But once some good thing is found, it should be taken away from the creators and transferred to responsible people in a control-lable process, to be integrated in the organization's standard operations.

There are many solutions used in practice for creativity and innovation. We describe four main approaches and five structures.

### 6.2.3.1. *Imitation and Adoption*

The organization tries to copy someone else's solution to avoid the pro-cess of creativity, or subcontracts the innovation to another body. It is a rational approach to reduce risks and costs. This is done by benchmarking, and often results in 'me-too' innovations. When the company uses a sub-contractor, that subcontractor may either copy or generate ideas. Finally, the external innovation can be bought (e.g. patent) or an innovative com-pany itself be absorbed. **So a fit solution is spotted in the environment, *abstracted in symbolic form as a model,* validated by authorities and then the model is implemented in the organization.**

### 6.2.3.2. *Innovation as Problem-solving*

In this perspective, innovation is seen as a possible solution to a prob-lem (e.g. shrinking sales, dissatisfied customers, accident). Organizational change is rolled top-down; a team dedicated to solving the problem is set up. This usually comes with some systematic analysis of the situation, a rational search for solutions (which can include the benchmarking and copy in the preceding section). In the case of organizational change, a committee including some top managers teams with change specialists (e.g. consultants) to implement the change. John Kotter proposes an eight-step model for leading change that is typical of the structured way many consultants operate.[10]

Depending on the nature of the change, the nature of the group in charge will change, and they may use various internal or external resources as a project structure. **Here the solution is *first imagined as a new model that is the variant of the current state, validated by authorities and implemented.*** In both process of modelling and imple-mentation there is distribution of labour. **At some point a reality test is made to test actual fit.**

---

[10] Create a sense of urgency, build a guiding coalition, form a strategic vision and initiatives, enlist a volunteer army, enable action by removing barriers, generate short-term wins, sustain acceleration, institute change (Kotter, 1996, 2007).

### 6.2.3.3.   *Participative Innovation*

This perspective relies more on collective intelligence, and tends to involve a large number of members of the organization in the process. It tries to **enrol users in the design process of new products, and includes stakeholders in organizational change**. It is not exactly bottom-up but more democratic in its spirit than the structured top-down approach presented in the previous section.[11] Process consultation (Schein, 1999) is a typical approach of this philosophy applied to organizational change. An advantage is to avoid the NIH ('Not Invented Here') syndrome (Katz & Allen, 1982), which creates resistance to implementation of innovations of external origin.

Process consultation considers that the 'client' (e.g. the organization, the end user, etc.) owns the problem and is best placed to find the solution. Therefore the role of the innovators (e.g. the consultant) is to help the client solve his problem by providing and monitoring adequate processes that help a solution emerge as a shared vision. This may include confrontation with specialists, creative sessions, real-life tests, etc.

Experimental reality (Jégou, 2009; Lahlou, 2009) is a particular kind of participative innovation, where users experiment a new product or service, in conditions close to real ones, before it is launched to the market. As Akrich showed (Akrich, 1988), **users can intervene on sociotechnical devices in four ways: displacement, customization, extension and hijack**. Therefore, predicting uses is difficult and it can be more useful to involve real users in the development process to better understand their actual practices and needs. Participative design and crowdsourcing would be applications for product design. There are many avatars of this philosophy; for example it can be run on a continuous basis with specific implements to bring interesting suggestions bottom-up (e.g. employee innovation competition, suggestion mailboxes, consumer suggestions) or be set on ad-hoc basis. Users are sometimes the best innovators. Companies more open to external innovation learn to look closely at what is produced by these horizontal networks, to capture positive externalities for their benefit. They also learn to elicit voluntary commitment of users, as a way to outsource part of their business (Beaudouin, 2011). Crowdsourcing refers to these forms of outsourcing activities outside the firm with the 'crowd'.

Avatars of this are the clubs of beta testers, invited to test and evaluate products before others. It is related to the idea of promoting lead users and building attachment between companies and an elite of users.

---

[11]  See Eric von Hippel on the role of lead users in developing innovation (Hippel, 2005).

The main issue of those approaches is how to process participation of external communities into the organisational structure; in other words, how to articulate two opposite social structures: the hierarchical organization of companies and the soft organization of online communities (O'Mahony & Lakhani, 2011). Experimental reality can also be applied for internal changes within the organization, by involving a team of employees in an experiment of organisational or management change.

In this process, **the organization is supported to find itself *a new model, of which the functional fit is checked by involving all stakeholders in the construction and choice process.*** Adoption is an emerging result from the actual fit.

### 6.2.3.4. *Mixed Approaches and Overview*

What is sketched in the previous sections are ideal types. **In practice every organization comes with specific mixes of the philosophies just described**; and often several approaches or structures coexist in the same organization and are frequently changed.

**Note that in the process of innovation there is almost always a phase of representation of what is planned**. This representation is submitted to the stakeholders (typically; funders, sponsors, authorities and sometimes those who will do the job) to get assent, clearance, sponsoring, buy-in. In that phase, the 'proposals' or projects' (that is often how they are called) are discussed, amended, selected or rejected. A typical process at that stage would be the selection based on a call for tender, where those who own the problem (or want to own the solution) try to collect proposals. The proponents usually have filled out a proposal form that explains how they intend to address the problem, and request resources for doing so in a given amount of time.

### 6.2.4. *Structures of Innovation Used in Organizations*

The innovation processes described are implemented through different systems, which are dedicated to innovation, either for a one-off or for processing a series of innovations. These structures can be

- **external structures:** a subcontractor and consultant is in charge of the project;
- **project structure:** internal or mixed team in charge of solving the problem with allocated budget and deadline;
- **internal innovation structures** (e.g. R&D);

- **user lab or 'test site':** a limited area of the organization implements the innovation; or
- **'open innovation'** (Chesbrough, 2006): R&D activity is redeployed: exploration of 'horizontal innovations' by users (Hippel, 2002), start-up acquisitions, call for external participation in innovation, involvement in networks of competitors to benefit from external knowhow... R&D is forced to go beyond the walls of the organization and collaborate with competitors, customers or other stakeholders.

As for the processes, there is a continuous bricolage and organizations oscillate between models, use one or another for different issues and more generally come up with a mix of these. New models and fads continually emerge in organizations and in the managerial literature (see generally the vast literature on the topic and Lahlou & Beaudouin, 2016, where these structures are more detailed). After comments from my colleagues I decided to shorten this chapter drastically to spare the reader the detail of the complex procedures and structures in use, considering that the reader's own experience in various innovation committees and projects is sufficient to make my point, which is the following: ***All organizational processes to manage innovation involve tight supervision and precautions to minimize the risks to damage the current structure.***

That is the rationale behind devolving innovation with structures that can be disrupted or automatically disbanded with a sunset rule at the deadline (project, horizontal innovation, subcontracting); behind limiting their impact to local or secluded units (R&D, test sites), and more generally behind adopting a progressive approach so as to make the changes reversible until they are vetted by the supervising authority.

In practice, all these reactionary precautions result that, although innovators are officially encouraged to create, the management of the organization resists their efforts. Therefore creators and innovators are victims of a double bind. Norbert Alter, a French sociologist who led innovation projects, describes in detail the 'innovation fatigue' that affects innovators as they live a continuous uphill battle against their own organization to move it. In the end, usually, 'The repeated experience of conflicting relations leads the actor to decide to stop his/her resources' (Alter, 1993b).

**This amounts to some selection process by trial and error, but an exploration that is not random and rather guided by plans, in a process always continuously evaluated and supervised by the institution. Again, a betterment loop; but tightly controlled by stakeholders. That is the essence of the evolution of installations.**

In the selection process, there is some labour division. Interestingly, that division of labour take forms that mix collaboration, competition and conflict. For example, participative innovation and innovation as problem-solving tend to be collaborative efforts to go forward. Still, what happens in the detail is a dialectic process in which each party defends some specific stakes, so the final result is an admissible compromise that none of the parties alone would have spontaneously reached. Although the participants may not see this dialectic process as 'labour division' but rather as a fight or struggle, from the higher perspective of the selecting authority this is more like realistically playing the pros and cons rather than simulating it on paper, which is probably the only way to do it, considering the complexity of the issues.

Finally, competition appears, for example, in the way all competitors benchmark each other and try to copy and outsmart each other. Again, this is not seen as labour division, but in an evolutionary perspective we could say that the sector is trying out many variants and selects which works best – and each competitor's performance is a test of the efficiency of its strategy, which is *in fine* adopted by others.

In practice, reality is often a mixture or combination of all these. The project mode may be collaborative inside, but fighting against its environment, and competing with similar projects inside or outside the organization.

Finally, in the implementation phase, the reality must match the project. It must also fit with the environment: Is this product technically feasible according to specifications? Does it meet solvable demand?

### 6.2.5. *Takeaway on Innovation in Organizations*

Innovation in organizations is therefore the result of an evolving compromise between what **exists and what could be done. The methods addressing the issue appear as a continuously changing bricolage without any one organization having found the magic bullet yet. Nevertheless the solutions they adopt have some common features.**

**The paradigm is of improvement, a move of the organization from the existing state of things towards a better state, or at least a state imagined and represented as better. It is again a form of betterment loop, where the base for recursivity is the current installation. The constraint here is that business must continue during transformation; furthermore, existing installations are often the basis of the new and part of its constituents. As we have seen, that introduces inertia and many**

constraints. On the other hand, that also brings capital, anchoring, installed basis, resources and a motivated community. More generally it brings the impetus, resources and agency of the organization.

Observation uncovers some interesting characteristics:

- The innovation process is not random; it is oriented and uses representations to guide the process. All new objects systematically exist both as material object and as external representations (project, blueprint, mental representation).
- The innovation process is distributed and results of several types of 'labour division' (collaboration, competition, confrontation); some form of negotiation, more or less cooperative, occurs in the selection of alternatives. *In fine*, the organization's authorities have the last say in selection.
- There is some confrontation of the result of the innovation with the real world (the market, the technology), and the final fate of the innovation depends on that fit.
- Attempt at evaluation and control by the organization and especially its authorities is continuous and the control is heavy (reporting, control of resources, etc.) There is also such control in all operations, even noninnovative, of an organization. But there the default decision (e.g. of decision boards) is to continue as usual, whereas in innovation the default is to stay the same.
- The innovation process relies on selection of adequate representations of the possible futures, and it tries to formalize it. That enables cooperation and limits as much as possible the negotiation between stakeholders, and between actors and reality, to a symbolic simulation phase where the possible new state is considered and evaluated for its functionality and impacts. This planning process also occurs for the process itself, where successive phases are considered. That is obvious in the 'design cycles' or phase 3 ('vision') of Kotter's formalization of the change process (see Section 6.2.3.2), and even more in the project cycles in the negotiation phase and at the various checkpoints where deliverables are compared to plans.

### 6.3.   Takeaway: Some Common Features of the Societal Selection Mechanisms

The innovation process in organizations is distributed; this distribution can take various forms: collaboration, competition, confrontation. In all these formats, a recursive trial-and-error process occurs.

But the specificity of these processes of trial and error is that they are not simply material experiments of a random variation. The variations are oriented by some goal or some representation of the problem. The confrontations usually occur before the change is actually implemented: that is the process of negotiation. That negotiation is based on the evaluation of the representation of the planned change. Possible changes are compared to the current situation on the basis of their costs and simulated outcomes. That is very different from 'natural' trial and error, where the reality test happens *after* the change has been implemented. That is much less costly. So there is a constructive loop from reality to representation and back, and a lot of selection, collaboration and competition occurs at the level of the representation, which is much less costly than doing it for real.

Progress in science is also a type of betterment loop, but of a different kind. Instead of being bottom-up from material installations, it attempts to build new models that can be embodied and guide design of institutions and objects. There, we saw that communication plays an important role; that collective intelligence is, in a distributed manner, the engine for gradual construction of marginal improvement of the fabrics of knowledge. We also noted that external representations (publications) are an essential component of the process of generation, selection and capitalization of the produced knowledge.

For our general model, in the two previous examples (science and innovation), we can note a few common characteristics.

### Betterment loop

The betterment loop is a process where 'variants' are confronted to the current state of the world, then selected based on their fit. While biological evolution could be considered a simple case of betterment loop, with humans betterment loops usually are dual and involve two sides: the *object* (reality, phenomenon) and the *model* humans make of this object in order to deal with it (e.g. mental representation, map, concept, external representation). New variants of the object are usually constructed based on the model, so results of selection of the fitter variants (what aspects are better) give directions for improving the model. In that innovative loop, both object and model are progressively bettered.

## Institutional control

The process takes place under tight institutional control. Individuals allowed to innovate are selected based on their credentials. There are evaluation and selection systems all along the process.

## Duality: material / symbolic

Often, the variants are first created into some symbolic representation (project) of 'what could be' and then confronted with the current state of the system ('what there is'). This results in all man-made objects existing simultaneously in two formats: reified (material form) and symbolic (representation).

## Dual testing

Both forms (material and symbolic) are challenged in the innovation process; but in different ways. The material form is confronted with empirical reality (e.g. in technical trials, or marketing tests), the immaterial form is confronted with the general cultural system (are the theories compatible with the current body of knowledge?). Furthermore, the immaterial form and material form must match (that is the object of feasibility and quality control in industry, and of experiments in science). Figure 6.2 summarizes the constraints on innovations.

The tests are not random trial and error; they are the trial of some goal-directed simulation: If we did so, would it fit? Is this variant an improvement? The variant is calculated, constructed, based on some model (the plan in innovation, the model in science) and these plans are compared to reality (experiments or empirical observations in science; production trials or market tests in industry). The authority in charge checks the quality of the match and the capacity of the innovation to be inserted in the current state of affairs. If both criteria are satisfied, then the innovation is absorbed – the structure 'incorporates it', just like individuals would embody the new competence that was found adaptive.

Deliberate innovation is far from straight Lamarckism,[12] which was the integration of habits into the organism's structure: here we see a *deliberate*

---

[12] Lamarck believed, as part of his general model, and based on his apt observations, that the physiological characteristics of animals functionally matched well their behavioural 'habits' (a term frequently used by Lamarck), that functional use would develop the organs and nonuse make them

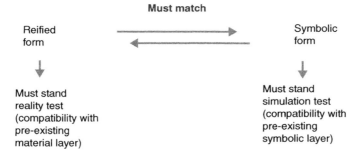

Figure 6.2. Constraints observed in innovation processes.

attempt to improve the system, with *intentional* exploration. Still, cultural systems also have a peculiarity, in relation to the ratchet effect described in Section 3.3 (see Glossary), by which *culture capitalizes on experience* and therefore these cultural systems have some Lamarckian aspect that natural biological systems do not exhibit.

The ratchet effect uses the symbolic form of representations (possibly specific to humans), by which information can be transferred to the next generation. Now, when one looks at how genotype is transmitted to the next generation in living organisms, and compares it to the reproduction of human systems, one cannot but be struck by the idea that gametes play a role similar to representations. They are transmitted, and when embodied become a behaviour factory. The physiochemical mechanisms of production, the time frame are different, but in essence the functional principle is similar. Genes, like components of representations, are encoded

disappear: 'First Law. In every animal which has not passed the limit of its development, a more frequent and continuous use of any organ gradually strengthens, develops and enlarges that organ, and gives it a power proportional to the length of time it has been so used; while the permanent disuse of any organ imperceptibly weakens and deteriorates it, and progressively diminishes its functional capacity, until it finally disappears. Second Law. All the acquisitions or losses wrought by nature on individuals, through the influence of the environment in which their race has long been placed, and hence through the influence of the predominant use or permanent disuse of any organ; all these are preserved by reproduction to the new individuals which arise, provided that the acquired modifications are common to both sexes, or at least to the individuals which produce the young'. (Lamarck [1809] 1963: 113). Therefore, after some time such modifications would be passed on to offspring; a hypothesis that has been rejected by the modern evolutionary synthesis where all information is transmitted through the genome. Recent findings in epigenetics, regarding the transmission of phenotype by various mechanisms that can foster or hinder the expression of genes, shed a new light on the transmission processes (Handel & Ramagopalan, 2010). In the same vein, the long-controverted Baldwin effect (Baldwin, 1896) states that learning an efficient response to the environment can bootstrap the selection of that response in the genome of the species. Indeed, in the population now exhibiting this (learned) trait, having it becomes a must.

interpretive competences that produce adapted responses to the environment and are transmitted within populations of subjects. This similarity between biological organisms and cultures comes naturally because biological organisms are one of the important components of our environments and therefore we are tempted to compare everything with them, – for example organizations and cities.

It is therefore no surprise that Richard Dawkins came up with a theory of 'memes', which he defines as elementary cultural elements that are replicated by communication between humans. His analogy with genes is explicit:

> Examples of memes are tunes, ideas, catch-phrases, clothes fashions, ways of making pots or of building arches. Just as genes propagate themselves in the gene pool by leaping from body to body via sperms or eggs, so memes propagate themselves in the meme pool by leaping from brain to brain via a process which, in the broad sense, can be called imitation. (Dawkins, 1976: 174)

But Dawkins' theory does not work very well except for some very specific cases (e.g. the commercial jingles and other small pieces that have a viral diffusion) because it misses the crucial fact that most representations are representations *of something*. For that reason their fate is attached to the fate of that *something* they represent.

We must be very careful with analogies; genes and representations are very different, as much as peas are different from pigeons. Nevertheless, **we can recognize in the reproduction of the installations (and of the behaviours they create) the general pattern of evolutionary systems based on some massively distributed process of trial and error with a recursive mechanism that enables some adaptive progression – the same mechanism we called a *betterment loop* in Section 5.5.**

There is another difference with biological evolution. Changes in human artefacts are not the results of random mutations; they are intentional. There is feedforward, a process in which action is determined by its final state as anticipated or aimed for by the subject; so it uses some kind of representation of the anticipated state. For example, there will be some engineering drawings and calculations of feasibility before a prototype is made.

Finally, the attempts to change we observe in installations use betterment loops, which are regulated by control systems, often by an external authority (a board of reviewers, a board of directors, the state department, the regulation agency, etc.)

The change process is risk averse; it avoids jeopardizing the survival of the current organization with the new implement. It usually does so by simulating what would be the possible consequences of change, in the safe realm of symbolic format: as plans, blueprints, in discussion, etc. For example, the costs and benefits are calculated to check whether the project is financially sound, etc. Then the result of the simulation is assessed, and usually this ends in a decision of whether or not construct the simulated entity for real. The assessment is often done by some external authority. In this evaluation, both mechanisms of simulation and control are combined.

In sum, the key selection mechanisms are:

- **compatibility of the new entity's forms with the existing entities (does it tile satisfyingly with the stock in its own realm?)**[13];
- **match between the reified and the symbolic form of the new entity;**
- **agreement for the form to exist granted by the authorities regulating its domain.**

The use of symbolic format and external representations facilitates the distribution and coordinating the generation and selection processes, as well as their storage and access for subsequent use. Furthermore, external representations afford capitalization of knowledge and the ratchet effect of culture.

The increased storage and transmission capacity provided by systematic use of symbolic external representations (e.g. through compulsory literacy instruction, information technologies, nurturing communities of scholars) accounts for the larger number and complexity of installations that large-scale societies create and manage, including massive systems (e.g. hospitals, an airports, submarines) that combine nested installations.

Let me make a few comments.

First, the evolution and selection criteria discussed here were extracted from a much larger body of material than the two cases used here (science and industry), and were primarily deduced from the analysis of the evolution of social representations (Lahlou, 2015).[14] But science and industry

---

[13] That is done through evaluations of functional satisficing in reality trials and thought experiments; but the betterment loop is an endeavour to go beyond the current level of satisfaction and reach a more satisfying state.

[14] Fritz Heider noted that science is ultimately a development of common sense, and therefore psychology is right to dig in common sense for research (Heider, 1958: 4–6).

are interesting illustrative cases of the selection mechanisms because they operate at a macro-level.

Second, the two (caricatured) cases just described are very different, apart from the commonalities discussed. They illustrate extremes of the societal reproduction process: one on the symbolic end (evolution of models and ideas) and the other on the material end (evolution of objects). When we look at installations that are more balanced, we probably see a combination of such processes. So for example the chairs used in 'a dinner' probably follow the reproduction process of industry, whereas diners' embodied interpretive processes also evolve according to more general politeness and linguistic customs and knowledge from the progress of dietetics, and family institutional rules incorporate societal evolution of family roles.

Third, the evolution of an installation as such is also dependent on local factors for it to remain functional as a bundle. Each change propagates in the three layers because they are all coupled in action.

The next chapter attempts a synthesis.

CHAPTER 7

# *The Evolution of Installations*

As the title suggests, this chapter attempts a synthesis of the mechanisms by which installations evolve in time. I must admit I feel dwarfed by the problem. The sophistication of the mechanisms and their number makes biological evolution (of which the principles are reminded at the beginning of this chapter) look almost simple in comparison.

Cultural evolution draws on a series of different mechanisms for producing new variants and selecting them. It is complex because these mechanisms not only apply locally to the existing situation (as in biology), but take into account the (simulated) anticipation of possible consequences and the results of past experience. These are made possible by symbolic representation systems and the use of 'external' representation techniques (language, documents, etc.)

There is a 'dual selection' making concurrent use of 'real' and 'simulated' experiments and tests for fitness; it is extremely efficient and reduces risk and waste. This dual selection is monitored by institutions. This monitoring ensures that local changes do not provoke negative externalities in the larger social system.

Finally, although installations' local functional processes evolve through the betterment loop, their component layers evolve also with their own rationale, partly independently of local installations. This results in installations evolving not only under their local conditions of fitness and efficiency, but also under the crossed impact of other installations.

Each of these mechanisms is easy to understand and to recognize in actual installations. It is their combination that makes the evolution of installations complex. The chapter ends with a simplified diagram that I tried to keep minimal.

**I apologize to the reader if this chapter is not always straight-forward: as for Simon's ant, the complexity is in the ground I tour, and I still have not found the best path.**

Before getting into theorizing the evolution of installations, I review the principles of Darwinian evolution because some apply here (Section 7.1). Section 7.2 presents an overview of the evolution mechanisms of installations. Section 7.3 looks at the evolution of embodied interpretive competences, Section 7.4 at the evolution of material artefacts and Section 7.5 at the evolution of institutions. Section 7.6 concludes this chapter with a quick synthesis.

## 7.1.   The Darwinian Principles of Evolution: Do They Apply to Installations?

Daniel Dennett summarized the conditions for evolutionary processes to apply:

> [E]volution occurs whenever the following conditions exist:

(1)  variation: there is a continuing abundance of different elements
(2)  heredity or replication: the elements have the capacity to create copies or replicas of themselves and
(3)  differential 'fitness': the number of copies of an element that are created in a given time varies, depending on interactions between the features of that element and features of the environment in which it persists. (Dennett, 1996: 343)

The idea behind the general theory of evolution, as it was elaborated for living organisms, can be summarized as follows: If there is a set of entities that reproduce, if there is some diversity among them and some entities reproduce more than others, those that survive and reproduce more will gradually become the majority.

Although the principle seems quite simple, the process that results in some entities producing more lasting copies than others may be less so. For biological organisms, this combines two distinct mechanisms, reproduction and selection, which determine the final reproduction rate at the next generation, depending on how many entities survive long enough to reproduce. Differential reproduction rates result from the generative capacity (e.g. fecundity) of the entities: some produce more copies than others. Selection in biological organisms results from environmental pressure: some manage to survive and reproduce, some don't. That is why, for example, some species manage to endure even though many individuals die before reproduction, because adults generate a sufficient amount of young.[1] Regarding differential fitness, intraspecific fit is just as important as environmental fitness, because what matters is final reproductive success and not simply survival.[2]

What is notable in biological evolutionary processes is that they are value-free. What matters is whether the species thrive or not, so the only 'value' is the capacity of the species to survive as a lineage, in adapting to its environment. What manages to thrive, thrives, for better or worse. There are no extra criteria involved; for example it does not matter whether the fact that one species 'A' thrives has negative impact on other species; if the other species need to manage to limit the growth of A, that is their own problem. As a result the whole picture is one of generalized struggle for life and not one of policed competition and concerted betterment.

We shall see that in the case of an installation, there are, in contrast, also other important selection factors that are *not* directly linked with this specific installation's fitness per se (regarding the behavioural efficiency of installations) but still have considerable impact, especially at the level of institutional control.

The evolutionary mechanisms of installations are somewhat different from those of biological species: in the latter case, because the individuals are mortal, the types that reproduce more finally crowd out those that reproduce less. So if we look longitudinally at a population, and consider that it is the same 'species' because the individuals are linked by genetic links in time, we see 'evolution' as the characteristics of the set, described in intension, change[3]: e.g. peacocks with larger tails, faster predators, better-protected preys, etc. But installations are not, like biological organisms, made of physical entities that reproduce as individual units; they are composite, and their components reproduce to some degree independently.

---

[1] See the example of yellow mud turtles (*Kinosternon flavescens*), whose mortality rate in the first year is 81%, mainly because of egg predation (Iverson, 1991).

[2] Another classic example is *Pavo cristatus*, where males ('peacocks') with showy feathers have more reproductive success because they are preferred by peahens. Even though showy feathers are a handicap against predators, the superior reproduction rate of showy-feathered individuals more than compensates for destruction by predators; this results in the genes for showy feathers being transmitted and the species as a whole having males with showy feathers. This effect is known as the sexy son hypothesis, or Fisherian runaway (Fisher, 1915).

[3] Naturally the question of where to draw the limits (since it is not, strictly speaking the 'same' population at different times) brings up many taxonomic questions; for example, what is the limit of a given species, a topic discussed among naturalists under the question of 'cladism'.

Does evolution theory apply to installations?

Each installation exists in many similar exemplars: there are billions of kitchens, of dinners, over a billion cars, hundreds of thousands of hospital wards, etc. The very nature of installations encourages some 'reproduction' of similar installations, as good solutions to similar problems. Similar reproduction and copy are also easier than redesign from scratch; atypical installations have more difficulty in emerging. This stereotypy is not random and abundance has its functional advantages: it is because installations are similar in their diverse local instances that they are so effective. I can, as a user, know how to behave in almost any kitchen, any hospital, etc., with only minor adjustments. We already touched that point when installations were presented as sets and 'paradigms' in Section 5.2.4.3.

Whatever the reason, we empirically observe that there exists large sets of similar installations; 'there is abundance of different elements' (Dennett's condition 1).

Clearly there are successive generations of installations, and the various exemplars are linked: in a given society, when one specific installation is improved, sooner or later others follow, further installations adopt the model. Consider any widespread installation, such as crossroads, telephones, bus stops, conferences, etc. When we look at the ones currently in operation in a given society, they are similar, yet they are also different from installations for the same purpose a few decades ago. For example current cars have a family resemblance but are different from the cars made fifty years ago. So there is obviously some kind of 'reproduction' (in space and time) but it is not as direct as the genetic reproduction of animals and plants.

Still, do installations 'have the capacity to create copies or replicas of themselves'? When we discussed reproduction in Chapter 5, we saw that installations are reproduced, indeed, but the capacity to reproduce cannot be attributed to installations alone, they need contribution from a larger environment. That seems to be quite a different case from animals. Nevertheless, when one thinks of the type of phenomena Dennett used as a basis for his model, biological organisms (e.g. pigeons or peas) one quickly realizes that similar issues occur there; they were simply neglected in the first approximation of the model. Indeed the reproduction of species is also in a more or less direct dependence to their environment, for example, because environment provides nesting affordances. That is much more important for some species than others, for example, flowering plants (angiosperms) need the cooperation of pollinators such as bees; other organisms, such as viruses, use another organism as reproductive scaffolding. The reproduction systems of living organisms are diverse, varied and amazingly complex; they involve behaviours as well as material structures. Compared to these, the reproduction system of installations is not particularly exotic, even though it is more exogenous to the individual entities.

So we can consider that Dennett's condition 2 (heredity or replication: the elements have the capacity to create copies or replicas of themselves) is also met for installations, if we accept that it is met for biological organisms.

Finally, differential fitness. Can we consider met Dennett's condition 3, 'the number of copies of an installation that are created in a given time varies, depending on interactions between the features of that installation and features of the environment in which it persists'?

Certainly some installations are more 'fit' than others: there is differential fitness. Some restaurants are better than others, as are some chiropractor's practices or basketball matches. In the reproduction process, this differential fitness results in the fact that the more fit installations tend to be more reproduced (in both meanings of reproduction: endurance and reconstruction of fit installations; copy and creation of new installations). That is what we call 'progress'. For example, consider crossroads and roundabouts.

> Crossroads were a major source of car accidents; modern roundabouts, introduced in 1906 by urbanist Eugène Hénard in Paris, proved considerably safer, because of fewer conflict points between vehicles (Figure 7.1), reduced speed, etc. (Transportation Research Board of the National Academies, 2010; Vanderbilt, 2008: 181–2).
>
> There were in 2016 about 32,000 of these roundabouts in France and 26,000 in the UK (RoundaboutsUSA, 2016), and these installations (physical setting, matching rules of the road and competence of drivers) are gradually replacing existing 'classic' crossroads in many countries.

Roundabouts are especially easy to describe and their short history is well documented, but we could make a similar historical analysis with installations for any activity, from tooth extraction to milking cattle or dancing. More generally, there is a widespread belief that new installations are, if not always an improvement on the previous, at least more fit to the current times; we generally tend to consider that the new versions (at least those that last) are 'better' than the previous.

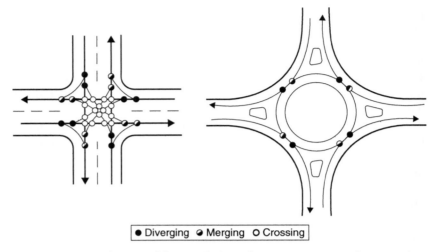

Figure 7.1. Crossroads vs roundabouts: vehicle conflict point comparison for intersections with single-lane approaches. (From Transportation Research Board of the National Academies, 2010: 106.)

It seems therefore that Dennett's condition 3 is met. We can conclude that an evolutionary approach is relevant to analyse the evolution of installations.

In fact, for most types of the objects we described above (behaviours, material objects, competences, installations) the three conditions of Dennett are met. What is tricky here is that these conditions are usually thought of with biological species in mind, as in Darwin's original theory (Darwin, 1859), where replication comes from inbreeding. Also, the 'copies' were meant in Dennett's definition as separate physical occurrences of the elements (e.g. different individuals). But, as Simondon warned, the evolution of objects is very different from the evolution of species (Simondon, 1989: 66–7).[4]

I will argue that installations evolve through their reproduction process under the condition of fitness to their environment, as for biological organisms; but I will also show their evolution principles differ somewhat from biological evolution.

The phenomena we study here differ from biological species in the following:

---

[4] Simondon notes that in living organisms the organ is not detachable from the species that *created* it, whereas in technical domain the part is detachable from the system that *produced* it.

- The reproduction of components of one kind (e.g. behaviours) depends upon the reproduction, or endurance, of components of the other kinds (e.g. competences, installations, but also of humans).
- The number of copies of an element can result from endurance in time, and not only reproduction in space: e.g. an installation's reproduction can be 'renewal' of the same physical entity rather than a separate occurrence (for example refit, renovation, reconditioning), as well as duplication (for example copy, mass production). It can even be a combination of both reproduction processes such as retrofitting a building or a car based on another model. That is different from the biological notions of reproduction and individual growth/development.
- The differential fitness does not simply depend on the environment, but on the reciprocal fit of the components of installation, which as we saw operate conjointly as a single functional unit, a coalescence.

Finally, the selection mechanisms are not only functional fitness of the entity within its environment. There are two extra selection mechanisms that have no equivalent in biological reproduction. Indeed there are, as I outlined in Section 6.3, *three* selection mechanisms:

- *Fitness*: **Compatibility of the new entity's forms with the existing entities (does the new entity tile satisfyingly with the stock in its own realm?)**
- *Dual matching*: **Match between the reified and the symbolic form of the new entity;**
- *Compliance-conformity*: **Agreement for the form to exist granted by the authorities regulating its domain.**

The first selection mechanism, fitness, seems very similar to biological species. But it is not that simple, as we shall soon see.

The most peculiar trait of installations is that they exist in dual formats: in a reified (material) form, and in symbolic (represented) form. These two forms are linked: the second form is the representation of the first; conversely, the first is the reification of the second. They generate each other in a chicken-and-egg fashion. The second selection mechanism (dual matching) is a consequence of that cycle.

Finally, the third mechanism (compliance-conformity) results from the supervision of the reproduction cycle by institutions, something that does not happen in biology.[5]

---

[5] Unless we accept that some deities oversee the whole process, a postulate that I exclude with Occam's razor: *Entia non sunt multiplicanda praeter necessitatem:* One should not introduce in a model entities which are logically redundant. I leave aside the case of domestic species.

## 7.2.    Overview of the Model

Evolution of installations takes the form of a *supervised dual selection process*.

Material objects and embodied interpretive structures evolve in parallel. These entities are separately selected for fitness, but they must also respect dual matching (the model and the material object it represents must match).

This coevolution is monitored by institutions, which impose compliance with process rules and conformity of the results with norms as selection criteria.

Furthermore, continuous adjustment occurs between the three layers of installations under the constraint of functional coherence (the installation must be operational to produce correct behaviour).

Let me outline the sections below. First I describe the *selection* mechanism in Section 7.2.1, then in Section 7.2.2 the mechanisms of *generation of new variants* (imagination in the symbolic realm and invention in the material realm).

### 7.2.1.    *Selection, Dual Selection and Supervised Dual Selection*

Before we go further I must illustrate these terms by an example to clarify the nature of the selection mechanisms.

Let us take the evolution of hats. The case involves at least three types of installations: hat shops, hat workshops and hats. Indeed hats themselves could be considered a limit case of small wearable installation[6]; I take this limit example because it is overly simple.

Hat-making (millinery) is an old industry. New hats are made after models of hats. Fabric is moulded on a 'block' that gives the shape to the crown, the part that fits the person's head. Although the details of the colour, fabric and decoration may change, the general shape still follows some standard model (e.g. Stetson, pillbox, Panama, etc.) The physical hat is made after the representation of such a hat model. There are therefore two forms of this particular hat: (a) the represented hat, the model hat in symbolic format (e.g. as described in linguistic form by the customer, or

---

[6] This raises the question of what are the narrower and larger limits of installations. Can an object be an installation? The response is: no. But if there is a bundle object/embodied competence/social rules which produces predictable behaviours, that can be an installation. Installation theory should not be taken as an instrument for reifying the world into a series of installations; rather as framework and tool to analyse and fix. If the theory helps modelling the phenomenon of interest in a useful and productive way, then it should be used. Otherwise, that means the theory is outside its domain of application. In the case of the hat, it seems to work. In the cases of cement, seagulls, electric networks, emails, adhesive tapes or hysteria it does not work.

drawn in a catalogue); and (b) the material hat (as made by the hatter and worn by the customer).

Let us now consider a candidate for evolution, an 'innovative hat'. This innovative hat will exist only if *both* its material and immaterial forms are satisficing. Each of these forms will be tested for fitness in its own realm.

First, let us consider the represented hat. While some materials are acceptable in our culture (say, beaver felt for a Stetson hat, or straw for a Panama hat – the plaited leaves of the *Carludovica palmate*) others are not, such as the skin of human babies. A respectable hatter will refuse an order of a hat made of the latter: a hat made of human skin does not fit with the psychological layer – where representations are evaluated for fit. That is a first type of selection, through simulation, in *thought experiment*. Our cultural value system denies baby skin the affordance to be hat material, even if that material would technically fit. Such a hat is no good to think about.

Let us now consider the physical hat. Suppose the hat was made of moulded then dried spaghetti: the first rainfall will demonstrate such a hat does not fit the physical layer satisfyingly.[7] Such a hat is no good to use. The spaghetti hat will be eliminated in the real-world empirical trial, in the realm of physical objects where objects are evaluated for fit against the material environment. Although our culture has a priori psychologically nothing against spaghetti being used to make hats, technically such material is not fit.

Only hats that will stand successfully *both* tests in their two forms (immaterial and material) will survive in the real world. That is what *dual selection* is: *passing the tests of fit both in the material and symbolic realms.*

There is more. The physical hat must match the represented hat, otherwise the customer will not be happy, or the hatter will not be able to make it. Only hats whose physical and representation forms match will reproduce, since one is made after the other. That is the *dual match* condition.

Finally, there is some external control. If the hats are judged by the public (or the arbiters of elegance, or the profession) as 'ugly', 'out of fashion' or 'offensive', they will not be worn or made, and therefore not be (re) produced. This can happen to hats that are perfectly functional in both forms, and whose forms meet the dual match condition; so it is another independent mechanism of selection. That is empirically observable in the fact that outdated hats are hardly seen in the public space; they decay in attics. That last control is a form of institutional selection.

---

[7] However disappointing that fact may appear to the faithful of Pastafarianism.

In most cases, that last institutional selection might seem benign to hats when it is the result of selection by fashion or good taste, but let me provide two examples of a stricter control by authorities.

**Case 1:** In 1925 Turkey, under Mustapha Kemal's ruling (aka Atatürk), wearing a fez was officially banned by law over the reform of secularization and Westernization of Turkey. In a speech, Atatürk described the fez as 'a symbol of neglect, bigotry, and hatred of progress and civilization.' Wearing the fez was considered an invitation to rebellion: as a result eight hundred and eight people were arrested and fifty-seven executed (Nereid, 2011). Those who tried wearing a fez under the Kemal regime soon enough discovered at their expense it did not fit the institutional layer at the time; it must have been hard times for fez makers in Turkey.

**Case 2:** Protection hats (helmets) are regulated by strict norms. The European Council Directive 89/686/EEC of 21 December 1989 on the approximation of the laws of the Member States relating to personal protective equipment lists the specifications of helmets for a range of activities, from firefighting and cycling to riding snowmobiles. Making or selling helmets that do not meet these requirements is prone to sanctions. In some countries or organizations, failing to wear these protections in certain circumstances (motorbike riding, car racing, construction sites, nuclear power plants, etc.) is also prone to sanctions.

Therefore, over time, hats or helmets that do not meet the approval of the authorities (whether they are the arbiters of elegance, dictators, regulation of commerce or Health and Safety committees) will not reproduce. That is *monitoring by institutions*. It hampers (in some cases fosters) the reproduction mechanism.

The combination of these selection pressures can quickly become complex. The selection processes may apply at various stages of the production and use of installations. The installation itself as a system, as well as the sector involved, must adapt to remain functional. The rules of millinery as a profession gradually adapt to practices; conversely, rulings of the trade influence actual practice. Consumer demand orients production and develops certain skills, while offer creates and mediates consumer demand and therefore generates embodied competences in hatters and customers. These adjustments are made gradually so that millinery and hat trade flourish, hatters are happy with their institutions, etc. Lobbying, marketing, courts of justice, consumer's voice and feedback, directly or through

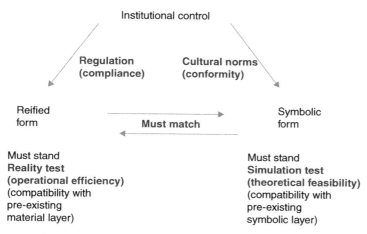

Figure 7.2. Selection mechanisms in the evolution of installations. Material and symbolic forms of objects must match each other. Each form must withstand the test of fitness in its own realm. Institutions control the compliance to regulations of reified forms and the conformity to norms of symbolic forms.

associations and mass media, contribute to the controversies, trade-offs and adjustments that take place in the process.

The example of hats may seem a poor illustration of installations; it was just given for a quick overview. *Mutatis mutandis*, the same applies to cocktail parties, religious services, public toilets or bakeries.

Now we have seen what the terms mean, we can come to a more generic description, which is schematized in Figure 7.2.

Objects are generated in two forms, material and symbolic (e.g. the hat and the representation of the hat). These two forms must match each other. But each form must also be considered fit in its own realm: according to the reality tests for the material form, and according to the thought experiments in the symbolic form. Institutions also exert control by eliminating the forms that are not compliant to regulations or do not conform to cultural norms.[8]

The three selection mechanisms that we have outlined (fitness test, dual match, compliance-conformity) operate simultaneously. Some of them are

---

[8] As Valsiner and Maslov note about a specific school of thought (but which is valid more generally): 'revolutionaries or terrorists attacking their own establishment are not allowed to emerge in the social system by way of its policies. In other words, social institutions are self-preserving, not suicidal' (Valsiner & Maslov, 2011).

in fact part of the reproduction cycle that we have seen in Section 5: that is the case in the lower part of Figure 7.2, where objects and their embodied competences reproduce each other. We have seen the processes illustrated in Chapter 6: scientific models must match the 'real' phenomena; products must be adapted to their use in real conditions.

Societal evolution is more complex than natural evolution because it *also* takes place in the symbolic realm. In nature, it often happens that species are selected in two different milieus, but they remain physical milieus. Take the dragonfly (suborder *Anisoptera*): this animal exists successively as aquatic larvae and then adult aerial insect, each generating the other during development and reproduction. The larva metamorphoses into the adult, and the adult generates the eggs that become the larvae. Just as the dragonfly is submitted to evolutionary pressures both as a larva in the aquatic medium and as a flying insect in the aerial medium, objects are submitted to a dual selection process in their embodied form (symbolic, the representation) and in their reified form (material, the artefact). The selective pressure of the two milieus of the dragonfly are different and have different impacts on the structure of the animal; but because each form of the dragonfly generates the other, some structural constraints are transmitted from one form to the other for the sake of continuity. The same goes for human artefacts (with some differences that I describe later).

In the case of material creatures such as the dragonfly, every failure to satisfice with the constraints of the milieu results in the death of the specific individual, and evolution has to restart from the previous state with another individual variant until more successful variants occur. There is no such thing as experimenting with a variant (a mutant dragonfly) 'in theory' to simulate 'if that would work better'. Every biological innovation is a matter of physical life or death for the individual mutant organism or its potential offspring.

But in the case of artefacts, although unsuccessful reified entities are actually costly failures, unsuccessful representations can be discarded at very little cost after evaluation in a thought experiment. I can think of a baby skin hat and immediately discard the idea, without having to make the hat if the thought experiment fails; another variant can be experimented fast and at very small marginal cost. Adding up the representational phase in the creation of artefacts therefore introduces a low-cost and fast selection based on simulation. As Dewey noted when discussing the virtues of communication, which includes here internal thought in the process of inquiry:

Events when once they are named lead an independent and double life. In addition to their original existence, they are subject to ideal
experimentation: their meanings may be infinitely combined and
re-arranged in imagination, and the outcome of this inner experimentation which is thought may issue forth in interaction with crude or raw
events ... In trying new combinations of meanings, satisfactory consequences of new meanings are hit upon; then they may be arranged in a
system ... (Dewey, 1929: 166; 194)

That selection by simulation escapes the deadly nature of natural selection
and speeds up the process.

By an intra-organic re-enactment of partial animal reactions to natural
events, and of accompanying reactions to and from others acquired in
intercourse and communication, *means-consequences are tried out in advance*
*without the organism getting irretrievably involved in physical consequences.*
Thought, deliberation, objectively directed imagination, in other words, is
an added efficacious function of natural events and hence brings into being
new consequences. (Dewey, 1929: 291; italics mine)

Jean-François Dortier suggested that 'imagination', the capacity to create
representations separately from perception and to manipulate them, is the
key explanation to human evolutionary success (Dortier, 2004): humans
are ideating machines ('machines à idées'), and that capacity is the product
and the engine of their coevolution with culture.

Indeed, the use of imagination to select appropriate solutions, *cognitive*
*selection*, is a major progress in efficiency; and the most adaptive aspect of
human intelligence. It is applied to behaviour, as Mead noted, but more
generally to any human production.

it is through this process of selective reaction –which can be selective only
because [reaction] is delayed – that intelligence operates in the determination of behavior. Indeed, it is this process which constitutes intelligence ...
Intelligence is essentially the ability to solve the problems of present behavior *in terms of its possible future consequences* as implicated on the basis of past
experience – the ability, that is, to solve the problems of present behavior
in the light of, or by reference to, both the past and the future; it involves
both memory and foresight. And the process of exercising intelligence is the
process of delaying, organizing, and selecting a response or reaction to the
stimuli of the given environmental situation (Mead [1934] 1972: 99–100;
italics mine).

Furthermore, as described in more detail in Section 7.3.3, humans have
developed external tools to enhance this cognitive selection by off-
loading some of that symbolic process of evaluation and simulation to
cognitive artefacts (with external forms of representations in language,

drawings, etc.) External representations enable to operate outside of the individual human mind the process of representation as 'making present'; this technique opens amazing possibilities, including social transmission and collaboration (Havelange, Lenay, & Stewart, 2003). The capacity provided by external representations to present and process a much larger amount of information than the human mind can hold in working memory, and to compare side by side the different options, multiplies these possibilities. For example, various potential versions of complex objects such as buildings or machines can be compared and selected on engineering drawings.

Humans have therefore invented a cultural system that is very efficient in selecting new fit variants for their artefacts – a massive improvement over biological evolution. It accounts for the extremely short time at geological scale it took our species to take over the planet since it invented culture.

### 7.2.2.    Generation Mechanisms: Drift, Crossed Impact and Innovation, with Examples

The previous section describes the selection mechanisms that constrain some characteristics of new variants, and eliminate unfit ones; this section considers how such variants, candidates for innovation, come into existence.

Changes are not all the same: some are big, some small. Some changes are initiated at the level of installations, some result from impacts of changes somewhere else. This results in three major types of evolution depending from the origin and nature of variation of changes: drift, crossed impact and innovation.

*Drift* is the cumulated result of small progressive changes and adjustments in the ordinary operation of installations, in their day-to-day reproduction cycle, wherever these changes are initiated.

*Crossed impact* is the result on a specific installation of a change in one of its layers that has been initiated somewhere else outside that installation, but which the installation must take into account and digest.

*Innovation* is the result of deliberate change at the level of the installation.

### 7.2.2.1.    Two examples: Parisian Café and Lecture
Let us illustrate with two installations: the Parisian café and the lecture.

### 7.2.2.1.1.    The Parisian Café    The Parisian café is an installation that provides drinks in a convivial ambiance. It provides its users with a setting

to spend some time in a public place, and serves as a convenient meeting place for sociability.

> Paris cafés are the meeting place, the neighbourhood hub, the conversation matrix, the rendez-vous spot, the networking source, a place to relax or to refuel – the social and political pulse of the city. (Wikipedia, June 2016)

The model emerged in the seventeenth century. 'Café Procope', still in activity at the time this book is written, started operations in 1686. This type of installation, which often has a terrace where consumers can watch the passers-by, has seen many variations during history; let us focus on a recent one. On 10 January 1991, was voted in France Law 91-32 relative to the struggle against tobacco consumption and alcoholism, also known as Évin law, after the then minister of health Claude Évin. This law takes into account the negative externalities of tobacco on health; it banned smoking from French public buildings.

Cafés adapted by asking the smokers to sit outside, on the terrace. This adjustment of the installation is a *crossed impact* of a change that occurred in the institutional layer. It was not initiated in the installations.

As a result, smokers would have to sit outside. Because this was uncomfortable in winter, cafés started installing radiant heaters on their terraces. That is *drift*, an internal adjustment of the installation to continue operating in satisfactory conditions. Another (unrelated) drift is growing use and advertising by cafés that they use 'fair-trade' coffee, following consumers' increased sensitivity to sustainability issues. There was also some *innovation* as companies specialized in providing equipment for restaurants designed artefacts for these specific installations: radiant heaters to heat in the open, or easily washable plaids designed for consumers sitting in the cold.

The same cause (banned smoking in buildings) had the effect of creating a new type of installation in airports: smoking areas, which are large glass boxes where smokers can come and smoke without leaving the building. That is an *innovation*, an installation specifically designed to perform a new function. In that case, the installation was purposefully designed after a plan, whereas in *drift* and *crossed impact* the modifications were rather minor adaptations of the previous model.

Of course, as for any typification, the limits may be blurry. For example, some cafés, aware of the costs (and stupidity) of heating open-air terraces, reorganized their installation by a major retrofit, enclosing the terrace with glass walls and making them glassed verandas for smoking areas.

Real cases are a combination of the three types of evolution, and the same installations gradually evolve over time as a result of these combined changes. For instance, the modern customer in a Parisian café may sit and work on her electronic tablet connected to the café's wireless Internet access, smoke an electronic cigarette while listening to a local radio with her earphones, sip a caffeine-free fair-trade coffee or a diet soda and pay with a mobile terminal. Two centuries ago, the same standard customer, dressed very differently, would read the morning paper (freshly bought from a 10-year-old street vendor) and drink absinth while smoking his cigar.

7.2.2.1.2.    *The Lecture*    That installation has the purpose of instruction by assembling a group of novices of approximately the same level of ignorance in the matter, and providing them with a description of the contents to be embodied by a teacher who is specialized in education, usually in a classroom. That type of installation is very ancient, and we shall only glance at some recent changes.

Various instruments were introduced so that the teacher could display contents and students take notes. The chalkboard and the school slate were introduced in the 1890s; the pencil around 1900, the ballpoint pen around 1940. With these instruments, transmission was mostly through the use of language, and the use of image was more limited; the students had to rewrite what the teacher said or wrote on the display. The generalization of copy machines since the 1960s enabled widespread use of syllabi and typed courses. The current state of the art with generalization of digital display on a large screen, and of students bringing in their own electronic devices, changed again the affordances. A common behaviour at the time this book is written is of teachers showing a (typically PowerPoint) presentation on the screen, while students take notes on their tablets, often on the basis of the same presentation that has been made available to them beforehand on some online learning platform (e.g. Moodle); live courses are video-recorded so students can review them as they prepare their exams.

The evolution of the lecture is a combination of crossed impact, drift and innovation. *Crossed impact* because the installation of new displays in the classrooms (screens, computers) is a transfer in the education domain of technologies that are so widespread that students and professors use them daily to manage information and therefore expect that the information management done in the lecture can tile with the rest of their logistics and habits. But this also has impact on the evaluation system: because information is ubiquitously available on digital platforms, exams tend to become more oriented at evaluating the students' capacity to recover knowledge and combine it in an efficient way rather than simply demonstrating they have memorized information in a linguistic format.

There is also *innovation*, with the creation of specific digital learning platforms that were designed purposefully for the lecture installation. These tools structure the contents by course and lectures, which is the way the lecture installation formats the delivery of knowledge.

Finally, there is also a *drift* resulting from the integration of all these changes, with the lecture delivery gradually becoming a composite process wherein teachers prepare and upload the presentations on Moodle before the lecture, students download it on their tablets to annotate it during the lecture, and students consult the downloaded presentations as well as the video recordings and any supplementary materials before exams. This drift changes the pace and type of the content delivered during lectures and also the interaction style of lectures, gradually changing their nature to empowering students to critically analyse the material available online rather than merely trying to make them memorize a series of contents. Because the installation evolved through drift, its funnelling properties were continuously preserved, and students or teachers behave in the 'new' correct way in lectures (except during technical system failures, against which disruptions they vigorously complain).

We now look in more detail at these three types of changes (drift, crossed impact, innovation) because they correspond to different selection mechanisms.

### 7.2.2.2. *Drift*

Depending on their importance, changes are not treated the same by the system. Small variants do not jeopardize the current installation; they simply result in accommodation in the course of ordinary operation. In the drift process, the changes are marginal and take place as part of the ordinary renewal of the installation. Usually, various components of the installation are renewed on a periodical basis; at the moment of renewal they are subjected to review by the stakeholders of the installation and a choice is made between the various alternatives available based on the state of the art and the zeitgeist. So the drift is a minor variation introduced in the standard cycle of reproduction of the same described in Chapter 5.

For example, in the café, customers may ask for a new type of drink that is not on the menu (say, organic apple juice), and then the owner may decide to change his menu and order from his suppliers the new drink in demand. In the same vein, he may implement a new type of payment (wireless) when changing his cash register. Consumers in turn will adapt (e.g. adopt a new habit: of paying wireless, or ordering organic drinks) as the affordance becomes available.

In the lecture, when display equipment is renewed the school may choose to order an interactive whiteboard or a tactile screen instead of a chalkboard or a video-projector. Students, knowing that the course is available on a digital learning platform, will adopt digital tablets instead of paper and pencil. It will become a norm that teachers upload their lecture material in advance, which will force those teachers who were not doing it already to comply. As a result, the new installations can operate as a coherent whole, where the embodied skills match the equipment, and where regulations reflect actual practice.

In the long run, because there is diffusion from one installation to another (through benchmarking, competition, copy), the more efficient or preferred installations may become the norm. This way, smart local adjustments between layers found in one place can generalize.

### 7.2.2.3.  *Crossed Impact*

Crossed impact results from the fact that installations are made from assembling components that each have some autonomy. Therefore a change in one layer that happened somewhere has a mechanical impact on others installations that share the same layer. This can happen in any of the layers.

Some of the components of installations are mobile. The human users, going from one installation to another, are like pollinating bees: they modify their representations in one installation and bring these representations to another. So if for example consumers become very aware of environmental risk at school, they will bring this embodied competence to all installations they go through, and this will force the other layers to adapt locally, by providing the right affordances or enabling their desired behaviour. For example, consumers who are more ecologically conscious may import these preferences in their orders at the café, and that will have on the menus offered the consequences described above. In the lecture, students and teachers come with the expectations that information processing is done digitally, rather than with pencil and paper. They will also expect wireless to be available in the lecture (it is even available in cafés!) and request it from the school authorities.

Humans are not the only components that circulate across installations. The material objects, which as we have seen are made in series, also diffuse change between installations. Stacking chairs, for example, may gradually be adopted in many places over nonstacking chairs; the same goes for drinks, glasses, dishwashers, etc. Sometimes, the installations have no choice. For example, they are forced to use the last version of a software or operating system for the computers, or change their machines, simply because their preferred choice has become unavailable or too expensive.

Finally, the institutional layer imposes top-down changes to a whole domain or area. For examples, regulations on employment will impact cafés in the way personnel is hired and managed. New methods of evaluation of academics will sway their efforts to publication and make them orient their teaching to leverage students' contribution to that purpose – for example, using them as easy accessible populations of subjects for experiments in psychology. This is in some universities facilitated by the obligation of psychology students to participate in experiments to get credit in their courses ('research participation obligation').

Such changes in turn have a ripple effect. Let us look at psychology lectures. The use of undergrad students as an easy source of empirical material in psychology experiments resulted in recent mainstream behavioural science being based mostly on a single homogeneous population. Jeffrey Arnett, analysing research papers in top journals in six subdisciplines of psychology, calculated that 94% of subjects samples were from Western industrialized countries (mostly North America and Europe), and in some journals most of this sample was made of psychology undergrad students (Arnett, 2008). Arnett notes humorously that some changes may be in order in the names of scientific journals, e.g. *Journal of the Personality and Social Psychology of American Undergraduate Introductory Psychology Students*. Indeed (Henrich, Heine, & Norenzayan, 2010) show how such sampling provides a biased, WEIRD (Western, Educated, Industrialized, Rich, and Democratic) account of human psychology. Which is what we teach to psychology students. There is here an interesting example of feedback loop on the content of what is done in the classrooms. As we can see, evolution is a complex process that includes many loops.

The crossed impact often comes from institutions, which regulate a domain that is larger than the installation itself. We saw above the example of health law on cafés. In the lecture the content of the programmes usually comes from outside the school itself: the things to teach (the technology or the scientific results) change because they are produced outside of the lecture. New norms on political correctness, the commercial relation with students who pay high fees, etc., change the style of delivery and select out behaviours such as corporal punishment, sarcasm or sexist jokes on the part of teachers; increased pressure on the job market and the higher level of formal diplomas required to get a job induce students to be increasingly anxious about the marks and therefore more careful if not instrumental in their communication with teachers.

Each layer has its own logic, based on the internal regulation processes and constraints on production, at its own level (availability or quality of the raw material, economic rationality, value systems and norms, coherence with international regulations, etc.) These logics inevitably impact the content and form of the new variants that are produced, which bear the mark of these constraints and in some way import them into the various installations in which they become part thereof. Note that the rationales of these constraints are specific to a given layer and not necessarily directly connected to the functional efficiency of a given installation to produce behaviour.

### 7.2.2.4.   *Innovation*

Innovation happens where there is a deliberate 'change operation' in the installation, a project with dedicated resources. The system then goes into explicit change mode; the general design of the installation is reconsidered in perspective of the installation's purpose. For example, the owner of the café decides on a major retrofit of the façade and terrace; a teacher sets up a new course.

Often, the decision is taken at some higher institutional level, and stakeholders of the local installations are delegated the task to implement the change, under supervision of the larger entity who acts as a sponsor and/ or censor. The township may decide to build a new gymnasium, the police to create a special force, the hospital to overhaul its emergency ward, the family to agree on a new rule for dinner. Often this is caused by the emergence of malfunction, obsolescence, failure or deficiency of the current installations: the old gymnasium is too small; there are terrorist attacks, patients catch nosocomial infections, the children keep using their smartphones while they eat. In most cases, usually a person or team is given the mission to come up with a representation (model) of the new installation; this representation is discussed with stakeholders and the authority makes a decision to implement it and provides the necessary resources.

I describe in Section 6.2 some of the most frequent forms innovation takes in industry, but *mutatis mutandis* the same occurs at the level of the entities in charge of an installation (family, local company, mayor) although it may be less formal and often more sketchy.

Now that we have seen separately the main forms of selection and generation, let us have a closer look at how they operate together in each of the layers of installations. The next sections describe the principles that govern the coevolution of the three layers, making use of the selection mechanisms highlighted in Chapter 6.

## 7.3. The Evolution of the Symbolic Layer, Embodied or Embedded

Fifty thousand years ago the coevolution of the embodied layer and objects was simpler than today. When Professor Eric Boeda taught me (the rudiments of) the art of carving flint to make a biface, I simply had to watch him do it, imitate him and listen to his instructions and guidance as I tried. I assume the first *Homo sapiens* proceeded in similar ways to learn new skills: there was only, on one side, the physical artefact, and on the other, in the bodies, some embodied competence, located in the brain, muscles and joints – as figured on the left side of Uexküll's functional loop. Objects and the matching embodied competence would coevolve as people would learn new skills and improve artefacts.

I must apologize to the reader, but the situation has become more complex and therefore more complicated to describe. Now most objects also have a symbolic representation inscribed on some media. Knives – the modern equivalent of flint bifaces – are pictured in catalogues, described in encyclopaedia, drawn in engineering drawings, coded in computer files, etc. We cannot ignore the role of these external representations in the evolution of installations. Because humans have augmented their embodied memory and mental processes with external, prosthetic artefacts, we must also include the latter in the picture. That is why we must also consider the evolution of a 'symbolic layer' rather than only of an embodied layer: the knowledge can be embedded in different substrata, embodied in humans or inscribed in physical media.

This section therefore describes the evolution of the content of the symbolic layer in its various forms and media. Section 7.3.1 describes the evolution of embodied competences in humans; Section 7.3.3 describes the evolution of external symbolic representations.

### 7.3.1. *Evolution of Embodied Representations and Interpretive Competences*

A quick reminder here. I have called for short 'lata' the (individual) embodied interpretive structures, the physical substratum of competences. Lata are the bodily section that produces coupling with a specific state-of-the-world and have usually been learned in connection with that state-of-the-world. Lata are, to repeat a metaphor I used in Section 5.2.3.2, what the wires are to the electric circuit.

Embodiment is the process of constructing lata in the course of life (through conditioning, education); interpretation is the process of mobilizing lata to act upon the world (perception-action loop). Of course, as interpretation is practice, each interpretation inevitably implies some reembodiment, therefore some marginal modification of the lata. Modifications also occur when the lata are mobilized in the mind in connection with other lata.

Lata do not remain unchanged in the minds of people as brute neuronal casts of their experiences. They undergo internal transformation as they are transferred into long-term memory, they are reshaped during sleep, they are transformed into symbolic description (when we put words on them), they connect to the rest of our experience and the rest of our culture. This process has been described as 'representation redescription' (Karmiloff-Smith, 1994).

> a specifically human way to gain knowledge is for the mind to exploit internally the information that it has already stored (both innate and acquired), by redescribing its representations or, more precisely, by iteratively re-representing in different representational formats what its internal representations represent. (Karmiloff-Smith, 1992: 15)

That was about embodied representations. But furthermore, representation redescription continues beyond the body. It occurs in communication, with others or even with self as internal dialogue, or when representations are embedded in external media such as books.

This redescription of representations into symbolic and more abstract forms (e.g. words) facilitates their capitalization, their critical analysis and transmission (Goody, 1977, 2000), and also their combination, which Gilles Fauconnier calls 'conceptual blending' (Fauconnier, 1994; Fauconnier & Turner, 2002). That is analogous to combining genes in biological reproduction.

Accidents may happen in redescription. In art, which is also a form of redescription in the material form, such accidents are key aspects of the creative process, sometimes they even reframe the project itself (Dubuffet, 1973). These accidents are similar to random mutations in biological evolution.

> Allow me to narrate an embarrassing personal example. I was struck by a paper by Lucy Suchman on office procedures (Suchman, 1983) describing how an accounting department checks that all is done correctly when paying an invoice, a paper I started citing in 1998. What is a procedure, in fact, for practitioners when getting the work done? In this paper Suchman

analyses in detail the conversations of an auditing clerk and the accounting supervisor about *one* specific case where some of the documents appeared to be missing. A core conclusion of that paper, addressed at computer scientists designing automated office systems, is that 'smooth flow' of office procedures 'is an outcome to which practitioners orient their work – it is not the work itself' (one should not mistake the procedure for a stepwise description of what actual work is). For many years I strongly recommended that paper to my students and colleagues, and here is in substance what I said: 'Suchman analysed *several cases* of invoice processing at Xerox accounting department and she showed that *not in one single case* did the actual work follow the procedure.' And I gave them the reference of the paper to read. That is a wrong account of the paper (my apologies); obviously some reconstruction I made. I don't know where this reconstruction came from. Was it from a brief discussion with Lucy Suchman at Xerox PARC in 1995? Or from her book (Suchman, 2007)? I doubt it – at least the book does not mention that research. It is just that this misinterpretation fitted better with my own experience and what I wanted to demonstrate. It is only recently, as I was trying to get an exact citation for this book, that I read the paper again and realized to my embarrassment that I had been wrong all those years.

Redescription incurs many biases that have been described in psychology. For example, a category of similar experiences tends to be manipulated through a prototype (Rosch et al., 1976), some typical features become more salient than others, representations are tainted with emotional, hedonic or moral values. A classic illustration of what memory does to experience is that eyewitnesses, when remembering a scene, distort it according to their prejudices and the stereotypical situation. Among other things 'the type of crime committed systematically affects whom eyewitnesses mistakenly identify' (typically, black or white suspect) (Osborne & Davies, 2012). False memories can be implanted by suggestions or simply reading an ad, and these memories combine with the existing experience memory of the individual (Loftus, 2004). There is also a familiarity bias: in an experiment where subjects were asked to cook a recipe in a university lab setting, then asked a week or two later what brands of ingredients they used, subjects declared remembering having used the most familiar brands (which were not in fact used, only less frequent brands had been made available) two times more frequently than accurate responses (Krug & Weaver, 2005). As Frederic Bartlett, a pioneer of memory studies, aptly noted 'the past operates as an organised mass rather than as a group of elements each of which retains its specific character' (Bartlett, 1932: 197). We cannot therefore expect that the representation of one object can be free of the influence of the rest of the subject's culture.

Memory encoding, after perception[9], continues in the same direction the remodelling work of anchoring the new into the old and making it fit with what's already there.

So, representations are subject to operations of redescription, translation, projection; but also as they become part of the subject's mental portfolio of resources they are liable to combination, symbolization and so on and so forth. These operations produce variants; this results in the set of individual representations being diverse, even though similar. This set therefore has the 'continuing abundance of different elements', which is the first condition for evolutionary laws to apply, according to Dennett. Such processes account for the mental chemistry that underlies weird creations such as the hat made of spaghetti or baby skin mentioned in Section 7.2.1. A more realistic and mundane example is available on the websites that describe new cocktails or dish recipes and where many recipes come in a number of variants. (On a single cooking website, I counted 527 recipes for pizzas in June 2016.)

The work of memory and imagination provides therefore the variants that are simulated and submitted to cognitive testing against the represented environment in thought experiment. For example, we might mentally simulate several possible alternative ways to go to a meeting, to see which will get us there on time. Dewey provides a nice introspective example of how he compared mentally using the car or taking the subway (including the time to find the station) and finally opted for the subway (Dewey, 1910: 68–9). The same process we use to compare existing alternatives can be used to compare hypothetical alternatives. Moles and Rohmer propose a detailed description of a very similar situation (a businessman leaving his tenth-floor Parisian flat to go to a meeting by train) and include the 'psychological costs' (waiting, anxiety, fear of failure, etc.) coming up with a 'generalized cost' of the considered action (Moles & Rohmer, 1976: 71–83).

Variants can come in various shades of detail and can be evaluated at different levels. A professional cook will select among his emerging ideas those that are likely to produce an acceptable dish. In modern societies, the competition between potential innovations is often organized in a systematic way, for example by a call for tender by research agencies, a suggestion box or a competition for innovative ideas in organizations. The mayor can have the idea of a new bridge, but the town council may dismiss it

---

[9] Which is already a 'top-down' process guided by previous experience, through the orientation of exploration according to expected patterns.

immediately. The idea can also be accepted as such, but under the provision of further examination: finally the model of a bridge architectural project will be evaluated by structural engineers for static and dynamic loading.

In their immaterial form, objects are more prone to manipulations than in concrete format. Although it is difficult to combine two physical hats into one, or to modify the shape of a material car, such operations are easy in their symbolic representations (speech, drawing, computer-aided design). In symbolic format, objects can undergo a lot of transformations fast and at low cost.

In parallel to modifications that take place at the individual level, it has been noted that memory and representations are under social influence, because memory needs to be anchored in social frames (Halbwachs [1925] 1994: 130) and socially constructed concepts.

In other words, the representations must be encoded into some socially constructed alphabet. To use a metaphor, a computer can only compute within the framework of its operating system. In the same way, humans can only think and perceive by combining elements that are in the framework of their cultural experience and concepts (Lahlou, 1990). Whorf is famous for highlighting the constraining influence of language into formatting experience (Whorf, 1956). Human symbolic system is more flexible than computer operating systems, but still the symbolic framework used remains a limiting factor; even though symbolic frameworks evolve in time, as Ignace Meyerson showed (Meyerson, 1948)[10]; nevertheless that is a limiting factor, it is also a constraint that contributes to the coherence of new concepts with the old.

So, the content of embodied representations evolves naturally because the medium in which it is inscribed, the body, is not a passive medium and because they get reinscribed in other media where they will also be subject to redescription. Representations of objects undergo a continuous rerepresentation, redescription and reinscription that is influenced by the process of human memory, by technologies of the mind, by conceptual blending, by social influence. As a result, these representations as a set over a population of users (and designers) of installations present a wide array of variants. This distribution of variants provides ground for evolution.

The variants, at an individual level in a thought experiment, or at a collective level in conversations or more formal evaluations, are selected

---

[10] Meyerson illustrates this with the evolution of the notions of 'object ' and 'person' in European and Indian cultures over history.

according to the cognitive selection processes listed in Section 6.3 earlier. The dual matching process provides comparison of the new symbolic variant to its material referent. We saw in Section 6.1 how science proceeds. Common sense also operates in a less systematic way, but the nature of the test remains similar: does the mental version enable us to describe and act upon the material referent in a satisficing manner? Is the model 'realist'?

### 7.3.2.    *Values and Worth*

Another selection occurs at the level of the fit of the new symbolic variant with the rest of the symbolic culture. This may sound vague, but the principles are 'is the new variant good to think about?' and 'is it better than the previous version?'

Let us take an example of the 'good to think'. Claude Fischler noted that in most cultures, people only eat a fraction of the species that would technically be edible. For example, in Europe insects are not eaten, although they are considered food in many other places; French people eat frogs and snails, which others cultures find disgusting, etc. As Fischler says: 'not all that is biologically edible is also culturally comestible' (Fischler, 1990: 37; my translation): to be comestible, the food must be compatible with the cultural system of cuisine, which rules the domain of eating in a given culture. Transgressing the rules of this system would have far-reaching implications on the nature of the self, as Fischler demonstrates, because the symbolic system is one single fabric. Objects and symbols are not just tokens in one single local function; they are also involved in other functions and processes as well, therefore the reason for one rule here in this domain might be a potential impact in another one elsewhere.[11] Something will not be 'good to think about' if its thought produces forbidden collateral impact. This has implications for the food industry and for the health authorities.

Now for the 'is the new variant better than the previous version?' Because humans are good at comparing things, that is an easy task as long as there is some criterion for comparison. This is where *value systems* come into play. The new version will be selected as more fit if it has more worth in the value system that is locally used. In a way, the selection test evaluates the potential increase in utility of the new version vs the existing one. But

[11] Refer to the examples provided by May Douglas of prohibition of specific foods for religious reasons (Douglas, 2001).

what is expected utility? That is the black box of economists, and often they are only able to record revealed preferences.

Boltanski & Thévenot, with their theory of 'economies of worth', bring in a useful framework in that respect (Boltanski & Thévenot [1991] 2006). Boltanski and Thévenot are interested in what general categories are used to characterize individuals, and how individuals can be compared to each other. They distinguish several 'orders of worth', which are principles of evaluation of action and serve to legitimate arbitration between protagonists in 'trials' ('épreuves').

The principles of evaluation are based on some resource, substance or property that is locally accepted as a common good by the persons involved. It can therefore be used as a common criterion for evaluation of 'how worthy' are different entities and justify the preference for one alternative against another. Orders of worth are connected with 'polities'. The polities (in French, 'cités') refer to a set of 'situations' where the same principles of worth are applicable. Here is a list of the polities and the source of worth in them[12]:

- 'inspired' (grace, creativity);
- 'domestic' (kin, care);
- 'fame' (reputation, opinion);
- 'civic' (citizenship, social contracts);
- 'industrial' (performance, productivity);
- 'market' (money, competitiveness).

Polities of worth, because the theory was mainly designed with the comparison of individuals, do not provide as such a formal value system to compare behaviours, objects or installations. But the vision behind them is powerful and applies to our problem.

It goes more generally with the idea that what is worthy in a situation is the resource that is useful in that situation for the activity concerned. Entities (persons, objects, actions, etc.) that possess more of this particular resource are more worthy in that situation. This idea has been expressed before in Talcott Parsons' 'generalized symbolic media of social interaction' (Parsons, 1963) or 'generalized media of interchange'. These media qualify the type of utility or interest entities provide in a given situation, for a given type of activity, their capacity to 'yield results'. For example, money is a good medium for an economic transaction; power for political decisions, love for bonding, etc.

---

[12] In their first version, there were six, later the polity of ecology was added.

Parsons distinguishes the following four primary subsystems in the general system of action and their generalized media of interchange (Parsons [1978] 1980: 393):

- economic system: money;
- political system: political power;
- societal community: influence;
- fiduciary system (cultural tradition): value-commitment.

There are also other domains where different generalized media are in currency, for example: science (truth); religion (faith); bonding: love.

The value attributed to the generalized symbolic media depends on actors' belief in their 'convertibility into 'real,' intrinsically valuable or meaningful commodities or relationship' (Turner, 1968). What is interesting is that because these media are symbolic, the evaluation process is not an ex post account of how useful that entity actually was, but an a priori cognitive assessment on how likely that entity might actually be worth in the activity sphere considered.

> Money, power, love, truth, and the other media are the way in which societal subsystems, firstly, regulate their internal functioning by contributing to its own differentiation and, secondly, find the way to interrelate with each other to produce co-ordinations between subsystems. (Chernilo, 2002)

As we see, although generalized media are somewhat similar to Boltanski and Thévenot's economies of worth, they also differ slightly from them. I am not interested in discussing the detail of taxonomies; there have been other attempts to list 'values' and the results vary (Cieciuch & Schwartz, 2012; D'Andrade, 2008; Schwartz, 1992; Schwartz & Bilsky, 1987); what matters is the idea that 'values' are not immanent and abstract moral categories that fall from the sky of metaphysics, but rather a functional criterion for assessing the differential worth of some entity in the perspective of some activity. That is why 'values' – or generalized media of interchange – are relevant to us here as selection criteria used in the evolution of installations. Indeed, installations or their components will be assessed in cognitive trials according to the values that matter for their functional purpose: supporting a specific activity.

For example, an industrial installation (e.g. a power plant, an assembly chain, a call centre) will be assessed (and variants selected) according to performance and productivity, whereas a domestic installation (e.g. the family dinner, a wedding) will be assessed on the scale of kin and good human relations, etc. As installations might involve several polities of subsystems of action, each installation may be evaluated on several scales of worth. For example, the Parisian café will be evaluated on profit and competitiveness, but also on good social ambiance. Of course, these evaluation scales may produce contradictory results, which is the general case in human affairs. That is why institutions, which prioritize some criteria over others, are so useful. Dewey distinguishes two types of valuation, valuation of ends (prizing) and valuation of means (appraising), but considers in the end that they are inseparable, and that the societal learning process (what I called the betterment loop) involves a combination of both in a historically constructed sequence of experiences:

> We commonly speak of 'learning from experience' and the 'maturity' of an individual or a group … When this process is examined, it is seen to take place chiefly on the basis of careful observation of differences found between desired and proposed ends (ends-in-view) and attained ends or actual consequences. Observation of results obtained, of actual consequences in their agreement with and difference from ends anticipated or held in view, thus provides the conditions by which desires and interests (and hence valuations) are matured and tested.' (Dewey, 1939: 29–30)

'Value' is an ambiguous term because it designates both a number and a dimension; e.g. ten pounds. It may be clearer to use 'worth' to designate the amount (ten pounds), 'value' for the number (ten) and 'value scale' or 'currency' (of worth) for the dimension (pounds).

Allow me to candidly extract the following takeaway from these erudite and complex theories: **there are different value systems for different situations or domains of activity, which are used to 'evaluate' the worth of an entity. The worth (the amount of desirability) of a given entity is linked to the agency it may provide in the local culture, as a fuel to transactions, and to its capacity to make 'the local system' (e.g. the community concerned) operate properly.**

**In other words, the worth of an entity is the position that is attributed to it on some value scale (currency). That position is attributed because of the belief of stakeholders that the entity will bring in useful functional resources for activity; the scale is chosen according to what is important in use for the social exchanges around that activity (e.g. efficiency in an industrial context, care in a family context, etc.)**

**The cognitive assessment of worth grounds the selection of new variants of entities (we select the components that appear to have more value). That is how value systems intervene in decision-making, and especially in selecting new components for installations. This entails**

that the choice is not directly of functional efficiency of the component, or cost efficiency, but it is mediated by a more general social construct, the value system and the main currencies in use in the context of choice. For example, again in an industrial context, a new workstation will be considered better mainly if it is more efficient, perhaps more healthy and safe, rather than because it is more aesthetic, cosy or famous.

Let us now summarize the evolution of lata and symbolic systems. Generation of new ideas comes from the transformation of individual experience through mental processes, as ideas are remodelled, redescribed and combined. That intellectual work produces new variants. In the selection phase, selection of fitter ideas then results in selecting the underlying lata, the inscribed flesh (and the embedded knowledge in symbolic format).

Selection is based on the fit with the real objects (dual match). It is also based on the operational quality of the representation. Finally it is also based on its compatibility and good form in the existing symbolic system so it can tile with the rest of the description system used in the culture (is this written in good English? Is this a correct (e.g. scientific, engineering) representation?)

Variants are compared on the criteria above with each other and with the older versions, based on the added value they are expected to bring. At this point, the expected result in functional terms (outcome of the resulting behaviour or production) is evaluated in simulation. The criteria used are the scales of value in the local polity of worth relevant for the installation (value system): Will this be more efficient (for a production system)? Does it produce more harmonious long-term interpersonal relationships (in the family polity)?, etc.

### 7.3.3.  *Evolution of External Representations*

Representations, thanks to symbolic format, do not need to exist only in an embodied form. They can also, like spores, be separated from the body that created them, be transmitted and then reembodied in another body. They can also be embodied in a nonliving form (e.g. document, object). Pea calls 'inscriptional systems' these external representations (Pea, 1993). Bachimont, in his general theory of the medium, considers that knowledge, as the capacity to reach a goal (see Glossary) can only proceed from an inscription on a physical medium (Bachimont, 2004: 77, 78). In that perspective, the human body is just one of the many possible media for the inscription of knowledge, each medium having its own inscription technique.

> All knowledge, understood as the ability to perform an action, is materially inscribed in some technical support of which the physical structure prescribes its use and the corresponding actions. (Bachimont, 2004: 77; my translation).

There is a continuous loop of reinscription of the representations between external media and embodied representations.

Thanks to the externalization, the body that creates material representations is not necessarily one single human: it can be a group (for example a party, an advertising company, a design team, a focus group). It can even be a machine (a copier, a camera, translation software, radar). Some competences cannot be easily separated from their substratum because they are difficult to translate into immaterial format, like riding a bicycle, or because they are so very dependant of the local resources. Tacit knowledge (Polanyi, 1958, 1967) is an example of the first type. 'Sticky information' (Hippel, 1994), a know-how that cannot easily be transferred from one company to another, is an example of the second. These, as Polanyi noted for tacit knowledge, can be passed on only by example from master to apprentice (Polanyi, 1958: 54), and I would add, as we saw in Section 5.2, 'in the context of the installation'.

In the course of reproduction, storage, transmission and evaluation, representations are for practical reasons transferred onto physical supports and that has considerable implications on their content and usability (Goody, 1977). They become 'external representations' encoded on a medium. We call these representations coded on media 'information', although that term is vague and does not clearly separate the content from the medium. The theory of communication (Shannon, 1948; Shannon & Weaver, 1963) provides a clear framework to distinguish the content from the medium, but it is rather a theory of transmission and says little about the interpretation of the message and the impact of the operations of coding on the content itself.

But as knowledge is translated and reinscribed onto another medium, some components are lost in translation, and some added. Detailed empirical analysis of communication of 'information' in actual practice shows that the contents are extracted from the media and subjected to a series of transformation processes. These processes, as well that those occurring upstream and resulting in coding the content in the message, are not transparent; they contribute to change the content.

Representations coded on media (external representations) are powerful because they transcend some cognitive limitations of humans. They can be compared, linked, classified beyond the limitations of human short-term memory. Graphic representation can combine on one single page very different things. Representations are also reified into objects, as described with the notion of 'mediating structures' (Hutchins, 1995a; see Glossary) but more generally into physical objects such as books and other 'cognitive artifacts' (Norman, 1991; see Glossary).

What is extremely interesting to note is that in practice the selection of new variants (e.g. decisions on projects, choice of a new model, a new theory) are in large-scale society almost always made based on the comparison of several variants in the form of external representations (list of specifications, drawings, blueprints, reports, etc.).

Indeed external representations have affordances that are very important for societal evolution: they are durable, they are transmittable, they are comparable and they are computable[13]

**Durable:** We still can use external representations made long ago (for example old literature, as used in this book, or the graphic representation of a watermill on a Roman sarcophagus mentioned in footnote 68 of Chapter 5). This enables good ideas to endure even if the environment at the time they were generated was not conducive of success. Famous examples include technological lineages that were extinct and then revived, like the electric car.[14]

**Transmittable:** They can travel independently of their authors, their original media or of the thing they represent; also they can do so in some dematerialized form which can travel fast and far, e.g. across the Internet.

**Comparable:** External representations can be put side by side and subjected to clinical systematic examination, far beyond what the very limited short-term human memory capacity. That characteristic is essential for selecting the fittest and literally multiplies the selection capacity.

[13] The properties of external representations make them a powerful instrument in scientific or administrative controversies. Latour, considering the properties of 'immutable mobiles', external representations or inscriptions, showed how their properties of being 'mobile but also immutable, presentable, readable and combinable with one another' can make them an instrument of movable proof that can be mobilized to persuade and win the argument in controversies distant in time and space from the phenomenon represented; hence becoming instruments of power and even domination (Latour, 1986).

[14] The first car to go faster than 100 km/h was a Belgian electric car, 'La jamais contente', and the record was set in 1899.

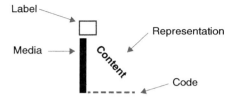

Figure 7.3. Composition of reified representations (documents, messages, etc.).
Adapted from Lahlou & Fischler, 1999: 116.

**Computable:** Finally, because they are in formal format, these external representations can be processed systematically by automata. This enables mass selection, for example as is done in computer simulation to explore multiple possible interpretations. Recent applications have been the victory of computer programmes over human champions in games of chess or Go, evolutionary robotics and the generalized use of computers in structural engineering, biotechnology and so on.

Without these properties, the ratchet effect would be limited to what a human can remember and process, and a lot would be lost in transmission.[15]

When we observe what people do with knowledge, in the process of generation or selection, we can see that a lot of the processing happens outside of the human mind, as Hutchins noted. Our studies showed that in offices, workers set up information-processing chains, where the representations coded on media are separated from their medium by the receiver and then processed mentally or with the help of various tools.

In practice (Figure 7.3), most information arrives in the form of a representation 'coded on media': some substratum (paper, screen, vocal message, etc.) contains, in symbolic format, some encoded representational content. This could be an email, an oral communication from a colleague, a book, an electronic spreadsheet, a video, a journal article, a number on a machine display, etc. These chunks of reified information usually arrive with a label appended, which facilitates dispatch and interpretation, e.g. by indicating the code that must be used to decode the message (think of the format indication at the end of a computer file name, the label on paper file, the title of a message, the emoticon in an email, etc.) The label is an indication of which installation is supposed to process the information.

---

[15] As Goody notes, in societies without writing, creative inventions get lost unless they prove immediately useful (Goody, 1977: 13–14)

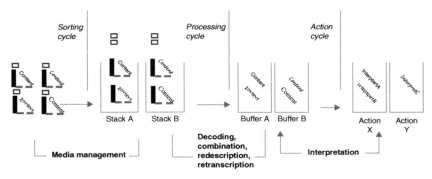

Figure 7.4. The documents processing cycle. *Left* to *right*: he documents arrive at the work station, they are sorted on the basis of their label and preview of content, the content is then decoded and processed for interpretation, they eventually lead to action. Adapted from Lahlou et al., 2002.

Recipients usually first decode the content from its media envelope, combine it with other information and interpret it into action. In that process, the contents are compared, recombined and finally reinscribed on some media to be archived and/or transmitted to other workers. Those processes play a role similar to that of gene transmission in the selection of biological organisms. Figure 7.4 provides a simplified view.

Although that seems pretty trivial to describe, it must be noted that in the process, the media and the coding systems bring a series of affordances and biases that may not have much to do with the content itself, but have an impact on the result. In the same way that the process of information management by the human body modifies the structure and content of representations, and therefore spontaneously creates variants – as described in Section 7.3.1, the information management process of externalized representations does modify the structure and content of representations.

That is not innocuous: the formal processes involved in coding, storage and distribution deeply influence the type of contents that are transmitted and who accesses them, and lead to differential exposure to the various generation and selection mechanisms. First, the system channels the transformations and decisions in the framework of the existing structure, respecting the labour division and the structure of command. This biases towards reproduction of the same, or at least minimizes the risks of changing the structure of the system itself.

Then the process colours the results (generation and diffusion) with the values of the system that filter content at every step of redescription. For example, a very bureaucratic and formal system may orient evolution of variants in a way that is different from an informal and distributed system. For example, when the content has to be put in forms and check boxes, only some dimensions are described, and the subject is often only given a restricted array of choice. Also, the labelling orients treatment (e.g. which department will evaluate, which procedures will be applied).

The encoding of phenomena into formal descriptions (language, graphic symbols, figures, etc.) is a projection into a matrix that has its own properties and is inevitably a distortion and often a reduction. For example, at the time this book was written, innovation projects in industry or government make massive use of presentation software called Microsoft PowerPoint; installed on more than one billion computers. PowerPoint has been widely criticized for reducing and biasing the contents presented (Beaudouin, 2008; Tufte, 2003), among other things by forcing the structure into a linear succession of simplistic bullet point lists.

I describe in Section 6.1 how the very format of scientific communication informs the whole process of science. The phenomenon is more general and applies to procedures also.

> In a study of contemporary cancer research, for example, Fujimura (1992) introduces the trope of the 'standardized package' in the service of understanding processes through which ordering devices and their enactments are made reproducible across research sites (see also Fujimura 1996). A standardized package incorporates both discursive (theoretical) and material (technological) practices. (Suchman, 2007: 194)

The same process of standardization and stabilization operates in organizations. The circuits and formats of the circulating information are a way to maintain the current structure in terms of delegation of decision, labour division and control, by assigning specific tasks and roles to recipients. This means that *only some forms of innovation are left open in the system*, and that the current structure of the organization itself, which is embedded in the format of information and not only in its content, is less prone to innovation.

An interesting example is the use of directed creativity, a widespread technique in organizations. Staff is assembled in 'creativity sessions', usually under the supervision of a creativity consultant. Everyone is asked to freely come up with new ideas, which are then collected and displayed on a wall. Participants are then asked to vote, by sticking anonymously stickers on their preferred ideas. The ideas with the most votes are kept, then some synthesis is attempted. In my experience, the results of such group creativity tend to turn into 'normative reduction': the smart innovative ideas are lost in the process because they get no votes or are destroyed when 'synthesized' with others. By definition, original ideas find little support because they diverge from the norm or are difficult to fit in. That is why democratic forms of managing innovation tend to be prone to some kind of regression to the mean, and the mean is the present state. Perhaps radical innovation is easier in tyrannical mode.

Nevertheless, the generativity of possible combinations is enough to create, here too, the 'continuing abundance of different elements' that is the first condition for evolutionary laws.

**As a takeaway from this section, we note that the external representations have a series of properties that make them handy for cognitive operations and enable a distributed, systematic processing with labour division, capitalization, transmission and evaluation. They are durable, transmittable, comparable and computable. That makes them ideal material for producing many variants that can be selected.**

**We note also that in the process of being externalized and embedded on media, representations re subjected to reductions, transformations and coding which project in them the current structure of the system or organization that produced them. Therefore external representations, even when they propose some innovation or change, naturally tend to be biased towards some implicit reproduction of the system which produced them.**

### 7.3.4.    *Takeaway on the Evolution of Interpretive Structures and External Representations*

**The embodied layer and external representations should be considered together because of the continuous transfers between the two.**

**Experience is capitalized into knowledge in the form of embodied lata, or representations encoded in external media. In both forms, this knowledge is subject to redescriptions and reformatting, which make it compatible with past knowledge.**

**This knowledge is then redescribed and recombined and this produces an abundance of new variants, which are then selected for use in practice. These various operations tend to bias the content towards the values and norms of the system that generates and evaluates the variants. This facilitates continuity and coherence (but tends by design to eliminate some variants).**

External representations present specific properties (durable, transmittable, comparable and computable) that make them especially handy for assessment, storage and transmission. Selection of new models is based on thought experiments where variants are evaluated for fitness to their functional purpose, but also where their worth is assessed based on values. Values are generalized currencies of utility in the local culture. A given model can be assessed on several values.

Overall, the evolution of knowledge follows an evolutionary process based on generation and selection. But the evolution of knowledge appears therefore more complex than the evolution of biological species. First, the generation is combinatory rather than merely reproductive. Second, the format of external representations used in the process of evaluation introduces biases in favour of coherence with the current state. Third, selection is based on simulation of potential impact rather than on actual trials in the real world. Fourth, the selection criteria used go beyond the local efficiency and involve more generic 'values', which are determined by the dominant forms of social exchange and stakes in the local culture.

## 7.4.  Genesis and Evolution of Objects

Our core interest as social scientists is not how material objects are designed, so we'll keep this section short; furthermore some of the topic has been partly covered in Section 6.2 about innovation. We are interested in how variants are generated, and selected. I describe the generation and selection mechanisms in the design cycle, and then sketch some of the generic laws that emerge from technological development.

Some objects are natural, like the sun and the moon, but most objects of our daily environment are constructed by the human hand: 'artefacts'. Look around you now, reader: unless you are reading in a primary forest, it is likely that most objects in your visible environment are man-made.

Artefacts are not randomly made, they follow a plan; their makers design and build them with a specific purpose in mind. These designs, unless in radical innovation that is the odd case, resemble previous objects with minor modifications.

Objects are made from their representation. Figure 7.5 focuses on the relevant section of the general process, and shows (in grey) the three selection processes to which new objects are subjected in their reified, material, form (dual matching with the symbolic representation, reality trial and compliance with institutional regulation).

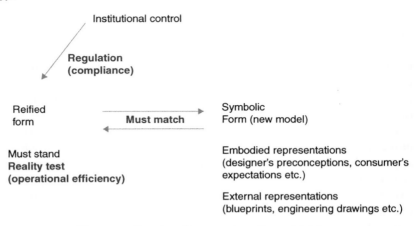

Figure 7.5. Genesis and construction of material objects.

In practice, there is a design cycle, in which, when the mental representation of the object is evaluated as good enough to be tried in the real world, the object is then reified into a material artefact. Often, as described in Section 7.3.3, there is an intermediary phase in which the object is externally represented in material media (engineering drawing, plan, etc.) because that facilitates construction of an object that matches the representation, especially if construction requires some division of labour. Based on the representation, a first version of the object is made. Then, the resulting artefact is confronted to a series of trials. Is it really feasible? Does it work? Does it produce the expected outcome? Is the object robust? Is it compatible with the current regulations?

For example, a new helmet is imagined, using a new material that is better for shock absorption. The prototype is compared against the concept and ideas: for example, is it technically feasible with the current tools, does the material enable it to keep the right shape (does it match the new model?). The prototype is also subjected to regulations (does it pass the crash tests?). It is subjected to reality tests in the actual installations for which it is designed (is it comfortable to wear?) and to a marketing test (do consumers like it?) In practice, selection trials may combine several tests in one: the consumer test is both a test of matching the consumer's expectations and of functional satisficing.

Based on these selection criteria, the object may be modified and rebuilt according to an amended representation, which results in an amended model, until a material solution that fits is obtained. The results of the reality test are a feedback to the representation, which can then be modified intentionally to correct the result.

In the course of that process, sometimes interesting and unexpected discoveries are made. For example, both the Post-it note and penicillin resulted from functional properties of material artefacts that were discovered during tests of objects designed with another purpose. Also, final users may sometimes come up with a different use of the artefacts made. Serendipity is a contributor to evolution of objects.

Recently there has been an increased effort to design objects according to the expectations of users and clients. A considerable amount of effort and resources are spent in 'market research', basically studies to understand what the client expects the object will be like. Conversely, once the object is made substantial amounts of resources are also spent into trying to influence the representation of the clients to make it match the object ('advertising', 'persuasion'), so the dual matching process does go both ways.

The human design process of oriented trial and error that combines selection at symbolic level and material level is more efficient than the natural biological evolution process. It took millions of years for natural evolution to produce adapted life forms. Natural evolution is limited by the length of a generation, because the physical reproduction process takes time. Also, the mutations are random. In contrast, in only a few hundred thousand years, humans, with the cultural evolution mechanism outlined in this chapter, have achieved a number of very complex systems. Stevens and Burley (1997) venture that there is a ratio of about 3,000 ideas for one successful commercial product; but most ideas do not even reach the reality test phase: in fact only one in 1,800 of raw unwritten ideas would get to that stage, and only 9 out of 3,000 reach some significant material testing phase (Figure 7.6).

As a result of this preselection, of which more than 95% is done in thought experiment (simulation with models), the success rate of innovative products on the market is evaluated to about 10% to 60% depending upon the sources. Castellion and Markham (2013) argue that the figure of 80% failure rate that is widespread in consultant's slides and press articles is an urban legend, and the real figure is around 40%. Statistics are difficult to make; it is hard to know exactly at which stage of development products considered in the studies are, so these figures should only be taken as an indication of magnitude. We must also note here that in the process, usually the initial ideas get modified according to intermediate discussions, tests and constraints – the selection process is not a fit-or-die one, but one of marginal improvement through feedback. But the final

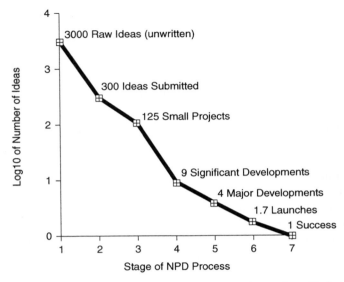

Figure 7.6. 'Universal industrial success curve' illustrating the number of 'substantially new product ideas' surviving between stages of the new product development process (from Stevens & Burley, 1997).

result remains the same: ***the bulk of the selection is done at the stage of simulation with models.***

Although this final market launch success ratio has sometimes been lamented as 'small' by marketers and industrialists, it should be compared to the rate of successful mutations in biological organisms, which is smaller by several orders of magnitudes as they evolve in random trial and error. As an illustration, it took about fifty years for microorganisms, among the fastest-adapting organisms, to become resistant to all antibiotics, even though they can develop resistance faster than by mere genetic mutation through exchange of plasmids. Colistin was a last-reserve antibiotic invented in 1952; it was authorised in animal farming in 1989. *Escherichia coli*, of which the generation time in vitro is 17 minutes, has only recently been found resistant to colistin after its widespread use in Chinese pig farms (Liu et al., 2016). Even if we take a generous twenty-four hours as a generation time for *E. coli* in vivo, that means it has taken about eight thousand generations to adapt, in over twenty years; to be compared with the couple of generations and few months needed to develop a new variant of an industrial product.

The hybrid evolution cycle of artefacts is very efficient because it anticipates in the simulation the potential failures of fit of new variants in their interaction with the various layers of the installations, and eliminates them at the simulation stage. That is made possible by the separation of the symbolic layer of knowledge from the material layer of objects and the use of representations. *So **we see here that the triple structure of installations, and especially the separation of the material and symbolic layer, is not only a factor of stability, but also an evolutionary advantage that enables faster and more economic evolution**.*

As stated above, the information management *process* has an impact on the structure and content of information. Technology is the science of craft; it is a system for systematically accumulating, storing and transferring knowledge and know-how about how to make artefacts. Technology also has discovered some laws of evolution of artefacts, which result from the properties of external representations, of constraints on production and general constraints of material efficacy.

Technologists have been able to identify 'lineages' in objects, which follow some inherited shape or principle, in a way very similar to animals species (Deforge, 1985). This results from the continuity of innovation based on functional design (e.g. front-load washing machine; Diesel engine), but also from the fact that once a functional principle is discovered, it can be stored as an external representation and saved for a later use. We already mentioned the example of the electric car (Section 7.3.3), a principle that was abandoned for almost a century before flourishing again.

Another law, the 'fusion of components' was described by Simondon and by Deforge (Deforge, 1985), a member of the École de Compiègne who developed the ideas of Simondon. Let us take the classic example of the radiator in a combustion engine, described in detail by Simondon (Simondon, 1989: 21–2) Early radiators were a separate part of the engine, with the sole function of evacuating the heat of the engine. As motors developed, the radiator became further and further integrated with other parts. Cooling fins were added to the valve area of the motor head, and at first their only function was to dissipate heat, but gradually they came to play a mechanical role, as ribs opposing deformation of the cylinder head under the pressure of gases. This results in a global structure that uses less material than the previous, and more efficient thermal dissipation because the cylinder wall is thinner. A similar evolution is visible on automobiles: the mudguards and fenders, which were separate parts of the body on early models, gradually became integrated into it (Deforge, 1985: 142–5)

There is a convergence towards a process of concretization, towards a leaner object where the various components are combined in such a way that each part can play several functional roles. This enables the object to meet economic constraints (less raw material, work, energy consumption) and technological requirements (the object must not be self-destructive, it must stay stable in operation as long as possible) (Simondon, 1989: 26, 34).

Conversely, the fusion of components, by reducing redundancy, also makes the system less resilient to failure and more resistant to change because an attempt to change one part of the system for one function may also impact other functions served by the same part.

Economics and technology organize the evolution of objects. The laws of technology apply to objects just as the laws of chemistry and physics apply to living organisms and their growth (Thompson, 1942). Such laws of technological evolution contribute to produce new variants in design; they express the pressure of mechanical and economic selection processes. These laws also operate in the evolution of installations.

### 7.4.1. *Takeaway on the Evolution of Objects*

**Objects are created and evolve through a design cycle. In this cycle, when the representation of the object is evaluated as 'good enough' to be tried in the real world, it is then reified into a material artefact. There is a spiral loop between the object and its representation; the latter is almost always inscribed in external representations (models). Both material version and represented version undergo a series of trials.**

**Material forms are tested in real-world experiments; models are tested in simulation (cognitive selection). The outcome is submitted to evaluation within the local value system of the activity, which results in selection. The selection is subject to institutional control.**

**Technology and production have their own laws (fusion of components, functional integration), which are somewhat independent of the worth in use for activity. The bulk of the selection is done on models, which is faster and more economical.**

### 7.5. The Regulation of Installations and the Evolution of Institutions

We have seen that embodied interpretation systems emerge from the practice with actual objects in the environment (or indirectly through systematic education); and conversely that actual objects are constructed from their representations. Therefore objects and their representations are taken in a chicken-and-egg reproduction cycle. We have also seen that institutions monitor the reproduction process by imposing their own selection procedures, through compliance and pressure to normality, on top of the fitness and matching tests that representations and material objects have to pass.

The regulation of institutions was described for *components* of installations at their two levels: education and control of new behaviours, construction of new objects and formalisation of representations. But are installations per se regulated as complete systems (rather than through their parts)? And do institutions also evolve? Section 7.5.1 addresses the first question, Section 7.5.2 the second.

### 7.5.1. *The Regulation of Installations*

Are there regulations at the level of the Parisian café, of the classroom, of the family dinner, rather than only regulations of juice bottles, work contracts, education programmes or cutlery norms? Who regulates installations?

Yes there are regulations at installation level. *Installations are regulated as such; they are regulated by stakeholders interested in their good operation, as well as by those who incur their externalities.*

Many people can have a say in the evolution of installations: those who have ownership on the material objects, those whose jurisdiction or power encompasses the physical space where the installation operates, those who have control over the humans who operate in the installations.

Initiatives may also come from other entities who incur or manage the externalities of the installation (for example the neighbours of the cafés, the students and their unions for the lectures, the doctor for the family dinners) but arbitration is usually done by those in charge of the installation. Indeed there are usually one or several bodies that have the authority, and/or responsibility, on an installation In our examples here the legal entities who own the café, the school[16] the family. These bodies may have a hierarchical structure: owner/manager; principal/teacher, parents/children, etc.

---

[16] For example, in the US education system, regulation of curriculum by states and school districts, teacher quality testing by districts and states and sometimes in tension, by teacher unions, and assessment of learning regulated, depending on grade level and subject, by the federal government or, largely, the states and local school districts (Roy Pea, personal communication, 2016).

The list above means that several different entities may regulate the same installation at different levels. The regulators may be nested, cooperative and/or competitive. For example, consider a fairground stall, say a shooting gallery. That installation may be regulated by the showman who runs the place (e.g. price, prizes, decoration, etc.), by the management of the fair (opening hours, noise level), by the laws of the country (type of guns allowed), etc. For the example of the lecture, the same: the teacher, the school, the state all impose their regulation; each with their own selection criteria. They also suggest or encourage modifications from their own perspective according to their own value system.

We showed in the previous sections how value systems and different evaluation metrics or processes can be used to select candidate alternatives for change. The mechanisms remain the same for installations as a whole, but what is selected now is the outcome of installations: the behaviour, the product of the behaviour, the impact of that behaviour in general. What is interesting here is that the selection process must now consider a compound, the installation, therefore it inevitably considers a combination of changes in the various layers, which each have their own selection criteria; also it considers impacts on various stakeholders, who usually have partly convergent, but also partly divergent if not opposing interests.

For example, the interests of the clients and the owner of a café are convergent in producing a harmonious service, but they diverge in interests for the distribution of costs. The interest of teachers and students converge in having a harmonious lecture but they diverge in the choice of evaluation procedure (marking) and course preparation. The interest of parents and children converge in having harmonious dinners but diverge in labour division (who prepares, who sets the table, etc.) Therefore, the selection of variants in installations is a compromise between stakeholders' interests; it is not only a technical but also a political process involving power struggles, conflicts, negotiation, controversies and governance issues.

At societal level, the coevolution of installations is monitored by domain-local communities of interest and stakeholders (users, providers, public authorities, etc.) who set the patterns of behaviour allowed in the public space. Because these stakeholders know the field, objects, representations and rules are adapted to behaviours. These stakeholders create institutions (see Glossary and Sections 4.4 and 5.4), which are both sets of rules to be applied to maintain order and foster cooperation, and communities of interest aware that they are playing in the same game. We describe the rules to maintain the installation in Section 4.4, but there are also rules to select evolution, and (political) rules to determine the criteria and processes that are used in such process.

For example, there are hierarchical rules for decision-making (one person or body is in charge of the final choice between alternatives: e.g. the boss), rules for building the case (a specific subunit may be in charge of making the evaluation, such as the audit supervisor, or the marketing department), rules for arbitration (vote, committee work), etc.

What is the evolutionary advantage of such institutions? Economy in transaction costs and avoidance of feuds.

Let us imagine that there are no institutions regulating the evolution of installations. Then, every time a new variant is proposed, all the stakeholders would fight to influence the choice in a direction that is favourable to what they perceive to be their own best interest. Although this may result in a choice that reflects the state of respective power of influence and agency of the parties involved at the time, it certainly creates substantial transaction costs, frustration of some parties based on outcomes being lower than anticipated, and in the course of the conflict durable antagonisms may occur that are an obstacle to future cooperation. Although such confrontations of interests are useful, their systematic repetition at every occasion of change is problematic. It slows evolution and creates collateral costs that may outweigh the benefits of betterment.

Now when there are institutions, they stabilize the state of things after such a struggle, and prevent the occurrence of new struggles, by avoiding change, or funnelling change according to the selection principles that were adopted (or enforced) at the outset of the last struggle. In this perspective, the processes of arbitration are in favour of keeping organisational cohesion and long-term relations, and this may select out some innovations that would be beneficial to only some or (more often than not) to the less powerful.

This logic of selection by institutions therefore appears not simply a rationale of making the installation as efficient as possible, but rather it is to minimize transaction costs and avoid open conflicts and other collateral damage resulting from confronting divergent interests. This does not mean that institutions do not try to optimize the efficiency of installations; of course they do and this is usually the official and primary purpose of institutions. But we must remain aware that avoiding collateral damage is a key factor in the selection process by institutions.

*What we must take away from this section is the following:*

- *there is regulation of evolution at the level of installations;,*
- *this regulation is done by the bodies officially in charge of these installations,*
- *the regulation usually involves arbitration between divergent interests of various stakeholders,*
- *although institutions strive to optimize the efficiency of the installation in its primary purpose (production of correct behaviour), an important aspect of the selection process is to stabilize the system and to avoid transaction costs and organizational negative externalities,*
- *therefore, the institutional regulation inevitably reflects the power balance between the stakeholders.*

### 7.5.2.     The Evolution of Institutions

Institutions themselves evolve, and this evolution has impact on installations. Indeed, institutions are what ultimately control the evolution of installations, so if one wants to change the installation one should take the control of institutions.

We should not be naive: institutions are not 'fair' by nature. They simply reflect the balance of power between the various stakeholders at a given point in time. Depending on how the arbitration is made, the 'power' can be the expression of different resources: finance (shareholder's assembly), persuasion (committee work, media campaigns), number (democratic vote), etc. This struggle for control (because in the end who controls installations controls behaviour) is visible to anyone who has been a member of boards or decision bodies. Apart from some rare exceptions of those who by some position of power or independence are protected from the impact of potential decisions, participants exhibit a strong tendency to advocate for the interests of their local community. The default attitude of participants in meetings is to make one's best efforts so that no decision is taken that would have a negative impact on one's constituency (department, unit, area, discipline, party, etc.), or on oneself.

When the power balance changes, those who have more agency attempt to change the institutions to match their own vision and approach. This is typically what happens during elections in democratic systems (at any level, from the government of a state to the steering committee in charge of the bar of the student's association). Some regimes of governance plan such renewal on a regular basis (elections), some others require more aggressive takeover (public companies); sometimes a revolution is necessary. Don't misunderstand me: I take no specific stand here other than descriptive; I don't mean that autocratic structures, or democratic structures, are better to run installations. There is no such thing as a best governance system in the absolute: it all depends on the evaluation criteria used, and institutions all strive to be as efficient as possible based on their own set of values.

We now can see better the evolutionary role of institutions as a social monitoring and control system overseeing the reproduction of installations to keep selection guided by the proper values.[17] This regulation of installations by institutions is also a regulation of the processes by which installations evolve. They supervise and frame that evolution process.

Through political struggle, individuals and groups come up with compromises that are then reified by institutions. In doing so, institutions bring stability and save transaction costs. We saw the classic definition of institutions (as a set of rules) is to regulate behaviour. In practice, institutions often do so by regulating installations, which in turn regulate behaviour.

Social construction is a complex evolutionary process, multilayered and path-dependant, where material objects and their representations evolve as two semiautonomous sets distributed over – and used by – populations of humans as scaffolding instruments to interpret the world and act upon it.

---

[17] Interestingly, the positive role of institutions in the long run has been rediscovered by evolutionary robotics. Evolutionary robotics simulate the evolution of organisms by trial and error, by modelling the system inside powerful computers, producing variants and computing the fitness in 'tournaments': fit individuals are then reproduced and their characteristics combined with the rest of the population. As a result, the characteristics of the population drift. Computing power enables that tournaments can be simulated 'in silico' thousands of times in a split second. Here is how Phil Husbands describes one of his successful models:

> An important part of this model is a population of Arbitrators, again initially randomly generated. The Arbitrators' job is to resolve conflicts between members of the other populations; their fitness depends on how well they achieve this. Each population, including the Arbitrators, evolve under the influence of selection, crossover and mutation … The Arbitrators are required to resolve conflicts arising when members of the other populations demand the same resources during overlapping time intervals … It should be noted that in early versions of the work to be described, the Arbitrators were not used. Instead fixed population precedence rules were applied. Not surprisingly, this and similar schemes were found to be too inflexible and did not give good results. Hence the Arbitrator idea was developed and has proved successful. (Husbands, 1994)

An intuitive idea here is that if there is no regulation by arbitrators, then the fitness for the specific subcompetition for scarce resources will become a major selective advantage, and may overwhelm the selective advantages that are required for an overall optimization of the population. An example would be in a competition between projects, say, in science, those proponents who have some better capacity to get access to funding sources or publication networks would see their projects chosen because of that selective advantage of 'nice project writing' rather than based on the quality of the project they submit. The role of the arbitration is to focus selection on the criteria that are relevant at a higher level.

Objects themselves are not passive; they are actants that contribute to the interactions with and between humans.

**Humans have constructed institutions as social instruments to control the reproduction and evolution of these sets of scaffolding instruments (installations), and institutions themselves evolve as a result of power struggle between communities. Politics organizes the evolutionary competition of institutions and their underlying communities.**

**The coevolution between artefacts and representations is done under monitoring and control of stakeholder communities, which use institutions as social and economic instruments to safeguard their interests. Institutions reflect the balance of power between stakeholders.**

### 7.6.    A Synthetic Schema of the Evolution of Installations

The closer examination of evolution of installations provides the following model.

There is a core replication mechanism in which practice reproduces the installation in day-to-day operation. In this mechanism, described in Chapter 5, each of the layers is reproduced by the two others.

(1)  Practice informs embodiment of the correct lata in humans, by guiding humans into performing the expected behaviour (through affordances and social regulation) and the natural biological mechanisms of learning imprint the corresponding lata into the nervous system and body.

(2)  Objects are continuously reconstructed after their embodied representations. In that process, external representations of objects (blueprints, etc.) are also constructed and facilitate transmission and endurance.

(3)  Institutions monitor these reproduction processes by organizing education, by creating norms of what behaviours are acceptable and enforcing them. They also ensure that there is compatibility between the various installations; conflicts are taken care of and compromises stabilized by rules.

The evolution of installations involves reproduction at the synchronic scale and change at the diachronic scale.

**Objects and their embodied representations reproduce in a chicken-and-egg fashion, representations being constructed through practice, and objects being constructed from their representation taken as a model. Each kind is subjected to a Darwinian selection process of fitness: objects in the arena of reality, and models in the symbolic**

world. Reality tests challenge the functional fitness of the installation and its components. Models are tested by simulation of their potential outcome, in thought experiments and through external representations (cognitive selection).

In cognitive selection the worth of new variants is based on the belief in what functional value the new variants bring in. Institutions monitor this dual selection cycle of reproduction by controlling what is allowed to exist in the public space. They add their own selection criteria of compliance to regulations and conformity with norms. In parallel, each layer independently evolves according to its own laws: this adds to the variation.

That reproduction cycle is resilient enough to small variations to remain quasi-stable. This quasi-stability still results in a gradual drift, where the installation undergoes marginal modifications for minor adjustments.

But more substantial modifications may also occur. These can happen through some local invention ('innovation'), made possible by the capacity of imagination and simulation that the symbolic system allows (e.g. discovery), or by the 'crossed impact' of a change that occurred elsewhere in the system and that induces a major change in one of the components of the installation. These may come, for example, from new institutional rules, reflecting a change in the balance of power.

Finally, the layers also have their internal logic that may bias the evolution or induce specific constraints. For example, the formatting imposed by the external representation process, or the laws of mass production and technology, have effects on which representations will be selected and what objects will be produced.

The core reproduction cycle, by adapting each layer to the two others under the constraint of functional efficiency, keeps the installation coherent across these bigger changes.

This results in an evolutionary spiral, where the core reproduction cycle gradually drifts but still keeps its short-term local capacity to reproduce through practice. Figure 7.7 shows this evolution of the components of the installation. The reader will notice that it is the same as Figure 7.2, which describes the core reproduction cycle; the sources of evolution of the core reproduction cycle were simply added on the outer rim.

The two mechanisms involved in evolution do not happen at the same time scale. The core reproduction cycle is on a daily scale, whereas the larger evolution is more observable on a yearly scale.

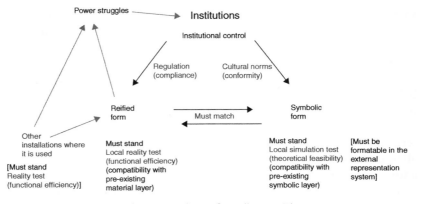

Figure 7.7. The long-term betterment loop of installations. The components must pass the various trials of the dual supervised selection systems for the local installation. In that process the material form of components must match their immaterial model. Each form is also separately evaluated in trials. Some external constraints on the components come from other installations to which these components participate; and from the necessity to take into account crossed impacts and externalities. Finally, higher-level systems of worth are imposed by institutions as extra selection factors.

**Finally, the installations themselves are the locus where the coalition of assembled elements is evaluated as a bundle: does the new version produce better results? That is assessed by the quality of the resulting behaviour.** Figure 7.8 pictures this evaluation of the new against the old by comparing their aesthetic results. In reality, that overall behavioural quality is measured along the worth scales in order in the local community, by the institutions in charge. Because there are many scales of worth, such judgement is usually the result of trade-offs and involves power struggles.

The system we have described shares some features with the biological evolution: for example, the selection of variants under various constraints of the milieu. But it also has specific features such as coherence-maintaining mechanisms that firmly anchor the new variant in the preexisting systems, anticipation capacities that can select variants based on their simulated outcome, 'external' information storage capacity that conserve and transmit representations (and can do so irrespective of their current level of fitness). This capacity to capitalize on the assets constructed during previous experience, combined with the cautious mechanisms of critical assessment of new variants before investing in them, generates sophisticated betterment

Figure 7.8. Short-term betterment loop of installations. The combination of components in the three layers in the new installation (*right*) produces a more harmonious behaviour (inside triangle) than the older version (*left*).

loops with multilayered and distributed storage and regulation. It makes the evolution of installations risk-averse and safe.

Also there are specific mechanisms related to the hybrid nature of installations that ensure the continuous match of its various components locally while allowing for some independence of the components from one another. For example, the investments in form in the process of model construction and in the format of the models and the monitoring and selection procedures.

One could conclude that this stringent selection mechanism, which we have seen at work in industrial innovation, would freeze installations, but that is not the case. In fact, that stringent selection must be considered in the light of the massive creativity allowed by the combinatory power of redescription and the technologies of the mind (external representations, literacy, etc.) That is the power of simulation. As a consequence, installations can evolve fast at historical scale. As a matter of fact, installations evolve much faster than biological species; we often see major changes of installations within the span of one human generation.

As a result, the three layers of the installations coevolve in a way that is more efficient and faster than the classic Darwinian selection mechanism solely based on trial and error and selection of the fittest. Even though installations evolve fast, their resilience, which also results from their multilayered regulation mechanisms, is remarkable.

This latter property, the resilience of the core reproduction cycle, is interesting in the perspective of the change agent who wants to change the system. Indeed, one can expect that the system will adapt dynamically to minor variations; therefore one does not have to deal up front with the whole complexity and can, to some extent, force a change in one layer and expect the system to drift gracefully if that change does actually have ecological worth and minimal negative externalities.

The next chapter illustrates some interventions to change installations.

# CHAPTER 8

# Redesigning Installations to Change Behaviour

**This section is more applicative. The examples provided in Chapters 2 and 3 showed how installation theory can be used for descriptive and analytic purposes; now we will see examples of its use in interventions.**

**Four examples are presented: a small-scale intervention in an academic department to foster communal activity, an intervention to increase water intake in Polish preschool children, the design of an installation for presentations in a meeting room and interventions to change social norms about incivility and violence in Colombia.**

**The reader who jumped directly to this chapter in the hope of getting straight to the 'how to' is advised to read Chapter 4 or at least Section 2.1 and Section 9.1, which are abstracts of the theory, because reading the following illustrations alone will not enable one to design interventions. It is necessary to know a minimum about the framework underlying these interventions.**

Sustainability for a system is the capacity to last in time (endurance); usually this implies that the internal structures of the system enable it to maintain as is, and that the relationship of the system to its environment has reached some quasi-stable state.

At the time of writing, sustainability has a political connotation and also refers to planet Earth's ecosystems (including the anthroposphere) and the ways to maintain them thriving and diverse. We are here interested in the endurance of installations, and of the behaviours that go with them. This may have impacts on global sustainability or not. Indeed some installations can be locally very enduring and still have a negative impact on the planet as an ecosystem. In fact, most human activities that use non-renewable resources fall into that category. A gold mine, a fishing boat, a coal power plant, for example, may not contribute to global sustainability; nevertheless as installations we must admit that they have endurance because they sustain the same set of behaviour for decades. Sustainability raises the issue of the scale of time and space considered. We focus here only on what makes an installation able to last in time and operate successfully. I trust the reader will have at heart also the larger interest of the planet.

A 'good' installation should closely support and monitor the desired activity at every step. Crucial steps should be supported and controlled by the three layers simultaneously. Of course there will be a trade-off between supporting every step with the three layers (heavy and costly) and supporting each step with only one layer at a time (cost-efficient but less resilient).

In practice, the way to go for betterment is to follow the current activity step by step in the installation, and analyse at each step what affordances and what competences are necessary to improve it. Affordances supporting the desired features should be made available and control implemented to avoid failure, risks and externalities. Rules indicating what is recommended and/or what is forbidden can be made, and one should make sure that some other agents will be present to enforce the rules if necessary. Relevant embodied competences should be present in participants according to their respective roles. When the competences are inadequate, training should be considered.

A high degree of freedom is provided by the fact that the same behavioural feature can be scaffolded by any of the three layers. Therefore, intervention can be opportunistic and target what seems the easiest layer to work on, given the available resources and the agency of the change agent.

Also, redesign of the installation can take advantage of distributed cognition and action, and a given part of the process can be executed by one or another human agent, or by a nonhuman actant such as a computer. Tim Kindberg and Armando Fox introduced the expression 'semantic Rubicon' to express the principle that some decisions and actions can be either at the initiative of the user or at the initiative of the automated system (Kindberg & Fox, 2002). That limit can be moved by the designer. Gapenne and colleagues (Gapenne, Lenay, & Boullier, 2002) distinguish four ways in which the technological systems can improve human/system coupling: supplementation, assistance, support and substitution; all these are possible paths for redesign. Control (monitoring and limiting user's action) is also always implicitly present in installations; its rigour and domain of application are design parameters.

When there are several possible ways to act at a given step, given the competences and affordances, then some ways may be better than others. It is therefore useful to have a clear vision of the worth criteria that are used to assess the alternatives.

Involving participants and stakeholders is a necessary aspect of intervention on installations, as it is for design in general (Bødker, Ehn, Sjogren, & Sundblad, 2000; Schuler & Namioka, 1993). First, participants better accept changes in which they had the opportunity to have their say. Second, in the long run, the installation works better if the participants are motivated, because their interest and motivation are the main drivers of their actions. Changes must therefore take these motivations into account. Third, negative externalities always bring problems and costs: it is therefore wise to include those who will be impacted by the changes to foresee and minimize collateral damage.

Finally, installations tend to evolve with their environment: the current changes are never the last ones; installations are always works in progress and one must design them so that future evolution is made simpler. This includes considering day-to-day maintenance and drift adaptation as functions of the installation that must be planned and facilitated. For example, when coding software, making good documentation and comments in the code makes future interventions easier; designing independent modules makes changes easier; using standard components rather than in-house development facilitates evolution, etc.

Good design is design that considers that the ordinary state of the system is a 'degraded state' with some degree of local failure on many minor aspects of the process. Terry Winograd's team provides an illuminating series of design principles in this regard for the case of augmented environments using advanced information technology. Two of them are especially relevant for installations (replace 'system' and 'workspace' with 'installation' in the following quote):

> '- The interactions should maximize the potential for 'fluency' of the users, reducing as much as possible the need to shift attention from the content of the work to the mechanism ...
>
> - The system should be loosely coupled and robust, so that failures and changes of individual elements are gracefully handled and do not disrupt the functioning of the overall workspace.'(Johanson, Fox, & Winograd, 2010: 31)

More generally, capacity not only for smooth operation but also for maintenance evolution must be implemented at design stage, since the life of an installation covers four stages: design, operation, maintenance and evolution. (Lahlou, 2007a).[1]

Although these comments may seem at first to have little to do with psychology and social science, on the contrary, the embodied layer of competences is crucial. As Lomov noted, the more automated the system, the more the operator must embody competences to be able to fix the inevitable failures (Lomov, 1963: 19–22); this includes having a good overall vision and models of the local subsystems and their relations.

Change agents should make sure that appropriate installations in the three layers (physical environment, embodied competences and relevant institutions) have been addressed. What is left to them is the strategy of how to create and distribute improvements. For example, one could start with the physical layer by procuring products, and then try to recruit some organizations so they take over the educative part of the installation. The fact that we have three possible levers for action enables us to be opportunistic in strategies, and to start with what is the most feasible at one given point of time from the perspective of the change agent.

This chapter therefore addresses the process of intentional change of installations. Starting in Section 8.1 with classic approaches in psychology and their application in groups and organizations (e.g. unfreeze-change-refreeze from Lewin to Schein), I show why efficient change process should be done hands-on, in actual situations. I then provide four examples, at micro-level in an academic department (Section 8.2), at micro-level in families but on a large scale (Section 8.3), at meso-level in an organization (Section 8.4) and at city level (Section 8.5). Then I provide a simple way to proceed in using installation theory to inform the change and redesign process (Section 8.6).

The section remains sketchy: I trust the readers will creatively adapt the principles to their own endeavours.

## 8.1.    Intervention and Change in Organizations

There is no such thing as a passive equilibrium. It results from the balance of competing forces. When a system has reached an equilibrium, it means there are active forces at work that maintain it in this state.

Therefore the forces that maintain the system in a stable state oppose some resistance to minor changes. The system may yield but then come

---

[1] The sustainability-conscious reader will notice that a good design from cradle to grave should also actually also include decommissioning and recycling.

back after a few oscillations, or even resist strongly any move in the phase space. Since most systems that we deal with when we want to change them have reached a quasi-stable state, we can almost take for granted the existence of this local attractor basin with a set of forces that maintain the system in it, and will actively resist attempts to change.

The intuition behind Lewin's change theory is that the system needs to be put away from this local attractor zone first (unfreeze), before it stabilizes into another zone. Another of Lewin's intuitions was that to move the system in one direction, because of this tensor system of opposing forces, there are two ways: either push stronger in one direction, adding to the forces in that direction, or simply lower the opposing forces, then the existing forces in the right direction will meet less resistance and the system will move.

The second approach (lowering the opposing forces) is obviously more efficient, because it spares the energy of the forces of resistance and does not need additional force in the direction of change.

But are there already forces that push in the right direction? The very dynamical nature of equilibria suggests that yes, one force or a set of forces combined do already push in that direction, otherwise the system would have gone 'backwards' already.[2] Therefore a key question becomes what are the forces that oppose change, and for what reason. 'Oppose' must not be understood here in an agonistic or conflictual way; that is of course the way they tend to be perceived by change agents, as 'resistance'; but in fact their nature is not to oppose change, and by the way, they were in place even before the change was considered; rather they try to push the system in an opposite direction for some valid reason. This mechanism must be understood. It may be, often, because these forces foster or defend the interests of some group. With this group a negotiation must take place to see how the new desired state would safeguard their interests in a different manner, or provide them fair compensation.

The vocabulary of 'forces' results from the mechanics physics that were used as a metaphor in Lewin's model, and this vocabulary chimes with our natural tendency to attribute agency and responsibility mainly to humans – the so-called fundamental attribution bias. A problem with this approach is that it tends to attribute the source of the problem to 'people' and generates suspicion, blame and conflicts.

---

[2] We assume here that we want to move the system in the same plane where forces maintain it. Of course there are other dimensions for which that strategy is not usable.

Installation theory incites us to a more objective approach and to look for the determinants of action, rather than for agonistic 'forces', to look into the affordances of objects, the embodied competences and external representations, and the institutions. As mentioned above, a systematic analysis of what component of what layer is instrumental in determining each section of the behaviour provides a map of the possible interventions and how they might impact the behaviour.

If we want to change the installation, regarding the social layer, institutions should be the objects of our analysis and the targets of our intervention to amend the rules so they foster appropriate behaviour, and foster social mechanisms that effect and enforce these rules. For the physical layer, it is a matter of designing the right affordances to support and channel that behaviour. Regarding embodied competences, instruction, training or simply experience can be considered to complement or correct the existing stock, but framing the first time a subject performs the behaviour is critical: that can be obtained by making the installation more resilient with increased redundancy between its layers.

## 8.2.   Micro-level: An Academic Department

A small-scale example, in a context well known to the academic reader, illustrates the principles of enabling change to foster collective intelligence in a department with a staff of forty-five. My original assessment, as I arrived as head of that department, coming from another organization, was that even though the people were very kind and got along together it lacked a common narrative, and that its teaching as well as its research was more the juxtaposition of individual initiatives than the result of collaborative projects and team work. That situation must be familiar to many colleagues in social sciences, where researchers are as easy to manage as a bunch of wild cats and suspicious of any authority that could interfere with their academic freedom (I include myself in the bunch). The idea was then to create an installation to produce collaborative behaviour, and to do this openly by involving participation in a double-loop learning (Argyris, 1976). I had in previous experiments found that changing the setting could solve collaboration issues that were rebellious to managerial intervention (Lahlou, 2008b).

After observing the setting for a year without taking any substantial decision, I suggested we create a staff coffee room, and this became a collective project. Clawing back a room, we created a physical space for the desired activity, in the form of a large and comfortable staff room, which was named for the founder of the department half a century before. One researcher chose a nice coffee machine; we bought comfy seats and put art on the wall and in a corner was a life-size standing picture of Freud with his cigar.

The physical setting was not enough; it needed the actual affordance for staff to meet and that was rendered difficult by different timetables and the fact that not everyone was on-site at the same moment. We created time for this activity by freeing teaching timetables on Tuesdays, securing the presence of staff and of our thirty-plus research students by moving research seminars and the PhD seminar on Tuesdays (institutional rules). In doing so, we created the affordance for regular informal meetings and brown-bag lunches, which partly eliminated some staff eating sandwiches alone in their offices. Of course, was not so easy because we had to relocate the previous users of the room and change routine timetables that had been in operation for decades, find the budgets, etc. It took a year.

In the collective discussion space opened, and through practice in these 'Research Tuesdays', a common research agenda and narrative (representations and practice, interpretation layer) was produced and a new dynamics of collective intelligence and collaboration emerged. For example, this led to the production of a paper coauthored by most academics of the department, which was a manifesto of common scientific goals and values (Howarth et al., 2013). This common narrative that clarified the positioning of the department was used many times in various internal reporting exercises and presentations of the department outside the institution.

Another output was more discussions about teaching, which resulted in the various Masters in the department, each of whom originally had their own core course, together creating a 'flagship course', which eventually became a common half of the core courses of the various Masters. The department gained a reputation of being a nice 'familial' place.

The takeaway is that some behaviours (here, collaboration) are very difficult if there is no supporting installation, that a minor intervention can have far-reaching consequences and is not so difficult to do when the culture considered is small scale.

Of course, the final result is never exactly as anticipated. Change is a long, distributed, process where actors and actants have their say. Results are also fragile and vulnerable to change of installations, such as a move in another building or change in leadership.

As Kurt Lewin articulated in a seminal paper on action research, the process is a spiral that has a lot to do with betterment loops:

> The first step then is to examine the idea carefully in the light of the means available. Frequently more fact-finding about the situation is required. If this first period of planning is successful, two items emerge: namely, an "overall plan" of how to reach the objective and secondly, a decision in regard to the first step of action. Usually this planning has also somewhat modified the original idea. In highly developed fields of social management, such as modern factory management or the execution of a war, this second step is followed by certain fact-findings...
>
> The next period is devoted to executing the first step of the overall plan. The next step again is composed of a circle of planning, executing, and reconnaissance or fact-finding for the purpose of evaluating the results of the second step, for preparing the rational basis for planning the third step, and for perhaps modifying again the overall plan. (Lewin, 1946: 37–8).

This led Lewin to state that 'we should consider action, research and training as a triangle that should be kept together for the sake of any of its corners.' (Lewin, 1946: 40). His approach has been popularized by this quote attributed to him that 'if you want to truly understand something, try to change it'.[3]

> Rational social management, therefore, proceeds in a spiral of steps each of which is composed of a circle of planning, action, and fact-finding about the result of the action. (Lewin, 1946: 38)

Although deliberate design can influence the natural mechanisms of social construction to some extent, it can do so only with the active participation of the stakeholders, and the emerging result is necessarily a product of compromise between local interests under objective constraints and power balance. Changing the installation is naturally easier if the change agents have a power position and agency: it is easier to foster change from the top because authority positions come with some control over the evolution of the installation (e.g. buying equipment, deciding training, enacting regulations: see Section 7.5).

### 8.3.   Micro-level on a Large Scale: Changing the Drinking Behaviour

Larger societal changes involve larger scale installations. Most changes are not deliberately monitored. They result from bottom-up processes, often

---

[3] I must say I still have not been able to find where Lewin wrote that phrase, if he ever did.

initiated by a problem to solve or the push of a specific group's interest. Government policies are an exception to this, but they find limitations in the capacity of governments to change all three layers.

In the state of the art, societal interventions at meso-level (a town, an organisation) are the ones that work best. Simon and colleagues (Simon et al., 2006, 2011) provide a successful example of fighting obesity by reinstalling a town to foster teenagers' physical activity. That is because by intervening on local, but collective, installations (e.g. a park, a theatre, a clinic, a school) one can impact the large population of users of that installation. Local cases can then become exemplars and inspire evidence-based policy (Campbell, 1971) – although generalization is not an easy task (Pawson, 2006).

I present here a slightly different case where we targeted a series of local installations, family homes, in one go. The problem we tackled was the insufficient intake of water by children, and connected with that the mechanism of building the habit of drinking sweetened drinks. The European Food Safety Authority (EFSA Panel on Dietetic Products, Nutrition, 2010) estimated that European children 4–8 years old have a typical average daily water intake (from all sources) of around 1,100 mL, significantly less than a recommended daily intake of 1,600 mL. Isabelle Guelinckx and colleagues, surveying 13 countries, showed the proportion of children not meeting EFSA adequate intake for total fluid intake ranged from 10% to more than 90% in some countries (Guelinckx et al., 2015). That situation is general: Adam Drewnowski and colleagues found that in the United States, 75% of children 4–8 years old fail to meet the water intake recommendations of the Institute of Medicine (Drewnowski, Rehm, & Constant, 2013). Humans have an innate preference for sweet taste (sweetness is a proximate signal for high calorie density), and beverage companies put on the market sweet drinks (sodas and fruit juice) that people, especially children, enjoy drinking.

But this is cause for concern: soft drinks have been identified as a contributor to child obesity (Ruyter, Olthof, Seidell, & Katan, 2012). As lifelong health-related behaviours may be established in early childhood (Umberson, Crosnoe, & Reczek, 2010), this also impacts adult obesity. It is therefore better to substitute plain water for soft drinks. Plain water contributes, without the extra calories, to hydration, which is a crucial factor for good health and performance. Dehydration hampers the cognitive performance (memory, attention and visual search tasks) of 6–7-year-olds, whereas a single additional drink of water can improve it (Edmonds & Jeffes, 2009). Similar benefits of hydration are observed in adults (Adan, 2012; Edmonds, Crombie, Ballieux, Gardner, & Dawkins, 2013).

The purpose of our intervention was to act on the three layers to increase plain water intake (vs sweet beverages). Poland was an especially good field to test the effects of intervention: Polish children are among the most dehydrated and drink a lot of sweet drinks. At the time of the survey, around 50% of children (3–6 years old) were drinking more than 800 mL of sweet beverages (hot sweet tea, juices and nectars) and less than 150 mL of water a day (Danone, 2010). In comparison to the EFSA guidelines, this suggests that they consumed too little liquid containing water overall, and proportionately too little plain water. We enrolled in the experiment 439 households in eight cities in Poland (Bydgoszcz, Gdańsk, Lublin, Łódź, Katowice, Kraków, Poznań, Warszawa; with a representative sample on age, socioeconomic categories and household size). Eligible families had children 3–6 years old who drank a maximum of 250 mL/day plain water, a minimum of 800 mL/day sweet hot or cold beverages, failing to meet EFSA adequate level of total water intake.

We tried to modify the embodied competences layer by providing specific information to the families with an online tutorial describing the benefits of water ('Information' treatment). The physical layer was modified by providing increased affordances for drinking with small water bottles (kid's size, 330 mL) freely delivered at home by the experimenter team (three bottles a day for three weeks, for a total of sixty-three bottles) ('Water affordance' treatment). The bottles were designed for small children to grasp, pick up and open themselves; the bottles were refillable. Finally we tried to intervene on the social layer by providing an online forum where the families could engage in community activities, discuss various ways of increasing water consumption and exchange experience, and possibly tips, good practice and rules ('Social Regulation' treatment). That was an attempt to constitute the participating families into a community of interest, and benefit from the group effects fostering long-term behavioural changes described by Lewin in his experiments on changing food habits (Lewin, 1943).

To compare the effects of the three layers, we designed an experimental plan that separated, as much as possible, the interventions on each layer. To follow the impact of our intervention we followed the families for a year, with six waves each of seven consecutive days of measures of liquid intake of parents and children. A control condition (no intervention) was given to eighty-seven families; this control sample was followed in the same way for comparison and eliminating factors external to our intervention such as seasonality, temperature, child maturation, etc. (see Lahlou, Boesen-Mariani, Franks, & Guelinckx, 2015 for details).

So in sum we have three conditions: Information (INFO), Water affordance (WATER), and Social Regulation (SR). Although these conditions are theoretically separable, we do not assume that the different influences are independent in actual phenomena. Indeed, they may each make different contributions at different points in the process of habit formation and maintenance. To spare sample size, and to make the experiment as realistic as possible (in what would be a national campaign), all families except the control started with the Information treatment (after a first period of pure observation to get baseline measures). At baseline, liquid intake was well below the recommended levels (EFSA Panel on Dietetic Products, Nutrition, 2010); children's mean consumption of plain water was less than 55 mL/day and parents' was less than 280 mL/day.

Then the sample was randomly separated into two groups. One had no further treatment. The other received the Water affordance. Finally, thirteen weeks after the intervention ended one subgroup from each was assigned to a Social Regulation condition, inviting them to join an online discussion forum in weeks 36–39, to share support in helping increase their children's water intake. So in total, we have five groups: Control, INFO only, INFO+SR; INFO+WATER; INFO+WATER+SR.[4]

All groups increased their intake over the twelve-month measurement period. The pattern also includes a sinusoidal trend. The general increase is probably due to maturation of children (increased intake) and possibly national campaigns for dietetics or bottled water. The sinusoid is seasonality: people drink more water in summer. Given these rather complex patterns, it is more informative to assess the *relative* changes within and between groups, rather than the absolute changes in consumption. Figure 8.1 presents the evolution in terms of their relations to each group's own starting point at the baseline (i.e., each group's baseline = 100%).

The two patterns noted here – a general increase in consumption over the twelve-month period overlaying a sinusoidal variation in consumption within that period – can be seen clearly by focusing first on the control group (*lower line*).

Note that the effect of social regulation is hardly visible on the global results. This may be because our forum was not very effective. First, interaction through the forum probably does not provide the same degree of

---

[4] There is no Social Regulation Only group (it would not make sense), nor groups with Water without Information; that would not make sense to the participants.

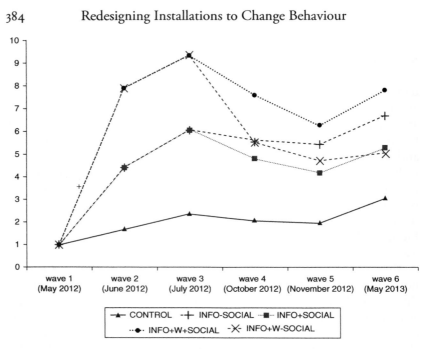

Figure 8.1. Evolution of plain water (tap water and bottled still water) in the various groups' intake during and after interventions.

commitment as do face-to-face interactions. Second, only a few of our participants were active users on the forum. For those who were, we noted a substantial increase in water consumption.

The visible presence of water bottles triggers water intake by children and by parents and reminds parents to encourage children's drinking. The effect of affordances is even more massive when the affordances (here small water bottles) are actually present (at month 3: 801% for children and 118% for parents in WATER+SR), but of course decreases when the affordance is discontinued (water bottles were no longer made available to the household after month 3), before stabilizing at the final measure.

Details of the analysis are presented elsewhere (Franks, Lahlou, Bottin, Guelinckx, & Boesen-Mariani, 2017). What we must remember of this intervention is that:

• affordances (WATER) have the strongest impact on changes, but they tend to have effect only as long as they remain present;
• social regulation (the online forum) has effects only for those who participated in the forum;

- information[5] does have an effect, but not as strong as affordances;
- the strongest (and lasting) impact is obtained through combined intervention at the level of the three layers.

So, overall, the interventions had a positive effect on water consumption. Participants increased their water intake, but the effect on overall liquid intake was minimal. The increase in water consumption came from substitution for soft drinks (a positive outcome for health).

Two rather trivial effects can be noted: affordances are especially efficient when they are present, but had a lasting effect when they were part of a complete installation. Also, social regulation had an influence only on those who participated. Nevertheless the behavioural changes produced (increased intake of plain water) lasted at least six months after the intervention, suggesting that some new habits were formed.

An analysis of a subsample with the SEBE method revealed some of the mechanisms by which this increase occurred. Parents intervened with various strategies, acting as gatekeepers of children's consumption. Analysis of video replay interviews illustrated this variation: following Information recommendations, they offer children water, also drinking it themselves as role models. Some parents intentionally put the water bottles in visible places so they would be reminded to drink; and indeed we observed on the tapes that the sight of the bottle as the parent walks by it actually triggers the parent to drink and/or propose water to children. That is confirmed in replay interviews.

The takeaway here is that installation theory facilitates the design of interventions, and that combining intervention at the level of the three layers can produce spectacular results. Testing interventions at small scale can give good insights to designing and rolling out national evidence-based interventions.

### 8.4. Meso-level: Experimental Reality and the LDC Case

A crucial problem in changing installations is that we seldom start from a blank slate, rather we must modify an existing system. Therefore a local change crosses existing representations, habits, rules etc. in the three layers

---

[5] We must note here that the information did not merely involve descriptive information about the nature and benefits of water consumption; it also offered behavioural prescriptions, tips for action and suggestions to parents on how to increase their child's water consumption. It seems likely, therefore, that the Information condition also already carried some of the normative force that was reinforced in the social regulation condition.

of the existing installations. To make the change sustainable potential obstacles (improperly called 'sources of resistance') must be identified and acceptable solutions found in building compromises with already installed reality and stakeholders. Because the system is complex, there are multiple feedback loops and indirect effects that are difficult to see and model. Often the impact of a local modification is difficult to simulate and predict; therefore only by trying the change 'for real' can we discover the nature of interdependence and pathways of interaction between stakeholders. That is what Lewin meant by saying 'if you want to truly understand something, to try to change it'.

In other words, complex installations often defy the 'thought experiment' capacity of designers and laboratory experiments, and it may be faster to try and see than to model and simulate. Of course, that is not completely true. In practice, in very complex situations, the change agent should consider combining the simulation with trial and error. What is too complicated to model and simulate can simply be tried out to see the results. In that process, the change agent can better 'truly understand the system' and inform further modelling along the way, as the role of components within each layer of the installation appears more clearly.

This finding is at the root of 'living laboratories', 'user laboratories' and the like. These labs try to combine the rigour of laboratory observation and the control of some variables with the introduction of a realistic situation (real users, mostly). User labs are a transient state: in the future the real world will be the lab, and scientific rigour will come in natural experiments through the use of embarked sensor and sophisticated observation protocols; interventions will replace lab experiments.

We used such a living lab to adapt a large corporation (Electricité de France, staff 120,000) to digitization. The idea was to create the 'offices of the future', and also later to digitize the production processes in generation plants (mostly nuclear). We applied the technique of 'experimental reality', that is, to experiment in a small part of the organization the new regimen in real operation conditions, then disseminate the new installation throughout the whole organization (Jégou, 2009; Lahlou, 2009; Lahlou et al., 2002). This multimillion project is a modern version of monitored 'natural experiments' (Lazurskii [1916] 1997). In practice, we constructed a whole experimental 'building of the future' (the K1 building), augmented with futuristic Information and Communication Technology (ICT), where actual (volunteer staff) users worked. The K1 building was fully armed for continuous observation.[6] The whole project became an administrative experimental unit, the Laboratory of Design for Cognition (LDC), that lasted a decade.

A wide range of new technologies and work processes were tested on this experimental population of workers, especially regarding distributed, ICT-augmented, collaborative work. The various layers of the installations were then modified to enable change, in a gradual problem-solving approach as difficulties and solutions emerged, involving all stakeholders in a garbage can theory style (Cohen, March, & Olsen, 1972), where potential solutions and problems were confronted by trial and error to find solutions that 'satisficed' stakeholders.

This building contained various types of workspaces, the most prominent being the RAO 'ICT-augmented' meeting room. RAO (standing for the French acronym for computer aided meetings) became a 'mother room' for other meeting rooms in the company: when solutions in RAO reached a satisfying level of usability, they were disseminated, preferably by viral diffusion (Lahlou, 2005). As dissemination was done, further improvement testing continued in the mother room, so new versions were issued to update the global organization as they were evaluated sustainable. This solves the 'never-endingness' issue of workplace design (technology and regulations continuously change), and enables inclusion, in a realistic way, of the distant/unexpected impacts of local changes, in cooperation with the multiple stakeholders.

For example, setting up systems that enable working from a distance raised a number of unexpected issues, which led to negotiations with the information technology division (bandwidth, servers, firewalls) Human Resources services (insurance, work contracts, time-stamping, equality), finance (which unit pays for common spending?), procurement (selecting equipment and vendors at corporate level), estates (videoconference meeting rooms, physical access, telework centres), etc. It also brought managerial changes (evaluation criteria for promotion of teleworkers, responsibility and delegation) and of course changed the worker's representation of what is the nature of a meeting, how to organize it and how to set an agenda, which involved training. Detailed description of the case, which started with twenty-five experimenters, then hundreds, then thousands, is presented in a monograph (Lahlou et al., 2012a): the list of more than eighty institutions and people credited is a sign of how complex such

---

[6] Video visit available at https://www.youtube.com/watch?v=GZVIpNgZqoo.

Figure 8.2. A view of the open space offices in the K1 building. The RAO meeting room, with the Tabec screen during a videoconference (*right*). A black and white version of this figure will appear in some formats. For the colour version, please refer to the plate section.

changes are.[7] Figure 8.2 provides a view of two areas of the ground floor of the K1 building: the open space and the RAO meeting room.

The reader has now become familiar with my somewhat obsessive taste to get into the details to show how the theory applies in practice. Indeed, general theoretical descriptions remain ambiguous, and the proof of a good theory is in its application. We shall see very concretely here the role of external representations (blueprints, plans, etc.), what matching the representation with reality means, reality tests and their examples, crossed impacts, etc. Because descriptions are long, let us simply illustrate here the process with a single installation within the RAO room, the 'Tabec' (electronic board). This example is described at length in Lahlou et al., 2012: 248–57.

(I must state here that I hesitated in providing the detailed description that follows, because this book is already too long and I felt I was abusing the reader's patience. But the interest of this lengthy description is to illustrate in detail what has been said about installation changes in the previous chapters, especially the relation between models and material prototype testing. It also illustrates the innovation processes in industry and the problems they meet. As for Hutchins' description of position fixing (Hutchins, 1995a), we can realize the nature of the process in creating and evolving an installation only when we can appreciate how much the devil is in the details, and how minute issues in the quality of the affordances,

---

[7] For another example at the same meso-scale with a testbed, see the CoVis project (Pea et al., 1997), which describes a similar entanglement of technology, competence learning and social and institutional issues.

or in the expectations of users, can have a major impact and reorient the project.)

The Tabec was a large (3.7 m × 1.3 m; 154 inches diagonal) electronic writable interactive screen. At the time the Tabec was designed (2000), the current commercial equivalents, Smart Boards, had much smaller screens and were bulky and very expensive. The first Smart Board to offer more than basic capabilities was actually introduced in 2001. So the Tabec addresses the need to have a large, cheap, interactive shared display for augmented meeting rooms. The Tabec was developed in four successive versions between 2000 and 2002, when it finally reached a stable state. Further improvements were mostly software and interface design for the videoconferencing functions.

The idea of a 'Tabec'[8] was first discussed in the fall of 2000 during the preparation for the interior design of the K1 building. The behaviour to support was 'conferencing' and 'meeting'. We wanted to have an interactive screen for shared display, with memorizing and printing capacity.

We briefly analyse the evolution of this installation from the beginning (version V-01) to the final version to illustrate the emergence of problems and solutions as a result of the effective participation of users in the design of the installation, in a typical betterment loop process.

Initially, we wanted several functionalities, resulting from the analysis of what the activity of a user 'at the board' in a meeting needed when making a presentation, annotating or illustrating, in short, doing what one usually does with a whiteboard but with the augmented capacities of display and recording offered by digitization.

(1) 'Touch' control of what is displayed on the board, e.g. switch from one slide to the next during a presentation, the presenter being on the stage ('at the board');
(2) recording of what is written on the screen with an erasable marker.

Available Commercial Off The Shelf ('COST') components were a classic video projector to show presentations, a then-new system to track the movements of the marker on the board with an ultrasound triangulation technique (Mimio®)and the (also then-new) wireless network to

---

[8] The acronym is a short for the French, Tableau-Ecran (Board-Screen). A very similar device, with back projection, had already been invented by Jim Hollan in his lab at the University of California, San Diego, where we saw it, so here is an example is a cross-transfer. Interestingly, at the moment of redesigning the Tabec we forgot to ask Jim's advice although we had excellent relations with him and his lab; this mechanism of reinventing the wheel seems to happen often in innovation (Lahlou, et al., 2012: 249).

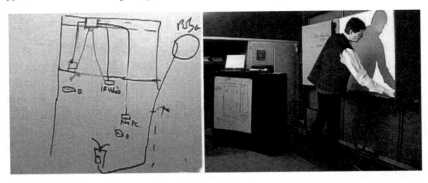

Figure 8.3. First draft of the Tabec (*left*). First prototype with direct projection (V-01) showing the problem of the user's shadow. (From Lahlou et al., 2012.) This picture and all the Tabec illustrations that follow are reproduced with the kind agreement of Lavoisier Publications, Paris. For the colour version, please refer to the plate section.

connect the system to users' computers. The Tabec was first imagined and sketched on a paperboard as a combination of these components, which we had tested separately in our quest to build the desired functionalities (Figure 8.3, *left*).

The prototyping of this initial version (V-01) proved easy, apart from the ordering of the components that were non-standard for the Procurement Division, and the impossibility to find a proper screen for back projection. Therefore a modified V-01 prototype was built and functional in a few weeks (Figure 8.3, *right*). Because we had not found the adequate screen, the projection was made from the front and the shadow of the presenter masked the screen when he wrote on it.

The conclusion of the first reality test of the V-01 version of Tabec was simple: the idea is good but should switch to rear projection. The problem was in the match between the physical characteristics of the screen and its model. We had hoped for a moment that direct projection would satisfice, but it had not.

This finding significantly changed the design blueprint of the meeting rooms, and thus the development of the K1 building. We decided to build a technical area about 3 m deep behind the semitransparent screen to allow for back projection The plan, presented on the right in Figure 8.4, figured at the top right the triangle representing the rear projector for the Tabec.

The architectural implications of the new design with a 3-m deep technical space behind the Tabec were substantial (Figure 8.4, *right*). An additional partition wall was introduced, with a full review of plans the

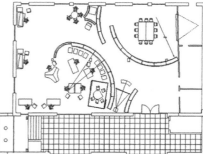

Figure 8.4. New blueprint of Tabec, with back projection (*left*). Architectural drawing of the K1 ground floor (*right*).The meeting room is on the upper right corner of the open space, with a folding table in the middle; the small room on the very top corner on the right, with a *dotted triangle* inside, is the technical room. The *dotted triangle* represents the projection from the video projector to the Tabec screen, which is now part of the wall between the technical space and the RAO meeting room. (From Lahlou et al., 2012a.)

construction site already in the making to insert the new technical space behind the meeting room, to accommodate the video projector; this to the despair of foremen and finance officers. Because the partition offered more space than the technical room alone, we took the opportunity to install a kitchen and an electrical equipment room.

We see in passing that every system specification of a component has an influence on many others, in terms of space, but also in other dimensions; here for the information technology architecture and networks. In terms of project management, it required changes, transfers of budgets between work packages, schedule adaptation, security and safety surveys, etc. These changes of course create tensions that require good institutional governance to manage gracefully.

Based on this model, a partition was installed and a hole carved in it to install a screen (in the meanwhile we had found some large semitransparent Plexiglas that first tests showed could be used as a screen).

Figure 8.5 shows the partition wall between the RAO meeting room and the technical room, before the screen is installed.

The impossibility to find COST semitransparent screens that meet the quality required for projection proved a major difficulty. Initially, we used a matted Plexiglas sheet, but it caused a big loss of light, especially on the edges, and the markers could not be erased easily. Frosted glass was unsuitable because it cannot be written on. Fresnel lens screens were very expensive and could not be written on either. The installation of special films on

Figure 8.5. Tabec V-02, *left*. The hole in the partition before the screen is installed, with the technical space, seen from the RAO room. *Right*: the same seen from the technical room. (From Lahlou et al., 2012.)

Figure 8.6. Prototype V-02 of the Tabec in use, seen from the RAO meeting room (*left*). Videoconferencing with a large TV (*right*). (From Lahlou et al., 2012a.)

classic glass also caused problems. Finally, we overcame the difficulty with a special order to a major glass company. This allowed us to achieve a large Tabec (Figure 8.6, *left*) at significantly lower cost, and much larger than tactile screens on the market. We determined the right size before drilling the hole by testing on moving platforms, taking into account the average size of users, the length of their arms and the limits of sensitivity of the device that identified the position of the marker.

However we then realized that the original dimensions were not really good.

Tabec V-02 version met the initial functional specifications: rear projection, 'touch' command of the projector, memorizing written comments on the screen. The prototype proved practical and simple to use, allowing its use in dozens of workshops and presentations.

Still, in actual use of the Tabec we found some limitations, preventing certain user tasks. Indeed, in the meanwhile, users had become familiar with other devices. One advantage of augmented environments is the ability to collaborate with remote participants through videoconferencing. In the V-02 version of Tabec, a 'large' additional TV screen (diagonal 102 cm – a massive device for the time [2000]) was set up to view remote participants. But this screen quickly appeared 'too small'. In most cases, the videoconferencing involved multiple remote sites whose display appeared too small on a 102-cm TV screen. Moreover, the participants, who were accustomed to the visual comfort afforded by the larger screen, resented the 'small' size and poor-quality TV picture (Figure 8.6, *right*).

The issues raised during the practical organization of work meetings during the period 2000–2001 led us to design a remote meeting management tool (KCR). That web tool combined live screen-sharing and videoconferencing and was an ancestor of what workers now routinely use on their laptops. That project had a crossed impact on the Tabec. Our initial specifications had not thoroughly considered the use of Tabec for multisite videoconferencing; it posed a series of software and hardware problems, particularly so that remote sites could also make notes and print them on their own site. I will not go into the details of how these were solved. Our goal in this section is simply to show that the design and evolution of even a seemingly simple feature (here rear projection on a large screen) is iterative, complex and difficult to predict. It involves drift, crossed impact and innovation.

So we decided to incorporate into the Tabec two 'sources' of images to promote holding meetings. The first was a computer workspace display. The second source was the videoconferencing device or the interface of the KCR (which included video and the meeting secretary's minutes-in-progress as well as a series of speech-turn-management and chat systems).

The V-03 version of Tabec required a larger screen and tiling these different sources. We ordered a larger screen (3.7 m × 1.3 m) and expanded accordingly the opening in the wall board to hold that massive and heavy screen (Figure 8.7), also solving the implied architectural problems in terms of structural engineering.

Our initial idea was to use two video projectors connected to a single computer source to view more information; we could be projecting a screen 3,000 pixels wide, rather than using two separate sources. However, this did not work for a technical reason: the images from different projectors have a different colour drift over time and the effect is unpleasant: the seam between the two images is very visible (Figure 8.8). In addition, the

Figure 8.7. Broadening the Tabec. Here we see the new screen attached for tests before the enlargement of the wall opening, visible in the back. This allows size comparison between Tabec V-02 and Tabec V-03. (From Lahlou et al., 2012a.) A black and white version of this figure will appear in some formats. For the colour version, please refer to the plate section.

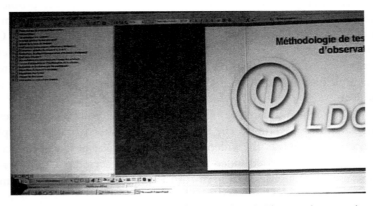

Figure 8.8. Double projection from a single source (V-03). The seam between the two sources (vertical line in the middle of the logo) is very visible and unpleasant. (From Lahlou et al., 2012.) A black and white version of this figure will appear in some formats. For the colour version, please refer to the plate section.

Mimio® system could no longer locate the markers on such a large area. Other systems we tried also encountered limitations (battery life, etc.) Despite the promises of manufacturers and improvement in successive version, usability was not satisfising. V-03, resulting from crossed impacts, had better specifications and matched the design external representation but failed the reality test.

Figure 8.9. Tabec V-04: Double projection from two independent sources (2002). (From Lahlou et al., 2012a.) A black and white version of this figure will appear in some formats. For the colour version, please refer to the plate section.

The obstacles created by the failure of the double projection led us to redesigning a system using two projections controlled by two independent sources (Figure 8.9), for which the identification of markers was managed separately.

That version was very usable and was the basis of dissemination in many other meeting rooms until the Tabec started using flat LED screens when they became affordable in large size. It then continued adapting by using different input devices that made it easier and easier to log in, connect to remote sites, input various types of data, write, record live, archive, etc. The RAO room continued to serve as the 'Mother of Augmented Rooms', where the new devices and uses were tested in real meetings before upgrading the system and disseminating it across the company (Lahlou et al., 2012). The RAO room inspired the design of the offices for the new EDF R&D facility in the Saclay cluster, partly because those in charge of the design and implementation of that new facility had participated in the LDC experiments,[9] an example of crossed impact through the mobility of persons (cf. Section 7.2.2.3). And of course at some point the in-house prototypes that were the Tabecs were replaced by off-the-shelf devices which performed similar functions with the lower cost of large production series.

Of course that device evolved faster than most of the usual installations, but that enables us to see in an accelerated mode the mechanisms described in Chapter 7.

[9] For example, the director of the new facility project had been an LDC test user for a decade, the company in charge of the space planning was a research partner of the LDC, the brief of the architect competition for the new facility was written by the architects of the LDC building, the director of R&D at the time the new facility project was launched was the direct sponsor of the LDC, etc.

The takeaway from the evolution of that installation is that every new change has ripple effects on the other layers, and that feeds the design spiral (e.g. users becoming used to large displays and asking for new functionalities). It is also quite reassuring to see that powerful solutions gradually build up even though they were difficult to foresee in the beginning (e.g. collaborative software). The external environment appears as a source of opportunities (new technologies, resources to address functional problems) more than a source of problems. External representations indeed appear at almost every step of the project in the form of sketches, plans, specifications, reports. Reality tests have unexpected outcome (e.g. the colour drift of projectors). The results of these tests can bring new ideas, which then are reified as blueprints, and then prototyped and tested.

Here appears something we hinted at in Chapter 7: there are specific places where people test new installations, and they are only deployed when they stand the test of reality and culture. In this specific case, the testers have access to large range of technical and financial agency (e.g. constructing a whole test building in nine months) as well as some exceptional leeway to test new stuff in a test area somewhat immune to common institutional control. We used to say familiarly that our lab was the place where we could 'play with fire' under the protection of a strong institutional firewall.

That distribution of labour for innovation is one more refinement of the cultural evolutionary system of societies; it spares the risk and burden to try out risky and costly solutions anywhere, and sets up optimal conditions for doing so; delaying dissemination until the new installations are evaluated fit.

## 8.5. Examples of Interventions Using Social Norms in Colombia

It is interesting to revisit some interventions with the installations grid, an exercise done by my colleague Paulius Yamin-Slotkus for some interventions he was involved with. The examples in this section are especially instructive in showing how the social layer can be approached in a creative way, leveraging social norms, media and narratives.

The experience of Antanas Mockus as mayor of Bogotá, Colombia (1995–1997 and 2001–2003), shows that behavioural change interventions that target several of the layers of installations can also be effective in a much bigger scale: a city of seven million people (Sommer, 2006; Tognato, 2016; Yamin-Slotkus, 2015).

With the objective of reducing the rates of murder and deaths in traffics accidents, the mayor's office designed and applied several interventions to build taboos and to increase people's capacity to regulate each other (placing a great emphasis on the citizens' responsibility on acting for a common objective). Although they were applied in specific spots of the city (in specific installations), the media broadcast them widely due to their novelty, potentiating in this way their pedagogical effect. Those included:

Against homicides:

- continuous reinforcing by the mayor and the programmes of the mayor's office of the slogan 'Life is Sacred';
- inscription in empty mausoleums in the Central Cemetery of Bogotá of this slogan and at the end of the year an event with many youngsters standing in the empty tombs of the mausoleum (one for each life spared due to homicide reduction that year);
- programme for voluntary handing over of weapons;
- symbolic vaccination campaigns against violence, where people were given some drops of water and they promised to solve their conflicts peacefully.

Against traffic accidents:

- in some intersections in Bogotá, mime artists were hired to regulate traffic by mocking those who didn't respect traffic norms;
- 'thumbs-up' and 'thumbs-down' cards were distributed so that people could peacefully approve or disapprove other people's behaviour in the city;
- bars and night clubs were limited to closing at 1 AM, together with messages about responsibility (because most traffic accidents were due to drunk driving).

Unfortunately, because those actions have not been systematically evaluated, the relationship of causality between them and their results is unclear. And yet, the results are impressive: the homicide rate in the city, considered one of the most dangerous in the world at the start of Mockus' first term as mayor, dropped from 82 per 100,000 inhabitants in 1993 to 25 in 2003. That is a 69% decrease in 10 years. In the same period, deaths in traffic accidents dropped by 55% (Mockus et al., 2009, drawn from official data).

If we now look at these interventions with installation theory, we can see that although some were symbolic, addressing the embodied layer and contributing to 'de-freezing' the situation, to use a Lewinian terminology, some others were direct interventions in installations to change the way they operate by addressing various layers, and therefore making participants experience another use. That is what was done with the mime artists who acted as vigilantes in intersections, night clubs closing early and having new informal rules or cards to facilitate the vigilante effect.

Yamin-Slotkus examined how this same approach was applied to reduce domestic violence rates in Barrancabermeja, a small city of Colombia founded around the biggest oil refinery in the country (Yamin-Slotkus, 2012). There, Mockus' team, together with the local mayor's office, the largest oil company in the country and civic organizations, designed and applied the following interventions (once again in specific installations but broadcast by the media):

- Declaration in a public event a zero-hour for domestic violence in the city. The event took place in one of the most important landmarks of the city with the attendance of local and national personalities, and was reinforced with continuous media campaigns (building a cultural taboo: social regulation).
- Actors performing in public spaces situations of domestic violence, without the people knowing they were actors. At the end of those surprise performances, bystanders were invited to share their experiences and possible solutions, and trained personnel gave them 'whistles against abuse' to use in case they witnessed a domestic violence situation (embodied competences, affordances).
- Training of local journalists on how to report domestic violence cases in a way that was compatible with this new narrative (embodied competences).
- The creation of a 24-hour telephone line to provide anonymous professional help for jealousy and stopping possible assaults of the callers (physical affordances, social regulation).
- Symbolic vaccination campaigns against violence, where people were given some drops of water and they promised to solve their conflicts peacefully (symbolic certification of embodied competences).
- Partnerships with popular artists to include in their songs messages against domestic violence (building and reinforcing the common narrative: social regulation).
- Visit of trained personnel to houses to distribute more 'whistles against abuse' and to give instructions on how to deal with domestic violence at home but also if they saw it in their neighbours, family and friends (providing affordances, building embodied competences, creating social regulation).

Here, as well, although it is not clear which interventions worked, the results on a city-wide scale are impressive: the rate of domestic violence cases in the city decreased by 30% in the first year of the implementation of the project (from 2010 to 2011), and by 50% in the second (from 2010 to 2012).

We can see here how the various initiatives against domestic violence addressed the three layers (physical: hotline and whistles; embodied: symbolic events and involvement; social regulation: training of specialized personnel). Mockus' humorous and light-touch approach, which proved efficient, shows how one can leverage the vigilante effect in a friendly manner. It also shows that there are many ways to design interventions beyond the classic media campaigns or edicting laws.

## 8.6. A General Practical Approach to Apply Installation Theory for Interventions

**Installation theory provides a general framework for analysing activity. A given activity (eating, shopping, working, etc.) is performed in a series of installations;** these installations can correspond to variants of the activity (e.g. going to the local bakery vs the butcher shop) or to segments of that activity (supermarket alleys vs supermarket cash desk).

**The three layers provide a grid to list, in a given installation, the local components relevant for activity, and what aspects of behaviour each component addresses.** For example, the chairs afford sitting, but also prepare a specific spatial distribution of participants; the embodied competence about how to position the fingers and the knife when one chops a shallot enables producing very small cubes without cutting one's hand; the rules of hygiene avoid germs to proliferate on the medication workstation.

**Looking at these scaffoldings and safeguards facilitates identifying the functional specifications of the installation and the quality parameters for the behaviour and its outcomes.**

There are many ways to use installation theory in the analysis phase, and the reader will creatively adapt it to her own methodology. I only briefly present the technique we most often use for quick analysis and redesign, based on using the SEBE technique.

**We follow, in the actual operation of the system considered for intervention, the course of action of one the participants in the installation through the complete activity.** For example, the client shopping in the shop, the maintenance operator making a round in the production plant, the mother preparing dinner, the bricklayer building a wall.

Activity theory enables us to spot the turns in the activity, when the actor goes from one action to the next. To each action is assigned a subgoal, using questioning based on activity theory (What is your goal at that moment? What are you trying to avoid?). We try to figure out, from the subcam tape and especially during the replay interview, the components of the installation that were instrumental in that turn. We use the installation theory framework to systematically explore the three layers: Had some affordance in the context suddenly become relevant? Was some rule activated? Was there feedback from another participant? Was it a decision by the actor based on previous experience or training?

We focus on the actions moments that are 'interesting', that is, especially impactful on the outcome of the behaviour or the well-being of the participants. Typically, we shall analyse the moment where things are considered not to be graceful and fluid by the operator: where it fails, where it rubs, where it is difficult, painful or unethical; where the participants feel uncomfortable, risky, dissatisfied, frustrated. With them we explore the reasons for problems, and what possible changes they would suggest to address the issue.

Again, we systematically explore, with the participants, the three layers of installation theory to see what easy redesign could address the issues noted, either by scaffolding the expected behaviour and outcomes or by making the undesired ones more costly, difficult or even impossible to perform.

The results of this investigation feed a design cycle. In each new stage of implementation we apply the same SEBE technique to inform further modifications and assess their effects: Is it getting better?

That is of course the general principle of investigation. The detailed practice includes supporting and leveraging the evolutionary processes that are sketched out in Chapter 7, and reinstalling the reproduction and resilience features described in Chapter 5. But this would be the subject of another book; and the readers now know enough to construct their own methods.

There are some caveats, though.

Installation theory facilitates the identification of what components of an installation sustain the activity as it is, and therefore where and how intervention might change the behaviour. Nevertheless experience shows that current components were seldom designed by chance; there are usually one or several reasons why things are like they are and

**it is unwise to implement changes without having understood these reasons.** Sometimes, the reasons are not valid any more. Sometimes they are still around and the changes might lead to undesired results. These may appear only once the change is made when the causal chains are complex. That brings us back to Lewin's statement that to fully understand a system, you must try to change it. That is why it is good practice to experiment with the changes at small scale and in a reversible manner.

**Fiddling with the rules is a tempting move, especially when the change agent is in power to do so. Intervening in the social layer raises issues about the relations of the local regulation with larger regulation** (e.g. labour law, trade law, health and safety regulation). **That may involve more stakeholders than one might think.** Regulation is a difficult endeavour, it raises very complex issues regarding the level at which regulations should apply. *In fine*, regulation is a social affair, and its rationale is inevitably linked to power balance, because regulation often boils down to arbitration between competing interests of different stakeholders, or trade-offs between proximal and ultimate effects. Subsidiarity (see Glossary) is a great principle, but as the weight of European or American federal regulations shows, it is not so easy to apply in practice.

There is a wealth of past research and accumulated wisdom in ethics and law, but also in people. Adding formal procedures or rules results in making installations complicated to use. **Sometimes, rather than adding formal rules, it is safer to implement a small social group to monitor the installation to make custom adaptation for special cases, whose decisions will have the same effect as would a huge set of rules.** Knowledge in societies is distributed over its members, and each individual is a living memory of many cases and former decisions. Committees, boards and meetings, as John Roberts (1964) aptly noted in his seminal paper on distributed cognition, are not only decision-making devices but also systems for information retrieval where members invoke their own networks and experiences to judge the matter at hand. Such bodies are capable of much more subtle decisions than rigid procedures, and they can be innovative to process new cases, which a procedure cannot.[10] As one can easily guess, the more 'new' cases the installation meets (typically in times of change) the

---

[10] As a general rule, involving more stakeholders is usually beneficial. That openness may induce more transaction costs in the beginning. But those stakeholders who have a different opinion or oppose would anyway have been in the way of the rollout of what is decided, because they are stakeholders, and their lack of cooperation at that later stage almost always incurs more cost and delay than a preliminary discussion at the stage where the model is being discussed.

more such flexible bodies prove useful. A single committee, or person 'in charge of' the installation, can make the installation leaner and more efficient and humane than a massive set of bureaucratic rules. Of course there must be some political safeguards put in place to protect against the possibility that such authorities would act in a foolish, self-interested, unfair or dangerous manner, which history has many times shown is a very real risk. But humans, despite their limitations and biases, remain the best element to make installations flexible and humane.

**In any case, change is never a simple and easy affair. What installation theory brings, apart from pointing at possible components to intervene on, is the knowledge that every behaviour can be modified by components in any of the three layers. This provides some choice as to which layer is the best target for intervention, taking into account opportunity windows and costs, but also the potential undesired effects that each level of intervention may bring along.**

We can now conclude with what installation theory brings, and its limits.

CHAPTER 9

# *Conclusion*

**To the brave reader who managed to read up to this point, a great thank you for your attention. To those who skipped a few chapters and come here to get the abstract, my apologies for being too long in the previous chapters – that is because the evolution of societies is indeed somewhat complex.**

**This chapter proposes a wrap-up of the theory (Section 9.1); then some final considerations (what I think of that theory myself) in Section 9.2 –and then you're through!**

## 9.1.  An Abstract of Installation Theory

'Installation' is a unit of analysis to study the determination of human behaviour in ecological conditions – in the everyday life of people in their natural setting (e.g. a family dinner, a dental practice, an escalator). Installations are entities that determine behaviour; installation theory provides a formal framework to analyse scientifically the bundle that common sense would call 'the person and the setting in a habitual situation'.

Installation theory has two aspects: synchronic and diachronic. The synchronic aspect describes what installations are, what their structure is and how they work at a given point of time. The diachronic aspect explains how installations evolve in time.

The synchronic aspect provides a framework to analyse a given installation. It is a pragmatic tool for description and understanding, it is a relatively simple model and comes as a synthesis of many other works in social science; its added value is its robustness and pragmatic usability for the scientist and the change agent. It tiles a series of other theories in a complete chain from social structure to individual behaviour and provides a single answer to two big questions in social science:

- *How is, in practice, constructed the continuous predictability and efficient control of the behaviour of millions of individuals, which in turn is necessary for smooth operation of societies?*
- *How can individual humans make sense on-the-fly of the rich, ambiguous and complex environments of society and take appropriate action (keeping in mind humans are cognitive misers)?*

The diachronic aspect of installation theory is more complex. Let us take the metaphor of the potter making a pot on a potter's wheel. Each turn of the wheel is a short cycle that keeps the flexible clay in a general cylindrical, symmetrical form, but the action of the hands of the potter gradually modifies that general shape. In installations also, the longer-term evolution mechanism is superimposed on the daily cycle of reproduction through practice.

Installation theory describes these two mechanisms. First, the short cycle by which installations *reproduce* in time and in space. In passing the theory provides a detailed answer to the old question of how practice reproduces structure and vice versa.

Second, installation theory proposes a new framework to describe the longer-term evolutionary mechanisms of installations, and more generally of human societies. These mechanisms are sophisticated because the components of the various layers of the installations evolve conjointly as an installation, but also independently.

Understanding these mechanisms is useful for the change agent because she will use the natural forces and mechanisms of evolution to tweak the process in the desired direction.

### 9.1.1.   *Installation Theory, Synchronic Aspects*

Installations are local, societal settings where humans are expected to behave in a predictable way. Installations consist of a set of components that simultaneously support and control individual behaviour. The installation is made of what Barker calls the 'behavioural setting' (the place, with its tools and artefacts and its behavioural standing rules – e.g. the dental clinic) *and* the embodied interpretive systems (aka 'lata') of the persons who take part in the activity: the subject, and the other participants (e.g. the patient and the dentist).

The components of an installation are distributed over the physical space (affordances), the subject (embodied interpretive systems; for short: 'competences') and the social space (institutions). These components assemble at the time and place of performance of the activity.

The different layers must be considered together because they geneti-cally were constructed *as a bundle*, to answer a specific problem. Each layer alone makes little sense unless it is connected with the others. See the example of road traffic: the physical road, the rules of the road, the compe-tences of drivers evolved together as transportation technology developed. The components of each layer are adaptations to a specific problem where the parameters are set by the other layers: what to afford, how to behave, what to control. For example, the competences of the drivers are adapted (when they learn how to drive) to the affordances of the vehicles, and to the rules of the road. The rules of the road are adapted to the characteris-tics of vehicles and human capacities (e.g. speed limits). The affordances (cars, intersections, road signs, etc.) are adapted to human competences and rules.

The parameters of one layer are the variables in another layer. That makes the layers interdependent.[1]

When the installation is assembled, it operates as a behavioural attractor: predictable behaviour sequences occur. Seen from the perspec-tive of the subject who enters the attractor, one feels prompted, empow-ered, supported, scaffolded and perhaps controlled into performing a specific behavioural sequence. The installation carries its own momen-tum; it induces the persons who step into it to become participants in a specific way.

That sequence is not rigid: in detail, it is never *exactly* the same behav-ioural sequence that occurs; what actually happens is each time adapted to the specifics of the subject, variations in the artefacts, etc.; the subject has some freedom of choice. For example, at the dentist, what surgical oper-ation actually occurs depends on the state of the dentition and character-istics of the patient, as well as on the dentist's own particularisms; in the café the customer may order tea or coffee. But the general envelope of the behaviour in a given installation roughly follows a certain script, and more importantly the outcome is (usually) attained: e.g. tooth cured, customer refreshed.

---

[1] The same interdependence goes between the individual level and the social level: the individual behaviours are such that their aggregation works in coalition. Because all vehicles follow a certain type of behaviour, the global traffic pattern is smooth. The social is resulting from the individual. Conversely, for the coalition to work, the individual behaviours must be guided to fit the aggregate problem. The behaviour that a given vehicle follows are determined by a social construction, the rules of the road. The individual is resulting from the social. In other words, the constraints that set the specific solution in one level (individual or collective) are themselves set by the border conditions in the other level. The parameters of one level are the variables in another level. The social and the individual are connected; they are a set of dual problems.

Installations have a dynamic of their own. That dynamic supersedes the subject's individual will, usually by nudging the behaviour under the radar of consciousness; if necessary by putting social pressure on the subject. Individuals find themselves performing a specific behaviour often without having even taken a conscious, explicit, decision to do so: their decision system has been bypassed because the material context affords only a few possible alternatives, because culture naturally pushes towards a specific one of these and because in any other case other participants or institutions put the person back on track. In installations we behave in 'channelled state'.

Installations ensure that each member of society behaves 'appropriately' in the situation (that is: in a way that is reliably predictable by other participants and stakeholders). They also save transaction costs and cognitive costs. Although installations do not cover every aspect of social life, they are ubiquitous.

Individual subjects still have leeway and can exert free will: they can act in slightly idiosyncratic ways within the installation as long as they stay within certain limits; they also have some choice of which installations they choose to enter.

Installation theory models the components of installations as distributed over three different layers: affordances in the material environment; representations and other interpretive systems embodied in the persons; social regulation exerted by other persons and institutions. These components assemble at the point of delivery, when the subject with embodied competences finds herself in the physical and social context socially designed to produce a specific behaviour. Then the subject is channelled into behaving 'normally', in the predicted way.

The *affordances* of an object are the pragmatic potential of this object as perceived by the subject: what the subject can do with it (or what the object can do to the subject). The affordances of an object are its agency relative to that subject. For example, the dentist's chair, with its headrest, has the affordance to keep the patient seated comfortably but also to maintain the patient's head in a stable position so the dentist can work properly.

Interpretive competences are the capacity, but also the semiautomatic process, by which the perception of a given object or situation triggers a conventional cultural interpretation. Embodiment implements this process in the individual's body as a paradigm of 'embodied interpretive systems', which produce perception-action loops. I have introduced the term 'lata' to name the biological structures in the flesh that are the support and engine for the interpretive systems, e.g. the synapses in the brain.

Lata are to competences what the material wiring is to an electric circuit. Lata are the physical substratum of symbolic sense-making and emotional and motor response. These lata are competences for action *inscribed* in the subject's flesh, especially in the nervous system. They offer a paradigm of potential interpretations which can be applied to situations which the subject can hereby assimilate to past experiences.

In a given situation, the subject mobilizes these competences to interpret, reason and act. For example, when asked by the stewardess what he wants to drink, the passenger mobilizes his linguistic competences to understand the question, compare the available choices with his acquired preferences, verbalize his choice, use his motor skills to take the glass and drink and finally use his digestive system to process the liquid. These embodiments not only are functionally efficient regarding goal achievement, they also include compliance to social rules; for example, the vehicle driver automatically pressing the brake pedal when seeing a red traffic light, or the tennis player moving his racket with a fine automatic adjustment of his muscles and joints that sends the ball according to the rules of the game.

There are many types of embodied competences: they are the embarked agency of the subject. Competences are dynamical processes because they couple the subject to her environment, by matching embodied patterns with 'pragmatic correspondents': objects in the environment that resonate with these lata.

Finally, the social layer is made of the institutions: the sets of behaviours that are expected in that specific installation. They come as a set of formal or informal rules. These rules exist in a 'social' realm, which is an interesting concept but difficult to pin down empirically because rules can come in various guises. In practice, the rules can be displayed in the environment (written in codes, laws, regulations, posts, signs, etc.); they can be enforced by other participants or objects that give feedback and feedforward to the individual. For example, the rule at the dentist's office is that the patient should obey the dentist and collaborate by providing feedback on what she feels, pay the dentist, etc. An institution is inseparable from the community that enforces it and from the material culture it operates in: the social and material system by which they are transmitted, publicized and enforced. Therefore installation theory remains open as to how the institution is enforced and the rules implemented. What matters is that the description of installation, and the interventions, should target the rules themselves, beyond the form their enforcement takes in a particular instance.

When a subject enters the installation, she is confronted with a set of physically possible behaviours, limited by the affordances. For example, a student enters a classroom to attend a lecture. She could stand, or sit, or keep walking around or jump over the tables, etc. Among those, only some are interpreted as psychologically relevant, because the embodied competences eliminate a series of alternatives. For example, she considers sitting, but only sitting on the chairs – even though tables also afford sitting. This selection occurs because the student's behaviour is goal-directed (attending lecture) and her representation of a lecture is that students should be seated on chairs. Finally, the time and duration of her stay in the lecture have been determined by institutional rules (here, the timetables) and if she does not behave according to expectations (e.g. chatting with her neighbour) she will get corrected (the teacher and other students may stare at her or make some remark). This third layer eliminated even more possible behaviours. As a result, all students behave according to the lecture script, and the expected behaviour occurs.

The three layers therefore act as a pruning system that cuts out most branches of behavioural possibilities and leaves the subject only a few alternatives, usually minor variants along a standard script. But the layers also act as scaffolding for the subjects' behaviour, enabling her find the right place and time to attend a lecture, keep other students from distracting her with chatting, etc.

These three realms to which the installation components belong are of different nature. They are also somewhat redundant. For example, the subjects will have embodied the social rules in their representations of the setting; rules can be built into affordances, etc. That should by no means worry the reader. This redundancy naturally comes from the way installations reproduce as an interaction between the various layers and coevolve as a bundle in practice.

*The redundancy also has essential functional value: it makes the installation resilient. This resilience enables the installation to produce appropriate behaviour even with incompetent or novice participants. This property is essential because novices learn in doing through practice in installations. That is how education occurs through practice; it is the mechanism by which societal reconstruction continuously occurs in its daily operation.*

The installation is a relevant unit of analysis because it makes behaviour predictive; its determination power tends to supersede all classic social and psychological variables. A given person entering the installation will behave in a predicable way; and that behaviour depends upon the roles assigned by the installation rather than by age, gender, social class, religion, etc. Bus passengers behave as bus passengers, dentist's patients as dentist's patients, etc. Again, that is more predictive than all classic dispositional or socioeconomic variables. As reasoning is situated, the local context plays a strong role in local decision and behaviour (Warde, 1997: 201–2). Free will can be exercised at a higher level (e.g. selecting values, determining goals, choosing a specific installation), and also at the fined-grained level of behavioural style within the limits of what is acceptable in the installation (e.g. choosing dishes from the menu).

There are important individual variations in behaviour even within an installation: the appropriate behavioural path is usually a standard script around which individual subjects vary according to their own characteristics, history, preferences, etc. Individual can also choose to behave in a way that does not respect the installation's well-threaded pathway, and to incur the physical, psychological and legal risks attached to such 'inappropriate' behaviours. The degree of leeway and slack left by installations is variable (e.g. choice of drinks in the plane vs choice of drinks at the duty-free shop); within a specific installation it will also vary: some parts of the script may be left very loose whereas some others are very tight (you *must* sit at a specific seat in the plane; you *must* pay at the cash register in the duty-free shop). On the other hand no one is forced to buy in the duty-free shop, or even to walk into it.

But when we want to perform a specific activity, usually there are in a society dedicated installations for this; that is where the experience of societies regarding that activity have capitalized, precisely to help us perform it satisfyingly.

Furthermore installations are a relevant unit of analysis because they are the locus of societal reproduction, where structure constructs practice and where practice regenerates structure. In installations, the functional and the structural transform into one another. That is the synchronic aspect of the theory.

### 9.1.2. *Installation Theory, Diachronic Aspects*

Evolution has two aspects: endurance and change. Entities continue to exist (endurance) in a continuously modifying form (change). The diachronic part of installation theory addresses these two aspects. First, endurance is the result of the synchronic operation of installations. Installations produce expected behaviour, as we saw. In turn, each correct execution reinforces and perpetuates the various layers of the installation. Every session at the dentist sustains the dentist's practice.

But over time this continuous reproduction is not exactly identical. There are drifts in the behaviour produced, crossed impacts between installations because components move across installations; there is also innovation, when humans deliberately change the installation. This produces over time different installations.

Let us first consider endurance. The synchronic aspect of installations describes how their structure reproduces practice. That is in fact precisely the function of installations. The continuous reproduction of behavioural sequences produces embodiment of the adequate competences and expectations in subjects. In turn, each subject can then act as a loyal vigilante, fixing and repairing installations or behavioural sequences, guiding fellow participants and educating novices.

Therefore the reproduction cycle of embodied competences is a cycle between practice and representation of that practice. This cycle is scaffolded by objects and fostered and supervised by communities. Installations, because they provide oriented feedback, produce operant conditioning of their users; they leverage the learning mechanisms of humans and reward appropriate behaviour and nip in the bud the inappropriate ones. In doing so, in the same movement they ensure synchronously that only adequate behaviours are performed, they train and condition the participants so they embody the adequate competences and rules for future correct behaviours.

The reproduction of objects (which make the physical layer) is a bit more complex: objects are made by humans, based on a representation of the object (cars or hats are made after a model of cars or hats). Objects exist in both immaterial format and in material format, just as many insects or plants have a cycle with alternation of generations: they exist in the form of larvae and in the form of adult (for plants, a diploid sporophyte stage and a haploid gametophyte stage). The reproduction of objects is also a cycle, because the representations of objects are made after the objects themselves. So that is a chicken-and-egg type of reproduction (representations create objects, objects create their representation). That cycle is also a drifting spiral because reproduction is not always strictly identical.

This reproduction of objects is done by individuals or organizations under the ruling of communities. Social regulation appears as a monitoring and control system on the reproduction cycle between objects and representations, ensuring that the local implements are coherent with the larger system.

The institutional rules may also evolve themselves as a result of the power struggle between the various stakeholders (this includes humans but also other actants).

Finally, we noted that the key factor for reproduction is the fitness with individual needs (does the process yield desired result?) and fitness with institutions (does this conform to the socially expected norm?). The first fit is directly sanctioned by the law of effect (good behaviour is rewarding and therefore reinforced). The second is indirectly sanctioned by the same: correct behaviour yields positive social feedback.

The reproduction system is active at several levels: micro-level, with installations, and macro-level, at the level of communities that rule a series of installations. Communities set up institutions that may rule various installations of diverse types (e.g., politeness rules, status hierarchies, language, money) and also set up, especially in large-scale societies, instructional systems. We insisted on the reproduction mechanisms taking place in installations, through practice; we showed how they are ubiquitous and continuous and therefore that their importance is paramount in the reproduction of society. These mechanisms also account for reproduction of knowledge and practice where there is no formal instructional system (informal knowledge, small-scale societies, etc.). But of course not *all* education and embodiment take place in practice within installations; installations are important but not the sole system for societal reproduction.

Let us now consider change. I described the *betterment loop* that many mechanisms used in human societal evolution seem to follow. That is especially the case for the evolution of installations. Betterment loop is a class of processes by which the new state of a system is based on a variation of the previous. That variant is selected according to comparison of its outputs with expectations and with the previous state of the system. There may be diverse criteria and metrics to evaluate if and how much a variant is better than the previous state. For an installation, usually these criteria are functional criteria: Does the installation produce a better behaviour? Or does it produce the same behaviour better: faster, cheaper, with less risk and so on? But the evaluation of innovative variants are also made along worth scales, which are proxies for more generic 'currencies' of worth that are in use in the local culture. Users of the installation, but also the owners of the installation, are those who make these evaluations. These betterment loops are recursive because they chain in a spiral of progress.[2] They are 'learning' loops because they are able to keep in memory previous states of the system.

[2] Note that 'progress' is a subjective notion and depends on what metrics are used. For example, much of what was labelled as progress in the past decades turned out to be problematic in its consequences on the natural environment and on social cohesion.

Some of these mechanisms have commonalities with the classic evolutionary theories that were set up to describe the evolution of biological organisms (that is, variation and selection of the fitter); but there are also other mechanisms, specific to human societies, that make the societal evolution faster and more efficient. Understanding these mechanisms informs social intervention to change behaviours by designing or redesigning installations.

These mechanisms are, like the classic evolutionary theory, based on producing variants and selecting 'better' ones for the evolution of installations. But the production of variants is not random. It is oriented from the start at producing a 'better' state of affairs somewhere. Then there are mechanisms that ensure that the variants are compatible with the current state of things. These mechanisms are embedded in the very production process of variants, because (a) these are usually a combination of existing objects, (b) the production of variants includes an external description phase in which the representation of the new must be expressed within the current symbolic and technical framework[3] and (c) the process of production of new variants is under the control of institutions, which ensure they both comply with regulations and conform to cultural norms and value systems.

The properties of external representations such as documents (durable, transmittable, comparable, computable) considerably leverage the technologies of the mind; they afford better labour division, simulation and evaluation of the variants. They account for the capitalization of knowledge, massive generation of potential variants and assessment of their potential impacts on the installation.

Then comes selection. This selection process is dual: the material form of entities is tested in reality (by actual confrontation to the real world, e.g. a physical prototype, a market test), and the symbolic form is tested by simulation in the symbolic realm (*thought experiments*, computer simulation etc.)

This design phase where variants are selected in the very process of their making (rather than testing the variants once they have occurred, as nature does with living beings) is a spiral. It belongs to betterment loops: minor variants are produced and selected on the basis of their fitness and on their capacity to tile with the current state of things. This selection occurs in the material implementation phase of the variants, but it also occurs in the conceptual phase (when the variant is created in the

---

[3] On plans, blueprints, etc.

form of an idea and submitted to evaluation in that form, as a simulation of its expected outcomes). The second selection process (simulation) is fast, economic and risk-free: it is usually applied before any physical prototype is realized.

The selection is based not only on local functional fitness in the installation, but also on its possible collateral impacts outside the installation. Institutions consider these externalities in their evaluation and selection. Different scales of worth and currencies can be used to evaluate the interest of a variant. These might correspond to different interests of various stakeholders. Institutions, which monitor the reproduction and evolution process, are precisely there to arbitrate the choices on the basis of the power relations between stakeholders.

In that process, the material form of components must constantly match their immaterial form as models, because models and the material form are taken in a continuous coreproduction cycle where each is generated after the other, each serving as a reference for the other.

Because installations are made of three semiautonomous layers, the evolution of a given component does not only depend on its functional effect in that installation. Its design and characteristics may be influenced by what happens in another installation. For example, some standard objects (chairs, computers) are used in various installations; their design is a compromise between the requirements of the various installations and their evolution is the result of the various influences they are submitted to locally in these diverse installations. Also, individual humans circulate between installations and their individual competences and embodied dispositions are therefore constructed within and for diverse installations. That produces combinations and trade-offs.

Furthermore, institutions usually care for more than one type of installation (think of a state or a city) and therefore the regulations are arranged to cover several installations.

Finally, each layer has its own technical (re)production logics and constraints, and that has an impact on the substance and form of the components. For example, most material objects now are mass-produced by industry; regulations tend to be explicit and bureaucratic (in the sense of anonymous and egalitarian).

These crossed effects and technical processes make the evolution of installations, which are composite entities, more complex than the natural evolution of biological creatures. The latter must evolve 'in one piece', reproducing as a whole organism and not as separate parts, as installations do.

The societies therefore appear as reproducing piecemeal, in a distributed manner in installations; – a bit like biological organisms continuously reconstruct new cells but within the same global structure. Installations are also, therefore, a place where evolution takes place; but the determinants of the evolution of installations are not purely local, because the components of installations also evolve with logics independent from one specific installation.

Overall, the evolution mechanisms of installations, which combine material and symbolic processes, appear faster and more economical than biological mechanisms. That is the secret of mankind's amazingly fast evolution at geological scale.

As installations are the entities that frame and regulate most basic behaviours in society, and channel a substantial if not a major part of human activity in large-scale societies, they can be considered the distributed infrastructure of culture. Installations are also the place where practice is reproduced. We can therefore suggest that installations are elementary components of society and culture; and that they are the means by which societies and culture reproduce. This perspective provides a new vision of the endurance and evolution of societies, where societies would reproduce piecemeal and in a distributed manner in installations rather than as a structural whole.

The model of installations and the understanding of installations' evolution facilitates interventions to change the world by changing installations. I provided some examples and the principles of intervention. The first step is to understand the goals, the value systems, and how at each step of behaviour each layer contributes to channel the behaviour of the participants. That can be done by following the behavioural trajectory of participants in the installation, using such techniques as SEBE.

The change agent can then consider interventions on components on any of the layers to curb the channelling in the desired direction. This should be done with the help of the stakeholders, using the classic know-how of action research, and in a careful and reversible manner in order to evaluate the collateral impacts of the changes before scaling up. Although interventions which target the three layers benefit from the resilience of good installations, interventions on one layer only can have effects that gradually modify the other layers. Therefore, using the installations approach provides more leeway and allows some opportunism in the targets of interventions.

## 9.2.   Considerations on Trees and Forests

Please allow me to share here some personal thoughts on the theory in its present state.

Social sciences have a more complicated task than natural sciences, not only because they must include in their field of observation the material world with which natural sciences deal but also because the units they study (humans) do not simply react to external stimuli, they act on their own will, and they do so on the basis of their own representation of the whole situation, of what they think others think, etc. On top of that, humans learn and imagine, so the causes of an event may reside in the past (experience) or in the future (anticipation) and not only in the present. Motivation, memory, reflexivity, specularity and simulation introduce substantial complexity in the dynamics of social systems.

But on the other hand, social science may not be as difficult as natural science. Whereas natural science deals with phenomena that have no designer, and tries to guess what natural laws could predict empirical phenomena, social science deals with a man-made society. In society, most of the objects we study do have a design and purpose; human concepts are at the root of their construction, and the human language, which we understand, is adapted to their description. Therefore the laws of design of the systems (or at least the motives and functions behind them) exist and are accessible to our intelligence.

To take a metaphor: a natural forest is difficult to describe in a simple way because the position of the trees results from a complex local history of seeds falling more or less randomly on the ground; but a man-made plantation of trees is easier to describe. That is because the latter follows a plan: it is usually single species (say, pines or palm trees) and systematically ordered by human design, usually as rows of evenly spaced trees. So man-made systems are rather easy to understand if we know their design principles and their purpose. To build on this metaphor of the plantation, all one needs is to find the right position from which the perspective makes the structure obvious (Figure 9.1).

The reader will judge whether I have found such a simplifying perspective to describe more easily the problem of the social determination of behaviour, an issue that has brought about many theories and models.

I think that because installations are frames designed to produce specific behaviour, behaviours are more simply described at the level of installations. We can easily deconstruct phenomena there, because *there* was a

Figure 9.1. A loblolly pine (*Pinus taeda*) plantation in the southern United States, seen from a perspective that reveals the alignment. Photo from USDA Natural Resources Conservation Service via Wikimedia Commons (cc-by).

construction indeed. And because installations are made by humans and for humans, they can be described easily by humans. That is what I tried to do in this book.

Nevertheless, as the reader may have noticed, it is not so simple. Installations also evolve in history, and their construction and evolution result from a complex series of mechanisms, some of which are independent and some of which are connected. There is no such thing as a general model of installations; no more than there is a general model of living beings. Installations are diverse in form, and each one has a path-dependent sociohistoric construction that depends upon the context in which it was grown, and upon its own history as well as upon the history of the culture that houses it. What installation theory provides is a general descriptive framework to analyse installations and a series of general mechanisms of installation endurance and evolution. Installation is not a theory of everything.[4] It is rather a framework for a first approach of a

---

[4] I know some people will be tempted to see 'installations' everywhere. Using a theory beyond its reasonable domain of application is a devilish temptation. Against it, one should always keep in mind Randolph Kirkpatrick's theory of the 'Nummolosphere'. This respectable scientist, conservator at the

given installation or activity and helps sorting the wood from the trees; it will help to structure analysis and interventions. Its added value for action is a simple model of the components distributed in three layers that makes the problem tractable.

But for more specific purposes, other theories, specialized or domain specific, should be used.

Beyond that simple and operational formulation, the originality of installation theory resides in making explicit the chain of links between social construction and individual behaviour. That chain had been announced in broad terms by other systemic theories in sociology, anthropology or neuroscience,[5] but never made fully explicit, especially in the specific way the conditioning of individuals takes place in everyday life: general descriptions lack operational detail, and detailed ones address only a single segment of the chain. Now that I have attempted to describe it at length, I understand why: that was probably as exhausting for the reader as for myself, and it is a frustrating process because a proper description in full detail would require tiling hundreds of theories in dozens of disciplines, from anthropology to neuroscience, through linguistics and a dozen shades of psychology.

Alas, *ars longa, vita brevis*, and the sea of publications is infinite. I am painfully aware of the immense amount of literature that I have neglected through ignorance, laziness and lack of time. I am also aware that my superficial knowledge of the history of several disciplines has inevitably made me underestimate, reduce or distort the content and reach of many a work I mobilized. Finally there are trade-offs in theory-making. Installation stays on the vague and large side of general investigation tools rather than on the detailed side of description and classification.

Perhaps someday someone will attempt a taxonomy of installations, as Barker attempted for the 'behavioral settings' of 'Midwest' with his two hundred and twenty 'genotypes', from 'Abstract and Title Company Offices' to 'X-Ray Laboratories' (Barker, 1968: 110–6). Such was not my purpose. I tend, in accordance to my mentor's early work (Cicourel, 1964), and as someone whose initial specialism is statistics, to be cautious against attempts to straitjacket complex phenomena into quantified grids. That

---

British Museum from 1886 to 1927, became so obsessed by Nummulites (small lenticular foraminifera whosefossils appear as small circles in sediments) that he came to believe that *all rocks* on the surface of Earth were formed by an accretion of Nummulites. (Kirkpatrick, 1912).

[5] For example, Aleksander Luria, after his mentor Vygotsky, considered that the higher-order functions of the brain were formed by the subject's interaction with the culturally constructed structures of the social world: they are 'sociohistorical in origin' (Luria, 1966: 32)

looks nice but, considering the state of our knowledge, it may be premature. In science as in life, doing well is not always doing good.

The installation is a smaller unit than society; it is dedicated to the production of a specific behaviour. That makes it a functional unit tractable for analysis. It is also immediately recognizable by members of a given culture, and therefore the analyst can discuss it with stakeholders in their natural language without having to infer complicated concepts in a scientific vernacular. Installations also usually come with institutions and communities who are in charge of it, so it is rather clear who has to be addressed when studying them or attempting to change them.

Another originality of installation theory comes from its epistemological transgression. Most previous theories would attempt to keep a single, coherent philosophical background and epistemic unity. Although many have already noted that there are material, psychological and social dimensions to their object, they would usually consider these as different perspectives on the same object, as dimensions to describe it scientifically. Installation theory makes a bold step and mixes impudently three layers of different ontological material to make a compound object that assembles at the point of delivery. For installation theory, the three layers are not three views of the installation: they are three actual *components* of the installation. The installation is an epistemic hybrid or chimera, part material (realism), part embodied (subjectivism), part social (constructivism). As a consequence installation theory seems to draw on several incompatible epistemologies: objectivist, phenomenological, relativist; or perhaps more sophisticated variants and hybrids.

I understand that hybridization may appear a problem for some colleagues. I don't think it is diriment; our desire to have everything in a coherent model is just one more (scientific) version of the eternal desire of humans for a single *Weltanschauung* that Freud described so well.[6] But the world is not designed after our formal philosophical systems. One single model cannot fit all scales of a phenomenon, sometimes it cannot even account for all aspects of the phenomenon at a single scale (see the issues that physics has with the description of the dual theoretical nature of light,

---

[6] 'In my opinion, then, a Weltanschauung is an intellectual construction which solves all the problems of our existence uniformly on the basis of one overriding hypothesis, which, accordingly, leaves no question unanswered and in which everything that interests us finds its fixed place. It will easily be understood that the possession of a Weltanschauung of this kind is among the ideal wishes of human beings. Believing in it one can feel secure in life, one can know what to strive for, and how one can deal most expediently with one's emotions and interests.' (Freud, 1932, 1999: 158)

as a wave and as a particle).[7] Let us for the sake of simplicity consider that the installations have three different dimensions for their components.[8] A model is just a model and a theory just a theory: their value resides in their usability. In psychology, we know that the same individual may use alternative versions of knowledge depending on the situation at hand; e.g. one may be an evolutionary biologist and believe in God, be a rationalist but have some superstitions, etc.[9] In art, using 'mixed media' has become acceptable only recently; perhaps it is now the turn of science to be more open to 'mixed ontologies'. Anyway, the proof is in the pudding: installation theory appears pretty robust on the field, whatever its hybrid origins; time will tell if that is indeed the case.

I must here say again a word about the three layers. Why three? Distinguishing three layers in the determination of behaviour is the result of many years of work on empirical data, trying to describe what are the factors which determine behaviour. There are infinite ways to categorize these determinants, that are of very diverse nature, and that is why there are so many theories. We could just as legitimately consider three, four or ten layers. In practice, two appeared too little, and with three there is already some redundancy. As we saw, redundancy is not a flaw of the model, it captures an essential aspect of the phenomenon which accounts for resilience. But most importantly three appeared convenient and robust in practice. I don't believe there is a strong ontological reason to distinguish three, but it is handy and fits well with operationalization of analysis and

---

[7] Almost a century after the 1927 Fifth Solvay Conference, where Albert Einstein and the realists lost against Niels Bohr and the instrumentalists, the debate on interpretation is still vivid and new alternative theories are presented. See, e.g. Gondran, 2014.

[8] For those who are sensitive to arguments of authority, epistemic mix has long been around for those who attempt to explain human action. See how Tomas and Znanecki describe 'social values' in their classic book: 'By a social value we understand any datum having an empirical content accessible to the members of some social group and a meaning with regard to which it is or may be an object of activity. Thus, a foodstuff, an instrument, a coin, a piece of poetry, a university, a myth, a scientific theory, are social values. Each of them has a content that is sensual in the case of the foodstuff, the instrument, the coin; partly sensual, partly imaginary in the piece of poetry, whose content is constituted, not only by the written or spoken words, but also by the images which they evoke, and in the case of the university, whose content is the whole complex of men, buildings, material accessories, and images representing its activity; or, finally, only imaginary in the case of a mythical personality or a scientific theory. *The meaning of these values becomes explicit when we take them in connection with human actions.*' (Thomas & Znaniecki, 1918: 21). When it comes to taking action, humans seem to care little about epistemological purity and draw opportunistically on what seems efficient on the moment. As a matter of fact, we build our mental life on a strange mix of naive realism, phenomenology and constructionism. See also Jana Uher's transdisciplinary philosophy-of-science paradigm (Uher, 2014a, 2014b, 2016a), which combines three epistemologically different kinds of properties of phenomena to study personality.

[9] 'Cognitive polyphasia' (Provencher, 2011).

intervention. The use of the three layers (physical affordance, embodied competences, social regulation) can be considered a refinement of activity theory, one that provides a framework to analyse in a systematic manner the 'conditions given' to the subject who strives to satisfy her motives and reach her goals in the world. Then, once we use that framework, when we want to analyse installations, they will naturally be described as made of three layers. That is a projection of the analytic framework rather than an ontological imperative. I suspect that would be true of any other model, whatever the number of layers.

I must warn that the notion of installation as I define it can appear deceptively simple. We tend to think of an installation as the physical setting where a particular installation assembles (e.g. a ticket booth). But the installation is made of three types of components, of which the physical layer is only one aspect. The dinner is a better example than the ticket booth. Furthermore, we observe only specific, local, instances of installations (e.g. *this* dinner). But, just as for social representations, what makes installations what they are is precisely that they exist in many similar individual occurrences, with repetition in time and space, and slight variation in instantiation. *An installation is in fact a triple paradigm*: of settings affording the practice, of competences enabling its interpretation, of regulation systems funnelling the behaviour.

The power of installations comes from their fit to the way humans construct, learn and regulate their behaviour. Humans learn how to act based on their experience of successful previous behaviours in given situations, which they repeat when encountering similar situations. Then they regulate locally their behaviour with the feedback and feedforward provided in the situation by the environment (material and social). What we learn in one situation will be usable in all situations similar: therefore, by standardizing situations, installations make our life simple. All dinners, all dental practices, all elevators are similar; what I have learned in a specific one can be used in any other similar.

The distribution of similar, replicated, local instances of a specific type of installation in a given society (the thousands of dinners, of dental practices), has another important aspect. Installations are a massive distributed education system; each local installation is a training station for its users; again, what I have learned in a specific one can be used in any other similar. That is how is managed in practice the immense task of installing similar competences in large-scale populations. As I showed, this training is possible because installations are resilient to incompetence, and can create embodied competences in previously incompetent users.

The redundancy of layers, which produces resilience, and the replication of similar local instances, which produces paradigmatic learning and functional efficiency, are essential aspects of installations.

Historically, installation theory was designed to analyse the rich data obtained with the subcam and the SEBE technique; therefore it was not intended as a 'capital-T Theory'. As my colleagues, students and I used it to analyse real cases, it appeared that installations were of interest to study the evolution of human-made systems.

I was happy to realize that installations are the unit where societal-reproduction-through-practice takes place. That was unexpected. But it makes sense that the structures that emerge to control behaviour have a deep connection with the nature of society as a socially constructed system that facilitates life in common. Because installations are small-scale, local and specialized devices, they cannot account for what is a society as-a-whole, but they shed light on the local mechanisms by which societies operate and endure.

It has often been theorized that practice reproduces social structure, but 'capital-T' Theories had remained vague as to how where and when exactly that reproduction happens in detail. It seems to me that installations are the main reproduction units of societies. I showed in detail how this happens, by following the chain from institutionalized social structures to embodied neural structures. That was a painful exercise, at times trivial and often cumbersome, but I think it had to be done and I hope it is convincing, even though sketchy and in places approximate. The idea that emerges – that societies do not reproduce as a whole through structure, but piecemeal in a distributed and subsidiary manner – will, I hope, go a long way. It has important political implications.

Encouraged by that unexpected success, I was then expecting to find that installations are the place where societal evolution takes place. It seemed a natural continuation of the distributed reproduction hypothesis. But as I tried to model that process by looking at actual cases, I realized I was wrong. As Chapter 7 shows, the evolution is a much more complicated process than small mutations in local installations, followed by survival of the fitter. There are transverse mechanisms of diffusion, retroaction and control; that is where we find strong macro-level structural constraints and a more systemic and sociological approach must kick-in.

But as a result, societal evolution is an extremely powerful mechanism. I have not finished describing it in detail, but I think the first sketch at local level yields interesting directions for further research. The three layers of installation theory proved very useful to clarify a complex series of interlocked mechanisms and unbundle the various forms of evolution that take place concurrently.

The simplicity of the three-layered installations model provided by the theory becomes especially handy when one wants to change installations and redesign them for the better. One simply has to follow one of the circulating objects (typically, a user, a practitioner or the product being processed) and look, at each step of the activity, what are the layers involved in the foster, switch or shunt of the course of action; and what their mechanism of influence is. Any segment of behaviour can then be related to what is its main cause of determination; this immediately points at what should be changed and how to modify the outcome. Naturally, nothing is simple and the changes might have unintended effects downstream or upstream, or impacts outside the installation domain, and these should be monitored. But again, there are three layers to scaffold, limit and compensate these effects, each of these offering windows of opportunities for design.

Installation theory was designed with applications in mind. In the trade-off between a beautiful theory and a robust theory, I have chosen the robust side. Installation theory is just a framework to support more local and precise, adapted theories and applications. I am confident the reader will use it for what it is: a simple but robust chassis to build more sophisticated vehicles, and leverage it to make a better world.

Some of my early readers expressed shock and dismay at how installation theory describes individuals as constrained and alienated, almost as if they had lost the capacity to use free will. I understand. That is the old debate between socialization and autonomy, between structure and agency. My answers to that gut reaction are threefold.

First, there is indeed structure and socialization; there are police and schools; installation theory is not responsible for that state of affairs, it only reveals it: don't shoot the messenger.

Second, we must be lucid: this continuous compliance is the price to pay to benefit from civilisation. What would you expect? That we can pack millions of primates in cities and get them to run these complex structures efficiently and peacefully without imposing on them some constraints? Installations capitalize knowledge, competences and resources painfully gathered and assembled by hundreds of generations. As the complexity of civilizations grows, the scaffolding and control grow in proportion. And we don't like being controlled. Still, obviously society does control us massively; it tries to influence our thoughts and deeds. That produces reactance, a tendency to resist and oppose (Brehm, 1966). What installation theory shows in its synchronous version is the huge benefit we get from compliance: the installations control but they also scaffold and enable cooperation on a massive level, empowering most of us to live a comfortable, safe and easy life compared with our ancestors'.

But the most important is this: installations regulate behaviour (that is, the overt expression of action); but they do not regulate desire, imagination or subjective experience. Subjects are actors, they play the system, they play with the system. There is leeway and slack within installations, and also some capacity of choice between installations. So there is autonomous agency – to a certain extent – that must be negotiated with the structure.

Then what installation theory shows in its diachronic version is that cultural evolution is very controlled, with many redundant mechanisms to ensure that the betterment loop does not jeopardize the accumulated capital of material and symbolic culture. It is precisely with this cautious, conservative approach that humanity managed to capitalize and develop knowledge and agency. One single big mistake and all the capital may be lost. And it is very long to reconstruct because the early phases are extremely slow.

That reactionary and cautious, stringent selection of potential innovations is compensated by the amazing generativity of imagination, leveraged by external representations and literacy, which propose continuously a massive array of potential innovative variants and recombinations. Only the enormous power of simulation, coupled with the labour division afforded by external symbolic representations, which enables assessing and pruning at low cost this mass of continuously generated variants, can enable selecting the most sustainable ones to improve installations in a controlled betterment loop. As a result, we benefit from continuously improved but resilient installations.

Finally, I must say something about nudging. Nudging can be described, in its present state, as trying to build installations mostly using the material affordances and some generic cognitive mechanisms, with occasional and indirect use of social norms. Nudging is currently more a list of tricks to influence choices and behaviour than a systematic framework. Because it comes with a philosophy of libertarian paternalism, nudging is reluctant to use the social layer, which has controlling aspects. In Sunstein's list of thirty-one 'freedom-preserving tools' or 'nudges' (Sunstein, 2016), only two involve social control and education, and they mildly do so. That is perhaps because behavioural science so far shows some reluctance to include social interaction in its analyses, and tends to cautiously remain within the limits of behavioural economics without stepping too far into politics and values. Overall, nudging lacks a general theoretical spine to structure a systematic approach in the design of interventions.

Installation theory does provide a general framework for *regulation* of behaviour and could be the theoretical spine for nudging.

As we have seen, the third layer, social, is very important in regulation. Of course that involves a political aspect, where stakeholders must make explicit their value systems, discuss, get involved in controversies and conflict, build compromises. But politics is an inescapable aspect of the life of primates like us; there is no such thing in reality as regulation purely through an economic market where individuals make their decisions and live their lives alone.

It may seem an unsavoury takeaway to our youthful and rebellious feelings that societal evolution should be so complicated, controlled and cautious, and that we must always face the Others and make political compromises, not to mention the stubbornness of the material world. Change is a slow, uphill, difficult, emotionally demanding and never-ending endeavour; it cannot be done alone and involves difficult interactions with Others who think different. Finally, change agents tend to get more blame than reward, even when they succeed.

But changing the world is also an exciting challenge; and anyway we should continue trying, however slow and cumbersome the process.

As I write this conclusion, the world is not so well and the future appears gloomy (Diamond, 2005; Meadows, Randers, & Meadows, 2002; Turner, 2008). But another world is always possible. Most of our current problems have a human origin, and where the problem is the solution is there too. So, as the motto of William the Taciturn, Prince of Orange (1533–1584) goes, 'Point n'est besoin d'espérer pour entreprendre, ni de réussir pour persévérer': 'Need not expect to undertake, need not succeed to persevere'.

# *Glossary*

ABDUCTION: A form of reasoning from effect to cause, where from 'B' one infers 'A' because, considering 'B,' 'A' appears plausible, probable, likely as a cause of 'B'. Abduction is looser than deduction, where if A then B (A is a sufficient condition for B). Abduction is not induction either, because it is looking for an explanation of 'B,' one that is satisficing, preferably 'the best explanation'. Abduction is difficult to define formally because, in its initial version by C. S. Peirce, it was intended to capture the creation of new hypotheses in the first stage of inquiry and not just a choice between various plausible ones (Fann, 1970).

ACTION: Consciously controlled motoric or mental move. (To contrast, in our version of activity theory, with *operation*, which is an automatic move occurring below the threshold of consciousness.)

ACTIVITY: What subjects do and how they make sense of it. Activity is goal-driven and subjectively experienced; it stems from the subjective perspective of the subjects in their 'phenomenological tunnels.' Activity includes the objective deeds of the subjects, but also their internal, covert, intentional and interpretative processes of thought.

ACTIVITY (IN RUSSIAN ACTIVITY THEORY) : Oriented trajectory from a given state ('conditions given') to a consciously represented expected state ('goal'), driven by internal motives (urge to reach some internal state of balance or satisfaction). The trajectory of activity is a succession of small problems to be solved ('tasks'), which can each be seen as reaching a local subgoal. Activity is subject-centric: performed from the perspective of the subject.

AFFORDANCE: 'Roughly, the affordances of things are what they furnish, for good or ill, that is what they *afford* the observer ... they are *ecological*, in the sense that they are properties of the environment *relative* to an animal ... Affordances do not cause behaviour but constrain or control it. Needs control the perception of affordances (selective attention) and also initiate acts. An observer is not "bombarded" by stimuli. He extracts invariants from a flux of stimulation'. (Gibson [1967] 1982)

ALGORITHM: A formalized step-by-step plan for a computational procedure. Algorithms usually begin with an input value and yield an output value in a finite number of steps. Algorithms are a special, tighter kind of procedure. A procedure is a particular method for performing a task based on a series of rules; algorithms are implementable and computable, they always halt and produce a result.

BEHAVIOUR: What subjects do, as described from the outside by an external observer. It is an external description of objective phenomena. In contrast, *activity* is what subjects do, experienced from their own perspective. In activity, the subject knows his goals and experiences emotions and consciousness; in behaviour the subject's goals and internal states of the subject are guesses by the external observer.

BETTERMENT LOOP: An *abductive* strategy for improving the standard solution to a problem or interpretation of a phenomenon. A model created through experience is used as a default model to deal with incoming cases considered 'similar'. This model is continuously updated with the results of new experience. The betterment loop considers whether a small variation based on 'educated guess' (abduction) would be a better interpretation; that solution is then tested and the result incorporated in the experience stock, eventually leading to changing the default solution for the improved variant. Regarding action-in-the-world *the betterment loop improves both the model used by the subject to act upon reality and the reality that is acted upon.*

COALITION: 'A coalition is not a system-plus-context. It is the minimal system that carries its own context. Finally, a coalition is, for us, the minimal organization that can properly be said to have functional integrity'. (Turvey et al., 1978)

COGNITIVE ARTEFACT: 'A cognitive artifact is an artificial device designed to maintain, display, or operate upon information in order to serve a representational function'. (Norman, 1991)

COMMON GROUND (IN CONVERSATION): '"X" is in common ground when two interactants each know "X," and each knows that the other knows "X." Mutual perspective taking, then, is the attempt to establish what is in common ground'. (Hotgraves, 2010:1406)

COMMUNITY: A group of humans with common interest (e.g. sharing a resource, a need or a territory) who recognize each other as members of the same group, are aware of their common fate and have developed some institutions and organization.

CONVENTIONS: Practices, routines, agreements, and their associated informal or institutional forms that bind acts together through mutual expectations. (Salais & Storper, 1992: 171) 'A regularity R in the behavior of members of a population P when they are agents in a recurrent situation S is a convention if and only if it is true that, and it is common knowledge in P that, in any instance of S among members of P, (1) everyone conforms to R; (2) everyone expects everyone else to conform to R; (3) everyone prefers to conform to R on condition that the others do, since S is a coordination problem and uniform conformity to R is a coordination equilibrium in S'.[1] (Lewis [1969] 2002: 58)

---

[1] That is not the final definition by Lewis, but it seems to me the clearest. Note the similarity with the notion of social norms by Bicchieri (2006: 11).

DOUBLE-BIND: A phenomenon discovered by Gregory Bateson and his group in Palo Alto, California, when studying family communication (Bateson, Jackson, Haley, & Weakland, 1956) and more clearly defined by Sluzki and Veron (1971). It is, in short, a situation of crossed-constraints that remains hidden to its victims. The subject feels summoned to take action. But acting in one direction is forbidden; and acting in another direction (or not acting) is forbidden also. Moreover, the problem is set in such a way that this double impossibility is hidden to the subject, who therefore feels restrained but without clearly understanding why.

DUAL SELECTION: Evolutionary process whereby the matching pairs (representation, object) are selected for fitness both in the symbolic realm of ideas, by thought experiments and controversies, and in the material arena of the world of action, by empirical trials. For example, a new product will be selected as an idea both during the conception phase in the research and development department of a company and as a material device in the field tests. These selections can chain in spiralling loops as the product evolves.

DYNAMICAL SYSTEM: Mathematical modelling whereby the evolution of a system (e.g. activity) is represented as a trajectory in a 'phase space': a multidimensional space where every possible state of the system is represented by a point.

ENACTION: 'The process by which a world is brought forth by the interaction or structural coupling between an embodied agent and its medium or environment; also the study of the manner in which a subject of perception creatively matches its actions to the requirements of its situation'. (Toscano, 2006) More simply: the emergent process by which perception and action emerge from the interaction between the subject and the environment.

FEEDFORWARD: 'The idea that the functional state of a still inactive processing system is modified in advance by the output of an earlier processing stage'. (Requin, 1980: 373) In other words, a preparation of the execution system (e.g. motor) to the anticipated conditions of performance. That (motor) process has some analogy with 'priming', an implicit memory effect in which some stimulus makes more readily available some elements for further cognitive processing, e.g. enabling faster recognition of these elements in the context.

FUNCTIONAL EXPLANATION IN SOCIOLOGY: According to Elster (1983: 57), 'An institution or a behavioural pattern X is explained by its function Y for group Z if and only if:

(1)  Y is an effect of X;
(2)  Y is beneficial for Z;
(3)  Y is unintended by the actors producing X;
(4)  Y or at least the causal relation between X and Y is unrecognized by the actors in Z;
(5)  Y maintains X by a causal feedback loop passing through Z'.

GOAL: A representation of the desired final state. The subject tries to reach her goals in the conditions given (the situation).

GROUNDED COGNITION: A concept that posits that during experience of a given situation, the brain captures internal states (e.g., cognitive, affective), bodily states (e.g., interoception, taste) and actions (e.g., executive, motoric) across the sensory modalities and integrates them with a situated conceptualization (or multimodal representation) stored in memory. Any element of a situated conceptualization can later serve as a cue for retrieving the rest of the situation (Barsalou 2008; 2009).

HABIT: A behaviour that is frequently repeated to the point it has become an routine and almost automatically occurs by default in specific situations.

HABITUS: 'The habitus is the product of the work of inculcation and appropriation necessary in order for those products of collective history, the objective structures (e.g. of language, economy, etc.) to succeed in reproducing themselves more or less completely, in the form of durable dispositions, in the organisms (which one can, if one wishes, call individuals) lastingly subjected to the same conditionings, and hence placed in the same material conditions of existence'. (Bourdieu [1972] 2013: 85)

HEURISTICS: Simple rules people use to make satisficing decisions or solve problems by using only a small amount of the available or potentially available information.

INSTALLATION: Specific, local, societal setting where humans are expected to behave in a predictable way. Installations consist of a set of components that simultaneously support and socially control individual behaviour. The components are distributed over the physical space (affordances), the subject (embodied competences) and the social space (institutions, enacted and enforced by other subjects). These components assemble at the time and place the activity is performed.

INSTITUTION: A set of behavioural rules applied by a group of individuals in a given context, and of which these individuals are aware.

INTERPRETIVE COMPETENCE: The capacity, but also the automatic process, by which the perception of a given object or situation triggers a conventional cultural interpretation. Embodiment implements this automatic process in the individual's body.

INVESTMENTS IN FORM: Standards, norms, codes, regulations, conventions, contracts, qualifications, brands and other types of immaterial investments; where investment is understood in the larger sense of 'a costly operation to establish a stable relation with a certain lifespan' (Thévenot, 1984: 11).

KNOWLEDGE: According to Bachimont, 'a piece of knowledge is the capacity to perform an action to reach a goal' (Bachimont, 2004: 65) ('une connaissance est la capacité d'exercer une action pour atteindre un but'). A knowledge can be embedded in various media supports: e.g. embodied in a human as a mental representation, inscribed in a document as a procedure.

LATA: (as opposed to data): From the passive past participle of the Latin verb *ferre*, to bear. Whereas data are what the environment brings to the subject in a given situation, lata are what the subject comes equipped with in her own body: representations, memories, skills, etc.

LEGITIMATE PERIPHERAL PARTICIPATION: 'By this we mean to draw attention to the point that learners inevitably participate in communities of practitioners and that the mastery of knowledge and skill requires newcomers to move toward full participation in the sociocultural practices of a community.' Legitimate peripheral participation 'provides a way to speak about the relations between newcomers and old-timers, and about activities, identities, artifacts, and communities of knowledge and practice. It concerns the process by which newcomers become part of a community of practice'. (Lave & Wenger, 1991: 29)

MEDIATING STRUCTURE: Information is propagated through a system in the form of representational states or 'mediating structures'. These structures include internal as well as external knowledge representations. 'Language, cultural knowledge, mental models, arithmetic procedures, and rules of logic are all mediating structures too. So are traffic lights, supermarkets layouts, and the contexts we arrange for one another's behavior. Mediating structures can be embodied in artifacts, in ideas, in systems of social interactions...' (Hutchins, 1995a: 290–1) The difference between a mediating structure and a representation is that a mediating structure is a *tool* that can process (display, store, transfer, transform, etc.) representational states. The mediating structure, independently of the human operator, does its local bit of the larger, distributed, work of information processing.

NUDGE: 'A nudge, as we will use the term, is any aspect of the choice architecture that alters people's behavior in a predictable way without forbidding any options or significantly changing their economic incentives. To count as a mere nudge, the intervention must be easy and cheap to avoid. Nudges are not mandates. Putting fruit at eye level counts as a nudge. Banning junk food does not'. (Thaler & Sunstein, 2008: 6)

OBJECT: For the observer, *what appears to act or is being acted upon as a unitary whole.*

OPERATION: Automatic, routinized move taking place beyond the threshold of consciousness (in contrast with action, which is conscious).

OPERANT CONDITIONING: The procedure wherein modifications of behaviour take place as an act of the consequences of behaviour (e.g. reinforcement or punishment). Operant behaviour is maintained by its consequences (and extinguished gradually if such consequences cease to follow). Operant conditioning contrasts with classical conditioning (respondent conditioning) wherein the conditioning of reflexive behaviours (reflex) are elicited by antecedent conditions (conditioned stimuli).

OPERATIONAL CLOSURE: 'A system that has operational closure is one in which the results of its processes are those processes themselves' (Varela et al., 1993: 139).

ORGANISM: 'dynamic agency acting in a very complex and unstable environment ... An organism is a complex, definitely coordinated and therefore individualized system of activities, which are primarily directed to obtaining and assimilating substances from an environment, to producing other similar systems, known as offspring, and to protecting the system itself and usually also its offspring from disturbances emanating from the environment'. (Wheeler, 1911).

ORGANIZATION (HUMAN): Sociotechnical entity combining people in an explicit structure with labour division to reach a goal.

PARADIGM: A set of entities that have some relation of functional equivalence. Initially, in traditional grammar, a paradigm is a 'list of forms from which we have to make a choice at a given point in the spoken chain' (Mounin, 1985: 7). A paradigm will be the set of units that can commute in a given situation; the array of alternative possibilities at this point.. For example, suffixes are a paradigm; so would be the various words describing 'places'. This notion was introduced by Ferdinand de Saussure: 'Thus a declensional paradigm is an associational grouping <which has the right to claim a unity>. Within this unity there is something which varies and something which does not vary; this is the character of all associational groups.' (Saussure [1909] 1997: 143a).

Because the notion of fit between element and structure is symmetrical, the set off elements that fit is equivalent to the structure in which it makes sense. The meaning has therefore extended to designate frameworks that subsume a set of elements that 'fit' in them (e.g. 'scientific paradigm'). I use the term in a sense close to the original: the set of entities that 'fit' in a given functional perspective; e.g. the paradigm of 'shower' subsumes all variants of behavioural sequences that produce the specific cultural type of hygienic practice we know under that name. Installations are paradigms.

PRECAUTIONARY PRINCIPLE: When some innovation is suspected to risk causing harm, the default public decision is to postpone authorization until the proponents bring the proof (typically scientific) that it is not harmful (to the public, the environment). The onus of the proof of harmlessness is on the activity proponent. Because there is no such thing as zero-risk, in practice the decision is based on the evaluation of 'proportionality' of potential risk/ cost to the benefits of the proposed action.

PREDMET: Predmet ('subjective object') is a notion deriving from Russian activity theory. It is an aspect of the object which, at a given moment, concerns the subject in his activity. It is therefore a production of the subject, inseparable from the subject in action, with an intentional perspective. The predmet incorporates the experiences of the subject throughout his history and evolves according to these experiences (dynamic stability). In particular, it can incorporate the achievements of cultural history. The predmet in its operation mediates the relation of the subject to the 'objective' object. It is a mixed entity that depends upon both the object and the subject (Nosulenko, 2008).

PRINCIPLE OF BOUNDED RATIONALITY: 'The capacity of the human mind for formulating and solving complex problems is very small compared with the size of the problems whose solution is required for objectively rational behaviour in the real world – or even for a reasonable approximation to such objective rationality'. (Simon, 1957: 198)

PROCEDURE: A set of steps based on a set of rules. In this book a procedure is how the activity is supposed to be executed as per the institution's formal rules of practice.

RATCHET EFFECT: The current state serves as a basis for the next; the system is prevented from going back. For Tomasello, a beneficial cultural trait or competence that has been acquired by some individuals of the population will, by imitation, be transferred to the rest of that population and not be lost; therefore the new generation starts from a higher tooth of the ratchet: culture is cumulative (Tomasello, 1999).

RATIONALITY: (substantive vs procedural): Herbert Simon made a distinction between two types of rationality:

'Behavior is substantively rational when it is appropriate to the achievement of given goals within the limits imposed by given conditions and constraints. Notice that, by this definition, the rationality of behavior depends upon the actor in only a single respect – his goals. Given these goals, the rational behavior is determined entirely by the characteristics of the environment in which it takes place'. (Simon, 1976: 130–1) 'Behavior is procedurally rational when it is the outcome of appropriate deliberation. Its procedural rationality depends on the process that generated it'. (Simon, 1976, 132)

In other words, in substantive rationality, the problem is defined in a bird's-eye, or third-person, perspective: there is a goal, and environmental conditions, that can be objectively described. Therefore the solution is which behaviour can ideally produce the goal. In contrast, in procedural rationality the behaviour is the result of the way the subject addresses the problem by using his own 'deliberating' processes.

RECURSION: (as used in this book): A process in which the future state of an object is defined based on the same process that contributed to creating its previous state. More formally, recursion is a process that at some point involves reiterating the whole constructive process itself. For example, calculating the next step based on the result of calculation for the current step, or the reflection of two parallel mirrors.

REGULATION (s): The most frequent meanings in social science literature are targeted rules, direct state intervention in the economy and 'all mechanisms of social control, by whomsoever exercised' (Baldwin, Scott, & Hood, 1998: 3). The third is the most relevant for us but too large to be operational. In this book, we adopt Black's definition: 'regulation is the sustained and focused attempt to alter the behaviour of others according to defined standards or purposes with the intention of producing a broadly identified outcome or outcomes, which may involve mechanisms of standard-setting, information-gathering and behaviour-modification' (Black, 2002), and use 'regulations' (plural) to designate specific instances of local rules.

REPISODE: A regularly occurring situation, no longer based on a clear local and temporal reference (Flick, 2000).

RESILIENCE TO INCOMPETENCE (OF PARTICIPANTS): An installation is resilient to incompetence if it is able to produce satisficing behavioural activity sequences even if the competence of participants is deficient.

ROLE (OF A PERSON): The set of behaviours that others can legitimately expect from a person (Stoetzel, 1963; my translation)

SCAFFOLDING: '[Scaffolding] refers to the steps taken to reduce the degrees of freedom in carrying out some task so that the child can concentrate on the difficult skill she is in the process of acquiring'. (Bruner, 1978: 19)

SEMANTIC RUBICON: 'The semantic Rubicon is the division between system and user for high-level decision-making or physical world semantics processing. When responsibility shifts between system and user, the semantic Rubicon is crossed'. (Kindberg & Fox, 2002)

SIMULATION: 're-enactment of perceptual, motor, and introspective states acquired during experience with the world, body, and mind'. (Barsalou, 2008)

STATUS (OF A PERSON): The set of behaviours a person can legitimately expect from others. (Stoetzel, 1963; my translation)

STIGMERGY: How individuals can effect the behaviour of others through the modification of artefacts. For example, how termites, by depositing building material at a specific place, induce others to build at the same place, which results in a column (Grassé, 1959). Stigmergy can also influence one's own activity (e.g. annotation, diaries).

STRUCTURE: (in structuration theory): 'Rules and resources, recursively implicated in the production of social systems. Structure exists only as memory traces, the organic basis of human knowledgeability. And as instantiated in action' (Giddens, 1984: 377); 'Structures refer to a virtual order of relations, out of time and space. Structures exist only in their instantiation in the knowledgeable activities of situated human subjects, which reproduce them as structural properties of social systems embedded in spans of time-space'. (Giddens, 1984: 304)

SUBSIDIARITY: A regulation principle in which issues are dealt with at the most immediate (or local) level that is consistent with their resolution. Decision and action are taken at local level unless issues cannot be dealt with at that local level, in which case they are then addressed at the higher level. That principle is especially applied in political governance.

TRANSLATION: (according to sociology of translation): 'By translation we understand all the negotiations, intrigues, calculations, acts of persuasion and violence, thanks to which an actor or force takes, or causes to be conferred on itself, authority to speak or act on behalf of another actor or force: "Our interests are the same", "do what I want", "you cannot succeed without going through me". Whenever an actor speaks of "us" s/he is translating other actors into a single will, of which s/he becomes spirit and spokesman'. (Callon & Latour, 1981: 279)

ZONE OF PROXIMAL DEVELOPMENT: The set of behaviours a learner can perform with the help of someone more skilled, but not without this help. (see Bruner, 1978; Vygotsky, 1978; Wood et al., 1976).

# References

Aarts, H., & Dijksterhuis, A. (2000). Habits as knowledge structures: Automaticity in goal-directed behavior. *Journal of Personality and Social Psychology*, *78*(1), 53–63.

(2003). The silence of the library: Environment, situational norm, and social behavior. *Journal of Personality and Social Psychology*, *84*(1), 18–28.

Abric, J.-C. (1994). *Pratiques sociales et représentations*. Paris: PUF.

(1999). *Psychologie de la communication*. Paris: Armand Colin.

(2003a). L'analyse structurale des représentations sociales. In S. Moscovici & F. Buschini (Eds.), *Les méthodes des sciences humaines* (pp. 375–392). Paris: PUF.

(2003b). La recherche du noyau central et de la zone muette d'étude des représentations sociales. In *Méthodes d'étude des représentations sociales* (pp. 59–80). Toulouse: érès.

(2003c). *Méthodes d'étude des représentations sociales*. Toulouse: érès.

Adan, A. (2012). Cognitive performance and dehydration. *Journal of the American College of Nutrition*, *31*(2), 71–78.

Agogué, M., Kazakçi, A., Hatchuel, A., Le Masson, P., Weil, B., Poirel, N., & Cassotti, M. (2014). The impact of type of examples on originality: Explaining fixation and stimulation effects. *Journal of Creative Behavior*, *48*(1), 1–12.

Ajzen, I. (1985). From intentions to actions: A theory of planned behavior. In J. Kuhl & J. Beckmann (Eds.), *Action control: From cognition to behavior* (pp. 11–39). Berlin, Heidelberg: Springer.

(1991). The theory of planned behavior. *Organizational Behavior and Human Decision Processes*, *50*(2), 179–211.

Ajzen, I., & Fishbein, M. (1980). *Understanding attitudes and predicting social behavior*. Englewood Cliffs, NJ: PrenticeHall.

Akrich, M. (1998). Les utilisateurs, acteurs de l'innovation. *Education Permanente*, *134*, 79–89.

Akrich, M., Callon, M., & Latour, B. (2006). *Sociologie de la traduction: textes fondateurs*. « Sciences sociales ». Paris: Mines Paris, les Presses.

Alderson, G. J. K., Sully, D. J., & Sully, H. G. (1974). An operational analysis of a one-handed catching task using high speed photography. *Journal of Motor Behavior*, *6*(4), 217–226.

Alexander, C., Ishikawa, S., Silverstein, M., Jacobson, M., Fiksdahl-King, I., & Angel, S. (1977). *A pattern language : Towns, buildings, construction.* New York: Oxford University Press.

Alexandrov, Y. I. (2008). How we fragment the world: The view from inside versus the view from outside. *Social Science Information, 47*(3), 419–457.

Alexandrov, Y. I., & Sams, M. E. (2005). Emotion and consciousness: Ends of a continuum. *Cognitive Brain Research, 25*(2), 387–405.

Allport, G. W. (1935). Attitudes. In C. Murchison (Ed.), *A handbook of social psychology* (Vol. 1, pp. 798–844). Worcester, MA: Clarck University Press.

Alter, N. (1993a). Innovation et organisation: Deux légitimités en concurrence. *Revue Française de Sociologie, 34*(2), 175–197.

(1993b). La lassitude de l'acteur de l'innovation. *Sociologie du Travail,* (4), 447–468.

Amabile, T. M. (1988). A model of creativity and innovation in organizations. *Research in Organizational Behavior, 10*, 123–167.

Anderson, M. L. (2003). Embodied Cognition: A field guide. *Artificial Intelligence, 149*(1), 91–130.

Anderson, N., Potocnik, K., Zhou, J., Potocnik, K., & Zhou, J. (2014). Innovation and creativity in organizations: A state-of-the-science review, prospective commentary, and guiding framework. *Journal of Management, 40*(5), 1297–1333.

Anglin, J. M. (1993). Vocabulary Development: A Morphological Analysis. *Monographs of the Society for Research in Child Development, Serial N° 238, 58*(10), 1–166.

Anonymous. (2014). Prison UK: An Insider's View: Perils and Pitfalls of Life After Prison. Retrieved April 3, 2016, from http://prisonuk.blogspot.fr/2014/08/perils-and-pitfalls-of-life-after-prison.html

Apostolidis, T. (2003). Représentations sociales et triangulation : enjeux théorico-méthodologiques. In J.-C. Abric (Ed.), *Méthodes d'étude des représentations sociales* (pp. 13–35). Saint-Agne: Erès.

Argyris, C. (1976). Single-loop and double-loop models in research on decision making. *Administrative Science Quarterly, 21*(3), 363.

Armitage, C. J., & Conner, M. (2001). Efficacy of the Theory of Planned Behaviour: A meta-analytic review. *British Journal of Educational Technology, 40*, 471–499.

Arnett, J. J. (2008). The neglected 95%: Why American psychology needs to become less American. *The American Psychologist, 63*(7), 602–614.

Asch, S. E. (1951). Effects of group pressure upon the modification and distortion of judgments. In H. Guetzkow (Ed.), *Groups, leadership and men* (pp. 177–190). Pittsburgh, PA: Carnegie Press.

Atkinson, J. W. (1957). Motivational determinants of risk-taking behavior. *Psychological Review, 64*(6), 359–372.

Attride-Sterling, J. (2001). Thematic networks: An analytic tool for qualitative research. *Qualitative Research, 1*(3), 385–405.

Avery, J. A., Kerr, K. L., Ingeholm, J. E., Burrows, K., Bodurka, J., & Simmons, W. K. (2015). A common gustatory and interoceptive representation in the human mid-insula. *Human Brain Mapping, 36*, 2996–3006.

Bachimont, B. (2004). *Arts et sciences du numérique: Ingénierie des connaissances et critique de la raison computationnelle. Mémoire de HDR.* Compiègne, France: Université de Technologie de Compiègne.

Bailey, H. N., DeOliveira, C. A., Wolfe, V. V., Evans, E. M., & Hartwick, C. (2012). The impact of childhood maltreatment history on parenting: A comparison of maltreatment types and assessment methods. *Child Abuse and Neglect, 36*(3), 236–246.

Baldwin, J. M. (1896). A new factor in evolution. *The American Naturalist,* (354, June 1896), 441–451.

Baldwin, R., Scott, C., & Hood, C. (1998). Introduction. In R. Baldwin, C. Scott, & C. Hood (Eds.), *A Reader on Regulation* (pp. 1–55). Oxford, UK: Oxford University Press.

Bandura, A. (1977). *Social Learning Theory* (Vol. 53). Englewood Cliffs, NJ: Prentice Hall.

(1978). Self-efficacy: Toward a unifying theory of behavioral change. *Advances in Behaviour Research and Therapy, 1*(4), 139–161.

(1986). *Social foundations of thought and action : A social cognitive theory.* Englewood Cliffs, NJ: Prentice-Hall.

(1991). Social cognitive theory of self-regulation. *Organizational Behavior and Human Decision Processes, 50*(2), 248–287.

Barabanschikov, V. (2007). La question de l'activité dans la psychologie russe. In P. Rabardel & V. N. Nosulenko (Eds.), *Rubinstein Aujourd'hui. Nouvelles Figures de L'activité Humaine* (pp. 41–81). Paris: Octarès et Maison des Sciences de l'Homme.

Barker, R. G. (1968). *Ecological psychology : Concepts and methods for studying the environment of human behavior.* Stanford, CA: Stanford University Press.

Barsalou, L. W. (1999). Perceptual symbol systems. *Behavioral and Brain Sciences, 22*(4), 577–660.

(2003). Abstraction in perceptual symbol systems. *Philosophical Transactions: Biological Sciences, 358*(1435), 1177–1187.

(2008). Grounded cognition. *Annual Review of Psychology, 59*(4), 617–645.

(2009). Simulation, situated conceptualization, and prediction. *Philosophical Transactions of the Royal Society B: Biological Sciences, 364*(1521), 1281–1289.

Bartlett, F. C. (1932). *Remembering. A study in experimental and social psychology* (Vol. 1). Cambridge, UK: Cambridge University Press.

Basso, F., Guillou, L., & Oullier, O. (2010). Embodied entrepreneurship: a sensory theory of value. In A. A. Stanton, M. Day, & I. M. Welpe (Eds.), *Neuroeconomics and the Firm* (pp. 217–232). Cheltenham, UK: Edward Elgar.

Basso, F., & Oullier, O. (2010). *Le Corps et les Prix.* ENS Cachan: Unpublished manuscript.

Basso, F., Petit, O., Le Bellu, S., Lahlou, S., Le Goff, K., Anton, J.-L., Nazarian, B., Cancel, A., & Oullier, O. (2017). *Taste at First (Person) Sight: Visual*

*Perspective Modulates Brain Regions Contributing to Taste and Reward Representations.* Working paper, LSE: London.

Basso, F., Robert-Demontrond, P., Hayek, M., Anton, J. L., Nazarian, B., Roth, M., & Oullier, O. (2014). Why people drink shampoo? Food imitating products are fooling brains and endangering consumers for marketing purposes. *PLoS ONE, 9*(9), e100368 https://doi.org/10.1371/journal .pone.0100368

Bataille, M. (2002). Un noyau peut-il ne pas être central? In C. Garnier & W. Doise (Eds.), *Les Representations Sociales, Balisage du Domaine d'Étude* (pp. 25–34). Montréal: Editions Nouvelles.

Bates, F. (1955). Position, role, and status: A reformulation of concepts. *Social Forces, 34*(1), 313–321.

Bateson, G. (1972). *Steps to an ecology of mind. Collected essays in anthropology, psychiatry, evolution, and epistemology* (Vol. 26). Northvale, NJ: Jason Aronson Inc.

(1979). *Mind and nature: A Necessary unity. Philosophy of Science.* New York: E.P. Dutton.

Bateson, G., Jackson, D. D., Haley, J., & Weakland, J. (1956). Toward a theory of schizophrenia. *Behavioral Science, 1*(2), 251–264.

Baudelaire, C. (1857). *Les fleurs du mal.* Paris: Poulet-Malassis et de Broise.

Bauer, M. W. (1991). Resistance to change – a monitor of new technology. *Systems Practice, 4*(3), 181–196.

(1995). Towards a functional analysis of resistance. In M. W. Bauer (Ed.), *Resistance to New Technology: Nuclear Power, Information Technology and Biotechnology.* (pp. 393–418). Cambridge, UK: Cambridge University Press.

Bauer, M. W., & Gaskell, G. D. (2000). *Qualitative researching with text, image and sound: A practical handbook for social research.* London: Sage Publications.

Beaudouin, V. (2008). PowerPoint : Le lit de Procuste revisité. *Social Science Information, 47*(3), 371–390.

(2011), Prosumer. *Communications, 88*(1), 131–139.

Becker, G. S. (1996). The economic way of looking at behavior: The Nobel lecture. *Essays in Public Policy, 101*(9), 385–409.

Becker, H. S. (1966). *Outsiders: Studies in the sociology of deviance.* New York: The Free Press.

Becvar-Weddle, A., & Hollan, J. D. (2010). Professional perception and expert action: Scaffolding embodied practices in professional education. *Mind, Culture, and Activity, 17*(2), 119–148.

Bedny, G., & Meister, D. (1997). *The Russian theory of activity: Current applications to design and learning.* Mahwah, NJ: Lawrence Erlbaum.

Beeler, J. A. (2012). Thorndike's law 2.0: Dopamine and the regulation of thrift. *Frontiers in Neuroscience, 6*(Aug), 1–12.

Berger, P. L., & Luckmann, T. (1966). *The social construction of reality; a treatise in the sociology of knowledge.* Garden City, NY: Doubleday.

Bernays, E. L. (1928). *Propaganda.* New York: Horace Liveright.

Bernstein, N. A. (1947). *On the construction of movements (О построении движений).* Moscow: Medgiz.

Berridge, K. C. (2007). The debate over dopamine's role in reward: The case for incentive salience. *Psychopharmacology, 191*(3), 391–431.

Berthoud, H.-R. (2006). Homeostatic and non-homeostatic pathways involved in the control of food intake and energy balance. *Obesity, 14 Suppl* 5(August), 197S–200S.

Berthoud, H.-R., & Morrison, C. (2008). The brain, appetite, and obesity. *Annual Review of Psychology, 59*(1), 55–92.

Bestor, C. (2003). Installation art: Image and reality. *ACM SIGGRAPH Computer Graphics, 37*(1), 16–18.

Bicchieri, C. (2006). *The Grammar of Society. The Nature and Dynamics of Social Norms.* Cambridge, UK: Cambridge University Press.

Billig, M. (1988). Social representations, objectification and anchoring: A rhetorical analysis. *Social Behaviour, 3,* 1–16.

Birch, L. L. (1999). Development of food preferences. *Annual Review of Nutrition, 19,* 41–62.

Birdwhistell R. L, (1971). Appendix 6: Sample Kinesic Transcription. In N.A. McQuown (dir.), The Natural History of an Interview, Chicago, Microfilm Collection of Manuscripts on Cultural Anthropology, Fifteenth Series. Chicago: University of Chicago, Joseph Regenstein Library, Department of Photoduplication, 1971, 1–29.

Bittner, E. (2005). Florence Nightingale in pursuit of Willie Hutton. In T. Newburn (Ed.), *Policing: Key Readings* (pp. xiv, 834). Cullompton, Devon: Willan Publishing.

Black, J. (2002). Critical reflections on regulation. *Australian Journal of Legal Philosophy, 27*(1), 1–36.

(2008). Forms and paradoxes of principles-based regulation. *Capital Markets Law Journal, 3*(4), 425–457.

(2010). The Rise, fall and fate of principles-based regulation. *London School of Economics. Law Society Economy Working Papers,* (17), 1–25.

Blake, J. (1999). Overcoming the "value-action gap" in environmental policy: Tensions between national policy and local experience. *Local Environment, 4*(3), 257–278.

Blau, P. M. (1964). *Exchange and power in social life.* New York: Wiley.

Bødker, S. (1991). Activity theory as challenge to system design. In H.-E. Nissen & Sanström (Eds.), *Information System Research: Contemporary Approaches and Emergent Traditions. Proceedings of the IFIP TC 8/WG 8.2 Working Conference* (pp. 551–564). Copenhagen: Elsevier.

Bødker, S., Ehn, P., Sjogren, D., & Sundblad, Y. (2000). Co-operative design – Perspectives on 20 years with "the Scandinavian IT Design Model." In *Proceedings of NordiCHI 2000, Stockholm, October 2000.* (pp. 1–12). CID Center for User Oriented Design.

Bohner, G., & Schwarz, N. (2001). The construction of attitudes. In A. Tesser & N. Schwarz (Eds.), *Intrapersonal Processes (Blackwell Handbook of Social Psychology)* (pp. 436–457). Malden, MA: Blackwell.

Boltanski, L., & Thévenot, L. (2006). *On justification : Economies of worth* (1st ed. French 1991). Princeton, NJ: Princeton University Press.

Bourdieu, P. (1979). *La distinction: critique sociale du jugement.* Paris: Les Editions de Minuit.

(2013). *Outline of a theory of practice {1st ed.French 1972)* (28th ed.). Cambridge: Cambridge University Press.

(2014). Men and machines. In K. D. Knorr-Cetina & A. V. Cicourel (Eds.), *Advances in Social Theory and Methodology. Toward an Integration of Micro- and Macro-Sociologies.* London: Routledge.

Bower, G. H. (1972). Mental imagery and associative learning. In L. Greeg (Ed.), *Learning and Memory* (pp. 51–88). New York: Wiley.

Bower, G. H., Black, J. B., & Turner, T. J. (1979). Scripts in memory for text. *Cognitive Psychology, 11*(2), 177–220.

Brehm, J. W. (1966). *A theory of psychological reactance.* New York: Academic Press.

Broady, M. (1966). Social theory in architectural design. *Arena (The Architectural Association Journal), 81*(898 [January]), 149–154.

Bronfenbrenner, U. (1979). *The ecology of human development: Experiments by nature and design.* Cambridge, MA: Harvard University Press.

Bruner, J. S. (1966). On cognitive growth. In *Studies in cognitive growth* (pp. 1–29). New York: John Wiley & Sons.

(1968). *Towards a theory of instruction (1st ed. 1966).* Cambridge, MA: Harvard University Press.

(1972). The nature and uses of immaturity. *American Psychologist, 27*(8, August), 687–708.

(1974). From communication to language – A psychological perspective. *Cognition, 3*(3), 255–287.

(1978). The role of dialogue in language acquisition. In A. Sinclair, R. J. Jarvelle, & W. J. Levelt (Eds.), *The Child's Concept of Language.* New York: Springer-Verlag.

(1984). *Savoir faire et savoir dire.* Paris: PUF.

(1987). Life as narrative. *Social Research, 54*(1), 11–32.

(1990). *Acts of Meaning. The Jerusalem-Harvard Lectures.* Cambridge, MA; Harvard University Press.

(1991). The narrative construction of reality. *Critical Inquiry, 18*(1), 1.

Brushlinskii, A. V., Kol'Tsova, V. A., & Oleinik, I. N. (1997). A brief sketch of the life and scientific activity of A. F. Lazurskii. *Journal of Russian and East European Psychology, 35*(2), 6–31.

Cabanac, M. (2003). *La cinquième influence, ou La dialectique du plaisir.* Québec: Presses de l'Université Laval.

Cabanac, M., Guillaume, J., Balasko, M., & Fleury, A. (2002). Pleasure in decision-making situations. *BMC Psychiatry, 2*, 7.

Callon, M. (1986). Some elements of a sociology of translation: domestication of the scallops and the fishermen of St Brieuc Bay. In J. Law (Ed.), *Power, Action And Belief: A New Sociology of Knowledge?* (pp. 196–223). London: Routledge.

(2001). Actor network theory. In N. J. Smelser & P. B. Baltes (Eds.), *International Encyclopaedia of the Social and Behavioral Sciences* (pp. 62–66). Elsevier.

Callon, M., & Latour, B. (1981). Unscrewing the big leviathan: How actors macro-structure reality and how sociologists help them do so. In K. Knorr-Cetina & A. V. Cicourel (Eds.), *Advances in Social Theory and Methodology: Toward an Integration of Micro- and Macro-Sociologies* (pp. 277–303). Boston: Routledge & Kegan Paul.

Campbell, D. T. (1971). Reforms as experiments. *Journal of Legal Education, 23*(1), 217–239.

Cangiano, G. R., & Hollan, J. D. (2009). Capturing and restoring the context of everyday work: A case study at a law office. In *Lecture Notes in Computer Science* (Vol. 5619) (pp. 945–954). Berlin: Springer-Verlag.

Cantor, G. (1874). Ueber eine Eigenschaft des Inbegriffs aller reellen algebraischen Zahlen ("On a Property of the Collection of All Real Algebraic Numbers"). *Journal Für Die Reine Und Angewandte Mathematik, 77*, 258–326.

Carlesimo, G. A., Lombardi, M. G., Caltagirone, C., & Barban, F. (2015). Recollection and familiarity in the human thalamus. *Neuroscience and Biobehavioral Reviews, 54*, 18–28.

Carver, C. S., & Scheier, M. F. (1982). Control theory: A useful conceptual framework for personality-social, clinical, and health psychology. *Psychological Bulletin, 92*(1), 111–135.

Castellion, G., & Markham, S. K. (2013). Perspective: New product failure rates: Influence of argumentum ad populum and self-interest. *Journal of Product Innovation Management, 30*(5), 976–979.

Challamel, M.-J., Lahlou, S., Revol, M., & Jouvet, M. (1985). Sleep and smiling in neonate: A new approach. In W. Koella, E. Ruther, & H. Schulz (Eds.), *Sleep 84* (pp. 290–292). New York: Gustav Fisher Verlag.

Chen, J., Papies, E. K., & Barsalou, L. W. (2016). A core eating network and its modulations underlie diverse eating phenomena. *Brain and Cognition, 110*, 20–42.

Cheng, Y., Meltzoff, A. N., & Decety, J. (2007). Motivation modulates the activity of the human mirror-neuron system. *Cerebral Cortex, 17*(8), 1979–1986.

Chernilo, D. (2002). The theorization of social co-ordinations in differentiated societies: The theory of generalized symbolic media in Parsons, Luhmann and Habermas. *The British Journal of Sociology, 53*(3), 431–449.

Chesbrough, H. (2006). Open innovation: A new paradigm for understanding industrial innovation. In H. Chesbrough, W. Vanhaverbeke, & J. West (Eds.), *Open Innovation: Researching a New Paradigm* (pp. 1–12). Oxford: Oxford University Press.

Chomsky, N. (1965). *Aspects of the theory of syntax.* Cambridge, MA: MIT Press.

Cialdini, R. B. (2009). *Influence. Science and practice* (5th ed.). Boston: Pearson Education.

Cialdini, R. B., Kallgren, C. A., & Reno, R. R. (1991). A focus theory of normative conduct: A theoretical refinement and reevaluation of the role of norms in human behavior. *Advances in Experimental Social Psychology, 24*, 201–234.

Cialdini, R. B., Reno, R. R., & Kallgren, C. A. (1990). A focus theory of normative conduct: Recycling the concept of norms to reduce littering in public places. *Journal of Personality and Social Psychology, 58*(6), 1015–1026.

Cicourel, A. V. (1964). *Method and measurement in sociology.* New York: Free Press, Macmillan.

(1974). *Cognitive sociology: language and meaning in social interaction.* New York: Free Press, Macmillan.

(1992). The interpenetration of communicative contexts: examples from medical encounters. In A. Duranti & C. Goodwin (Eds.), *Rethinking Context* (Vol. 50, pp. 291–311). Cambridge, UK: Cambridge University Press.

(2002). *Le raisonnement médical.* Paris: Seuil.

(2012). Origin and demise of socio-cultural presentations of self from birth to death: Caregiver "scaffolding" practices necessary for guiding and sustaining communal social structure throughout the life cycle. *Sociology, 47*(1), 51–73.

Cieciuch, J., & Schwartz, S. H. (2012). The number of distinct basic values and their structure assessed by PVQ–40. *Journal of Personality Assessment, 94*(3), 321–328.

Clark, A. (1997). *Being there: Putting brain, body, and world together again.* Cambridge, MA: MIT Press.

Clark, H. H., & Marshall, C. R. (1981). Definite reference and mutual knowledge. In A. K. Joshi, B. L. Webber, and I. A. Sag (Eds.), *Elements of discourse understanding* (pp. 10–63). Cambridge: Cambridge University Press.

Clark, H. H., & Wilkes-Gibbs, D. (1986). Referring as a collaborative process. *Cognition, 22,* 1–39.

Clémence, A. (2002). Catégorisation sociale et représentation sociale : Commentaires sur le texte de Lacassagne, Salès-Wuillemin, Castel & Jébrane (2001). *Papers on Social Representations, 11,* 2.1–2.4

Clot, Y., Faïta, D., Fernandez, G., & Scheller, L. (2001). Entretiens en auto-confrontation croisée: une méthode en clinique de l'activité. *Education Permanente, 146*(1), 17–25.

Coase, R. H. (1937). The nature of the firm. *Economica, 4,* November (16), 386–405.

(1960). The problem of social cost. *Journal of Law and Economics,* (3), 1–44.

Cochin, Y., & Dupont, F. (1995). *La relation de service et la clientèle en difficulté. HN-51 95-003.* Clamart, France: EDF Direction des Etudes et Recherches.

Codol, J.-P. (1969). Note terminologique sur l'emploi de quelques expressions concernant les activités et processus cognitifs en psychologie sociale. *Bulletin de Psychologie Sociale, 23,* 63–71.

Cohen, M. D., March, J. G., & Olsen, J. P. (1972). A garbage can model of organizational choice. *Administrative Science Quarterly, 17*(1), 1–25.

Cole, M. (1984). The zone of proximal development: when culture and cognition create each other. In J. Wertsch (Ed.), *Culture, Communication and Cognition: Vygotskian Perspective.* Cambridge: Cambridge University Press.

Cole, M., Hood, L., & McDermott, R. (1997). Concepts of ecological validity: Their differing implications for comparative cognitive research. In

M. Cole and Y. Engeström (Eds.), *Mind, Culture, and Activity: Seminal Papers from the Laboratory of Comparative Human Cognition* (pp. 48–58). Cambridge: Cambridge University Press.

Cordelois, A. (2010). Using digital technology for collective ethnographic observation: an experiment on "coming home." *Social Science Information, 49*(3), 445–463.

Coutu, W. (1951). Role-Playing vs. Role-Taking: An Appeal for Clarification. *American Sociological Review, 16, April*(2), 180–187.

Cranach, M. von, & Kalbermatten, U. (1982). The Ordinary interactive action: theory, methods and some empirical findings. In M. von Cranach & R. Harre (Eds.), *The Analysis of Action* (pp. 115–160). London: Cambridge University Press.

Crews, W., & Young, R. (2013, June 5). Twenty years of non-stop regulation. *The American Spectator*. Arlington, VA.

D'Andrade, R. G. (2008). *A study of personal and cultural values. American, Japanese, and Vietnamese.* New York: Palgrave, MacMillan.

D'Anna, C., Zechmeister, E., & Hall, J. (1991). Toward a meaningful definition of vocabulary size. *Journal of Literacy Research, 23*(1), 109–122.

Dahlgren, G., & Whitehead, M. (1991). *Policies and strategies to promote social equity in health. Background document to WHO – Strategy paper for Europe.* Stockholm: Institutet för Framtidsstudier.

Damasio, A. R. (1989). Time-locked multiregional retroactivation: A systems-level proposal for the neural substrates of recall and recognition. *Cognition, 33*, 25–62.

Danone. (2010). *TNS-OBOP uses and attitudes survey. Unpublished data for Danone.* Warsaw, Poland.

Darnton, A. (2008a). *GSR behaviour change knowledge review – Reference report: An overview of behaviour change models and their uses.* London: Government Social Research.

(2008b). *Practical Guide : An overview of behaviour change models and their uses.* London: Government Social Research.

Darwin, C. (1859). *On the Origin of Species by Means of Natural Selection, or the Preservation of Favoured Races in the Struggle for Life.* London: John Murray.

(1872). *The expression of the emotions in man and animals.* London: John Murray.

Daucé, E. (2010). Systèmes dynamiques: Propriétés générales et définitions. Retrieved November 5, 2010, from http://emmanuel.dauce.free.fr/sdsc/node3.html

Davis, K. (1948). *Human society.* New York: Rinehart and Company.

Davis, R., Campbell, R., Hildon, Z., Hobbs, L., & Michie, S. (2015). Theories of behaviour and behaviour change across the social and behavioural sciences: a scoping review. *Health Psychology Review, 9*(3), 323–344.

Dawkins, R. (1976). *The selfish gene.* Oxford: Oxford University Press.

Dawnay, E., & Shah, H. (2005). *Behavioural economics : Seven principles for policymakers.* London: New Economics Foundation.

de Araujo, I. E., & Simon, S. A. (2009). The gustatory cortex and multisensory integration. *International Journal of Obesity, 33* (Suppl 2), S34–S43.

Deforge, Y. (1985). *Technologie et génétique de l'objet industriel.* Paris: Maloine.

Dennett, D. C. (1996), Darwin's Dangerous Idea: Evolution and the Meanings of Life. London: Penguin Book.

Dent, E. B., & Goldberg, S. G. (1999). Challenging "resistance to change." *The Journal of Applied Behavioral Science, 35*(1), 25–45.

Dessalles, J.-L. (2007). *Why we talk – The evolutionary origins of language* (2nd ed.). Oxford: Oxford University Press.

Deutsch, M., & Gerard, H. B. (1955). A study of normative and informational social influences upon individual judgement. *The Journal of Abnormal and Social Psychology, 51*(3), 629–636.

Dewey, J. (1896). The reflex arc concept in psychology. *Psychological Review, 3,* 357–370.

(1910). *How we think.* Boston: D. C. Heath & Co.

(1929). *Experience and nature* (Vol. 1). London: George Allen & Unwin.

(1939). Theory of valuation. *Political Research Quarterly.* Chicago: University of Chicago Press.

Diamond, J. (2005). *Collapse. How societies choose to fail or succeed.* New York: Penguin Books.

Dieckmann, P., Clemmensen, M., & Lahlou, S. (2016). Medication dispensing from a "work as done" perspective. Paper presented at the Fifth Resilient Health Care Net meeting, Hindsgavl Castle, Middelfart, Denmark, August 15–17, 2016.

(2017). *How the medication room dispenses the medication. An ethnographic study of facilitators and obstacles. Working paper.*

Dijkstra, K., Kaschak, M. P., & Zwaan, R. A. (2007). Body posture facilitates retrieval of autobiographical memories. *Cognition, 102*(1), 139–149.

Doise, W., & Palmonari, A. (1986). Caractéristiques des représentations sociales. In W. Doise & A. Palmonari (Eds.), *L'étude des représentations sociales. Textes de base en Psychologie* (pp. 12–33). Neuchâtel, Paris: Delachaux et Niestlé.

Dortier, J.-F. (2004). *L'homme, cet étrange animal. Au origines du langage, de la culture et de la pensée.* Auxerre: Sciences Humaines Editions.

Douglas, M. (2001). *Purity and danger. An analysis of concepts of pollution and taboo (1st ed. 1966).* London: Routledge.

Douglas, M. T. (1986). *How institutions think.* New York: Syracuse University Press.

Dourish, P. (2006). Re-space-ing place : "Place" and "space" ten years on. *Computing,* 299–308.

Drewnowski, A., Rehm, C. D., & Constant, F. (2013). Water and beverage consumption among children age 4–13y in the United States: Analyses of 2005–2010 NHANES data. *Nutrition Journal, 12*(85).

Drobes, D. J., Miller, E. J., Hillman, C. H., Bradley, M. M., Cuthbert, B. N., & Lang, P. J. (2001). Food deprivation and emotional reactions to food cues: Implications for eating disorders. *Biological Psychology, 57*(1–3), 153–177.

Dubuffet, J. (1973). *L'homme du commun à l'ouvrage.* Paris: Gallimard.

Duque, L. F., Toro, Jo. A., & Montoya, N. (2010). Tolerancia al quebrantamiento de la norma en el area metropolitana de Medellín, Colombia. *Opiniao Publica, Campinas, 16* (1), 64–89.

Durkheim, E. (1912). *Les formes élémentaires de la vie religieuse* (1968, 5ème ed.). Paris: PUF. Collection "Bibliothèque de philosophie contemporaine."
  (1982). *The rules of the sociological method* (1st ed. 1895 French). New York: The Free Press.

Duveen, G., & Lloyd, B. B. (1993). An ethnographic approach to social representations. In G. M. Breakwell & D. V Canter (Eds.), *Empirical Approaches to Social Representations* (pp. 90–109). Oxford: Oxford University Press.

Edelman, G. M. (2004). *Wider Than the Sky. The Phenomenal Gift of Consciousness.* New Brunswick and London: Yale University Press.

Edmonds, C. J., Crombie, R., Ballieux, H., Gardner, M. R., & Dawkins, L. (2013). Water consumption, not expectancies about water consumption, affects cognitive performance in adults. *Appetite, 60*(1), 148–153.

Edmonds, C. J., & Jeffes, B. (2009). Does having a drink help you think? 6–7-Year-old children show improvements in cognitive performance from baseline to test after having a drink of water. *Appetite, 53*(3), 469–472.

EFSA Panel on Dietetic Products Nutrition and Allergies (NDA) (2010). Scientific opinion on dietary reference values for water. *EFSA Journal, 8*(3), 1459.

Eibl-Eibesfeldt, I. (1967). *Éthologie – Biologie du comportement.* Paris: Éditions Scientifiques, Naturalia et Biologia,.

Einstein, A. (1949). Remarks to the essays brought together in this co-operative volume. In P. A. Schilpp (Ed.), *Albert Einstein: Philosopher-Scientist* (pp. 665–688). New York: MJF Books.

Elfenbein, H. A. (2014). The many faces of emotional contagion: An affective process theory of affective linkage. *Organizational Psychology Review, 4*(4), 326–362.

Elster, J. (1983). *Explaining technical change. Studies in rationality and social change.* Cambridge: Cambridge University Press.
  (2007). *Explaining social behaviour. More nuts and bolts for the social sciences.* Cambridge: Cambridge University Press.

Enfield, N. J. (2013). *Relationship thinking. Agency, enchrony, and human sociality.* Oxford: Oxford University Press.

Engel, A. K. (2010). Directive minds: How dynamics shapes cognition. In J. Stewart, O. Gapenne et E.A. Di Paolo (dir.), *Enaction: Toward a New Paradigm for Cognitive Science* (pp. 219–243). Boston: The MIT Press.

Engeström, Y. (2000). Activity theory as a framework for analyzing and redesigning work. *Ergonomics, 43*(7), 960–74.

Engeström, Y., & Bannon, L. (2009). What is activity theory ? Retrieved August 2, 2015, from http://www.psicopolis.com/psycosphere/whatsactiv.htm

Ericsson, K. A., & Simon, H. A. (1996). *Protocol analysis: verbal reports as data* (rev. ed.). Cambridge, MA: MIT Press.

Estes, W. K. (1961). Dynamics of choice behaviour. *Behavioral Science, 6*(3), 177–184.

Evans, S. (2015). *Virtual selves in virtual worlds: Towards the development of a social psychological understanding of the self in contemporary society.* PhD Thesis. London: London School of Economics.

Everri, M., Fruggeri, L., & Molinari, L. (2014). Microtransitions and the dynamics of family functioning. *Integrative Psychological and Behavioral Science*, *48*(1), 61–78.

Everri, M., & Sterponi, L. (2013). Identity development is distributed; specifically, it emerges from the texture of different interactive configurations occurring in families. In *Proceedings of the REID Conference "Revisiting Identity: Embodied communication across time and space". Örebro University, Sweden, October 22–24, 2013.* Springer.

Ewoldsen, D. R., Rhodes, N., & Fazio, R. H. (2015). The MODE model and its implications for studying the media. *Media Psychology*, *18*(3), 312–337.

Eymard-Duvernay, F., & Thévenot, L. (1983). *Les investissements de forme: leurs usages pour la main d'oeuvre* (Vol. N°1878/432). Malakoff, France: INSEE.

Fang, L. (2014). Where have all the lobbyists gone? *The Nation*, Feb 19, 2014.

Fann, K. T. (1970). *Peirce's theory of abduction.* The Hague: Martinus Nijhof.

Fauconnier, G. (1994). *Mental spaces. Aspects of meaning construction in natural language* (1st ed. 1985). Cambridge: Cambridge University Press.

Fauconnier, G., & Turner, M. (2002). *The way we think. Conceptual blending and the mind's hidden complexities.* New York: Basic Books.

Fauquet-Alekhine, P. (2016a). Risk assessment for subjective evidence-based ethnography applied in high risk environment. *Advances in Research*, *6*(2), 1–13.

(2016b). Subjective ethnographic protocol for work activity analysis and occupational training improvement. *British Journal of Applied Science & Technology*, *12*(5), 1–16.

Fazio, R. H. (1990). Multiple processes by which attitudes guide behavior: The MODE model as an integrative framework. In M. P. Zanna (Ed.), *Advances in Experimental Social Psychology,* vol. 23 (pp. 75–109). New York: Academic Press.

Festinger, L. (1957). *A theory of cognitive dissonance.* Stanford, CA: Stanford University Press.

Festinger, L., Riecken, H. W., & Schachter, S. (1956). *When prophecy fails.* Minneapolis: University of Minnesota Press.

Fischler, C. (1990). *L'homnivore.* Paris: Editions Odile Jacob.

Fishbein, M., & Ajzen, I. (1975). *Belief, attitude, intention, and behavior: An introduction to theory and research.* Reading, MA: Addison-Wesley.

Fisher, J. D., Fisher, W. A., Bryan, A. D., & Misovich, S. J. (2002). Information-motivation-behavioral skills model-based HIV risk behavior change intervention for inner city high school youth. *Health Psychology*, *21*(2), 177–186.

Fisher, R. A. (1915). The evolution of sexual preference. *The Eugenics Review*, *7*(3), 184–192.

Flament, C. (1962). L'analyse de similitude. *Cahiers du Centre de Recherche Operationnelle (Bruxelles)*, *4*, 63–97.

(1994). Structure, dynamique et transformation des représentations sociales. In J.-C. Abric (Ed.), *Pratiques Sociales et Représentations* (pp. 37–57). Paris: PUF.

(2007). Conformisme et scolarité : Les représentations sociales du travail et du non travail chez les jeunes non qualifiés des quartiers défavorisés. *Les Cahiers Internationaux de Psychologie Sociale*, *1*(73), 3–10.

Fleck, L. (1979). *Genesis and development of a scientific fact* (1st ed. 1935 German). Chicago: University of Chicago Press.

Flick, U. (2000). Episodic interviewing. In G. Gaskell (Ed.), *Qualitative Researching with Text, Image and Sound* (pp. 75–92). London: Sage Publications.

(2007). *Designing qualitative research* (Vol. 1). London: Sage Publications.

Foucault, M. (1975). *Surveiller et punir : Naissance de la prison*. Paris: Gallimard NRF.

Franks, B. (2011). *Culture and cognition. Evolutionary perspectives*. Basingstoke, UK: Palgrave Macmillan.

Franks, B., Lahlou, S., Bottin, J. H., Guelinckx, I., & Boesen-Mariani, S. (2017). Increasing water intake in pre-school children: a year-long randomised controlled longitudinal field experiment assessing the impact of information, water availability, and social regulation. *Appetite*, 116, 205–214.

Freud, S. (1895). Project for a scientific psychology. In J. Strachey, A. Freud, A. Tyson, & A. Strachey (Eds.), *The Standard Edition of the Complete Psychological Works of Sigmund Freud, Volume I (1886–1899)* (pp. 283–398). London: Vintage [reprint 1999].

(1923). The ego and the id. In J. Strachey, A. Freud, A. Tyson, & A. Strachey (Eds.), *The Standard Edition of the Complete Psychological Works of Sigmund Freud, Volume XIX (1923–1925)* (pp. 3–68). London: Vintage [reprint 1999].

(1925). Negation. In J. Strachey, A. Freud, A. Tyson, & A. Strachey (Eds.), *The Standard Edition of the Complete Psychological Works of Sigmund Freud, Vol. XIX (1923–1925)* (pp. 233–240). London: Vintage [reprint 1999].

(1926). Psycho-analysis. In J. Strachey, A. Freud, A. Tyson, & A. Strachey (Eds.), *The Standard Edition of the Complete Psychological Works of Sigmund Freud, Volume XX (1925–1926)* (pp. 259–270). London: Vintage [reprint 1999].

(1932). New introductory lectures on psychoanalysis. Lecture 35: The Question of a Weltanschauung. In J. Strachey, A. Freud, A. Tyson, & A. Strachey (Eds.), *The Standard Edition of the Complete Psychological Works of Sigmund Freud, Volume XXII (1932–1936)* (pp. 158–184). London: Vintage [reprint 1999].

Fried, I., Mukamel, R., & Kreiman, G. (2011). Internally generated preactivation of single neurons in human medial frontal cortex predicts volition. *Neuron*, 69(3), 548–562.

Gallese, V., Fadiga, L., Fogassi, L., & Rizzolatti, G. (1996). Action recognition in the premotor cortex. *Brain*, (119), 593–609.

Gapenne, O., Lenay, C., & Boullier, D. (2002). Defining categories of the human/technology coupling: theoretical and methodological issues. *Adjunct Proceedings of the 7th ERCIM Workshop on User Interface for All*, 197–198.

Garfinkel, H. (1964). Studies of the routine grounds of everyday activities. *Social Problems*, 3(11), 225–250.

Geertz, C. (1973). *The interpretation of cultures. Selected essays*. New York: Basic Books.

Gibbons, F. X., Gerrard, M., & Lane, D. J. (2003). A social reaction model of adolescent health risk. In J. Suls & K. A. Wallston (Eds.), *Social Psychological*

*Foundations of Health and Illness* (pp. 107–136). Malden, MA:Blackwell Publishing Ltd.

Gibson, J. J. (1950). *The perception of the visual world.* London: Houghton Mifflin.

(1963). The useful dimensions of sensitivity. *American Psychologist,* (18), 1–15.

(1979). *The ecological approach to visual perception* (2015 ed.). New York: Psychology Press.

(1982). Notes on affordances (unpublished manuscript, 1967). In E. Reed & R. Jones (Eds.), *Reasons for Realism. Selected Essays of James J. Gibson* (pp. 401–418). London: Lawrence Erlbaum Associates.

Giddens, A. (1984). *The constitution of society: Outline of the theory of structuration.* Berkeley: University of California Press.

Gigerenzer, G. (2008). Why heuristics work. *Perspectives on Psychological Science, 3*(1), 20–29.

Gigerenzer, G., & Brighton, H. (2009). Homo heuristicus: Why biased minds make better inferences. *Topics in Cognitive Science, 1*(1), 107–143.

Girard, R. (1985). *Deceit, desire, & the novel. Self and other in literary structure* (1st ed. 1965 French). Baltimore: The Johns Hopkins University Press.

Glăveanu, V. P. (2012). Habitual creativity: Revising habit, reconceptualizing creativity. *Review of General Psychology, 16*(1), 78–92.

Glăveanu, V. P., & Lahlou, S. (2012). Through the creator's eyes: Using the subjective camera to study craft creativity. *Creativity Research Journal, 24*(2–3), 152–162.

Gobbo, A. (2015). *The making of consumer decisions: Revisiting the notions of evaluation and choice by reconstructing consumer habits through subject evidence-based ethnography.* PhD Thesis. London: London School of Economics.

Goethe, J. W. von. (2005). *Elective affinities* (1st ed. German 1809). London: Penguin Books.

Goffman, E. (1959). *The presentation of self in everyday life.* New York: Doubleday Anchor Books.

(1961a). *Asylums: Essays on the Social situation of mental patients and other inmates.* New York: Anchor Books.

(1961b). *Encounters. Two studies in the sociology of interaction.* Harmondsworth, Middlesex, England: Penguin Books Ltd.

(1967). *Interaction ritual: Essays on face-to-face behaviour.* New York: Anchor Books.

(1969). *Strategic interaction.* Philadephia: University of Pennsylvania Press.

(1971). *Relations in Public: Microstudies of the Public Order.* New York: Basic Books.

(1974). *Frame analysis: An essay on the organization of experience.* London: Harper & Row.

Goldstein, K. (1995). *The Organism: A Holistic Approach to Biology Derived from Pathological Data in Man (1st ed. 1934).* New York: Zone Books.

Goldstein, N. J., Cialdini, R. B., & Griskevicius, V. (2008). A room with a viewpoint: Using social norms to motivate environmental conservation in hotels. *Journal of Consumer Research, 35*(3), 472–482.

Goldstein N. J & Cialdini R. B. (2009). Normative influences on consumption and conservation behaviors. In M. Wänke (dir.), *Social Psychology of Consumer Behavior* (pp. 273–296). New York: Psychology Press.

Gondran, M. (2014). *Mécanique quantique. Et si Einstein et de Broglie avaient aussi raison ?* Paris: Editions Matériologiques.

Goodwin, C. (1995). The negotiation of coherence within conversation. In M. A. Gernsbacher & T. Givon (Eds.), *Coherence in Spontaneous Text* (Vol. 31, pp. 117–137). Amsterdam/Philadelphia: John Benjamins Publishing Company.

Goody, J. (1977). *The domestication of the savage mind.* Cambridge: Cambridge University Press.

(2000). *The power of the written traditions.* Washington, DC: Smithsonian Institution Press.

Grassé, P.-P. (1959). La théorie de la stigmergie: Essai d'interprétation du comportement des termites constructeurs. *Insectes Sociaux, 6*(1), 41–80.

Grice, P. H. (1975). Logic and conversation. In P. Cole & J. L. Morgan (Eds.), *Syntax and Semantics, Vol. 3, Speech Acts* (pp. 41–58). New York: Academic Press.

Guala, F. (2012). Reciprocity: Weak or strong? What punishment experiments do (and do not) demonstrate. *Behavioral and Brain Sciences, 35*(1), 1–15.

Guelinckx, I., Iglesia, I., Bottin, J. H., De Miguel-Etayo, P., González-Gil, E. M., Salas-Salvadó, J., Kavouras, S. A., Gandy, J., Martinez, H., Bardosono, S., Abdollahi, M., Nasseri, E., Jarosz, A., Ma, G., Carmuega, E., Thiébaut, I., & Moreno, L. A. (2015). Intake of water and beverages of children and adolescents in 13 countries. *European Journal of Nutrition, 54*, 69–79.

Guimelli, C. (1994a). *Structures et transformations des représentations sociales.* Neuchâtel: Delachaux et Niestlé.

(1994b). Transformation des représentations sociales, pratiques nouvelles et schèmes cognitifs de base. In C. Guimelli (Ed.), *Structures et transformations des représentations sociales* (pp. 171–198). Neuchâtel: Delachaux et Niestlé.

(1998). Differentiation between the central core elements of social representations: Normative and functional elements. *Swiss Journal of Psychology, 57*(4), 209–224.

Halbwachs, M. (1994). *Les cadres sociaux de la mémoire (1ère ed 1925).* Paris: Albin Michel.

Halmos, P. R. (1974). *Naive set theory* (1st ed. 1960). New York: Springer Science+ Business Media, LLC.

Hamilton, W. H. (1932). Institution. In E. R. A. Seligman & A. Johnson (Eds.), *Encyclopaedia of the Social Sciences, Vol. 8* (pp. 84–89). New York: Macmillan.

Handel, A. E., & Ramagopalan, S. V. (2010). Is Lamarckian evolution relevant to medicine? *BMC Medical Genetics, 11*, 73.

Hardin, G. J. (1968). The tragedy of the commons. *Science, New Series, 162*(3859– Dec. 13), 1243–1248.

Harré, R. (1984). Some reflections on the concept of "social representation." *Social Research, 51*(4, Winter), 927–938.

Harrison, S., & Dourish, P. (1996). Re-place-ing space: The roles of place and space in collaborative systems. *Proceedings of the 1996 ACM Conference on Computer Supported Cooperative Work – CSCW '96 7*, 67–76.

Hartkopf, V., Loftness, V., & Aziz, A. (2009). Towards a global concept of collaborative space. In S. Lahlou (Ed.), *Designing User Friendly Augmented Work Environments. From Meeting Rooms to Digital Collaborative Spaces* (pp. 63–85). London: Springer.

Hatchuel, A., Le Masson, P., & Weil, B. (2011). Teaching innovative design reasoning: How concept–knowledge theory can help overcome fixation effects. *Artificial Intelligence for Engineering Design, Analysis and Manufacturing, 25*(1), 77–92.

Hatchuel, A., & Weil, B. (2009). C-K design theory: An advanced formulation. *Research in Engineering Design, 19*(4), 181–192.

Haugtvedt, C. P., Herr, P., & Kardes, F. R. (2008). *Handbook of consumer psychology. Marketing and consumer psychology series*. New York: Lawrence Erlbaum Associates.

Havelange, V., Lenay, C., & Stewart, J. (2003). Les représentations : mémoire externe et objets techniques. Intellectica 35, 115–131. *Intellectica, 35*, 115–131.

Hayek, F. A. von. (1952). *The sensory order. An inquiry into the foundations of theoretical psychology*. Chicago, IL: University of Chicago Press.

Hazlehurst, B., McMullen, C. K., & Gorman, P. N. (2007). Distributed cognition in the heart room: How situation awareness arises from coordinated communications during cardiac surgery. *Journal of Biomedical Informatics, 40*(5), 539–551.

Headland, T. N. (1990). Introduction: A dialogue between Kenneth Pike and Marvin Harris on emics and etics. In T. N. Headland, K. L. Pike, & M. Harris (Eds.), *Emics and Etics: The Insider/Outsider Debate* (pp. 13–27). Newbury Park, CA: Sage.

Headland, T. N., Pike, K. L., & Harris, M. (1990). *Emics and etics: The insiders/outsiders debate. Frontiers in Anthropology*, Volume 7. (p. 226). Newbury Park, CA: Sage.

Hebb, D. O. (2002). The organization of behavior a neurpsychological theory (1st ed. 1949). Mahwah, NJ and London: Lawrence Erlbaum Associates.

Heider, F. (1958). *The psychology of interpersonal relations*. New York: John Wiley & Sons.

Henrich, J., Heine, S. J., & Norenzayan, A. (2010). The weirdest people in the world? *The Behavioral and Brain Sciences, 33*(2–3), 61–83–135.

Heptonstall, B. (2015). *Cognitive de-biasing strategies in medicine: A Subject evidence-based ethnography approach*. MSc Thesis. London: London School of Economics.

Herzlich, C. (1969). *Santé et maladie, analyse d'une représentation sociale*. Paris: Mouton.

Hetzel-Riggin, M. D., & Meads, C. L. (2011). Childhood violence and adult partner maltreatment: The roles of coping style and psychological distress. *Journal of Family Violence, 26*(8), 585–593.

Himmelweit, H. T., & Gaskell, G. D. (1990). *Societal psychology: Implications and scope*. London: Sage.

Hippel, E. von. (1994). "Sticky information" and the locus of problem solving: Implications for innovation. *Management Science, 40*(4), 429–439.

(2002). Horizontal innovation networks. *MIT Sloan School of Management Working Paper*, (4366–2), 1–27.

(2005). *Democratizing innovation*. Cambridge, MA: MIT Press.

Hobbes, T. of M. (1651). *Leviathan or the matter, forme, & power of a commonwealth ecclesiasticall and civill*. London: Andrew Crooke.

Hodgson, G. M. (2006). What are institutions? *Journal of Economic Issues (Association for Evolutionary Economics), 40*(1), 1–25.

Hollan, J. D., Hutchins, E. L., & Kirsh, D. (2002). Distributed cognition: Toward a new foundation for human-computer interaction research. In J. M. Carroll (Ed.), *Human-Computer Interaction in the New Millennium* (pp. 75–94). New York: ACM Press.

Horner, V., & Whiten, A. (2005). Causal knowledge and imitation/emulation switching in chimpanzees (Pan troglodytes) and children (Homo sapiens). *Animal Cognition, 8*(3), 164–181.

Hotgraves, T. (2010). Social psychology and language words, utterances, and conversations. In S. T. Fiske, T, D. T. Gilbert, & G. Lindzey (Eds.), *Handbook of Social Psychology* (pp. 1386–1423). New York: John Wiley & Sons.

Hovland, C. I., Irving, L. J., & Kelley, H. H. (1953). *Communication and persuasion: Psychological studies of opinion change*. New Haven. CT: Yale University Press.

Howarth, C. S., Campbell, C., Cornish, F., Franks, B., Garcia-Lorenzo, L., Garcia-Lorenzo, Lucia Gillespie, A., Gleibs, I., Goncalves-Portelinha, I., Jovchelovitch, S., Lahlou, S., Mannell, J., Reader, T., Tennant, C. (2013). Insights from societal psychology: The contextual politics of change. *Journal of Social and Political Psychology, 1*(1), 364–384.

Hunt, E., & Agnoli, F. (1991). The Whorfian hypothesis: A cognitive psychology perspective. *Psychological Review, 98*(3), 377–389.

Husbands, P. (1994). Distributed coevolutionary genetic algorithms for multi-criteria and multi-constraint optimisation. *Evolutionary Computing, 865*, 150–165.

Hutchins, E. L. (1995a). *Cognition in the wild*. Cambridge, MA: MIT Press.

(1995b). How a cockpit remembers its speed. *Cognitive Science, 19*, 265–288.

Huxley, A. (2011). The doors of perception (1st ed. 1954). *In The Doors of Perception; including Heaven and Hell*, London, Thinking Ink, pp. 1-41

Itani, J. (1957). On the acquisition and propagation of a new food habit in the natural group of the Japanese monkeys at Takasi-Yama. *Primates, 12*, 84–98.

Iverson, J. B. (1991). Life history and demography of the yellow mud turtle, Kinosternon flavescens. *Herpetologica, 47*(4, Dec.), 373–395.

Jahoda, G. (1977). In pursuit of the emic-etic distinction: Can we ever capture it? In Y. H. Poortinga (Ed.), *Basic Problems in Cross-Cultural Psychology* (pp. 55–63). Amsterdam and Lisse: Swetz and Zeitlinger B.V.

James, W. (1890). *Principles of psychology*. New York: Holt.

Jégou, F. (2009). Co-design approaches for early phases of augmented environments. In S. Lahlou (Ed.), *Designing User Friendly Augmented Work Environments. From Meeting Rooms to Digital Collaborative Spaces.* (pp. 159–190). London: Springer.

Jevons, W. S. (1871). *The theory of political economy.* London: Macmillan & Company.

Jinha, A. E. (2010). Article 50 million: an estimate of the number of scholarly articles in existence. *Learned Publishing, 23*(3), 258–263.

Jodelet, D. (1989). Les représentations sociales: un domaine en expansion. In D. Jodelet (Ed.), *Les Représentations Sociales* (pp. 31–61). Paris: Presses Universitaires de France.

(1991). *Madness and social representations: Living with the mad in one French community* (1st ed. French 1989). Berkeley: University of California Press.

(2013). Encounters between forms of knowledge. *Papers on Social Representations, 22*(9), 1–2.

Joffe, H. (1995, August). Social representations of AIDS: Towards encompassing issues of power. *Papers on Social Representations.*

Johanson, B., Fox, A., & Winograd, T. A. (2010). The Stanford Interactive Workspaces Project in. In S. Lahlou (Ed.), *Designing User Friendly Augmented Work Environments.* (pp. 31–61). Berlin: Springer.

Johnson-Laird, P. N. (1983). *Mental models: Towards a cognitive science of language, inference, and consciousness.* Cambridge: Cambridge University Press.

Jonassen, Z. (2016). *Good practices of replay interviewers: An explorative study of their understanding of the interview setting, attitude, and behaviour.* MSc Thesis. London: London School of Economics.

Jones, E. E., & Harris, V. A. (1967). The attribution of attitudes. *Journal of Experimental Social Psychology, 3*, 1–24.

Joulé, R.-V., & Beauvois, J.-L. (2002). *Petit traité de manipulation à l'usage des honnêtes gens.* Grenoble: Presses Universitaires de Grenoble.

Jullien, F. (1995). *The propensity of things: Toward a history of efficacy in China* (1st ed. French 1992). New York: Zone Books.

Kahneman, D. A. (2011). *Thinking, fast and slow.* New York: Farrar, Straus and Giroux.

Kahneman, D. A., Slovic, P., & Tversky, A. (1982). *Judgment under uncertainty: Heuristics and biases.* Cambridge: Cambridge University Press.

Kahneman, D. A., & Tversky, A. (1974). Judgment under uncertainty: Heuristics and biases. *Science, New Series, 185*(4157), 1124–1131.

Kalampalikis, N. (2006). Des noms et des représentations. *Cahiers Internationaux de Psychologie Sociale, 53*, 20–31.

Kalampalikis, N., & Apostolidis, T. (2016). La perspective socio-génétique des représentations sociales. In G. Lo Monaco, S. Delouvée, & P. Rateau (Eds.), *Les Représentations Sociales.*(pp. 69–84). Bruxelles: De Boeck.

Kalampalikis, N., Bauer, M. W., & Apostolidis, T. (2013). Science, technology and society : The social representations approach. *Revue Internationale de Psychologie Sociale, 26*(3), 5–9.

Kaptelinin, V. (2013). Activity theory. In M. Soegaard & R. F. Dam (Eds.), *The Encyclopedia of Human-Computer Interaction,* 2nd Ed. Aarhus, Denmark: The Interaction Design Foundation. Retrieved August 2, 2015, from https://www.interaction-design.org/literature/book/the-encyclopedia-of-human-computer-interaction-2nd-ed/activity-theory.

Karmiloff-Smith, A. (1992). Beyond modularity. A developmental perspective on cognitive science. Boston: MIT Press.

(1994). Precis of beyond modularity: A developmental perspective on cognitive science. *Behavioral and Brain Sciences, 17,* 693–745.

Katok, A., & Hasselblatt, B. (1996). *Introduction to the modern theory of dynamical systems.* Cambridge: Cambridge University Press.

Katz, R., & Allen, T. J. (1982). Investigating the not invented here syndrome: A look at the performance, tenure, and communication patterns of 50 R&D project groups. *R&D Management, 12*(1), 7–19.

Kawai, M. (1965). Newly acquired pre-cultural behavior of the natural troop of Japanese monkeys on Koshima Islet. *Primates, 61,* 1–30.

Killgore, W. D. S., Young, A. D., Femia, L. A., Bogorodzki, P., Rogowska, J., & Yurgelun-Todd, D. A. (2003). Cortical and limbic activation during viewing of high- versus low-calorie foods. *NeuroImage, 19*(4), 1381–1394.

Kindberg, T., & Fox, A. (2002). System Software for ubiquitous computing. *IEEE Pervasive Computing, 1,* 70–81.

Kirkpatrick, R. (1912). *The nummulosphere. An account of the organic origin of the so-called igneous rocks and of abyssal red clays.* London: Lamley & Co.

Klein, G. A., & Calderwood, R. (1991). Decision models: some lessons from the field. *IEEE Transactions on Systems, Man, and Cybernetics, 21*(5), 1018–1026.

Kobayashi, M., Takeda, M., Hattori, N., Fukunaga, M., Sasabe, T., Inoue, N., Nagai, Y., Sawada, T., Sadato, N., Watanabe, Y. (2004). Functional imaging of gustatory perception and imagery: "Top-down" processing of gustatory signals. *NeuroImage, 23*(4), 1271–1282.

Kollmuss, A., & Agyeman, J. (2002). Mind the gap: Why do people behave environmentally and what are the barriers to pro-environmental behaviour. *Environmental Education Research, 8*(3), 239–260.

Koppensteiner, M. (2013). Motion cues that make an impression. Predicting perceived personality by minimal motion information. *Journal of Experimental Social Psychology, 49,* 1137–1143.

Koppensteiner, M., & Grammer, K. (2010). Motion patterns in political speech and their influence on personality ratings. *Journal of Research in Personality, 44*(3), 374–379.

Korzybski, A. (1933). A non-Aristotelian system and its necessity for rigour in mathematics and physics sanity, *Science and Sanity, suppl.* III, 747–761.

Kotler, P., & Keller, K. L. (2009). *Marketing management, 13th edition.* Upper Saddle River, NJ: Prentice-Hall.

Kotter, J. P. (1996). *Leading change.* Boston: Harvard Business School Press.

(2007). Leading change: Why transformation efforts fail. *Harvard Business Review, 85*(1), 96–103.

Kringelbach, M. L., O'Doherty, J., Rolls, E. T., & Andrews, C. (2003). Activation of the human orbitofrontal cortex to a liquid food stimulus is correlated with its subjective pleasantness. *Cerebral Cortex*, *13*(10), 1064–1071.

Kringelbach, M. L., & Radcliffe, J. (2005). The human orbitofrontal cortex : Linking reward to hedonic experience. *Nature Reviews. Neuroscience*, *6*(September), 691–702.

Kroese, F. M., Evers, C., & De Ridder, D. T. D. (2009). How chocolate keeps you slim. The effect of food temptations on weight watching goal importance, intentions, and eating behavior. *Appetite*, *53*(3), 430–433.

Krug, K. S., & Weaver, C. a. (2005). Eyewitness memory and metamemory in product identification: Evidence for familiarity biases. *The Journal of General Psychology*, *132*(4), 429–445.

Kuhn, T. S. (1977a). Objectivity, value judgment, and theory choice (c 1973). In *The Essential Tension: Selected Studies in Scientific Tradition and Change* (pp. 320–329). Chicago: University of Chicago Press.

(1977b). Second thoughts on paradigms (c 1974). In *The Essential Tension. Selected Studies in Scientific Tradition and Change* (pp. 293–319). Chicago: University of Chicago Press.

(1996). *The Structure of Scientific Revolutions* (c 1962). *University of Chicago Press* (3rd ed.). Chicago: University of Chicago Press.

Kuutti, K. (1991). Activity theory and its applications to information systems research and development. In H.-E. Nissen (Ed.), *Information Systems Research*. (pp. 529–549). Amsterdam: Elsevier Science Publishers.

La Boétie, E. de. (1993). *Discours de la servitude volontaire ou le Contr'un (1ere ed 1575)*. Paris: Flammarion.

Laan, L. N., van der, de Ridder, D. T. D., Viergever, M. A., & Smeets, P. A. M. (2011). The first taste is always with the eyes: A meta-analysis on the neural correlates of processing visual food cues. *NeuroImage*, *55*(1), 296–303.

LaBar, K. S., Gitelman, D. R., Parrish, T. B., Kim, Y. H., Nobre, A. C., & Mesulam, M. M. (2001). Hunger selectively modulates corticolimbic activation to food stimuli in humans. *Behavioral Neuroscience*, *115*(2), 493–500.

Lahlou, S. (1990). *Eléments de formalisation pour une théorie de l'évolution des systèmes: la système-compatibilité. Cahiers de recherche*. Paris: Crédoc.

(1992). Si je vous dis « bien manger », à quoi pensez-vous ? *Consommation et Modes de Vie*, (69, Juin–Juillet), 2–4.

(1995). *Penser manger. Les représentations sociales de l'alimentation*. Paris: École des Hautes Études en Sciences Sociales.

(1998). *Penser manger : alimentation et représentations sociales*. Paris: PUF.

(1999). Observing cognitive work in offices. In N. Streitz, J. Siegel, V. Hartkopf, & S. Konomi (Eds.), *Cooperative Buildings. Integrating Information, Organizations and Architecture* (LCNS Vol. 1670, pp. 150–163). Heidelberg: Springer.

(2000). Attracteurs cognitifs et travail de bureau. *Intellectica*, *30*, 75–113.

(2003). L'exploration des représentations sociales à partir des dictionnaires. In J.-C. Abric (Ed.), *Méthodes d'Étude des Représentations Sociales* (pp. 37–58). Toulouse: érès.

(2005). Cognitive attractors and activity-based design: Augmented meeting rooms. In *Human Computer Interaction International. 2005*(Vol. 1). Las Vegas.

(2006). L'activité du point de vue de l'acteur et la question de l'inter-subjectivité : huit années d'expériences avec des caméras miniaturisées fixées au front des acteurs (subcam). *Communications*, (80), 209–234.

(2007a). Human activity modeling for systems design: A trans-disciplinary and empirical approach. In *Engineering Psychology and Cognitive Ergonomics* (Vol. 4562 LNAI, pp. 512–521). Berlin: Springer.

(2007b). The activity of teleconferencing | L'activité de réunion à distance. *Réseaux, 144*(5), 59–101.

(2008a). *L'Installation du monde. De la représentation à l'activité en situation.* Aix-en-Provence: Université de Provence.

(2008b). Supporting collaboration with augmented environments: design and dissemination issues. In P. Dillenbourg, J. Huang, & M. Cherubini (Eds.), *Interactive Furniture Supporting Collaborative Work/ Learning* (pp. 75–93). Berlin: Springer Verlag.

(2009). Experimental reality: Principles for the design of augmented environments. In S. Lahlou (Ed.), *Designing User Friendly Augmented Work Environments. From Meeting Rooms to Digital Collaborative Spaces* (pp. 113–158). London: Springer.

(2010a). Contexte et intention dans la détermination de l'activité : une nouvelle topique des motivations. *Intellectica, 53–54*(1–2), 233–280.

(2010b). Digitization and transmission of human experience. *Social Science Information, 49*(3), 291–327.

(2011a). How can we capture the subject's perspective? An evidence-based approach for the social scientist. *Social Science Information, 50*(3–4), 607–655.

(2011b). Socio-cognitive issues in human-centred design for the real world. In G. Boy (Ed.), *The Handbook of Human-Machine Interaction* (pp. 165–188). Burlington, UK: Ashgate.

(2012). Innovation, social representations, and technology. In R. Permanadeli, D. Jodelet, & T. Sugiman (Eds.), *Alternative Production of Knowledge and Social Representations* (pp. 73–86). Jakarta, Indonesia: University of Jakarta Press.

(2014). Difusão de representações e inteligência coletiva distribuída. In *Teoria das Representações Sociais: 50 anos* (pp. 72–132). Rio de Janeiro: TechnoPolitik Editora.

(2015). Social representations and social construction: The evolutionary perspective of installation theory. In G. Sammut, E. Andreouli, G. Gaskell, & J. Valsiner (Eds.), *Handbook of Social Representations* (pp. 193–209). Cambridge: Cambridge University Press.

(2017). How agency is distributed. In N. J. Enfield & P. Kockelman (Eds.), *Distributed Agency* (pp. 221–232). Oxford: Oxford University Press.

Lahlou, S., & Abric, J.-C. (2011). What are the "elements" of a representation? *Papers on Social Representations, 20*, 20.1–20.10.

Lahlou, S. & Beaudouin, V. (2016). Creativity and culture in organizations. In *The Palgrave Handbook of Creativity and Culture Research* (pp. 475–498). London: Palgrave Macmillan UK.

Lahlou, S., Boesen-Mariani, S., Franks, B., & Guelinckx, I. (2015a). Increasing water intake of children and parents in the family setting: A randomized, controlled intervention using installation theory. *Annals of Nutrition and Metabolism, 66*(3), 26–30.

Lahlou, S., Dieckmann, P., Zhang, M., & Heptonstall, B. (2017). Decision making in the ICU: a video ethnographic study Working paper. London: LSE.

Lahlou, S., & Fischler, C. (1999). Le traitement de l'information par le bureau. *Technologies, Idéologies, Pratiques, 65,* 109–127.

Lahlou, S., Le Bellu, S., & Boesen-Mariani, S. (2015b). Subjective evidence-based ethnography: Method and applications. *Integrative Psychological and Behavioral Science, 49*(2), 216–38.

Lahlou, S., Marsal, F., Peyre, L., Wattrelot, S., & Yvon, F. (1995). Le petit déjeuner. Représentations et comportements. *Cahiers de Recherche CREDOC, 75.*

Lahlou, S., Nosulenko, V. N., & Samoylenko, E. S. (2002). Un cadre méthodologique pour le design des environnements augmentés. *Social Science Information, 41*(4), 471–530.

(2012a). *Numériser le travail. Théories, méthodes et expérimentations.* Paris: Lavoisier, coll. EDF R&D.

Lahlou, S., Urdapilleta, I., Pruzina, I., & Catheline, J.-M. (2012b). Changing behaviour:Representation, practice and context. The case of obesity. In *European Congress on Obesity (ECO 2012).* Lyon, France, May 9–12.

Lally, P., Van Jaarsveld, C. H. M., Potts, H. W. W., & Wardle, J. (2010). How are habits formed: Modelling habit formation in the real world. *European Journal of Social Psychology, 40,* 998–1009.

Lamarck, J.-B. de. (1963). *Zoological philosophy, an exposition with regard to the natural history of animals* (c 1809 French). New York: Hafner Publishing Company.

Laplanche, J., & Pontalis, J.-B. (1973). *The language of psycho*-analysis.Translated by Donald Nicholson-Smith (Vol. 94). London: The Hogarth Press and the Institute of Psycho-Analysis.

Lashley, K. (1951). The problem of serial order in behavior. In L. A. Jeffress (Ed.), *Cerebral Mechanisms in Behavior: the Hixon Symposium* (pp. 112–146). New York: Wiley.

Latour, B. (1986). Visualisation and cognition: Drawing things together. In J. Kuklick (Ed.), *Knowledge and Society: Studies in the Sociology of Culture Past and Present* (Vol. 6, pp. 1–40). Greenwich, Conn: JAI Press.

(1987). *Science in action: How to follow scientists and engineers through society.* Cambridge: Harvard University Press.

(1993). Le "pédofil" de Boa Vista – montage photo-philosophique. In *Petites leçons de sociologie des sciences* (pp. 171–225). Paris: La Découverte.

(1996). On actor-network theory. A few clarifications plus more than a few complications. *Soziale Welt, 47,* 369–381.

(2013). *An inquiry into modes of existence. An anthropology of the moderns* (Vol. 53). Cambridge, MA: Harvard University Press.

Latour, B. & Woolgar, S.(1986). *Laboratory life: The construction of scientific facts.* Princeton, NJ: Princeton University Press.

Lave, J. (1988). *Cognition in practice: Mind, mathematics and culture in everyday life*. Cambridge: Cambridge University Press.

Lave, J., & Wenger, E. C. (1991). *Situated learning: Legitimate peripheral participation*. Cambridge: Cambridge University Press.

LaVerne-Masayesva, J. (1978). *Aspects of Hopi grammar*. Cambridge, MA: MIT Press

Lawrence, P. T. (1964). How to deal with resistance to change. *Harvard*, (May-June), 49–57.

Lazurskii, A. F. (1997). The natural experiment (1916). *Journal of Russian and East European Psychology*, *35*(2), 32–41.

Le Bellu, S. (2011). *Capitalisation des savoir-faire et des gestes professionnels dans le milieu industriel : Mise en place d'une aide numérique au compagnonnage métier dans le secteur de l'énergie*. PhD Thesis. Bordeaux: *Ecole Nationale de Cognitique*.

Le Bellu, S., Lahlou, S., & Le Blanc, B. (2009). Comment capter le savoir incorporé dans un geste métier du point de vue de l'opérateur ? *Information Sciences for Decision Making*, (36).

Le Bellu, S., Lahlou, S., & Nosulenko, V. N. (2010). Capter et transférer le savoir incorporé dans un geste professionnel. *Social Science Information*, *49*(3), 371–413.

Le Bellu, S., Lahlou, S., Nosulenko, V. N., & Samoylenko, E. S. (2016). Studying activity in manual work: A framework for analysis and training. *Le Travail Humain*, *79*(1), 7–28.

Le Fort, L., Pasteur, J., & Depaul, J.-A.-H. (1878). Suite de la discussion sur la désarticulation de la hanche et le pansement des plaies. *Bulletin de l'Académie de Médecine, 2e série,*(19 mars 1878), 264–285.

Lebart, L., Salem, A., & Berry, L. (1998). *Exploring textual data*. Dordrecht: Kluwer Academic Publisher.

Leeds-Hurwitz Wendy (1987). The social history of the natural history of an interview: A multidisciplinary investigation of social communication. *Research on Language & Social Interaction*, 20(1–4): 1–51.

Lem, S. (1976). Ijon Tichy's eleventh voyage. In *The Star Diaries* (1st ed. Polish 1971) (pp. 41–70). New York: Continuum Books, Seabury Press.

Lenay, C. (2012). Separability and technical constitution. *Foundations of Science*, *17*(4), 379–384.

Leontiev, A. N. (1961). The intellectual development of the child. In *Soviet Psychology. A Symposium* (pp. 55–78). New York: The Philosophical Libray.

(1976). *Le développement du psychisme. Problèmes*. Paris: Editions sociales.

(1978). *Activity, consciousness, and personality*. Englewood Cliffs, NJ: Prentice-Hall.

Leroi-Gourhan, E. (1965). *Le geste et la parole*. Paris: Albin Michel.

Lévi-Strauss, C. (1962). *La pensée sauvage*. Paris: Plon.

Lewin, K. Z. (1935). *A dynamic theory of personality: Selected papers*. New York: McGraw-Hill.

(1936). *Principles of topological psychology*. New York: McGraw-Hill.

(1943). Forces behind food habits and methods of change. *Bulletin of the National Research Council, 108*(October), 35–65.

(1946). Action research and minority problems. *Journal of Social Issues*, *2*(4), 34–46.

(1948). *Resolving social conflicts: Field theory in social science*. New York: Harper & Brothers.

(1959). Group decision and social change (1st ed. 1947). In T. M. Newcomb & E. L. Hartley (Eds.), *Readings in Social Psychology* (pp. 197–211). New York: Henry Holt.

(1999). Intention, will and need (1 st ed. 1926). In M. Gold (Ed.), *A Kurt Lewin Reader. The Complete Social Scientist* (pp. 83–115). Washington, DC: American Psychological Association.

Lewin, K. Z., & Grabbe, P. (1945). Conduct, knowledge, and acceptance of new values. Journal of Social Issues, 1(3), 53–54.

Lewis, D. (2002). *Convention. A Philosophical Study (1st ed. 1969)*. Wiley-Blackwell.

Lewontin, R. C. (2000). *The triple helix : gene, organism, and environment*. Cambridge, MA: Harvard University Press.

Lheureux, F., Rateau, P., & Guimelli, C. (2008). Hiérarchie structurale, conditionnalité et normativité des représentations sociales. *Les Cahiers Internationaux de Psychologie Sociale*, *77*, 41–55.

Libby, L. K., & Eibach, R. P. (2011). Visual perspective in mental imagery: A representational tool that functions in judgment, emotion, and Self-insight. *Advances in Experimental Social Psychology* (1st ed., Vol. 44). Amsterdam: Elsevier Inc.

Libet, B., Gleason, C. A., Wright, E. W., & Pearl, D. K. (1983). Time of conscious intention to act in relation to onset of cerebral activity (readiness potential). *Brain, 106*(3), 623–642.

Linton, R. (1945). *The cultural background of personality*. Oxford: Appleton-Century.

Littré, E. (1885). Installation. In *Dictionnaire de la Langue Française*, Tome 3 (p. 117). Paris: Hachette.

Liu, Y. Y., Wang, Y., Walsh, T. R., Yi, L. X., Zhang, R., Spencer, J., Doi, Y., Tian, G., Dong, B Huang, X., Yu, L. F., Gu, D., Ren, H., Chen, X., Lv, L., He, D., Zhou, H., Liang, Z., Liu, J. H., Shen, J. (2016). Emergence of plasmid-mediated colistin resistance mechanism MCR-1 in animals and human beings in China: A microbiological and molecular biological study. *The Lancet Infectious Diseases, 16*(2), 161–168.

Loewenstein, G. F., Weber, E. U., Hsee, C. K., & Welch, N. (2001). Risk as feelings. *Psychological Bulletin, 127*(2), 267–286.

Loftus, E. F. (2004). Memories of things unseen. *Current Directions in Psychological Science, 13*(4), 145–147.

Lomov, B. F. (1963). *Man and technology (Outlines in Engineering psychology)*. Washington DC: JPRS 22300. US Dept of Commerce.

(1982). The Problem of Activity in Psychology. *Soviet Psychology*, 21, 55–91.

Lomov, B. F., Belyaeva, A., & Nosulenko, V. N. (1985). Психологические исследования общения (Psychological Research on Communication). Moscow: Nauka.

Lorenz, K. (1935). Der Kumpan in der Umwelt des Vogels: der Artgenosse als auslösendes Moment sozialer Verhaltungsweisen. *Journal Für Ornithologie*, *83*(37–215), 289–413.

Luria, A. R. (1966). *Higher cortical functions in man* (1st ed. Russian 1962). New York: Consultant Bureau Enterprises & Basic Books.

Lyle, J. (2003). Stimulated recall: A report on its use in naturalistic research. *British Educational Research Journal*, *29*(6), 861–87.

Mack, A., & Rock, I. (1988). *Inattentional blindness*. Cambridge, MA: MIT Press.

Marková, I. (2008). The epistemological signicance of the theory of social representations. *Journal for the Theory of Social Behaviour*, *38*(4), 461–487.

Marková, I. (2012). Method and Explanation in history and in social representations. *Integrative Psychological and Behavioral Science*, *46*(4), 457–474.

Maslow, A. H. (1943). A theory of human motivation. *Psychological Review*, *50*(4), 370–396.

Masson, E. (2001). *Les formes du manger: représentations de pratiques alimentaires contemporaines*. PhD thesis. Paris: EHESS.

Mauss, M. (1990). *The Gift. The form and reason for exchange in archaic societies* (1st ed. French 1924). London: Routledge.

McKinlay, A., & Potter, J. (1987). Social representations: A conceptual critique. *Journal for the Theory of Social Behaviour*, *17*(4), 471–487.

McLuhan, M. (1994). *Understanding media. The extensions of man (c1964)*. Cambridge, MA: MIT Press.

Mead, G. H. (1972). *Mind, self, and society from the standpoint of a social behaviourist* (1st ed 1934). Chicago: University of Chicago Press.

Meadows, D. H., Randers, J., & Meadows, D. L. (2002). *Limits to growth. The 30-year update*. London: Earthscan.

Meeus, W. H., & Raaijmakers, Q. A. W. (1995). Obedience in modern society: The Utrecht studies. *Journal of Social Issues*, *51*(3).

MESNR-DEPP. (2014). *L'éducation nationale en chiffres, 2014*. Paris.

Meyerson, I. (1948). Discontinuités et cheminements autonomes dans l'histoire de l'esprit. *Journal de Psychologie*, *XLI*, 273–289.

Milewski, A. V., Young, T. P., & Madden, D. (1991). Thorns as induced defenses: Experimental evidence. *Oecologia*, *86*(1), 70–75.

Milgram, S. (1963). Behavioral study of obedience. *Journal of Abnormal Psychology*, *67*(4, Oct 1963), 371–378.

   (1965). *Obedience*. Pennsylvania State University Films in The Behavioral Sciences.

   (1974). *Obedience to authority: An experimental view*. London: Tavistock Publications.

Mill, J. S. (1999). *On liberty* (1st ed 1859). *Educational Philosophy and Theory*. Peterborough, Ontario, Canada: Broadview.

Miller, G. A. (1956). The magical number seven, plus or minus two: Some limits on our capacity for processing information. *The Psychological Review*, *63*(2), 81–97.

Miller, G. A., Galanter, E., & Pribram, K. H. (1960). *Plans and the structure of behavior*. New York: Holt, Rinehart and Winston.

Minsky, M. L. (1985). *The society of mind.* New York: Simon and Schuster, Touchstone Books.

Mirdal, G. M. (1984). Stress and distress in migration: Problems and resources of Turkish women in Denmark. *International Migration Review, 18*(4), 984–1003.

Mironenko, I. a. (2013). Concerning interpretations of activity theory. *Integrative Psychological and Behavioral Science, 47*(3), 376–393.

Mislevy, R. J. (2010). Design under constraints: The case of large-scale assessment systems. *Measurement: Interdisciplinary Research & Perspective, 8*(1994), 199–203.

Mockus, A. (2002). Convivencia como armonizacion de ley, moral y cultura. *Perspectivas, XXXII*(1, Marzo), 19–37.

Mockus, A., García, M., Sánchez, E., Rodríguez, V. M., Melo, J. O., Castro, C., Martínez, L. F., Patiño, O., Bromberg, P., Murrain, H., Cabra, E. S., Osorio, C. C. (2009). *Cultura ciudadana en Bogotá: nuevas perspectivas.* Bogotá: Secretaría de Cultura, Recreación y Deporte, Cámara de Comercio de Bogotá, Fundación Terpel, Corpovisionarios.

Mockus, A., Murraín, H., & Villa, M. (Eds.). (2012). *Antípodas de la violencia. Desafíos de cultura ciudadana para la crisis de (in)seguridad en América Latina iii.* Washington DC: Banco Interamericano de Desarrollo.

Moles, A., & Rohmer, É. (1976). *Micropsychologie et vie quotidienne.* Paris: Denoël.

Moliner, P. (1993). ISA: L'induction par scénario ambigu. Une méthode pour l'étude des représentations sociales. *Revue Internationale de Psychologie Sociale, 2,* 7–21.

   (1994). Les méthodes de repérage et d'identification du noyau des représentations. In C. Guimelli (Ed.), *Structures et Transformations des Représentations Sociales* (pp. 199–232). Neuchâtel: Delachaux et Niestlé.

Monnas, L. (1988). Loom widths and selvedges prescribed by Italian silk weaving statutes 1265–1512: A preliminary investigation. *Bulletin de Liaison du Centre International d'Étude des Textiles Anciens,* (66), 35–44.

Morin, E. (2008). *La méthode* (Tomes I et 2). Paris: Seuil.

Morris, J. S., & Dolan, R. J. (2001). Involvement of human amygdala and orbitofrontal cortex in hunger-enhanced memory for food stimuli. *The Journal of Neuroscience: The Official Journal of the Society for Neuroscience, 21*(14), 5304–10.

Moscovici, S. (1961). *La psychanalyse, son image et son public. Etude sur la représentation sociale de la psychanalyse.* Paris: PUF.

   (1972). Theory and society in social psychology. In J. Istrael & H. Tajfel (Eds.), London: Academic Press in cooperation with the European Association of Experimental Psychology.

   (1976). *La psychanalyse son image et son public* (2eme éd. revue). Paris: PUF.

   (1984). Le domaine de la psychologie sociale. In S. Moscovici (Ed.), *Psychologie Sociale* (pp. 5–24). Paris: P.U.F.

   (2008). *Psychoanalysis: Its image and its public.* Cambridge: Polity.

Moscovici, S., Lage, E., & Naffrechoux, M. (1969). Influence of a consistent minority on the responses of a majority in a color perception task. *Sociometry*, *32*(4), 365–80.

Mounin, G. (1963). *Les problèmes théoriques de la traduction*. Paris: Gallimard.

(1985). *Semiotic praxis: Studies in pertinence and in the means of expression and communication. New York: Plenum Press*. New Yorkn: Plenum Press.

Neisser, U. (1976). *Cognition and reality*. San Francisco: W.H. Freeman.

(1978). Perceiving, anticipating, and imagining. In H. Feigl, G. Maxwell, & C. Wade Savage (Eds.), *Minnesota Studies in the Philosophy of Science. Volume IX: Perception and Cognition. Issues in the Foundations of Psychology* (pp. 89–105). Minneapolis: University of Minnesota Press.

Nereid, C. T. (2011). Kemalism on the catwalk: The Turkish hat law of 1925. *Journal of Social History*, *44*(3), 707–728.

Neumann, J. von, & Morgenstern, O. (1944). *Theory of games and economic behavior*. Princeton, NJ: Princeton University Press.

Nevile, M. (2015). The embodied turn in research on language and social interaction. *Research on Language and Social Interaction*, *48*(2), 121–151.

Nickerson, R. S. (1998). Confirmation bias: A ubiquitous phenomenon in many guises. *Review of General Psychology*, *2*(2), 175–200.

Niedenthal, P., & Barsalou, L. (2005). Embodiment in attitudes, social perception, and emotion. *Personality and Social Psychology Review*, *9*(3), 184–211.

Norman, D. A. (1988). *The design of everyday things*. New York: Basic Books.

(1991). Cognitive artifacts. In J. M. Carroll (Ed.), *Designing Interaction: Psychology at the Human Computer Interface*. (pp. 17–28). New York: Cambridge University Press.

Nosulenko, V. N. (2008). Mesurer les activités numérisées par leur qualité perçue. *Social Science Information*, *47*(3), 391–417.

Nosulenko, V. N., Barabanshikov, V. A., Brushlinsky, A. V., & Rabardel, P. (2005). Man–technology interaction: some of the Russian approaches. *Theoretical Issues in Ergonomics Science*, *6*(5), 359–383.

Nosulenko, V. N., & Rabardel, P. (2007). *Rubinstein aujourd'hui. Nouvelles figures de l'activité humaine*. Toulouse: Octarès – Maison des Sciences de l'Homme.

Nosulenko, V. N., & Samoylenko, E. S. (2001). Evaluation de la qualité perçue des produits et services : approche interdisciplinaire. *International Journal of Design and Innovation Research*, *2*(2), 35–60.

(2009). Psychological methods for the study of augmented environments. In S. Lahlou (Ed.), *Designing User Friendly Augmented Work Environments. From Meeting Rooms to Digital Collaborative Spaces* (pp. 213–236). London: Springer.

O'Mahony, S., & Lakhani, K. R. (2011). Organizations in the shadow of communities. *Research in the Sociology of Organizations: Communities and Organizations*, *33*(July), 3–36.

Ochs, E., Pontecorvo, C., & Fasulo, A. (1996). Socializing taste. *Ethnos*, *61*(1–2), 7–46.

Ochs, E., & Schieffelin, B. B. (2012). The theory of language socialization. In A. Duranti, E. Ochs, & B. B. Schieffelin (Eds.), *The Handbook of Language Socialization* (pp 1–22). Oxford: Wiley-Blackwell.

Ochs, E., & Shohet, M. (2006). The cultural structuring of mealtime socialization. *New Directions for Child and Adolescent Development*, (111), 35–49.

Oddone, I., Re, A., & Briante, G. (1981). *Redécouvrir l'expérience ouvrière. vers une autre psychologie du travail ?* Paris: Editions sociales.

OECD/ITF. (2014). Road Safety Annual Report, data from 2012. Paris.

Ogilvy, D. M. (1983). *Ogilvy on advertising*. Toronto: John Wiley and Sons.

Olson, R. G. (2010). Technology and science in ancient civilizations. Santa Barbara, Denver, Oxford: Greenwood.

Omodei, M. M., Wearing, A. J., & McLennan, J. (2002). Head-mounted video and cued recall: A minimally reactive methodology for understanding, detecting and preventing error in the control of complex systems. In C. W. Johnson (Ed.), *Proceedings of the 21st European Annual Conference of Human Decision Making and Control*. GIST Technical Report G2002.1, Glasgow: Department of Computer Science, University of Glasgow.

Osborne, D., & Davies, P. G. (2012). Eyewitness identifications are affected by stereotypes about a suspect's level of perceived stereotypicality. *Group Processes & Intergroup Relations*, *16*(4), 488–504.

Oshanin, D. A. (1973). Предметное действие и оперативный образ (Physical action and operative image). Moscow-Voronej: Leningrad State University. AA Zhdanov. Academy of Pedagogical Sciences Institute of General and Pedagogical Psychology.

Oshlyansky, L., Thimbleby, H., & Cairns, P. (2004). Breaking affordance. In *Proceedings of the Third Nordic Conference On Human-Computer Interaction – NordiCHI '04* (pp. 81–84). New York: ACM Press.

Ouellette, J. A., & Wood, W. (1998). Habit and intention in everyday life: The multiple processes by which past behavior predicts future behavior. *Psychological Bulletin*, *124*(1), 54–74.

Oullier, O., & Basso, F. (2010). Embodied economics: How bodily information shapes the social coordination dynamics of decision-making. *Philosophical Transactions of the Royal Society of London. Series B, Biological Sciences*, *365*(1538), 291–301.

Ouwehand, C., & Papies, E. K. (2010). Eat it or beat it. The differential effects of food temptations on overweight and normal-weight restrained eaters. *Appetite*, *55*(1), 56–60.

Panofsky, E. (1939). *Studies in iconology*. Oxford: Oxford University Press.

Paradise, R., & Rogoff, B. (2009). Side by side : Learning by observing and pitching in cultural practices in support of learning. *Ethos*, *37*(1), 102–138.

Parsons, T. (1954). *Essays in sociological theory* (1st ed. 1949). Glencoe, IL: The Free Press.

(1963). On the concept of influence. *The Public Opinion Quarterly*, *27*(1), 37–62.

(1964). *The social system* (1st ed. 1951). Glencoe, IL: The Free Press.

(1980). Action theory and the human condition (1st ed. 1978). *Social Forces* (Vol. 58). New York: The Free Press.

Patriotta, G. (2003). Sensemaking on the shop floor : Narratives of knowledge in organizations. *Journal of Management Studies*, *40*(2), 349–375.

Pavlov, I. P. (1927). *Conditioned reflexes: An investigation of the physiological activity of the cerebral cortex. Translated by G. V. Anrep*. Oxford: Oxford University Press.

Pawson, R. (2006). *Evidence-based Policy: A Realist Perspective*. London: Sage.

Pea, R. D. (1985). Integrating human and computer intelligence. In E. L. Klein (Ed.), *Children and Computers. New Directions for Child and Adolescent Development* (Vol. 28, pp. 75–96). San Francisco: Jossey-BAss.

    (1993). Practices of distributed intelligence and designs for education. In G. Salomon (Ed.), *Distributed Cognitions. Psychological and Educational Considerations* (pp. 47–87). Cambridge: Cambridge University Press.

    (1994). Seeing what we build together: Distributed multimedia learning environments for transformative communications. *Journal of the Learning Sciences*, *3*(3), 285–299.

    (2004). The social and technological dimensions of scaffolding and related theoretical concepts for learning, education, and human activity. *Journal of the Learning Sciences*, *13*(3), 423–451.

Pea, R. D., Gomez, L. M., Edelson, D. C., Fishman, B. J., Gordin, D. N., & O'Neill, D. K. (1997). Science education as driver of cyberspace technology development. In K. C. Cohen (Ed.), *Internet Links for Science Education. Student-Scientist Partnerships* (pp. 189–220). New-York: Springer.

Petty, R. E., & Cacioppo, J. T.(1986). *Communication and persuasion. Central and peripheral routes to attitude change*. New York: Springer Verlag.

Phelps, J. M., Strype, J., Le Bellu, S., Lahlou, S., & Aandal, J. (2016). Experiential learning and simulation-based training in Norwegian police education: Examining body-worn video as a tool to encourage reflection. *Policing*, (June), 1–16.

Phillips, D. P., & Carstensen, L. L. (1986). Clustering of teenage suicides after television news stories about suicide. *New England Journal of Medicine*, *315*(11), 685–9.

Piaget, J. (1926). *La représentation du monde chez l'enfant*. Paris: Alcan.

    (1955). Les stades du développement intellectuel de l'enfant et de l'adolescent. In P. A. Osterrieth, J. Piaget, R. de Saussure, J. M. Tanner, H. Wallon, Zazzo, R., Inhelder, B., Rey, A. (Eds.), *Le problème des stades en psychologie de l'enfant: Symposium de l'Association de psychologie scientifique de langue française, Genève 1955* (pp. 33–42). Paris: PUF.

Pike, K. L. (Ed.). (1967). *Language in relation to a unified theory of structure of human behavior*. The Hague, Netherlands: Mouton.

Polanyi, M. (1958). *Personal knowledge: Towards a post-critical philosophy*. London: Routledge & Kegan Paul.

    (1967). *The tacit dimension*. Garden City, N Y: Anchor Books.

Poon, E. G., Keohane, C. A., Yoon, C. S., Ditmore, M., Bane, A., Levtzion-Korach, O., Moniz, T., Rothschild, J. M., Kachalia, A. B., Hayes, J., Churchill, W. W., Lipsitz, S., Whittemore, A. D., Bates, D. W., Gandhi, T. K.

(2010). Effect of bar-code technology on the safety of medication administration. *New England Journal of Medicine, 362 (May 6*(18), 1698–1707.

Posner, M. I., & Snyder, C. R. R. (1975). Attention and cognitive control. In R. L. Solso (Ed.), *Information processing and cognition: The Loyola symposium* (pp. 55–85). Hillsdale, NJ: Lawrence Erlbaum.

Potter, J., & Edwards, D. (1999). Social representations and discursive psychology: From cognition to action. *Culture & Psychology, 5*(4), 447–458.

Potter, J., & Litton, I. (1985). Some problems underlying the theory of social representations. *British Journal of Social Psychology, 24*(2), 81–90.

Potter, J., & Wetherell, M. (1987). *Discourse and social psychology : Beyond attitudes and behaviour*. London: Sage.

Prinz, W., Beisert, M., & Herwig, A. (Eds.). (2013). *Action science. Foundations of an emerging discipline*. Cambridge, MA: MIT Press.

Prochaska, J. O., Wright, J. A., & Velicer, W. F. (2008). Evaluating theories of health behavior change: A hierarchy of criteria applied to the transtheoretical model. *Applied Psychology, 57*(4), 561–588.

Provencher, C. (2011). Towards a better understanding of cognitive polyphasia. *Journal for the Theory of Social Behaviour, 41*(4), 377–395.

Puntambekar, S., & Hübscher, R. (2005). Tools for scaffolding students in a complex learning environment : What have we gained and what have we missed ? *Educational Psychologist, 40*(1), 1–12.

Puntambekar, S., & Kolodner, J. L. (2005). Toward implementing distributed scaffolding: Helping students learn science from design. *Journal of Research in Science Teaching, 42*(2), 185–217.

Quervain, D. J. de, Fischbacher, U., Treyer, V., Schnyder, U., Buck, A., & Fehr, E. (2013). The neural basis of altruistic punishment. *Science, 305*(5688), 1254–1258.

Ramón y Cajal, S. (1895). Les nouvelles idées sur la structure du système nerveux chez l'homme et chez les vertébrés. Paris: C. Reinwald.

Rasmussen, J. (1983). Skills rules and knowledge, other distinctions in human performance models. *IEEE Transactions on Systems, Man, and Cybernetics, 13*(3), 257–266.

(1985). The role of hierarchical knowledge representation in decision-making and system management. *IEEE Transactions on Systems, Man, and Cybernetics, SMC-15*(2), 234–243.

Rausch de Traubenberg, N. (1970). *La pratique du Rorschach*. Paris: PUF.

Reader, T. W., & Gillespie, A. (2013). Patient neglect in healthcare institutions: a systematic review and conceptual model. *BMC Health Services Research, 13*(1), 156.

Reason, J. T. (1990). The contribution of latent human failures to the breakdown of complex systems. *Philosophical Transactions of the Royal Society, 327*(1241), 475–484.

(2000). Human error: Models and management. *BMJ (Clinical Research Ed.), 320*(7237), 768–70.

Reinert, M. (1983). Une méthode de classification descendante hiérarchique : Application à l'analyse lexicale par contexte. *Les Cahiers de l'Analyse des Données, Vol VIII*(n° 2), 187–198.

(1987). Classification descendante hiérarchique et analyse lexicale par contexte: Application au corpus des poésies d'Arthur Rimbaud. *Bulletin de Méthodologie Sociologique*, (13, Janvier), 53–90.

Requin, J. (1980). Towards a psychobiology of preparation for action. In G. E. Stelmach & J. Requin (Eds.), *Tutorials in Motor Behaviour* (pp. 373–398). Amsterdam: North-Holland Publishing Company.

Reymond, P., & Lahlou, S. (1996). *Coupure et ratios. Une étude de terrain sur les relations entre coupure pour impayé et ratios de trésorerie dans 3 Centres EDF-GDF Services*. Clamart, France: EDF Direction des Etudes et Recherches.

Rieken, J. C. (2013). *Making situated police practice visible: A study examining professional activity for the maintenance of social control with video data from the field*. PhD Thesis. London: London School of Economics.

Rieken, J. C., & Lahlou, S. (2010). *Theories, protocols and techniques used to elicit and record the production of know-how by experts*. London: London School of Economics/ISP.

Rieskamp, J., & Otto, P. E. (2006). SSL: A theory of how people learn to select strategies. *Journal of Experimental Psychology: General, 135*(2), 207–236.

Rimal, R. N., & Real, K. (2005). How behaviors are influenced by perceived norms: A test of the theory of normative social behavior. *Communication Research, 32*(3), 389–414.

Ritti, T., Grewe, K., & Kessener, P. (2007). A relief of a water-powered stone saw mill on a sarcophagus at Hierapolis and its implications. *Journal of Roman Archaeology, 20*, 138–163.

Rix, G., & Biache, M.-J. (2004). Enregistrement en perspective subjective située et entretien en re situ subjectif : une méthodologie de constitution de l'expérience. *Intellectica*, 363–396.

Rizzolatti, G., & Craighero, L. (2004). The mirror-neuron system. *Annual Review of Neuroscience, 27*, 169–192.

Rizzolatti, G., Fadiga, L., Fogassi, L., & Gallese, V. (1996). Premotor cortex and the recognition of motor actions. *Cognitive Brain Research, 3*(131–141).

Roberts, J. M. (1964). The self-management of cultures. In W. Goodenough (Ed.), *Explorations in Cultural Anthropology: Essays in Honor of George Peter Murdock* (p. 433–454.). New York: McGraw-Hill.

Rocheblave-Spenlé, A.-M. (1969). *La notion de rôle en psychologie sociale*. Paris: PUF.

Rogers, R. W. (1975). A protection motivation theory of fear appeals and attitude change. *Journal of Psychology, 91*, 93–114.

Rogers, Y. (2008). 57 varieties of activity theory. *Interacting with Computers, 20*, 247–250.

Rogoff, B. (1998). Cognition as a collaborative process. In W. Damon, D. Kuhn, & R. S. Siegler (Eds.), *Cognition, Perception and Language: Vol. 2. Handbook of Child Psychology (5th ed.)* (pp. 679–744). New York: Wiley.

(2003). *The Cultural Nature of Human Development*. New Haven, CT: Oxford University Press.

Rolls, E. T. (2000). The orbitofrontal cortex and reward. *Cerebral Cortex, 10*(3), 284–294.

Romer, P. M. (2015). Mathiness in the theory of economic growth. *American Economic Review: Papers & Proceedings, 105*(5), 89–93.

Roqueplo, P. (1990). Le savoir décalé. In L. Sfez, G. Coutlée, & P. Musso (Eds.), *Technologies et Symboliques de la Communication. Colloque de Cerisy* (pp. 75–80). Grenoble: Presses Universitaires de Grenoble.

Rosch, E., Mervis, C. B., Gray, W. D., Johnson, D. M., & Boyes-Braem, P. (1976). Basic objects in natural categories. *Cognitive Psychology, 8*, 382–439.

Rosenbaum, D. A., Cohen, R. G., Jax, S. A., Weiss, D. J., & Wel, R. van der. (2007). The problem of serial order in behavior: Lashley's legacy. *Human Movement Science, 26*(4), 525–554.

Rosenstock, I. M. (1964). Historical origins of the health belief model. *Health Education Monographs, 2*(4), 328–335.

Rosenthal, R. (1966). *Experimenter effects in behavioural research*. New York: Appleton-Century-Crofts.

Ross, L. (1977). The intuitive psychologist and his shortcomings: Distortions in the attribution process. In L. Berkowitz (Ed.), *Advances in Experimental Social Psychology* (Vol. 10, pp. 173–220). New York: Academic Press.

RoundaboutsUSA. (2016). History of the Modern Roundabout. Retrieved May 13, 2016, from http://www.roundaboutsusa.com/history.html

Rousseau, J.-J. (1796). *Du contrat social, ou principes du droit politique*. Leipsic: Gerard Fleisher.

Rubinstein, S. L. (1922). Le principe de l'activité du sujet dans sa dimension créative. In P. Rabardel (Ed.), *Rubinstein Aujourd'hui. Nouvelles figure de l'activité humaine.* (pp. 129–140). Toulouse: Octarès – Maison des Sciences de l'Homme.

Rumelhart, D. E., & Norman, D. A. (1978). Accretion, tuning and restructuring: Three modes of learning. In J.W Cotton & R. Klatzky (Eds.), *Semantic Factors in Cognition* (Vol. 15, pp. 36–53). Hillsdale, NJ: Lawrence Erlbaum.

Runde, V. (2005). Set theory. In *A Taste of Topology* (pp. 5–22). Berlin: Springer-Verlag.

Russell, B. (1908). Mathematical logic as based on the theory of types. *American Journal of Mathematics, 30*(3), 222.

Ruyter, J. C. de, Olthof, M. R., Seidell, J. C., & Katan, M. B. (2012). A trial of sugar-free or sugar-sweetened beverages and body weight in children. *New England Journal of Medicine, 367*(15), 1397–1406.

Sacks, H. (1992). *Lectures on conversation.* (G. Jefferson, Ed.) (Vol. I & II). Cambridge: Blackwell.

Sacks, H., Schegloff, E. A., & Jefferson, G. (1974). A simplest systematics for the organization of turn taking for conversation. *Language, 50*(54, Part 1), 696–535.

Salais, R., & Storper, M. (1992). The four "worlds" of contemporary industry. *Cambridge Journal of Economics, 16*, 169–193.

Salamone, J. D., Correa, M., Farrar, A., & Mingote, S. M. (2007). Effort-related functions of nucleus accumbens dopamine and associated forebrain circuits. *Psychopharmacology, 191*(3), 461–482.

Salisbury, J. of, & McGarry, D. D. (1955). *The Metalogicon of John of Salisbury: A Twelfth-Century Defense of the Verbal and Logical Arts of the Trivium.* Berkeley: University of California Press.

Sanford, N., Sherif, M., & Bruner, J. S. (1957). On perceptual readiness *Psychological Review, 64*(2), 123–152.

Saussure, F. de. (1997). *Saussure's Second Course of Lectures on General Linguistics* (1908–1909). From the Notebooks of Albert Riedlinger and Charles Patois. Oxford: Pergamon.

Schaff, A. (1969). *Introduction à la sémantique.* Paris: Anthropos.

Schank, R. C., & Abelson, R. P. (1975). Scripts, plans, and knowledge. *Proceedings of the 4th International Joint Conference on Artificial Intelligence – Volume 1.* San Francisco: Morgan Kaufmann Publishers Inc.

(1977). *Scripts, plans, goals and understanding.* Hillsdale, NJ: Lawrence Erlbaum Associates.

Schegloff, E. A. (1982). Discourse as an interactional achievement. Some uses of 'uh huh" and other things that come between sentences. In D. Tannen (Ed.), *Georgetown University Roundtable on Language and Linguistics: Analyzing Discourse and Talk* (pp. 71–93). Washington DC: Georgetown University Press.

Schein, E. H. (1960). *Brainwashing.* Cambridge, MA: Center for International Studies.

(1999). *Process consultation revisited. Building the helping relationship.* Reading, MA: Addison-Wesley Longman, Inc.

Schildkrout, E. (2004). Inscribing the body. *Annual Review of Anthropology, 33*(1), 319–344.

Schneider, B., & Pea, R. D. (2013). Real-time mutual gaze perception enhances collaborative learning and collaboration quality. *International Journal of Computer-Supported Collaborative Learning, 8*(4), 375–397.

(2014). Toward collaboration sensing. *International Journal of Computer-Supported Collaborative Learning, 9*(4), 371–395.

Schonhardt-Bailey, C., Yager, E., & Lahlou, S. (2012). Yes, Ronald Reagan's rhetoric was unique – but statistically, how unique? *Presidential Studies Quarterly, 42*(3), 482–513.

Schuler, D., & Namioka, A. (Eds.). (1993). *Participatory design. Principles and practices.* Hillsdale, NJ: Lawrence Erlbaum Associates.

Schumpeter, J. A. (1962). *Capitalism, socialism, democracy* (1st ed. 1942). New York: Harper Torchbooks.

Schütz, A. (1944). The stranger : An essay in social psychology. *The American Journal of Sociology, 49*(6), 499–507.

(1962). *Collected papers. Volume I., The problem of social reality.* (M. Natanson, Ed.). The Hague: Martinus Nijhoff.

(1970a). *Collected papers. Volume III, Studies in phenomenological philosophy.* (I. Schutz, Ed.). The Hague: Martinus Nijhof.

(1970b). Some structures of the life-world. In (I. Schutz, Ed.), *Collected Papers, Volume III, Studies in Phenomenological Philosophy* (pp. 116–132). The Hague: Martinus Nijhoff.

(1976a). Collected paperspapers, Volume II. Studies in Social Theory. (A. Briodersen, Ed.). The Hague: Martinus Nijhoff.

(1976b). The dimensions of the social world (1932). In A. Brodersen (Ed.), *Collected Papers. Volume II. Studies in Social Theory* (pp. 20–63). The Hague: Martinus Nijhoff.

(1976c). The social world and the theory of social action (1960). In A. Brodersen (Ed.), *Collected Papers. Volume II. Studies in Social Theory* (pp. 3–19). The Hague: Martinus Nijhoff.

(1996). *Collected papers. Volume IV.* (H. Wagner, G. Psathas, & F. Kersten, Eds.). Dordrecht: Springer-Science+Business Media, BV.

(2011). *Collected papers. Volume V. Phenomenology and the social sciences.* (L. Embree, Ed.). Dordrecht: Springer.

(2013). *Collected papers. Volume VI. Literary reality and relationships.* (M. Barber, Ed.). The Hague: Springer.

Schwartz, S. H. (1977). Normative influences on altruism. *Advances in Experimental Social Psychology, 10*(C), 221–279.

(1992). Universals in the content and structure of values: Theory and empirical tests in 20 countries. In M. P. Zanna (Ed.), *Advances in Experimental Social Psychology* (pp. 1–65). New York: Academic Press.

Schwartz, S. H., & Bilsky, W. (1987). Toward a universal psychological structure of human values. *Journal of Personality and Social Psychology, 53*(3), 550–562.

Sémelin, J. (2007). *Purify and destroy: The Political uses of massacre and genocide* (c 2005, French). New York: Columbia University Press.

Shannon, C. E. (1948). A mathematical theory of communication. *The Bell System Technical Journal, 27*(July, October 1948), 379–423, 623–656.

Shannon, C. E., & Weaver, W. (1963). *The mathematical theory of communication.* Urbana, IL: The University of Illinois Press.

Sherif, M. (1935). A study of some social factors in perception. *Archives of Psychology, 27*(187).

Shin, A. C., Zheng, H., & Berthoud, H.-R. (2009). An expanded view of energy homeostasis: neural integration of metabolic, cognitive, and emotional drives to eat. *Physiology & Behavior, 97*(5), 572–580.

Shteingart, H., Neiman, T., & Loewenstein, Y. (2012). The role of first impression in operant learning. *Journal of Experimental Psychology: General, 142*(2), 476–488.

Simon, C., Schweitzer, B., Triby, E., Hausser, F., Copin, N., Kellou, N., Platat, C., Blanc, S. (2011). Promouvoir l'activité physique, lutter contre la sédentarité et prévenir le surpoids chez l'adolescent, c'est possible : les leçons d'ICAPS. *Cahiers de Nutrition et de Diététique, 46*(3), 130–136.

Simon, C., Wagner, A., Platat, C., Arveiler, D., Schweitzer, B., Schlienger, J. L. J., & Triby, E. (2006). ICAPS: A multilevel program to improve physical activity in adolescents. *Diabetes & Metabolism, 32*(1), 41–49.

Simon, H. A. (1955). A behavioral model of rational choice. *The Quarterly Journal of Economics, 69*(1), 99–118.

(1957). *Models of man, social and rational: Mathematical essays on rational human behavior in a social setting*. New York: John Wiley and Sons.

(1976). From substantive to procedural rationality. In S. J. Latsis (Ed.), *Method and Appraisal in Economics* (pp. 129–148). Cambridge: Cambridge University Press.

(1996). *The sciences of the artificial*. Cambridge, MA: MIT Press.

Simondon, G. (1989). *Du mode d'existence des objets techniques (1ère éd. 1958)*. Paris: Aubier.

(2013). *L'individuation à la lumière des notions de forme et d'information (1ère éd. 1958)*. Grenoble, FR: Jérôme Millon.

Skinner, B. F. (1938). *The behavior of organisms: An experimental analysis*. New York: Appleton-Century-Crofts.

Slovic, P., Finucane, M., Peters, E., & MacGregor, D. G. (2002). The affect heuristic. In T. Gilovich, D. Griffin, & D. A. Kahneman (Eds.), *Heuristics and biases: The psychology of intuitive judgment* (pp. 397–420). Cambridge: Cambridge University Press.

Sluzki, C. E., & Veron, E. (1971). The double bind as universal pathogenic situation. *Family Process, 10*(4), 397–410.

Small, D. M. (2010). Taste representation in the human insula. *Brain Structure and Function, 214*(5), 551–561.

Smith, A. (1976). The theory of moral sentiments (1st ed. 1759). In *The Glasgow Edition of the Works and Correspondence of Adam Smith (Vol. 1, pp. 1–342)*. Oxford: Clarendon Press.

Smith, E. R., & Semin, G. R. (2004). Socially situated cognition: Cognition in its social context. *Advances in Experimental Social Psychology, 36*(53–117).

(2007). Situated social cognition. *Current Directions in Psychological Science, 16*(3), 132–135.

Snow, J. (1855). *On the mode of communication of cholera*. London: John Churchill.

Sommer, D. (Ed.). (2006). *Cultural agency in the Americas*. Durham, NC: Duke University Press.

Soon, C. S., Brass, M., Heinze, H.-J., & Haynes, J.-D. (2008). Unconscious determinants of free decisions in the human brain. *Nature Neuroscience, 11*(5), 543–545.

Spaargaren, G. (2011). Theories of practices: Agency, technology, and culture. Exploring the relevance of practice theories for the governance of sustainable consumption practices in the new world-order. *Global Environmental Change, 21*(3), 813–822.

Spaargaren, G., & Vliet, B. Van. (2000). Lifestyles, consumption and the environment: The ecological modernization of domestic consumption. *Environmental Politics, 9*(1), 50–76.

Sperber, D. (1996). *La contagion des idées*. Paris: Odile Jacob.

Sperber, D., & Wilson, D. (1986). *Relevance: Communication and cognition*. Oxford: Blackwell.

Sperry, R. W. (1952). Neurology and the mind-brain problem. *American Scientist, 40*(2), 291–312.

Spindler, G., & Spindler, L. (1989). There are no dropouts among the Arunta and the Hutterites. In H. T. Trueba, G. Spindler, & L. Spindler (Eds.), *What Do Anthropologists Have to Say About Dropouts?* (pp. 7–15). New York: Falmer Press.

Stafford, C. (2004). Learning economic agency in China and Taiwan. *Taiwan Journal of Anthropology, 2*(1), 1–10.

(2007). What is going to happen next? In R. Astuti, J. Parry, & C. Stafford (Eds.), *Questions of Anthropology. London School of Economics Monographs on Social Anthropology (76)* (pp. 55–75). Oxford: Berg.

Stangeland, H. (2016). *Technology-enhanced learning in operative policing: Expert illustration videos and subjective evidence-based ethnography (SEBE) as learning tools among Norwegian police novices.* MSc Thesis. London: London School of Economics.

Stanovich, K. E., & West, R. F. (2000). Individual differences in reasoning: implications for the rationality debate? *Behavioral and Brain Sciences, 23*(5), 645–665–726.

Stern, P. C., Dietz, T., Abel, T., Guagnano, G. A., & Kalof, L. (1999). A value-belief-norm theory of support for social movements: The case of environmentalism. *Research in Human Ecology, 6*(2), 81–97.

Stevens, G. A., & Burley, J. (1997). 3,000 raw ideas equal 1 commercial success! *Research Technology Management, 40*(3), 16–27.

Stoetzel, J. (1963). *La psychologie sociale.* Paris: Flammarion.

Strong, E. K. (1925). *The psychology of advertising.* New York: McGraw Hill.

Suchman, L. A. (1983). Office procedure as practical action: Models of work and system design. *ACM Transactions on Information Systems, 1*(4), 320–328.

(1987). *Plans and situated actions. The problem of human-machine communication.* Cambridge: Cambridge University Press.

(1988). Representing practice in cognitive science. *Human Studies,* 11, 305–325.

(2007). *Human-machine reconfigurations: Plans and situated actions.* Cambridge: Cambridge University Press.

Sunstein, C. R. (2016). The council of psychological advisers. *Annual Review of Psychology, 67,* 713–737.

Susi, T., & Ziemke, T. (2001). Social cognition, artefacts, and stigmergy: A comparative analysis of theoretical frameworks for the understanding of artefact-mediated collaborative activity. *Cognitive Systems Research, 2*(4), 273–290.

Sutton, R. S., & Barto, A. G. (1998). *Reinforcement Learning: An introduction.* Cambridge, MA: MIT Press.

Sykes, D., & Matza, G. M. (1957). Techniques of neutralization: a theory of delinquency. *American Sociological Review, 22*(6), 664–670.

Tajfel, H. (1970). Experiments in intergroup discrimination. *Scientific American, 223*(5), 96–102.

(1974). Social identity and intergroup behaviour. *Social Science Information,* (13), 65–93.

(1982). Intergroup behaviour. *Annual Review of Neuroscience, 33,* 1–39.

Tajfel, H., & Turner, J. C. (1979). An integrative theory of intergroup conflict. In W. G. Austin & S. Worchel (Eds.), *The Social Psychology of Intergroup Relations* (pp. 33–47). Monterey, CA: Brooks-Cole.

Tankard, M. E., & Paluck, E. L. (2016). Norm perception as a vehicle for social change. *Social Issues and Policy Review, 10*(1), 181–211.

Tannenbaum, M. B., Hepler, J., Zimmerman, R. S., Saul, L., Jacobs, S., Wilson, K., & Albarracín, D. (2015). Appealing to fear: A meta-analysis of fear appeal effectiveness and theories. *Psychiatric Bulletin, 141*(6), 1178–1204.

Thaler, R. H., & Sunstein, C. R. (2008). *Nudge: Improving decisions about health, wealth, and happiness.* New Haven, CT: Yale University Press.

Theureau, J. (1992). *Le cours d'action: Analyse sémio-logique, essai d'une anthropologie cognitive située.* Bern: P. Lang.

Thévenot, L. (1984). Rules and implements: Investments in form. *Social Science Information, 23*(1), 1–45.

Thomas, H. D., & Anderson, N. (1998). Changes in newcomers' psychological contracts during organizational socialization: A study of recruits entering the British army. *Journal of Organizational Behavior, 19*, 745–767.

Thomas, W. I., & Znaniecki, F. (1918). *The Polish Peasant in Europe and America. Monograph of an immigrant group* (Vol. I). Boston: Richard A. Badger. The Gorham Press.

Thompson, D. W. (1942). *On Growth and Form* (c1917). Cambridge: Cambridge University Press.

Thorndike, E. L. (1911). *Animal intelligence. Experimental Studies.* New York: Macmillan.

Tognato, C. (Ed.). (2016). *Cultural agents reloaded. The legacy of Antanas Mockus.* Cambridge, MA: Harvard University Press.

Tomasello, M. (1999). *The cultural origins of human cognition.* Cambridge, MA: Harvard University Press.

Tomasello, M., Kruger, A. C., & Ratner, H. H. (2010). Cultural learning. *Behavioral and Brain Sciences, 16*(3), 495.

Tomkins, S. S. (2008). *Affect imagery consciousness: The complete edition.* New York: Springer.

Toomela, A., & Valsiner, J. (2010). *Methodological thinking in psychology: 60 years gone astray?* Charlotte, NC: Information Age Publishing.

Toscano, A. (2006). Enaction. In J. Protevi (Ed.), *Dictionary of Continental Philosophy* (pp. 169–170). New Haven, CT: Yale University Press.

Transportation Research Board of the National Academies. (2010). *Roundabouts : An Information Guide. Second Edition.* Washington, D.C.

Traynor, I., Kuraś, B., Ricard, P., Fariza-Somolinos, I., Cáceres, J., & Zetterin, M. (2014, May 8). 30,000 lobbyists and counting: Is Brussels under corporate sway? *The Guardian.*

Triandis, H. (1977). *Interpersonal behaviour.* Monterey, CA: Brooks-Cole.

Tucker, A. W. (2001). A two-person dilemma, unpublished note, Stanford University, May, 1950. In *Readings in Games and Information* (p. 7). Malden, MA: Wiley-Blackwell.

Tufte, E. (2003). PowerPoint is evil. *Wired Magazine*, (September 11).

Tulving, E. (1972). Episodic and semantic memory. In E. T. W. Donaldson (Ed.), *Organization of Memory* (pp. 381–403). New York: Academic Press.

(2002). Episodic memory: From mind to brain. *Annual Review of Psychology*, (53), 1–25.

Turner, G. (2008). A comparison of the limits to growth with thirty years of socio-economics and the environment. *CSIRO Working Paper Series*, (June)52.

Turner, J. C., & Oakes, P. J. (1986). Reference to individualism, interactionism and social influence. *British Journal of Social Psychology*, *25*, 237–252.

Turner, J. C., & Reynolds, K. J. (2012). Self-categorization theory. In P. A. M. Van Lange, A. W. Kruglanski, & E. T. Higgins (Eds.), *Handbook of Theories of Social Psychology* (pp. 399–418). London: Sage Publications, Ltd.

Turner, T. (1968). Parsons' concept of "generalized media of social interaction" and its relevance for social anthropology. *Sociological Inquiry*, *38*(2), 121–134.

Turvey, M. T., & Shaw, R. E. (1979). The primacy of perceiving: An ecological reformulation of perception for understanding memory. In L. G. Nilsson (Ed.), *Perspectives on Memory Research: Essays in Honor of Uppsala University's 500th Anniversary* (pp. 122–167). Hillsdale, NJ: Lawrence Erlbaum.

Turvey, M. T., Shaw, R. E., & Mace, W. (1978). Issues in the theory of action: Degrees of freedom, coordinative structures and coalitions. In J. Requin (Ed.), *Attention and Performance VII* (pp. 557–595). Hillsdale, NJ: Lawrence Erlbaum.

Tversky, A., & Kahneman, D. A. (1979). Prospect theory: An Analysis of decision under risk. *Econometrica*, *47*(2), 263–291.

Tzu, S. (2009). *The art of war*. Pax Librorum.

Uexküll, J. von. (1992). A stroll through the worlds of animals and men. A picture book of invisible worlds (1st German ed. 1934). *Semiotica*, *89*(4), 319–391.

Uher, J. (2014a). Conceiving "personality": Psychologist's challenges and basic fundamentals of the transdisciplinary philosophy-of-science paradigm for research on individuals. *Integrative Psychological and Behavioral Science*, *49*(3), 398–458.

(2014b). Developing "personality" taxonomies: Metatheoretical and methodological rationales underlying selection approaches, methods of data generation and reduction principles. *Integrative Psychological and Behavioral Science*, *49*(4), 531–589.

(2016a). Exploring the workings of the psyche: Metatheoretical and methodological foundations. In J. Valsiner, G. Marsico, N. Chaudhary, T. Sato, & V. Dazzani (Eds.), *Psychology as the Science of Human Being: The Yokohama Manifesto* (pp. 299–324). Heidelberg: Springer.

(2016b). What is behaviour? And (when) is language behaviour? A metatheoretical definition. *Journal for the Theory of Social Behaviour*, *46*(4), 475–510.

Uher, J., Werner, C. S., & Gosselt, K. (2013). From observations of individual behaviour to social representations of personality: Developmental pathways, attribution biases, and limitations of questionnaire methods. *Journal of Research in Personality, 47*(5), 647–667.

Umberson, D., Crosnoe, R., & Reczek, C. (2010). Social relationships and health behavior across the life course. *Annual Review of Sociology, 36*(1), 139–157.

UNESCO. (2015). *UNESCO science report. Towards 2030.* Paris.

Valsiner, J. (2006). *Culture in minds and societies: Foundations of Cultural psychology.* Worcester, MA: Sage.

(2009a). Cultural psychology today: Innovations and oversights. *Culture & Psychology, 15*(1), 5–39.

(2009b). Integrating psychology within the globalizing world: A requiem to the post-modernist experiment with Wissenschaft. *Integrative Psychological and Behavioral Science, 43*(1), 1–21.

Valsiner, J., & Maslov, K. (2011). The theoreticians' digest. *Journal of Russian and East European Psychology, 49*(2), 16–22.

Van den Bos, R., & de Ridder, D. (2006). Evolved to satisfy our immediate needs: Self-control and the rewarding properties of food. *Appetite, 47*(1), 24–29.

Van den Bulck, J. (2008). Childhood "contagion" through media: where is the epidemiologic evidence? *Epidemiology (Cambridge, Mass.), 19*(2), 280–281.

Van der Laan, L. N., de Ridder, D. T. D., Viergever, M. A., & Smeets, P. A. M. (2011). The first taste is always with the eyes: A meta-analysis on the neural correlates of processing visual food cues. *NeuroImage, 55*(1), 296–303.

Van Lawick-Goodall, J. (1968). The behaviour of free-living chimpanzees in the Gombe Stream Reserve. *Animal Behaviour Monographs, 1*, 161–311.

Vanderbilt, T. (2008). *Traffic. Why we drive the way we do (and what it says about us).* New York: Alfred A. Knopf.

Varela, F. J., Thompson, E., & Rosch, E. (1993). *The embodied mind. Cognitive science and human experience.* Cambridge, MA: MIT Press.

Veldhuizen, M. G., Albrecht, J., Zelano, C., Boesveldt, S., Breslin, P., & Lundström, J. N. (2011). Identification of human gustatory cortex by activation likelihood estimation. *Human Brain Mapping, 32*(12), 2256–2266.

Vermersch, P. (1994). *L'entretien d'explicitation.* Paris: ESF.

Vlek, C. (2000). Essential psychology for environmental policy making. *International Journal of Psychology, 35*(2), 153–167.

Vlek, C., Jager, W., & Steg, L. (1997). Methoden en strategieën voor gedragsverandering ter beheersing van collectieve risico's [Methods and strategies for behaviour change aimed at managing collective risks]. *Nederlands Tijdschrift Voor de Psychologie, 52*, 174–191.

Vrabcová, T. (2015). *I would never eat that back home. Analysing changes in food habits among Canadian and Chinese students in London: Subjective evidence-based ethnography.* MSc Thesis. London: London School of Economics.

Vygotsky, L. S. (1978). *Mind in society: The development of higher psychological processes.* (M. Cole, V. John-Steiner, S. Scribner, & E. Souberman, Eds.). Cambridge, MA: Harvard University Press.

Wagner, W., Duveen, G., Farr, R., Jovchelovitch, S., Lorenzi-Cioldi, F., Markova, I., & Rose, D. (1999). Theory and method of social representations. *Asian Journal of Social Psychology*, 2, 95–125.

Wallner-Liebmann, S., Koschutnig, K., Reishofer, G., Sorantin, E., Blaschitz, B., Kruschitz, R., Unterrainer, H. F., Gasser, R., Freytag, F., Bauer-Denk, C., Mangge, H. (2010). Insulin and hippocampus activation in response to images of high-calorie food in normal weight and obese adolescents. *Obesity*, *18*(8), 1552–1557.

Wang, G. J., Volkow, N. D., Telang, F., Jayne, M., Ma, J., Rao, M., Zhu, W., Wong, C. T., Pappas, N. R., Geliebter, A., Fowler, J. S. (2004). Exposure to appetitive food stimuli markedly activates the human brain. *NeuroImage*, *21*(4), 1790–1797.

Warde, A. (1997). *Consumption, food and taste: Culinary antinomies and commodity culture*. London: Sage.

Warren, W. H. J. (1984). Perceiving affordances: visual guidance of stair climbing. *Journal of Experimental Psychology. Human Perception and Performance*, *10*(5), 683–703.

Weber, M. (1949). *The methodology of social sciences*. Glencoe, IL: The Free Press.

Wells, G. L., & Petty, R. E. (1980). The effects of over head movements on persuasion: Compatibility and incompatibility of responses. *Basic & Applied Social Psychology*, *1*(3), 219–230.

Wendling, T. (2010). Us et abus de la notion de fait social total. *Revue du MAUSS*, *36*(2), 87.

Wenger, E. C. (1998). *Communities of practice: Learning, meaning, and identity*. Cambridge: Cambridge University Press.

(2000). Communities of practice and social learning systems. *Organization*, *7*(2), 225–246.

Wenger, E. C., McDermott, R., & Snyder, W. M. (2002). *Cultivating communities of practice*. Boston: Harvard Business Press.

Wertsch, J. (1981). *The concept of activity in Soviet psychology*. Armonk, NY: M.E. Sharpe.

Wheeler, W. M. (1911). The ant-colony as an organism. *Journal of Morphology*, *22*(2), 307–325.

Whitehead, A. N., & Russell, B. (1962). *Principia mathematica* (2nd ed.). Cambridge: Cambridge University Press.

Whiten, A. (1999). Parental encouragement in gorilla in comparative perspective. Implications for social cognition. In S. U. T. Parker, H. L. Miles, & R. W. Mitchell (Eds.), *The Mentality of Gorillas* (pp. 342–366). Cambridge: Cambridge University Press.

Whorf, B. L. (1956). *Language, thought, and reality: Selected writings of Benjamin Lee Whorf.* (J. B. Carroll, Ed.). Cambridge, MA: Technology Press of Massachusetts Institute of Technology.

Williamson, O. E. (2007). Transaction cost economics: An introduction. *Economics Discussion Paper*, March 1, 0–33.

Wilson, M. (2002). Six views of embodied cognition. *Psychonomic Bulletin & Review*, *9*(4), 625–636.

Wilson, R. A., & Foglia, L. (2015). Embodied cognition. In E. N. Zalta (Ed.), *The Stanford Encyclopedia of Philosophy* (Spring 2016).

Wise, R. A. (1982). Neuroleptics and operant behavior: The anhedonia hypothesis. *The Behavioral and Brain Sciences*, *5*(1), 39–87.

Wittgenstein, L. (1921). *Tractatus logico-philosophicus* (2001 ed.). London: Routledge. (1953). *Philosophical investigations* (3rd ed. 1986). London: Basil Blackwell.

Wolpert, D. M., Doya, K., & Kawato, M. (2003). A unifying computational framework for motor control and social interaction. *Philosophical Transactions of the Royal Society of London B: Biological Sciences*, *358*(1431).

Wood, D., Bruner, J. S., & Ross, G. (1976). The role of tutoring in problem solving. *Journal of Child Psychology and Psychiatry and Allied Disciplines*, *17*, 89–100.

Wood, W., Quinn, J. M., & Kashy, D. A. (2002). Habits in everyday life: Thought, emotion, and action. *Journal of Personality and Social Psychology*, *83*(6), 1281–1297.

Wundt, W. (1912). *An introduction to psychology*. London: George Allen & Unwin.

Yamin-Slotkus, P. (2012). *"An Engaged Pedagogy of Everyday Life." Master's thesis*. Goldsmiths College, London.

(2015). Politics (and mime artists) on the street. In T. Henri & S. Fuggle (Eds.), *Return to the Street.* (pp. 135–145). London: Pavement Books.

Zechmeister, E., Chronis, A., Cull, W., D'Anna, C., & Healy, N. (1995). Growth of a functionally important lexicon. *Journal of Literacy Research*, *27*(2), 201–212.

Zhang, M. (2015). *How is the decision-making distributed in a complex dynamic system? An explorative study of air management teams in the intensive care unit using subjective evidence-based ethnography*. MSC Thesis. London: London School of Economics.

Zittoun, T., & Gillespie, A. (2015). Internalization: How culture becomes mind. *Culture & Psychology*, *21*(4), 477–491.

# Index

475